D0378977

Lovecraft

OTHER BOOKS BY L. SPRAGUE DE CAMP

Fiction

THE ARROWS OF HERCULES

THE BRONZE GOD OF RHODES

THE CARNELIAN CUBE
(with Fletcher Pratt)

THE CASTLE OF IRON
(with Fletcher Pratt)

THE CLOCKS OF IRAZ

CONAN
(with Robert E. Howard & Lin Carter)

CONAN OF CIMMERIA
(with Robert E. Howard & Lin Carter)

CONAN OF THE ISLES
(with Lin Carter)

CONAN THE ADVENTURER
(with Robert E. Howard)

CONAN THE AVENGER
(with Björn Nyberg & Robert E. Howard)

CONAN THE BUCCANEER
(with Lin Carter)

CONAN THE FREEBOOTER
(with Robert E. Howard)

CONAN THE USURPER
(with Robert E. Howard)

CONAN THE WANDERER
(with Robert E. Howard & Lin Carter)

DIVIDE AND RULE

THE DRAGON OF THE ISHTAR GATE

AN ELEPHANT FOR ARISTOTLE

THE FALLIBLE FIEND

THE FANTASTIC SWORDSMEN
(anthology)

GENUS HOMO (with P. Schuyler Miller)

THE GLORY THAT WAS

THE GOBLIN TOWER

THE GOLDEN WIND

A GUN FOR DINOSAUR AND OTHER IMAGINATIVE TALES

THE HAND OF ZEI

THE INCOMPLETE ENCHANTER
(with Fletcher Pratt)

LAND OF UNREASON
(with Fletcher Pratt)

LEST DARKNESS FALL

A PLANET CALLED KRISHNA

THE RELUCTANT SHAMAN AND OTHER FANTASTIC TALES

ROGUE QUEEN

THE SEARCH FOR ZEI

SOLOMON'S STONE

THE SPELL OF SEVEN (anthology)

SWORDS AND SORCERY (anthology)

THE TOWER OF ZANID

THE TRITONIAN RING

WALL OF SERPENTS
(with Fletcher Pratt)

WARLOCKS AND WARRIORS
(anthology)

Non-fiction

THE ANCIENT ENGINEERS

CITADELS OF MYSTERY
(with Catherine C. de Camp)

THE CONAN GRIMOIRE
(symposium, with George H. Scithers)

THE CONAN READER

THE CONAN SWORDBOOK
(symposium, with George H. Scithers)

DARWIN AND HIS GREAT DISCOVERY
(with Catherine C. de Camp)

Lovecraft
A BIOGRAPHY

By L. Sprague de Camp

1975
DOUBLEDAY & COMPANY, INC.
GARDEN CITY, NEW YORK

Library of Congress Cataloging in Publication Data
De Camp, Lyon Sprague, 1907–
Lovecraft.
Bibliography: p. 477
1. Lovecraft, Howard Phillips, 1890–1937—Biography.
PS3523.O833Z59   813'.5'2 [B]
ISBN 0-385-00578-4
LIBRARY OF CONGRESS CATALOG CARD NUMBER 74-9483

ACKNOWLEDGMENTS

Grateful acknowledgment is made to the following for permission to quote these copyrighted or unpublished selections:

To Stephen Birmingham for the quotations from his book *The Late John Marquand*, © 1972 by Stephen Birmingham.

To the *Brown Alumni Bulletin* for the quotation from the article "The Day He Met Lovecraft," © 1972 by the Brown Alumni Bulletin.

To Lin Carter for the quotation from his poem *Beyond*, © 1968 by the Terminus, Owlswick, & Ft Mudge Electrick Street Railway Gazette.

To Doubleday & Company, Inc., for the quotations from *Exiles and Fabrications*, by Winfield Townley Scott; copyright © 1961 by Winfield Townley Scott; reprinted by permission of Doubleday & Company, Inc.

To Drake Douglas for the quotation from his book *Horror!*, © 1966 by Drake Douglas.

To Farrar, Straus & Giroux for the quotations from *Classics and Commercials: A Literary Chronicle of the Forties*, by Edmund Wilson; © 1950 by Edmund Wilson.

To Alfred Galpin for the quotation from his article "Memories of a Friendship," in *The Shuttered Room and Other Pieces*, by H. P. Lovecraft *et al.*, © 1959 by August Derleth, and for quotations from personal letters.

To Forrest D. Hartmann, executor of the estate of August W. Derleth, for the quotation from the article "A Memoir of Lovecraft," by Rheinhart Kleiner, in *The Arkham Sampler*, I, 2 (Spring, 1948), © 1948 by August Derleth; reprinted by permission of Arkham House, Sauk City, Wis.

To the Harvard University Press for the quotation from *Henry Adams: The Major Phase*, by Ernest Samuels, © 1964 by the President & Fellows of Harvard College.

To Daniel Hoffman for the quotation from his book *Poe Poe Poe Poe Poe Poe Poe*, © 1972 by Daniel Hoffman.

To the International Universities Press, Inc., for the quotation from *The Nonhuman Environment*, by Harold F. Searles, © 1960 by Harold F. Searles.

To Richard E. Kuhn, executor of the estate of Carolyn Dorman Smith Wakefield, for the quotations from the poems *To Howard Phillips Lovecraft* and *H.P.L.*, by Clark Ashton Smith, © 1937 by Weird Tales, Inc. and 1959 by August Derleth respectively.

To Frank Belknap Long for the quotation from a personal letter.

To Samuel Loveman for the quotations from personal letters and for that from his poem *Bacchanale*, © 1936 by Samuel Loveman.

To *The Magazine of Fantasy and Science Fiction* for the quotation from a book review by Avram Davidson, © 1962 by the Mercury Press, Inc.

To Ethel Phillips Morrish for the quotations from numerous letters by Howard Phillips Lovecraft.

To Edgar Hoffmann Price for the quotation from his article "The Man Who Was Lovecraft," in *Something About Cats and Other Pieces*, by H. P. Lovecraft, © 1949 by August Derleth.

To J. Vernon Shea for the quotations from his article "H. P. Lovecraft: The House and the Shadows," © 1966 by Mercury Press, Inc.

To Helen Sully Trimble for the quotation from her letter to August Derleth, © 1969 by August Derleth.

To Colin Wilson for the quotation from his book *The Strength to Dream* (*Literature and the Imagination*), © 1962 by Colin Wilson.

For the use of photographs, permission is gratefully acknowledged to Colonel E. W. Barlow, Irving Binkin, the Brown University Library, Gerry de la Ree, Glenn Lord, and Emil Petaja.

To the memory of the Three Musketeers of Weird Tales:

ROBERT E. HOWARD,
H. P. LOVECRAFT, and
CLARK ASHTON SMITH

PREFACE

For two reasons, I never knew H. P. Lovecraft. First, I started seriously writing fiction only during the year following his death in 1937. Second, I seldom read *Weird Tales*, almost his only professional outlet, until nearly a decade later. Alas! in the summer of 1932 I was in Boston, an hour from his home, taking graduate courses at M.I.T. Had I but known. . . .

During the period 1946–60, I learned about Lovecraft little by little. I also learned about other members of the Lovecraft-*Weird Tales* circle, especially Robert E. Howard. While I enjoyed Lovecraft's fiction, Howard's stories came closer to the kind of swashbuckling adventure-fantasy that I most enjoy reading and writing. Later, I became involved in completing, rewriting, and editing a number of Howard's unpublished tales; but that is another story.

A few years ago, I gathered material on Lovecraft and his colleagues for a series of magazine articles, "Literary Swordsmen and Sorcerers." In this project, I had help and encouragement from August W. Derleth of Sauk City, Wisconsin, who had more or less single-handedly kept Lovecraft's name alive and his books in print since Lovecraft's death.

Knowing that Derleth intended to write a full-length biography of Lovecraft, I had no thought of attempting such a task. Derleth, however, died suddenly on July 4, 1971, his biography unwritten.

Since I had amassed many letters and publications by and about Lovecraft, it seemed logical for me to undertake the work.

It appeared to me that, even if I had not known Lovecraft, I had one advantage over Lovecraft's friend Derleth. Whereas Derleth admired Lovecraft to the point of idolatry, I felt that I could approach my subject more objectively. Whether I was right in so thinking is for the reader to judge.

The more I delved into Lovecraft's life, the more fascinating I found him. I saw in him certain of my own shortcomings, in what I hope is exaggerated form. To read of his many mistakes and misadventures gives me a "there-but-for-the-grace-of-God" feeling.

I do not pretend completely to understand H. P. Lovecraft. It is hard for one who is future-oriented rather than past-oriented, is rather indifferent to physical surroundings, has never experienced homesickness, and has no special nostalgia for the scenes of his youth, to comprehend a man who suffered actute, lifelong homesickness for his grandfather's house on Angell Street. In other ways, too, his nature and mine were far apart.

In my judgment, the average author is not a very interesting subject for biography. Most writers pound away at their typewriters, year in and year out, save when their families drag them off for a few weeks of enforced vacation.

That is not to say that authors find life dull. They are often enthusiastic about their trade. But their fascinating adventures and discoveries mostly take place inside their own heads and so are not available to the biographer.

On the other hand, an author's autobiography may be very interesting, since he can discuss his mental processes and emotional experiences. Although Lovecraft never wrote a real autobiography, he did the next best thing. He put his personal history and intimate thoughts into letters, of which he wrote an incredible number: 100,000 according to one estimate. While many of these have disappeared, thousands still exist in the archives of Brown University, in private collections, and in published form.

For my sins, I have read thousands of these letters, the great majority in Lovecraft's original scribbly longhand. If he had not spent so much time on letters, he might have achieved more

worldly success; but then I could not have written about him
in such detail.

In preparing this book, I have had the generous help of
many colleagues and Lovecraft fans. I am particularly indebted to:

Irving Binkin, for letting me use the Philip Jack Grill collection
of Lovecraftiana and furnishing me with photocopies of hundreds
of pages of letters and amateur publications, and the photograph
of the Lovecraft family;

The Brown University Library, for the use of copies of numerous
letters, publications, and photographs by, of, and about H. P. Lovecraft;

My wife, Catherine Crook de Camp, for taking time from
her own professional writing to edit my manuscript;

Frank Belknap Long, for reviewing a large part of the manuscript and submitting to lengthy interviews about his reminiscences
of Lovecraft;

Ethel Phillips Morrish (Mrs. Roy A. Morrish), Lovecraft's
cousin and heir, for giving permission to quote *ad libitum* from Lovecraft's letters and for giving background information on the
Phillips family;

Sam Moskowitz, for letting me use his priceless collection of
old pulp magazines, including *Weird Tales* and the Munsey magazines; and

Henry L. P. Beckwith, Kenneth W. Faig, Jr., Donald M. Grant,
and Barton Levy St. Armand, who showed me around Providence
and Rhode Island, read and criticized part or all of the manuscript, and answered many questions about Lovecraft and his
milieu.

I am also grateful to the following for help of various kinds,
such as answering questions, granting permission to quote, and
making available copies of letters, publications, and photographs:
Forrest J. Ackerman, Janet Jeppson Asimov, Jacques Bergier, Edward
P. Berglund, Robert Bloch, Harry Brobst, Lin Carter, Edward Sher-
man Cole, Willis Conover, William L. Crawford, Gerard B. Crook,
Gerry de la Ree, Arthur P. Demers, the late August Derleth, the Rev.
John T. Dunn, Steve Eng, Christopher Evans, Jacques Ferron, Harry
O. Fischer, Robert M. Fisher, Alfred Galpin, Theodore Grieder and

Richard J. Schaubeck, Jr., of the New York University libraries, Robert C. Harrall, Forrest D. Hartmann, Robert W. Kenny, Lawrence Kunetka, Jerry A. Lawson, Fritz Leiber, Maurice Lévy, Glenn Lord, Samuel Loveman, Richard Mohr, Harry O. Morris, Jr., Dirk W. Mosig, Vrest Orton, Emil Petaja, Edgar Hoffmann Price, W. Peter Sax, James Schevill, Stuart D. Schiff, Richard F. Searight, J. Vernon Shea, Roy A. Squires, John H. Stanley and the late Christine D. Hathaway of the Brown University Libraries, Kenneth J. Sterling, Wilfred B. Talman, Oswald Train, Sheldon and Helen Wesson, George T. Wetzel, and Sheila J. Woodward.

L. Sprague de Camp
Villanova, Pennsylvania
August, 1974

CONTENTS

xvi   CONTENTS

Lovecraft

One

COLLEGE HILL

Where bay and tranquil river blend,
And leafy hillsides rise,
The spires of Providence ascend
Against the ancient skies,

And in the narrow winding ways
That climb o'er slope and crest,
The magic of forgotten days
May still be found to rest.[1]

LOVECRAFT

In a big, rambling, three-story clapboard house with fifteen rooms, in Providence, Rhode Island, lived Whipple Van Buren Phillips with his wife and two unmarried daughters. The third floor, whence gables and dormer windows faced in all directions, housed four servants. The house stood on spacious grounds with well-kept walks, arbors, trees, an orchard, and a fountain, and behind the house a barn sheltered the Phillips carriage and three horses.

Besides the amenities of upper-class American life of the 1890s, the house at 454 Angell Street[2] included a library of 2,000 books, some of them centuries old. Whipple Phillips and his wife Robie were both well-read. Robie Phillips, who had had for her time a good education, developed an interest in astronomy and collected books on the subject.

To this house, in late spring or early summer of 1893, came the Phillipses' middle daughter, Susie Phillips Lovecraft, with her two-year-old son Howard.

Susie had been living with her husband, Winfield Scott Lovecraft, in the suburbs of Boston; but the husband had gone violently insane and had been placed in a mental institution. The shock of her husband's breakdown, apparently, started Susie on a mental decline, which continued until she died eighteen years later. Between his indulgent grandparents and aunts and his neurotic mother, young Howard Lovecraft had a very odd upbringing indeed.

In later years, H. P. Lovecraft liked to talk of his mother's accomplishments: her singing and piano-playing, her painting, and her knowledge of French. People who knew her after her husband's death, however, spoke differently. Albert A. Baker, the family lawyer, called her a "weak sister." The psychiatrist at Butler Hospital, which she entered in 1919 for her final illness, termed her "a woman of narrow interests who received, with traumatic psychosis, an awareness of approaching bankruptcy."[3]

Without her husband, Susie became obsessed by the idea that little Howard was all she had. Since her narrow interests were now concentrated on her son, she protected, coddled, pampered, and indulged the boy to a degree that even the staunchest advocate of permissive upbringing might deem excessive. From the Victorian rocking chair in which she used to rock him to sleep while singing airs from *Pinafore* and *The Mikado*, she had the ornamental knobs planed off lest he hurt himself on them. Furthermore:

> On their summer vacations at Dudley, Massachusetts . . . Mrs. Lovecraft refused to eat her dinner in the dining room, not to leave her sleeping son alone for an hour on the floor above. When a diminutive teacher friend, Miss Sweeney, took the rather rangy youngster for a walk, holding his hand, she was enjoined by Howard's mother to stoop a little lest she pull the boy's arm from its socket. When Howard pedaled his tricycle along Angell Street, his mother trooped beside him, a guarding hand upon his shoulder. This vigilance increased rather than relaxed, the older Howard grew. . . .[4]

Susie let her son eat what he pleased. As a result, he became an avid consumer of sweets and ice cream at the expense of healthier foodstuffs, and he never did get over childish aversions to sea food and some common vegetables. She let him rise and go to bed when he liked, so that he became a noctural creature seldom seen in the daytime. When he was seven, she confiscated a copy of H. G. Wells's novel, *The Island of Dr. Moreau*, lest its gruesomeness harm his delicate nerves.

Equally unfavorable to the boy's development was the fact that Susie Lovecraft had ardently wished for a girl; she had started a hope chest for one. Hence, she persistently favored the character-istics of her son considered feminine. She dressed him in a Lord Fauntleroy suit and deliberately tried to feminize him. As a result of his mother's suggestions, the infant Lovecraft for a while insisted: "I'm a little girl."[5]

He was a brown-eyed tot with long golden curls. When the Lovecrafts had boarded with a family named Guiney in Massachu-setts, these curls had led Mrs. Guiney to call him "Little Sunshine." Susie made him keep those curls for six years, although he began to complain about them at the age of three. For a while, Susie appeased him by showing him pictures from the eighteenth-cen-tury *Spectator*, depicting grown men in long hair and short pants like his. This started his lifelong enthusiasm for the Baroque Era but did not reconcile him to the curls. At last, when he was six, she yielded to his plaints. Weeping bitterly, she had his hair cut.[6]

At the same time, strangely enough, she avoided all physical contact with the small boy and told people that he was ugly. Long afterwards, Lovecraft confessed to his wife that his mother's attitude towards him had been "devastating." His Aunt Lillian told a friend of his "that they had been very foolish in the super-protection that they had thrown about the boy, even to his thirtieth year."[7] By then, however, it was too late to do much about it.

Howard Lovecraft was, furthermore, a very precocious child with an amazing memory. He knew his letters at two, was reading at three, and was writing at four. He soon began reading his way through the Phillips library. This combination of peculiar heredity, bizarre upbringing, and early bookishness combined to produce the mass of contradictions that was Lovecraft.

Howard Phillips Lovecraft (1890–1937) commands attention from any lover of imaginative fiction, not only because of his highly original stories, his wide influence, and his key position in the genre, but also because of the strange personality that resulted from his unusual background. He embodied more contradictions than one would think could be crammed into a single human being.

When Lovecraft died, he was almost unknown outside a small circle of friends, correspondents, and connoisseurs of fantastic fiction. Not a single book of his stories had been professionally published, although friends had made abortive amateur efforts to print such books. The book *Rhode Island, a Guide to the Smallest State*, issued in the year of his death by the Federal Writers' Project, does not mention Lovecraft in its chapter on Rhode Island's writers. Neither does the *Providence Journal's* tourist brochure *Seeing Providence*. Lovecraft deemed himself an utter failure, a "total loss."

Yet, thirty-odd years later, Lovecraft's works are selling by the hundreds of thousands. Collectors pay $30 to $100 for each of his letters. He had been the subject of a play and of at least five masters' theses.

Lovecraft has been translated into half a dozen foreign languages and hailed, especially in the Latin countries, as the compeer of Edgar Allan Poe. A Spanish writer, José Luís García, has pronounced Lovecraft one of the ten greatest writers of all time. Michel de Ghelrode in Belgium ranks him as one of America's four greatest writers, the others being Poe, Bierce, and Whitman. Stephen Vincent Benét has joined Jean Cocteau and André Billy of France in praise of Lovecraft's work.[8] On Sunday, August 5, 1973, the newspaper *La Opinión* Buenos Aires devoted its entire cultural supplement to Lovecraft.

Lovecraft lamented his own lack of accomplishment; yet all his life he threw up self-made barriers between himself and his goals. He condemned affectations and poses but was himself the very prince of poseurs. He liked to consider himself an aged recluse, writing his aunts as "My darling daughter" and "My dear grandchild" and signing his letters "Grandpa."

He affected the language, attitudes, and even spelling ("antient," "publick," "ask'd") of an eighteenth-century English Tory, or at least of a Colonial Loyalist. He laced his letters with exclamations of "God save the King!" When his friend Morton taxed him with being a poseur, he blandly replied: "But isn't it an artistic pose?"[9]

Once he visited the monument to the first Colonials to fall in the Revolution, in Lexington, Massachusetts. Asked if he had felt an emotional reaction, he replied:

"I certainly did! I drew myself up and cried in a loud voice: 'So perish all enemies and traitors to His lawful Majesty, King George the Third!' "[10]

A philosophical materialist, he had a sound knowledge of the sciences and a profound respect for the scientific method. Yet he was full of pseudo-scientific racial theories. He rhapsodized on "the infinite superiority of the Teutonic Aryan" and "the lusty battle-cry of a blue-eyed, blond-bearded warrior,"[11] although he himself was as unlike a stalwart Viking marauder as one can imagine.

Despite his talk of being a bloodthirsty berserker and his stories of ghouls, cannibalism, and rotting corpses, he was so squeamish that, when he caught a mouse, he threw away trap and all rather than touch the tiny cadaver. Long a belligerent nationalist and militarist, he was so overcome with remorse when, as a youth, he shot a squirrel that he never hunted again.

Most people whose political views change begin as liberals or radicals and grow conservative with age; Lovecraft started as an ultraconservative and became a Socialistic liberal and a fervent admirer of Franklin D. Roosevelt.

Lovecraft wrote: ". . . my hatred of the human animal mounts by leaps and bounds the more I see of the damned vermin," and his wife said: "I think he hated humanity in the abstract."[12] Yet, for a self-proclaimed misanthrope, he gathered a marvelous lot of devoted friends. All his friends described him as one of the kindest, most generous, and most unselfish persons they had known.

Until the last few years of his life, Lovecraft was ethnocentric to the point of mania. In the abstract, he hated all foreigners, immigrants, and ethnics, calling them "twisted ratlike vermin from the ghetto" and "rat-faced, beady-eyed oriental mongrels."[13] When he was rooming in Brooklyn and learned that his neighbor was a Syrian, he reacted like a man who finds a rattlesnake in his bathtub.

Yet, when Lovecraft came to know members of these hated ethnoi, he always proved as kind, courteous, friendly, generous, and affectionate towards them as he did towards Anglo-Saxons. For all his oft-proclaimed antipathy to Jews, he married one and numbered another among his closest friends. In his last years, Lovecraft dropped practically all his ethnic phobias and denounced the very opinions he had earlier flaunted.

Lovecraft gave good advice on literary matters but failed to take it himself. He advised apprentice poets to avoid affectations, such as archaic words and spellings, while himself composing in the style of the days of good Queen Anne. He urged them to shun "Baroque excesses," although critics found his own works crammed with such excesses.

He warned one young friend against the delusion that the world owed him a living because of his literary talents and artistic tastes.[14] But all his life, Lovecraft acted as if he were owed such a living. He played the impoverished aristocrat who would not compromise his gentlemanly principles for vulgar mercenary reasons.

He inveighed against "mawkish sentimentality"[15] in fiction; but if anyone was mawkishly sentimental about his own childhood and the mementos of it, it was HPL.

Lovecraft detested sexual irregularities and deviations. Yet his own approach to sex was so prissy and inhibited that, combined with his high voice and what even a close friend has called his "mincing manner,"[16] some have wondered about his sexual orientation, too.

While he undoubtedly loved Sonia, the wife of his short-lived marriage, the real love affair of his life was with the city of Providence; that is, with the material city—the houses and streets —not with the people, for whom he cared little and few of whom even knew he existed. This passion kept him fixed in Providence nearly all his life, although he suffered from a rare ailment that made him hypersensitive to the cold of Yankee winters.

One critic called Lovecraft "a complex blend of neurasthenic invalid and Nordic superman; of arrogant poseur and lonely misfit; of cosmic fantaisiste and rigorous scientific materialist; of scholar, scoffer, and seeker; of life hater, and lover who never found object worthy of his love, or who never found himself worthy to offer love, save in the indirect guise of these torrential, compulsive letters which both clamor for and repel that affection which was . . . simply his due as a human being."[17]

This picture is not wrong so far as it goes, but it errs in selection. It omits Lovecraft's many positive qualities, such as his keen intelligence, vast knowledge, artistic sensitivity, strict personal probity, charm, courtesy, and kindness.

Lovecraft's peculiarities make him sound like an unattractive freak. Yet people who met him, prepared to dislike him, found themselves captivated. In 1920, a fellow amateur journalist, George Julian Houtain, called upon him at home and wrote:

> Somehow I had never been ambitious to meet Lovecraft—I had an impression that he was heavy and ponderous. . . . He is apparently all those things I detest—yet, from the minute I met him, I liked Howard P. Lovecraft immensely.[18]

So there we have him: a man of outstanding virtues and egregious faults; a man both lovable and hateable, depending upon which side of his complex nature one views; a man born out of his time; the writer of stories about which opinions differ to a fantastic degree; a man whose powerful influence on his genre of literature contrasts utterly with the paltry recognition accorded him in his lifetime.

The city of Providence, for which Lovecraft had such a singular platonic passion, is an attractive place, especially for those who like Colonial architecture, old-fashioned Yankee atmosphere, and early hours. The local speech is typical eastern New England American.

Rhode Island is the smallest of the fifty states in area, with a mere 1,248 square miles, 181 of them under water. It embraces the large, deeply indented Narragansett Bay, in which rise several islands. The colony eventually took its name from the largest of these islands.[19]

Banished from Massachusetts for heresy in 1636, Roger Williams and four companions settled on the site of Providence. Williams was one of the first men in Christendom fully to embrace the principle of religious freedom. He welcomed Quakers when Massachusetts was hanging them along with witches and pirates. He even invited "Papists, Infidels, Turkes, and Iewes"[20] to settle in the colony without fear.

Although the Rhode Islanders cultivated a low religious temperature, they clung to the Puritan virtues of thrift, commercial enterprise, and hard work. When in 1762 a company of actors set up a theater in Providence, a town meeting persuaded the Assembly to legislate them out of town, not because their plays were immoral but because: "So Expensive Amusements and idle Diversions, cannot be any good Tendancy among us, especially at this Time, when this Colony as well as others, is labouring under the grievous Calamity of an uncommon Drought, and a very great Scarcity of Hay and Provisions."[21]

At its northern end, Narragansett Bay forks. The eastern fork is the Taunton River; the western, the so-called Seekonk River— actually the estuary of the Blackstone River. Providence stands on the west side of the Seekonk. Besides being the capital of the state, it is a manufacturing town and a minor seaport. Its population has ranged, during this century, between a fifth and a quarter of a million.

The little Providence River, now mostly bridged over, cuts through the city to empty into the Seekonk. Paralleling the Providence River, the tracks of the Penn Central Railroad and Interstate Route 95 run along low ground through the middle of the town.

The Penn Central station faces a large central plaza, bedight with statues and other monuments. South and west of this plaza extends the main business district, where tall office buildings have begun to dwarf the relics of the eighteenth and nineteenth centuries. A little over a quarter mile north of the station stands the Rhode Island State House, built of marble and white granite in 1895–1901, with columns and central dome.

The vale through which the river, the railroad, and the highway run is flanked by two hills, in addition to smaller heights elsewhere. To the west rises Federal Hill, large in area and gentle in slope. Its population has long been heavily Italo-American. To the east stands the smaller but steeper College Hill, where the houses form a living museum of Colonial and Federalist architecture. College Hill occupies a blunt peninsula, about a mile across, formed by the junction of the Providence and Seekonk rivers. Above its steep western slope, Brown University crowns the hill.

Benefit Street, stretching along the side of the hill west of the campus, is noted for its red-brick and wooden-frame Colonial houses. No. 88 is the Sarah Helen Whitman house, built in the 1780s and named for the irresistible widow who dwelt there in the 1830s and 40s. Hither in 1848, the last year of his life, came Edgar Allan Poe for a hectic courtship of Mrs. Whitman. She agreed to marry him if he gave up drinking; he promised but soon reneged and was given his congé.

Crossing Benefit Street at right angles is Angell Street, on which Lovecraft lived for thirty-one of his forty-six years. It climbs up one side of College Hill, crosses through the Brown campus, and slopes down the other side. Except for some of the office buildings and the superhighway through the center of town, Providence looks much as it did in Lovecraft's time.

During Lovecraft's boyhood (1890–1910) the people of Providence were divided along class lines much like those of nearby Boston. The crust of this society was made up of Old Americans: persons of long-settled Northwest European descent, mostly Anglo-Saxon Protestants. Among them, "more emphasis is placed on duty, probity, good manners, and quiet accomplishment than on money or show."[22]

Thrift stood high in their scale of virtues. In a wealthy household, a moderate shabbiness of person and property was not only tolerated but even admired as showing the owner's thrift. As a Bostonian in John P. Marquand's novel *The Late George Apley* (1936) advises his son:

> Your Great-uncle William's house has always seemed to me a part of him and, therefore, not subject to change. The plainness of the furnishings, the draughtiness of its halls, the worn tines of the forks on his dining table, and the darns in his table linen have been to me of his characteristics and an intimation of inherent worth. Your Great-uncle William, if he wished, could live with the ostentation of the *nouveau riche*; but he does not wish it. He has a dislike for external show, which is shared by others who are accustomed to money. He still goes to his place of business on the trolley cars. He buys perhaps one suit a year. . . . In commenting on this you must not forget his generosity to others. . . .

In economic matters, this ruling class adhered to an extreme pro-capitalist conservatism, of the sort that led Marquand's fictional George Apley to inveigh against "such Socialistic nonsense as an income tax and old age pensions."[23] At the bottom of this heap was a mass of immigrants and ethnics, largely Italian, Irish, Portuguese, and Jews of various antecedents. There was animosity between the upper and lower groups, especially when the ethnics began clawing their way up into positions that the Old Americans viewed as theirs

by right of descent. One critic has described the turn of the nineteenth and twentieth centuries in Boston thus:

> It was a period that was very English Colonial in feeling, and
> where the concept of Society, in the English sense, was not only
> accepted but stressed. One talked seriously of who the people of
> Quality were, who were the gentry and who were not. Both blood
> and breeding mattered. Anything English was admired. . . . Most
> important, there were Upper and there were Lower classes, and
> each class dressed and spoke and acted its part.

Among Old Americans, the most highly regarded were those
who had inherited wealth. While money was always good, inherited
money was better than earned money. The belief was that by
growing up with money instead of having to scrounge for it, one
was more likely to learn the superior code of behavior that distinguished gentlefolk.

Below this upper-upper class were the Old Americans who,
starting from little or nothing, had made money, or those who had
once had money but had it no longer. Lovecraft's maternal ancestors,
the Phillips family, fell into this lower-upper class. An acquaintance
described them as "old fashioned gentlefolk which meant considerable in the old aristocratic Providence East Side neighborhood
prior to World War I."[24]

Like the rest of the nation, New England has felt the mixing,
leveling, homogenizing forces of the twentieth century. Hence, much
of the former social stratification has been blurred and broken up.
But old attitudes die hard. In New England, one still meets a quiet
pride of class, caste, and Old American ancestry; a tradition of
wealth artfully hidden behind a shabby-genteel façade; and a high
regard for thrift, sobriety, industry, prudence, and probity.

Like most upper-class New Englanders, the Phillipses were
ancestor-conscious. Lovecraft, who sometimes hunted for ancestral
tombstones in the graveyards of western Rhode Island, liked to
claim that his mother's family were derived from some of the more
eminent Phillipses of Rhode Island and thence from titled British
ancestors. A genealogist, however, reports that Lovecraft's connections
are doubtful. Here are the main, well-established facts about Lovecraft's forebears.

West of Providence, the land rolls away in a series of low,

rounded hills. The land was once cleared of the forest primeval for farming; but, within the present century, most of the farms have been given up and the land has gone back to dense, scrubby second growth.

Fifteen miles west of Providence, on the Connecticut border, lies the "town" (that is, township) of Foster. Here in the hamlet of Moosup Valley lived the Phillips farming family, and here, on November 22, 1833, was born Whipple Van Buren Phillips.

At fourteen, Whipple Phillips was orphaned when his father, Jeremiah Phillips, perished in a mill accident; he caught his coat-tails in the machinery. Young Whipple Phillips ran a store in Moosup Valley; he invented a fringe-trimming machine and made money from it. In 1855, he and his younger brother James fell in love with two local girls, Robie Alzada Place and her cousin Jane Place. Said Whipple to James:

"You take Jane and the farm, while I take Robie and go to Providence to seek my fortune."[25]

Whipple Phillips was a hearty, energetic, enterprising, extro-verted man who had a long and checkered but, on the whole, successful business career. He operated a sawmill and engaged in the coal and real-estate business in the village of Greene, which he named for the hero of the Revolutionary War. In 1874, having sold out his local interests, he settled in Providence. He served in several public offices and joined every organization in sight, becoming a prominent Mason.

Whipple Phillips also picked up a fair degree of culture. He twice visited Italy and acquired a taste for Italian art. In late years he was a large, stout man with a big white walrus mustache.

Whipple and Robie Phillips had five children, four girls and a boy. The three girls who survived childhood were Lillian Dolores (1856–1932); Sarah Susan (called "Susie," 1857–1921); and Annie Emeline (1866–1941). Lillian, a plain woman whose short, hooked nose and eyeglasses gave her an owlish look, was quiet, shy, timid, calm, and cheerful. Susie, despite a prominent nose and a long chin, was considered the beauty of the family. She had vague artistic leanings but was foolish and unrealistic. Annie, a small, fairly good-looking woman, had more spunk and common sense than either of her sisters.

All three girls were well-educated at finishing school. Lillian showed a lively interest in literature and science. Susie could play the piano and sing, and both she and Lillian were competent painters.

Whipple Phillips's son Edwin E. Phillips (1864–1918) married in 1894 but left no children. He worked with his father but quarreled with him shortly before Whipple's death and was therefore treated less generously in the will than his sisters, with whom he later reëstablished friendly relations.

Of the three Phillips sisters, the first to marry was the middle one, the pretty but featherbrained Susie. On June 12, 1889, at St. Paul's Episcopal Church in Boston, she wedded Winfield Scott Lovecraft, a traveling salesman for the Gorham Silver Company of Providence. She was thirty-one and he, thirty-five.

This Lovecraft was a foppishly dressed, handsome man with a luxuriant mustache. Although born in Rochester, New York, he spoke with so audible a British accent that acquaintances remembered him as a "pompous Englishman."[26]

Winfield Lovecraft's grandfather, Joseph Lovecraft, had been a native of Devonshire, England, whose father had lost his property. In 1827, Joseph Lovecraft migrated to the United States with his wife and six children and settled in Rochester. One of the children, George Lovecraft (1815–95) married Helen Allgood, also of British parentage, and reared two girls and a boy. Born in 1835, the boy, like many boys of his time, was named for a popular hero—in this case, General Winfield Scott of the Mexican War. As Winfield Lovecraft grew up, his parents, conscious of their British background, insisted that he speak in the English manner.

Winfield Scott Lovecraft's parents moved to Mount Vernon, New York, and young Winfield Lovecraft went to work for Gorham. He seems to have been an able salesman, but little is known about him.

Following the marriage, the not-so-young couple rented quarters in Dorchester, Massachusetts, south of Boston, since most of Winfield Lovecraft's business was at that time in Boston. Before the birth of their only child, fourteen months later, Susie Lovecraft returned to her father's home in Providence. There, on August 20, 1890, Howard Phillips Lovecraft—in his time, the only American known to have borne the Lovecraft name—was born.

Two

BENT TWIG

By a route obscure and lonely,
Haunted by ill angels only,
Where an Eidolon named Night,
On a black throne reigns upright,
I have reached these lands but newly
From an ultimate dim Thule—
From a wild weird clime that lieth, sublime,
Out of SPACE—*out of* TIME.[1]

POE

Since Winfield Lovecraft's principal business was in Boston, he set about buying a lot in that region and contracting for a house. In the spring of 1892, when Howard was a year and a half old, the family moved. Their movements for the next year are uncertain. According to Lovecraft, the family rented temporary quarters in Dorchester and took a vacation in Dudley, Massachusetts.

They also boarded for about seven weeks, in June and July, at the Guiney house in Auburndale, Massachusetts, a crossroads suburb near the Stony Brook Reservoir. The Guiney family consisted of the poetess Louise Imogen Guiney (1861–1920), a scholarly spinster in her early thirties, and her mother, the widow of an Irish-born Civil War general. In 1892, the Guineys were hard-pressed. Louise

was scraping a living by writing poems and articles for local papers
and by proofreading and other forms of casual editing.

Forty years later, Lovecraft said that his mother had been a
friend of Louise Guiney and that the Lovecrafts had stayed at the
Guineys' for six months, through the winter of 1892–93. Louise
Guiney's letters for 1892, however, show that Lovecraft's memory
had deceived him. They indicate that, so far from being Susie's close
friend, Louise disliked the Lovecrafts and resented their presence.
She wrote: "Two confounded heathen are coming to BOARD this
summer." "There are two and a half of them, as I said all atrocious
Philistines, whom I hate with enthusiasm." "Our cussed inmates
here, praise the Lord, go next month." "The unmentionables are
gone, and we are our own mistresses again."[2]

The reasons for Louise's dislike of the older Lovecrafts are not
hard to guess. She was a complete scholar and intellectual, well-read
in the European literature of several preceding centuries, literate in
French and Italian, and indifferent to the practical sides of life.
By "Philistines" she meant prosaic, conventional, unintellectual, com-
mercial-minded persons. The Lovecrafts may have been a respectable
bourgeois couple; but, being intellectual lightweights, they probably
bored Louise stiff.

Louise's relations with the infant Howard Lovecraft, however,
seem to have been more friendly. She taught him Mother Goose
and Tennyson's *Maud*. She coached him, when she asked him:
"Whom do you love?" to reply: "Louise Imogen Guiney!" She
also taught him to make rhymes. Since Louise had already published
several books of poems and essays, eminent literary visitors came to
the house. Lovecraft sat on the knee of Dr. Oliver Wendell Holmes.

In later years, Lovecraft's earliest memories were of the vacation
at Dudley and of his stay at the Guineys':

> I recall the house with its frightful attic water-tank & my
> rocking-horses at the head of the stairs. I recall also the plank walks
> laid to facilitate walking in rainy weather—& a wooded ravine, & a
> boy with a small rifle who let me pull the trigger while my mother
> held me. . . . My first *clear* & *connected* memories centre in Au-
> burndale—the shady streets, the bridge over the 4-tracked B. & A.
> R. R. with the business section beyond, the Guiney house in Vista
> Ave., the poetess's great St. Bernard dogs, the verse-reciting session
> at which I was made to stand on a table & spout Mother Goose &
> other infantile classics. . . .

Because of Lovecraft's extreme youth (he was not quite two) at the time he knew Louise Guiney and the shortness of the time he lived with her, it would be rash to credit any of his later attitudes to her. Still, one cannot help being struck by the similarities between the two. Moreover, Lovecraft was precociously aware and intelligent and had an amazing memory, reaching back into his second year.

Like Lovecraft in later life, Louise Guiney despised commercialism and cared little about money. Like him, she was an ardent Anglophile. Like him, she rejected the modern world and professed allegiance to earlier times. Like his, her outlook was sexless.

Although an able writer, she preferred, rather than earn a good living, to spend her time on scholarly monographs about forgotten seventeenth-century poets. She wrote much verse. (I regret to say that I find her poetry dull and saccharine; to Lovecraft it was unintelligible.)

During this period, Winfield Lovecraft seems to have played a normal husband-and-father rôle. H. P. Lovecraft recalled that he used to go up to his father when the latter was seated, resplendent in black coat and vest, striped trousers, wing collar, and Ascot tie. He would slap Winfield on the knee and cry: "Papa, you look just like a young man!"[3]

I do not know where the Lovecrafts lived during the fall and winter of 1892-93, but in any case this ménage did not long endure. In April, 1893, when Howard Lovecraft was two and a half, Winfield Lovecraft went to Chicago on a business trip. "Alone in his hotel room, he suddenly began crying out that the chambermaid had insulted him and that his wife was being assaulted on the floor above."[4] He was put under restraint and returned to the East. Since his hallucinations came more and more often, he was declared legally incompetent, committed to the guardianship of the lawyer Albert A. Baker, and placed in a mental institution.

This state of affairs continued for five years until, on April 25, 1898, Winfield Lovecraft was admitted (or readmitted) to Butler Hospital in Providence, in a condition of advanced cerebral disease or "general paralysis of the insane." On July 19th aged forty-four, he died. The cause of death was listed on his death certificate as "general paresis."

Today, "paresis" implies the disorders resulting from an advanced case of syphilis. Writers on H. P. Lovecraft have therefore assumed that Winfield Lovecraft died of syphilis, although in the 1890s "paresis" was still used as a general synonym for "paralysis."

In 1958, the psychiatrist and former *Weird Tales* writer Dr. David H. Keller wrote an article arguing that not only did Winfield Lovecraft die of syphilis but that he had also transmitted it to his wife, so that H. P. Lovecraft suffered all his life from congenital, hereditary syphilis.

Another psychiatrist, Kenneth Sterling, who had known H. P. Lovecraft personally, vehemently disagreed. Keller's medical ideas, he said, were obsolete. Winfield Lovecraft's syphilis was not proved; paralysis like his could have causes other than syphilis. Even if Winfield Lovecraft was syphilitic, H. P. Lovecraft would have had only an outside chance of incurring the disease.

Physicians tell me that, from the meager data, they think that Winfield Lovecraft probably, but not certainly, had syphilis. He died before the development of the Wassermann test in 1907. While Winfield Lovecraft may not have been the roué he has sometimes been pictured, it is safe to say that for a handsome, dashing traveling salesman, marrying at thirty-five, to have had no previous sexual experience would be unusual. On the other hand, neither Susie nor her son, for all their oddities, ever showed syphilitic symptoms.

The best conclusion we can reach is that, while Winfield Lovecraft probably died of syphilis, the likelihood of Howard Phillips Lovecraft's having been syphilitic appears to be negligible.

It is not known whether H. P. Lovecraft ever knew of the alleged cause of his father's affliction. He never spoke or wrote of any such thing, calling the breakdown "a complete paralysis resulting from a brain overtaxed with study & business cares."[5]

Practically nothing is known of the personal relationship between Winfield and Susie Lovecraft. H. P. Lovecraft once spoke of his mother as a "touch-me-not." He indicated that she had almost no physical contact with him after his early childhood.[6]

On this small foundation, Lovecraftians have reared an imposing structure of speculation. Susie, they say, must have been sexually frigid. (Why shouldn't she be, growing up in an era when many young ladies first learned the facts of life on their wedding nights and suffered a dreadful shock?) So Winfield Lovecraft, finding his wife at best a grimly acquiescent sexual partner, sought his amusement elsewhere and thus picked up his syphilis.

This is only guesswork. Still, HPL's queasy attitude towards sex must have come from somewhere, and his mother is the likeliest source. Probably Susie, like many wives of her generation, deemed sex a bestial, disgusting business to which women were condemned by the mysterious decrees of God to submit for the purpose of breeding children.

Such a view of sex was not strange in late nineteenth-century New England. As Henry Adams explained: ". . . any one brought up among Puritans knew that sex was sin. . . . American art, like the American language and American education, was as far as possible sexless. Society regarded this victory over sex as its greatest triumph. . . ."[7]

So the projected Lovecraft house was never built. Shortly after the onset of Winfield Lovecraft's madness, Susie and her son moved back to her father's house in Providence.

Here, Whipple Phillips overshadowed the rest of his family: his wife, a "serene, quiet lady of the old school";[8] his oldest daughter Lillian, learned but shy and timid; his middle daughter Susie, now sunk in sorrow; and his youngest daughter, Annie, lively and socially active. Phillips enjoyed the Italian paintings and mosaics he had bought in his European travels. He wore mosaic cuff links, one showing the Colosseum and the other the Forum. He was usually genial, save when harassed by one of his frequent headaches. His daughter Susie inherited his tendency to migraine and passed it on to her son.

Phillips had formed a youthful taste for weird and macabre fiction. His favorites had been the Gothic writers of the late eighteenth and early nineteenth centuries: Mrs. Anne Radcliffe, Matthew Gregory Lewis, and Charles Maturin. Seeing that his grandson showed similar interests, Whipple Phillips amused the lad with ghost stories and weird tales that he made up. He told of "black woods, unfathomed caves, winged horrors . . . old witches with sinister cauldrons, and 'deep, low, moaning sounds.'"[9]

To cure the boy of fear of the dark, Phillips led him about the unlighted house at night. This indoctrination was so successful that, for the rest of his life, Lovecraft preferred night as the time to be up and abroad.

Whipple Phillips was one of the organizers of the Owyhee Land and Irrigation Company, which had ambitious plans for damming the Snake River in Idaho, near the Snake's junction with the Bruneau. Phillips often traveled to Idaho, whence he wrote his grandson from the town of Mountain Home.

H. P. Lovecraft was strongly influenced, not only by his mother but also by the books he read. A born bookworm, he was affected more by the printed word than by his peers. In fact, for his first thirty years, his impressions and opinions of the world were mainly formed from books.

When Lovecraft was a tot, Susie read him the usual fairy tales. Soon he was reading voraciously. One of the first books he read was Grimm's *Tales*.

At five, he followed this with a junior edition of *The Arabian Nights*. He at once fell in love with the glories of medieval Islâm and spent hours playing Arab. He "made my mother fix up an Oriental corner with hangings and incense-vessels in my room."[10] He collected oriental pottery and proclaimed himself a Muslim.

An older relative playfully suggested that he call himself by the pseudo-Arabic name of "Abdul Alhazred." He did and, moreover, put the name to literary use later. "Alhazred" is probably derived from "Hazard," the name of an old Rhode Island family connected with the Phillipses.

One effect of dabbling in non-Christian traditions was to make Lovecraft skeptical of the faith of his fathers. Before he reached his fifth birthday anniversary, young Lovecraft announced that he no longer believed in Santa Claus. Further private thought convinced him that the arguments for the existence of God suffered the same weaknesses as those for Santa.

At five, Lovecraft was placed in the infant class of the Sunday school of the venerable First Baptist Meeting House on College Hill. The results were not what his elders expected. When the feeding of Christian martyrs to the lions came up, Lovecraft shocked the class by gleefully taking the side of the lions. He wrote:

The absurdity of the myths I was called upon to accept, and the sombre greyness of the whole faith compared with the Eastern magnificence of Mahometanism, made me definitely an agnostic; and caused me to become so pestiferous a questioner that I was permitted to discontinue attendance. No statement of the kind hearted and motherly preceptress had seemed to me to answer in any way the doubts I honestly and explicably expressed, and I was fast becoming a marked "man" through searching iconoclasm.[11]

Home again among his beloved books, the young heathen, now six, plunged into Classical mythology:

Always avid for fairy lore, I had chanced upon Hawthorne's "Wonder Book" and "Tanglewood Tales", and was enraptured by the Hellenic myths even in their Teutonised form. Then a tiny book in the private library of my elder aunt—the story of the Odyssey in "Harper's Half-hour Series"—caught my attention. From the opening chapter I was electrified, and by the time I reached the end I was for evermore a Graeco-Roman. My Bagdad name and affiliations disappeared at once, for the magics of silks and colours faded before that of fragrant templed groves, faun-peopled meadows in the twilight, and the blue beckoning Mediterranean, that billowed mysteriously out from Hellas into the reaches of haunting wonder where dwelt Lotophagi and Laestrygonians, where Aeolus kept the winds and Circe her swine, and where in Thrinacian pastures roamed the oxen of radiant Helios. As soon as possible I procured an illustrated edition of Bullfinch's "Age of Fable", and gave all my time to the reading of the text, in which the true spirit of Hellenism is delightfully preserved, and to the contemplation of the pictures, splendid designs and half-tones of the standard classical statues and paintings of classical subjects. Before long I was fairly familiar with the principal Grecian myths and had become a constant visitor at the classical art museums of Providence and Boston. I commenced a collection of small plaster casts of the Greek masterpieces, and learned the Greek alphabet and the rudiments of the Latin tongue. I adopted the pseudonym of "Lucius Valerius Messala"—Roman and not Greek, since Rome had a charm all its own for me. My grandfather had travelled observingly through Italy, and delighted me with long, first-hand accounts of its beauties and memorials of ancient grandeur. I mention this aesthetic tendency in detail only to lead up to its philosophical result—my last flickering of religious belief. When about seven or eight I was a genuine pagan, so intoxicated with the beauty of Greece that I acquired a half-sincere belief in the old gods and nature spirits. I have in literal truth built altars to Pan, Apollo, and Athena, and have watched for dryads and satyrs in the woods and fields at dusk. Once I firmly thought I beheld some kind of sylvan creatures dancing under autumnal oaks; a kind of "religious experience" as true in its way as the subjective ecstasies of a Christian. If a Christian tell me he has *felt* the reality of his Jesus or Jahveh, I can reply that I have *seen* hoofed Pan and the sisters of the Hesperian Phaëthusa.[12]

For a time, young Lovecraft imagined that his ears were growing points and that horns were sprouting from his forehead. He was sorry that wishing failed to turn his feet into hooves. When he first read about Rome, a sense of personal connection seized him, so that whenever he thought of the ancient world he pictured himself as a Roman.

The Germans have a word, *Wundersucht,* for this mystical sense of the reality of magic and the supernatural, which is often evoked in childhood by sights and sounds. I suppose that many have this feeling in youth. With most, I daresay, it dwindles and dies beneath the stresses of daily life.

Some, however, keep it or at least the memory of it. Some seek to recover it by going into mysticism and occultism. Some become writers of imaginative fiction. One who did both, the Welsh fantasist Arthur Machen (1863–1947) explained it: "This, then, was my process: to invent a story which would recreate those vague impressions of wonder and awe and mystery that I myself had received from the form and shape of the land of my boyhood and youth. . . ."[13]

A growing person passes through stages when he is prepared to accept certain ideas, if they are forcefully presented just then. He may, as it were, snap shut on them, like a molested bivalve, and cling to them with a tenacity out of proportion to their merit. We all know of such sudden conversions, say, to Christianity or to Marxism; but the phenomenon may take many other forms.

So it was with Lovecraft. His skeptical view of the supernatural —his nontheism—and his love of the Classical world were not the only lasting passions formed in his childhood. Another was Anglophilia—a passion for everything English. He took the Tory or Loyalist side in the American Revolution:

> . . . some inner force set me at once to singing "God save the King" and taking the opposite side of everything I read in American-biased child books on the Revolution. My aunts remember that as early as the age of three I wanted a British officer's red uniform, and paraded around the house in a nondescript "coat" of brilliant

crimson, originally part of a less masculine costume, and in picturesque juxtaposition with the kilts which to me represented the twelfth Royal Highland Regiment. Rule, Britannia! Nor can I say that any major change has ever taken place in my emotions. . . . All my deep emotional loyalties are with the race and the empire rather than with the American branch—and if anything, this Old Englandism is about to become intensified as America grows more and more mechanised, standardized, and vulgarised—farther and farther removed from the original Anglo-Saxon stream which I represent.[14]

Anglophilia persisted throughout Lovecraft's life; hence his demonstration in Lexington. He could, he said, have claimed British citizenship on the basis of his paternal grandfather's birth.

During the First World or Kaiserian War, Lovecraft bitterly hated President Wilson for not taking the United States into the war on the British side at once instead of clinging to neutrality for two and a half years. At various times, Lovecraft urged that the United States (or at least New England) rejoin the British Empire. When others sang *America*, he sang *God Save the King*; when they sang *The Star-Spangled Banner*, he sang the eighteenth-century English drinking song *To Anacreon in Heaven*, whose tune Francis Scott Key had appropriated.

Connected with this sentiment was an obsession with the British Empire, as it was not in Lovecraft's time but in the eighteenth century:

At home all the main bookcases in library, parlours, dining-room, and elsewhere were full of standard Victorian junk, most of the brown-leather old-timers . . . having been banished to a windowless third-story trunk-room which had sets of shelves. But what did I do? What, pray, but go with candles and kerosene lamp to that obscure & nighted aërial crypt—leaving the sunny downstairs 19th century flat, and boring my way through the decades into the late 17th, 18th & early 19th century by means of innumerable crumbling & long-f'd tomes of every size & nature—Spectator, Tatler, Guardian, Idler, Rambler, Dryden, Pope, Thomson, Young, Tichell, Cooke's Hesiod, Ovid by Various Hands, Francis's Horace & Phaedrus &c. &c. &c . . . golden treasures, & thank gawd I have 'em yet as the *main* items in my own modest collection.

As a small child, Lovecraft showed a precocious ability to memorize poetry and at six began composing rhymed jingles. These, he said later, were so bad that even he was aware of their faults and

set about improving himself. He learned his rules of versification
from Abner Alden's *Reader* of 1797, which his great-grandfather had
used as a schoolbook and which he found in the attic in 1897.
Lovecraft

> . . . conceived the childish freak of transporting myself altogether
> into the past; so began to choose only such books as were very old—
> with the 'long f' . . . and to date all my writings 200 years back—
> 1697 instead of 1897 and so on. . . . Before I knew it the eighteenth
> century had captured me more utterly than ever the hero of 'Berke-
> ley Square' was captured; so that I used to spend hours in the
> attic poring over the long-s'd books banished from the library down-
> stairs and unconsciously absorbing the style of Pope and Dr. John-
> son as a natural mode of expression.[15]

Lovecraft disliked Fielding's bawdiness; while aware of that side
of eighteenth-century life, he deplored it and as far as he could
ignored it. On the other hand, he embraced eighteenth-century
rationalism, which confirmed him in his atheistic materialism.

Such a flight into the past is not unique. Louise Guiney and
Arthur Machen idealized the seventeenth and earlier centuries.
Henry Adams thought of himself as having been "born an eighteenth-
century child." Few outside of mental institutions, however, have
carried out the charade with Lovecraft's rigor. When indulging his
eighteenth-century pose, he used archaic pronunciations like *me* for
"my" and *sarvent* for "servant." He tried to purge his speech of
post-Colonial words and expressions. As a result, he could say:

> I think I am probably the only living person to whom the ancient
> 18th century idiom is *actually* a prose & poetic mother-tongue. . . .
> the naturally accepted norm, & the basic language of reality to
> which I instinctively revert despite all objectively learned tricks.
> . . . I would actually feel more at home in a silver button'd coat,
> velvet small-cloaths, three-corner'd hat, buckled shoes, Ramillies
> bob wig, Steenkirk cravat, & all that goes with such an outfit from
> sword to snuff-box, than in the plain modern garb that good sense
> bids me wear in this prosaick aera. I've always had subconscious
> feeling that everything since the 18th century is unreal or illusory
> —a sort of grotesque nightmare or caricature. People seem to me
> more or less like ironic shadows or phantoms—as if I could make
> them (together with all their modern houses & inventions & per-
> spectives) dissolve into thin aether by merely pinching myself
> awake & shouting at them, "Why, damn ye, you're not even born,
> & won't be for a century & a half! God save the King, & his Colony
> of Rhode-Island & Providence-Plantations!"

For the rest of Lovecraft's life, eighteenth-century England and Republican Rome remained his favorite historical periods. Although he admired Gothic architecture, the Middle Ages gave him "a pain in the neck." He loved the Baroque, he said, because it was the last pre-mechanical period—the last era before the Industrial Revolution— and so, to his way of thinking, the most truly "civilised" of all.

In the grip of this Baroque obsession, Lovecraft began grinding out pseudo-Georgian couplets, in imitation of Addison, Dryden, Pope, and their colleagues. At eleven, he bound up a manuscript book with the erudite title of *Poemata Minora* and dedicated it "To the Gods, Heroes, and Ideals of the Ancients." One poem, *Ode to Selene or Diana*, began:

> *Take heed, Diana, of my humble plea;*
> *Convey me where my happiness shall last—*
> *Draw me against the tide of time's rough sea,*
> *And let my spirit rest amidst the past.*[16]

While this stanza certainly expresses Lovecraft's outlook, the loss of most of these poems in a warehouse, years later, does not seem an unbearable tragedy.

When his elder aunt married Franklin Chase Clark, Lovecraft found a fellow-enthusiast for such poetry. Doctor Clark was a scholarly physician who made unpublished verse translations of Homer, Virgil, Lucretius, and Statius and who corrected and encouraged young Lovecraft's attempts at Georgian prose and poetry.

Lovecraft's pagan gods had not yet finished equipping him with crotchets. The Phillipses were teetotalers. Lovecraft said: "In my own family, wine has been banished for three generations; and only about a quarter of the conservative homes of this section retain any use of it."

In January, 1896, Lovecraft's grandmother, that "serene, quiet lady" Robie Place Phillips, died. Since mourning was taken seriously in those days, the Phillips girls donned black attire, which "terrified & repelled me [Lovecraft] to such an extent that I would surreptitiously pin bits of bright cloth or paper to their skirts for sheer relief. They had to make a careful survey of their attire before receiving callers or going out!"[17]

During the ensuing period of gloom, the five-year-old Lovecraft got hold of a book called *Sunlight and Shadow* by John B.

Gough, a temperance crusader. The book teemed with such forthright dicta as "There is no trade so damaging to the community, so dangerous to the people, and so hardening to the dealer, as the trade in intoxicating liquors. . . . but for the drink curse, the number of criminals would be so small that at least two thirds of the convict prisons would be empty. . . ." Beer "feeds the sensual and beastly nature. Beyond all other drinks it qualifies for deliberate and unprovoked crime."

Gough also stood for strict Sabbath observance and denounced the mounting of photographs in albums. His Prohibitionist exhortations found a ready believer in young Lovecraft, who became an ardent, lifelong Dry. He boasted of having never tasted liquor and, thirty years after his conversion by Gough, assured his correspondents that "The existence of intoxicating drink is certainly an almost unrelieved evil from the point of view of an orderly and delicately cultivated civilisation; for I can't see that it does much save coarsen, animalise, & degrade." He also said: "I am nauseated by even the distant stink of any alcoholic liquor."[18] But since he attended, without visible distress, many parties where liquor was served, the statement was probably defensive rhetoric rather than fact.

Three

NIGHT-GAUNTS

Out of what crypt they crawl, I cannot tell,
But every night I see the rubbery things.
Black, horned, and slender, with membraneous wings,
And tails that bear the bifid barb of hell.
They come in legions on the north wind's swell
With obscene clutch that titillates and stings,
Snatching me off on monstrous voyagings
To grey worlds hidden deep in nightmare's well.[1]

LOVECRAFT

Realizing that Howard Lovecraft was a somewhat odd child, Susie Lovecraft curtailed her mourning. The somber garb appeared to make the boy nervous.

Young Lovecraft had little to do with the neighborhood children, although some of them later remembered him as lurking behind shrubbery and jumping out to scare them. He disliked games, because they seemed so purposeless. "Amongst my few playmates I was very unpopular, since I would insist on playing out events in history, or acting according to consistent plots. . . . The children I knew disliked me, & I disliked them. . . . Their romping & shouting puzzled me. I hated mere play & dancing about—in my relaxations I always desired *plot*."

When he was seven, his mother tried to enter him in a dancing class. He balked and, having already picked up a smattering of Latin, quoted Cicero in the original: *"Nemo fere saltat sobrius, nisi forte insanit!* [Almost nobody dances sober, unless he happens to be insane]."[2] So Susie gave up the idea.

One day a neighbor, Mrs. Winslow Church, saw with alarm a large grass fire in a nearby field. She went out and found that young Lovecraft had set it. When scolded for endangering others' property, he replied: "I wasn't setting a big fire. I wanted to make a fire one foot by one foot." Thus was foreshadowed his adult passion for accuracy.

Sometimes Lovecraft's second cousin Ethel Phillips, two years his senior, was brought over from Foster to give him some companionship. She found him willing to play, in a vague sort of way, but surprisingly inept. There was a swing on the property, but Lovecraft did not even know how to swing on it until she showed him.[3]

During these pre-school years, Lovecraft dragged his mother on many long walks. Although walking was the nearest he ever came to any athletic sport, he had the normal boy's enthusiasm for railroads and played train in the yard with express wagons, wheelbarrows, and packing cases.

Indoors, he built model villages on table tops, with houses of wood or cardboard, trees, and hedges. Larger public buildings were made of blocks, and these model cities were peopled by toy soldiers. He enacted the entire history of such places, including their growth and decay or destruction.

Often he tried, with the help of a synchronous historical chart, to reënact the story of a real place, either Roman, Baroque, or modern. After a week or so, he would tire of a model and replace it by another. Sometimes he built a toy railroad system, for which his indulgent elders furnished an abundance of trains, tracks, and accessories.

At five or six, he wrote one of his first stories, "The Little Glass Bottle." This juvenile trifle, less than two hundred words long, begins: " 'Heave to, there's something floating to the leeward' the speaker was a short stockily built man whose name was William Jones. He was the captain of a small cat boat. . . ." The floating object turns out to be a bottle containing a note, which reads: " 'I am John Jones who writes this letter my ship is fast sinking with a treasure on board I am where it is marked* on the enclosed chart'"

The captain and his crew sail to the place east of Australia shown on the chart. A diver fetches up another bottle, this time of iron. It holds another note: "'Dear Searcher excuse me for the practical joke I have played on you but it serves you right . . .'" Captain Jones, understandably vexed, exclaims: "'I'd like to kick his head off!'"

No great work of art, the story shows, by its mere existence, that its youthful author was already apprenticing himself in the storytellers' trade. Another early effort, which no longer exists, was "The Noble Eavesdropper," about "a boy who overheard some horrible conclave of subterranean beings in a cave."[4]

If Lovecraft was an odd child, his mother showed signs of becoming even odder. In fact, she gave evidence that Lovecraft's peculiarities were largely her doing. She got the idea that, for all his genius, her boy was ugly. She even told neighbors that he "was so hideous that he hid from everyone and did not like to walk upon the streets where people could gaze at him. . . . because he could not bear to have people look upon his awful face."[5]

In truth, young Lovecraft was a perfectly normal-looking child. As he matured, he showed in exaggerated form his mother's prominent nose and long chin. Despite his "lantern jaw," he was rather personable in his bony way.

The child was, however, aware of his mother's opinion, and this knowledge doubtless encouraged his nocturnal habits. It also contributed to his shyness and timidity towards women. Before Sonia Greene became his fiancée, he said to her:

"How can any woman love a face like mine?"

Late in life, he wrote: "Nobody among my progenitors was as rotten-looking as I am. . . . I am a sort of parody, or caricature, facially of my mother & maternal uncle."

According to Lovecraft, in childhood he suffered from a tendency to chorea (St. Vitus's dance), which manifested itself in uncontrollable facial tics and grimaces. As chorea minor usually does, this nervous disorder disappeared in time; but it may have laid the foundation for Susie's obsession.[6] Furthermore, chorea minor is now held to be a result of rheumatic fever, which often recurs periodically.

It is therefore highly likely that Lovecraft suffered one or more bouts of rheumatic fever.

Susan did not neglect her son's culture. She took him to his first play at six. He acquired a toy theater, to which he added cardboard scenery and characters of his own make. He penciled programs, like one headed:

DRURY-LANE THEATRE
Nov.ʳ 1779
The Company prefents a Comedy by Mr.
Sheridan, intitul'd
THE CRITICK;
OR, A TRAGEDY REHEARS'D

During the Christmas season of 1897, when Lovecraft had just turned seven, he saw a Saturday matinée of Shakespeare's *Cymbeline* at the Providence Opera House. Enraptured, he at once added Shakespearean plays to his repertory. He read lines and moved toy figures about his miniature stage.

Susie also took her son to symphonic concerts. When he seemed to show interest in music, she hired a violin teacher, Mrs. Wilhelm Nauck. The results at first were promising; the pupil had an excellent sense of time and pitch. For two years, from 1897 to 1899, he dutifully sawed away on his junior-sized fiddle and became adept enough to play a solo by Mozart before an audience of friends and neighbors.

Never one to submit easily to tedious discipline, Lovecraft came more and more to hate the drudgery of violin practice. Despite the classical exposure, he remained indifferent to Bach, Beethoven, and Brahms. The only music that he really liked consisted of current popular tunes, such as *In the Shade of the Old Apple Tree*, *Sweet Adeline*, and *Bedelia*, or the music of operettas like those of Gilbert and Sullivan.

When, at nine, Lovecraft developed a nervous condition that led to withdrawal from school, the family physician recommended stopping the violin lessons. Lovecraft never played the violin again. Classical music, with a few exceptions like Wagner's *Ride of the Valkyries* and Saint Saëns's *Danse Macabre*, which he liked for their associations, remained a blind spot. He sometimes wished that he could appreciate such music. His indifference to it is curious in view of his eighteenth-century fixation, since during that century, of all the arts, music made the most striking advances.

The boy was also taken to plays by Wilde and Pinero. Lovecraft was not taken to the circus, because the family thought that his nerves could not endure the crowds, the smells, and the loud noises.[7] In later years, sinus troubles blunted his hypersensitivity to odors, and he gradually overcame his fear of loud noises. But he never got rid of his terror of crowds.

In 1897, Lovecraft's Aunt Annie married Edward Francis Gamwell (1869–1936), who had been an instructor in English at Brown and then managing editor of the *Atlantic Medical Weekly* of Providence. At the time of his marriage, Gamwell was city editor of the *Chronicle* of Cambridge, Massachusetts. He lived the rest of his life in Cambridge and in Boston, where he worked as editor, advertising agent, and free-lance writer.

In 1893, Annie bore a son, Phillips Gamwell, and in 1900 a daughter who lived a few days only. In 1916 her son, an amiable, promising youth, died of tuberculosis. Meanwhile Edward Gamwell had become a heavy drinker. Annie left him to return to Providence, where she worked at several jobs including librarian.

In the 1890s, Aunt Lillian (who at one time taught school) became engaged to Dr. Franklin Chase Clark (1847–1915), who had been a pupil of Oliver Wendell Holmes. Clark, however, could not marry while he had aged parents to support. He and Lillian Phillips were not united until 1902, when she was forty-five and he, fifty-four. Not surprisingly, they had no children.

On July 19, 1898, Winfield Scott Lovecraft, aged forty-four, died in Butler Hospital. After a private funeral, he was buried in Swan Point Cemetery, next to the Butler Hospital grounds. His death had little effect on Howard Lovecraft, to whom his father remained a shadowy figure.

Winfield Lovecraft left an estate of $10,000—a respectable legacy for the time. He also left his son his fine raiment: his black coats and vests, striped trousers, Ascot ties, and silver-headed walking stick. H. P. Lovecraft not only kept these garments but also, when he grew into them, wore them, although by that time they were long out of date.

In the fall of 1898, Lovecraft, going on eight, entered the primary school on Slater Avenue, north of Angell Street.[8] Being somewhat nearsighted, he began wearing eyeglasses and continued to do so off and on all his life. In 1925, finding the glasses irritating to his nose and ears, he took to going without them most of the time, donning them only when he wished a clear view of something distant, as at a play or a lecture.

During the school year of 1899–1900, Susie Lovecraft withdrew her son from the Slater Avenue School, supposedly for illness. Speaking of this withdrawal, Lovecraft's friend Cook said: "I shall always believe that it was his mother and not he that was sick—sick with fear of losing her sole remaining link to life and happiness."

There does seem to have been more to it than Susie's neurotic fear that her genius of a son was too nervous and sensitive to bear the rigors of public schooling. Perhaps this was the time of his rheumatic fever. A quarter-century later, Lovecraft wrote:

> . . . my hypersensitive nerves reacted on my bodily functions to such a degree as to give the appearance of many different physical illnesses. Thus I had a very irregular heart action—badly affected by physical exertion—and such acute kidney trouble that a local practitioner would have operated for stone in the bladder had not a Boston specialist given a sounder diagnosis & traced it to the nervous system. . . . Then, too, I had frightful digestive trouble—all, probably, caused by malfunctioning nerves—besides atrocious sick-headaches that kept me flat 3 or 4 days out of every week. I still have headaches now and then—of the unexplained sort known as migraine—though they don't compare with what I used to have.

He was also subject to terrifying dreams, which he described, the brackets being Lovecraft's:

> When I was 6 or 7 I used to be tormented constantly with a peculiar type of recurrent nightmare in which a monstrous race of entities (called by me "Night-Gaunts"—I don't know where I got hold of the name) used to snatch me up by the stomach [bad digestion?] & carry me off through infinite leagues of black air over the towers of dead & horrible cities. They would finally get me into a grey void where I could see the needle-like pinnacles of enormous mountains miles below. Then they would let me drop—& as I gained momentum in my Icarus-like plunge I would start awake in such a panic that I hated to think of sleeping again. The "night-gaunts" were black, lean, rubbery things with horns, barbed tails, bat-wings, and *no faces at all*. Undoubtedly I derived the image

from the jumbled memory of Doré drawings (largely the illustrations to "Paradise Lost") which fascinated me in waking hours. They had no voices & their only form of real torture was their habit of tickling my stomach [digestion again] before snatching me up & swooping away with me. I somehow had the vague notion that they lived in the black burrows honeycombing the pinnacle of some incredibly high mountain somewhere. They seemed to come in flocks of 25 or 50, & would sometimes fling me one to the other. Night after night I dreamed the same horror with only minor variants—but I never struck those hideous mountain peaks before waking.[9]

In most respects, young Lovecraft seemed physically normal, but he obviously suffered from what are now called psychosomatic ills, aggravated by his mother's nervous fears and apprehensions. He shed oblique light on his boyhood conditions in a later story, wherein he told of a fictional character much like himself:

He was the most phenomenal child scholar I have ever known, and at seven was writing verse of a sombre, fantastic, almost morbid cast which astonished the tutors surrounding him. Perhaps his private education and coddled seclusion had something to do with his premature flowering. An only child, he had organic weaknesses which startled his doting parents and caused them to keep him closely chained to their side. He was never allowed out without his nurse, and seldom had a chance to play unconstrainedly with other children. All this doubtless fostered a strange secretive inner life, with imagination as his one avenue of freedom.[10]

Whatever the reason—neurotic illness, bullying, his mother's frantic over-protectiveness, or some combination of these—he was taken out of school. At first he was taught at home by his mother, his grandfather, and his Aunt Lillian. Then tutors, including one A. P. May, were hired.

Lovecraft was out of school for over two years. During this time, in addition to his tutorial lessons, he read voraciously. He read the boys' adventure novels of authors like George A. Henty, Edward S. Ellis, and Kirk Munroe. He devoured the adventures of a pair of fictional detectives, Old King Brady and Young King Brady, in *Secret Service* and other dime novels.

"Then," he recollected, "I struck EDGAR ALLAN POE!! It was my downfall, and at the age of eight I saw the blue firmament of Argos and Sicily darkened by the miasmal exhalations of the tomb!"

Poe remained his lifelong enthusiasm and the strongest single influence upon him. He also learned about sex:

> In the matter of the justly celebrated "facts of life" I didn't wait for oral information, but exhausted the entire subject in the medical section of the family library . . . when I was 8 years old—through Quain's Anatomy (fully illustrated and diagrammed), Dunglinson's Physiology &c. &c. This was because of curiosity & perplexity concerning the strange reticences & embarrassments of adult speech, & oddly inexplicable allusions & situations in standard literature. The result was the very opposite of what parents generally fear—for instead of giving me an abnormal & precocious interest in sex (as *unsatisfied* curiosity would have done), it virtually killed my interest in the subject. The whole matter was reduced to prosaic mechanism—a mechanism which I rather despised or at least thought non-glamourous because of its purely animal nature & separation from such things as intellect & beauty—& all the drama was taken out of it.[11]

He was still reading writers of the seventeenth and eighteenth centuries and their translations of Graeco-Roman classics. These inspired him to attempt an epic in the same style. Called *The Poem of Ulysses, or the New Odyssey*, it began:

> *The night was dark, O reader Hark, and see Ulysses' fleet;*
> *All homeward bound, with Vict'ry crowned, he hopes his spouse to*
>   *greet;*
> *Long hath he fought, put Troy to naught, and levell'd down its walls,*
> *But Neptune's wrath obstructs his path, while into snares he falls . . .*[12]

Lovecraft also resumed his experiments in prose. One such effort is "The Secret Cave or John Lees Adventure" (1898), beginning:

> "Now be good children," said Mrs. Lee "While I am away & don't get into mischief." Mr. & Mrs. Lee were going off for the day & to leave the two children John 10 yrs old & Alice 2 yrs old "Yes" replied John. . . .

To make a short story shorter, John and Alice explore the cellar. A wall gives way, revealing a tunnel. They enter the tunnel and find a small box. When they try to dig into the end of the tunnel, water bursts in, drowning the sister. John escapes with the corpse and the box. When the latter is opened, ". . . they found it to be a *solid* gold chunk worth about $10,000 enough to pay for anything but the death of his sister. End."[13]

In 1898 or 1899 came "The Mystery of the Grave-Yard or 'A Dead Man's Revenge.'" HPL's narrative technique had developed to the point of dividing the story into twelve chapters—but these are only about fifty to a hundred words long. Still, the story, over five hundred words of it, shows more staying power on the author's part:

> It was noon in the little village of Mainville, and a sorrowful group of people were standing around the Burns's Tomb. Joseph Burns was dead. (When dying, he had given the following strange order:— "Before you put my body in the tomb, drop this ball onto the floor, at a spot marked "A"." He then handed a small golden ball to the rector.) . . .

The rector, Mr. Dobson, follows orders but disappears. Dobson's daughter calls the police station and cries "'Send King John'! King John was a famous western detective." The kidnapper flees, but he and his minions are arrested as they are about to take ship for Africa. At the trial, Dobson reappears, telling of his imprisonment in a vault beneath the tomb. It was a plot on the part of the dead man and his brother against Dobson.[14]

Caves, crypts, cellars, and tunnels featured Lovecraft's fiction all his life. One more story survives from this juvenile period: "The Mysterious Ship," subtitled "The Royal Press 1902." Lovecraft was beginning to think of the mechanics of publishing.

This story, less than five hundred words, is divided into nine chapters. Some of these, however, are only a sentence or two long, so that the existing work is an outline rather than a story.

It tells of the kidnapping of three men by a villainous Latin, who takes them to the Arctic in a submarine. "At the N. Pole there exists a vast continent composed of volcanic soil, a portion of which is open to explorers. It is called 'No-Mans Land.'"[15] The polar regions, like underground chambers and passages, held a lasting fascination for Lovecraft.

The young author neatly printed these stories by hand and bound the pages together. He wrote other stories, too, but at eighteen looked them over and found them so repulsive that he destroyed all but a few rescued by his mother. They were, he said, written "in a Johnsonese that only a pedant of the 1810 period could equal." The stories were actually no worse than most such puerile efforts, but authors are wont to take a hypercritical view of their own juvenilia.

Before Lovecraft went further in his fictional apprenticeship, a new interest seized him. The Phillips library included a Webster's Unabridged Dictionary of 1864. In those days, Webster's Unabridged had a rear section wherein the illustrations appearing in the body of the text were repeated, grouped in categories. In 1898, Lovecraft pored over these pictures.

The mythological section drew him first, and his interest in astronomy was first stimulated by the Classical myths attached to the constellations. Then he immersed himself in "antiquities, mediaeval dress & armour, birds, animals, reptiles, fishes, flags of all nations, heraldry, &c. &c." He became hypnotized by the section on "Philosophical and Scientific Instruments" and avidly studied the cuts of "retorts, alembics, aeolipiles, cryophori, quadrants, anemometers, crucibles, telescopes, microscopes, & what not else." To the boy, these instruments had magical meaning, for he had come upon pictures of similar devices in fairy tales of alchemists and astrologers.

The chemical instruments so beguiled him that he resolved to have his own laboratory. In March, 1899, a cellar room was put at his disposal. His Aunt Lillian bought him some simple apparatus and a copy of *The Young Chemist* by Prof. John Howard Appleton of Brown University, a friend of the family. Soon Lovecraft was happily puttering in his crypt, making smokes, stenches, and an occasional minor explosion and drawing alchemical symbols on the walls.[16]

By the fall of 1902, aged twelve, Lovecraft was thought well enough to go back to school. He entered the sixth grade at the Slater Avenue School. Here he continued for two years, with withdrawals for "nerves" and the help of tutors to make up lost time.

He now succeeded in being a more social being than at almost any time in his life. He apparently suffered some bullying and teasing, to combat which he assumed a "tough guy" pose. The boys nicknamed him "Lovey," which he understandably hated. He recalled:

> I had some fairly rough fights (from which I would not retreat, but in which I almost always got the worst except when I managed to frighten my foe through a dramatically murderous expression & voice) till I was 16 or 17 . . . the "by God, I'll kill you!" stuff.

Still, he made some friends, notably the brothers Chester Pierce Munroe (1889–1943) and Harold Bateman Munroe (1891–1966); the three Banigan brothers, whose family gave him two tiny green statuettes of Irish antiquity; and several others. He persuaded his friends to help him to build a model village in a nearby vacant lot. The boys formed a "Slater Avenue Army," "whose wars were waged in the neighbouring woods, & though my dramatic suggestions were not always accepted with perfect tolerance, I managed to get along with my 'fellow-soldiers' fairly well. . . ." He and Chester Munroe claimed the joint title of the worst boys in the Slater Avenue School, "not so actively destructive as merely antinomian in an arrogant & sardonic way—the protest of individuality against capricious, arbitrary & excessively detailed authority."[17]

Having become an avid reader of Sherlock Holmes, Lovecraft joined his friends in a "Providence Detective Agency":

> Our force had very rigid regulations, & carried in its pockets a standard marking equipment consisting of a police whistle, magnifying-glass, electric flashlight, hand cuffs, (sometimes plain twine, but "handcuffs" for all that!) tin badge, (I have mine still!!) tape measure, (for footprints) revolver, (mine was the real thing, but Inspector Munroe (aet 12) had a water squirt-pistol while Inspector Upham (aet 10) worried along with a cap-pistol) & copies of all newspaper accounts of desperate criminals at large—plus a paper called "The Detective", which printed pictures & descriptions of outstanding "wanted" malefactors. Did our pockets bulge & sag with this equipment? I'll say they did!! We also had elaborately prepared "credentials"—certificates attesting our good standing in the agency. Mere scandals we scorned. Nothing short of bank robbers and murderers were good enough for us. We shadowed many desperate-looking customers, & diligently compared their physiognomies with the "mugs" in *The Detective*. . . . Our headquarters were in a deserted house just out of the thickly settled area, and there we enacted, and "solved", many a gruesome tragedy. I still remember my labours in producing artificial "bloodstains on the floor!!!"[18]

Lovecraft also formed the percussion section of another boyish group, the Blackstone Military Band. While he beat the drum with his hands, he worked the cymbals with one foot and the triangle-beater with the other, at the same time blowing the zobo, a little brass horn held in the teeth.

He engaged with his friends in secret orgies of smoking. Having thus proved his manhood, at fourteen he gave up tobacco for good.

In later life, he claimed that he found tobacco smoke nauseous; "To me the ultimate horror on earth is a smoking car."

In 1900, Lovecraft was given a bicycle, the first of three that he owned. In 1913, during a race with another boy, he took a bad spill and broke his nose. In later life he was sensitive about the damage to the member, although his photographs show no visible harm to it. He also had a black cat, Nigger-Man, to whom he was devoted. Altogether, he remembered these years as the happiest time of his life.

Amid these normal boyish activities, Lovecraft continued his intellectual progress. He read all the novels of Jules Verne that he could get his hands on. His interest in chemistry widened to include geography and astronomy. He was introduced to astronomy by his Aunt Lillian's long-outdated textbooks on the subject. At twelve, he began adding his own up-to-date astronomical books to the collection. The library also included books inherited from several lines of forebears, going back to the eighteenth century, when printers still used the "long *s*" (*f*).

In 1899, Lovecraft began a handwritten periodical, the *Scientific Gazette*, of which he made one original and (usually) four carbon copies for family and friends. Soon he "discovered the myriad suns and worlds of infinite space." Then the *Scientific Gazette* was joined by the *Rhode Island Journal of Astronomy*. Both were published intermittently to 1909. The *Scientific Gazette* was devoted largely to chemistry, consisting for the most part of paraphrases of passages from Lovecraft's chemical textbooks. The other publication contained facts about the positions of the heavenly bodies, notices of Lovecraft's own astronomical observations, and summaries of newspaper stories of such events as the discovery of Jupiter's eighth satellite in 1908.

In February, 1903, Lovecraft got his first telescope. This was a 99-cent instrument with papier-mâché tubes, from a mail-order house. The following July, his mother gave him a better 2.25-inch telescope, with 50- and 100-power eyepieces, costing $16.50. For $8.00 he had a tripod mount made by a local craftsman. In 1906 he acquired his third telescope, a three-inch refractor, from Montgomery Ward, for $50. He still had this device, battered and corroded, more than thirty years later.

From 1903 on, Lovecraft spent many nights stargazing. Another academic friend of the family, Prof. Winslow Upton of Brown University, gave him the run of the Ladd Observatory, located on one of the highest points of College Hill a mile from the Phillips home. Here he was allowed to look through the twelve-inch refractor. Lovecraft spent many hours peering into the eyepiece of a telescope; he claimed his later habit of cocking his head to the side resulted from this activity.

He also got a microscope, two spectroscopes, and a spinthariscope for observing the effect of radioactivity. Had events not interfered, Lovecraft might well have become an adult scientist or at least a teacher of science.

From 1900 on, the Phillipses suffered mounting financial troubles. The failure of the dam on the Snake River in Idaho put Whipple Phillips's Owyhee Land and Irrigation Company in peril. Under Phillips's energetic direction, a second dam was begun. This, too, collapsed, bringing the Owyhee Company to the verge of ruin. Whipple Phillips, the president and treasurer of the company, resolutely instituted drastic economies at home.

At first young Lovecraft, carefully sheltered from stress, hardly noticed. When the groom was dismissed and the horses and carriage were sold, he rejoiced in having the whole barn to himself, to use as a playroom and clubhouse:

> My array of toys, books, and other youthful pleasures was virtually unlimited; and I doubt if I ever thought of such a thing as varying prosperity or the instability of fortune. The poor were simply curious animals about whom one spoke insincerely and to whom one gave money, food, and clothing . . . like the "heathen" about whom the church people were always talking. Money as a definite conception was wholly absent from my horizon.

But Lovecraft had liked the horses and later regretted that they had been sold before he had a chance to learn to ride. As more servants were let go, a hint of impending doom at last reached even HPL's unworldly consciousness; "my spirits were dampened by a vague sensation of impending calamity." Aunt Lillian had married Doctor Clark on April 10, 1902, leaving the big house to Whipple Phillips, his widowed daughter, and his grandson.

Then, on the evening of Sunday, March 27, 1904, Whipple

Phillips was visiting a political crony, Alderman Gray. There he was seized by a "paralytic shock."[19] The following day, shortly before midnight, he died, aged seventy, at his home.

He left $5,000 to each of his three daughters and $2,500 to each of his two grandsons, Howard Phillips Lovecraft and Phillips Gamwell. HPL also fell heir to his grandfather's collection of guns. The rest of Whipple Phillips's estate was to be distributed equally among his four children, but aside from some interests in Rhode Island quarries there was not much to distribute.

Without Phillips's driving force to keep it going, the Owyhee Land and Irrigation Company was soon liquidated, and the mansion at 454 Angell Street was sold. It became a rookery of physicians' offices and, in 1961, was torn down to make way for an apartment-house development.

Four

SPOILT GENIUS

O'er the midnight moorlands crying,
Through the cypress forests sighing,
In the night-wind madly flying,
    Hellish forms with streaming hair;
In the barren branches creaking,
By the stagnant swamp-pools speaking,
Past the shore-cliffs ever shrieking;
    Damn'd demons of despair.[1]

                                        LOVECRAFT

Susie Lovecraft and her adolescent son moved to a house three
blocks east of the Phillips mansion: Number 598–600 Angell Street.
They rented the ground floor, which bore the number 598. Although
the new quarters had five rooms, besides the use of attic and basement, the move gave young Lovecraft a staggering shock:

> For the first time I knew what a congested, servantless house
> —with another family in the same house—was. There was a vacant
> lot next door (although even that was later built up—during my
> adulthood), which I promptly exploited as a landscape garden and
> adorned with a village of piano-box houses, but even that failed to
> assuage my nostalgia. I felt that I had lost my entire adjustment to
> the cosmos—for indeed what was HPL without the remembered
> rooms & hallways & hangings & staircases & statuary & paintings

. . . & yards & walks & cherry-trees & fountain & ivy-grown arch & stable & gardens & all the rest? How could an old man of 14 (& I surely felt that way!) readjust his existence to a skimpy flat & new household programme & inferior outdoor setting in which almost nothing familiar remained? It seemed like a damned futile business to keep on living. . . . My home had been my ideal of Paradise & my source of inspiration—but it was to be profaned by other hands. Life from that day has held for me but one ambition —to regain the old place & reëstablish its glory—a thing I fear I can never accomplish.[2]

To crown Lovecraft's sorrow, about this time his beloved cat, Nigger-Man, disappeared.

What a boy he was! I watched him grow from a tiny black handful to one of the most fascinating & understanding creatures I've ever seen. He used to talk in a genuine language of varied intonations —a special tone for every different meaning. There was even a special "prrr'p" for the smell of roast chestnuts, on which he doted. He used to play ball with me—kicking a large rubber sphere back at me from half across the room with all four feet as he lay on the floor. And on summer evenings in the twilight he would prove his kinship to the elfin things of shadow by racing across the lawn on nameless errands, darting into the blackness of the shrubbery now & then, & occasionally leaping at me from ambush & then bounding away again into invisibility before I could catch him.[3]

In his intense territoriality, Lovecraft was rather catlike himself; he once said: "I have a veritably feline interest in & devotion to places." Perhaps Nigger-Man disliked the move as much as his master did and simply refused to stay in the new quarters. In any case, Lovecraft never kept another pet.

For most young people, adolescence is a time of stress, when thoughts of suicide are common. It hit the over-protected Lovecraft with devastating force:

No more tutors—high-school next September which would probably be a devilish bore, since one couldn't be as free & easy in high school as one had been during the brief snatches at the neighbourly Slater Ave. school. . . . oh, hell! Why not slough off consciousness altogether? The whole life of man & of the planet was a mere cosmic second—so I couldn't be missing much. The *method* was the only trouble. I didn't like messy exits, & dignified ones were hard to find. Really good poisons were hard to get—those in my chemical laboratory (I reestablished this institution in the basement of the new place) were crude & painful. Bullets were spattery and unreliable. . . . Well—what tempted me most was the warm, shallow, reed-grown Barrington River down the east shore of the bay. I used to go there on my bicycle & look speculatively at it. (That summer [of 1904] I was always on my bicycle—wishing to be away from home as much as possible, since my abode reminded me of the home I had lost.) How easy it would be to wade out among the rushes & lie face down in the warm water till oblivion came. There would be a certain gurgling or choking unpleasantness at first—but it would soon be over. Then the long peaceful night of non-existence. . . . what I had enjoyed from the mythical start of eternity till the 20th of August 1890.

What revoked this plan was not so much the normal urge of self-preservation as another strain in Lovecraft's nature: intellectual curiosity. Where most people lust for the physical pleasures of food, drink, and sex, Lovecraft lusted for knowledge:

And yet certain elements—notably scientific curiosity & a sense of world drama—held me back. Much in the universe baffled me, yet I knew I could pry the answers out of books if I lived & studied longer. Geology, for example. Just *how* did these ancient sediments & stratifications get crystallised & upheaved into granite peaks? Geography—just *what* would Scott & Shackleton & Borchgrevingk find in the great white antarctic on their next expeditions . . . which I could—if I wished—live to see described? And as to history—as I contemplated my exit without further knowledge I became uncomfortably conscious of what I didn't know. Tantalising gaps existed everywhere. When did people stop speaking Latin & begin to talk Italian & Spanish & French? What on earth ever happened in the black Middle Ages in those parts of the world other than Britain & France (whose story I knew)? What of the vast gulfs of space outside all familiar lands—desert reaches hinted by Sir John Mandeville & Marco Polo. . . . Tartary, Thibet. . . . What of unknown Africa? I knew that many things which were mysteries to me were not such to others. I had not resented my lack of a solution as long as I expected to know some day—but now that the idea of *never knowing* presented itself, the circumstance of frustrated curiosity became galling to me. Mathematics, too. Could a gentleman properly die without having demonstrated on paper why the square of the hypotenuse of a right triangle is equal to the sum of the squares of the other two sides? So in the end I decided to postpone my exit till the following summer.

High school, however, proved a pleasant surprise:

Well—that fall I found high-school a delight & stimulus instead of a bore, & the next spring I resumed publication of the *R. I. Journal of Astronomy*, which I had allowed to lapse. . . . The Hope

Street preceptors quickly *understood* my disposition as "Abbie" [Hathaway, principal of the Slater Avenue School] had never understood it; & by *removing all restraint*, made me apparently their comrade & equal; so that I ceased to think of discipline, but merely comported myself as a gentleman among gentlemen. I had nothing but the pleasantest of relations with the Hope Street faculty during my four years' stay there.

Although Lovecraft took no part in sports or other extracurricular activities, he got along well enough with his fellow-students. For one thing, he found that, in dealing with bullies, fierce faces and bloodthirsty threats were less effective, for a dub at fighting, than a façade of bland, quiet imperturbability. He practiced this objective, unemotional pose so thoroughly that as an adult he actually thought of himself as a man virtually without emotions—a thinking machine or disembodied intelligence. Some of his fellow-students said later that they had tried to make friends with him but were rebuffed by his air of cold indifference. Others remembered him as "crazy as a bedbug."

In fact, Lovecraft was not coldly unemotional at all. His emotions—his loves and hatreds, his enthusiasms and disgusts—were quite as strong as others'. But he had kept a stiff upper lip so long that he found it hard to express his emotions openly.

During his first high-school year (1904–05), Lovecraft did well scholastically, with an average grade of 81. His best subject was Latin (87) and his poorest, algebra (74).[4] He remembered the period as one of intellectual excitement and discovery.

First-year *physics* opened problems connected with the nature of visible phenomena & the operation of the universe which my earlier chemistry & astronomy had not even suggested. . . . was it possible that educated men knew things about the basic structure of the cosmos which invalidated all my confidently-held concepts? And god! what a surprise *history* was proving! The whole pageantry of the *Byzantine Empire*, & its hostile connexion with that gorgeous Islam which my early Arabian Nights & my later astronomical studies . . . had made close to me, swept unheralded on my sight—& for the first time I heard of the lost Minoan culture which Sir Arthur Evans was even then busily digging up in Crete. Assyria & Babylonia, too, stood out with greater impressiveness than ever before—& I heard at last of the eternal query of *Easter Island*. What a world! Why, good god, a man might keep busy forever, even in an uncongenial environment, learning new things. . . .

Sample of H. P. Lovecraft's handwriting, from a letter

During this year, Lovecraft was absent eighteen days and late seventeen. There have been guesses about his persistent tardiness. It has been supposed, for instance, that he loitered on his way to school to avoid bullying or because of general misanthropy.[5] But such surmises are not really necessary. Throughout his early life, he had little sense of time and could never be counted upon to meet an appointment promptly.

In the spring of 1905, the fourteen-year-old Lovecraft made another try at fiction. The story was "The Beast in the Cave," a little over 2,000 words long. This is a fairly adult short story, with a simple plot and a florid, Latinistic style derived from Poe. If not up to commercial standards, it is miles ahead of Lovecraft's juvenile efforts. It begins:

"The horrible conclusion which had been gradually obtruding itself upon my confused and reluctant mind was now an awful certainty. I was lost, completely, hopelessly lost in the vast and labyrinthine recesses of the Mammoth Cave."

The narrator tells his sensations of doom and congratulates himself on the stoical spirit in which he prepares to meet his fate. Then: "All at once, however, my attention was fixed with a start as I fancied that I heard the sound of soft approaching steps on the rocky floor of the cavern. . . . in an instant my delight was turned to horror as I listened; for my ever acute ear, now sharpened in an even greater degree by the complete silence of the cave, bore to my benumbed understanding the unexpected and dreadful knowledge that these footfalls were *not like those of any mortal man.* . . . when I listened carefully, I seemed to trace the falls of *four* instead of *two* feet."

The narrator's torch gives out. For several pages, the mysterious footfalls stalk him. At last he hurls a stone, which fells the creature. Soon he stumbles upon the guided party from which he had become separated. They find a dying quadruped, which at first they take to be an ape, scantily furnished with straggling white hair. On closer examination, they discover that "The creature I had killed, the strange beast of the unfathomed cave, was, or had at one time been a MAN!!!"[6]

The story (dated April 1, 1905) shows several fictional characteristics of Lovecraft as an adult writer. There is stress on mood and atmosphere rather than on action. There is the heavy hand of Poe, including one of Poe's worst fictional vices: the lavish use of typographic eccentricities (capitals, italics, and multiple exclamation points) to lend force to his narrative.

Finally, the story shows Lovecraft's perennial fascination with caves and similar places. As a boy, he had a poor sense of balance and a mild acrophobia, but he overcame this fear by walking on walls and trestles. He said that he suffered neither from claustrophobia nor from agoraphobia, but:

> I have, however, a *cross betwixt the two*—in the form of a distinct fear of *very large enclosed spaces*. The dark carriage-room of a stable—the shadowy interior of a deserted gas-house—an empty assembly-room or theatre-auditorium—a very large cave—you can probably get the idea. Not that such things throw me into visible & uncontrollable jittery spasms, but that they give me a profound & crawling sense of the sinister—even at my age [of forty-six].[7]

In "The Picture" of 1907, Lovecraft definitely set his course towards the fantastic; at this time, he said, his literary taste was for "phantasy or nothing":

> I had a man in a Paris garret paint a mysterious canvas embodying the quintessential essence of all horror. He is found clawed & mangled one morning before his easel. The picture is destroyed, as in a titanic struggle—but in one corner of the frame a bit of canvas remains. . . . & on it the coroner finds to his horror the painted counterpart of the sort of claw which evidently killed the artist.

"The Alchemist" of 1908 runs to about 2,700 words. A French aristocrat, heir to an ancient castle, also inherits an ancient curse. A former comte had slain a local wizard, Michel Mauvais, wrongly suspecting him of having done away with his son, who turned up alive. The wizard's son, Charles Le Sorcier, pronounced the curse:

> *May ne'er a noble of thy murd'rous line*
> *Survive to reach a greater age than thine!*

He then threw poison into the face of the then comte, who at once expired, and fled. Thereafter, the heir to the title always died by one means or another at the age of thirty-two.

The time of the narrator-hero, Comte Antoine de C——, approaches. This unheroic protagonist is a typical fictional hero of the Romantic Era of the early nineteenth century: a sensitive, ineffectual creature who swoons with excitement. Orphaned early, Antoine was reared by an aged servitor, Pierre, in whom one critic has seen a resemblance to Whipple Phillips.[8]

Exploring a deserted part of his castle, the hero finds a trapdoor leading to a crypt. In the crypt he encounters a "mysterious stranger":

> . . . a man clad in a skull-cap and long mediaeval tunic of dark colour. His long hair and flowing beard were of a terrible and intense black hue, and of incredible profusion. His forehead, high beyond the usual dimensions; his cheeks, deep-sunken and heavily lined with wrinkles. . . .

While the apparition is boasting of how he murdered the narrator's ancestors one by one, the hero throws his torch at him and faints. When he comes to, his dying antagonist reveals the fact that any alert reader would already have guessed:

> "Fool", he shrieked, "Can you not guess my secret? . . . Have I not told you of the great elixir of eternal life? Know you not how the secret of Alchemy was solved? I tell you, it is I! I! I! **that have lived for six hundred years to maintain my revenge.** FOR I AM CHARLES LE SORCIER!"[9]

The story—capitals, bold-face type, and all—is still elementary pastiche-Poe, but the author is enlarging his command of fiction. Lovecraft also wrote other stories in early adolescence; but, with the few exceptions noted, all of them perished in his literary housecleaning of 1908.

At the end of the 1904–05 school year, Lovecraft dropped out of high school and stayed out all the following year. The reason is not known, although in later years he spoke of a "nervous breakdown" in 1906.

During this year he was not inactive. In fact, 1906 saw his first appearance in print. On June 3d, there appeared in the *Providence Journal* a letter by Lovecraft, in which, as a scientific materialist, he denounced astrology. Two months later, the *Scientific American* published a letter from him, urging that astronomical observatories undertake a coöperative program of searching for a trans-Neptunian planet.

Regular astronomical articles soon followed. One series appeared in a local weekly, the *Pawtuxet Valley Gleaner*, published in West Warwick, Rhode Island. Lovecraft admitted that this paper accepted his articles because Whipple V. Phillips had been a big man in those parts.

The other series, which ran simultaneously with the foregoing, was a monthly column in the *Providence Evening Tribune*. Professor Upton had been contributing astonomical articles to the rival *Providence Journal* since 1893, and the *Tribune* was doubtless glad to field a matching feature—especially if, as was almost surely the case, Lovecraft demanded no pay.

When Lovecraft returned to school, his columns afforded him some small triumphs. For one, the boys stopped calling him "Lovey" and began addressing him as "Professor." The columns also gave him a delicious chance to score off one of his teachers:

> My English teacher was an old lady named Mrs. Blake, who had a pleasant though slightly cynical disposition. She annoyed me with a certain doubt of the *originality* of my compositions. One day she called me to her desk & asked me if a certain essay of mine . . . were not copied from a magazine article; to which I replied, that I had taken it *verbatim* from a rural paper! Upon her waxing wroth, I produced the clipping—with the prominently printed heading "By H. P. Lovecraft"!!!

The *Tribune* pieces were mainly ephemerides; that is, simple tables of the main astronomical facts for the following month: the times of sunrise and sunset, the phases of the moon, the positions of the planets, and the like. The contributions to the *Gleaner*, on the other hand, were more extensive. They bore such titles as "Is Mars an Inhabited World?"; "Is There Life on the Moon?"; "Are There Undiscovered Planets?"; and "Can the Moon Be Reached by Man?" Lovecraft presciently voted "no" on the first two and "yes" on the others. In discussing a journey to the moon, however, he did not foresee the use of rocket power to get there. The methods that he proposed were to be shot from a gun, anti-gravity, and some kind of "electrical repulsion," the latter two yet to be discovered.

In his article about life on Mars, Lovecraft attacked the theories of the eminent Bostonian astronomer Percival Lowell, brother of President Abbot L. Lowell of Harvard University. Percival Lowell had popularized the idea that the faint streaks on the surface of Mars, which he and some other astronomers saw through their telescopes, were canals (or at least belts of vegetation bordering canals) dug by intelligent Martians to bring water from the polar caps to the rest of their arid planet. The theory was incorporated in many science-fiction stories, including Edgar Rice Burroughs's Martian novels.

In 1907, Percival Lowell lectured at Sayles Hall in Providence. Before the lecture, Professor Upton saw Lovecraft in the crowd and, much to HPL's embarrassment, introduced him to Lowell as an active astronomical journalist:

> With the egotism of my 17 years, I feared that Lowell had read what I had written! I tried to be as noncommittal as possible in speaking, and fortunately discovered that the eminent observer was more disposed to ask me about my telescope, studies, etc., than to discuss Mars.[10]

The *Gleaner* went out of business around the end of 1906. Lovecraft continued in the *Tribune* until mid-1908, when these columns also ceased. For five and a half years, Lovecraft published no more scientific articles.

He also continued to bring out the *Scientific Gazette* and the *Rhode Island Journal of Astronomy* for friends and kinsfolk. Now the papers were hectographed in editions of twenty-five copies. For a while in 1905, Lovecraft's friends Chester and Harold Munroe issued rival papers. The boys got together in presenting juvenile shows, with lantern-slide talks and conjuring acts.

Late in 1905, Lovecraft persuaded his mother to buy him a small hand printing press. For half a year, he advertised himself in his hectographed publications as a printer of cards at five cents a dozen. Whether he ever got any orders, the record sayeth not.

In the spring of 1906, Lovecraft offered the press for sale. He was trying to organize a Providence Astronomical Society, which left him no time for printing; on January 25, 1907, he lectured the Boys' Club of the First Baptist Church on astronomy. He also wanted the money for more astronomical instruments. In any case, he was never handy with machines.

At this time, also, Lovecraft had an attack of premature social consciousness:

> I was a great reformer then—(in my own mind), and had high ideas about uplifting the masses. I came across a superficially bright Swedish boy in the Public Library—he worked in the "stack" where the books were kept—and invited him to the house to broaden his mentality (I was fifteen and he was about the same,

though he was smaller and seemed younger.) I thought I had uncovered a mute inglorious Milton (he professed a great interest in
my work), and despite maternal protest entertained him frequently in my library. I believed in equality then, and reproved
him when he called my mother "Ma'am"—I said that a future
scientist should not talk like a servant! But ere long he uncovered
qualities which did not appeal to me, and I was forced to abandon
him to his plebeian fate. . . . He left the library (by request) and
I never saw him more.

Lovecraft liked guns. He cherished the collection of rifles and
pistols that he had inherited and added to it a series of .22 rifles,
which he took into the country to shoot. Laws against carrying and
shooting firearms were fewer and laxer then than now. Lovecraft
later said that he had become quite a good shot until, around 1910,
eye trouble forced him to quit. "The lore of hunting allured me, and
the feel of a rifle was balm to my soul; but after killing a squirrel
I formed a dislike for killing things which could not fight back,
hence turned to targets. . . ."

Later, Lovecraft sold or gave away the entire collection piece
by piece, save for one flintlock musket, which he kept as an antique.

On July 6, 1906, Lovecraft acquired a used Remington typewriter. He never, however, took the next logical step: to learn to
type by touch. All his life, he typed with his two forefingers, as did
many writers of his generation like H. L. Mencken.

What with Lovecraft's impractical mother and his amateur-
gentleman complex, he never really grasped the idea that there are
right and wrong ways of doing things; and that one saves oneself
much grief by learning the right way. A modern writer who does not
know how to type with all his fingers is like a cowboy who cannot
ride a horse. But the stubbornly archaistic Lovecraft stuck to the
writing habits of an earlier day, like a Babylonian scribe of the
Hellenistic Era clinging to his clay tablets and stylus and decrying
this newfangled system of pen and papyrus.

This 1906 Remington stayed with Lovecraft all his life. When
it wore out, he had it rebuilt. But this occured only at long intervals,
since he could only rarely afford such costly repairs. In his twenties,
he typed his letters in the daytime but wrote them in longhand at
night so as not to disturb people by the noise.

He came to hate typing more and more, saying: "I think I am
constitutionally lazy, for mechanical activity bores and fatigues me

Every man ought to be able to dig up a job somehow through cleverness or persistence is evil though its exaltation of the merely shrewd, calculative, & grasping qualities] — I certainly don't think (as Belknap actually does nowadays!) that such a worker ought to receive as much recompense as a high-grade man whose services are infinitely more important, & involve an infinitely greater expenditure of personal energy. The notion of setting up the crude factory hand as an <u>ideal cultural type</u>, & adapting all the institutions of civilisation to conform to his crudest tastes, is simply crazy or criminal — or both. So likewise is the Marxian doctrine which condemns all disinterested intellectual & aesthetic endeavours, & demands that all human activities be conducted with the material advancement — physical & economic — of the group in mind .... a doctrine which would exile characters like Newton, Einstein, Baudelaire, Poe, Eddington, Darwin, James Branch Cabell, Harry Clarke, ... & you & Howard Wandrei & Klarkash-Ton & grandpa Ech-Pi-El — & little Belknap himself, if he only knew it! To my mind such a doctrine is simply beneath contempt — it forms no part of any civilisation worthy of the name. And yet not only the communists, but even (albeit to a less grotesque & destructive extent) the Nazis are thoroughly permeated with it. So, too, though less extremely & dogmatically, are the united Republican capitalists — tradesman-minded poltroon bounders that they are — of the dying American plutocracy (which dates, in its present aggravated form, from about 1870). Well — I spit upon all social schemes which do violence to the natural instincts of sensitive & civilised inheritors of the great Graeco-Roman tradition. I repudiate any putrid synthetic "culture" which frowns upon sheer beauty, intellectual integrity, & the reasonable refinements necessary to the comfort of civilised & sensitive people. I hold that the cure of <u>economic</u> evils should be confined to the <u>economic</u> field, & that no excuse exists for a general transvaluation of human values & an attack on the traditions & refinements natural to our race &

Sample of H. P. Lovecraft's handwriting, from a letter

immeasurably." Throughout his life, he increasingly displayed (to quote a modern scientist) "the curious general hatred of machines to be found in some modern intellectuals, who yearn nostalgically for the cruelty, drudgery and squalor of a world without machinery."[11] Gradually, Lovecraft went back to a fountain pen for everything except the final drafts of manuscripts. After 1923, nearly all his personal letters were in longhand. Some of his stories were never submitted in his lifetime because he so dreaded the ordeal of typing and could never afford to hire a typist.

Lovecraft wrote very fast and went to much trouble to get fountain pens that would flow freely under the lightest pressure. His longhand was fairly good in his youth, but as he got older it became smaller, more scribbly, and harder to read; although, like being hanged, one can get used to it. Hence, one of his later correspondents took the word "hermit" in a letter for "haircut." Another wondered what "orianfolots" were; Lovecraft had meant to write "orientalists." The mother of a correspondent, glancing at a letter from HPL, asked in all seriousness if it was written in Arabic.

When his correspondents complained, he defended his illegible handwriting as a case "of that lordly contempt for the obvious, which hath ever been the mark of superior parts." If he took the time to write legibly, "I couldn't get all my MSS. & letters written." Besides he said, people used to be able to read handwriting of all kinds before the typewriter spoiled them.

In 1907, Lovecraft got his first camera: a two-dollar No. 2 Brownie. This was a simple little box camera with a fixed focus and a single shutter speed. Although he kept this camera all his life and took occasional pictures with it and with the vest-pocket Kodak he later owned as well, he never attempted the higher forms of photography.[12] He did not even take a camera on his later antiquarian trips. Like other modern machinery, he viewed the camera with suspicion, disdain, and grudging admission of its utility.

In September, 1906, the sixteen-year-old Lovecraft reëntered the Hope Street High School, taking a full course. For the first term, his marks were adequate: English 90; algebra, 75; drawing, 85; Latin grammar, 85; Latin texts, 90; Greek texts, 85; plane geometry, 92; and physics, 95.

As before, algebra proved his most difficult subject. This fact cast a shadow over his plans for the future. He had assumed that he would graduate from Hope Street High, enter Brown University, major in astronomy, and become a professor like Upton. Now he began to fear that his weakness in algebra might defeat this aim, since a practicing astronomer needs a facile command of the major branches of mathematics. Like many young people, he had been drawn to an occupation by its glamour without realizing the drudgery involved in its practice.

For the school year of 1907–08, Lovecraft took a reduced course, consisting only of chemistry, intermediate algebra, and physics. Although he got good marks even in algebra, he dropped that subject after the first quarter. At the end of the year, with only two and a half years of high school completed, he withdrew for good.

In his later letters, Lovecraft several times spoke of his graduation from high school; for example: "I liked it [high school], but the strain was too keen for my health, and I suffered a nervous collapse immediately after graduating, which prevented altogether my attending college."[13] The "nervous collapse" may have been real enough but was not the primary cause of his failure to attend college. He never did graduate from high school and could only have done so with a year and a half of further study. With his school record, he could not have entered Brown University even if his health had permitted and if the family could have afforded it.

In later years, Lovecraft sometimes made light of this educational failure: "After all, a cultivated family is the best school, and I am singularly complacent about the training this young man did not get." This was bluff; in a more candid moment he wrote: "Of my non-university education, I never cease to be ashamed; but I know, at least, that I could not have done differently."[14]

This failure looms as one of the most important events in Lovecraft's life, for it did as much as anything to determine his future. In several letters, Lovecraft told of his "nervous collapse." For instance:

In those middle years, the poor devil was such a nervous wreck that he hated to speak to any human being, or even to see or be seen by one; and every trip to town was an ordeal. . . . In those days I could hardly bear to see or speak to anyone, & liked to shut out the world by pulling down dark shades & using artificial light. . . . I'd hate to think of the amount of high-school lore which slipped out of my mind during the five years following '08. My health did not permit me to go to the university—indeed, the steady application to high-school gave me a sort of breakdown.[15]

He spoke of headaches, indigestion, lassitude, fatigue, depression, and inability to concentrate. Symptoms like these can be caused by any of many ailments, such as hypotension (low blood pressure), hypoglycemia (low blood sugar), hypothyroidism (low thyroid-gland function), and several infections by microörganisms. Some physicians say that an idle, useless existence, such as Lovecraft led for the next decade, is enough by itself to cause the symptoms of which he complained. The medical science of 1908 was not up to coping with Lovecraft's infirmity, whatever it was.

Lovecraft may have suffered from the form of hypoglycemia called hyperinsulinism, or excessive production of insulin by the pancreatic gland. Although it is, in a way, the opposite of diabetes, the victim must avoid sugars as assiduously as does the diabetic. If he takes in a massive dose of sugar, as by eating candy, his overactive pancreas floods his bloodstream with too much insulin. Then he goes into insulin shock, with the symptoms that Lovecraft described.

Now, Lovecraft was notoriously fond of sweets. He consumed vast quantities of chocolate and ice cream; he so saturated his coffee with sugar that a sticky mass was left in the cup. If he was hyperinsulinic, such a practice was guaranteed to cause a collapse of the kind he told about.

Furthermore, according to his letters, Lovecraft had always been sensitive to cold. We cannot be sure how things were in this respect during his boyhood and adolescence. In any event, this condition either appeared after or was vastly aggravated by his breakdown of 1908.

He seems to have developed a rare, little-understood affliction called poikilothermism. The victim loses the normal mammalian ability to keep his body's temperature constant, regardless of changes in the ambient temperature. His body assumes the temperature of its surroundings, as if he were a reptile or a fish.

For the rest of his life, Lovecraft was comfortable only at temperatures over 80° F. When the air was in the nineties and others were melting in the heat, he felt fine and full of energy. Below 80° he felt worse and worse. At 70° he was stiff and sniffling. At 60° he was miserable. On the few occasions when he was caught out of doors with the temperature below 20°, he collapsed into unconsciousness and was rescued by passers-by. This weakness confined him to his house practically all winter, save during the rare warm spells. To aggravate his plight, he disliked heavy winter clothing, finding it burdensome.

Poikilothermism, I am told, can be caused either by abnormalities, such as tumors, in the hypothalamic region at the base of the brain or by hypothyroidism, which also brings lassitude, fatigue, and depression. In fact, a combination of hypoglycemia and hypothyroidism would account for all of Lovecraft's major physical symptoms. It is interesting to speculate that, possibly, regular doses of thyroid extract and a sugar-free diet might have restored him to normal life during the critical years from the ages of seventeen to twenty-nine.

Another clue to Lovecraft's disorders is furnished by his extraordinary memory. He seems to have had total recall of almost everything from the age of three. If asked about a gathering that had taken place years before, he could identify the place, the exact date, the names of those present, and tell who said what to whom. A psychiatrist tells me: "Photographic memory has been noted in some instances at least to be associated with considerable limitation of emotional freedom, capacity to grieve etc.—which in turn accentuates the difficulty of dealing with even ordinary strains and losses. Adolescence is a considerable strain *per se*."

There is also a story that, at fifteen, Lovecraft sustained a bad fall in a house under construction. But I do not have enough details to guess whether this fall was related to his later ills.[16]

A growing body of medical opinion views breakdowns of Lovecraft's type as the result of congenital defects in the victim's biochemical organization. These weaknesses, in turn, are thought to be hereditary and to predispose the individual to such a malfunction when triggered by some environmental stress or stimulus. Such stresses were furnished by Lovecraft's peculiar home, family, and schooling.

Whatever is the true, exact connection among HPL's apparent poikilothermism, his ravenous appetite for sweets, his hypoglycemic symptoms, his eidetic memory, his probable rheumatic fever, and his breakdown of 1908, we shall probably never know. The enigma is further complicated by the fact that, when Lovecraft speaks of spells of youthful poor health, we can never be sure whether, in any one case, something was really wrong with him or whether the ill was foisted upon the unfortunate youth by his neurotic mother.

From 1909 to 1914, Lovecraft turned from adolescent to adult; but his life during this period is an almost utter blank. Apparently he sat at home, day after day, staying up most of the night and in bed all morning, reading voraciously, writing reams of Georgian poetry, and doing little else.

This pattern is not rare. A shy, timid youth, highly intelligent and precociously intellectual, suddenly drops out of the educational race, turns his back on the world, and holes up. It is a collapse less of nerves than of will, of motivation. If allowed, the victim may idle his whole life away. If made to work, he settles for some petty job far below his capacities. While the affliction is familiar to psychiatrists, the cause and cure are not certainly known.

Susie Lovecraft, though, evidently thought that the poetic genius she attributed to her son excused him from earning a living. When preparation for this was most urgently needed, she put no pressure on him to bestir himself.

One factor in Lovecraft's long idleness was his indoctrination by his mother in "ideals and and unbroken traditions as the base for a proper self-respect and a gentleman's attitude of delicacy and mutual non-encroachment. . . .";[17] in other words, how to be a gentleman. What kind of gentleman she urged him to be we can guess from the qualities he showed later. He exemplified the Victorian ideal of a gentleman: polite, dignified, poised, imperturbable, tasteful, fastidious, obliging, honest, truthful, chaste, chivalrous, upright, and aware of his class superiority.

Most of these are still considered virtues; but Susie's training did not include the idea of learning to make a living. To a Victorian gentleman, talking about money and work would seem vulgar, as would prying into others' affairs or using strong language in a lady's presence.

It is said that the mother of King George III told him: "George, be king!" and that many of this well-meaning but far from brilliant monarch's troubles stemmed from trying to obey her. Likewise, Susie Lovecraft in effect told her son: "Be a gentleman!" She succeeded in making him into a lifelong snob, who spangled his letters with insolent gibes at the "ignorant rabble" or "vulgar herd."

Lovecraft tried to live up to his mother's ideal of a gentleman and frankly called himself such: ". . . a gentleman respects a cat for its independence." or ". . . it goes against the grain for a gentleman to charge money for a favour extended to a friend." Those who did not measure up to this standard were loftily dismissed: Oscar Wilde was never "what one likes to call a gentleman," and "there was always something a bit bourgeois and tradesmanlike about the thrifty sage"—Benjamin Franklin. His mother neglected, apparently, to tell him that a gentleman does not praise himself and that, therefore, he who says "I am a gentleman" implies by so doing that he is no such thing.

In his last years, Lovecraft tried to change these attitudes. In his last months, however, he still wrote: "I despise trade & haggling & competition."[18] If one is a dub at trade and a feeble competitor, it is some comfort to affect to "despise" trade and competition.

There have been two different meanings to "gentleman." One is a person with the virtues—politeness and so on—listed above. The older meaning, which obtained in the Baroque Era and earlier, was one belonging to a hereditary social class, below the nobility but above the merchants, farmers, and workers. While members of this class naturally liked to think of themselves as having all the listed virtues, the main qualification for this rank was to have inherited enough property so as not to have to work. Many such gentlemen kept busy in such genteel occupations as law, medicine, politics, war, science, or religion. But to earn a living by work outside the list of permitted occupations barred one from the gentry. A gentleman took pride in his ignorance of plebeian tasks.

With the breakup of the medieval class system in the Industrial Revolution, "gentleman" came less and less to mean a member of this hereditary class and more and more to mean a man of politeness, dignity, and the rest. But Lovecraft never—at least, until the last years of his life—distinguished the two meanings. He not only tried to practice the gentlemanly virtues but also to live as if he possessed a secure, gentlemanly income as well.

The Lovecraftian ideal of a gentleman was passive, static, and unambitious, out of tune with the kinetic, competitive spirit of most of twentieth-century America. The true function of a gentleman, in Lovecraft's antiquated view, was not to *do* anything—to achieve or accomplish any aim—but simply to *be*—to display the attitudes, strike the poses, and obey the rules of his station. To such a gentleman, the question "And what do you *do*?" were meaningless. Lovecraft wrote: ". . . my ideal is to be an absolutely passive & non-participating spectator. . . ." and:

A far greater net return from life can be obtained through a repudiation of the overspeeded modern ideal, & a return to the sane classic principles of old which recognise the superiority of *being* over *doing*, & emphasise the necessity of *civilised leisure* & of an easy-going reflective & savouring process if one is to extract any solid or enduring satisfaction from the events of existence. The 18th century had the right idea. . . .[19]

Such elegant idleness, however, calls for an independent income. Gentlemen of earlier times had this by definition. A modern writer says:

. . . about the turn of the century there were in England about a quarter of a million persons with no specific occupations, idlers, *not* unemployed. . . . among my friends in London, there are two hard-working elderly gentlemen whose Victorian fathers never did a stroke of work in their lives. They just got up late, went to the barber, then to the club, playing billiards in the afternoon, cards in the evening. They were quite happy to let other people do their work for them while they lived on their family fortunes.[20]

Such folk were widely tolerated and often admired. In Europe, such a gentleman was called a *flaneur*, a *boulevardier*, or a *bon vivant*. P. G. Wodehouse affectionately satirized the class. Detective-story writers took its members as models for their amateur sleuths, such as Lord Peter Wimsey or (in America) Philo Vance. In his play *Loyalties* (1922), Galsworthy asks his audience to sympathize with a young gentleman who, losing his money, is thereby forced to steal and kills himself when caught; his going to work is never even suggested.

In the United States, the non-working gentleman was never so popular. He was likely to be called by the unflattering terms of "lounge lizard" or "playboy."

During this century, such a life of idleness has come more and more to be viewed as unworthy, contemptible and, worst of all, boring. Those who practiced it have felt increasingly guilty. Now the aristocratic tabu on showing an interest in money has largely disappeared. So we have well-heeled pretenders to extinct thrones who sell airplanes or otherwise keep the wheels of industry turning. An Anglo-Irish lord is fixing up a ruined castle as a tourist attraction; a maharaja's son represents an American industrial association in India.

In later years, Lovecraft actually worked hard, but he gave the impression of idleness by his talk of himself as a "gentleman dilettante" and by his poverty. His talk, however, was just hot air, while his poverty was the result less of indolence than of ineptness in managing his time and his business affairs. He strove to make a virtue of this very ineptness.

In truth, Lovecraft's ideal of the non-commercial gentleman had never been practical. Not even in the days of swords and periwigs could a gentleman be so loftily detached from thoughts of money. If he did not take care of his property, he might, like Galsworthy's hero, awaken to find that he no longer had it.

So Lovecraft's pose of belonging to the squirearchy of a bygone day not only pretended to a style of life far beyond his means but also one that, even if he could have swung it, was coming into growing disfavor. His rôle-playing was therefore as futile as the attempt of that *ingenioso hidalgo*, Don Quixote de la Mancha, to revive the glories of chivalry.

Such progress as Lovecraft later achieved towards becoming a mature, normal human being, tardy and imperfect though this was, he achieved on his own. Long afterwards, he ruefully realized what this eccentric domestic regime had done to him:

> If I were young again, I would take some clerical training fitting me for lucrative work. . . . It's my mistake that I never thought about money when I was young. There was no immediate want then, & I always thought it would be easy to slip into some modestly paying niche when the need might arise. . . . Today [1936] I would jump at any *regular position* paying $10.00 per week or more. . . .[21]

But, as Lovecraft sadly added, "46 is 46." The stream of time not only bore him along in its irresistible course but also bore him downward, from better to worse, from richer to poorer, from the life of a happy spoiled child to that of a gifted but unhappy and thwarted adult. Hence one of his wishes as an adult was somehow to vanquish time or turn it backwards. He wished to improve his lot by rowing back up the stream of time to the childhood that he remembered as happy.

But time is strictly a one-way stream. The woman who wrote

> *Backward, turn backward, O Time, in your flight,*
> *Make me a child again just for tonight!*[22]

never claimed that Time had obeyed her. Moving back up the stream of time occurs only in science-fiction stories. Lovecraft, too, discovered that method of temporal voyaging.

Five

HAUNTED HOUSE

Miniver loved the days of old
*   When swords were bright and steeds were prancing;*
The vision of a warrior bold.
*   Would set him dancing.*

Miniver sighed for what was not,
*   And dreamed, and rested from his labors;*
He dreamed of Thebes and Camelot,
*   And Priam's neighbors.*[1]

ROBINSON

Several writers have called Lovecraft an "eccentric recluse"; although, during the last decade of his life, he was hardly more eccentric or more reclusive than most professional writers. Outside of New York City and arty places like Taos and Carmel, most writers lead rather reclusive lives, because there are so few other writers within visiting distance with whom they can talk shop. Their daily lives consist of sitting at home in their old clothes, pounding their type-writers, often keeping odd hours, ignoring many business-class con-ventions, and never being sure of their income. Hence to their bourgeois neighbors they seem eccentric.

During the five years after he left high school, however, Love-craft was indeed an eccentric recluse. At an age when most young men are learning a trade or a profession or seeking employment, he sat at home, did no useful work, and seldom spoke to anyone but his mother. Many years later, he reminisced: "In my own younger days, I often pulled out of a breakdown by withdrawing entirely from external contacts and vegetating for a period either largely in bed or in an easy-chair with dressing-gown and slippers."

When he did venture forth, he walked with a quick, jerky, bird-like stride: head down, shoulders hunched, and eyes fixed on the ground before him. He seldom recognized those whom he passed. A neighbor remembered him thus:

> As a little girl I was scared to death of him, for he used to walk rapidly up and down Angell Street at night just as a group of us were playing Hare and Hounds at the corner of Angell and Paterson Streets. His appearance always frightened me. He was certainly the neighborhood mystery. He would never speak to any of us, but kept right on with his head down. Once in a while I would pass him in the day but never could get him to say hello. . . .

Lovecraft continued to suffer from the mysterious collapse that had overwhelmed him in 1908:

> . . . the deadly fatigue and lethargy which accompany a state of health such as that under which I have been staggering for ten years or more [he wrote in 1918]. At times the very effort of sitting up is insupportable, and the least added exertion brings on a sort of dull tiredness which shews itself in the lagging brilliancy and occasional incoherence of my literary and epistolatory productions. . . . I am only about half alive—a large part of my strength is consumed in sitting up or walking. My nervous system is a shattered wreck, and I am absolutely bored and listless save when I come upon something which particularly interests me.[2]

During this torpid period, Lovecraft was not quite so inactive as his words imply:

> I busied myself at home with chemistry, literature, & the like; composing some of the weirdest & darkest fiction even written by man! . . . I shunned all human society, deeming myself too much of a failure in life to be seen socially by those who had known me as a youth, & had foolishly expected great things of me.

Lovecraft did not altogether abandon his efforts at formal education. He took a correspondence course in chemistry. He had kept up his chemical laboratory work and in 1908 suffered a vicious phosphorus burn on one finger. Doctor Clark saved the finger, but the member was a little stiff and heavily scarred on the palm side thereafter.

After the chemistry course, however, Lovecraft's interest in chemistry tapered off. He explained:

> Between 1909 & 1912 I tried to perfect myself as a chemist, conquering inorganic chemistry & qualitative analysis with ease, since they had been the favourite pastimes of my youth. But in the midst of *organic* chemistry, with its frightfully dull theoretical problems, & involved cases of isomerism of hydrocarbon radicals— the benzene ring—&c., &c., &c., — — — — I found myself so wretchedly bored that I positively could not study for more than fifteen minutes without acquiring an excruciating headache which prostrated me completely for the rest of the day.

In response to his mother's growing nervousness about his experiments with explosive and poisonous substances, Lovecraft dismantled his basement laboratory. So chemistry joined astronomy among the possible careers whence Lovecraft's intolerance of boredom and pathological loss of will debarred him. Long afterwards he confessed: "I wanted the glamour & mystery & impressiveness of the sciences without their hard work."

He made a stab at the pictorial arts, drawing pen-and-ink sketches of landscapes and painting marine subjects in watercolors. Then he gave this up, too. For the rest of his life he vehemently protested that, much as he would have loved to be able to draw and paint, he completely lacked aptitude for it:

> On my maternal side I inherited a love of art. My mother is a landscape painter of no little skill, whilst my eldest aunt is still more expert in this direction, having had canvases hung in exhibitions at the Providence Art Club—yet despite *their* genius, *I* could not draw anything better than the junk you have so often beheld in my letters. I tried my best, but the gift was *absolutely wanting.* . . .[3]

In fact, the lively little pen sketches of himself, of old houses, and of cats, with which he decorated his letters, and the maps and sketches in his treatise on Quebec, show real pictorial talent. Had he put his mind to it and undergone formal training, he might have become a passable illustrator. But he was averse to the constraints of formal training and never grasped the need for it in any skilled occupation. The lack was not of talent but of volition. He said so himself in a letter:

> It is my weakness that I can't conform to rules and restrictions very well. I have to learn and do things in my own way—as dictated by my especial interests and aptitudes—or not at all.

It is easy to see how a child, coddled, spoiled, and isolated as Lovecraft was, might later find it hard to accept the fact that some boredom and drudgery are normal conditions of life. He exemplifies a psychologist's statement: "A high degree of intelligence is often accompanied by a temperamental aversion from continuous work, by a lack of persistence and perseverance." Perhaps Lovecraft entertained an illusion of romantics like Poe, that the true artistic genius was too pure of soul and too delicate of sensibility to need, or even to tolerate, the discipline of learning mere technique.

He also said: "With *languages* I had failed equally,"[4] whereas he was a fair self-taught linguist. In school he had acquired a good knowledge of Latin and a smattering of Greek, and he later picked up a reading knowledge of French and Spanish. It probably salved his ego to say that he did not do something because it was completely impossible for him than to confess that he lacked determination.

He collected stamps but in 1915 gave the collection to his younger cousin, Phillips Gamwell. He also undertook to tutor young Gamwell in algebra and geometry. He found that he had forgotten much of what he had learned of these subjects and had to brush up to keep ahead of his pupil. He tried writing detective stories but did not persevere in the genre. In addition:

> Chemical writing—plus a little historical and antiquarian research—filled my years of feebleness till about 1911, when I had a reaction toward literature. I then gave my prose style the greatest overhauling it has ever had; purging it of some vile journalese and some absurd Johnsonism.[5]

This overhauling of his style was only partly effective, as his pedantic, Latinistic early essays in amateur publications show. Still in the grip of his Anglophile and Baroque obsessions, he persisted in his literary Briticisms ("colour," "shew," "connexion") and archaisms ("smoak," "ask'd").

His main occupation during his fallow period, however, was reading. He read the Bible through. He read novels by H. G. Wells and Jules Verne; Verne's *Journey to the Centre of the Earth* inspired a lifelong interest in Iceland. He read Shakespeare aloud to his mother, delivering some dramatic scenes with such *brio* that the neighbors thought the Lovecrafts were quarreling.

His love of Poe inspired him to read Poe's precursors, the Gothic writers of the late eighteenth and early nineteenth centuries:

Walpole, Maturin, Beckford, and Mrs. Radcliffe. But Poe remained his ideal.

He took to reading magazines, among them three of the chain published by Frank A. Munsey: *The Argosy, All-Story Magazine,* and *The Cavalier* (later combined with *All-Story*)—all precursors of the so-called pulp magazines, which flourished mightily in the 1920s and 30s. Like their later imitators, the Munsey magazines were all-fiction periodicals providing escape literature to a largely male readership. From time to time, these periodicals published science fiction or fantasy. Lovecraft read *All-Story* from its first issue, since it often ran tales of the weird type that to him was the ultimate in fiction.

In 1911 a Westerner in his thirties, who had tried being a bookkeeper, a cowboy, and a railroad detective with little success, became disgusted with a story he had read and swore that even he could do better. The result was a novel of adventure on Mars. The author, Edgar Rice Burroughs (1875–1950) sent the story to *All-Story Weekly* (as it was then called) under the name of "Normal Bean," Burroughs's little joke. In 1912, the story appeared as "Under the Moons of Mars," by "Norman Bean" (a typographical error) in the form of a six-part serial.

A great success, the story was published as a book, *A Princess of Mars,* in 1917. It was the first of ten Martian novels by Burroughs about the valiant, chivalrous, and invincible John Carter of Virginia and his mate, the red-skinned, egg-laying Martian princess Deja Thoris.

Burroughs followed this novel with another in *All-Story:* "Tarzan of the Apes," the most successful of all of his sixty-odd books. An avid reader of Burroughs's stories when they appeared in the Munsey magazines, young Lovecraft praised them highly. When he was older and more sophisticated, he changed his mind, dismissing Burroughs's works as "cheap pulp stuff." He missed the point of Burroughs's fiction. The stories were excellent in their way—but as juvenile, not adult, fiction. When Lovecraft was no longer a juvenile, they enthralled him less.

Beginning with the issue of January 1, 1916, *All-Story Weekly* ran a serial by Victor Rousseau (the pseudonym of Victor Rousseau Emmanual) which probably influenced Lovecraft. This was "The Sea Demons," about a race of amphibious, semihuman creatures who come out of the sea to invade England. When alive, they are completely transparent except for their eyeballs and hence virtually invisible. The popeyed, scaly, web-fingered minions of Cthulhu, in Lovecraft's later stories, may be derived from Rousseau's gelatinous mer-folk.

During his long torpor, Lovecraft did not think himself ill-used: "My family are as delightful and kind as any family could be—my mother is a positive marvel of consideration—but none the less I am not thought any particular credit socially—I am awkward and unpleasing." He blamed himself for his shortcomings; early letters abound in statements like: "I have always had a sort of sensation of unpopularity—knowing how odd and utterly boresome I am."[6]

In reading Lovecraft's statements of his own uselessness and unworthiness, one must bear in mind a psychiatric dictum: "To be excessively modest is to be egocentric." Winfield Townley Scott wrote about Lovecraft as a "mama's boy" and a "fearful and selfish young man." Timid and over-mothered Lovecraft surely was, but "selfish" is hardly the right word. Self-centered and introverted, yes; but always, when jarred out of his perennial trance, kind, obliging, as generous as he could be, and willing to blame himself rather than others.

Still, like many intellectual introverts, he was so wrapped up in his own thoughts that he was largely unaware of those about him. He thought about himself and his emotions, about his physical surroundings, about the world and the universe, and about abstract questions. As for individual human beings, he did not mean to treat them ill; he just did not think about them. As he put it, "I have always been tremendously sensitive to the *general visual scene* . . . while relatively indifferent to people."

One so detached from and indifferent to worldly matters and so egregiously unable to adapt himself realistically to his environment is said to have a "schizoid" personality (not to be confused with the form of insanity called schizophrenia). Such a person is also likely to be shy, seclusive, over-sensitive, to avoid close or competitive human relationships, and to be individualistic to the point of eccentricity. All of this perfectly fits Lovecraft.

For several decades, psychologists and psychiatrists have argued whether or not there was a connection between the schizoid personality on one hand and the possession of a creative mind, like that of scientists, inventors, artists, writers, and other intellectuals, on the other. While the question cannot yet be considered settled, some do believe that there is such a connection—that people with creative minds tend to have schizoid personalities, or conversely that schizoids are more likely to be creative than the general run of mankind.

The Lovecraft home became odder and odder. Susie was a hypersensitive whose least discomfort became a major crisis. A toothache made her shriek. Although she regretted, in a vague, ineffectual way, the extreme one-sidedness of her son's development (". . . my mother deems me a rural barbarian indeed . . ."), she aggravated the trend by encouraging Lovecraft to stay in and the rest of the world to stay out.[7] One of Lovecraft's later correspondents has written:

> In my correspondence with Lovecraft, I once cited George Kelly's play, *Craig's Wife*, as bad psychology in that Mrs. Craig, although passionately interested in her home to the exclusion of everything else, including her husband, none the less never permitted visitors inside that house; this quirk seemed to me unnatural, for I thought it was only feminine for a woman to want to show off her possessions. But Lovecraft upheld Kelly's characterization of Mrs. Craig, writing that he had known just such women. I didn't realize at the time that he meant his mother. For Mrs. Lovecraft, instead of wishing to exhibit her brilliant son, also discouraged visitors.

Another neighbor, Clara L. Hess, was invited into the house but did not find the atmosphere cozy:

> Although of a younger generation, I knew Howard's mother better than I knew Howard who even as a young boy was strange and rather a recluse, who kept by himself and hid from other children, because, as his mother said, he could not bear to have people look upon his awful face. She would talk of his looks (it seemed to be an obsession with her) which would not have attracted any particular attention if he had been normal as were the other children in the community. They, because of the strangeness of his personality, kept aloof and had little to say to him.
>
> I first remember meeting Mrs. Lovecraft when I was a very little girl at the home of the late Mr. and Mrs. Theodore [read, "Whipple"] Phillips on Angell Street where I visited often. At that time Mrs. Lovecraft [then Susie Phillips] was living on the corner of Angell Street and Elmgrove Avenue [at 454 Angell Street]. She was very pretty and attractive, with a beautiful and unusually white complexion. . . . She was an intensely nervous person.

Later when she moved into a little downstairs flat in the house on Angell Street around the corner from Butler Avenue I met her often on the Butler Avenue cars, and one day after many urgent invitations I went to call on her. She was considered then to be getting rather odd. My call was pleasant enough but the house had a strange and shutup air and the atmosphere seemed weird and Mrs. Lovecraft talked continuously of her unfortunate son who was so hideous that he hid from everyone and did not like to walk the streets where people could gaze at him.

When I protested that she was exaggerating and that he should not feel that way, she looked at me with a rather pitiful look as though I did not understand about it. . . . Surely it was an environment suited for the writing of horror stories but an unfortunate one for a growing youth who in a more wholesome environment might have grown to be a more normal citizen.

Howard used to go out into the fields back of my home to study the stars. One early fall evening several of the children in the vicinity assembled to watch him from a distance. Feeling sorry for his loneliness I went up to him and asked him about his telescope and was permitted to look through it. But his language was so technical that I could not understand it. . . .

After a time one did not meet Mrs. Lovecraft very often. . . . Sometimes when going around the corner to mail a letter on an early summer evening, one would see a dark figure fluttering about the shubbery of her house, and I discovered that it was Mrs. Lovecraft.

I remember the aunts who came to the little house on Angell Street often, as I recollect, quiet, determined little New England women, quite different from Mrs. Lovecraft, although Mrs. Lovecraft was a very determined person herself. I remember Mrs. Lovecraft spoke to me about weird and fantastic creatures that rushed out from behind buildings and from corners at dark, and that she shivered and looked about apprehensively as she told her story.[8]

It is not surprising that HPL should write about "shunned houses" with spooky atmospheres, when he himself had so long dwelt in one. Nor need we look further than Susie Lovecraft's hallucinations of "weird and fantastic creatures" for the source of Lovecraft's malign alien entities, waiting to snatch the earth away from the rule of man.

The haunted-house feel of the place had not changed a few years later, when Lovecraft began to emerge from his shell. In September, 1917, his friend in amateur journalism, W. Paul Cook, called upon him for the first time. Cook, a printer by trade, reminisced:

I was bound from New York to Boston, and broke my trip in Providence purposely to see Lovecraft. . . . Arriving at the address on Angell Street which later was to be the best known address in Amateur Journalism, I was met at the door by Howard's mother and aunt. Howard had been up all night studying and writing, had just gone to bed, and must under no circumstance be disturbed. If I would go to the Crown hotel, register, get a room and wait, they would telephone when, and if, Howard woke up. . . . It was essential that I be in Boston early that evening, which allowed me about three hours in Providence, but there was a train leaving in half an hour which I could catch if I kept moving. I had a life-like picture of myself hanging around Providence until His Majesty was ready to receive me! . . . I was part way to the sidewalk and the door was almost latched when Howard appeared in dressing gown and slippers. Wasn't that W. Paul Cook and wasn't it understood that he was to be seen immediately on his arrival? I was almost forcibly ushered [in] by the guardians of the gate and into Howard's study. Even then when Howard thought it advisable to assert himself his wishes ruled, although it was with extreme reluctance and anxiety that he was permitted to contact a harsh world. But to cross him would sap his strength. (I really should not use that word "contact" here. Howard hated it. "I hope," I said, "you will excuse me for using that word." "Well, I won't," said Howard. He would admit to no elasticity or natural growth in our language. . . .)

In later life, Lovecraft came around to admitting that usage—at least, the usage of fastidious writers like Cabell and Wharton—was the final authority for correctness in English. Cook continued:

That day for about an hour and a half I listened to a monologue—more properly a lecture. Howard had but recently heard of Amateur Journalism. . . . As a newcomer he of course knew all about what was the matter with it. . . . Every few minutes Howard's mother, or his aunt, or both, peeped into the room to see if he had fainted or shown signs of strain. . . .[9]

Under this regime, Lovecraft became a lifelong hypochondriac—although he neglected his health and forwent medical attention. The willing prisoner of his hallucinated mother, he understood, long afterwards, what had been done to him. He and his friend Price were arguing by letter over a story by their young colleague Derleth. Lovecraft said:

I don't think the non-escape of the rebellious daughter is at all unlifelike. People do get bound & paralysed like that—helpless in the face of a family feeling which overshadows everything else. One sees it often amongst the ancient New England stock. It is, of course, lamentably unwholesome, & we may thank the modern age for removing much of the basis of this type of psychosis.

It is obvious to whom Lovecraft referred.

Lovecraft was not, however, completely isolated. He remained close friends with Chester Munroe and often visited the Munroe house. Their father, Addison P. Munroe, recalled:

> Howard was a most peculiar character, a recluse with a brilliant mind but many strange ideas. He invariably stayed up all night and slept all day. At the time I saw much of him, probably no power on earth could have induced him to sleep in any bed but his own. He was diffident and shy, and while I would not say he had an inferiority complex, I would say that he lacked self-confidence. Not being around in the daytime, he met few people and his circle of acquaintances was small. He was not at ease with the other sex and was only at his best when with a few chosen male friends.
>
> He lived but a few houses distant from our home and was quite frequently over here with our sons. I remember that we had a room fixed up in our basement for the boys to use as a club room, which was a popular place with Howard. The club, so called, consisted of about a half-dozen of the neighborhood boys, around twenty years of age, and when they had a so-called "banquet," improvised and usually self-cooked, Howard was always the speaker of the evening and my boys always said he delivered addresses that were gems.
>
> Occasionally I would have an opportunity to talk with him and he always surprised me with the maturity and logic of his talk. I remember one time in particular, when I was a member of the R. I. Senate, 1911–1914, we had several important measures before that body; Howard, being over here one evening, started to discuss some of these measures, and I was astounded by the knowledge that he displayed in regard to measures that ordinarily would be of no interest to a young fellow of twenty.[10]

In 1916, Chester Munroe moved to the South, went into the hotel business, and did not return to Providence for many years. His brother Harold became a sheriff and finally a parole and probation counselor. The other members of the circle grew away from Lovecraft, so that he rarely saw them.

Still, Lovecraft was not left entirely alone. For, in his middle twenties, his health improved and he developed new interests.

In his early twenties, Lovecraft looked much as he did throughout life. He was just under five feet, eleven inches tall, with broad but stooped shoulders, and (save for a few years in the early 1920s) lean to gauntness, with a size fourteen neck that seemed thin to support his large head. He had dark eyes and hair (which later turned mousey gray) and a long face with an aquiline nose. His salient feature was a very long chin—a "lantern jaw"—below a small, pursed-up mouth, which gave him a prim look.

He parted his hair on the left and kept it cut short, almost in a crew cut. He justified this coiffure on the ground that eighteenth-century gentlemen wore their hair thus under their wigs.

Ingrown hairs on his face bothered him all his life. The only cure for this condition is to grow a beard; but, as a devotee of the clean-shaven Baroque Era, Lovecraft hated all facial hair; he said: "I'd as soon think of wearing a nose-ring as of growing a mustache. . . ." Later, when some of his young literary protégés grew mustaches (or, worse yet, goatees) he carped at them in letter after letter, urging them to take off the offending growths.

His skin was pale from his nocturnal habits. Cook reported that "he never liked to tan, and a trace of color in his cheeks seemed somehow to be a source of annoyance. He was the only person I ever met to be ashamed of a coat of tan." Perhaps this was part of his archaistic pose. Before the Industrial Revolution, pallor was deemed aristocratic. Since most proletarians labored out of doors, a tan was the stigma of a plebeian occupation. In any case, Lovecraft got over this quirk late in life, when he found how much good the sunshine of Florida did him.

He had long, pale, slender hands and small feet. Because of his poikilothermism, his hands were colder than people expected. To shake hands with him was a little like shaking hands with a corpse.

In dress, he was clean and neat but ultraconservative in taste. In his twenties, he affected an aggressively old-fashioned appearance: "a sedulous cultivation of premature elderliness and sartorial antiquarianism manifesting itself in stiff bosom shirt, round cuffs, black coat and vest and grey striped trousers, standing collar and black string tie, &c—with austere and reticent manners to match."[11] He also donned black bow ties and high-buttoned shoes and carried an old-fashioned change purse. He wore his father's elegant nineteenth-century garments until they wore out.

Even after he gave up this affectation, however, he remained conservative in dress. He preferred dark suits without patterns, and black or navy-blue neckties, either plain or with minute polka dots. Any bold pattern or bright color he rejected as "too youthful."

To Lovecraft in his twenties, it was unthinkable to appear in company without his coat or to go out hatless. He felt about such deshabille as did the man in Marquand's novel:

> "One morning, as Tim, the coachman, came up with the carriage . . . my father, who had not gone down to his office at the usual early hour . . . came out with us to the front steps. I could not have been more than seven at the time, but I remember the exclamation he gave when he observed the brownstone steps of the house across the street.
>
> "'Thunderation,' Father said, 'there is a man in his shirt sleeves on those steps.' The next day he sold his house for what he had paid for it and we moved to Beacon Street."

Lovecraft's voice was high-pitched, with the flat, nasal quality often heard in New England. When he sang, it was a clear, sweet tenor. About 1907 he owned an Edison recording machine, into which he sang tenor solos. He even thought of a singing career, but the record "reminded me so much of the wail of a dying fox-terrier that I very carelessly happened to drop it soon after it was made."

When he spoke, especially with emphasis, his voice became harsh. When he heard a phonograph recording of his own voice, he described it as a "raucous squawk." He smiled easily but laughed seldom, and his laugh has been described as a "harsh cackle."[12]

When excited, he tended to stutter. His normal pronunciation was that of cultivated Rhode Island, rhyming "farce" and "grass"; "scarf," "laugh," and "half"; and "aren't," "aunt," and can't." His normal speech tended, like his writing, to be pedantically polysyllabic; he was the kind who, instead of "I'm going to get a drink," would say: "I shall endeavor to procure liquid refreshment."

With strangers, his manner was shy, stiff, and over-formal; but, when he knew people well enough to unbend with them, he became a charming conversationalist. His celebrated eighteenth-century-gentleman pose was assumed in a playful, whimsical spirit and not taken seriously.

Late in 1909, an attack of measles "damn near finished me." From then on, aside from his psychoneurotic weakness, his health was fairly good, especially considering his odd hours, unbalanced diet, and lack of regular exercise. He disliked the attentions of physicians and dentists and visited them only at long intervals. He looked normal, and the doctors could find nothing definitely wrong with him.

When he was thirty, a fellow amateur journalist, a Brooklyn lawyer named George Julian Houtain, called on him at his home and shortly thereafter saw him at an amateur journalists' convention. Houtain reported in his magazine:

> Lovecraft honestly believes he is not strong—that he has an inherited nervousness and fatigue wished upon him. One would never suspect in his massive form and well constructed body that there could be any ailment. . . . I came to the conclusion that he is willing to overcome this and would but he isn't allowed to do so, because others in his immediate household won't permit him to forget this hereditary nervousness. As it is Lovecraft is a mental and physical giant, not because of, but in spite of these conditions.

In a letter, Lovecraft plaintively defended his invalidism:

> If you received G. J. Houtain's Zenith you will see how I impress a stranger—as a husky, pampered hypochondriac, tied down to indolence by indulgent relatives, and by false notions of heredity. If Houtain knew how constant are my struggles against the devastating headaches, dizzy spells, and spells of poor concentrating power which hedge me on all sides, and how feverishly I try to utilise every available moment for work, he would be less confident in classifying my ills as imaginary.

The term "psychosomatic illness" had not yet come into general use, but Lovecraft grasped the concept. Much later, he wrote:

> The more we know of psychology, the less distinction we are able to make betwixt the functional disorders known as "mental" & those known as "physical." Nothing is more unfortunate than a neurotic temperament, & I am just enough inclined that way myself to sympathise deeply with anyone else who suffers from shadowy depressions. Many times in my youth I was so exhausted by the sheer burden of consciousness & mental & physical activity that I had to drop out of school for a greater or lesser period & take a complete rest free from all responsibilities. . . .

Lovecraft's idiosyncratic tastes in food certainly did not promote his health. Towards food in general he was indifferent, despising gourmanderie and priding himself on a spare diet. He thought that his brain worked better when it was slightly starved.

Despite his mother's efforts to stuff him, he watched his weight, trying to keep below 150 pounds. Leanness, he thought, was aristocratic. He objected strongly when he saw that his friend Cook, a small man but a hearty eater, was putting on weight. On Thanksgiving Day, 1911, he could not be bothered with getting up to attend the feast to which he and his mother had been bidden at the Clarks'. Instead, he wrote Susie a jingle:

> If, as you start toward Lillies' festive spread,
> You find me snoring loudly in my bed,
> Awake me not, for I would fain repose,
> And through the day in quiet slumber doze.
> But lest I starve, for lack of food to eat,
> Leave here a dish of Quaker Puffed Wheat,
> Or breakfast biscuit, which, it matters not,
> To break my fast when out of bed I've got.
> And if to supper you perchance should stay,
> Thus to complete a glorious festive day,
> Announce the fact to me by telephone,
> That whilst you eat, I may prepare my own.[13]

He disliked milk and fat, abhorred sea food, and was picky about vegetables, disliking string beans and asparagus. He had a passion for cheese ("How can anybody dislike *cheese?*" he wrote), for ice cream, for coffee with four to eight spoonfuls of sugar in each cup, and for candy. A caller once found Lovecraft's bathtub full of empty candy boxes. In 1927, he and his friends Donald Wandrei and James Morton stopped at Mrs. Julia A. Maxfield's Ice Cream Parlor in Warren, Rhode Island, which advertised thirty-two flavors of ice cream.

"Are they all available?" asked Lovecraft.

"No," said the waiter, "only twenty-eight today, sir."

"Ah, the decay of modern commercial institutions!" sighed Lovecraft. Each of the three ordered a double portion in a different flavor and traded parts of his serving with the others, so that each got three flavors with each serving. Wandrei soon dropped out, but Morton and Lovecraft continued triumphantly through the whole twenty-eight flavors, consuming more than two quarts of ice cream apiece at one sitting.

Lovecraft had a genuine horror of sea food. Any attempt to make him eat it, he said, would cause instant vomiting. When somebody quietly set before him a salad containing sea food, he at once put it aside, convinced by its smell that whatever it was made of had spoiled.

When Edgar Hoffmann Price visited Lovecraft in 1933, he took his guest to Pawtuxet so that Price could enjoy its famed steamed-clam dinner. Lovecraft ordered for Price and said: "While you are eating that God-damned stuff, I'll go across the street for a sandwich; please excuse me." Lovecraft rarely swore. He saved his "damns" for state occasions, of which the sight of a person eating that "horrible stuff" was one. It is no coincidence that the monsters of his later stories resemble combinations of various denizens of an aquarium, given colossal size and malignant intelligence.

Lovecraft's hatred of sea food has been related to an alleged fear and dislike of the sea. He often used the sea, along with cold, wet, and darkness, as a symbol of evil in his stories. He once told Donald Wandrei: "I have hated fish and feared the sea and everything connected with it since I was two years old."[14] Such aversions can be the result of becoming painfully sick just after eating the food in question—whether or not the food was the cause—and this may have been the case with Lovecraft.

As far as the sea is concerned, this was mere histrionics. Lovecraft spent most of his life in port cities. Most of his travels were to seaports, and he delighted in the few steamship voyages he took into the open sea.

Although he never owned a pet after Nigger-Man's disappearance, Lovecraft doted on cats. He said: "I have no active dislike for dogs, any more than I have for monkeys, human beings, tradesmen, cows, sheep, or pterodactyls." Other remarks about dogs, however, as "noisy, smelly, pawing, slobbering, messy" and "panting, wheezing, fumbling, drooling," imply an active dislike. The mention of pawing and slobbering points to a distaste for physical contact with other creatures, which Lovecraft probably got from his mother.

He made friends with all the neighborhood cats wherever he lived and got them in the habit of calling on him by keeping catnip mice for them to play with. He lavishly praised their beauty, grace, self-sufficiency, and other supposed aristocratic qualities: "Dogs, then, are peasants and the pets of peasants, cats are gentlemen and the pets of gentlemen."[15] When he visited Cook, and a kitten went to sleep in his lap, he sat up all night rather than disturb the animal.

Other physical attributes of Howard Phillips Lovecraft were his immunity to poison ivy and his ability to go without sleep for long periods. When he met Price in New Orleans in 1932, they spent a straight twenty-eight hours in talk, sight-seeing, and socializing. At the end of that time, Price was glad to collapse into bed. When he awoke, eight hours later, it was to see Lovecraft, who had not yet retired, busily writing notes on his trip.

Besides the psychological explanations that have been given for Lovecraft's nocturnal habits—that night stimulates the imagination, or that he took to heart his mother's claim that he was "hideous" —there may have been a metabolic factor. Visitors reported that Lovecraft seemed wan and weary by day but came brightly alive as night approached. Most of his writing was done at night. When he did work in the daytime, he simulated night by pulling down the shades and turning on the electric light. Starrett wrote:

> . . . he was his own most fantastic creation—a Roderick Usher or C. Auguste Dupin born a century too late. Like his heroes in Poe's gigantic nightmare, he fancied himself as a cadaverous, mysterious figure of the night—a pallid, scholarly necrologist—and cultivated a natural resemblance until it was almost the real thing, although he was first and last a "literary cove."

One of his longtime friends, Alfred Galpin, remembered his early impressions of Lovecraft thus:

> All who met Howard, so far as I can tell, no matter how strange they may have found him at first, liked him spontaneously and cordially. He was certainly one of those persons whose unsociable ways—if and when he was unsociable—were due to a sense of isolation from people among whom he might find himself thrown by chance, without any sense of communion; but when he felt himself in congenial company, he had a boyish charm and enthusiasm which completely overshadowed his well-known physical peculiarities: the strange half dead, half arrogant cock of his head weighed down by its enormous jaw, the rather fishy eyes belied by his animated and friendly manner when he began to speak—but with what a strange high-pitched voice!

Profoundly shy, Lovecraft practiced a gentlemanly reserve and imperturbability until it came naturally to him. When angered, he merely became more coldly polite. This ideal of complete emotional self-control may have contributed to his dislike for people of Mediterranean origin, with their more vivacious, extroverted cultural tradition.

He thought of himself as a kind of disembodied intellect, undistracted by human passions: "I shall never be very merry or very sad, for I am more prone to analyse than to feel. What merriment I have is always derived from the satirical principle, and what sadness I have, is not so much personal, as a vast and terrible melancholy at the pain and futility of all existence. . . ."[16]

Later, he showed that inside the old Lovecraft there had been quite a different one struggling to get out: gregarious, garrulous, charming, warm-hearted, and physically fairly active. This Lovecraft did succeed in emerging—but only part way, and too late to make much difference in the over-all pattern of his life. Then he sadly confessed: "I vastly regret the absence of traditional accomplishments—fencing, horsemanship, military service, &c. &c. caused by my early ill health & lack of appreciation of the quality of well-roundedness."

In his fallow period, Lovecraft said, he had been extravagant: "Up to 1910 or 1915 there was no one more recklessly careless of expenditures than I—even though the big collapse in family fortunes had come as far back as 1904. My mother used to say that I was absolutely ruined as a handler of money, & utterly spoiled as an endurer of poverty."

Although Susie may have said these things, it is hard to see what Lovecraft could have spent much money on—a few pieces of astronomical and chemical apparatus before 1912, and thereafter books and magazines. He had no automobile, traveled nowhere, and never owned a large wardrobe. The usual vices of gluttony, drink, gambling, and fornication were not his. From his later twenties on, he certainly led a life of stringent economy, saving all his old safety-razor blades to resharpen them on a patent sharpener.[17]

Had Lovecraft continued along the path he had marked out during his torpid years, he would have lived as one of the most obscure of mortals and probably died, as did both parents, in a hospital for those of unsound mind. Instead, during the years 1913–17 he gradually awoke and began the slow, painful process of rejoining the human race.

During this time, he resumed his astronomical newspaper articles. He began to build up a circle of correspondents. He entered the amateur journalism movement and acquired personal friends to replace the scattered chums of his boyhood. And he read a certain book. This book sent him off on a bizarre pseudo-scientific tangent, which took him twenty years to correct and which has furnished his bitterest critics with ammunition ever since.

Six

AMATEUR SUPERMAN

Why are base foreign boors allow'd to dwell
Amongst the hills where Saxon greatness fell;
Live their low lives, themselves in filth degrade
As monkeys haunt a palace long decay'd? . . .
The village rings with ribald foreign cries;
Around the wine-shops loaf with bleary eyes
A vicious crew, that mock the name of "man,"
Yet dare to call themselves "American."[1]

LOVECRAFT

In 1913, the health of the twenty-two-year-old Lovecraft improved, albeit he long continued to describe himself as "practically a nervous wreck, unable to attend to anything regularly, or to keep definite engagements." He complained of fatigue and lassitude and of feeling already middle-aged. "Adulthood," he wrote, "is hell."[2]

Nonetheless, he began to emerge from his seclusion, like a hibernating insect testing the air of spring with a cautious antenna. The first sign of his emergence was a 1,300-word letter, in what he himself called "quaint Queen-Anne prose," to *The Argosy*. The letter denounced the works of the popular author Fred Jackson. This man's sin had been to write love stories:

Whilst I am not wishful to be unduly censorious of any author, I must own that the Jacksonesque style of narrative inspires in me far less of interest than of distaste, and must express my wonderment at the extraordinary favour accorded its originator by the publishers of *The Argosy* and *Cavalier*. . . .

There is a numerous set of people whose chief literary delight is obtained in the following of imaginary nymphs and swains through the labyrinthine paths of amorous adventure, and who deem an account of an affection won or lost quite as exciting and entertaining as that of a kingdom saved or destroyed.

To such as these are the fictions of Jackson well suited; but these, methinks, are not the average readers of *The Argosy*. The latter prefer, I am sure, a sprightlier sort of story, where acts of valor are more dwelt upon than affairs of Venus. For mine own part, I have ever preferred the Aeneid of Virgil to the Ars Amatoria of Ovid.

Apart from the mere choice of subject, let me venture to describe the Jacksonine type as trivial, effeminate, and, in places, coarse.

The author remarks the costumes of his heroines with the minute attention of a mantua-maker and describes the furnishings and decorations of their apartments like a housewife or chambermaid.[3]

And so on for two full columns. As for the "coarseness" of Jackson's "erotic fiction": compared to that of today, all magazine fiction was then as mild as milk toast. But so strongly had Lovecraft been sexually inhibited that any treatment of this basic division of the species made him uncomfortable.

The letter brought a spate of replies. The fact that Lovecraft had complained of Jackson's "outlandish words" gave his critics an opening:

If he would use a few less adjectives and more words which the general public are familiar with than labyrinthine, laureled, luminary, lucubration, and many others. . . .

I get sore at people like H. P. L. I will pay his fifteen cents a month if he will quit reading *Argosy*. Jackson is great. . . . I am a cow-puncher, and certainly would like to loosen up my .44-six on that man Lovecraft. Yours for luck. Excuse pencil, as ink is scarce at the Bijou Ranch.[4]

Unsuppressed, Lovecraft replied with a forty-six-line poem, *Ad Criticos:*

What vig'rous protests now assail my eyes?
See Jackson's satellites in anger rise!
His ardent readers, steep'd in tales of love,
Sincere devotion to their leader prove;
In brave defense of sickly gallantry,
They damn the critic and beleaguer me. . . .
Scrawl on, sweet Jackson, raise the lover's leer;
'Tis plain you please the fallen public ear.
As once, in Charles the Second's vulgar age,
Gross Wycherly and Dryden soil'd the stage,
So now again erotic themes prevail,
However loud the sterner souls bewail. . . .[5]

The war of words continued through 1914. Inspired by *Ad Criticos*, some readers put their comments into verse. John Russell, a Scotchman living in Tampa, Florida, wrote:

Lovecraft has dropped from rime to prose,
To shew that what he knew, he knows.
I say that really to my view
'Twas little that he even knew. . . .
He says a novel he will write,
Our ardent passions to enlight.
Each reader then will have to carry
The latest published dictionary.[6]

In the issue of October, 1914, the editor set aside a section of "The Log Book" with the subtitle: "Fred Jackson, Pro and Con," and filled it with letters for and against Jackson and Lovecraft. Meanwhile Lovecraft, amused by Russell's rhymed rejoinders, had written him and struck up a friendship. They sent in a pair of joint poems. Russell's was *The End of the Jackson War:*

Indulgent sir, pray spare an inch or two,
And print the carping critics' joint adieu.
So long it is since we began the fray
That readers swear we've filched your Log away!
Forgive, we beg, the sinners that presume
To fill with venomed verse such precious room. . . .
But fiercest feuds draw sometimes to their ends,
And ancient foemen live to meet as friends:
So do we now, conjoin'd in lasting peace,
Lay down our pens, and mutual slander cease.
What sound is this? 'Tis but a joyous yell
From thankful thousands, as we say farewell.

Lovecraft composed *Our Apology to E. M. W.*:

> *'Tis the voice of the knocker,*
> *Just hear him complain:*
> *"Here's Lovecraft and Russell,*
> *With verses again.*
> *I really do think*
> *It is a disgrace*
> *The way they use up*
> *Your valuable space.*
> *The Log-Book is just*
> *For critical use,*
> *And not, as they think,*
> *For sarcastic abuse.*
> *So please, Mr. Editor,*
> *Tell them to quit,*
> *Or they will both finish*
> *By thinking they're IT."*
>
> *Don't vex yourself more,*
> *My dear E. M. W.,*
> *For we'll never again,*
> *With our verses trouble you.*[7]

The controversy died, but Lovecraft kept on writing to *Argosy* and *All-Story*. A letter in the latter states his fictional preferences: "In the present age of vulgar taste and sordid realism it is a relief to peruse a publication such as *The All-Story*, which has ever been and still remains under the influence of the imaginative schools of Poe and Verne. . . ."

His last letters in the Munsey magazines, in 1919–20, praised the adventure-story writer Francis Stevens, one of his favorites along with Zane Grey and Edgar Rice Burroughs. He also worked in a dig:

"Why not have one of your able corps of writers give us a bang-up good story without the hugging and kissing end? There is such a thing as being fed up with the love business."[8]

Poor Lovecraft, who had never had a date with a girl, had never been alone with one, and had not been kissed even by his mother since childhood! Those last two letters in *Argosy* were signed "Augustus T. Swift," for Lovecraft had taken to the lavish use of pseudonyms. This name combined the term "Augustan Age," applied to the reign of Queen Anne (1704–14), with the surname of one of its luminaries. Lovecraft was then a busy contributor to amateur journals. Often having two or more pieces in a single issue, he used pen names to avoid the appearance of monopolizing their space. Besides Augustus T. Swift, he also appeared as Lawrence Appleton, John J. Jones, Humphrey Littlewit, Archibald Mainwaring, Henry Paget-Lowe, Ward Phillips, Richard Raleigh, Ames Dorance Rowley, Edward Softly, Lewis Theobald, Jr., Albert Frederic Willie, and Zoilus.

All but the last are good Old American names, some from Lovecraft's family tree. This use of pseudonyms has given Lovecraft's bibliographers some knotty problems. Hence all of Lovecraft's writings may never be completely identified.[9]

While the Jackson War raged, Lovecraft, who had kept up his astronomical notebook, revived his newspaper feature. Beginning January 1, 1914, the *Providence Evening News* carried his monthly astronomical column. This feature ran without a break until May, 1918. Then, as Lovecraft put it, "the paper was sold to the Democrats" and "a change of management produced a demand for a changed style to which I refused to accede."[10] Another series of eighteen astronomical articles appeared in 1915 in the Asheville, North Carolina, *Gazette-News*. Lovecraft's connection with this paper was probably effected by his boyhood friend Chester Munroe, then living in Asheville.

The articles in the *News* ran 1,400 to 1,800 words each. They usually appeared on the first day of the month but sometimes a few days one way or the other. They gave the bald astronomical facts—the phases of the moon and the positions of the constellations and the planets—but much else as well.

Lovecraft retold the old myths about the planets and the constellations, quoting ancient poems by Aratos, Manilius, and Ovid, as translated by Dryden, Addison, and other Baroque writers. He also included a few of his own poems. He eloquently lectured his readers on the history of astronomy and the philosophy of science:

Above the southeastern horizon in fierce gorgeousness crawls the Scorpion, with its brilliant fire-red star Antares; a fitting portent of the flaming scenes which await our warriors on the Hun-infested plains of France. Scorpio is the most spectacular and characteristic of the summer groups, and will blaze radiantly in the months to come. West of Scorpio, and reaching completely to the meridian, the uppermost parts of Centaurus line the horizon. The entire group, including its brightest stars, is never visible in this latitude. Alpha Centauri, the brightest star of this constellation, is the nearest of our stellar neighbours, lying at a distance of 25,000,000,000,-000 miles from the solar system. That so vast an interval in terrestrial terms should be reckoned as infinitesimally small in terms of siderial space, is an eloquent testimony to the unbounded magnitude of the visible universe, to say nothing of the stupendous conception of absolute infinity. The consideration of boundless space and time is indeed the most thought-provoking feature of astronomical science. Humanity with its pompous pretensions sinks to complete nothingness when viewed in relation to the unfathomed abysses of infinity and eternity which yawn about it. The entire period of existence of mankind, or of the sun and solar system, or of the visible universe itself, is but an inconsequential instant in the history of the whirling spheres and ether currents that compose all creation; a history which has neither beginning nor ending. Man, so far from being the central and supreme object of Nature, is clearly demonstrated to be a mere incident, perhaps an accident, of a natural scheme whose boundless reach relegates him to total insignificance. His presence or absence, his life or death, are obviously matters of utter indifference to the plan of Nature as a whole. Even the vast universe we behold is but an atom in the absolutely unlimited expanse which stretches away on all sides. . . . A recent writer has attempted a portrayal of astronomical infinity in blank verse, describing a dream or vision in this fashion:

> Alone in space, I view'd a feeble fleck
> Of silvern light, marking the narrow ken
> Which mortals call the boundless universe.
> On ev'ry side, each as a tiny star,
> Shone more creations, vaster than our own.
> As on a moonless night, the Milky Way
> In solid sheen displays its countless orbs
> To weak terrestrial eyes, each orb a sun;
> So beam'd the prospect on my wond'ring soul;
> A spangled curtain, rich with twinkling gems.
> Yet each a mighty universe of suns—
> And all the universe in my view
> But a poor atom in infinity.

The "recent writer" is Lovecraft himself. Another time he dwelt, with gloomy relish, on eventual running down of the universe:

It is a fundamental principle of the science of physics, that neither matter nor energy may be created or destroyed. Since the stars and nebulae are constantly distributing energy in the form of light and heat, and since they cannot create more to replace that which they are losing, it follows that some day their activity must all be dissipated into infinity as unvariable waves of radiant heat, too feeble to produce any perceptible effects. The resulting scene of desolation will be terrible indeed. A vast sepulchral universe of unbroken midnight gloom and perpetual arctic frigidity, through which will roll, dark and cold, suns with their hordes of dead, frozen planets, on which will lie the dust of those unhappy mortals who will have perished as their dominant stars faded from the skies.

While writing his columns, Lovecraft locked horns with another *News* contributor, the astrologer Hartmann. In one of his early columns, Lovecraft declared:

> It is with regret that the writer notes at the present time a rather virulent epidemic of astrological quackery in this city. Belief in the fortune-telling power of the stars and planets is of course superstition of the grossest sort, and a most incongruous feature of this enlightened age; yet astrology is a plague which has proved most difficult to eradicate, and only too many persons of indifferent education are still the dupes of its absurd pretentions.
>
> Since it is practically impossible under our existing laws to prosecute and punish astrologers who do not use the mails in plying their nefarious trade, we must attack the evil at another point, and seek to undermine astrology by diffusing astronomical truth, and thus lifting the public above the range of the charlatans who now flourish because of the general condition of ignorance.[11]

Lovecraft also contributed articles titled "Science versus Charlatanry" and "The Falsity of Astrology." When Hartmann continued to publish his Babylonian pseudo-science, Lovecraft remembered the campaign of Dean Jonathan Swift against the astrologer Partridge. In 1708, Swift issued a pamphlet, under the pseudonym of "Isaac Bickerstaff," which astrologically predicted the death of Partridge among others. When the date had passed, Swift issued another pamphlet, announcing that Partridge had died as foretold. The pamphlet convinced many, and Partridge had a terrible time proving that he still lived.

Burlesquing Hartmann, Lovecraft ran articles as "Isaac Bickerstaffe, Jr.," wherein he made ever more fantastic predictions, as that the earth would be blown up in A.D. 4952 but that mankind would be saved by hopping a passing comet to Venus. But alas for Lovecraft's hopes of educating the public out of belief in astrology! Rational men have been trying to do that ever since Marcus Tullius Cicero, but the hoary superstition still thrives.

Lovecraft bore the banner of scientific materialism all his life. In 1917, a "correspondent pretended to have dreams parallel to certain ones of my own which I had mentioned," by way of arguing an occult or telepathic sympathy between Lovecraft and the correspondent. Lovecraft made up fake dreams, of which he sent the correspondent splendidly detailed descriptions. Sure enough, the correspondent came back with equally impressive accounts of dreams that he had had, paralleling those that Lovecraft had concocted but had never dreamed at all.

As a result of the war of words over Fred Jackson, Lovecraft discovered amateur journalism, which goes back a century as an organized hobby. Many well-known persons, including Benjamin Franklin, Robert Louis Stevenson, and Thomas Edison, have in their youth printed magazines and journals of their own and their friends' authorship, for fun rather than for money.

The hobby, however, greatly expanded with the invention, in the later 1860s, of several makes of small, cheap printing presses. Amateur publishers began exchanging their publications, as science-fiction fans did from the 1930s on.

Americans are notoriously the world's most avid organizers. Cast a few away on a desert island, and their first act will be to draw up a constitution, elect officers, and appoint committees. Hence amateur journalists, like the nation's other hobbyists, got together and organized. A National Amateur Press Association was founded in 1870–71 but in 1874 expired for lack of interest. A second club of the same name was formed in 1876 and steadily grew.

Many amateur journalists were frustrated writers, frustrated printers, or frustrated politicians. They competed, feuded, and intrigued with the zeal and craft of candidates for public office. They recruited new members, telling them that their writings were too good for commercial outlets. As Lovecraft put it:

Amateur journalism is a pastime, but it is more than a common pastime. It is at bottom a spontaneous striving for untrammelled artistic expression on the part of those unable to speak as they choose through the recognized literary channels; and as such it possesses the fundamentals which make for permanent endurance.[12]

Amateur publications varied vastly in format and in quality. Many got no further than Vol. I, No. 1. They often exasperate the researcher by omitting such details as dates or page numbers. Many have been printed on paper of such poor quality that now, half a century or more later, it is crumbling into dust.

For many, amateur journalism was an agreeable, harmless hobby, not too costly and not altogether unconstructive. Like other hobbyists, however, some took their avocation more seriously than their vocations. They became immersed in amateur journalism to the exclusion of other interests. For several years, Lovecraft fell into this class.

In the 1890s, writers of letters to readers' columns in boys' magazines formed the United Amateur Press Association. It was not hatched as a rival to the NAPA, because the founders did not know about the older organization. Relations between the two groups were usually friendly, although hostility flared up whenever somebody proposed that the two societies unite.

Both associations went through storms, with accusations of election fraud and of illegal official actions. Officials were ousted; members were expelled; associations fissioned like amebae. The UAPA split into two factions in 1900 and, after these had been reunited, into three in 1905.

In 1912, after a contested UAPA election, the winner, Harry Shepherd, expelled the runner-up, Helene E. Hoffman, from the association on grounds of insurrection. Miss Hoffman then pronounced herself the true, legal president and set up her own faction as a rival organization, with Edward F. Daas as official editor and Maurice Winter Moe, a Wisconsin schoolteacher, as official critic. The critic's job was to read all the members' amateur journals sent in for distribution and to write articles for the official organ tactfully criticizing them.

Thus, in 1914, there were two groups, each calling itself the United Amateur Press Association. The factions even published two official organs of the same title, *The United Amateur*.

Then Daas noted the exchange of letters between Lovecraft and John Russell in *The Argosy*. Thinking that such literary zest ought not to go to waste, he got in touch with both. He called on Lovecraft on his way to New York for a meeting of the Blue Pencil Club, the New Yorkese local amateur journalistic society. He urged both Lovecraft and Russell to join his faction of the UAPA. Edward H. Cole of Somerville, Massachusetts, long active in both NAPA and UAPA, sent Lovecraft a bundle of amateur papers to criticize. (In 1916, Cole married Miss Hoffman. Three years later, Mrs. Cole died in a minor surgical operation.) Lovecraft replied:

> It is not likely that my first efforts on the critical board will attain the high standard which you set, yet I hope that I may not win your unqualified condemnation. My aim shall be for justness, simplicity, and charity, rather than for brilliancy or the display of literary attainments, and I shall look upon your own luminous reviews rather as models than as objects of rivalry.
>
> While I can scarcely expect my laboured prose and ponderous heroic couplets to meet with approbation from one so correct in his tastes, I shall await with eagerness the impartial verdicts of the REVIEWER on several literary attempts of mine which are shortly to appear in various amateur publications. My ideal in English is the restoration of eighteenth-century dignity and regularity both in prose and in verse; an ideal which very few share with me, and which will probably provoke much caustic sarcasm. . . .

After some experience as an official critic of amateur publications, Maurice W. Moe came to the cynical conclusion that such criticism was "vain, ineffective, & superfluous," because "the ordinary mind can never be influenced by mere advice, more or less mingled with flattery; and that on the other hand, real criticism arouses so much antagonism on the part of the subject that its purpose is entirely defeated." Lovecraft, however, continued to serve on boards of critics and to write columns of amateur criticism all the rest of his life, in hope of raising national standards of literature.

Although Lovecraft attained great influence in amateur journalism, he never succeeded in converting his fellow-hobbyists to eighteenth-century usage. He had, however, been showering amateur papers with essays and Baroque poems. Since non-paying publications always have trouble in filling their space with literate material, the amateur publishers were delighted to print the poems, although Lovecraft himself had begun to have doubts about them.

These poems included eulogies of his new friends in amateur

journalism, praise of England and the British Empire, denuncia-
tions of Germany, and insipid Georgian pastorals such as *To Spring*:

> *Arise, ye swains! for fair Aurora's light*
> *Shews the wild geese in scurrying matin flight;*
> *In shifting ranks their silent course they take,*
> *And for the valley marshland quit the lake:*
> *Tho' loose they fly, in various modes arrang'd,*
> *Their eyes are steady, and their goal unchang'd. . . .*[13]

And so on for a page and a half. Lovecraft had apparently
never heard a flock of wild geese on the wing. His poems found
ready acceptance because, while the longer ones are the best in-
somnia cures I know of, they still looked good by comparison with
the competition. One has no idea of the quantity of bad poetry
that has been written until one has gone through the files of the
amateur periodicals. Moreover, in some of his shorter pieces, when
he got away from his periwigged models, Lovecraft displayed a
pleasant wit:

THE NYMPH'S REPLY TO THE MODERN BUSINESS MAN

> *If all the world and love were young,*
> *And I had ne'er before been "stung",*
> *I might enough a dullard prove*
> *To live with thee and be thy love.*
>
> *But promised "autos", Love's rewards,*
> *Turn out too often to be Fords;*
> *And though you vaunt your splendid yacht—*
> *'Tis but a rowboat, like as not!*
>
> *Your silks and sapphires rouse my heart,*
> *But I can penetrate your art—*
> *My seventh husband fool'd my taste*
> *With shoddy silks and stones of paste! . . .*
>
> *So, dear, though were your pledges true*
> *I should delight to dwell with you;*
> *I still must as a widow rove,*
> *Nor live with thee, nor be thy love!*[14]

Soon after joining the UAPA, Lovecraft was told of a local
society of amateurs, the Providence Amateur Press Club. He reported to Cole:

As Miss Hoffman has doubtless informed you, the members are
recruited from the evening high school, and are scarcely repre-

sentative of the intellectual life of Providence. Their environment
has been distinctly plebeian, and their literary standards should
not at this time be criticised too harshly. . . .

Their President, Victor L. Basinet, is a socialist of the extreme type, whose opinions have been formed through contact with
the most dangerous labour agitators in the country. He is, however,
a man of much native intelligence, and I strongly hope that the
influence of the press association may help to modify his conception of society. The Official Editor, John T. Dunn, is a wild Irishman with the usual offensive Popish and anti-English views; but
he is of very fair education, and fired by real literary ambition. Of
course, there is much frivolity in some of the members, which
detracts from the dignity of the meetings. . . .[15]

In early 1915, Lovecraft worked on two projects: the first issue
of the official organ of the PAPC, *The Providence Amateur*, and
the first issue of his own amateur periodical, *The Conservative*. For
The Providence Amateur he furnished a long poem, describing the
members of the club in more flattering terms than in his letter to
Cole:

To The
Members Of The United Amateur Press Ass'n
From The
Providence Amateur Press Club.

Before you all, in apprehension stand
The timid members of a new-formed band.
With awkward pen, but eager of success,
Our sev'ral failings must we here confess;
Let critics treat us with a kindly sense,
And frown not on our inexperience.
As President above the others set,
Firm in his rule, see gifted Basinet,
By his bright genius all the club was made;
In every act his wisdom is displayed.
In broadest sympathy, he seeks to lend
A pitying ear to all, and all befriend;
With fearless mien he scorns oppressive laws,
And stands a champion of the people's cause. . . .

After describing seven other members, Lovecraft finished with
becoming modesty:

Gaze last on H. P. L., whose bookish speech
But bores the auditors he tries to teach:
Whose stiff heroics ev'ry ear annoy;

Whose polysyllables our peace destroy.
The stilted pedant now can do no worse,
For he it is that writ this wretched verse![16]

Although appalled by the slovenly English of members whose writings he corrected, Lovecraft continued with the Providence Amateur Press Club for two years. Its Irish-American members ruffled him with anti-British tirades. The sight of Irishmen "using the United States . . . as a weapon against their lawful King and Empire" infuriated the Anglophile Lovecraft, who refused on principle to wear anything green on St. Patrick's Day. The fact that, in the twelfth century, Pope Adrian IV had given Ireland to Henry II of England—as if it had been his to give—got no sympathy for the Irish from HPL. In 1918 he wrote:

> My last attempt [at uplift] was in 1914–16, when I laboured with a "literary" club of Micks who dwelt in the dingy "North End" of the city. The brightest of them was an odd bigoted fellow named Dunn, two years older than I. He hated England & was violently pro-German—& I was foolish enough to waste time trying to convert him—as if an Irishman could reason!!

"Bigoted Irishman" was one of Lovecraft's regular ethnic pejoratives, which suggests the old platitude about pots and kettles. Nonetheless, Lovecraft ghost-wrote for Dunn a long poem for Dunn's sister to recite upon her graduation from the Rhode Island Hospital's School of Nurses.

The club published one more issue of *The Providence Amateur*, dated February, 1916, with an editorial and two poems by Lovecraft. In 1917, Dunn went to jail rather than register for the draft, and the club became inactive. Dunn eventually took holy orders. Long afterwards, Father Dunn, M.F., reminisced about Lovecraft: "He told me that he would think of a piece to write and he would stay up to finish it even if it took till six in the morning. He had an income and he did not have to get up as we did to go to work."[17]

Meanwhile, Lovecraft concentrated on his own paper, which continued intermittently for eight years. The first number of *The Conservative* (April, 1915), of which 210 copies were printed, shows the editor's (or the printer's) inexperience, but later numbers were well-designed.

The first page of this issue bore a long poem ridiculing simplified spelling. Spelling reform was a pet peeve of Lovecraft. His only defense of English orthography—the most irregular, chaotic, and difficult of any European language—was to assert that it was established usage, which ought not to be tampered with.

On the second page of this *Conservative* begins an astonishing editorial, "The Crime of the Century." This composition sheds light on the most controversial of all of Lovecraft's attitudes:

The present European war, occurring as it does in an age of hysterical sentimentality and unsound political doctrines, has called forth from the sympathizers of each set of belligerents an un-exampled torrent of indiscriminate denunciation. . . .

That the maintenance of civilization rests today with that magnificent Teutonic stock which is represented alike by the two hotly contending rivals, England and Germany, as well as by Austria, Scandinavia, Switzerland, Holland, and Belgium, is as undeniably true as it is vigorously disputed. The Teuton is the summit of evolution. That we may consider intelligently his place in history we must cast aside the popular nomenclature which would confuse the names "Teuton" and "German," and view him not nationally but racially. . . .

Though some ethnologists have declared that the Teuton is the only true Aryan, and that the languages and institutions of the other nominally Aryan races were derived alone from his superior speech and customs; it is nevertheless not necessary for us to accept this daring theory in order to appreciate his vast superiority to the rest of mankind.

Tracing the career of the Teuton through mediaeval and modern history, we can find no possible excuse for denying his actual biological supremacy. In widely separated localities and under widely diverse conditions, his innate racial qualities have raised him to preeminence. There is no branch of modern civilization that is not of his making. As the power of the Roman Empire declined, the Teuton sent down into Italy, Gaul, and Spain the re-vivifying elements which saved those countries from complete destruction. Though now largely lost in the mixed population, the Teutons are the true founders of all the so-called Latin states. Political and social vitality had fled from the old inhabitants; the Teuton only was creative and constructive. After the native elements absorbed the Teutonic invaders, the Latin civilizations declined tremendously, so that the France, Italy, and Spain of today bear every mark of national degeneracy.

In the lands whose whole population is mainly Teutonic, we behold a striking proof of the qualities of the . . . race. England and Germany are the supreme empires of the world. . . . United

States history is one long panegyric of the Teuton, and will continue to be such if degenerate immigration can be checked in time to preserve the primitive character of the population.

The Teutonic mind is masterful, temperate, and just. No other race has shown an equal capability for self-government. . . .

The division of such a splendid stock against itself, each representative faction allying itself with alien inferiors, is a crime so monstrous that the world may well stand aghast. Germany, it is true, has some appreciation of the civilizing mission of the Teuton, but has allowed her jealousy of England to conquer her intellectual zeal, and to disrupt the race in an infamous and unnecessary war.

Englishmen and Germans are blood brothers, descended from the same stern Woden-worshipping ancestors, blessed with the same rugged virtues, and fired with the same noble ambitions. In a world of diverse and hostile races the joint mission of these virile men is one of union and co-operation with their fellow-Teutons in defense of civilization against the onslaughts of all others. There is work to be done by the Teuton. As a unit he must in times to come crush successively the rising power of Slav and Mongolian, preserving for Europe and America the glorious future that he has evolved. . . .[18]

As this outburst shows, Lovecraft had been converted to the myth of the blue-eyed Nordic Aryan superman, later made notorious by Adolf Hitler.

Now, let me point out several things. First of all, this opinion, so far from being eccentric, was widespread, popular, and respectable in the United States of that time, especially among upperclass Old Americans and even more especially among New Englanders of this type. Secondly, Lovecraft came by it naturally, since it fitted the outlook of his time, place, and class; his Anglo-Saxonism no more proves him a monster than would a medieval Christian's belief in witchcraft. Thirdly, this opinion was held by not a few learned men of the time. Thus Herbert Spencer, the British sociologist whose ideas were enormously influential in the 1890s, was an Aryanist; so was Henry Cabot Lodge, one of the ablest and most scholarly politicians of the time and, like Lovecraft, a belligerent nationalist. Lastly, Lovecraft later abandoned this view, although it took him many years to do so.

We live at a time when a racist is deemed, among advanced thinkers, worse than a murderer. "Racist" has become an all-purpose pejorative, as "Red" and "Fascist" have also been. Yet ethnocentrism (to give racism its technical name) is one of the oldest and most universal of human traits. People have always tended to like and to trust most those most like themselves. Only in recent decades has disapproval of ethnocentrism become widespread, and such disapproval is anything but universal.

To give examples, the name by which primitive men call members of their own tribe often means something like "real human beings." Herodotos noted that the ancient Persians

> . . . honor most their nearest neighbors whom they esteem next to themselves; those who live beyond these they honor in the second degree; and so on with the remainder, the further they are removed, the less the esteem in which they hold them. The reason is, that they look upon themselves as very greatly superior in all respects to the rest of mankind, regarding others as approaching in excellence in proportion as they dwell nearer to them. . . .

Aristotle explained that, whereas Europeans were brave but stupid and Asiatics clever but cowardly, it was only right that the Greeks, who alone of mankind combined valor with intelligence, should conquer and enslave the rest. Not long ago, an anthropologist on the steppes of Central Asia was told by a Kirghiz shepherd that the Kirghiz were the best of all men; they had the best hearts, and "the heart is what really matters."[19]

Now the pendulum has swung the other way, largely under the influence of Marxism, which for political, non-scientific reasons is dogmatically egalitarian and environmentalist. A scientist who tries to find out whether the races do in fact differ in ability is persecuted. He gets anonymous threats and is howled down when he lectures. The howlers may be ethnics who fear that his tests may make them look bad or Marxists to whom the absolute equality of races is an article of faith.

It is obvious that the races differ physically. Some are larger and stronger than others. The Nilotic Negroes are the world's best high jumpers because of their great stature. Eskimos and Fuegian Indians can withstand cold, and Tibetans and Quechuas altitude, better than other men. Races differ in susceptibility to various diseases.

Nobody, however, yet knows whether the races also differ in mental ability. Perhaps they do; perhaps not. The evidence is inconclusive and contradictory. Some inherent mental differences among the races, like those between the sexes, probably exist, but nobody yet knows for sure what they are.

Since such differences, if they exist, are heavily masked by wide variations among individuals and by the effects of social environments, and since no tests now known can distinguish between the hereditary and the environmental differences among populations, there is no present way to settle the question. Hence everybody feels free to issue self-serving dogmata on the subject.

Before (let us say) 1915, most Old Americans were what would today be called "racists." In the nineteenth century, they were known as "nativists," hostile to everyone not of Anglo-Saxon Protestant origin. To them, it was obvious that the white race was superior to all others and that the highest type of white was the Anglo-Saxon. At that time, the world-wide power of the English-speaking peoples lent color to the view. The nativists or Anglo-Saxonists thought it only natural that there should be a fixed social and economic hierarchy, with themselves at the top. They feared being swamped by immigrants of inferior, non-Anglo-Saxon stock:

> The influx of a large immigrant population from peasant countries in central and southern Europe, hard to assimilate because of rustic habits and language barriers, gave color to the notion that immigration was lowering the standard of American intelligence; at least so it seemed to nativists who assumed that a glib command of English is a natural criterion of intellectual capacity.

Hence the fictional George Apley advises his undergraduate son:

> I have been greatly worried by your mention of this fellow-student named Alger. It is all very well to be democratic and pleasant to an acquaintance who sits beside you in the classroom, by alphabetical accident. I have no wish to limit your circle of acquaintance, as acquaintances are valuable and instructive, but you must learn as soon as possible that friendship is another matter. Friends must be drawn from your own sort of people, or difficulty and embarrassment are apt to be the result.[20]

Lovecraft's aunt, Annie Gamwell, while a person of some excellent qualities, was socially a snob and economically ultraconservative. She and his mother would have perfectly understood George Santayana's Nathaniel Alden, their fictional Bostonian contemporary (in his novel *The Last Puritan*) when Alden chides his younger brother:

> I think I ought to tell you, Peter, that I don't approve of your intimacy with persons of inferior education and a lower station in life. Of course, we all believe in democracy, and wish all classes to enjoy the greatest possible advantages: but we shall never help the less fortunate to rise to our own level, if we sink away from it ourselves. Your undesirable friendships have already affected your language and manners. . . . The same influence might in time affect your morals, not to speak of your prospects. . . .

In those days, ethnic prejudice was so rife that it seemed the natural order of things. Barbed ethnic jokes, usually directed against the Negro, the Jew, and the Irishman, were a staple of humorous magazines, the vaudeville stage, and party conversation. Ethnic stereotypes were the stock in trade of practically all popular fiction writers. The writers and their readers took it for granted that all Scots were thrifty, Irishmen funny, Germans arrogant, Negroes childish, Jews avaricious, Latins lecherous, and Orientals sinister. Popular writers like John Buchan and Cutcliffe Hyne took sneering digs at the Jews as a matter of course.

The static, hierarchial outlook usual among nineteenth-century gentlefolk is out of tune with the spirit of today. One who holds it is likely to be called a snob, a racist, or a stuffed shirt. The late Winfield Townley Scott, who studied Lovecraft, also wrote: "An unimaginative thing in any human being, snobbery is crippling in an artist."

Still, such a view had, in its time, advantages for those who accepted it. Such an individual never had an "identity crisis." When people were more closely tied to their birthplaces, their kin, and the social milieux into which they were born, a man might be poor or unlucky or oppressed, but at least he could say: "I am a Roman citizen," or "I am of the Nayyar caste," or "I am a MacDonald of the Isles," or "I am a Carter of Virginia, suh." He knew who he was and how he was expected to behave in the rôle for which fate had cast him.

While Lovecraft's "Anglo-Saxon gentleman" pose may from one point of view seem not only self-conceited but also pitiful, it did give him the strength to resist the world's slings and arrows. He knew perfectly well who he was and how he should conduct himself.

Time and experience, however, taught Lovecraft many hard lessons. In one of his last letters, he said: "Yuggoth, but I'd pay blackmail to keep some of my essays & editorials of 20 or more years ago from being exhumed & reprinted!"[21] I have little doubt that he had in mind "The Crime of the Century" among other youthful vagaries.

In Lovecraft's generation, feelings towards Negroes reached a pitch that few today can appreciate. In 1913, *All-Story Cavalier Weekly* printed a story by a liberal Southern clergyman, "A Gentleman of the New South," with a black hero. Vassar Hamilton of Birmingham, Alabama, wrote in:

> You printed something which was an insult to the Southern people, and I want to correct you right here for it.
> We, the people of the South, do not call negroes "ladies" and "gentlemen," but "coons" and "shines." We do not love and marry these shines as Yankees do. . . . Do you think that the people in the South will buy one of your magazines after the way you have insulted their country? . . . I know you will not print this in your next magazine, for you don't want the Southern readers to know that some one has noticed your insult to our South and to our most beloved Confederate veterans.

In the 1920s, Southerners were still writing letters to editors protesting the prefixing of "Mr." to Negroes' names or capitalizing the word "Negro." Feeling in the North was only relatively less strong; Theodore Roosevelt was widely and furiously denounced in 1901 for having had Booker T. Washington to lunch at the White House.

Lovecraft had his share of these sentiments, as is shown by the following doggerel of July, 1905:

DE TRIUMPHO NATURAE

The triumph of Nature
Over Northern Ignorance

The northern bigot with false zeal inflam'd
The virtues of the Afric race proclaim'd;
Declar'd the blacks his brothers and his peers,
And at their slavery shed fraternal tears;

Distorted for his cause the Holy World,
And deem'd himself commanded by the Lord
To draw his sword, whate'er the cost might be
And set the sons of Æthiopia free. . . .

And so on for two more stanzas. Eight years later, Lovecraft
was still airing such sentiments:

On the Creation of Niggers

When, long ago, the gods created Earth
In Jove's fair image Man was shaped at birth.
The beasts for lesser parts were next designed;
Yet were they too remote from humankind.
To fill the gap, and join the rest to Man,
Th'Olympian host conceiv'd a clever plan.
A beast they wrought, in semi-human figure,
Filled it with vice, and called the thing a NIGGER.[22]

Lovecraft also defended the motion picture *The Birth of a
Nation*, produced by David Wark Griffith in 1914. The picture made
cinematic history by its scale and advanced techniques; but Griffith,
an unreconstructed Southerner, portrayed the Ku Klux Klan as a
band of selfless heroes defending their womenfolk against the
bestial blacks.

Besides the general ethnocentrism of Old Americans of his
time, Lovecraft came under the influence of a book, which sent
him off on a pseudo-scientific tangent. This was Houston Stewart
Chamberlain's *Grundlagen des Neunzehnten Jahrhunderts*, a 1,200-
page treatise published in Germany in 1899. In 1912, an English
translation appeared as *Foundations of the Nineteenth Century*, and
thence Lovecraft got his belief in the Aryan superman.

The Aryan myth arose as follows. Early in the nineteenth century, scholars discovered that most of the languages of Europe belonged to the same family as those of Iran, Afghanistan, and most
of India.

During the next hundred years, history, linguistics, and archaeology have revealed that, before 2000 B.C., a cattle-raising, semi-
nomadic folk in Poland or the Ukraine tamed the horse. These
people and their descendants set out in their rattling chariots and,
with this terrifying new weapon, conquered their neighbors, made
themselves a ruling class, imposed their language and some of their

customs on their subjects, and finally intermarried with them. Their descendants conquered more adjacent tribes, and so on until they had spread their language, their horses, their bronze swords, and their sky gods from Portugal to Ceylon. The original language split up into many tongues, which nonetheless retained similarities of words and grammar.

The conquerors of Iran and India about 1500 B.C. called themselves Ārya, "nobles." When scholars realized the kinship of languages as far apart as Icelandic, Armenian, and Bengali, they called this group of languages the Aryan family. Later linguists, however, preferred the term "Indo-European."

We do not know the physical type of the original Aryans, if so I may call the horse-tamers and their near descendants. Since the Alpine type—stocky, broad-headed, with medium to dark coloring—predominates today where the taming probably took place, it is a fair guess that they were Alpines. In any case, the Aryans created no civilizations, although they overthrew several in their path. As far as science can tell, there is not and probably never has been an "Aryan race." And, whatever the Aryans' original racial type, it soon disappeared by intermarriage with the more numerous conquered.

The greatest of the scholars who solved the Indo-European linguistic problem was the German philologist Max Müller. In a careless moment, Müller alluded to the "Aryan race." He later corrected himself, saying: "To me, an ethnologist who speaks of an Aryan race, Aryan blood, Aryan eyes and hair, is as great a sinner as a linguist who speaks of a dolichocephalic dictionary of a brachycephalic grammar. . . . If I say Aryans, I mean neither blood, nor bones, nor hair, nor culture. I mean simply those who speak an Aryan language."

But the harm had been done. The "Aryan race" was seized upon by a French diplomat and writer, Comte Arthur Joseph de Gobineau. In the 1850s, Gobineau wrote a book, *Essai sur l'inégalité des races humaines* [*The Inequality of Human Races*]. He undertook to prove that the white race was the only one with creative ability and that the Aryan, which Gobineau identified as the tall, long-headed, blond, blue-eyed Nordic type of northern Europe, was the best kind of white.[23]

Gobineau naturally classed himself as one of the Aryans, who as the Germanic Franks had conquered Gaul around A.D. 500 and made themselves the French aristocracy. France had ruined herself, he said, by destroying these "best people" in the French Revolution. It was no coincidence that Gobineau was himself a French aristocrat.

While Gobineau's anthropology was pre-Darwinian, tracing all men from Adam, others soon adapted Gobineau's theses to evolutionary theory. All deemed themselves Aryans, since nobody has ever written a book to prove his own ethnos inferior.[24] Some Frenchmen agreed with the idea of Aryan civilizers but averred that the Aryans had been, not Nordics, but sturdy Alpines like most Frenchmen. In Italy, Sergi said that both were wrong; the Aryans had been gifted Mediterraneans like Sergi.

Gobineau was followed by Houston Stewart Chamberlain. The son of a British admiral, Chamberlain was educated in Switzerland and Germany and became a German citizen. A frail little neurotic with hallucinations of being haunted by demons, he also became a son-in-law of Richard Wagner and a friend of Kaiser Wilhelm II.[25]

Chamberlain's *Foundations* is a dreadful farrago of windy, rambling, tendentious, verbalistic nonsense. The author undertakes to prove the superiority of the "Teutonic Aryan" by a circular argument. Anybody he likes, such as Julius Caesar (a brunet) or Jesus (of whose appearance nothing is known) is proved a Teutonic Aryan by his virtues, and the virtues of all these Teutons prove Aryan superiority. While "mixtures" like the Germans are good, "mongrels" like the Jews are bad, and one tells the difference by "spiritual divination." Little Teutonic girls know the difference by instinct and cry when a Jew enters the room. If science disagrees, so much the worse for science:

> What is clear to every eye suffices, if not for science, at least for life. . . . One of the most fatal errors of our time is that which impels us to give too great weight in our judgments to the so-called "results" of science.[26]

These delusions were popularized in the United States by Madison Grant (*The Passing of the Great Race*, 1916) and Lothrop Stoddard (*The Rising Tide of Color Against White World Supremacy*, 1920). These writers accepted the standard division of Europeans, worked out by Ripley and others, into Nordics, Alpines, and Mediterraneans. The Nordics—tall, long-headed, blond, and blue-eyed—dwelt in the north; the Alpines—broad-headed, of medium height and stocky build, and of medium to dark coloring—in the central and eastern parts; and the Mediterraneans—short, slight, long-headed, and dark of eyes and hair—in the south.

Then Grant and Stoddard argued that the Alpines were stolid, stupid, cowardly peasants. Mediterraneans were artistic and intellectual but frivolous and untrustworthy. Only Nordics were brave, wise, and true. The bloodstream of the Nordic Aryans must be guarded against intermixture with the lesser breeds, lest civilization, whereof the Nordic was the originator and prime mover, perish from the earth.

These books were widely read. Although utterly unscientific, they influenced the immigration law of 1924. An Anti-Immigration League saw to it that their claims received wide circulation.

History and anthropology, as now understood, tell quite a different story. Northern Europe, the Nordic homeland, was a notably backward, barbarous place down to a thousand years ago. All the main advances of civilization had theretofore been made by swarthy southerners and yellow-skinned easterners. Only in the last few centuries have circumstances enabled the northern Europeans to catch up with and sometimes to surpass their southern neighbors in culture and power. And there is no reason to think that the recent northern European preëminence will prove any more lasting than the earlier dominance of the Arabs or the Mongols.

The Nordic-Aryan myth had already been debunked by the American economist William Z. Ripley in *The Races of Europe* (1899). Ripley divided the white or Caucasoid race into the Nordic, Alpine, and Mediterranean sub-races or types. Ripley's classification is still valid if we remember that all three types occur in differing proportions throughout Europe, that most Europeans do not fit any one ideal type but show a mixture of traits, and that one can divide up Europe's population along different but equally plausible lines.

Lovecraft once said: "To be a member of a pure-blooded race ought to be the greatest achievement in life!" This was one of his silliest statements. As far as is known, there has never been a truly "pure-blooded race" on earth. The different branches of mankind have never, with trivial exceptions like the Easter Islanders, been completely isolated one from the other for many centuries at a time. There has always been some mixing going on, and the great civilizations have been the products of mixed folk.

Therefore, there is no reason to think that the main subdivisions of the Caucasoid race have ever existed in pure form; nor has there ever been a pure blond race. All that happened is that blondness—an evolutionary adaptation to the sunless clime of northern Europe—became much commoner there, where under primitive conditions the pale coloring that went with it helped in survival, than it did elsewhere, where it was harmful.

Lovecraft, apparently, never read Ripley. It is practically certain that he read Chamberlain, because of resemblances in wording between his racial writings and Chamberlain's. "The Crime of the Century," in fact, reads like a paraphrase of parts of Chamberlain. Lovecraft is known to have read Grant and probably Stoddard, too; but their books appeared only after the first *Conservative*.

Lovecraft's Aryanism has done his reputation lasting harm. Yet Lovecraft had only shown a common human failing. Most people embrace beliefs, not because of compelling evidence or ironclad logic, but because the beliefs comfort them and make them feel superior. Lovecraft's falling for Chamberlain's nonsense proves, not that he was an evil man, but that he was given to the nativist prejudices of his time, place, and class, and that he was much less objective, astute, and judicious than he liked to think.

A high-school dropout who never did earn all his modest living expenses, Lovecraft keenly felt his failure as a student and as a self-supporting adult. He stopped frequenting the Ladd Observatory because he could not bear to go there as an outsider instead of as the student and then the professor of astronomy that he had hoped to be.[27] So the Aryan cult was made to order for him. If he could not excel as an individual, at least he could belong to a superior breed of man. He learned better, but it took him a long time.

Seven

WASTED WARRIOR

With our swords we have contended!
When the Vistula we enter'd
With our ships in battle order
We unto the hall of Woden
Sent the bold Helsingian foemen.
Then our sword-points bit in fury;
All the billows turned to life-blood
Earth with streaming gore was crimson'd;
Reeking sword with ringing note
Shields divided; armour smote.[1]

ANONYMOUS (translated by Lovecraft)

In 1915, Lovecraft survived an attack of chicken pox and lost the only remaining adult male kinsman who might have served as a model for him. This was his elder aunt's husband, Dr. Franklin Chase Clark, who at sixty-eight died of an apoplectic stroke on April 26th.

With the scholarly doctor gone, there was nobody to counter the effects on Lovecraft of his mother's smothering affection. Not, probably, that it would have made much difference by then. At twenty-four, Lovecraft's character had already been set.

The second issue of Lovecraft's *Conservative* (July, 1915) led off with a poem, *Dream of the Golden Age*, by one of Lovecraft's pen pals, a Kansan cowboy-poet of scanty education but some natural talent, named Ira Albert Cole. Lovecraft's main contribution was "Metrical Regularity": an attack on free verse, which was beginning to edge out fixed-form verse as the preferred poetic medium:

> Most amusing of all the claims of the radical is the assertion that true poetic fervour can never be confined to regular metre; that the wild-eyed, long-haired rider of Pegasus must inflict upon a suffering public in unaltered form the vague conceptions which flit in noble chaos through his exalted soul . . .[2]

Stripped of its rhetoric, Lovecraft's piece did have a point, considering what has befallen poetry since he wrote. There followed an editorial, wherein Lovecraft nailed his colors to the masthead:

> The Conservative will ever be found an enthusiastic champion of total abstinence and prohibition; of moderate, healthy militarism as contrasted with dangerous and unpatriotic peace-preaching; of Pan-Saxonism, or the domination by the English and kindred races over the lesser divisions of mankind; and of constitutional or representative government, as opposed to the pernicious and contemptible false schemes of anarchy and socialism.[3]

Lovecraft also took on a fellow-amateur, Charles D. Isaacson of Brooklyn, New York, publisher of *In a Minor Key*. Isaacson was what we should call a left-liberal, full of benevolence and altruism carried to a naïve extreme. His pacifism was of the purest, non-resisting kind. He was sure that "war was promoted by a mere handful of perverts" and that if the "people" of one of the warring nations would only lay down their arms and refuse to fight, the "peoples" of all the other belligerents would do likewise, and peace would prevail.

Isaacson praised pacifism, Socialism, and the poetry of Walt Whitman; he denounced militarism, conscription, racial prejudice, and the movie *The Birth of a Nation*, whose "backers," he said, "should be flogged." He was strong for freedom of expression—except for periodicals like *Life* (not the late picture magazine but its humorous predecessor) and *The Menace*, which vilified the Jews. These journals he would have suppressed.

Lovecraft's reply, "In a Major Key," praised Isaacson's literary merits but went on:

> Charles D. Isaacson, the animating essence of the publication, is a character of remarkable quality. Descended from the race that produced a Mendelssohn, he is himself a musician of no ordinary

talent, whilst as a man of literature he is worthy of comparison with his co-religionists Moses Mendez and Isaac D'Israeli. But the very spirituality which gives elevation to the Semitic mind, partially unfits it for the consideration of tastes and trends in Aryan thought and writings, hence it is not surprising that he is a radical of the extremest sort.

In 1915, few Old Americans would have thought it in bad taste or hitting below the belt to use a man's ethnic background as an argument against his ideas. Lovecraft went on about Whitman, a *bête noire* because he had not only made free verse popular but also had several times alluded pointedly to sexual intercourse. In the middle of his essay, Lovecraft printed an eighteen-line poem beginning:

> *Behold great* Whitman, *whose licentious line*
> *Delights the rake, and warms the souls of swine.*
> *Whose fever'd fancy shuns the measured pace,*
> *And copies Ovid's filth without his grace . . .*

Lovecraft continued in the same haughty tone:

Mr. Isaacson's views on racial prejudice, as outlined in his "*Minor Key*", are too subjective to be impartial. He has perhaps resented the more or less open aversion to the children of Israel which has ever pervaded Christendom, yet a man of his perspicuity should be able to distinguish this illiberal feeling . . . from the natural and scientifically just sentiment which keeps the African black from contaminating the Caucasian population of the United States. The negro is fundamentally the biological inferior of all White and even Mongolian races, and the Northern people must occasionally be reminded of the danger which they incur by admitting him too freely to the privileges of society and government. . . . the Ku-Klux-Klan, that noble but much maligned band of Southerners who saved half of our country from destruction. . . . Race prejudice is a gift of nature, intended to preserve in purity the various divisions of mankind which the ages have evolved. . . .

The Conservative dislikes strong language, but he feels that he is not exceeding the bounds of propriety in asserting that the publication of the article entitled "The Greater Courage" is a crime which in a native American of Aryan blood would be deserving of severe legal punishment. This appeal to the people to refuse military service when summoned to their flag is an outrageous attack on the lofty principles of patriotism which have turned this country from a savage wilderness to a mighty band of states. . . .[4]

In a temperate reply, Isaacson defended Whitman, peace, racial tolerance, and democracy. He also used an *ad hominem* argument, with surer aim than his young adversary:

> There comes a musty smell as of old books with the reading of the Conservative; the imagination unconsciously rushes to the days of Raleigh, Elizabeth and Lovelace. . . .
> I have said that Mr. Lovecraft's writings smell of the library. They are literary. They are of the play-world. Everything is so unreal about everything in the Conservative's writings.[5]

Isaacson had put his finger on Lovecraft's main weakness as a thinker. Although erudite, Lovecraft was wont to pontificate on subjects of which he had the merest literary smattering, without the correctives of firsthand knowledge or worldly experience. The friends to whom he expounded his half-baked notions were usually too awed by his learning to contradict him. His long seclusion had instilled in him "that haste to form judgments and that lack of critical sense in testing them, which are often the result of self-education conducted by immense and unsystematic reading."

By happenstance, Lovecraft had come upon writings advocating Aryanism, Prohibition, and militant nationalism. As if an angel had spoken to him, he had instantly and fervently embraced these doctrines, without any notion of how weak, inconclusive, and controvertible the arguments over such questions really were.

Furthermore, one cannot always be sure of how seriously to take Lovecraft's more outrageous opinions. He confessed that, for the sake of argument, he often assumed "whatever opinion amuses me or is the opposite to that of the person or persons present." His letters, he said later, were merely "shooting his mouth off . . . on subjects which none but the special student can rightly handle."

The third *Conservative* carried an article by Lovecraft, "The Allowable Rhyme," noting that the rules had been tightened since Alexander Pope rhymed "shy" with "company" and "join" with "line."[6] The rest of the issue held two more outbursts. "The Renaissance of Manhood" begins:

> After the degrading debauch of craven pacifism through which our sodden and feminised public has lately floundered, a slight sense of shame seems to be appearing, and the outcries of [the] peace-at-any-price maniac are less violent than they were a few

months ago. . . . Why any sane human being can believe in the possibility of universal peace is more than the CONSERVATIVE can fathom.

At this time, many people still romanticized war. They imagined battles fought with bands and banners, and cavalry charging with lance and saber. The full disillusion that followed the First World War did not take effect until the 1920s, when realistic accounts of the grimy butchery of trench warfare became current.

The other *Conservative* article, "Liquor and Its Friends," commences:

> While a cynical press, disgusted at the political acts of Mr. William J. Bryan, applaud in servile glee each motion of his successor, Robert Lansing, Prime Minister of the United States [*sic*], and presumably a man desirous of bettering our country, has just restored the disgusting presence of liquor at American state dinners.[7]

Lovecraft had much to learn.

Despite growing disillusion with his Baroque verse, Lovecraft continued to grind it out. He excused his poems on the ground that they were the best he could do:

> Some of my creaking couplets have this day appeared in "The Pinfeather". . . . When I view them with my critical eye, I find difficulty in abstaining from that severity which I usually deplore in reviewers. One might wonder why I try to dabble in numbers when I can produce no better results than this, but I suppose a strain of native perversity is responsible for such futile pursuit of the Nine.

> I am certainly a relic of the 18th century both in prose and in verse. My taste in poetry is really defective, for I love nothing better than the resounding couplets of Dryden and Pope. . . .

> Impromptu verse, or "poetry" to order, is easy only when approached in the coolly *prosaic* spirit. Given something to say, a *metrical mechanic* like myself can easily hammer the matter into technically correct verse. . . .[8]

To prove his point, Lovecraft took ten minutes to reel off a ten-line poem, *On Receiving a Picture of Swans*, inspired by a post card:

> *With pensive grace, the melancholy Swan*
> *Mourns o'er the tomb of luckless Phaëthon. . . .*

followed by another of thirty-two lines, *To Charlie of the Comics*, a tribute to Charlie Chaplin's early films:

> You trip and stumble o'er the sheet
> That holds your lifelike image.
> You shuffle your prodigious feet
> Through love-scene, chase or scrimmage. . . .

Although he said that in 1916 he had suffered another "nervous collapse,"[9] throughout 1916–17 Lovecraft began to lead a more active life. He became a regular movie-goer, even though he said that, because of cost, movies "must be suited to the groveling taste of the mindless & promiscuous rabble." Much as he admired Charlie Chaplin, "The atmosphere of squalor too often clouds the merit of the Chaplin plays. After a time, the fastidious eye tires of looking at rags & dirt" and prefers "the breezy, captivating antics" of Douglas Fairbanks, Sr., which at least had "a certain wholesomeness."[10] When in January, 1917, Fay's Theater in Providence ran a contest for critiques of the picture *The Image-Maker of Thebes*, Lovecraft won the prize of $25, despite the fact that his review was a roast.

To mid-1917, Lovecraft published *The Conservative* on a quarterly basis. The fourth issue of Volume I and the four issues of Volume II contain more material by Lovecraft's colleagues and less by himself than before, because other amateurs had begun to send him poems, essays, and stories to print.

The essays praise the British Empire and set forth the Tory side of the American Revolution. They denounce Germany and pro-German Irish-Americans. Lovecraft contributed similar pieces and assailed modern art, T. S. Eliot's poetry, and the idea of a writers' union.

In his letters, Lovecraft still gave vent to Chamberlain's Aryanist rant:

> Science shows us the infinite superiority of the Teutonic Aryan over all others, and it therefore becomes us to see that his ascendancy shall remain undisputed. Any racial mixture can but lower the result. The Teutonic race, whether in Scandinavia, other parts of the continent, England, or America, is the cream of humanity. . . .

After his outburst in the first *Conservative*, however, Lovecraft published only one more Aryanist blast. This was *The Teuton's Battle Song*, in *The United Amateur*:

The mighty Woden laughs upon his throne,
And once more claims his children as his own.
The voice of Thor resounds again on high,
While arm'd Valkyries ride from out the sky:
The Gods of Asgard all their pow'rs release
To rouse the dullard from his dream of peace. . . .

And so on for sixty lines. Lovecraft added an "Author's Note":

> The writer here endeavours to trace the ruthless ferocity and incredible bravery of the modern Teutonic soldier to the hereditary influence of the ancient Northern Gods and Heroes. . . . Whilst we may with justice deplore the excessive militarism of the Kaiser Wilhelm and his followers, we cannot rightly agree with those effeminate preachers of universal brotherhood who deny the virtue of that manly strength which maintains our great North European family in its position of undisputed superiority over the rest of mankind, and which in its purest form is today the bulwark of Old England.[12]

Thereafter Lovecraft published nothing more on the glories of the Teutonic Aryan. Perhaps he found it awkward to be pro-Teuton and anti-German at the same time.

After Volume II of *The Conservative*, other interests competed more and more for Lovecraft's time. Hence Vols. III, IV, and V consist of but a single issue each, appearing in July of 1917, 1918, and 1919 respectively. The 1918 *Conservative* had three essays by Lovecraft, which have been reprinted. "The Despised Pastoral" defends that genre of poetry. "Time and Space" stresses the insignificance of man and the universe. And "Merlin Redivivus" deplores the rise of Spiritualism and other occultisms, which accompanies any great war.

While the 1919 issue consisted mainly of contributions from Lovecraft's fellow-amateurs, a couple of editorials showed that Lovecraft still maintained his jingoistic, ultracapitalistic views. "The League" is a sneering attack on the brand-new League of Nations:

> Endless is the credulity of the human mind. Having just passed through a period of indescribable devastation caused by the rapacity and treachery of an unwisely trusted nation which caught civilisation unarmed and unawares, the world purposes once more to adopt a policy of sweet trustfulness, and to place its faith again in those imposing 'scraps of paper' known as treaties and covenants. . . . Warfare, whose minimising is the avowed object of the proposed league, is something which can never be abolished altogether. As

the natural expression of such inherent human instincts as hate, greed, and combativeness, it must always be reckoned with. . . .

In fairness to Lovecraft, the League proved almost as ineffectual as he predicted. Lovecraft's other editorial, "Bolshevism," took a predictable tone:

> The most alarming tendency observable in this age is a growing disregard for the established forces of law and order. Whether or not stimulated by the noxious example of the almost sub-human Russian rabble, the less intelligent element throughout the world seems animated by a singular viciousness, and exhibits symptoms like those of a herd on the verge of stampeding. Whilst long-winded politicians preach universal peace, long-haired anarchists are preaching a social upheaval which means nothing more or less than a reversion to savagery or medieval barbarism. . . .[13]

If one did now know otherwise, one would picture the author of these words as a stout old tycoon, standing in the window of his club to watch the rabble outside and deploring the radicalism of all United States Presidents since William McKinley.

Amateur journalism taught Lovecraft little new about writing, since in knowledge of literature he was already far ahead of most amateurs. It did, however, give him something he desperately needed: a circle of friends. Amateur journalists wrote to submit contributions for his journal or to discuss amateur business. Many of these correspondents became pen pals; some like Cole, Cook, Daas, Houtain, and Kleiner called upon the recluse of Providence.

When Cook appeared at the Lovecraft home in the fall of 1917, Lovecraft was taken aback at first by his visitor's "antique derby hat, unpressed garments, frayed cravat, yellowish collar, ill-brushed hair, & none too immaculate hands." But he soon decided that Cook's encyclopedic conversation more than made up for his lack of trigness. Lovecraft gave Cook the contract for printing his *Conservative*.

Susie Lovecraft did not like Cook but did take to another caller: Rheinhart Kleiner (1892–1949), a lanky, bushy-haired Brooklynite who worked as an accountant for the Fairbanks Scale Company among other jobs and later served as a justice of the peace. Kleiner met Lovecraft in 1916, when he and other amateurs were on their way to Boston for a convention. They took ship to

Providence and there changed to the train. Somebody telephoned Lovecraft, who came to the station to greet them. Kleiner reminisced:

"He was still somewhat young in looks then, and, as I thought, of a very prepossessing appearance. What struck me was his extreme formality of manner, and the highly complimentary style of his approach. . . ."

Next year, Kleiner visited Lovecraft:

I was greeted at the door of 598 Angell Street by his mother, who was a woman just a little below average height, with graying hair. . . . She was very cordial and even vivacious, and in another moment she had ushered me into Lovecraft's room. In those days he had not overcome a certain tenseness of manner. . . .

I noticed that every hour or so his mother appeared in the doorway with a glass of milk, and Lovecraft drank it. Something was said about a cup of tea for me, but by that time I had become aware of the heat in the room and thought it might be a good idea to suggest that we take a short walk. I digress sufficiently to say that the room in which I sat was fairly small and lined around three sides with books, mostly old ones.

Although Lovecraft said he had no interest in rare books as such, he had inherited an impressive ancestral collection of old volumes. Besides his bound files of eighteenth-century periodicals, he had about one hundred books published before 1800, including several seventeenth-century books and one from 1567. His most valuable single item, he said, was a copy of Cotton Mather's *Magnalia Christi Americana* of 1702.

On the wall near his desk were small pictures of Robert E. Lee, Jefferson Davis, and one or two others. An almanac hung against the wall directly over his desk; it was a *Farmer's Almanac* with which he had been familiar for many years.

Collecting old *Farmer's Almanacs* was a longtime hobby of Lovecraft, who took Kleiner on one of the antiquarian walks for which he became known. They strolled for miles about Providence, while Lovecraft pointed out old buildings and told of their history and architecture.

On our way back to his home, and while we were still downtown, I suggested stopping at a cafeteria for a cup of coffee. He agreed, but took milk himself, and watched me dispose of coffee and cake, or possibly pie, with some curiosity. It occurred to me that this visit to a public eating-house—a most unpretentious one—might have been a distinct departure from his usual habits. . . .

It has always seemed to me that Lovecraft's fundamental instincts were entirely normal. Removed from the repressive sick-room atmosphere of his home and the attendance of his mother or his aunts, he blossomed out astonishingly. Furthermore, he had a real knack for making himself liked.[14]

In later years, Lovecraft said he disliked milk, save when mixed with coffee or cocoa. He also drank vast amounts of coffee, although he would drink Postum or other coffee substitutes with equal relish.

In 1914, Daas, who had recruited Lovecraft into amateur journalism, put him in touch with Maurice Winter Moe (1882–1940). Moe taught high-school English, first in Appleton and, from 1920 on, in Milwaukee. He was a learned man, a Semitist who read cuneiform, and also a devout Presbyterian and an elder in his church.

Moe introduced HPL by letter to two more friends. One was Ira A. Cole, the cowboy-poet of Kansas. The other was one of Moe's former pupils, a tall, husky, rumpled young intellectual named Alfred Galpin (b. 1901).

Another friend was James Ferdinand Morton (1870–1941). Morton, a native of Littletown, Massachusetts, was like Lovecraft a man of old New England family, being a grandson of the Rev. Samuel Francis Smith, composer of the words of "America." Morton was a short, stout man, with bushy, graying red hair and a mustache. His mild eccentricities included wearing an ordinary felt hat with the uncreased crown standing up, like that of a derby. A graduate of Harvard, Morton had worked as a newspaper reporter and then become a professional lecturer. The New York Board of Education had lately hired him to lecture, and he did professional genealogy on the side.

Like Lovecraft, Morton was a man of prodigious erudition, abstemious habits, and many hobbies and enthusiasms. These included amateur journalism, genealogy, mineralogy, puzzle-solving, Negro rights, and Henry George's Single Tax movement. The last two led the ultraconservative Lovecraft to describe Morton as one who had "wasted a magnificent brain on radical nonsense."[15]

Finally, there was Sam Loveman, a young bookseller of Cleveland

who had been active in amateur journalism around 1907 but had
dropped out. A little older than Lovecraft, Loveman was good-
looking despite large ears and early baldness. Originally trained as
an accountant, he served in the U. S. Army during the First World
War, in the course of which his wife died in childbirth. He had considerable poetic talent, with a bent for Classical Greek themes. His
colorful, musical verse, which Lovecraft admired from 1915 on, tends
towards the sensitive and sentimental, full of butterflies, flowers, and
tears. The poem *Bacchanalia* (dedicated to the most un-bacchanalian
Lovecraft) begins:

> *A flagon is filled for the vintage guest,*
> *The grapes are crushed at the brim;*
> *The young lord loosens his loric vest,*
> *Violets bound on his brow and breast—*
> *And the revel is all for him,*
> *The revel is all for him.*

From first acquaintance, Lovecraft found Loveman congenial.
Loveman had let his UAPA membership lapse, and Lovecraft wrote
Kleiner:

"Loveman has become reinstated in the United through me.
Jew or not, I am rather proud to be his sponsor. . . . His poetical
gifts are of the highest order. . . . His variety of ideas, facility of
expression, & background of classical & antiquarian knowledge, place
him in the front rank." Elsewhere he called Loveman "a glorious
pagan—and a Jew by race."[16]

This friendship was one of the most contradictory things in
Lovecraft's paradoxical life. When he met Loveman in New York
in 1922, he wrote: "Loveman is utterly delightful—refined, delicate,
sensitive, and aesthetic; though he does his best to conceal his
artistic predelictions beneath a modest exterior of commonplace good-
fellowship. . . . His modesty is incredibly extreme. . . . Loveman
makes language a thing of music, line, colour. . . ."[17]

Of all his friends, Lovecraft showed the warmest affection for
Loveman. At the same time, as he revealed with Isaacson, he
entertained the Judaeophobia common among Old Americans of
his generation, such as the great Henry Adams. In Lovecraft's twenties and thirties (despite August Derleth's efforts to whitewash him)
this phobia grew to an active hatred. He wrote letters lavishly praising Loveman's intelligence, honor, and other virtues, and at the same

time vilifying Jews in general. One letter reverses the usual arguments for ethnic tolerance:

> Nothing is more foolish than the smug platitude of the idealistic social worker who tells us that we ought to excuse the Jew's repulsive psychology because we, by persecuting him, are in a measure responsible for it. This is damned piffle. . . . We despise the Jew not only because of the stigmata which our persecution has produced, but because of the deficient stamina . . . on his part which permitted us to persecute him at all! Does anybody fancy for a moment that a Nordic race could be knocked about for two millennia by its neighbors? God! They'd either die fighting to the last man, or rise up and wipe out their would-be persecutors off the face of the earth!! It's *because* the Jews have allowed themselves to fill a football's role that we instinctively hate them. Note how much greater is our respect for their fellow-Semites, the Arabs, who *have* the high heart—shewn in courage . . . which we emotionally understand and approve.

Had Lovecraft lived to witness the Arab-Israeli wars of the last quarter-century, he might have found the experience educational. He concocted an unusual excuse for hating Jews: that they were responsible for Christianity—a Judaic heresy—and Christianity had destroyed Classical paganism, which Lovecraft admired.

Today such opinions would place a man in the right-wing lunatic fringe, although the New Left has lately made similar noises about "Zionist imperialists." In the 1910s and 20s, however, such views were common among American gentiles. They did not then have quite the sinister connotation that they do now, after Auschwitz and Dachau.

For all his self-image as an objective, coldly analytical thinker, Lovecraft had never learned to distinguish between objective fact and subjective reaction. If one says that X is "good, right, beautiful, noble" or "bad, wicked, ugly, vile," one says nothing significant about X. One merely exposes one's own attitudes towards X. When Lovecraft called Jewish culture (about which he knew practically nothing) "repulsive,"[18] he was not making a factual statement about Jews. He was only expressing his emotions towards what, in his ignorance, he imagined Jewish culture to be. It seems not to have occurred to him that some features of this culture, such as sobriety, sexual puritanism, bookishness, and a wry, self-mocking humor, were precisely his own qualities.

When Lovecraft became close friends with Sonia Greene, he

sometimes asked her, in a puzzled way, how anyone could display Loveman's manifest virtues and still be a Jew. He was doing what those of strong ethnic prejudices often do to justify their bias. Having resolved to dislike an ethnos, when they meet an obnoxious member of the group they say he is "typical" of the whole. When they encounter another member whom they cannot help admiring and liking, they say that he must be a rare exception.

Most writers are, I think, less ethnocentric than the average man, because their reading has exposed them to many points of view. This is especially true of science-fiction writers. After one has coped with the problem of the spider-men of Sirius, no human being seems alien. Lovecraft, however, continued to write in this xenophobic vein for nearly twenty years, long after most American intellectuals had given up such attitudes. Not until his last decade did he much modify his views.

As a result of his growing circle of acquaintances, Lovecraft's correspondence swelled fantastically. It has been guessed that he wrote at least 100,000 letters, totaling at least ten million words. His letters to Clark Ashton Smith alone averaged about 40,000 words a year. He usually had fifty to a hundred correspondences going at once; these included a number of old ladies to whom his personation of an omniscient philosopher was convincing. He averaged eight to ten letters a day; when he fell behind, he raised the figure to fifteen. Most letters were four to eight pages long, but some ran to sixty or seventy pages.

Lovecraft tried to answer all the letters he received in the same day; a delay of more than a week or two in answering brought profuse apologies from him. Hence he spent about half his working time on letters. He realized that this immense correspondence used up time that could have been spent more profitably. He often vowed to reduce the volume, but he never did. A gentleman, he plaintively pleaded, simply *couldn't* be so rude as to answer a friendly letter curtly, late, or not at all.

Lovecraft gave other pretexts for letter-writing: he had no congenial friends in Providence, he said, so letters were his substitute for social life. He wrote: ". . . epistolatory expression is with me largely replacing conversation, as my condition of nervous prostration becomes more and more acute. I cannot bear to talk much now. . . ." ". . . an isolated person requires correspondence as a means of seeing his ideas as others see them, and thus guarding against the dogmatisms and extravagances of solitary and uncorrected speculation. . . ." He said that, no matter how often he met a man, he never felt that he really knew him until he had corresponded with him.[19] But when he lived in New York and had a circle of congenial friends there, he continued his compulsive letter-writing.

In later life, Lovecraft had a fair number of close friends, whose company he enjoyed—at least, up to a point. With the world at large, however, he really preferred correspondence to personal contact. For years he corresponded with Bertrand K. Hart, the literary editor of the *Providence Journal*; but, whenever Hart tried to meet him, Lovecraft found some excuse for not seeing him. Apparently, his shyness made him fear to meet even the most benevolent stranger, whereas he had no inhibitions about writing.

The fact was that Lovecraft loved to write letters and had no self-discipline in matters of time. For all his admiration for the Baroque Era, he never took to heart the words of one of its great letter-writers, the fourth earl of Chesterfield:

> There is nothing which I more wish that you should know, and which fewer people do know, than the true use and value of time . . . nobody squanders away their time, without hearing and seeing, daily, how necessary it is to employ it well, and how irrecoverable it is if lost. . . . I knew a gentleman, who was so good a manager of his time, that he would not even lose that small portion of it, which the calls of nature obliged him to pass in the necessary-house; but gradually went through all the Latin poets, in these moments.[20]

When Lovecraft became a traveler, he kept up his correspondence. He wrote picture post cards in a tiny, almost illegible hand, which covered not only all the message area on the back of the card but most of the address section as well, leaving barely space enough for the address. Exasperated postal employees sometimes charged the full letter rate by affixing postage-due stamps to Lovecraft's post cards.

For stationery, he used anything handy. When he visited a hotel, he helped himself to its letterhead stationery. He even used the backs of incoming letters, which he seldom filed or saved.

Addressees were meticulously addressed as "Esq." instead of

plain "Mr." In the letter proper, Lovecraft at first saluted his correspondent formally, as "Dear Mr. Bloch:—". When he knew the man better, he sometimes addressed him by surname only, in the British manner: "Dear Bloch:—", or by initials: "Dear A.W.:—" for August W. Derleth. Later he might use a phonetic respelling of the addressee's name or initials: "Bho-Blôk" for Robert Bloch and "Jehvish-Ei" for J. Vernon Shea. Clark Ashton Smith's solidly Anglo-Saxon name became "Klarkash-Ton," which looks like something from the planet Yuggoth.

For his friends, Lovecraft devised whimsical nicknames. Sometimes he merely Latinized names: "Mortonius" for Morton and "Belknapius" for Frank Belknap Long. Others were "Two-Gun Bob" for Robert E. Howard of Texas; "Malik Tawus" or "the Peacock Sultan" for E. Hoffmann Price, the writer of oriental stories; "M. le Comte d'Erlette" for Derleth; "Jonckheer" for Dutch-descended Wilfred B. Talman; and "Satrap Pharnabazus" (a Persian governor of Greek Classical times) for Farnsworth Wright, editor of *Weird Tales*.

Among fellow-weirdists, Lovecraft often used imaginative headings instead of the usual return address and date. Thus one finds letters headed: "Tomb 66—Necropolis of Thun. Hour of the Rattling of the Nether Grating"; or "Nameless Ruins of Iath—Hour of the Lambent Glow around the Sealed Tower"; or "Kadath in the Cold Waste: Hour of the Night Gaunts." This complicates the biographer's task of dating the letters.

When Lovecraft ended a letter, he might sign off with "Most cordially & sincerely yrs., H. P. Lovecraft." With intimates, he used the eighteenth-century "Yr. Obt. Servt., HPL," or some playful signature like "Éch-Pi-El" of "Grandpa Theobald." In some early letters, he captured the eighteenth-century style with astonishing fidelity:

> E. Sherman Cole, Efq.,
> Eaft Redham, Mafs.
>
> My dear Sir:—
>   I beg to acknowledge with gratitude y^r favour of the 14th ult., & to exprefs my regret at ye tardinefs of my reply. . . .

Others are full of current slang, puns, and other *jeux d'esprit*. These letters are learned, charming (save when he ranted), fas-

cinating, and—especially for a man who prided himself on aristocratic reticence—very self-revealing. One can follow his triumphs and
disasters almost day by day. He discourses on anthropology, architecture, astronomy, cosmology, esthetics, fiction writing, history, occultism, philosophy, politics, prosody, religion, science, sociology,
and travel. One is always coming upon learned disquisitions on
unusual subjects: What was the speech of the people of Britain
after the withdrawal of the Roman legions? Why do clocks have
"IIII" for "four" instead of "IV"? When in the eighteenth century
did men stop wearing wigs?

In 1916, Moe proposed that he, Ira Cole, Lovecraft, and one
other form a round-robin letter group. Lovecraft urged Kleiner as
the fourth member and called the club the Kleicomolo, after the
first syllables of the members' names. The joint letter went Cole-
to-Moe-to-Kleiner-to-Lovecraft-to-Cole. As each received the package, he took out his own previous letter and added a new one before
sending the package on.

The Kleicomolo flourished for two years. Then Cole was converted by a Pentecostal evangelist, heard voices, became a Holy
Roller preacher, and dropped out of amateur journalism. When
Cole quit, Lovecraft enlisted Galpin in Cole's place and called
the club the Gallomo. Kleiner and Moe, however, soon gave up.

In 1918, Lovecraft was told of a revival in British amateur
press activity. Through a British amateur named McKeag, he joined
the British Amateur Press Club. By 1921 he had organized an Anglo-
American round-robin correspondence club among amateur journalists, called the Transatlantic Circulator. He used this group as a
sounding board for his early stories, sending the manuscripts around
the circuit with requests for criticism.

When some members roasted one of Lovecraft's stories, he sent a
long letter with the next issue, defending his fiction. He did not,
he protested, write about ordinary folk because they did not
interest him. He did not write for the masses and would be
satisfied if only a few discriminating readers liked his work. In
September, 1921, he bade the group farewell.

Thus Lovecraft formed another lifelong habit, of sending
his fiction to friends for comment before submitting it for sale.
For a tyro at writing, this is sound procedure, if one can find

some candid, knowledgeable friend who is also serving his literary apprenticeship.

A writer who so submits a manuscript must accept criticism gracefully and not let it unduly perturb him. Lovecraft learned not to argue back but never did learn not to let criticism disturb or discourage him. To the end of his days, he sent each story to half a dozen friends and then, if one of them did not like it, fell into lethargic despair and talked of giving up writing altogether.

To endure the disappointments of his trade, a writer needs toughness, resilience, and a fair degree of egotism. Lovecraft lacked these. He was foolish to go on showing his manuscripts around, since in full maturity he knew more about literary techniques than his friends. They could tell him nothing useful, and their criticisms only quashed what little self-confidence he had.

But HPL never learned. Despite his talk of being an unemotional thinking machine, he remained an emotional, hypersensitive man with a fragile ego, childishly eager for praise and utterly crushed by blame.

Lovecraft's letters for 1915–21 contain the same pleas for nationalism, militarism, Aryanism, and Prohibition that appeared in his editorials and the same digs at ethnics: ". . . the alienised suburbs where reigns Hebrew, Italian, and French-Canadian squalor." The letters also discuss Lovecraft's philosophical outlook. He never wavered from the nontheism that he had embraced in childhood:

> I fear that all theism consists mostly of reasoning in circles, and guessing or inventing what we do not know. If God is omnipotent, then why did he pick out this one little period and world for his experiment with mankind?[21]

Lovecraft did not, however, altogether condemn organized religion. Like Strabon the geographer and Niccolò Machiavelli, he thought that religion, even if untrue, served a useful purpose in comforting and regulating the simple-minded. It was one of "the harmless little devices whereby we may trick ourselves into believing we are happy. . . ." "Whatever the faults of the church, it has never yet been surpassed or nearly equalled as an agent for the promotion of virtue." "The honest agnostic regards the church with respect for what it has done in the direction of virtue. He even supports it if he is magnanimous. . . . The good effects of Christianity are neither to be denied, nor lightly esteemed, though candidly I will admit I think them overrated."[22]

Lacking any supernatural belief, Lovecraft's own philosophy was an urbane, materialistic futilitarianism, incongruously combined with an austere asceticism of personal conduct. He defended this atheistic puritanism as "artistic." Since "Our human race is only a trivial incident in the history of creation," and "In a few million years there will be no human race at all," human affairs should not be taken seriously. "With Nietzsche I have been forced to confess that mankind as a whole had no goal or purpose whatever. . . . What man should seek, is the pleasure of non-emotional imagination—the pleasures of pure reason, as found in the perception of truths."

He maintained the fiction that he was himself unemotional: "I am sure that I, who hardly know what an emotion is like . . . am far less vexed than he who is constantly straining after new sensations. . . ."[23] Shakespeare's Hamlet, he said, was not mad or even neurotic. Hamlet had merely realized the futility of all human affairs and was therefore no longer motivated to take any action, good or ill.

Few aspects of Lovecraft's thought afford a fairer target for ridicule than his armchair militarism. From the safety of his rabbit-hole in Providence, he ferociously snarled bloodthirsty boasts and threats:

> . . . the decadent cowardice responsible for the propagation of peace ideas. Peace is the ideal of a dying nation; a broken race. . . .

> . . . shall we ever be such women as to prefer the emasculate piping of an arbitrator to the lusty battle-cry of a blue-eyed, blond-bearded warrior? The one sound power in the world is the power of a hairy muscular right arm!

> I am naturally a Nordic—a chalk-white, bulky Teutonic killer of the Scandinavian or North-German forests—a Viking—a berserk killer—a predatory rover of the blood of Hengist and Horsa—a conqueror of Celts and mongrels and founder of Empires—a son of the thunders and the arctic winds, and brother to the frosts and the auroras—a drinker of foemen's blood from new-picked skulls. . . .[24]

All the while, this inept, ineffectual, unathletic man was leading the most secluded, inactive, unadventurous, unwarlike life possible.

(He stopped sneering at Celts when he learned that one of his own ancestors had been named Casey.) His inactivity, however, was not entirely his doing.

Oppressed by his uselessness, Lovecraft made one serious effort to escape his mother's coddling. On April 6, 1917, the United States declared war on the German Empire. The next month, Lovecraft applied for enlistment in the National Guard. He passed the cursory physical examination by keeping his mouth shut about his medical history and was accepted as a private in the Coast Artillery.

When Susie Lovecraft heard, she "was almost prostrated with the news." There were scenes, and she and the family physician persuaded the Army to annul the enlistment. When conscription loomed, Lovecraft wrote: "My mother has threatened to go to any lengths, legal or otherwise, if I do not reveal all the ills which unfit me for the army."

When his draft questionnaire arrived, Lovecraft discussed it with the head of the local draft board. Knowing Lovecraft's history, this doctor, a family friend and a distant kinsman, told him to class himself as V, G—totally unfit. When Lovecraft protested, the doctor said he did not think Lovecraft could stand military life; so the board would not pass him. Lovecraft sadly wrote:

> If my health could have borne me along, I half believe I should have been at least a non-commissioned officer by this time, for I intended to study hard indeed. I half thought, that if I could hold out long enough, I might obtain even a commission. . . . But I suppose, as the doctor said, that I have no real idea of what a soldier has to undergo physically in even the smoothest camp or barrack life. At any rate, he decided that a man who cannot stay up all day as a civilian, is not exactly a General in the making.[25]

How an actual enlistment would have worked out is unknown. As Lovecraft wrote: "It would either have killed me or cured me." He obviously suffered from real psychosomatic ills, and in both world wars the Army gave medical discharges to thousands of recruits with similar weaknesses. On the other hand, good soldiers have been made from equally unlikely material; and Lovecraft, as Kleiner said, blossomed amazingly when he got away from the domination of his mother and aunts.

As it was, while two million other Americans were put into olive drab for the War to End War, poor Lovecraft was left feeling more "useless" and "desolate and lonely" than ever. He would, he said, have tried for the medical corps, whose physical qualifications were lower, "were it not for the almost frantic attitude of my mother; who makes me promise every time I leave the house that I will not make another attempt at enlistment!"[26] It never seems to have occurred to him that, since he was an adult, his mother had no power to "make" him do anything. And so ended Lovecraft's career as a warrior, Nordic or otherwise.

Eight

GHOSTLY GENTLEMAN

In fact, Penniless Edgar [Poe] lived his life in one rôle especially bitter in a country like ours, where despite the magnitude of the star under which we are born, status is thought to be achieved rather than prescribed. That rôle is the Disinherited Aristocrat. Especially bitter, yet especially attractive too. How many Americans have found, in the face of their personal failures (in business, in love, in life) a great consolation in the knowledge that, were truth and justice seen to, they would be acknowledged as—the Lost Dauphin of France; or Napoleon; or the true Earl of Renwick; or the rightful McLeod of Skye.[1]

HOFFMAN

After his rejection by the Army, Lovecraft found that he did, indeed, have something left to live for: his amateur journalism. He took this hobby seriously, for it gave him a chance to exercise his literary bent in a genteel, non-commercial way.

From 1915 to 1925, he had over a hundred essays and articles published in amateur periodicals, including his own *Conservative*. A typical Anglophile verse, *Britannia Victoria*, begins:

> *When Justice from the vaulted skies*
> *   Beheld the fall of Roman night,*
> *She bade a nobler realm arise*
> *   To rule the world and guard the right:*
> *She spake—and all the murm'ring main*
> *Rejoicing, hailed Britannia's reign!*

When that appeared in *The Inspiration* for April, 1917, the British, hard-pressed in France, needed all the encouragement they could get. Lovecraft also composed a "Temperance Song," whose first stanza reads:

> *We are a band of brothers*
> *Who fight the demon Rum.*
> *With all our strength until at length*
> *A better time shall come.*
>
> (CHORUS)
> *Hurrah! Hurrah! for Temperance, Hurrah!*
> *'Tis sweet to think that deadly drink*
> *Some day no more shall mar!*[2]

This verse did not sound so silly in the 1910s as it did later, when the "experiment noble in motive" had turned out disastrously. Prohibitionists were making rosy but plausible promises that, if only drink were nationally forbidden, we should all become healthy, wealthy, and wise overnight. Many intelligent people believed these predictions.

If Lovecraft was not paid for these amateur contributions, at least he was printed and so became known outside his own family circle. For that matter, he seems never to have thought about being paid. When someone suggested that he seek commercial outlets for his writings, Lovecraft was aristocratically shocked. What, a gentleman ask *money* for the products of his creative art? "I write to please myself only," he said, "and if a few of my friends enjoy my effusions I feel well repaid."

As a result of his labors for amateur journalism, Lovecraft soon became one of the best-known figures in this small field. In July, 1917, the UAPA (or rather, the Cole-Hoffman faction thereof) held its convention in Chicago. There they elected Lovecraft, who had served as one of their vice-presidents, to the presidency. Lovecraft was not there; in fact, he had never yet attended a convention.

Lovecraft can hardly have failed to be pleased. Once he got into the job, however, he underwent the disillusionment that attends most such offices: the torrent of paper work, the complaints to be answered, the sniping among factions, the endless record-keeping.

For instance, the president had to choose "laureate judges" from among the members. These judges yearly conferred the title of "laureate" upon the amateurs who had, they thought, published the best magazines or had written the best articles, stories, and poems. Such a scheme encouraged politicking and charges of bias and favoritism.

Soon, Lovecraft found himself "bored and harassed" by his new duties, but he stuck it out. He also decided to join the rival NAPA, although he knew that some of the more partisan members of the UAPA would disapprove.

Lovecraft was glad when, in 1918, Kleiner succeeded him, while he became chairman of the board of directors. Then Kleiner fell ill, and Lovecraft soon found himself saddled with as much administrative work as before. For five years following the death of Helene Hoffman Cole, on March 25, 1919, Lovecraft remained the principal moving spirit of her faction of the UAPA.

In 1919, fed up with Byzantine politics and teacup tempests, he declared he was "through with amateur journalism," which had brought him "only slights and insults." He repeated this threat several times during the next decade but—as with his vows to cut down his correspondence—failed to carry it out. In fact, when the 1922–23 president of the NAPA, William B. Dowdell, resigned his post in the middle of his term, Lovecraft let himself be appointed president of the NAPA to serve out the rest of Dowdell's term.

In 1920, when Alfred Galpin was president of Lovecraft's faction of the UAPA, Lovecraft became official editor of that group and held the post for five years. After he ceased active work for the faction in 1925, the group soon died a natural death.

Now Lovecraft began to experiment with other kinds of writing. He did not completely cease his wooden Georgian couplets; one of his last major efforts was a ten-page narrative poem, *Psychopompos*, which he composed in 1917–18. It is a conventional werewolf tale, beginning:

> *In old Auvergne, when schools were poor and few,*
> *And peasants fancy'd what they scarcely knew*
> *When lords and gentry shunn'd their monarch's throne*
> *For solitary castles of their own,*
> *There dwelt a man of rank, whose fortress stood*
> *In the hush'd twilight of a hoary wood . . .*

Nevertheless he came to esteem his work in this genre less and less. As he listed his seventy-seven poems published up to April, 1918, he commented: "What a mess of mediocre and miserable junk."[3]

This disillusionment finally stimulated him to get away from eighteenth-century conventions. Kleiner encouraged him to try light verse. One result was the mildly amusing *The Poet of Passion:*

> Pray observe the soft poet with amorous quill
> Waste full half a sheet on vague inspiration.
> Do not fancy him drunk or imagine him ill
> If he wails by the hour of his heart's desolations:
>   'Tis but part of his trade
>   To go mad o'er a maid
> On whose beautiful face he his eyes ne'er hath laid—
> And the fond ardent passion that loudly resounds,
> May tomorrow in Grub Street bring two or three pounds.[4]

This gibe at love poetry would come with better grace from one who had shown normal sexual interests. Since, up to then, Lovecraft had never been in love, the poem looks like a rationalization of his own shortcomings—in other words, a case of sour grapes.

A few years later, however, he published an unmistakable (if faintly humorous) love poem of his own. It appeared in *The Tryout* for January, 1920, under a pseudonym: *To Phillis,* "with humblest possible apologies to Randolph St. John, Gent.", by "L. Theobald, Jun.":

> Ah, Phillis, had I but bestow'd the art
> Upon my verses, that I vainly gave
> To fond designs and schemes to win your heart
> And tributes that abas'd me as your slave;
> If that fine fervour that I freely pour'd
> In suppliance at your feet and liv'd in rhyme
> And the soft warmth wherewith my soul ador'd
> Been sav'd in numbers for applauding Time;
> Had all th' affection, spent on you alone,
> Provok'd my fancy to poetic flights:
> Fill'd my rapt brain with passions not my own,
> And wafted me to dizzy lyric heights;
> The scanty laurels of this feeble quill,
> BELIEVE ME, KID, would sure be scantier still!

This trifle gives one to think: was it a mere literary exercise, as was the previous *Laeta: A Lament?* Or had Lovecraft been casting sheep's eyes upon some young woman whom he lacked the nerve to approach openly? Could it have been his fellow-amateur and ghosting client Winifred Virginia Jackson, with whom he had quite—for him—a close friendship? But who "Phillis" was, or whether she existed at all, we shall probably never know.

In trying to escape from his eighteenth-century poetic prison, Lovecraft also wrote a number of verses in imitation of Poe. The only nineteenth-century poets for whom he had any use were Poe and Swinburne, and Poe he esteemed the more highly. The other great Victorian poets, like Longfellow and Tennyson, left him cold. One of his pastiches on Poe was *Nemesis*, beginning:

> *Through the ghoul-guarded gateways of slumber,*
>   *Past the wan-mooned abysses of night,*
> *I have lived o'er my lives without number,*
>   *I have sounded all things with my sight;*
> *And I struggle and shriek ere the daybreak, being driven to madness*
>   *with fright.*[5]

Despite a good, swinging rhythm, *Nemesis* (probably inspired by Poe's *Ulalume*) is not only painfully derivative but also uses the galloping anapestic metre. This is fine for Browning's "Boot, saddle, to horse, and away!" but unsuited to Lovecraft's somber subject.

Lovecraft did better with *Despair*, whose first stanza is quoted at the head of Chapter IV. In his increasing freedom from poetic restrictions, he even brought himself to try some Poe-esque blank verse, entitled *Nathicana:*

> *It was in the pale garden of Zais;*
> *The mist-shrouded gardens of Zais,*
> *Where blossoms the white nephalot,*
> *The redolent herald of midnight.*
> *There slumber the still lakes of crystal,*
> *And streamlets that flow without murm'ring;*
> *Smooth streamlets from caverns of Kathos*
> *Where broodeth calm spirits of twilight.*

The narrator tells how there he loved "The garlanded, white Nathicana; The slender, black-hair'd Nathicana"; until "the cursed season of Dzannin" came and turned everything red, driving the narrator mad. Losing his maiden, he is now brewing

> *A draught that will banish the redness;*
> *The horrible coma call'd living.*
> *Soon, soon, if I fail not in brewing,*
> *The redness and madness will vanish,*
> *And deep in the worm-peopled darkness*
> *Will rot the base chains that have bound me. . . .*[6]

This effort (some of which echoes Poe's *For Annie*) suffers from the same faults as *Nemesis*, but at least Lovecraft was trying something new. Anything was better than the leaden Georgian couplets on which he had wasted so much of his youth.

In any event, Lovecraft soon stopped writing original poetry. For nearly a decade, he produced hardly any verse at all.

For some years, Lovecraft had convinced himself that he had no bent for fiction. He wrote: "I wish that I could write fiction, but it seems almost an impossibility."[7]

Around 1915, his friends W. Paul Cook and George W. Macauley urged him to try his hand again at fiction. In 1917, he began work in the field that was to bring him fame: weird fantasy. His short story "The Tomb" was printed in the March, 1922, issue of *The Vagrant*, the amateur magazine that Cook published in New Hampshire. A little over 4,000 words long, this is a competent but uninspired story of the kind that *Weird Tales* published throughout its existence. It may have been suggested by Walter de la Mare's *The Return*. The opening sentence is a cliché of such fiction:

> In relating the circumstances which have led to my confinement within this refuge for the demented, I am aware that my present position will create a natural doubt of the authenticity of my narrative.

The narrator, Dudley, tells how as a solitary, dreamy boy he was fascinated by the discovery of the burial vault of an extinct New England family in the woods near his home. Obsessed by a wish to enter the tomb, he finds a key, which admits him, and takes to spending nights in the vault. The spirits of the vanished Yankee gentlefolk invade his mind, until he speaks their kind of archaic English. When finally committed to an asylum, he is told that he never entered the tomb at all but suffered hallucinations of having done so. The echoes of Lovecraft's own past are obvious.

"The Tomb" was followed by "Dagon," published before the other in *The Vagrant* for November, 1919. More original than its predecessor, this 2,300-word story sets the pattern for most of Lovecraft's later tales. It has the same leisurely first-person narrative by a man—usually a reclusive, ineffectual, scholarly bachelor like Lovecraft—who comes upon some anomaly, some apparent violation of natural law.

There follows a long, slow, moody build-up, with little or no dialogue. At last, the narrator—who usually takes a passive attitude towards the looming disaster—makes the shattering discovery that the anomaly is real after all. The discovery leaves him either facing death or broken in health and mind.

"Dagon" tells of the narrator's capture by a German sea raider in the First World War. He escapes in a lifeboat but then grounds on a stretch of sea bottom suddenly raised above the surface by a seismic convulsion. Floundering through mud and slime, the narrator finds carvings of gigantic fish-men, one of whom presently emerges alive from the sea. The narrator escapes and returns to civilization but remains obsessed by horror. The Thing, he is sure, means to track him down and destroy him. . . .[8]

During the next few years, Lovecraft began his career as a gentleman fictioneer. He kept a "commonplace book" in which to jot down ideas for stories. Here are some of these notes:

> A very ancient colossus in a very ancient desert. Face gone—no man hath seen it.

> Castle by pool or river—reflection fixed thro' centuries—castle destroyed—reflection lives to avenge destroyers weirdly.

> Rats multiply and exterminate first a single city & then all mankind. Increased size and intelligence.

> Ancient cathedral. Hideous gargoyle. Man seeks to rob—found dead. Gargoyle's paw bloody.

> Subterranean region beneath placid New England village, inhabited by (living or extinct) creatures of prehistoric antiquity & strangeness.[9]

By 1920, the results of his storytelling pleased him enough to write:

> I am glad that you find merit in my fictional attempts, and I wish I had not dropped fiction in the nine years between 1908 and 1917. . . . I am at present full of various ideas, including a hideous novel to be entitled *The Club of the Seven Dreamers.*

Never written, *The Club of the Seven Dreamers* was one of Lovecraft's false starts. In 1918, Lovecraft planned a new amateur magazine *Hesperia*, to be devoted to fiction; but this never materialized. In 1919, he and Moe discussed an abortive plan to collaborate on a series of stories, under the joint pseudonym of "Horace Philter Mocraft." In 1922 came another stab at a novel, *Azathoth.* Lovecraft succeeded in composing only five-hundred-odd words, beginning:

When age fell upon the world, and wonder went out of the minds of men; when grey cities reared to smoky skies tall towers grim and ugly, in whose shadow none might dream of the sun or of Spring's flowering meads; when learning stripped Earth of her mantle of beauty, and poets sang no more save of twisted phantoms seen with bleared and inward-looking eyes; when these things had come to pass, and childish hopes had gone away for ever, there was a man who travelled out of life on a quest into spaces wither the world's dreams had fled.[10]

This fragment shows the mark of the man who, next to Poe, had the greatest influence on Lovecraft's writing: Lord Dunsany. Although Lovecraft never finished *Azathoth*, he used the same concept in some of his later stories, so the world lost nothing by his failure to finish this rudiment.

Through 1918, Lovecraft jogged along. His astronomical column in the *Providence Evening News* ended in May. He read Fenimore Cooper and reread Nathaniel Hawthorne's stories. He heard lectures at Brown University. And he sold a poem, *The Marshes of Ipswich*, to *The National Magazine*; this is the first money he is known to have earned in his life.

He wrote a learned article, "The Literature of Rome," for *The United Amateur* (November, 1918) and a 1,500-word story, "Polaris," which appeared in the December, 1920, issue of Galpin's *The Philosopher*. "Polaris" begins:

Into the north window of my chamber glows the Pole Star with uncanny light. All through the long hellish hours of blackness it shines there. And in the autumn of the year, when the winds from the north curse and whine, and the red-leaved trees of the swamp mutter things to one another in the small hours of the morning under the horned waning moon, I sit by the casement and watch that star. Down from the heights reels the glittering Cassiopeia as the hours wear on, while Charles' Wain lumbers up from behind the vapour-soaked swamp trees that sway in the night wind. . . .

And it was under a horned waning moon that I saw the city for the first time. Still and somnolent did it lie, on a strange plateau between strange peaks. Of ghastly marble were its walls and towers, its columns, domes, and pavements. . . .

The narrator is suffering from ancestral memory. He imagines himself a citizen of "Olathoe, which lies on the plateau of Sarkia,

betwixt the peaks Noton and Kadephonek," in the land of Lomar.
The city is threatened by "the Inutos; squat, hellish yellow fiends
who five years ago appeared out of the unknown west to ravage the
confines of our kingdom. . . ."

Since the narrator, a student of the mysterious Pnakotic manuscripts, is "feeble and given to strange faintings when subjected to
stress and hardships," he is not thought fit to fight these proto-
Eskimos hand to hand. Instead, his friend General Alos posts him in
the vital watchtower of Thapnen, to warn the army of the approach
of the Inutos. But sleep overcomes him, and he awakens in his
modern incarnation.

> And as I writhe in my guilty agony, frantic to save the city
> whose peril every moment grows, and vainly trying to shake off
> this unnatural dream of a house of stone and brick south of a
> sinister swamp and a cemetery on a low hillock, the Pole Star, evil
> and monstrous, leers down from the black vault, winking hideously
> like an insane watching eye which strives to convey some message,
> yet recalls nothing save that it once had a message to convey.[11]

As with many of Lovecraft's stories, this little tale has a strong
impact on first reading, even though later thought enables one to
pick it to pieces. For instance: What commander would put only a
single sentry in so vital a post? How does "ghastly marble" differ
from any other kind? How does a star wink "hideously"?

Stuffing a narrative with adjectives and adverbs like "uncanny,"
"hellish," "weirdly," "hideously," "evil," "eldritch," "shocking," and
"sinister" was Lovecraft's worst fictional vice. Such rhetorical extravagance may impress the naïve reader and cajole him into a
receptive mood, but a more sophisticated reader is soon irritated by
it.

The reason is that all such words denote, not physical facts,
but the narrator's emotional reaction to facts. It is not that all adjectives are objectionable; a moderate use of them gives the story
color. But adjectives like "horrible" and "ghastly," which merely
convey the mental state of the author or his fictional narrator,
slow the story down without enhancing it. As my colleague Lin
Carter, in criticizing Lovecraft's early story "The Nameless City,"
puts it:

> The story is overwritten, over-dramatic, and the mood of
> mounting horror is applied in a very artificial manner. Rather than
> creating in the reader a mood of terror, Lovecraft *describes* a

mood of terror; the emotion is applied in the adjectives—the valley in which the city lies is "terrible"; the ruins themselves are of an "unwholesome" antiquity; certain of the altars and stones "suggested forbidden rites of terrible, revolting, and inexplicable nature." Of course, if you stop to think about it, such terms are meaningless. A stone is a stone, a valley is a valley, and ruins are merely ruins. Decking them out with a variety of shuddery adjectives does not make them intrinsically shuddersome.

This excess of modifiers is simply a beginner's bad writing, such as one expects in freshman English themes. Poe did much of it, for in his day it was considered "fine writing"; but standards have changed. To the young Lovecraft, however, Poe could do no wrong. So Lovecraft ignored the changes in fictional techniques since Poe's time, just as he long ignored those in poetry since Dryden and Pope.

Nonetheless, the primary purpose of a story is not to be dissected by a reflective critic but to absorb and entertain a reader on first contact. From this point of view, "Polaris" may be counted a modest success.

Some Lovecraftians have classed "Polaris" among Lovecraft's "Dunsanian" fantasies—those written during the years when Lovecraft was most completely under Dunsany's spell. Lovecraft, however, wrote "Polaris" before he had ever read anything by Dunsany.

In 1918, Lovecraft learned that some of his fellow-amateurs would pay him to revise their writings. His friends urged him to make a career of revision, and he wrote Galpin:

> By the way, that good lady [a Mrs. Arnold] recently sent two pieces for revision at professional rates—better than anything from her pen which I had previously seen. . . . Speaking of clients—you and Miss Durr will be satisfied at last. I am a real labouring man! In other words, I have undertaken to make a thorough & exhaustive revision of Rev. D. V. Bush's long prose book—now called "Pike's Peak or Bust". . . . I do not see how the fellow manages to get on so in the world. He is, literarily, such a complete d—— fool!

Thus Lovecraft became a ghost-writer. Thereafter, ghosting remained his chief gainful occupation; his own fiction was only a sideline. During his last decade, I estimate that at least three fourths of his earned income came from ghosting.

Most of his "revision" work consisted merely of the correction of errors of spelling, punctuation, and grammar, with some improvement of style. But sometimes, when a story aroused his imagination, he rewrote the whole thing, using more of his ideas than of the original author's.

Despising commercialism and having little sense of his worth, he charged below what the market might have borne. His charges at the beginning averaged about an eighth of a cent a word. In later life, he asked much more than this. In 1933, he listed his current rates as follows:

H. P. Lovecraft—Prose Revision Rates
Reading only—rough general remarks

1000 words or less	0.50
1000–2000	0.65
2000–4000	1.00
4000–5000	1.25
20¢ for each 1000 wds over 5000	

Criticism only—analytical estimate in detail without revision

1000 words or less	1.50
1000–2000	2.00
2000–4000	3.00
4000–5000	3.75
60¢ for each 1000 wds over 5000	

Revision & Copying—Per page of 330 words

(a) Copying on typewriter—double space, 1 carbon. No revision except spelling, punctuation, & grammar—   0.25
(b) Light revision, no copying (prose improved locally—no new ideas)—
                                                                       0.25
(c) Light revision typed, double-space with 1 carbon—   0.50
(d) Extensive revision, no copying (thorough improvement, including structural change, transposition, addition, or excision—possible introduction of new ideas or plot elements. Requires new text or separate MS.) In rough draught longhand—   0.75
(c) Extensive revision as above, typed, double space, 1 carbon—   1.00
(f) Rewriting from old MS., synopsis, plot-notes, idea-germ, or mere suggestion—i.e. "ghost writing". Text in full by reviser—both language & development. Rough draught longhand—   2.25
(g) Rewriting as above, typed, double space, 1 carbon—   2.50

Special flat rates quoted for special jobs, depending on
estimated consumption of time & energy.

The last item, for which Lovecraft quoted $2.50 a page, is complete ghost-writing. Lovecraft was asking about three quarters of a cent a word for such work. But these figures represented a mere hope. In practice he seems to have accepted much lower prices than those he quoted.

On some jobs, he got as much as one quarter of a cent a word. Adolphe de Castro's 18,500-word novelette "The Last Executioner," however, which Lovecraft rewrote for $16, was sold to *Weird Tales* for $175. Lovecraft made less than one tenth of a cent a word on the deal. In 1933 he was rewriting an 80,000-word novel for $100, or one eighth of a cent a word.[12]

Since Lovecraft was a painstaking worker, this was a starvation wage for the time he spent. It is no wonder that he was never really able to make a living from his revision.

Moreover, he often had trouble in collecting even his modest fees. He could have made more had he haggled with and dunned his clients, but he would not behave in such an "ungentlemanly" way. Sometimes he even sent back checks that he did not think he had earned. When one of his last clients asked him how much he would charge her for a major job, he assured her that anything she offered would suit. In dealing with so unmercenary a ghost, his clients were not over-generous.

Still, ghost-writing gave Lovecraft his first earned income. He later said that he could get along on $15 a week and only wished he could always count on getting that much from his clients. Actually, he earned more than that in later years but saved the surplus for travel and postage. Though always poor, he was never in danger of starving, since his aunts, with whom he lived after his mother's death, could always tide him over a lean spell.

David Van Bush, one of Lovecraft's first ghosting clients, remained his largest single source of earned income for nearly a decade. Bush lectured for the New Thought movement. This movement had been founded in the late nineteenth century by followers of Phineas P. Quimby, who died in 1866 after a career as a "magnetic healer." Quimby's most celebrated patient was Mary Baker Eddy, before she launched her own somewhat similar doctrine of Christian Science.

Author of small books with titles like *Applied Psychology and Scientific Living*, *Practical Psychology and Sex Life*, and *Character Analysis (How to Read People at Sight)*, the stocky, burly, blue-eyed, sharp-nosed, balding Bush had an aggressive, professionally

"magnetic" manner and poetic ambitions without poetic talent. A
passage and a poem from his book *Grit and Gumption* will show
why Lovecraft called him a "literary damned fool":

> Genius consists in mustering your pepper. Every man has a
> certain amount of pepper in his system. Yes, you have. The hook-
> worm's got you if you have no pepper in your constitution. Even
> though you think that you have no pepper and the hook-worm
> has got you yet you have a chance to muster what pepper you
> have. . . .

And the poem, *Just Boost and Make 'Er Go:*

> *Don't have a face so glum and long*
> *   You look like a baboon*
> *But have a grin upon your chin*
> *   Like that upon the moon.*
> *So with a smile meet ev'ry foe;*
> *   Just boost 'er up and make 'er go!*[13]

Bush published his inspirational booklets and traveled about
lecturing. In June, 1922, Lovecraft attended one of his lectures
in Boston. The speaker gave a dramatic impersonation of a man
in delirium tremens, complete with pink snakes.

With time, Lovecraft disliked Bush more and more. In 1921,
after he had been ghosting for Bush for three years, he complained
of being "swamped with the drivel of that indescribable monstrosity
Bush."

Bush might be everything that Lovecraft despised: a loud-
mouthed, aggressive, vulgar, mercenary, successful spiritual racket-
eer, pandering to the weaknesses of the simple and the tender-
minded by bellowing platitudes and psychological half-truths from
the lecture platform. But Bush, unlike many clients, paid well and
promptly; so Lovecraft stuck it out.

During this period, Lovecraft ghosted two stories for an
amateur poet, Winifred Virginia Jackson—or perhaps I should say
he collaborated with her, since it is unlikely that any money changed
hands. Both tales appeared in amateur magazines under the double
pseudonyms of "Lewis Theobald, Jr., and Elizabeth Neville Berkeley."
Both are so Lovecraftian in style that they have been reprinted in
collections of Lovecraft's stories.

Miss Jackson, said Lovecraft, had no talent for prose. She

furnished him with ideas, around which he wrote the stories—or rather, vignettes. Both tales are merely little dream-narratives without formal structure, of about 3,000 and 2,500 words respectively.

In "The Crawling Chaos," the narrator tells how a physician, treating him for plague, gave him an overdose of opium. When he recovers consciousness,

> For a moment my surroundings seemed confused, like a projected image hopelessly out of focus, but gradually I realised my solitary presence in a strange and beautiful room lighted by many windows. . . .

The narrator steps out and finds that the house in which he awakened stands on a high, narrow point of land:

> On either side of the house there fell a newly washed-out precipice of red earth, whilst ahead of me the hideous waves were still rolling frightfully, eating away the land with ghastly monotony and deliberation.

The narrator flees inland, taking his adjectives with him. Entering a woodland, he meets a troop of divine-looking youths and maidens who, in Dunsanian language, invite him to come with them:

> In Teloe beyond the Milky Way and the Arinurian streams are cities all of amber and chalcedony. And upon their domes of many facets glisten the images of strange and beautiful stars. . . .[14]

In company with these luminous beings, the narrator rises into the firmament. Looking back, he sees the earth undergoing a vast convulsion. A chasm opens, the oceans pour into it and turn to steam, and the earth blows up.

"The Green Meadow" is even dreamier. A meteor falls in Maine. It proves to contain a book made of unknown materials and bearing a narrative in Classical Greek. The narrator tells of finding himself on a grassy floating island off the shore of an ocean, with a sinister forest on the landward side and a large floating mass, the Green Meadow, on the other. His island is borne by a current towards an abyss. As it nears the Green Meadow, he hears a song from invisible singers:

> And then, as my island drifted closer and the sound of the distant waterfall grew louder, I saw clearly the *source* of the chanting, and in one horrible instant remembered everything. Of such

things I cannot, dare not tell, for therein was revealed the hideous solution of all which had puzzled me; and that solution would drive you mad, even as it almost drove me. . . .[15]

Lovecraft did another collaboration, published in *The United Amateur* (September, 1920) as "Poetry and the Gods," by "Anna Helen Crofts and Henry Paget-Lowe." Since this sounds much less like Lovecraft than the other two, we may infer that Miss Crofts (if that was really her name) had done more of its actual writing. The prose has a feminine ring foreign to Lovecraft.

The story is a limp little fantasy wherein Marcia, "attired simply, in a low-cut evening dress of black," reads a piece of free verse and is at once visited by Hermes, winged sandals and all. The god carries Marcia off to Olympus. There Zeus tells her what a good girl she is and warns her to watch for the new messenger, whom he will soon send to earth.

During the First World War, Susie Lovecraft's mental state declined. Her neighbor Clara Hess wrote:

> The last time I saw Mrs. Lovecraft we were both going "down street" on the Butler Avenue car. She was excited and apparently did not know where she was. She attracted the attention of everyone. One old gentleman acted as if he were going to jump out of the car every minute. I was greatly embarrassed as I was the object of all of her attention.[16]

Spells of hysteria and depression became more and more acute. In January 1919, Susie went to visit her elder sister, Lillian Clark, leaving her younger one, Annie Gamwell, in charge of the house. Annie had left her husband and moved back to Providence. Susie's illness and absence distressed the twenty-eight-year-old Lovecraft until he could not eat; nor write, except with a pencil. He called on Susie every day; otherwise, he said, he was useless for anything.

On March 13, Susie was admitted to Butler Hospital for the Insane, where her husband had died twenty-one years before. Here she told everyone who would listen about her wonderful son, "a poet of the highest order." This son was not in good shape himself; he wrote:

> My nerve strain seems now to be manifesting itself in my vision— I am frequently dizzy & cannot read or write without a blurring of sight or a severe headache. Existence seems of little value, & I wish it might be terminated.[17]

Susie lingered two years in the hospital. Lovecraft often visited his mother. When kept away, he wrote her long letters. She sent him gifts: ". . . the small primroses—which still adorn this apartment—the Weekly Review, the banana, and that most captivating cat picture. . . ."[18]

It looks like a normal picture of a filial son and his invalid mother, but he never seems to have visited her *inside* the hospital. He met her on the grounds, usually at a place called "the Grotto." They strolled about the spacious, parklike Butler Woods overlooking the Seekonk River, but the hospital records list no visits by him inside the buildings. This fact is confirmed by a letter he wrote in 1925, when his wife was in the hospital in Brooklyn, and he visited her daily. He wrote that, until then, "I had never seen the interior of such an institution at any great length."

Lovecraft's avoidance of the hospital has caused speculation. As I have noted, Winfield Townley Scott dismissed Lovecraft as "a fearful and selfish young man." It seems unlikely, however, that this is the whole explanation. Lovecraft did often visit his mother. Futhermore, Lovecraft's reaction to his mother's death was certainly that of a devoted son.

Simple selfishness seems an inadequate answer; but we lack clues to any other: whether he was kept away by sensitivity to hospital smells, or unconsciously resented his disastrous upbringing, or doctor's orders, or some other reason, which has vanished down the remorseless gullet of time.

During the two years of his mother's hospitalization, Lovecraft, despite his spells of wretchedness, expanded his interests. He had hardly finished swearing off amateur journalism when he found himself official editor of the Cole-Hoffman faction of the UAPA. After the death of Helene Hoffman Cole, this group was called the "Lovecraft UAPA."

Lovecraft got out *The Conservative*, Vol. V, No. 1 (July, 1919)—which, however, proved the last issue for nearly four years. He wrote for other amateur publications, especially *The United Amateur* and *The National Amateur*.

An article in *The Silver Clarion* was titled, with self-conscious modesty, "The Brief Autobiography of an Inconsequential Scribbler." It begins with Lovecraft's arch disclaimer of having much to tell about: "Since the earthly career of a secluded and non-robust individual is seldom replete with exciting events, my readers must not expect the following chronicle to possess much which will hold their attention or awaken their interest. . . ." He tells of childhood and youth and of his joining the UAPA. "I have endeavoured to support the most purely literary and progressive elements in Amateurdom, and to aid in a revival of that conservatism and classicism which modern literature seems dangerously prone to reject."[19]

An article, "Idealism and Materialism: A Reflection," sets forth Lovecraft's Machiavellian attitude towards the supernatural. It starts with one of his verbosely irritating poses of superiority: "Human thought, with its infinite varieties, intensities, aspects, and collisions, is perhaps the most amusing yet discouraging spectacle on our terraqueous globe. . . ." The writer then gives a conventional anthropological account of how primitive man personified natural forces and so invented gods.

Lovecraft divides idealists into "two classes, theological and rationalistic." The former are the followers of religions; the latter, idealistic atheists who, believing in the perfectibility of man, attack religion in the hope that its overthrow will lead to such perfection. "Just as the theist forgets that his faith may be fallacious though its effects be good, so does the idealistic atheist forget that his doctrine may have ill effects though it be true."

The materialist, on the other hand, "sees the infinity, eternity, purposelessness, and automatic action of creation, and the utter, abysmal insignificance of man and the world therein. . . . Looking beyond the bald facts of atheism, he reconstructs the dawn of the human mind and perceives that its evolution absolutely necessitates a religious and idealistic period. . . ."[20] As for people who *know* the truth of their particular dogma, Lovecraft cites his own childhood, when he *knew* that the gods of Classical mythology existed.

Lovecraft read Schopenhauer (whose pessimism matched his own), Nietzsche, and Freud. He admired Nietzsche's reduction of human morals to an anthropological, materialistic basis but did not take the great German windbag very seriously: ". . . let me state clearly that I do not swallow him whole. His ethical system is a joke. . . ."[21] Freud, he thought, was on the right track, albeit he had reservations about some of Freud's theories.

He also began more stories. Early in 1919, he wrote "Beyond the Wall of Sleep"—like "The Tomb," a story showing more promise than performance. It begins wordily:

I have often wondered if the majority of mankind ever pause to reflect upon the occasionally titanic significance of dreams, and of the obscure world to which they belong. Whilst the greater number of our nocturnal visions are perhaps no more than faint and fantastic reflections of our waking experiences—Freud to the contrary with his puerile symbolism—there are still a certain remainder whose immundane and ethereal character permit of no ordinary interpretation, and whose vaguely disquieting effect suggests possible minute glimpses into a sphere of mental existence no less important than physical life, yet separated from that life by an all but impassable barrier.

The narrator tells of being an intern at a mental hospital. A patient, Joe Slater, is sent there after being acquitted of murder on grounds of insanity. Slater is a drooling, drunken degenerate from the backwoods, who sometimes acts as if possessed by a different and much more intelligent personality. He mumbles about "green edifices of light, oceans of space, strange music, and shadowy mountains and valleys."[22]

Convinced that Slater is experiencing life on another plane, the narrator rigs up an apparatus to put himself into rapport with Slater. When both sleep, the narrator, too, lives in that other dimension. He meets Slater's alter ego, his "brother of light." This gaseous being explains that he must go to Algol, the "demon star," to destroy an enemy. Slater dies, and sure enough a nova blazes up near Algol.

Lovecraft also experimented with "prose poems." These are sketches or vignettes of a few hundred words, which make up for lack of plot by lush, poetical language. Prose poems were popular with nineteenth-century French Decadents, who liked to hint at sins too frightful to be put into words. Lovecraft had read Huysmans and perhaps other Decadents. His first prose poem, "Memory," shows the influence of some of Poe's short fantasies, such as "The Conversation of Eiros and Charmion." It begins:

In the valley of Nis the accursed waning moon shines thinly, tearing a path for its light with feeble horns through the lethal foliage of a great upas-tree. And within the depths of the valley, where the light reaches not, move forms not meant to be beheld. Rank is the herbage on each slope, where evil vines and creeping plants crawl amidst the stone of ruined palaces, twining tightly about broken columns and strange monoliths, and heaving up marble pavements laid by forgotten hands. And in trees that grow gigantic in crumbling courtyards leap little apes. . . .

The Genie of the moonbeams asks the Daemon of the Valley, who built these ruins? The Daemon replies:

"I am Memory, and am wise in the lore of the past, but I too am old. These beings were like the waters of the river Than, not to be understood. Their deeds I recall not, for they were but of the moment. Their aspect I recall dimly, it was like that of the little apes in the trees. Their name I recall clearly, for it rhymed with that of the river. These beings of yesterday were called Man."[23]

Lovecraft wrote three more prose poems for amateur journals: "Nyarlathotep" (1920), "Ex Oblivione" (1921), and "What the Moon Brings" (1923). Such compositions are pleasant little things to read but cannot be classed as any author's major works. Like many of Lovecraft's stories, "Nyarlathotep" originated in a dream. It begins:

Nyarlathotep . . . the crawling chaos . . . I am the last . . . I will tell the audient void . . .

I do not recall distinctly when it began, but it was months ago. The general tension was horrible. To a season of political and social upheaval was added a strange and brooding apprehension of hideous physical danger; . . .

And it was then that Nyarlathotep came out of Egypt. Who he was, none could tell, but he was of the old native blood and looked like a Pharaoh. . . . Into the lands of civilisation came Nyarlathotep, swarthy, slender, and sinister, always buying strange instruments of glass and metal and combining them into instruments yet stranger. . . .

Nyarlathotep comes to the narrator's city with an electrical demonstration-show, which also includes a movie, showing "hooded forms amidst ruins, and yellow evil faces peering from behind monuments." At the end, the audience straggles out into open country in a blizzard. Everything disintegrates into chaos:

And through this revolting graveyard of the universe the muffled, maddened beating of drums, and thin, monotonous whine of blasphemous flutes from inconceivable unlighted chambers beyond Time; the detestable pounding and piping whereunto dance slowly, awkwardly, and absurdly the gigantic, tenebrous ultimate gods—the blind, voiceless, mindless gargoyles whose soul is Nyarlathotep.

That concluding sentence (which Lovecraft paraphrased in "The Dream-Quest of Unknown Kadath") has always reminded me of one of the noisier night clubs. The work originated in a dream, wherein Lovecraft got from Sam Loveman a letter, telling him:

> Don't fail to see Nyarlathotep if he comes to Providence. He is horrible—horrible beyond anything you can imagine—but wonderful.

The story followed the dream up to the point where Lovecraft "was drawn into the black yawning abyss between the snows,"[24] at which point in the dream he screamed and awoke. The name "Nyarlathotep" is a hybrid. *Hotep* is ancient Egyptian for "contented" or "satisfied"; *nyarlat* is probably an echo of some African place name, such as Nyasaland.[25]

In September, 1919, Lovecraft read *Time and the Gods*, by Lord Dunsany. "The first paragraph arrested me as with an electric shock . . ." Bowled over, Lovecraft began to read Dunsany's other books and was delighted to learn that Dunsany himself was to lecture at the Copley-Plaza Hotel in Boston early in November.

With three other amateur journalists, Lovecraft attended, arriving early enough to get front-row seats. He reported:

> Dunsany entered late, accompanied and introduced by Prof. George Baker of Harvard. He is of Galpinian build—6 ft. 2 in. in height, and very slender. His face is fair and pleasing, though marred by a slight mustache. In manner he is boyish and a trifle awkward; and his smile is winning and infectious. His hair is light brown. His voice is mellow and cultivated, and very clearly British. . . . Dunsany first touched upon his ideals and methods; then hitched a chair up to his reading table, seated himself, and commenced reading his short play, *The Queen's Enemies*.

To Lovecraft, any mustache "marred" its wearer's face. Edward John Moreton Drax Plunkett, Eighteenth Baron Dunsany (1878–1957), was sometimes called the worst-dressed man in Ireland. His usual lecture costume was a suit of shapeless, baggy tweeds into whose pockets he had stuffed a few penciled notes. He spoke fluently, with little histrionics but with the faintest trace of Irish lilt in his British public-school English.

Temperamental, vigorous, versatile, sporting, and poetically sensitive, Dunsany was an Anglo-Irish peer, writer, soldier, poet, sportsman, and world traveler—the kind of lord that many would like to be if they had a chance. Besides roaming the world, hunting foxes in the British Isles and wild goats in the Sahara, winning the chess and pistol championships of Ireland, serving as a British officer in the Boer and First World wars, associating with William Butler Yeats and the Abbey Theatre in the Irish renaissance, and making an abortive entry into politics, Dunsany also wrote sixty-odd books of stories, plays, poetry, and autobiography—mostly with a quill pen.

Dunsany alternated between a Regency house in Kent and a Norman castle in County Meath, an hour's drive from Dublin. The castle was modernized about two centuries ago. As Lady Dunsany once said: "If you're going to modernize a castle, the eighteenth century is the best time to do it." Behind the bookcases in the great library are a priest hole and a secret stair left over from the days of persecution of Catholics, before the Dunsanys converted to Protestantism.

Dunsany strongly influenced twentieth-century fantasy writers. He adapted heroic fantasy, revived by William Morris in the 1880s, to the short-story form—albeit he also wrote novels. A religious skeptic, he invented whole pantheons of deities to reign over his imaginary worlds. These were not gods of the abstract, perfectionistic kinds favored by theologians, but the kind that men believed in during the childhood of the race, endowed with human vanity, jealousy, capriciousness, vindictiveness, and cruelty. Lovecraft called Dunsany's writing "Unexcelled in the sorcery of crystalline singing prose, and supreme in the creation of a gorgeous and languorous world of iridescently exotic vision," which is pretty iridescent prose in itself.

After the lecture, the monocled peer "was encircled by autograph-seekers. Egged on by her aunt, Miss Hamlet almost mustered up courage enough to ask for an autograph, but weakened at the last moment. . . . For mine own part, I did not seek a signature; for I detest fawning upon the great." The last sentence is merely a rationalization of Lovecraft's shyness.

Alice Hamlet, one of Lovecraft's fellow-amateurs, "could not quite give up the idea of an autograph"[26] and wrote Dunsany a note inclosing gifts, including an autograph letter by Lincoln. Dunsany sent a courteous reply. Lovecraft wrote a sixty-four-line poem, *To Edward John Moreton Drax Plunkett, Eighteenth Baron Dunsany*. Composed in his worst eighteenth-century style, it appeared in C. W. Smith's *The Tryout*:

> *As when the sun above a dusky wold*
> *Springs into sight, and turns the gloom to gold,*
> *Lights with his magic beams the dew-deck'd bow'rs,*
> *And wakes to life the gay responsive flow'rs;*
> *So now o'er realms where dark'ning dulness lies,*
> *In solar state see shining PLUNKETT rise! . . .*

Miss Hamlet sent a copy of *The Tryout* to Dunsany, who replied:

Dec. 1 1919

My dear Miss Hamlet:—
I must thank you very much for sending me so magnificent a tribute, and—whether I deserve it or not—I am most grateful to the author of that poem for his warm and generous enthusiasm, crystallised in verse. Such tributes make me very humble, for I begin to wonder if I can have deserved them and I feel that I owe to such kind friends my very greatest efforts in the future, to try to justify my place in their appreciation. I am very glad to hear that "A DREAMER'S TALES" was able to fulfill the purpose for which it was required. Thank you very much for writing me.

Yours very sincerely,
Dunsany

Congratulations to Mr. Lovecraft.

Dame Gossip.[27]

The last line was probably by Lady Dunsany.
Both in person and as a fellow-author, Dunsany had a stunning impact on Lovecraft. For a while he even edged out HPL's long-time idol Poe. Dunsany was everything that Lovecraft would have liked to be. The appeal of an authentic British peer, who not only wrote exquisite fantasy but was also an accomplished, engaging, attractive person, was overwhelming.
The episode launched Lovecraft on a spate of Dunsanian

stories. It was fictionally the most productive period of his life. During 1917–21, he turned out at least seventeen stories, not counting collaborations.

The first—or one of the first—of his Dunsanian tales was "The White Ship," written just after the lecture. A little under 3,000 words, this dream-narrative begins: "I am Basil Elton, keeper of the North Point light that my father and grandfather kept before me. . . ." The narrator speaks of the "white-sailed argosies" that used to pass his lighthouse but now seldom do. He tells that:

> Out of the South it was that the White Ship used to come when the moon was full and high in the heavens. Out of the South it would glide very smoothly and silently over the sea. . . .

At last, Elton boards the ship, which cruises past fantastic lands. It stops at paradisiacal Sona-Nyl, where "there is neither time nor space, neither suffering nor death; and there I dwelt for many aeons."

Bored with perfection, Elton urges the captain to go on to Cathuria, "which no man hath seen, but which all believe to lie beyond the basalt pillars of the West." When they pass the Pillars, they find themselves rushing towards a cataract, "wherein the oceans of the world drop down to abysmal nothingness." Over they go, and Elton awakens to find his light out and a ship breaking up on the rocks.

In later years, Lovecraft disliked "The White Ship," which he said "makes me sick whenever I think of it!" It was, he said, "mawkish & namby-pamby."[28] This is over-severe. "The White Ship" is far from his best story; but others suffer even more from the faults of which he complained.

"Arthur Jermyn" (1920) is a science-fiction horror story, starting with the resounding statement: "Life is a hideous thing, and from the background behind what we know of it peer demoniacal hints of truth which make it sometimes a thousandfold more hideous."

Arthur Jermyn, who combines a sensitive, poetic nature with an apelike appearance, is heir to a baronetcy with a history of abnormality. His ancestor, Sir Wade Jermyn, had explored the Congo in the eighteenth century. Sir Wade had returned with fantastic tales of a ruined city inhabited by a vanishing white race. He also brought back a wife, whom he kept secluded. He took her back to Africa on subsequent trips, from the last of which he returned without her. Shortly thereafter, he was put in the madhouse.

Arthur Jermyn goes to Africa and hunts up the lost city, finding only scanty remnants. He hears tales of a stuffed white goddess who had been a fetish of the vanished dwellers. After he returns to England, an acquaintance sends him the goddess. When Jermyn opens the crate, he finds the mummy of an ape-woman, who is his own great-great-great-grandmother, Sir Wade's mysterious wife.

The story belongs to the lost-race sub-genre, very popular when "Arthur Jermyn" was written. H. Rider Haggard and Edgar Rice Burroughs used the idea over and over. Alas! the airplane has now been so perfected that hardly a square mile of the earth's surface has not been seen from the air. So the lost race and the lost city have dropped out of fiction, since there is no place left where they can plausibly hide.

For once Lovecraft told his story in simple, straightforward prose, uncluttered by modifiers like "ghastly" and "eldritch." When, a few years later, Edwin F. Baird bought "Arthur Jermyn" for *Weird Tales*, Lovecraft was furious because Baird changed the title to "The White Ape." This, said Lovecraft, gave away the dénouement. In fact, I doubt if many readers would have been surprised by the climax, whichever title was used.

You may wonder: Why do people like to read stories of horror, terror, disaster, doom, and despair? Many obviously do. If one reads fiction for the pleasure of stirring up synthetic, vicarious emotions, the emotions of horror and so forth are as legitimate as the pleasanter ones of sympathy, excitement, triumph, love, and laughter. Joseph Addison, one of Lovecraft's eighteenth-century idols, thought the matter through over two and a half centuries ago:

> The two leading Passions which the more serious Parts of Poetry endeavour to stir up in us, are Terror and Pity. And here, by the way, one would wonder how it comes to pass, that such Passions as are very unpleasant at all other time, are very agreeable when excited by proper Descriptions. . . .
>
> If we consider, therefore, the Nature of this pleasure, we shall find that it does not arise so properly from the Description of what is Terrible, as from the Reflection we make on our selves at the time of reading it. When we look on such hideous Objects, we are not a little pleased to think we are in no Danger of them. We

consider them at the same time, as Dreadful and Harmless; so that the more frightful Appearance they make, the greater is the pleasure we receive from the Sense of our own Safety. In short, we look upon the Terrors of a description, with the same Curiosity and Satisfaction that we survey a dead Monster.

"Arthur Jermyn" was followed by "The Cats of Ulthar." In this charming little fable, Lovecraft combined his Dunsanian style with his love of cats:

> It is said that in Ulthar, which lies beyond the river Skai, no man may kill a cat; and this I can verily believe as I gaze upon him who sitteth purring before the fire. For the cat is cryptic, and close to strange things which men cannot see. He is the soul of antique Aegyptus, and bearer of tales from forgotten cities in Meroë and Ophir. He is the kin of the jungle's lords, and heir to the secrets of hoary and sinister Africa.[29]

In that village dwell an old couple who like to trap and kill their neighbors' cats. One day a caravan of dark, Gypsylike strangers passes through the town. Among them is an orphan boy, Menes, whose only companion is a small black kitten. This kitten vanishes.

Menes prays to his own gods, and the caravan departs. That night, all the cats of Ulthar disappear. Next day they are back, placid and well-fed. Of the old couple, all that remains is a pair of skeletons.

"The Doom that Came to Sarnath," written about the same time, is an excellent little Dunsanian fantasy:

> There is in the land of Mnar a vast still lake that is fed by no stream, and out of which no stream flows. Ten thousand years ago there stood by its shore the mighty city of Sarnath, but Sarnath stands there no more.

Before the days of Sarnath had stood the gray stone city of Ib, "peopled with beings not pleasing to behold." Hating the froglike Ibites, the Sarnathians destroyed them. On the thousandth anniversary of the destruction of Ib, King Zokkar of Sarnath throws a great feast, to which he bids other princes. But at midnight. . . . Lovecraft was surprised when he later learned that there was an Indian city named Sarnath, since he thought he had made up the name.

Also written at this time is a 2,500-word horror story, "The Statement of Randolph Carter." Lovecraft had been arguing by mail with Loveman about horror stories, and early in December he got a letter on the subject from Loveman.

The night after receiving the letter, Lovecraft had a nightmare, in which he went with Loveman on a mysterious nocturnal mission. Soon after, he wrote the story.

The narrator, whose name appears in the title only, is called "Randolph Carter," while the Loveman of the dream becomes "Harley Warren." The story starts:

> I repeat to you, gentlemen, that your inquisition is fruitless. Detain me here forever if you will; confine or execute me if you must have a victim to propitiate the illusion you call justice; but I can say no more than I have said already.

The "gentlemen" are investigating Harley Warren's disappearance. Warren, it transpires, is a student of occult lore. On the night in question, Carter goes with Warren, who carries a lantern, a portable telephone set, and a book written in unknown characters. Carter bears a lantern and two shovels. They go to "an ancient cemetery; so ancient that I trembled at the manifold signs of immemorial years."

They pry up a granite slab, disclosing a black hole, into which Warren prepares to descend. Despite argument, he refuses to let Carter go with him, saying: ". . . I couldn't drag a bundle of nerves like you down to probable death or madness." Then down he goes, unreeling the telephone cable. After an ominous silence, Warren speaks through the telephone:

"God! If you could see what I am seeing! . . . it's terrible—monstrous—unbelievable!"

After further exclamations, Warren cries: "Carter! for the love of God, put back the slab and get out of this if you can! Quick!—leave everything else and make for the outside—it's your only chance! Do as I say, and don't ask me to explain!"

Warren utters several similar warnings, with rising excitement. He ends with a shriek of *"Beat it!"* Then silence. . . .[30]

The story (first published in Smith's *Tryout*) is an effective minor effort, despite an excess of rhetoric. "Randolph Carter," who reappears in several later stories, is a fictional idealization of Lovecraft himself, much as Conan the Cimmerian, the gigantic prehistoric barbarian adventurer, is an idealization of his creator, Robert E. Howard.

Carter is depicted as a dreamy, scholarly, aristocratic, and rather ineffectual Bostonian bachelor. He has two things that Lovecraft vainly longed for: enough money to live like a gentleman, and a military record; he has served in the French Foreign Legion. He dabbles in forbidden lore but, when drastic action is called for, becomes paralyzed with fright—"inert in the chains of stark horror." The Foreign Legion must have been glad to see the last of him. Doubtless Lovecraft, who had never been in such straits, imagined that a nervous person like himself would be thus paralyzed. People who knew him, however, assure me that Lovecraft would have faced a dire peril in a worthy manner.

Later in 1920, Lovecraft had another spurt of creativity. The first story was "The Tree": a minor effort using Classical lore. Two sculptors, Kalos and Musides, are close friends until the tyrant of Syracuse asks them to compete in making a statue for him. Thereupon Musides poisons Kalos. Later, Kalos has his revenge when a limb of the huge tree that grows out of his tomb falls upon Musides' house.

At about this time, Lovecraft wrote the better-known "Celephais." Like "The White Ship," "Celephais" is a dream-narrative; Lovecraft's dream world was taking more definite form. The story combines Dunsanian flavor, the geography of "The Cats of Ulthar," and Lovecraft's own outlook:

> In a dream Kuranes saw the city in the valley, and the seacoast beyond, and the snowy peak overlooking the sea, and the gaily painted galleys that sail out of the harbour toward distant regions where the sea meets the sky. In a dream it was also that he came by his name of Kuranes, for when awake he was called by another name. Perhaps it was natural for him to dream a new name; for he was the last of his family, and alone among the indifferent millions of London, so there were not many to speak to him and to remind him who he had been. His money and lands were gone, and he did not care for the ways of the people about him, but preferred to dream and write of his dreams. What he wrote was laughed at by those to whom he shewed it, so that after a time he kept his writings to himself and finally ceased to write.

Kuranes' favorite dream haunt is the city of Celephais in the valley of Ooth-Nargai. After adventuring in this dream world, Kuranes is unable to return to Celephais. He resorts to narcotics to dream more intensely; when *in extremis* he again finds his city:

> And Kuranes reigned thereafter over Ooth-Nargai and all the neighbouring regions of dream, and held his court alternately in Celephais and in the cloud-fashioned Serennian. He reigns there still, and will reign happily for ever, though below the cliffs at Innsmouth the channel tides played mockingly with the body of a tramp who had stumbled through the half-deserted village at dawn; played mockingly, and cast it upon the rocks by ivy-covered Trevor Towers, where a notably fat and especially offensive millionaire brewer enjoys the purchased atmosphere of extinct nobility.[31]

Lovecraft's model for "Kuranes" is plain as a pikestaff. As art, the story is praiseworthy, but the notes of self-pity and of wishful thinking may mar some readers' pleasure. Still, all fiction writers put themselves into their stories in one guise or another. Whom does one know half so well as oneself?

"From Beyond" (1920) is a conventional horror-fantasy or science-fiction horror story about a mad scientist who develops a machine that enables him to see into another dimension. He lures the narrator into joining him in an experiment, meaning to have the narrator devoured by a Thing from Outside.

"The Temple" (1920), of over 5,000 words, is in the form of a memoir by a German submarine commander, placed in a bottle. The Graf von Altberg-Ehrenstein tells how he sank a British freighter. A dead crewman from the sunken ship is washed up on the submarine. In his pocket is a youth's head carved in ivory, which exerts a malign influence.

An explosion cripples the submarine. The ship is haunted by swarms of uncanny dolphins. The crew either die, or go mad, or mutiny and are shot, until only the commander is left. The ship settles to the bottom amid the ruins of Atlantis, and the Graf determines to end his life exploring these ruins in a diving suit.

The story is mediocre; the various uncanny phenomena never make a coherent pattern. Interesting is Lovecraft's portrayal of the German officer, who speaks of "my iron German will," "I am always a German, and was quick to notice two things," "I am a Prussian and a man of sense." It is, of course, a hostile caricature—yet not so much as to strain credulity, for there have been many such Germans. The irony is that Lovecraft failed to see that, when he spoke of Anglo-Saxon Aryan superiority, he sounded like that himself.

"The Terrible Old Man" (around the end of 1920) is a competent little thousand-word fantasy—a conventional story of how three thieves go to rob an old sea captain of peculiar powers, and how the three meet violent ends.

The story is notable for three things. First, it is reminiscent of Dunsany's "The Probable Adventure of the Three Literary Men" and "How Nuth Would Have Practiced His Art Upon the Gnoles" and his play "A Night at the Inn," and probably modeled on them. Second, it is laid in Lovecraft's New England town of Kingsport. This is an imaginary doublet of Marblehead, Massachusetts; Lovecraft used it in later stories.

Finally, the story has one of those hostile snarls at "aliens" which, for the next decade, formed a leitmotif of Lovecraft's fiction. His three thieves are Angelo Ricci, Joe Czanek, and Manuel Silva, who "were not of Kingsport blood; they were of that new and heterogeneous alien stock which lies outside the charmed circle of New England life and traditions. . . ."

"The Music of Erich Zann" (1921) is often deemed one of Lovecraft's best stories. The narrator tells how, as a poor student in an unnamed French city, he took a cheap room in one of the decrepid old houses on the rue d'Auseil. His neighbor in the garret overhead is a mute old German musician, whose weird tunes the narrator hears. When the narrator strikes up an acquaintance, the mute lets him listen to his playing but stops him from looking out his shuttered and curtained window, which should command a view of the city. Zann also refuses, with signs of terror, to play the weird tunes the narrator has heard below.

One night the narrator hears a disturbance in the musician's room and comes in to help. Zann tries to write out an explanation of his secret. Then the unearthly strains are heard through the window. Zann snatches up his violin and begins feverishly playing. A tempest breaks the window, blows out the candles, and snatches away Zann's manuscript. When the narrator looks out, he sees only blackness. . . .

When somebody asked Lovecraft, who had never been abroad, how he described the atmosphere of Paris so well, he said he had indeed been there—in a dream, in company with Poe.

"The Nameless City" (1921) is the first story of what was later called the Cthulhu Mythos group. The narrator tells of a ruined city in the Arabian desert:

> There is no legend so old as to give it name, or to recall that it was ever alive; but it is told of in whispers around campfires and muttered about by grandmas in the tents of the sheiks so that all the tribes shun it without wholly acknowledging why. It was of this place that Abdul Alhazred the mad poet dreamed on the night before he sang this unexplainable couplet:
>
> > *"That is not dead which can eternal lie*
> > *And with strange aeons even death may die."*

Thus Lovecraft's childhood nickname, "Abdul Alhazred," was put to use. Exploring the ruins, the narrator finds carvings and mummies of a race of small, civilized dinosaurs. When he starts out from a tunnel, he is forced back by a shrieking wind, in which he thinks he hears the voices of the spirits of the former dwellers. As he struggles to the surface, against the sky he sees "a nightmare horde of rushing devils; hate-distorted, grotesquely panoplied, half transparent devils of a race no man might mistake—the crawling reptiles of the nameless city."[32]

Although not professionally published until after Lovecraft's death, the story is rather good of its kind. Like many of Lovecraft's tales, it was based upon a dream.

"The Other Gods" (1921), a very effective short fantasy, goes back to the dreamland of "The Cats of Ulthar." It begins: "Atop the tallest of earth's peaks dwell the gods of earth, and suffer no man to tell that he hath looked upon them." But then:

> In Ulthar, which lies beyond the river Skai, once dwelt an old man avid to behold the gods of earth; a man deeply learned in the seven cryptical books of earth, and familiar with the Pnakotic manuscripts of distant and frozen Lomar. His name was Barzai the Wise, and the villagers tell of how he went up a mountain on the night of the strange eclipse.

Apparently Lomar is not, as assumed in "Polaris," in the remote past of the waking world; instead, it is part of the dream world. Barzai and the young priest Atal climb forbidden Hatheg-Kla. Near the top, Barzai sprints ahead. As Atal gets higher, gravity seems to be pulling him up instead of down. Above, Barzai shrieks:

> "The other gods! The other gods! The gods of the outer hells that guard the feeble gods of earth! . . . Look away. . . . Go back. . . . Do not see! Do not see! The vengeance of the infinite abysses. . . . That cursed, that damnable pit. . . . Merciful gods of earth, I am falling into the sky!"[33]

"The Quest of Iranon" is a feeble fable of Lovecraft's dream world. Wearing a crown of vine leaves and a tattered purple robe, Iranon wanders about, singing for his supper and seeking, but never finding, the magical city of Aira. The story is impaired by the same note of self-pity heard in "Celephais." Lovecraft is, in effect, arguing that persons of his exquisite artistic sensitivity should be allowed to spend their lives in idle reverie and be supported while doing so.

"The Outsider" (1921) is often considered one of Lovecraft's best stories, although I do not personally care for it. In this, I seem to agree with the author, who called it "too glibly *mechanical* in its climactic effect, & almost comic in the bombastic pomposity of its language. . . . It represents my literal though unconscious imitation of Poe at its very height." The story is in fact so Poesque that some think it could have been passed off as a newly discovered story by Poe. Its opening paragraphs are almost a paraphrase of those of Poe's "Berenice."

The narrator tells how he grew up all alone: "I know not where I was born, save that the castle was infinitely old and infinitely horrible, full of dark passages and having high ceilings where the eye could find only cobwebs and shadows." Surrounded by a dense forest, this castle is full of bats, rats, moldy books, and moldering skeletons. What the poor fellow lived on is not stated.

At last the narrator climbs the castle's one tall black tower for a view. At the top, he is amazed to find that, instead of a lofty vantage point, he has merely reached the surface of the earth.

He bursts out, wanders the countryside, and finds another castle. Inside, gaily-dressed people are making merry, but all scream and run at the sight of him. In what looks like a doorway, he sees a ghoulish monstrosity, "the putrid, dripping eidolon of an unwholesome revelation." When he touches the thing, he finds that it is his own reflection in a mirror, and that he is the ghoul.

The sources of this story seem obvious. One is Poe's "The Masque of the Red Death." Another is Hawthorne's *The Journal of a Solitary Man*. In this work, Hawthorne noted an idea for a story in which he was walking in New York. He was astonished when people screamed and ran at the sight of him until he looked in a mirror and learned that "I had been promenading Broadway in my shroud!"

The title of "The Outsider" is significant. Lovecraft was, as he admitted, a self-made outsider. Now, the outsider—the hermit, the prophet, the visionary, the eccentric—has a hard time. He enjoys life only to the extent that he can give up ordinary mundane pleasures without missing them.

With his ascetic, viceless life, Lovecraft did pretty well at suppressing his lusts; but he never achieved a total, Buddhistic extinction of desire. He passionately wanted some things denied him: to recover and restore his grandfather's house; to travel to the West and to the Old World; to be a landed gentleman with enough income to support that rôle. So his life as an outsider, never very happy, had stretches of downright misery.

"The Moon-Bog" (1921) is a mediocre story of supernatural horror. It tells of an Irish-American who buys an estate in Ireland and plans to drain a haunted bog. But the bog-spirits turn the landowner and all his imported workers into frogs or otherwise dispose of them.

Following his mother's incarceration in March, 1919 was an inactive year for Lovecraft. Even though his aunts tried to take his mother's place in pampering him, he found it hard to get used to Susie's absence.

In 1920, he became livelier. He wondered if he could teach in a night school; his nocturnal hours, he said, ruled out daytime teaching. His new ghosting clients, he found, would pay him to correct their fiction.

In the spring, the amateur journalists Daas, Houtain, and Kleiner visited him. Then the Boston amateurs, comprising the Hub Club, planned a convention from July 3d to 10th. Lovecraft went.

Theretofore Lovecraft had rarely budged from home. He had not been out of Rhode Island in the three years before the Dunsany lecture and had not spent a night away from home since October, 1901, when he was eleven. At that time, his mother had taken him away for a vacation at a summer resort; but the boy's "nervous nostalgia forced a speedy return."[34]

At Boston, Lovecraft had a fine time. There were his fellow-amateurs Cook, Kleiner, and others. Lovecraft even clowned a little, burlesquing his eighteenth-century pose and telling the others he "was quite willing to be a regular Hooligan—for a day." Despite his apparent solemnity, Lovecraft had a lively sense of humor of the deadpan or poker-faced kind.

The first night, Lovecraft went home to Providence, to return the next day. Then others persuaded him to stay overnight in Boston. On the 6th, he set out with Alice Hamlet, "chaperoned by Mrs. Thompson [Miss Hamlet's aunt, as if Lovecraft ever needed chaperoning] and escorted by Mr. White" on a tour of the Boston metropolitan area. Later, Mrs. Thompson and Miss Hamlet took Lovecraft to their home in Dorchester for the night, since he was finding the noise of the convention house a trial and "had to have a quiet room by himself."

On August 7th, he was back in Boston for a picnic of the Hub Club. He had been invited by Edith Dowe Miniter, since the 1880s a leader in Massachusetts amateur journalism. Meanwhile he had received three UAPA laureateships at once: one for "The White Ship" and the others for an essay and an editorial.

Rain forced the picnickers to eat under cover, but the weather cleared enough to allow a mass hike in the Middlesex Fells Reservation. Mrs. Miniter gathered enough bay to construct a wreath for Lovecraft. She made him wear the thing in honor of his laureateship for the rest of the day.

On September 5th, he was back again for the Hub Club conference, where he met James F. Morton for the first time. HPL read a "long & tedious" speech in what he called "a dull monotonous fashion" and "pompous style,"[35] and was persuaded to sing.

Visiting Boston became a habit. On February 22, 1921, wearing a new suit from a factory outlet store, he braved the New England winter for a conference at Quincy House. The afternoon's topic was "What You Have Done for Amateur Journalism, and What Has

Amateur Journalism Done for You." Lovecraft read a paper, "What Amateurdom and I Have Done for Each Other." He told of his own entry into the field and of his aims as chairman of the Department of Public Criticism:

> What I have done for Amateur Journalism is probably very slight, but I can at least declare that it represents my best efforts toward . . . aid to the aspiring writer. . . . What I did was to commence a definite campaign for the elevation of the literary standard. . . . I undertook a fairly extensive amount of private criticism, and offered my services to any person wishing the revision of manuscripts of magazine copy. . . . When I entered amateurdom, I unfortunately possessed the delusion that I could write verse; a delusion which caused me to alienate my readers by means of many long and execrably dull metrical inflictions. . . .
>
> Happily, I can be less reserved in stating what amateurdom has done for me. . . . Amateur Journalism has provided me with the very world in which I live. Of a nervous and reserved temperament, and cursed with an aspiration which far exceeds my endowments, I am a typical misfit in the larger world of endeavour. . . . In 1914, when the kindly hand of amateurdom was first extended to me, I was as close to the state of vegetation as any animal well can be—perhaps I might best have been compared to the lowly potato. . . .
>
> What amateurdom has brought me is a circle of persons among whom I am not altogether an alien—persons who possess scholastic leanings, yet who are not as a body so arrogant with achievement that a straggler is frowned upon. . . . What I have given Amateur Journalism is regretably little; what Amateur Journalism has given me is—life itself.

Lovecraft reported to his mother: "My own remarks were received with a surprising amount of applause, which naturally gratified me immensely." At dinner, the talk became political, with Lovecraft defending Harding Republicanism.

Among the many amateurs whom Lovecraft met was a tall, strikingly handsome woman of vigorous personality, Sonia Haft Greene. Kleiner introduced them on the deck of a harbor boat taking them to a beach. Mrs. Greene hoped to publish her own amateur journal. Of Lovecraft, she later wrote: "I admired his personality but, frankly, at first not his person."

Lovecraft gave Mrs. Greene a sales talk on the merits of the UAPA. He promised to write her and to send her samples of his own and others' work in amateur journalism.

He had prepared another speech for the evening, on "'The Best Poet." When his turn came, he laid aside his script and, to his own surprise, spoke fluently *ex tempore*, with jokes and asides. The talk "evoked fairly thunderous applause."[36]

Lovecraft attended another amateur meeting on March 17th, where everyone was supposed to prepare some act with an Irish flavor, in honor of St. Patrick's Day. Lovecraft wrote "The Moon Bog" for the occasion and read it aloud.

Soon afterwards, the sixty-three-year-old Susie Lovecraft required a gall-bladder operation. The operation seemed successful. Five days later, however, she said that she wanted to die, because "I will only live to suffer." The next day, May 24, 1921, she died of "cholecystitis chalangitis"[37]—inflammation of the gall bladder and the bile duct.

During Susie's last illness, her sister Lillian Clark visited her, but apparently her son did not. Not knowing how long Susie was confined to her bed before her operation, we cannot tell whether this was purposeful or not; he may have been home with a nervous collapse.

Susie's death could possibly have been good for Lovecraft, by forcing independence and self-sufficiency upon him. It did not, because he had two loving aunts, ready, willing, and eager to take up Susie's burden. Thus Lovecraft lost whatever chance he had of escaping his rôle of mama's boy; he merely became his aunts' boy instead.

Nine

JOURNEYMAN FANTASIST

Be eloquent in praise of the very dull old days
    which have long since passed away,
And convince 'em, if you can, that the reign of Good Queen Anne
    was Culture's palmiest day.
Of course you will pooh-pooh whatever's fresh and new,
    and declare it's crude and mean,
For Art stopped short in the cultivated court
    of the Empress Josephine.[1]

W. S. GILBERT

Susie's death hit Lovecraft hard:

> Psychologically I am conscious of a vastly increased aimlessness and inability to be interested in events; a phenomenon due partly to the fact that much of my former interest in things lay in discussing them with my mother and securing her views and approval.

> . . . I am contemptuous of myself for continuing to live without the least valid excuse for prolonging so dismal a farce. I seldom awake without disgust at the necessity of remaining conscious another 16 or 17 hours before I can find oblivion again; and shall sooner or later be sensible enough to take steps toward a sleep of more merciful permanence.

He also abused the rest of mankind as "wolves, hyaenas, swine, fools, and madmen."[2]

Winfield Scott Lovecraft had left an estate of $10,000. Howard Phillips Lovecraft's grandfather, Whipple Van Buren Phillips, had willed $5,000 to his daughter Susie and $2,500 to his grandson. A sister of Winfield Scott Lovecraft, Mary Louisa Lovecraft Mellon, had died in 1916, leaving her nephew Howard Phillips Lovecraft $2,000.

Since Howard Phillips Lovecraft was his mother's sole heir, capital totaling at least $19,500 had been bequeathed him, either directly or through his mother. Of this, $12,000 came from his father and paternal aunt and $7,500 from his maternal grandfather. His mother probably received some additional money from the sale of the Phillips estate.

Some of this capital had been used by Lovecraft and his mother for living expenses. Some had been lost in a stock deal into which Susie had been inveigled by her brother, Edwin Phillips, in 1911. And much, doubtless, had been consumed by the two years of Susie's hospitalization.

In the early 1920s, Lovecraft used to say that his and his aunts' capital came to $20,000, and that this sum would have to last the three their lifetimes. Although $20,000 in 1921 had several times the buying power of that amount today—perhaps $60,000 or $70,000— the sum did not mean affluence for three people unable to earn a living and compelled to live on the interest and sometimes to dip into capital. Moreover, when Lovecraft mentioned this $20,000, he was discussing the Phillips estate; he may not have included the legacies from his father's side in this estimate of the family's capital.

In any case, the nephew and his aunts lived on a tight budget. About his income during the years he dwelt with Sonia in New York, she wrote: "His aunts, out of his share of the Phillips estate, were supposed to send him $15 a week; but while I provided for him they sent him only $5 and that not always readily." At $15 a week, the annual income due Lovecraft from his investment must have been about $750 to $780 a year. Assuming 6 per cent as most probably the rate of interest at that time, Lovecraft's personal capital in 1921 appears to have been about $12,500 or $13,000.

To reconcile these figures, we must assume either that the total worth of Lovecraft and his aunts was more than $20,000, because he had not included his own Lovecraft money, or else that Lovecraft had nearly two thirds of the total, leaving less than

$10,000 for the two aunts together. I think the former alternative is the right one.

The best estimate that I can make from this scanty record is that the total capital of the three was about $25,000; and that, of this, Lovecraft had about half. Besides the $5,000 apiece they got from Whipple Phillips, the aunts probably received legacies from other sources—Lillian Clark from her husband and Annie Gamwell from her son, who, like Howard Phillips Lovecraft, had received $2,500 under Whipple Phillips's will. They also shared in the proceeds from the sale of 454 Angell Street.

Lovecraft's main—perhaps his only—investment was in the form of promissory notes dating from 1911, secured by a mortgage on a quarry worked by an Italo-American, Mariano de Magistris. De Magistris seems to have paid his interest regularly. In the 1920s, Lovecraft liked to allude to this source of income, since it gave him the illusion of being a landed gentleman.

Although, in the early 1920s, Lovecraft may have had more money than either aunt, he never did earn enough to meet his modest expenses. Hence, except during the two years when his wife subsidized him in New York, he kept nibbling at his capital. That he was aware of this ominous trend is shown by the note of financial foreboding in his late letters. When he died, his capital was down to three notes valued at $500, whence the income was probably about $30 a year.[8] His money was nearly all gone. The other notes had presumably been paid off or sold, and the money spent. One might say that, while Lovecraft was never actually destitute, he died just in time to avoid that fate.

When Lovecraft spoke of his aunts' and his capital, he seems—fatalistically or realistically—to have assumed that he would never become a big earner. He did work, often quite hard, and he did earn some money. He did make spasmodic efforts to find jobs.

His efforts, however, were fatally handicapped, first by his failure either to get special training in youth or to build up an employment record in his twenties, and second by his gentleman complex. This tabu limited his choice of occupations to "genteel" ones and led him to view as vulgar the whole idea of money-making.

Thorstein Veblen pointed out, in *The Theory of the Leisure Class* (1899), that ostentatious indifference to money is part of the old aristocratic pose. One affected it to prove that one belonged to the propertied class and so had no need to worry about such things. When, however, the self-proclaimed aristocrat was in fact poor:

> Wherever the canon of conspicuous leisure has a chance undisturbed to work out its tendency, there will therefore emerge a secondary, and in a sense spurious, leisure class—abjectly poor and living a precarious life of want and discomfort, but morally unable to stoop to gainful pursuits. The decayed gentleman and the lady who has seen better days are by no means unfamiliar phenomena even now. This pervading sense of the indignity of the slightest manual labour is familiar to all civilised peoples. . . . In persons of delicate sensibility, who have long been habituated to gentle manners, the sense of the shamefulness of manual labour may become so strong that, at a critical juncture, it will even set aside the instinct of self-preservation.

When Susie died, Lovecraft's elder aunt, Lillian Phillips Clark, moved into the house at 598 Angell Street. For the next three years, Lovecraft lived with his aunts—usually with both, except when Annie Gamwell was away on a vacation or on a temporary job.

After his mother's death, Lovecraft vegetated in bathrobe and slippers, doing little but write letters. After three weeks, even his indulgent aunts urged him to bestir himself. They pointed out that, during Susie's last illness, Lovecraft had received an invitation to call upon a new and promising member of the UAPA. This was a retired lady professor, M. A. Little, of Haverhill, Massachusetts.

On June 9th, Lovecraft called on Miss Little. He also visited the eminent amateur publisher Charles W. Smith, another resident of Haverhill. At this time, Smith was a small, gray-bearded man of sixty-nine. He had been publishing since 1888 and issuing *The Tryout* since 1914, and he continued publishing for nearly three decades more.

Miss Little decided to go with Lovecraft to meet Smith, who welcomed them heartily to a "dilapidated old cottage" cluttered with the souvenirs and litter of decades. He was just setting up Lovecraft's story "The Terrible Old Man" to print in a forthcoming *Tryout*.

On July 4th, Lovecraft attended the annual convention of the NAPA in Boston. There, W. Paul Cook was presented a loving cup. Assigned the task of responding to the toastmaster, Lovecraft merely gabbed in a mildly humorous vein: "Since I have nothing to say, it behooves me to say it as tastefully as possible. . . ."

Lovecraft also did ghost-writing for Bush. On August 8th, he got a telephone call from his boyhood friend Harold Bateman Munroe, now a deputy sheriff. Munroe invited Lovecraft on an automobile trip to places near Taunton, Massachusetts, which they had frequented as boys, because Munroe had business there. Off they went in Munroe's new Model T. At Great Meadow Hill, Lovecraft rejoiced to find the old clubhouse intact. He later remarked that Munroe

> . . . does not miss youth as I do. For him the dull routine of adult life is perfectly adequate—yet I would trade any two of my adult & intellectual Boston "sprees" of today for one short hour as a boy of 17 or 18 with the old "gang". . . .[4]

Lovecraft now received a request from his fellow-amateur G. J. Houtain for a series of six connected horror stories to run in Houtain's new professional magazine, *Home Brew*. Houtain promised to pay $5.00 per story or $30 altogether. This came to a quarter of a cent a word—a rock-bottom price, but Lovecraft had to start somewhere.

Lovecraft found irksome the discipline of writing a connected series of stories, of predetermined length. He grumbled about "the burthen of hack labour" and "the arid waste of ochreous commercialism." But the stories were written.

Houtain called the series "Grewsome Tales," but they were later republished under the collective title of "Herbert West—Reanimator." The first instalment, "From the Dark," appeared in the first issue of *Home Brew* in January, 1922. The Herbert West of the stories is always reviving corpses and getting into trouble in consequence. In the last tale, "The Tomb Legions,"

> It was West who first noticed the falling plaster on that part of the wall where the ancient tomb masonry had been covered up. . . . Then I saw a small black aperture, felt a ghoulish wind of ice, and smelled the charnel bowels of putrescent earth . . . just then the electric lights went out and I saw outlined against some phosphorescence of the nether world a horde of silent toiling things. . . . They were removing the stones quietly, one by one, from the centuried wall. And then, as the breach became large enough, they came out into the laboratory in single file; led by a stalking thing with a beautiful head made of wax. A sort of sad-

eyed monstrosity seized on Herbert West. West did not resist or
utter a sound. Then they all sprang at him and tore him to pieces
before my eyes, bearing the fragments away into that subterranean
vault of fabulous abomination.[5]

Of all Lovecraft's stories, those comprising "Herbert West—
Reanimator" are perhaps the most forgettable. Yet they played a
part in Lovecraft's professional career. Houtain paid promptly for
the first two but kept Lovecraft waiting months for the rest of the
money.

During 1921, Lovecraft continued to correspond with Sonia
Greene, whom he had met at the convention in Boston in February.

Sonia was born on March 16, 1883, to a young Jewish couple,
Simyon and Racille Shifirkin, at Itchno, near Konotop, Tchernigov
Province, the Ukraine. Sonia's grandfather, Moisieh Haft, had opposed the match on the ground that the Shifirkins were not orthodox
enough.

Simyon Shifirkin ran a store in Itchno, without much success
because of the peasants' hatred of Jews. Once the locals, by circulat-
ing rumors of a pogrom, persuaded the Shifirkins to flee to Konotop,
whereupon they looted the store.

When Simyon was called up for military service, the Tsar's
officers regularly extorted kickbacks from the recruits' meager pay.
They also compelled them to write their relatives, begging for
money, which the officers took. Stubborn privates were beaten and
imprisoned until they became reasonable.

After his military service, Simyon Shifirkin proposed to seek his
fortune in western Europe. Racille's father insisted that the young
couple be divorced, and Racille remained at home. Simyon departed, vowing to send for her and their small daughter as soon as he
got established. But his letters came less and less often and finally
stopped. Racille resumed the name of Haft.

Racille's brothers emigrated to England and did well as an
auditor and a salesman in Liverpool. They sent for Racille, who
came with Sonia and opened a dressmaking shop. When some friends
she had known in Russia looked her up on their way to America, she
joined them, leaving Sonia in the Baron de Hirsch School near Liverpool.

In the United States, Racille married a widowed shopkeeper of

Elmira, New York, named Solomon Moseson, who called himself
Samuel Morris. In 1892, aged nine, Sonia was brought from England
and put in school in Elmira.

Morris proved a disagreeable tightwad with a tyrannical mother.
When Sonia was thirteen, he demanded that she be put to work,
since he was tired of supporting another man's child. Thus Sonia
was apprenticed to a milliner.

Two years later, when Sonia was working as a milliner in New
York, she met a twenty-five-year-old salesman, also of Russian-
Jewish origin, who had changed his name to Stanley Greene. She
became engaged to him; but Greene, too, proved a dubious bar-
gain: bossy, violent-tempered, and insanely jealous. The Haft girls
seem to have shown singularly bad judgment in picking husbands.
Sonia tried to break the engagement. By weeping and pleading on
his knees, Greene persuaded the sixteen-year-old girl to go through
with the wedding.

Sonia bore two children, a boy who died in infancy and a girl,
Florence Carol. Greene philandered and loafed, letting Sonia support him, until she divorced him; she said he was a "mild mental
case." Sonia settled in New York with her daughter Florence, her
mother Racille, and the two children whom Racille had borne to
Morris before she left him.

During Sonia's engagement, to improve her mind, Greene encouraged her to read widely in European literature. As a result,
Sonia became an energetic self-improver. In 1917 she met James F.
Morton, who introduced her to Walker's Sunrise Club. This was a
dinner and lecture club of which she became a habituée. While rising in the business world as a saleswoman and designer of women's
hats, she went to night school to perfect her English.

About 1920, Morton asked if he might use Sonia's apartment
for a meeting of the Blue Pencil Club, the New York society of
amateur journalists. It was his turn to entertain them, and his place
was too small. Thus Sonia encountered amateur journalism. Soon,
she attended the convention in Boston at which she met H. P.
Lovecraft.

At this time, she was earning nearly $10,000 a year as a sales-
woman and workshop manager for Ferle Heller's clothing shop in
Manhattan. This was a princely salary for a man in 1921 and a

fabulous one for a woman. Since shedding Greene, Sonia had had other suitors, including Morton.

Then Sonia joined the UAPA. In a fit of generosity, she gave $50 to the treasury of the official organ, *The United Amateur*. As editor, Lovecraft was overjoyed by this windfall. "Mrs. G.," he wrote, "has an acute, receptive, and well-stored mind. . . ." "Beneath the exterior of romantic spoofing and rhetorical extravagance she has a mind of singular scope and activity, and an exceptional background of Continental cultivation."[6]

A tall, well-built, handsome brunette of regal presence—"Junoesque," some called her—Sonia looked much younger than her age. Sam Loveman remembered her as "one of the most beautiful women I have ever met, and the kindest."

Although she had lived in the United States since the age of nine, Sonia showed all the extroversion, volatility, impulsiveness, and compulsive generosity common among pre-Revolutionary Russians. She was vigorous, enterprising, aggressive, strong-willed, and could not "keep still for two consecutive seconds." Her culture had nothing to do with her "Continental background" but had been gained by hard, purposeful study, including courses at Columbia. When, during a business trip, she dropped in on her fellow-amateur Alfred Galpin in Madison, Wisconsin, to urge him with passionate fervor "to Write, to Do, to Create," he "felt like an English sparrow transfixed by a cobra."

Her volubility led Lovecraft to describe her as "that learned but eccentric human phonograph." Otherwise he lavished praise upon her:

> Mme. G. is certainly a person of the most admirable qualities, whose generous and kindly cast of mind is by no means feigned, and whose intelligence and devotion to art merit the sincerest approbation. The volatility incidental to a Continental and non-Aryan heritage should not blind the analytical observer to the solid worth and genuine cultivation which underlie it.[7]

Learning that Sonia had an adolescent daughter, Lovecraft discreetly inquired whether this daughter would like a date with one of his younger single friends. Sonia assured him that Florence had no use for highbrows like Kleiner.

In fact, Sonia and her daughter did not get on well. Lovecraft once described Florence as a "flapper . . . pert, spoiled, and ultra-independent . . . hard boiled . . ." but otherwise ignored her. Sonia insisted on a life of strenuous self-improvement, and the daughter resisted. A few months after Sonia's marriage to Lovecraft, Florence left home, worked as a stenographer, went to Paris, and married a young American. She was soon divorced but, as "Carol Weld," remained in Paris seven years as a correspondent for Hearst. She did not see her mother again until Sonia was in her eighties.

Derleth described Sonia as "a woman of great charm and personal magnetism"; Cole, as "genuinely glamorous with powerful feminine allure." A greater contrast between the outgoing Sonia and the primly inhibited Lovecraft would be hard to find.

Still, they did have things in common besides amateur journalism. Sonia had literary ambitions, albeit these never got very far; her writings were gushy. Like Lovecraft (and curiously in view of her success in business) she professed a contempt for "commercialism." Like Lovecraft, she had a high, rigid standard of morals and manners. Some of her ideas were a little odd—for instance, she thought that no gentleman carried a pocket knife.

In the summer of 1921, Sonia struggled to get out the first number of her amateur journal *The Rainbow*, which appeared in October. Lovecraft sent her a long, philosophical letter, which she published as an article, "Nietzscheism and Realism."

This article says little about Nietzsche but much about Lovecraft's politics. Unlike Nietzsche, he did not believe a permanently good government possible "among the crawling, miserable vermin called human beings." Like Aristotle, Lovecraft thought that all forms of government—monarchy, aristocracy, democracy, and ochlocracy (mob rule)—contained the seeds of their own destruction. He favored a moderate aristocracy, because such a regime made possible the creation of works of art, which were all that made life worth living. He did not mean any such absolutist regime as that of the tsars and the kaisers:

> A tolerable amount of political liberty is absolutely essential to the free development of the mind, so that, in speaking of the virtues of an aristocratic system, the philosopher has in view less a governmental despotism than an arrangement of well-defined traditional social classes, like those of England and France.[8]

Lovecraft was not, however, so strict a stratificationist as this passage suggests. Not long before, he had written an essay,

"Americanism," for *The United Amateur*. Herein, along with Anglo-Saxon glorification, warnings against non-Nordic immigration, and an attack on "political criminals like Edward, alias Eamon, de Valera," he asserted:

> But the features of Americanism peculiar to this continent must not be belittled. In the abolition of fixed and rigid class lines a distinct sociological advance is made, permitting a steady and progressive recruiting of the upper levels from the fresh and vigorous body of the people beneath.

If this seems to contradict the previous statement about "traditional social classes," that is merely one more proof of the ability of the human mind to hold two mutually exclusive ideas at once.

Others amateurs, too, were persuaded to contribute to Sonia's magazine. Galpin furnished an article: "Nietzsche as a Practical Prophet," while Morton, Kleiner, and Loveman sent in poems.

On Sunday, September 4, 1921, Sonia stopped at Providence on a business trip and telephoned Lovecraft. He took her on a long sight-seeing walk around the city and up College Hill to his house. There he presented her to Lillian Clark. The meeting went well:

> Both seemed delighted with each other, and my aunt has ever since been eloquent in her praise of Mme. G., whose ideas, speech, manner, aspect, and even attire impressed her with the greatest of favourableness. In truth, this visit has materially heightened my aunt's respect for amateurdom—an institution whose extreme democracy and occasional heterogeneity have at times made it necessary for me to apologise for it.

Having entertained Lovecraft and his aunt for lunch at the Crown Hotel, Sonia suggested inviting several leading amateurs, including Lovecraft and Loveman, to New York. She would undertake to find quarters for them.

This was the first of several visits between Sonia and Lovecraft during the next few months. Once he showed her the display of glass flowers in the Musuem of Comparative Zoology at Harvard. When they visited in Boston or elsewhere outside of Providence, Lovecraft made a point of their staying at different hotels. On several occasions, they dined at a Greek restaurant in Boston, which Lovecraft liked because of the murals of Classical scenes.

Next June, Sonia stopped in Providence when both aunts were at home with Lovecraft. He reported that Annie Gamwell "likes her immensely despite a racial and social chasm which she doesn't often bridge."[9] Sonia's charm could thaw even that monument of Old American class-conscious self-esteem, Annie Emeline Phillips Gamwell.

During the thirteen months from December, 1921, to December, 1922, Lovecraft wrote the rest of the "Herbert West" stories, the prose poem "Nyarlathotep," and the abortive "Azathoth." He contributed editorials and articles to the amateur press, including the article "A Confession of Unfaith" in *The Liberal* for February, 1922.

This article told of Lovecraft's own mental development: his loss of faith in Christianity, his flirtations with Islâm and Classical paganism, and his growth into a materialistic atheist. He described his outlook as

> . . . a cynicism tempered with immeasurable pity for man's eternal tragedy of man's aspirations beyond the possibility of fulfilment.
> The war confirmed all the views I had begun to hold. . . . With me democracy was a minor question, my anger being aroused primarily by the audacity of a challenge to Anglo-Saxon supremacy. . . . I am . . . a warm partisan of Anglo-American reunion; my opinion being that the division of a single culture into two national units is wasteful and often dangerous. In this case my opinion is doubly strong because I believe that the entire existing civilisation depends on Saxon dominance.[10]

He wrote other stories. At the end of 1921, he composed "The Picture in the House," a simple horror tale without fantastic trappings. It begins ominously:

> Searchers after horror haunt strange, far places. For them are the catacombs of Ptolemais, and the carven mausolea of the nightmare countries. They climb the moonlit towers of ruined Rhine castles, and falter down black cobwebbed steps beneath the scattered stones of forgotten cities in Asia. . . . But the true epicure in the terrible, to whom a new thrill of unutterable ghastliness is the chief end and justification of existence, esteems most of all the ancient, lonely farmhouses of backwoods New England; for there the dark elements of strength, solitude, grotesqueness and ignorance combine to form the perfection of the hideous.

The narrator tells how he was bicycling on a mission of genealogical research through Miskatonic Valley. This valley was named
for an imaginary river, on which Lovecraft placed his ghoulish town
of Arkham. Caught by a thunderstorm, the narrator seeks shelter in
a decrepid old farmhouse. Inside, he finds a lusty, white-bearded,
ragged oldster speaking an archaic dialect:

> "Ketched in the rain, be ye?" he greeted. "Glad ye was nigh
> the haouse en' hed the sense to come right in. I calc'late I was
> asleep, else I'd a heerd ye. . . ."[11]

On a table lies a copy of *Regnum Congo* (1598) by Francesco
Antonio Pigafetta, one of Magellan's company on the first voyage
round the globe. Lovecraft says the book was "written in Latin
from the notes of the sailor Lopez."[12]

The old man gloats over an illustration of a Congolese butcher
shop, with the butcher cheerfully cleaving a human corpse into
marketable portions. Then a drop of blood, trickling down from the
room overhead, falls on the open page. The narrator falls into a
Lovecraftian fear-paralysis until a bolt of lightning destroys the
house, "bringing the oblivion which alone saved my mind." How the
lightning demolished the house without demolishing the narrator is
not clear.

"The Hound" (1922) is an effective, if over-adjectived, bit of
grue belonging to the Cthulhu Mythos canon, which was now taking
definite form.

The narrator tells how, for the sake of new sensations, he and
his friend St. John went in for decadence in a big way. In a crypt
under the old English mansion where they dwelt alone, they installed a museum of horrors, decorated with the proceeds of grave-
robbing: corpses mummified, stuffed, or otherwise preserved; skulls,
skeletons, tombstones, and similar cheerful bric-a-brac.

In robbing the grave of a ghoul in the Netherlands, they get an
amulet bearing the symbol of a winged hound: "the thing hinted
at in the forbidden 'Necronomicon' of the mad Arab Abdul Alhazred; the ghastly soul-symbol of the forbidden corpse-eating cult
of inaccessible Leng, in central Asia." Thereafter they are haunted by
the hound, or the ghoul, or both, until St. John is torn to pieces. . . .

The fictitious *Necronomicon*, a book of portentous spells for summoning dire entities from other worlds and dimensions, became a major element in Lovecraft's later stories of the Cthulhu Mythos. The name was probably suggested by that of the *Astronomica* of Manilius. This was a Roman astrological poem of the first century of the Christian Era, quoted by Lovecraft in his newspaper columns.

Lovecraft's stories are enlivened by references to many books of scientific, historical, and occult lore. Some of these books exist, some are merely legendary, and some like the *Necronomicon* were made up by Lovecraft. In "Polaris" and "The Other Gods," Lovecraft created the *Pnakotic manuscripts* (or *fragments*), which remained part of the canon of imaginary books in the Cthulhu Mythos. In the latter story, he brought in the *Seven Cryptical Books of Earth*, which in "The Dream-Quest of Unknown Kadath" acquired the more impressive title of the *Seven Cryptical Books of Hsan*.

Real books include Scott-Elliot's *The Story of Atlantis and the Lost Lemuria* (1896, 1930), Joseph Glanvil's *Sadducismus Triumphatus* (1681), and many others. Legendary books include the *Book of Thoth* and the *Book of Dzyan*. The *Book of Thoth* first appeared in an ancient Egyptian tale, *The Story of Setnau Khaemuast*, known from a Ptolemaic papyrus but probably much older. According to this novel, this book of mighty spells was originally penned by the Egyptian ibis-headed god of wisdom, Teḥuti or Thoth. When the papyrus was published early in this century, fantasy writers seized upon the *Book of Thoth* as a prop for their stories. Thus it plays a rôle in Sax Rohmer's *Brood of the Witch Queen* (1924).

The *Book of Dzyan* was concocted by Helena Petrovna Blavatsky, founder of Theosophy, in her *Secret Doctrine* (1888). This treatise, a mass of fakery and plagiarism, consists mainly of quotations from the *Dzyan* (pronounced something like "John") interspersed with her own commentaries and diatribes. Although Mme. Blavatsky said that the *Dzyan* was originally written in Atlantis in the lost Senzar language, it is actually paraphrased without credit from an English translation of the ancient Sanskrit *Rig-Veda*.

In "Hypnos" (1922) the narrator is again living in an old English mansion with a single friend, with whom he investigates the world of dreams by means of drugs. The friend explores further than the narrator and returns in terror at what he has seen. There-

after he dreads the constellation Corona Borealis. In time, a beam
of red light from that part of the sky strikes the friend as he lies
asleep. Next day, all that is left of the friend—who the authorities
say never existed—is a sculptured head, like that of the narrator in
his youth.

Late in 1922, Houtain persuaded Lovecraft to write another
serial, in four independent parts. This was "The Lurking Fear,"
which began in the January *Home Brew* and ran monthly, the instalments averaging 2,000 words each.

"The Lurking Fear," like "Herbert West," is only competent
hack work. The narrator investigates mysterious disappearances and
depredations among the farmers near the deserted Martense mansion
on Thunder Mountain, presumably in New York State. The Mar-
tenses had been an eccentric Dutch family, who left Nieuw Amster-
dam after the British took it in 1664 and renamed it New York.

The local people, a "degenerate squatter population" of "mongrels," give only confused accounts of attacks by devils. The narrator
and two helpers spend a night in the mansion. During the night,
the assistants are carried off. The narrator tries again with a journalist
friend named Munroe, who is killed.

The narrator proves himself a most incompetent investigator:
always falling asleep on watch, or being paralyzed with terror, or
screaming, or losing his mind. "I believe that my mind was partly
unhinged by events. . . ." ". . . though no sane person would have
tried at that time, I forgot danger, reason, and cleanliness in my
single-minded fever. . . ." "My brain was as great a chaos as the
earth. . . ." "After that I recall running, spade in hand . . . leaping,
screaming, panting, bounding. . . ." ". . . I understood and went
delirious. . . ."[13] Hardly the sort of person one would want as a
comrade in a tight fix.

Sonia urged Loveman to come to New York to look for a
better job. On April 1, 1922, he came. Sonia turned her apartment
over to him and stayed with a neighbor. On the 5th, Sonia, Loveman,
Morton, and Kleiner all spoke over the long-distance telephone to
Lovecraft in Providence, urging him to join them. On the 6th, Lovecraft took the train to New York, the farthest he had ever been from
home. He shared Sonia's apartment with Loveman.

There followed a memorable week. Lovecraft foregathered with Morton, Kleiner, and Houtain. He met Frank Belknap Long, a young aspirant writer of weird stories. Long had won a prize contest in a boys' magazine and, on the strength of his winning story, had been recruited into the UAPA. When he published another tale in *The United Amateur*, Lovecraft wrote him.

Long proved a small, dark-haired youth of twenty, a student at New York University's School of Journalism and the son of a successful dentist. Like Loveman and Lovecraft, he had literary and poetic ambitions. A heart murmur had led his parents to coddle him in a manner not unlike, though less extreme than, Lovecraft's early home life. Sensitive, esthetic, and unworldly, he was given to intense but passing enthusiasms for hobbies, interests, and beliefs.

Lovecraft walked his friends' feet sore, doing the sights of New York: the Woolworth Building, the financial district, and parts of Brooklyn. Lovecraft was enchanted by the sight of Manhattan's skyline at dusk:

> Out of the waters it rose at twilight; cold, proud, beautiful; an Eastern city of wonder whose brothers the mountains are. It was not like any city of earth, for above purple mists rose towers, spires, and pyramids which one may only dream of in opiate lands beyond the Oxus; . . .

The slums of the lower East Side, however, aroused Lovecraft's xenophobia:

> . . . these swine have instinctive swarming movements. . . . a bastard mess of stewing mongrel flesh without intellect, repellant to eye, nose, and imagination—would to heaven a kindly gust of cyanogen could asphyxiate the whole gigantic abortion, end the misery, and clean out the place.

While such a description of the immigrant poor sounds shocking today, it was not unusual among Old Americans in Lovecraft's childhood. Nativism, with hatred of foreigners and immigrants, was a major factor in American thought and politics through the latter half of the nineteenth century and the early years of the twentieth. Nativist speakers expressed themselves quite as strongly as Lovecraft, even using his favorite pejorative "mongrel." From the 1850s to the 90s, the Irish were called "a mongrel mass of ignorance and crime and superstition"; the Czechs, "depraved beasts, harpies, decayed physically and spiritually." Of Poles and Russians it was said: "Let us whip these Slavic wolves back to the European dens from which they come, or in some way exterminate them." So Lovecraft's anti-ethnic sentiments were not original with him—merely a little out of date.

Lovecraft met the neighbor who was putting Sonia up and made up to the neighbor's cat. Laughing, Sonia said: "What a lot of perfectly good affection to waste on a mere cat—when a woman might highly appreciate it!"

"How can any woman love a face like mine?" asked Lovecraft.

"A mother can, and some who are not mothers would not have to try very hard."

They laughed, and Lovecraft went on stroking the cat. It would seem that Sonia already had her eye on Lovecraft as her man.

The climax came with a dinner in an Italian restaurant on Forty-ninth Street. It was Lovecraft's first experience with Italian food, and he did himself proud on minestrone, spagetti with meatballs, and Parmesan cheese. He balked only at the wine, saying he had never tasted alcohol and did not intend to start now. He did, however, form a lasting taste for Italian food, especially for spaghetti. After dinner they went to Nikita Balieff's Russian review, *Chauve Souris*, with its celebrated *March of the Wooden Soldiers*.

Next morning, April 13th, Loveman and Lovecraft bade fare-well to Sonia at Grand Central: Loveman to take a train to Cleveland; Lovecraft, one to Providence.

During the following months, Lovecraft continued to write about "the futility of all effort" and to say that "Nowadays I am active only in order to kill boredom." Nonetheless, he was fairly lively.

Sonia stopped on her way to a fair at Magnolia, Massachusetts, a small resort between Gloucester and Salem, where she was to represent her firm. At her invitation, Lovecraft went to Magnolia to visit her. As they walked the esplanade in the moonlight, they heard a "peculiar snorting, grunting noise, loud in the distance." Sonia said:

"Oh, Howard, here you have the setting for a really strange and mysterious story."

"Go ahead and write it," he replied.

"Oh, no, I couldn't do it justice."

"Try it. Tell me what the scene pictures in your imagination."[14]

Sonia sat up that night and wrote an outline of a story. When Lovecraft saw it the next day, he was so enthusiastic that Sonia impulsively kissed him.

Utterly disconcerted, Lovecraft blushed, then turned pale. When Sonia kidded him about being so flustered, he explained that he had not been kissed since infancy.

He did, however, undertake to revise the story—or perhaps to write it from a mere outline. "The Horror at Martin's Beach," competent but undistinguished, appeared under Sonia's name in *Weird Tales* for November, 1923. As with "Arthur Jermyn," the editor changed the title—this time to "The Invisible Monster," which gave away the plot. The story is reminiscent of Fitz-James O'Brien's "What Was It?" and Ambrose Bierce's "The Damned Thing," save that the menace is not a humanoid being but a sea monster of supernatural powers.

At the end of July, Lovecraft set out on the visit he had promised to make to Galpin and Loveman in Cleveland. When Galpin had first urged it, Lovecraft had demurred on the grounds that his aunts would object: ". . . any serious attempt would rend ₰598 with civil war."

But he went anyway, learning the acrobatics of changing clothes in a Pullman berth. He did not like the landscape of Ohio. The villages, he said, were "insufferably dismal," right out of Sinclair Lewis's *Main Street*.

When he got off at the 105th Street Station, Galpin rushed upon him. Lovecraft said:

"So this is my son Alfredus!"

"It sure is," said Galpin, vigorously shaking hands.

Galpin's house was around the corner from Loveman's. The three had a fine literary weekend, with some juvenile roughhousing, while Galpin's family were away. Galpin, who had ambitions to be a composer, made fruitless efforts to convert Lovecraft to classical music by taking him to a concert and giving him a record of Chopin's *Nocturne in G*.

As usual when away from his womenfolk, Lovecraft blossomed: "I have no headaches or depressed spells—in short, I am for the time being really alive & in good health & spirits." He even modified his antique rules of dress to buy a belt and soft collars and to go without either hat or vest. "Can you picture me vestless, hatless, soft-collared, and belted, ambling about with a boy of twenty, as if I were no older? . . . When I hit New York again I shall resume the solemn manner and sedate vestments befitting my advanced years. . . ." (He was about to turn thirty-two.)

Loveman introduced Lovecraft to members of his literary circle. One was (Harold) Hart Crane (1899–1932), who in his short life earned a repute as a major poet. Like Lovecraft, Crane had a monster-mother—sexually frigid, foolish, possessive, erratic, and un-predictable. Crane himself, when sober, was a man of great charm—a fascinating talker and a born storyteller.

Crane was, however, a drunkard and an active homosexual, who cruised bars to pick up sailors and was sometimes beaten up for his pains. Because of his charm, he was always being asked to people's houses. When he got drunk, however, he became an appalling guest. He would run naked through the house, screaming threats and obscenities; he chased one hostess with a boomerang, trying to brain her. Or he would break up his host's furniture, or throw it out the window. During Lovecraft's visit to Cleveland, however, Crane was on good behavior.

Another member of the circle was Gordon Hatfield, with whom Crane was feuding; the two spent the evening needling each other. Unlike Crane, Hatfield proclaimed his deviation by patently effeminate mannerisms. Lovecraft later wrote: "Have you seen that precious sissy that I met in Cleveland. . . . I didn't know whether to kiss it or kill it!"[15]

Lovecraft also learned of Loveman's pen pal Clark Ashton Smith (1893–1961), some of whose letters and drawings Loveman showed him. Smith led almost as reclusive a life, in rural north-central California, as Lovecraft did in Providence. Save for a few visits to San Francisco and Carmel, where he was a protégé of the bohemian poet George Sterling, Smith spent nearly all his life near Auburn, California.

Smith's English father had bought a tract of hilly woodland a mile from Auburn and there practiced chicken farming with but meager success. Both of Smith's parents were around forty when Smith was born.

Smith early resolved to be a poet. He dropped out of school in the eighth grade and educated himself by such heroic measures as reading the whole encyclopedia and the unabridged dictionary. Like Lovecraft, he suffered long spells of unidentified illness.

During his early decades, Smith hated Auburn, calling it a "pestilential hell-hole." He had a long series of love affairs with married women in the town. Of the Three Musketeers of *Weird Tales*—Lovecraft, Smith, and Howard—Smith was the only one on whose normal male sexuality nobody ever cast any doubt.

As Smith's health improved, he learned that, in twentieth-century America, one cannot make a living writing poetry. So he engaged in casual labor: woodcutter, fruit picker, miner, typist, and night editor of a local paper.

Smith's poetry began appearing in 1910 in newspapers, magazines, and small volumes like *The Star-Treader* (1912), *Odes and Sonnets* (1918), and *Ebony and Crystal* (1922). In 1920, he composed a celebrated long poem, *The Hashish Eater:*

> Bow down: I am the emperor of dreams;
> I crown me with the million-colored sun,
> Of secret worlds incredible, and take
> Their trailing skies for vestment, when I soar,
> Throned on the mounting zenith, and illume
> The spaceward-flown horizons infinite . . .[16]

Like Lovecraft, Smith sometimes wrote of the effects of narcotics but vigorously denied having tried any himself. Both said they had all the nightmares they needed without drugs.

When Smith's poetry first appeared, western publications hailed him as a boy genius, the compeer of Milton, Byron, Keats, and Swinburne. His older colleagues Bierce, Sterling, and De Casseres pronounced him the leading American poet of his day. One wonders: Whatever happened to Smith's poetry, so lavishly praised when it appeared? One might think it had all been buried with its author, as was said of the composer Rubinstein's music. Of today's connoisseurs of poetry, most have never even heard of Smith.

There was nothing wrong with Smith's verse, most of which is either weird-fantastic or love poetry. It is vivid, stirring, evocative, colorful in a lush *fin-de-siècle* way, superimaginative, and technically polished. But public taste ever changes unpredictably, so that there is really no such thing as progress in the arts. In recent decades, American poetry, under the influence of Eliot, Pound, and others, has gone off in a direction quite different from Smith's. Most of Smith's poetry is in fixed forms like the sonnet, whereas nearly all contemporary American poetry (so-called) is in free verse.

The advantage of this formless "verse" is that it is easy. It is lazy man's poetry, or poetry in rough draft. Anybody, even a child or a computer, can do it, and in fact have done it. This makes it popular, since in today's climate of superegalitarianism—when an orangutan in the Topeka zoo wins a prize in a painting contest—it is thought that, if a task cannot be done by everyone, it ought not to be done at all. To do or admire that which requires outstanding talent, arduous effort, and austere self-discipline is elitism, and that is considered a very wicked thing.

By 1922, Smith had become well known in California as a poet, having spoken before ladies' clubs; he did not begin the weird fantasies, for which he is mainly remembered, until several years later. He also dabbled in drawing, painting, and sculpture.

In pursuing the plastic and graphic arts without formal training, Smith erred. In these arts, as in boxing among sports, the gap between the amateur and the professional yawns wide and the self-taught man has little chance. Hence Smith's carvings and drawings remained at best talented primitives.

Lovecraft wrote to Smith from Cleveland, expressing enthusiasm for his verse, drawings, and watercolors. Thus began a correspondence that lasted all of Lovecraft's life.

Lovecraft spent over a fortnight in Cleveland. On the way home, he stopped in New York, where Sonia again put him up. An excellent cook, she made an apple pie for Lovecraft's aunts. Sonia and he urged the aunts to come for a visit, and Annie Gamwell came for part of October.

Lovecraft visited institutions like the great American Museum of Natural History. He hunted down remnants of Colonial architecture like the Jumel mansion in Washington Heights. Morton shared his enthusiasm for these outings, but they bored Long. Lovecraft and Long composed a poem beginning:

To Zara
By Edgar Allan Poe (?)
Inscribed to Miss Sarah Longhurst—June 1829

I look'd upon thee yesternight
Beneath the drops of yellow light
That fell from out a poppy moon
Like notes of some far opiate tune. . . .

They "concocted an account of an 125-year-old hermit from Maine, who had in his possession an undiscover'd poem of Poe's." Galpin, to whom they sent this fabrication, did not believe that the poem was really Poe's. He praised it highly, however, as by one of Poe's best imitators—until he learned who had really composed it. Then he found flaws in it.

Lovecraft ghosted for Bush, who had now tripled Lovecraft's pay to a dollar for every eight lines of execrable verse that Lovecraft revised. He met a friend of Morton: Everett McNeil, who had had success as a writer of boys' adventure novels but who in old age had come upon hard times. Lovecraft declined to call upon his father's kin in New York, being sure they were "prim, pious, conventional, unimaginative" folk.[17]

Back in Providence, Lovecraft settled into his routine. Early in January, he stayed in Boston as the guest of Edward H. Cole and lectured a meeting of the Hub Club on Dunsany. He toured Salem and Marblehead and wrote rhapsodies on their antique beauties; Marblehead he called a "fantastic dream."

Lovecraft was becoming a connoisseur of Colonial architecture. He wrote that architecture was the greatest art; other human ideals and aspirations were meaningless. "I have ceased to admire character—all I value in any man are his manners, accomplishments, and choice of cravats."

He spoke up for Fascism, in the original sense of Mussolini's Italian dictatorship: ". . . there is no earthly reason why the masses should not be kept down for the benefit of the strong. . . . What does the condition of the rabble matter?" Since Lovecraft knew that he could hardly be counted among the "strong," this should not be taken too literally. It was probably just one more explosion of outrageous opinion, adopted *pro tem.* to strike an attitude or stir up an argument.

Lovecraft noted that Ernest Dench, of the Blue Pencil Club,

was organizing an amateur journalists' tour of England. He said: "The only reason I don't save like hell to get in on Dench's tour is that I simply couldn't come back, once I saw the ancient glories and monuments of my race."[18] This was, I am sure, mere pretense; the real reason he did not try to go was lack of money.

After Cervantes, around 1600, murdered the medieval romance by burlesquing it in *Don Quixote*, imaginative fiction was unpopular for a century and a half. A few seventeenth-century writers like Cyrano de Bergerac, Swift, and Fontenelle composed an occasional story of a marvelous voyage, a trip to the moon, or extraterrestrial visitors, all of which would today be classed as science fiction.

During the eighteenth century, fantasy, long moribund, reëntered the stream of European literature through three channels: the oriental fantasy narrative, which first appeared in the form of Galland's translation into French of *The Arabian Nights*; the Gothic novel, brought from Germany to England by Horace Walpole with his *Castle of Otranto* (1764); and the child's fairy tale, originally based upon traditional peasant tales, many of which were collected and published in the early nineteenth century by Andersen and the Grimm brothers.

At the same time, Walter Scott launched the modern historical novel with his *Waverly* (1814) and its many successors. Although people had long written stories of the days of yore—Homer's *Iliad* for example—Scott was the first to realize that the past had differed in many ways from the present and that these differences of costume and custom could be exploited for their entertainment value.

Many nineteenth-century writers did an occasional imaginative story, such as Dickens's *A Christmas Carol*, which introduced the theme of time travel. Edgar Allan Poe was especially active in the imaginative field. Besides his Gothic horror tales and detective stories, he wrote of marvelous voyages, aerial travel, trips to the moon, the revival of mummies, alchemy, and other fanciful themes.

Translated into French in the 1850s by Baudelaire, Poe's stories came to the notice of Jules Verne, then an unsuccessful young Parisian lawyer, stockbroker, and playwright. Inspired, Verne became the world's first full-time science-fiction writer, composing nearly a hundred novels. In the 1890s, Verne was followed in Great Britain by H. G. Wells. Where Verne had stayed close to existing technology, Wells freely invented anything that would provide a basis for a thrilling story: invisibility, anti-gravity, man-eating plants, and invaders from Mars.

In the 1880s, William Morris, the versatile British artist, decorator, poet, reformer, publisher, and novelist, created modern heroic fantasy. In his pseudo-medieval novels like *The Well at the World's End*, Morris combined the antiquarian romanticism of Scott and his imitators with the supernaturalism of Walpole and *his* imitators. After Morris, Dunsany adapted heroic fantasy to the short-story form.

Around the turn of the nineteenth and twentieth centuries, many general-circulation magazines, both in Britain and in America, ran science-fiction or fantasy stories. From 1890 to 1920, the imaginative stories of H. G. Wells and Arthur Conan Doyle usually appeared in these journals before they were published as books. Before 1919, however, there had never been a periodical devoted to imaginative fiction.

In 1919, Street & Smith Publications launched a pioneer magazine of fantasy and science fiction: *Thrill Book*. This magazine appeared semi-monthly, beginning with the issue of March 1, 1919, and continued for sixteen issues, to October 15, 1919. Then a combination of editorial inexperience and a printers' strike put *Thrill Book* out of business.

The idea of a magazine of imaginative fiction next occurred to J. C. Henneberger, publisher of the successful *College Humor*. A long-time fan of Poe, Henneberger was inspired to start *Weird Tales* by Poe's lines:

> *From a wild weird clime that lieth, sublime*
> *Out of* SPACE—*out of* TIME.

Henneberger hired Edwin F. Baird, a mystery writer, to edit *Weird Tales* and its companion *Detective Tales* in Chicago. The first issue of *Weird Tales*, with a cover picture of a man and a woman writhing in the grip of a giant octopus, appeared with the date of March, 1923. While the magazine ran both science fiction and fantasy, it published more of the latter.

Henneberger also read Lovecraft's serials in *Home Brew*. Thinking them too good for the company they kept, he made inquiries. Soon Lovecraft was being urged by his friends to submit stories to this new market. But, reported Cook, "he was actually impatient. Who ever said he wanted a market?" To Lovecraft, writing was still something a gentleman did for his own and his friends' entertainment, with no thought of money.

About April, Lovecraft let himself be persuaded to send Baird five manuscripts. His covering letter would be hard to beat for negative salesmanship:

> My dear Sir:
> Having a habit of writing weird, macabre, and fantastic stories for my own amusement, I have lately been simultaneously hounded by nearly a dozen well-meaning friends into deciding to submit a few of these Gothic horrors to your newly founded periodical. . . .
> Of these the first two are probably the best. If they be unsatisfactory, the rest need not be read. . . .
> I have no idea that these things will be found suitable, for I pay no attention to the demands of commercial writing. My object is such pleasure as I can obtain from the creation of certain bizarre pictures, situations, or atmospheric effects; and the only reader I hold in mind is myself.
> My models are invariably the older writers, especially Poe, who has been my favorite literary figure since early childhood. Should any miracle impel you to consider the publication of my tales, I have but one condition to offer; and that is that no excisions be made. If the tale cannot be printed as it is written, down to the very last semicolon and comma, it must gracefully accept rejection. Excision by editors is probably the one reason why no living American author has any real prose style. . . . But I am probably safe, for my MSS. are not likely to win your consideration. "Dagon" has been rejected by —— —— [name, probably *Black Mask*, deleted by Baird], to which I sent it under external compulsion—much as I am sending you the enclosed.

Lovecraft had done everything to assure rejection of his stories: the haughty tone, the art-for-art's-sake pose, the deprecation of his own work, and the mention of a previous rejection. He all but begged Baird to return his manuscripts.

All editors know that much of the material submitted to them has already been sent elsewhere, but it is tactless to rub it in. Moreover, it is poor strategy to submit more than one piece to an editor at a time. If he gets several from the same author, he is likely to pick the best and reject the rest, even though they may be better than other materials he is currently buying.

It therefore says something for Baird's objectivity and sense of humor that he bought all five stories and several more that Love-craft sent him. He published Lovecraft's letter with a wry note: "Despite the foregoing, or because of it, we are using some of Mr. Lovecraft's stories, and you will find his 'Dagon' in the next issue of WEIRD TALES."[19]

Of the eleven issues of *Weird Tales* from October, 1923, to February, 1925, Lovecraft appeared in nine, once with a poem and the other times with stories. (Several issues appeared a month late.) This fact has given the impression that 1923–25 was a very productive period for Lovecraft. Actually, his greatest spurt of production had been earlier, in 1918–22; but from 1923 to 1925 *Weird Tales* printed the earlier stories in rapid succession. Of the stories printed, about half were in public domain, having been previously published in uncopyrighted amateur magazines. Baird generously paid for them anyway.

Lovecraft was dismayed to hear that, while Baird liked the stories, he "could not consider their acceptance till I sent them in double-spaced typing. I am not certain whether or not I shall bother. I need the money badly enough—but ugh! how I hate typing! Maybe I'll try *Dagon* alone—following with others only in case of definite acceptance. I abhor labour."[20]

Evidently, besides his innocence about the customs of the publishing world, Lovecraft had not yet faced up to the need of earning a living. In some ways he never did.

Ten

BASHFUL LOVER

And every one will say
As you walk your flowery way,
"If he's content with a vegetable love which
would certainly not suit me,
Why, what a most particularly pure young man
this pure young man must be!"[1]

W. S. GILBERT

During 1923, despite renewal of his vows to quit amateur journalism, Lovecraft attended meetings of amateur journalists. He enjoyed visits from Morton and Moe, whom he took on walking tours. When showing Providence to visitors, Lovecraft would stop every now and then before some Colonial relic or some sylvan scene and cry: "Where but in Providence could you find. . . ." whatever he wished his friend to admire.

He suffered from spells of headache, depression, and misanthropy, causing him to write: "The natural hatefulness and loathsomeness of the human beast may be overcome only in a few specimens of fine heredity and breeding. . . ."[2] Indulging his aris-

tocratic fantasy, he spoke in his most affected, haughty, supercilious
vein of giving up writing:

> I am well-nigh resolved to write no more tales, but merely to
> dream when I have a mind to, not stopping to do any thing so vulgar
> as to set down the dream for a boarish Publick. I have concluded,
> that Literature is no proper pursuit for a gentleman; and that writ-
> ing ought never to be consider'd but as an elegant Accomplishment.

Lovecraft's attitude towards earning a living recalls that of
Arthur Machen (ryhmes with "blacken"), after Poe and Dunsany
the most important literary influence on Lovecraft. Machen wrote
that "this curse of getting a livelihood remains profoundly un-
natural to man. . . ."

A native of the Welsh border country, Machen was a dreamy,
impractical man and a slow and painful writer. He never made a
decent living from his writing or from anything else, although he
tried clerking, teaching, reporting, and acting.

Despite some irritating mannerisms and the vague inconclu-
siveness of many stories, Machen's work is a necessity to any connoisseur of fantasy. His favorite subject is the survival in Britain, in
caves, cults, and covens, of pagan magic and fertility worship and
of the spirits to whom these rites were addressed.

Lovecraft ignored Samuel Johnson's homely eighteenth-century advice: "No man but a blockhead ever wrote except for money."
When a fellow pulp-writer, Hugh B. Cave, called Lovecraft's attention to this dictum, Lovecraft dismissed it as "Philistine." But Lovecraft also wrote: "I suppose it is absurd for me to try to write . . . yet
. . . I could not help scribbling if I wished."[3]

Lovecraft got out two more issues of *The Conservative*, in
March and July 1923. These were his last, and he did not give
them volume numbers; they were simply Nos. 12 and 13. They contained poems from Loveman and Morton, articles by Galpin and
Long, and editorials by Lovecraft.

These editorials dealt mainly with literary criticism. Lovecraft's
tone was mild, save where he described T. S. Eliot's "disjointed and
incoherent 'poem' called 'The Waste Land,'" as "a practically meaningless collection of phrases, learned allusions, quotations, slang, and
scraps in general; offered to the public (whether or not as a hoax)
as something justified by our modern mind with its recent comprehension of its own chaotic triviality and disorganisation." I daresay

that others have felt the same way about *The Waste Land* but have hesitated to say so because of Eliot's prestige.

In August, Lovecraft called upon a family in Providence, named Eddy, with whom he had long been in contact by letter. Around 1918–19, Susie Lovecraft had gone to a suffragette meeting. There she met a Mrs. Clifford Martin Eddy, whose son, C. M. Eddy, Jr., had literary ambitions. Learning of Lovecraft's ghosting business, Mrs. Eddy put her son and his recent bride, Muriel Gammons, in touch with the Lovecrafts by telephone.

Answering the 'phone, Susie had raved about her gifted son. He would, she said, be glad to correspond with the Eddys, but he hated the telephone along with all modern machinery.

The Eddys met Lovecraft for the first time on a hot Sunday afternoon in August, 1923. In response to an invitation, he appeared on their doorstep "in a neat grey suit, white shirt, and black necktie; he wore a Panama hat. . . ."[4] They shook his frigid hand and listened incredulously as he said that he had enjoyed the three-mile walk from his home with the temperature near 100°. He made friends with the Eddy cat and gratefully accepted a cup of hot coffee, with cream and four spoonfuls of sugar.

The Eddys became the only real friends, outside of his aunts, whom for many years Lovecraft had in Providence. On subsequent visits, he often arrived late in the evening and stayed to the small hours. He read his stories aloud to the Eddys. Sometimes, for the three Eddy children, he brought a box of broken pieces of chocolate bar, or broken crackers, which he bought for almost nothing.

In November, 1923, Clifford Eddy and Lovecraft went on a hunt for a rumored Dark Swamp near Chepachet, Rhode Island. Lovecraft hoped that it would give him background for a weird story. Although they hiked for seventeen miles, they failed to find the swamp; but Lovecraft made notes on the dialect of the country folk, which he later used. (Cook, however, said that Lovecraft's "Yankee dialects" were mainly the products of Lovecraft's imagination; if they ever existed, they were extinct in Lovecraft's time. A letter by Lovecraft hints that he got them from James Russell Lowell's *Bigelow Papers*.)

Such a Dark Swamp did exist, north of Foster Town in the northwest part of the state. A few years after Lovecraft's and

Eddy's search, this swamp was submerged beneath the Ponaganset Reservoir.

Lovecraft passed some of his ghosting assignments on to Eddy. He revised several of Eddy's stories, which were later sold to *Weird Tales*. In return, Muriel Eddy typed some of Lovecraft's manuscripts. Of the tales revised by Lovecraft, "The Ghost Eater" (*Weird Tales*, April, 1924) starts with the hackneyed opening of a traveler caught in a storm, who finds a strange house in the woods. The authors worked a switch on the werewolf plot.

"The Loved Dead" (*Weird Tales*, May–June–July, 1924), although nominally by Eddy, was largely Lovecraft's work. It is a nonfantastic but gruesome tale of necrophilia, whose narrator gets his fun out of snuggling up to corpses. It begins with a thinly disguised account of Lovecraft's boyhood:

> My early childhood was one long, prosaic and monotonous apathy. Strictly ascetic, wan, pallid, undersized, and subject to protracted spells of morbid moroseness, I was ostracised by the healthy, normal youngsters of my own age. They dubbed me a spoil-sport, an "old woman", because I had no interest in the rough, childish games they played, or any stamina to participate in them, had I so desired.[5]

Since the narrator's love of death is not fulfilled by his work as an undertaker, he becomes a mass murderer to satisfy his craving. The story so horrified readers in some towns that legal action was brought to bar *Weird Tales* from newsstands. Unnerved, the editor and the publisher were wary thereafter of stories with more than a slight seasoning of grue.

During 1923, Lovecraft continued his acquaintance with Sonia Greene. The friendship flowered into a courtship, in which Sonia later admitted that she "was the aggressor." According to her, "It was after that vacation in Magnolia that our more intimate correspondence began which led to our marriage. H. P. wrote me of everything he did, everywhere he went: sometimes filling 30, 40, even 50 pages with his fine writing. Then he decided to break away from Providence."[6]

Whoever first suggested marriage, the subject of married life in New York arose between them. Sonia wrote that, after Lovecraft and Mrs. Gamwell had returned home from their visit in 1922:

. . . I was not ashamed to write him how very much I missed him. His appreciation of this led us both to more serious ground. . . .

Meanwhile his letters indicated his desire to leave 'Providence and settle in New York. Each of us meditated the possibilities of a life together. Some of our friends suspected. I admitted to friends that I cared very much for Howard and that if he would have me I would gladly be his wife. But nothing definite was decided.

Having now seen something of the wider world, Lovecraft was getting a little tired even of his beloved Providence. Cleveland, he had found, "is much more intellectually alive than Providence, where all artistic manifestations are confined to artificial & quasi-Victorian society groups." He wrote Clark Ashton Smith: "Like you, I don't know anyone who is at all congenial here; & I believe I shall migrate to New York in the end."[7]

By early 1924, it was settled that Lovecraft and Sonia should marry when possible. Lovecraft refused to tell his aunts of their engagement, saying he preferred to surprise them. The probable reason is that he was afraid of a painful scene. Sonia sent Lovecraft substantial gifts in money and stamps.

Through 1923, Lovecraft wrote three stories. The first was "The Festival," a minor story of the Cthulhu group. As in "The Nameless City," there is no dialogue but a slow build-up to a climax of horror.

The narrator comes to the fictitious New England city of Kingsport in response to a tradition that he shall celebrate Yuletide with his kin. He joins a throng of silent, hooded folk streaming into a nighted church and follows them down into a crypt. There, strange rites take place. A horde of bat-winged, web-footed things appear, and the people ride off on them. . . . Lovecraft not only mentions Abdul Alhazred but also tells of a copy of Abdul's *chef d'oeuvre*, the accursed *Necronomicon*, in the library of Miskatonic University at the fictional city of Arkham.

"The Rats in the Walls," a horror tale, is one of Lovecraft's best-known stories. The narrator, de la Poer, is an American of English descent. Despite rumors of a curse on the place, he buys and restores the crumbling English mansion of his ancestors. He moves in with seven servants and nine cats, the senior cat called "Nigger-Man" like Lovecraft's boyhood pet.

The curse takes the form of the scuttling of an army of invisible rats, which de la Poer and the cats alone can hear. De la Poer and his associates find an ancient altar in the cellar. When this is moved, it discloses a passage into a huge cavern. There they find evidence—including an army of human skeletons in pens—of a cannibal cult that used the site from prehuman times. The narrator goes mad:

> Now they have blown up Exham Priory, taken my Nigger-Man away from me, and shut me into this barred room at Hanwell with fearful whispers about my heredity and experiences. . . . They are trying, too, to suppress most of the facts concerning the priory. When I speak of poor Norrys they accuse me of a hideous thing, but they must know that I did not do it. They must know it was the rats; the slithering scurrying rats whose scampering will never let me sleep; the daemon rats that race behind the padding in this room and beckon me down to greater horrors than I have ever known; the rats they can never hear; the rats, the rats in the walls.[8]

Not counting the series "Herbert West—Reanimator" and "The Lurking Fear," "The Rats in the Walls" at 8,000 words was Lovecraft's longest tale up to then. For once, Lovecraft sold it to *Weird Tales* without first offering it to the amateur magazines.

The next tale, "The Unnamable," he gave to Cook to publish in the final number of his *The Vagrant*. But Cook sustained financial reverses and bad health; he suffered from chronic appendicitis, but a morbid fear of surgery kept him from coping with it. Hence his long-planned last *Vagrant* did not come out until 1927. In the meantime, Lovecraft sold the story to *Weird Tales*, where it appeared in 1925.

"The Unnamable" is an unimpressive little yarn of about 3,000 words, suggested by a passage in Cotton Mather's book of supernatural marvels, *Magnalia*. The narrator, Randolph Carter, tells of an argument with an unimaginative friend about a protean monster, supposed in a legend to lurk in a deserted house. They find the house and, in the dark, are attacked by the monster.

On February 3, 1924, Lovecraft wrote a long letter to Edwin F. Baird, who had urged him to do more stories for *Weird Tales*. Besides complaining of Henneberger's non-payment for the stories that *Weird Tales* had bought, he gave Baird an autobiographical account of himself. Of his current outlook he said:

> My daily life is a sort of contemptuous lethargy, devoid alike of virtues and vices. I am not of the world, but an amused and sometimes disgusted spectator of it. I detest the human race and its pretences

and swinishness. . . . It is damned odd that I, a nearly six-foot
chalk-white Nordic type—the type of the master-conqueror and man
of action—should be as much of a brooding analyst and dabbler in
impressions as any ox-eyed, sawed-off Mediterranean brunet. . . .
I am sure I would rather be a general than a poet. . . . safe preference, since I shall never be either. Futility and ineffectiveness are
my keynote. I shall never amount to anything, because I don't care
enough about life and the world to try. . . .⁹

The picture given by this mixture of candor and affectation,
of snobbery and despair, of shrewd self-knowledge and fallacious
racial fantasy, is not promising for a man about to enter the demanding relationship of matrimony.

Still, despite Lovecraft's arch futilitarianism, he did have hopes
of earning a living. Following a suggestion by Baird, Sonia took
samples of Lovecraft's work to the office of a magazine called *The
Reading Lamp*, to see if that publication would like to hire Lovecraft as a reviewer. The editor, Miss Tucker, seemed enthusiastic.

Changes impended in *Weird Tales*, since the magazine had lost
Henneberger thousands of dollars. He was looking for a new editor,
because the job of editing both *Weird Tales* and *Detective Tales*
seemed to be too much for Baird.

Henneberger had also made contact with Harry Houdini (pseudonym of Ehrich Weiss), the famous conjuror, escape artist, and
exposer of Spiritualist mediums. Houdini furnished the plots for two
stories, ghost-written for him and published in *Weird Tales*. Henneberger urged Houdini to write a regular column for his magazine.
Since Houdini knew little about writing, it was proposed that Lovecraft collaborate.

Announced in the issue of March, 1924, the column, "Ask
Houdini," appeared only in the next issue for that year. But Lovecraft composed a tale, "Imprisoned with the Pharaohs," on the basis
of suggestions by Houdini. The story, ostensibly by Houdini in the
first person, tells in eldritch-horror style of his being seized by a gang
of Arabs at night near the Sphinx of Giza and lowered down a burial
shaft. At the bottom, he finds a horde of indescribable monstrosities
performing unspeakable obscenities.

Lovecraft wrote a rough draft of "Imprisoned with the Pharaohs" in longhand and typed the final version. Then, on Sunday,
March 2, 1924, he took the 11:09 train to New York to meet and
marry Sonia. He had not yet told his aunts what he had in mind.

While awaiting the train, he dozed off, scrambled aboard, and found he had left the final draft of the manuscript in the station. Fortunately, he had the longhand rough draft with him.

In New York, he spent the night in Sonia's apartment at 259 Parkside Avenue, Brooklyn, with Miss Tucker of *The Reading Lamp* as chaperone. Next morning, he went to the office of *The Reading Lamp*, where Miss Tucker let him borrow one of her typists to try to re-create the final draft of "Imprisoned." Before it was half done, he had to rush away to join Sonia and to get the marriage license and ring. According to Sonia:

> In the matter of details—securing the license, buying the ring, etc. —he seemed to be jovial. He said one would think he was being married for the 'nth time, he went about it in such a methodical way.
>
> The man at the marriage bureau thought I was the younger. I was 7 years Howard's senior, and he said nothing could please him better: that Sarah Helen Whitman was older than Poe, and that Poe might have met with better fortune had he married her.[10]

They repaired to St. Paul's Chapel at Broadway and Vesey streets, in the financial district. Lovecraft insisted on a ceremony in that church, not because he had been converted to Episcopalian theology but because the church dated from 1776, and Admiral Lord Howe, George Washington, and other Baroque notables had worshiped there.

And there, on the afternoon of March 3, 1924, the Rev. George Benson Cox pronounced Howard Phillips Lovecraft and Sonia Haft Shifirkin Greene man and wife.

Writers on Lovecraft have speculated on the reasons for the union of this oddly assorted couple. Muriel Eddy thought that Sonia had proposed to Lovecraft and that he had been too much of a gentleman to say "no." James Warren Thomas surmised that Lovecraft's main motive had been to get a cook, a housekeeper, and a secure source of income all at once. Doctor Keller supposed that Lovecraft wished to escape his aunts' domination and their atmosphere of genteel decay, while Sonia wanted a gifted writer to help her to realize her literary ambitions. Professor St. Armand thought that Lovecraft was affected by the parallels between himself and Sonia on one hand and Poe and Mrs. Whitman on the other. August Derleth suggested that Sonia had the notion that, as in the old story of George Bernard Shaw and Isadora Duncan, she and Lovecraft could engender a child combining her beauty with his intellect.[11]

As far as one can judge, Lovecraft and Sonia were simply in love. Love has been making fools of the wise, and people have been falling in love with unsuitable mates, ever since Helen eloped with Paris of Troy and probably a long time before that.

At least, Sonia had been warned. Early in their romance, Lovecraft gave her a copy of George Gissing's autobiographical novel *The Private Papers of Henry Rycroft* (1903), telling her to read it if she wished to know what sort of man she was getting.

This story takes the form of a rambling memoir by an English writer and journalist, who has retired on a small legacy and is idling away his remaining years alone in the country. He tells how he hated his journalism. He has been married, but his blank silence about his wife suggests that he hated the married state, too. He analyzes himself at length:

> I am no friend of the people. As a force, by which the tenor of the time is conditioned, they inspire me with distrust, with fear; as a visible multitude, they make me shrink aloof, and often move me to abhorrence. For the greater part of my life, the people signified to me the London crowd, and no phrase of temperate meaning could utter my thoughts. . . . [A man may be fine as an individual, but] mass him with his fellows in the social organism, and ten to one he becomes a blatant creature, without a thought of his own, ready for any evil to which contagion prompts him.

> I had in me the making of a scholar. With leisure and tranquillity of mind, I should have amassed learning. Within the walls of a college, I should have lived so happily, so harmlessly, my imagination ever busy with the old world. . . . That, as I can see now, was my true ideal; through all my battlings and miseries I have always lived more in the past than in the present.

> Let me tell myself the truth. Do I really believe that at any time of my life I have been the kind of man who merits affection? I think not. I have always been much too self-absorbed; too critical of all about me; too unreasonably proud. Such men as I live and die alone, however much in appearance accompanied.

> For of myself it might be said that whatever folly is possible to a moneyless man, that folly I have at one time or another com-

mitted. Within my nature there seemed to be no faculty of rational self-guidance. Boy and man, I blundered into every ditch and bog which lay within sight of my way. . . . "Unpractical" I was called by those who spoke mildly; "idiot"—I am sure—by many a ruder tongue. And idiot I see myself whenever I glance back over the long, devious road. Something, obviously, I lacked from the beginning, some balancing principle granted to most men in one or another degree. I had brains but they were no help to me in the common circumstances of life.

. . . in all practical matters I am idle and inept.[12]

The resemblance to Lovecraft is uncanny. Since Lovecraft recognized this likeness, it seems as though, despite his tall talk of his Nordic blood, Aryan culture, and Anglo-Saxon gentility, he really knew his own shortcomings painfully well.

The question of Lovecraft's sexuality has stirred much interest. Some writers have called him "sexless." Others have surmised that he might have been a homosexual or at least a latent one. They have cited his indifference to heterosexual relationships; the lack of women in his stories, whose leading characters are often a single male narrator and one close male friend; and his many friendships with younger men, some of whom either were overt homosexuals or had tendencies in that direction.

"Latent homosexuality," however, is a vague, slippery concept. Moreover, the charge of "latent homosexual tendencies" has become such a fad that it is leveled at almost any notable whose love life is at all unusual.

According to what I read, many or most males pass through a phase in adolescence when, if subjected to homosexual influences, they can be drawn into homosexual experiences. Most of these become normally heterosexual; but some, depending upon the strength of the influences upon them, grow up homosexual or bisexual. In this sense, many or most males are latent homosexuals. How Lovecraft would have reacted to homosexual influences during adolescence we cannot tell. Practically speaking, he was subject to no sexual influences at all until he met Sonia. He insisted that:

As a matter of fact—although of course I always knew that paederasty was a disgusting custom of many ancient nations—I never heard of homosexuality as an actual instinct till I was over thirty. . . .

When the kids talked or acted dirtily I could have told them more than they tried to tell me—although (such was the state of Victorian formal medicine) my knowledge was restricted wholly to *normal* sex. I was middle-aged & married before I ever knew that there was such a thing as *instinctive* homosexuality. . . .[13]

In one letter, he made plain his own feelings toward homosexuality:

So far as the case of homosexualism goes, the primary & fatal objection against it is that it is naturally . . . repugnant to the overwhelming bulk of mankind. . . . For instance, I hate both physically normal adultery (which is contemptible sneaking treachery) & paederasty—but while I might enjoy (physically) or be tempted toward adultery, I simply could *not* consider the abnormal state without physical nausea.

That this was Lovecraft's honest opinion is confirmed by a letter he wrote to Robert Barlow in the last year of his life. Like several of Lovecraft's young protégés, Barlow became an active homosexual. His homosexuality, however, may not have developed until after Lovecraft's death; at least, Lovecraft apparently never knew of his young friend's deviation.

In the letter in question, Lovecraft criticized a story that Barlow had written about an artist who develops a strong attachment to a prizefighter. Lovecraft found this incredible:

There is not the slightest reason in the world why any sane & mature artist should wish to see or talk with a cheap & undistinguished prize fighter. And if some tragic disease or malformation gave the artist an abnormal interest, he would naturally spend all his time in fighting & eradicating the disease—not in displaying or encouraging it as a lower-grade character might.

Typically, Lovecraft was pontificating on something of which he knew little. Many artists, considered "great," have done things that Lovecraft would have disapproved. The graphic and plastic arts, especially, seem to have a higher-than-average attraction for homosexuals. Lovecraft went on:

And when it comes to making a thorough fool of oneself over women—hell! Compare the millions of high-grade men who *don't* with the relatively insignificant number who *do!* . . . This petty smirking and bridling is merely cheap unrestraint—perfectly normal, but aesthetically ignominious. We'd all *like* to kiss pretty girls till our dying day—but we know damn well that it would be only a repellant & sordid mockery except with the very few women who really have affection for us when we are young.

We need not belabor Lovecraft's lapses of logic; but it is incredible that Lovecraft should have written this letter, confessing to a yearning to kiss pretty girls, if he either had been a homosexual or had known that Barlow was one.

Sexual difficulties like repression, insufficiency, impotence, and inversion are not rare among writers. One may cite Carlyle, Dostoyevsky, E. T. A. Hoffmann, D. H. Lawrence, T. E. Lawrence, Nietzsche, Strachey, and T. H. White. Whether such troubles are commoner among authors than in the general populace, I know not.

There may, however, be a connection between these writers' sexual peculiarities and the fact that, like Lovecraft, several of them preached authoritarianism, militarism, racism, supermanism, and other doctrines classed by one writer as "heroic vitalism."[14] This was notoriously the case with Carlyle, D. H. Lawrence, and Nietzsche. Such vicarious blood-and-guts heroism seems to be a favored form of compensation for sickly, frail, and nervously unstable types, like the demon-haunted Houston Stewart Chamberlain, who glorified the "Teutonic Aryan."

Lovecraft certainly suffered from enough sexual repression to account for his erotic behavior. We cannot now prove whether one or more of the other tendencies cited above also complicated his life. But it would not be sound reasoning to drag in an unknown cause where there is a known cause that is enough by itself to account for the phenomenon.

On the basis of known evidence, homosexuality on Lovecraft's part seems, like hereditary syphilis, to be so very unlikely that, while not completely disprovable, it may be safely ignored. What is remarkable is the fact that, considering his peculiar upbringing and his mother's attempt to feminize him, he did *not* become an overt homosexual.

The main factor in Lovecraft's sexuality was an intense antisexual prejudice and inhibition, which he almost certainly got from his mother. It resulted from her general attitudes, her refusal to touch him after infancy, and her description of him as "hideous."

In addition, his sexual drive seems to have been low. He was surely speaking of himself when, writing in later life of the problems of a period of transition in sexual morals, he said: "In these transitional days the luckiest persons are those of sluggish eroticism who can cast aside the whole muddled business & watch the squirming of the primitive majority from the side-lines with ironic detachment."[15] As to which factor—his mother's influence or some physical insufficiency—contributed the more to his sexual inertia, we cannot tell; but the combination was evidently too much for his male sexuality.

In any case, he grew up with so powerful an anti-sexual inhibition that for most of his life it swamped any sexual proclivities, normal or otherwise. He carried his anti-sexual puritanism to ludicrous extremes. When Cook published a harmless story about an artist's model who posed in the nude, Lovecraft wrote a long, sizzling letter, castigating Cook for this "horrifying example of decadence in thought and morals." He also wrote: "Eroticism belongs to a lower order of instincts, and is an animal rather than a nobly human quality." "As for Puritan inhibitions, I admire them more every day. They are attempts to make life a work of art. . . ."[16]

Yet, if we sample the attitudes of Lovecraft's time and place, he no longer seems so freakish. Henry David Thoreau was as anti-sexual as Lovecraft:

> We are conscious of an animal in us, which awakens in proportion as our higher nature slumbers. It is reptile and sensual, and perhaps cannot be wholly expelled. . . . Chastity is the flowering of man; and what are called Genius, Heroism, Holiness, and the like, are but various fruits which succeed it. Man flows at once to God when the channel of purity is open. . . .

Or consider Marquand's fictional George Apley, when he settles down for man-to-man talk with his son on sex:

> "You know and I know that all this idea of sex is largely 'bosh.' I can frankly say that sex has not played a dominant part in my life, and I trust that it has not in yours. No right-thinking man permits his mind to dwell upon such things, and the same must be true of women. And now this is enough of this unsavoury subject."[17]

One can only wonder how an Apley ever managed to breed a son at all. While Lovecraft kept his own sexual life on the straight and narrow, he early gave up the thought of imposing his morality on others. In 1921 he wrote Kleiner:

In considering the origin of my opinions I have recently wondered whether or not my anti-erotic views are too hasty; formed from mere subjective prejudice rather than accurate or impersonal observation. . . . Thus I am coming to be convinced that the erotic instinct is in the majority of mankind far stronger than I could ever imagine without wide reading and imagination; that it relentlessly clutches the average person—even of the thinking classes—to a degree which makes its overthrow by higher interests impossible. . . . The only remedy would seem to lie in the gradual evolution of society out of the puritan phase, and the sanctioning of some looser morality of hetairism.

Lovecraft felt that the begetting of families might be a civic duty, but pleasure had nothing to do with it:

It is ever the part of the exemplary citizen to sustain with equanimity his share in the production of the coming generation; a responsibility so reprehensibly shirkt by some, that the foreigners are likely to ingulph us in but a few years unless checkt by legislation & the Ku Klux Klan.

In later years, some of Lovecraft's young literary protégés like Long and Derleth used to write him, boasting of their successes with the girls. The result was often a letter patiently preaching a strict sexual morality. For example, Lovecraft argued that permissiveness in fornication would logically lead to demands for similar liberty in sodomy, incest, and bestiality. These would be justified as "honest and progressive."[18] Nations and cultures that allowed such freedoms, he thought, were on the road to decadence and decay. Current social trends suggest that, perhaps, Lovecraft was not altogether wrong.

When Lovecraft first knew Sonia, she wrote him asking his thoughts on love. The reply was a lengthy sermon, such as a celibate philosopher might have addressed to a young disciple about to wed:

The mutual love of man and woman for one another is an imaginative experience that consists of having its object bear a certain special relation to the aesthetic-emotional life of its possessor. . . .
Youth brings with it certain erogenous and imaginative stimuli bound up in the tactile phenomena of slender, virginally-postured bodies and visual imagery of classical aesthetic contours symbolizing a kind of freshness and Springtime immaturity which is very beautiful but which has nothing to do with domestic love.
No conservative man or woman expects such extraordinary physical exaltation except for a brief period in extreme youth; and

any high grade person can soon transfer his or her physical needs to other fields when middle age approaches; other forms of stimulation mean much more than sex-expression to such persons, so that they hardly give it more than a cursory thought. . . .

This is merely one more eloquent rationalization of Lovecraft's own qualities, desires, and limitations. One may wonder how a man with this tepid, abstract, sluggish conception of love made out after marriage.

As it happens, we have some idea. Sonia wrote to Derleth: "As a married man he [Lovecraft] was an adequately excellent lover but refused to show his feelings in the presence of others." She confided to Frank Long's mother that Lovecraft (who had foresightedly read some books on sex) could indeed "perform."

On another occasion, she also said he was sexually "adequate—but little else." When Derleth visited her in 1953, she told him: "Howard was entirely adequate sexually, but he always approached sex as if he did not quite like it."[19] Each time, she said, she had to take the initiative.

I infer that, during the months following his marriage, Lovecraft performed his husbandly duties adequately if without much enthusiasm. One is reminded of the Victorian Englishman who prefaced the consummation of his marriage by telling his bride: "I now have a very unpleasant duty to perform."[20]

Seemingly, Lovecraft's physical sexual equipment was normal or nearly so. On the other hand, either because of his maternal tabu, or his low sexual drive, or both, he was content to resume a celibate life. After he and Sonia separated, he seems not to have missed his marital relations. In fact, he declined a chance to resume them when she made a last effort to win him back. Poor Lovecraft; poor Sonia!

Eleven

QUIXOTE IN BABYLON

Had I not been thus prolix, you might
either have misunderstood me altogether,
or, with the rabble, have thought me mad.
As it is, you will easily perceive that I am
one of the many uncounted victims of the
Imp of the Perverse.[1]

POE

When Poe wrote of the "Imp of the Perverse," he meant that urge, which comes betimes upon the most rational of men, to do something foolish, self-thwarting, contraproductive, or self-destructive, even when one knows better. It is the Imp that urges us to make public scenes, to quarrel with those who can do us the most good, to bet our all, or to play Russian roulette. When we stand near a cliff or a skyscraper window, the Imp whispers: "Go on, jump!" It is that which leads us to call a man like Lovecraft "his own worst enemy." Poe, who struggled with the Imp all his life, explained how it works:

We have a task before us which must be speedily performed. We know that it will be ruinous to make delay. . . . We glow, we are consumed with eagerness to commence the work, with the anticipation of whose glorious result our whole souls are on fire. It must, it shall be undertaken to-day, and yet we put it off until to-morrow; and why? There is no answer, except that we feel *perverse*, using the word with no comprehension of the principle. To-morrow arrives, and with it a more impatient anxiety to do our duty, but with this very increase arrives, also, a nameless, a positively fearful, because unfathomable, craving for delay. . . . The clock strikes, and is the knell of our welfare. At the same time, it is the chanticleer-note to the ghost that has so long overawed us. It flies—it disappears—we are free. The old energy returns. We will labor *now*. Alas, it is *too late!*

Lovecraft, too, was haunted by the Imp. Its true nature I must leave to psychiatrists, who have some plausible explanations. But more than once, we shall detect its shadowy form behind Lovecraft's shoulder.

The newlywed Lovecrafts had meant to leave at once on a one-day honeymoon but found themselves too exhausted. The following afternoon, "after changing the name card in the door of Parkside and notifying tradesmen of the new cognomen," they took the train to Philadelphia and put up at the Robert Morris. Lovecraft gleefully reported that "Signing the register 'Mr. and Mrs.' was quite easy despite total inexperience!"

To meet the deadline on the Houdini collaboration, they had to complete the typing of the manuscript. They found a public stenographer's office at the Hotel Vendig and, for a dollar, rented a typewriter. For three hours, Sonia sat dictating from the longhand draft while Lovecraft typed with two fingers.

Then, said Sonia, "we were too tired for honeymooning or anything else."[2] Sonia may have been disconcerted to find that Lovecraft, when most men had switched to pajamas, staunchly adhered to the long nineteenth-century nightshirt.

Next day, they took a bus tour of Philadelphia. They finished typing "Imprisoned with the Pharaohs" and mailed it to the offices of *Weird Tales*. Within three weeks, Lovecraft received $100 for his work. He insisted on spending all the money on a wedding ring with a circle of diamonds, assuring the doubtful Sonia that "there would be more where that came from."

Back in Brooklyn, Sonia went back to her millinery shop, while Lovecraft cast about for means of getting the "more where that came from." Some time before, Sonia's former employer Ferle Heller had gone out of business. Sonia and two woman partners rented a shop on Fifty-seventh Street in Manhattan to sell hats. To launch this project, Sonia sold some stock to finance a trip to Paris. There she bought hats and materials to use in copying them. The shop, however, failed to profit, because the customers could not meet the high prices.

During the early weeks of his marriage, Lovecraft's letters bubbled with high spirits. He gave the effect of the happy bridegroom, who had captured his love, proved his manhood, and was about to conquer the world:

> Two are one. Another bears the name of Lovecraft. A new household is founded!
>
> In other words, Old Theobald is hitting the high spots on a partnership basis, the superior nine-tenths of the outfit being the nymph whose former name has just been canned in favour of mine own on the doorplate at the above address.
>
> I wish you could behold Grandpa this week, getting up regularly in the daytime, bustling briskly about. . . . And all with a prospect of regular literary work—my first real job—in the offing!
>
> My general health is ideal. S. H.'s [Sonia's] cooking . . . is the last word in perfection. . . . She even makes *edible* bran muffins! . . . And—*mirabile dictu*—she is at least *trying* to make me stick to the Walter Camp exercises known as the "Daily Dozen"! . . . So far I haven't had a headache since the wearing off of the old one induced by the Houdini-Henneberger rush. Decidedly, Old Theobald is alive as he was never alive before![3]

The "regular literary work" was the proposal that Miss Tucker hire him as a reviewer for *The Reading Lamp*. While considering this, Miss Tucker suggested that Lovecraft start a non-fiction book on such weird survivals as witchcraft and haunted houses in America. She would try to sell it as his literary agent. Lovecraft began to gather materials.

Lovecraft poured praise on his bride. He credited her with rescuing him from eventual suicide:

> The more active life, to one of my temperament, demands many things, which I could dispense with when drifting sleepily and inertly along, shunning a world which exhausted and disgusted

me, and having no goal but a phial of cyanide when my money should give out. I had formerly meant to follow this latter course, and was fully prepared to seek oblivion whenever cash should fail or sheer ennui grow too much for me; when suddenly, nearly three years ago, our benevolent angel S. H. G. stepped into my circle of consciousness and began to combat the idea with the opposite one of effort, and the enjoyment of life through the rewards which effort will bring.

He told how Sonia had inspired him with "the need to 'get up and get'. . . . New York! Of course! Where else can one be alive when he has no vitality of his own and needs the magic spur of external inducement to active life and effective toil?"

They had decided not to let bourgeois prejudices about money stand in their way. Sonia's apartment would cost no more if he dwelt there than if he did not, and he hoped to pay his share of expenses soon. He apologized for not telling his aunts of his plans for marriage, giving as an excuse his "hatred of sentimental spoofing, and of that agonisingly indecisive 'talking over' which radical steps always prompt among mortals. . . ."

It is pitiable that such high hopes should fail so utterly, especially when it seems as though Lovecraft *almost* made the grade. He might have, had not a combination of personal shortcomings, wrong decisions, and bad luck conspired to defeat him. Despite Sonia's devotion, the habits and attitudes of thirty-three years were not easily changed.

Complications soon beset the Lovecraft-Greene ménage. Sonia's financial situation worsened. Since the Fifty-seventh Street shop was not doing well, she left it and opened a hat business of her own, in a small shop that she had previously rented and fitted out in Brooklyn. Here, alas, the customers could even less well afford fancy women's hats.

Then there was Lovecraft's continuing childish dependence upon his aunts. Instead of banking in New York, he continued to let his aunts manage his money and to dole him out the interest from his mortgage notes. Whenever he got a check from *Weird Tales* or elsewhere, he mailed it to his aunts, so that they could cash it and mail him back the cash. When his shoes or other garments needed repairs, he mailed them to his aunts, so that they could have the work done in Providence and send them back to him.

For two years, he wrote long letters to Lillian Clark on an average of once a week and sometimes oftener, besides less frequent letters to Annie Gamwell. The letters to Mrs. Clark deal in often tedious detail with the minutiae of daily life. They tell of his food, his clothes, his sight-seeing walks, and his meetings with his friends. If less intellectually stimulating than some of his letters, they give an almost day-by-day account of his doings in New York.

In return, Lillian Clark sent Providence newspapers and bushels of clippings to her nephew, thus keeping the silver cord unfrayed. Lovecraft never did take to heart that phrase in the marriage ceremony about "forsaking all others." In his first letter to Mrs. Clark after his marriage, he urged both aunts to come and live with him:

> Now to get you folks in on the celebration! You—and this is already an irrevocable dictum of Fate—are going to live here permanently. No negative decision will be accepted, and if you don't come voluntarily you'll be kidnapped! And that goes for A. E. P. G. [Annie Gamwell] too. . . .[4]

The aunts did not accept the offer. That spring, however, Annie Gamwell came to visit, since she also wanted to see friends in New Jersey. Sonia wrote Annie a letter gushing with cordiality:

> Darling,—
> . . . I'm so glad you can come! . . . My dear, I do hope you can stay a long time! . . . I just can't wait until you get here. . . .
>
> Lovingly yours, SONIA

Lovecraft added a note promising sight-seeing tours and asking that more of his clothes be sent. He also had many household furnishings shipped from Providence, claiming that "I could not live anywhere without my own household objects around me—the furniture my childhood knew, the books my ancestors read, and the pictures my mother and grandmother painted." Friends were surprised at the lengths to which he went to bring Providence with him to Brooklyn. A few unwanted furnishings in Providence—a folding bed, a bureau, and a gas plate—were given to the Eddys, and Lovecraft abandoned his celestial globe.

Still, Lovecraft was enjoying life. He bought souvenir models of the Woolworth Building and the Statue of Liberty, explaining:

"I like N. Y. so well that I am going to lug some of it home with me."[5]

A further strain on the marriage, Sonia found, was caused by her husband's peculiar habits and outlook. Though she might try to put the best face upon it, he was a pretty tepid lover. He never used the word "love"; his idea of verbal love-making was to say: "My dear, you don't know how much I appreciate you." His efforts at affectionate physical contact consisted of wrapping his little finger around hers and grunting, "*Unh!*"

Lovecraft tried to change his nocturnal hours. In May, when Morton invited him to a literary club meeting, Lovecraft said he could not come unless Sonia were up to coming, too, adding: "She generally has to hit the hay early, and I have to get home in proportionate time, since she can't get to sleep until I do. . . ."

Little by little, however, Lovecraft slipped back into his old habits "of staying up most of the night as when he and Sam Loveman visited me [Sonia], and when his aunt, Mrs. Gamwell, came to visit us, while I had to get up early, prepare and serve breakfast, prepare his lunch and then go back to work."[6]

There are sound reasons for a writer's working late at night. Most writers need to be left for long hours without interruptions. Interrupt the writer, and it may take him a quarter or half hour to get back into his groove. So, to keep him from composing anything at all, one need only interrupt him every quarter hour or so.

Late at night, neither the telephone nor the doorbell rings. No neighbors, salesmen, deliverymen, or collectors for worthy causes appear on the doorstep. The children, if any, are in bed instead of asking Daddy to come out and play or to drive them to the movies.

On the other hand, if the writer belongs to the average family, such hours put a strain on the other members, compelled by their jobs, schooling, marketing, and other necessities to keep a conventional schedule. To solve this dilemma, some writers rise at four in the morning and do most of their work before breakfast.

Lovecraft's vagueness was calculated to madden any brisk, prompt, efficient person. Sonia wrote:

> Sometimes I'd have him meet me after work and we'd dine in some fashionable restaurant, then go to a show or movie and sometimes to a comic opera. He had no conception of time. Many times I would stand waiting for him in some lobby or on a street corner

when the temperature would be as low as 30 and sometimes below; without exaggeration, I often stood there from three quarters to one hour and a half waiting for him.

His xenophobia also surfaced. He told Sonia "that whenever we had company he would appreciate it if 'Aryans' were in the majority."[7] When he gave vent to savage remarks against Jews, Sonia would remind him that, after all, she herself came of the "alien hordes" against which he railed. Then Lovecraft would complacently say: "You are now Mrs. H. P. Lovecraft of 598 Angell Street, Providence, Rhode Island,"[8] as if that somehow removed the stigma.

Lovecraft liked the Colonial relics of New York but not its rushing, motley, ill-mannered crowds. The longer he lived there, the more intense became his xenophobia. Sonia tried to reason him out of it, pointing out that every ethnos contained people of all kinds and that each had its share of saints and scoundrels.

> Later H. P. assured me he was quite "cured." But . . . whenever we found ourselves in the racially-mixed crowds which characterize New York, Howard would become livid with rage. He seemed almost to lose his mind. And if the truth must be known, it was this attitude toward minorities and his desire to escape them that eventually prompted him back to Providence. . . . He referred chiefly to Semitic peoples: "beady-eyed, rat-faced Asiatics," he called them. In general, all foreigners were "mongrels."[9]

When Lovecraft's shortcomings as man and husband are set out in cold type, he does not sound lovable. Yet we have the word of many who knew him that he was. In personal relations always kind, courteous, and obliging, he was also a fascinating conversationalist, with interesting ideas on almost any subject. Years later, Sonia remembered him as "a marvelous person. He was 'as wise as a serpent and as gentle as a dove,' when circumstances or the occasion prompted it; yet he was not of a calculating turn of mind, and never sought for the main chance."[10]

Despite these strains, the marriage jogged along amicably for half a year. Sonia gave Lovecraft spending money, soothing his pride by telling him: "You'll pay it all back with interest, I'm sure."

The money he got from Sonia, and the occasional payments from his aunts, from ghosting clients, or from *Weird Tales*, Lovecraft spent frugally. Now and then he bought books, sometimes to give to Sonia or to his friends. He also gave money to other amateur journalists—"gentle grafters," Sonia called them—who wrote him begging letters, even though he had to deprive himself to do so.

At Sonia's suggestion, they called each other "Socrates" and "Xantippe." She fed him up:

> When we were married he was tall and gaunt and 'hungry-looking'. I happen to like the apparently ascetic type but H. P. was too much so even for my taste, so I used to cook a well-balanced meal every evening, make a substantial breakfast—(he loved cheese soufflé!—rather an untimely dish for breakfast) and I'd leave a few (almost Dagwoodian) sandwiches for him, a piece of cake and some fruit for his lunch (he loved sweets) and I'd tell him to be sure to make some tea or coffee for himself. All this of course, while I still held my buyership in New York. . . .

As a result, Lovecraft's weight, which in the last few years had already risen above the 140s, increased to nearly two hundred pounds. Sonia thought he "looked and felt marvelous" at that weight.

Still hoping to become a solid family man, Lovecraft joined Sonia in buying two lots in Yonkers. They planned some day to build, on the larger lot, a house big enough for them and for Lovecraft's aunts, while they held the smaller lot as a speculation. In late July, Lovecraft wrote the Homeland Company of Yonkers, pleading inability to keep up the payments of $100 a week. Apparently the realty company agreed to carry the Lovecrafts, for several years later Sonia still had title to the lots and arranged for her half-brother to sell first one and then the other for her.

Lovecraft took Sonia on long antiquarian walks and haunted New York's great museums. As he said: "What's the use of living in a big town if you don't use the advantages thereof?"[11]

During this time, both Lovecraft and Sonia felt that each were yielding to the other in every possible way: a phenomenon not unknown among married couples. Sonia wrote:

> I effaced myself entirely and deferred to him upon all matters and domestic problems regardless of what they were in order to remove or reduce if possible some of the complexes he might have had. Even to the spending of my own earned money I not only consulted him but tried to make him feel that he was the "Head of the House".

Meanwhile, Lovecraft described his own status thus:

> I am reduced to a state of the most compleat obedience; & never respond to a connubial admonition but by saying, in the most domestick manner imaginable, "Yes, My Dear!"

Lovecraft had hardly begun his married life in Brooklyn when upheavals occurred in *Weird Tales*. Henneberger was now heavily in debt, owing at least $43,000 and perhaps as much as $60,000. Henneberger and Baird, his editor, parted with acrimony. The issues of the magazine for May and June, 1924, failed to appear.

Taking over as editor, Henneberger managed (with editorial help from Otis Adalbert Kline, a young pulp writer and literary agent) to get out a double-sized "anniversary issue" for May, June, and July, 1924. This might have been the last issue had not the notoriety of the Eddy-Lovecraft story, "The Loved Dead," and the ensuing efforts to ban the magazine given *Weird Tales* a new lease on life.

In casting about for a new editor, Henneberger thought of Lovecraft. In March he wrote from Chicago, sounding out Lovecraft on the possibility. Instead of being delighted, Lovecraft was appalled, writing Frank Long:

> Grandpa means to settle down here and do some intensive cash-corraling in local pastures unless . . . a thunderbolt comes out of *Weird Tales's* office and lands me in ugly, modern, crassly repellant CHICAGO. . . . damn the possibility! . . . This honest but uncouth Henny writes that he is making a radical change in the policy of *Weird Tales*, and that he has in mind a brand-new magazine to cover the field of Poe-Machen shudders. This magazine, he says, will be "right in my line," and he wants to know if I would consider moving to CHICAGO to edit it! O gawd, O Montreal! It may be a flivver, but your Grandma is urging me to take it up if it definitely materialises and is accompanied by the requisite guarantees. This I can hardly contemplate without a shiver—think of the tragedy of such a move for an aged antiquarian just settled down in enjoyment of the reliques of venerable New-Amsterdam! SH wouldn't mind living in Chicago at all—but it is Colonial atmosphere which supplies my very breath of life. I would not consider such a move, big though the proposition would be if genuine, without previously exhausting every sort of rhetorick in an effort to persuade Henneberger to let me edit at long distance. One trouble is, that the damned thing might fail after a few issues, leaving me

stranded in uncongenial Western scenes. . . . You can bet your
Grandpa'll look sharply into anything of the sort before contem-
plating it seriously! But it may be all hot air anyway.[12]

So Lovecraft gave Henneberger a noncommittal reply. Although
Henneberger has written: "I offered him the editorship of Weird
Tales," I have not found any other evidence that Lovecraft was
actually offered the editorship of *Weird Tales*, or that he refused
to move to Chicago, or that he turned down any genuine offer of
an editorship. Henneberger, however, made many trips to New York,
in the course of which he had several meetings with Lovecraft; and
Henneberger was a great talker. So an offer of the editorship of
Weird Tales may have occurred during these meetings. In any case,
by the time Henneberger got around to making Lovecraft a hard-
and-fast proposal, he no longer controlled *Weird Tales*, which by
then had a new editor.

Another man whom Henneberger had considered as a replacement for Baird was Farnsworth Wright, who had belonged to Lovecraft's faction of the UAPA. A native of San Francisco then living in
Chicago, Wright had sold several stories to *Weird Tales*. He was a
tall, gaunt Shakespearean scholar who suffered from Parkinson's
disease. This affliction caused his fingers to twitch so uncontrollably
that he had to type his signature on letters.

To settle the claims and counter-claims among Henneberger,
his business manager John Lansinger, Edwin Baird, and another em-
ployee named William Sprenger, a complex deal was worked out.
By the end of September, Lansinger and Baird, doing business as
the Collegiate Publishing Company, owned *Detective Tales*. Sprenger
and Wright were part owners of the Popular Fiction Publishing
Company, the publisher of *Weird Tales*, with Sprenger as business
manager and Wright as editor. Henneberger was still the nominal
publisher but was not to receive any profits until the debt was paid
off. After another lapse of three months, *Weird Tales* resumed
regular publication with the issue of November, 1924.

In September, Henneberger came to New York, full of talk of
his projected new periodical, for which he considered the name
Ghost Stories. He assured Lovecraft that he was definitely hired as
full-time editor of the new magazine. His salary was to be $40 a
week, later to be raised to $100.

Henneberger promised the first payment by September 26. The

date came and went without the money. For two months, Henneberger kept Lovecraft dangling, promising and promising. He gave Lovecraft some minor work to do, such as editing a collection of jokes.

At last, in November, Henneberger gave up for lack of financial backing. His proffered editorship had proved "hot air" after all. Owing Lovecraft for minor editorial work, Henneberger paid him off with a $60 credit at a bookstore. On the 9th, Lovecraft went with Long to the store and chose eighteen books, plus one as a gift to Long. Those that Lovecraft picked for himself were mainly by Dunsany and Machen, together with several on Colonial America, one on Rome, and a copy of Beckford's old Gothic-oriental novel *Vathek*.

Two of Lovecraft's traits call for explanation. One was his neophobia—his fear and hatred of change. The other was his fanatical attachment to certain physical, material things.

Sonia said: "He hated everything new and unfamiliar; whether it was wearing apparel, a city, or a face. However, when he became accustomed to the novelty of anything, at first he accepted it gingerly, then he embraced it. . . . He hated making new friends but when once made, he was loyal." (A bit overstated, perhaps, but true in general.) He got worked up over the destruction of any old building. One of his grudges against ethnics was that they had occupied old sections of Providence and wrought changes there.

This quirk is not hard to account for. Lovecraft had started life as a spoiled little rich boy. But then his life to the time of his marriage was one long downward slope, as the money dwindled and, in worldly achievement, he fell further and further behind the men he had known as a boy. While others went on to glory, he was mired in a swamp of paralyzing neuroses and genteel decay. He admired those who succeeded and wistfully wished that he could have done likewise.

Therefore, everything seemed to get better as one went backward in time. Since Lovecraft had no belief in a heaven-bound immortal soul to comfort him, everything would doubtless get worse as one went forward.

As a psychiatrist has put it, for everyone with pleasant childhood memories, "the land of his youth is a golden land. . . ."

Happiness, therefore, lay in trying to hold back the tide of time by preserving everything—houses, customs, costumes, and institutions—surviving from days of yore.

Moreover, Lovecraft clung to his household furnishings (most of them not Colonial but Victorian) with what his wife called "morbid tenacity."[13] He refused to move to the Midwest because it lacked Colonial atmosphere. To the ambitious, mobile young American of the 1970s, such a reason is lunacy; but to Lovecraft it mattered intensely.

One could consider Lovecraft's passion for his furnishings as merely a by-product of his neophobia, but there may be more to it than that. Harold F. Searles, the psychiatrist whom I just quoted, explains the attachment of children to pet teddy bears, security blankets, and similar objects. These things he calls "transitional objects," because they help the child to make the transition from complete dependence on its parents to a normal, self-reliant relationship with its peers—classmates, sweethearts, neighbors, friends, and associates in adult work and play.

A child without such objects tends to remain excessively attached to its parents. The transitional object weans it away from such dependence. Then:

> The concreteness of the child's thinking suggests that for him, as for the member of the so-called primitive culture and for the schizophrenic adult, the wealth of nonhuman objects about him are constituents of his psychological being in a more intimate sense than they are for the adult in our culture. . . .

In the normal person, according to Doctor Searles, love of things gradually matures into love of persons, and the motive power for this change is the growth of sexuality in adolescence. This is not to say that a mature adult ceases to care for his parents or is indifferent to heirlooms and to souvenirs of his childhood. But to find life not worth living without such relics, as Lovecraft did, means that one's process of maturation has halted in the teddy-bear stage. Considering the intense sexual repression under which Lovecraft was reared, Doctor Searles's theory, that sexuality is the means for getting one out of the transitional-object stage, makes sense:

> Those persons who . . . fail to make this final achievement of normal adolescence apparently continue throughout their lives to identify themselves more with Nature than with mankind. Toward

Nature they experience a passionately close relationship, toward mankind they have a misanthropic attitude; their fellow men seem alien to them.[14]

If one defines "Nature" as "the scenery of New England, especially Providence," one has the essence of Lovecraft, who, despite the closeness of his many personal friendships, "hated humanity in the abstract" and insisted that his real interest in life was "the general visual scene."

Miss Tucker, the editor of *The Reading Lamp*, decided not to hire Lovecraft, and the non-fiction book that she urged him to write get nowhere. Henneberger's new magazine aborted, so there was nothing for it but that Lovecraft should hunt for a job. Starting in late July, 1924, he made the rounds of New York employment agencies and called upon the employers to whom they sent him.

Sitting for hours in offices and then being interviewed by strangers was torture. Lovecraft was skittish about confronting new faces and knew that no gentleman boasted of his own abilities or tried to "sell himself." After a morning of such encounters, physically and psychologically exhausted, he would spend the afternoon walking in a park or visiting a museum to "get the taste out of my mouth." Furthermore, he met one insuperable obstacle right at the start:

Lack of commercial experience is a beastly obstacle—everybody is polite & complimentary enough, but it's tough work leading 'em up to the hiring-point!

Lovecraft had many things against him: his old-fashioned, shabby-genteel appearance; his shy, stiff manner with strangers; his pedantic way of speaking; even his high voice. Employers might have overlooked these things, but they could not overlook the fact that a man almost thirty-four years old had never held a single job. Asked for his employment record, he had none. Had he been fifteen years younger, his lack of experience would not have bulked so large, since nobody expects a mere stripling to have had wide experience. As it was, more than one personnel officer must have wondered whether this odd fellow had spent the last fifteen years in a mental institution.

He wrote letters of self-recommendation to circulate among publishers. We have the rough draft of one:

Dear Sir:—

If an unprovoked application for employment seem somewhat unusual in these days of system, agencies, & advertising, I trust that the circumstances surrounding this one may help to mitigate what would otherwise be obtrusive forwardness. The case is one wherein certain definitely marketable aptitudes must be put forward in an unconventional manner if they are to override the current fetish which demands commercial experience & causes prospective employers to dismiss unheard the application of any situation-seeker unable to boast of specific professional service in a given line.

The notion that not even a man of cultivation & good intelligence can possibly acquire rapid effectiveness in a field ever so slightly outside his own routine, would seem to be a naive one; yet recent events have shown me most emphatically what a widespread superstition it is. Since commencing two months ago, a quest for work for which I am naturally & scholastically well fitted, I have answered nearly a hundred advertisements without gaining so much as one chance for satisfactory hearing—& all, apparently, because I cannot point to previous employment in the precise industrial subdivision represented by the various firms. Faring thus with the usual channels, I am at last experimentally taking the aggressive.

The situation of which I am in search, & which I believe your establishment might afford, is one where the services of an author, reviser, re-writer, critic, reviewer, correspondent, proofreader, typist, or anything else even remotely of the sort, are required. In these lines I am prepared to display a mature & effective proficiency despite the fact that I have never been systematically employed by another; yet am willing, in deference to custom & necessity, to begin most modestly, & with the small remuneration which novices usually receive. What I wish is an initial foothold; after that I am confident that my work will speak for me.

I am by vocation a writer & reviser—composing original fiction, criticism, & verse, & with exceptionally thorough experience in preparing correct & fluent text on subjects assigned, or meeting the most difficult & intricate problems of re-writing & constructive revision, prose & verse. For over seven years I have handled nearly all the writing of a very prominent American author, editor, & lecturer; including several books & many poems which have subsequently achieved no little popularity in traversing the rounds of the press. I have also edited & revised books for others, & can if desired submit samples of this as well as of less extensive work—published stories, reviews, association organs which I have edited, & the like.

This free-lance industry, however, is obviously uneven & uncertain; & I am now—being married & settled in New York—extremely desirous of exchanging it for a regular & permanent salaried connection with any responsible enterprise of not too dissimilar nature. That I can adequately fill any ordinary position involving English composition & rhetoric, literary creativeness, & familiarity with typographical forms & practices, seems very clear to me. Experience in the details of any one commercial enterprise I may lack, but I nevertheless believe that I have assets of at least equal value in an ability to compose vividly, fluently, correctly from outlines, notes, or suggestions, & in such qualities as quick & discriminating perception, orthographical accuracy, stylistic fastidiousness, & a keenly developed sense of the niceties of English usage. As regards these qualities, I am willing to take any sort of practical examination such as composing continuous text from hints or synopses submitted, or reading proof under your supervision, with reference to speed & freedom from errors.

I am thirty-four years of age, & of cultivated native ancestry. My education, while not including the university or a professional translator's knowledge of modern languages, is that of a gentleman, & embodies all the essentials of liberal culture, literary technique, disciplined observation, & balanced conservatism. With this equipment—ordinary as it is—I cannot doubt but that I am capable of filling some position offered by such organisations as yours, even though lack of earlier employment form a fictitious barrier. Round pegs find round holes, square pegs find square holes. And by the same token, albeit with rather greater difficulty, I am sure that there must somewhere be a corresponding hole for such a peg as proverbial metaphor may dub trapezohedral!

Hoping—rashly or not—to hear from you & to receive a fuller opportunity for displaying my industrial qualifications, I am

Very truly yours,

HPL[15]

A worse approach to a prospective employer would be hard to imagine. Not surprisingly, this extraordinary letter produced no jobs.

Lovecraft had the qualifications for an adequate employment résumé, had he known how to write it without the verbosity, rhetoric, pedantries, and redundancies of this example. In another such letter, he told his prospective employer, a printer, not to fear that Lovecraft, because of his pure Anglo-Saxon ancestry, would take a snobbish attitude towards other employees not so fortunate. In this, Lovecraft was the one who needed a ghost-writer.

He ran an ad in the classified section of the *New York Times:*

WRITER AND REVISER, free-lance, desires regular and permanent salaried connection with any responsible enterprise requiring literary services; exceptionally thor-

ough experience in preparing correct and
fluent text on subjects assigned, and in
meeting the most difficult, intricate and extensive problems of rewriting and constructive revision, prose or verse; would also
consider situation dealing with such proofreading as demands rapid and discriminating
perception, orthographical accuracy, stylistic
fastidiousness and a keenly developed sense
of the niceties of English usage; good typist; age 34, married; has for seven years
handled all the prose and verse of a leading
American public speaker and editor. Y 2292
Times Annex.

Lovecraft evidently did not know what constituted a good
typist. The "leading American public speaker" was David V. Bush,
for whom he was still ghosting.

Lovecraft's efforts did land him a job, but one for which he
was about as ill-suited as a man could be. He answered a help-
wanted ad by a company in Newark. On July 23d, he went there
and found that the job was that of "canvassing salesman to introduce the service of the Creditors' National Clearing House, a
Boston firm with a Newark branch, whose specialty . . . is the
collection of slightly overdue accounts before they develop into
bad habits." Lovecraft was to sell the services of this debt-collection
agency on a straight commission basis.

Lovecraft was hired, took home and filled out a sheaf of forms,
attended a salesman's meeting, and was heartened when the sales
manager announced that Lovecraft's revised version of the standard
sales talk would be adopted by the branch. He also met "the head
of the Newark branch, a crude but well-meaning fellow named
William J. Bristol, who seems to display traces of Levantine heritage."

Next week, Lovecraft spent two exhausting and fruitless days,
tramping the streets of Greater New York and calling on prospects.
The best prospects, he learned, were in the garment industry, which
was in the hands of "the most impossible sort of persons." Then
Bristol took Lovecraft on a tour to show him how these things
were done:

> I had not walked far when my guide became very candid about the
> tone of the business, and admitted that a gentleman born and
> bred has very little chance for success in such lines of canvassing

salesmanship . . . where one must either be miraculously magnetic and captivating, or else so boorish and callous that he can transcend every rule of tasteful conduct and push conversation on bored, hostile, and unwilling victims.[16]

Lovecraft was relieved at being allowed to resign without giving a week's notice. Charmed by Lovecraft, "honest Bristol" opened his heart. His real ambition, he confided, was to get back into insurance. For this, being aware of his own crudity, he would need the help of a gentleman like HPL. Meanwhile, he hired Lovecraft to ghost a letter of application for a managership in some insurance company. It seemed as though the gods were determined to make a ghost-writer of Lovecraft.

He did not yet give up. Doggedly, he continued to make the rounds of employment agencies and publishers. His friends tried to help. Loveman, who arrived in New York on another job hunt in August, thought he could get Lovecraft the editorship of catalogues at the Anderson Galleries, but somebody else got the job. Lovecraft thought for a while that he had a good chance at an editorship of a trade journal, *The Haberdasher*; but that, too, evaporated.

Harry Houdini, whom Lovecraft had now met, also offered to help. He gave Lovecraft a letter to Brett Page, head of a newspaper syndicate. Page was cordial but had nothing. The only jobs for which Lovecraft was qualified, he said, were those of reader for a publishing house or assistant editor on a trade journal. This was much what Lovecraft himself had concluded; but none of the publishers to whom he had applied, in person or by letter, had seen fit to hire him.

By the end of the year, Lovecraft had made exhausting if inept efforts to find a job. Despite the fact that, under President Coolidge, the country was fairly prosperous and jobs were not hard to find, Lovecraft achieved no results save for a few more ghost-writing clients. For a retiring, unworldly man who had spent so much of his life in sickly, secluded, self-indulgent idleness, Lovecraft's effort was herculean. His friend Kleiner thought:

. . . that Lovecraft had nothing to gain from a commercial connection. His job was to write stories, and he should have been allowed to continue as he was doing. But the situation in which he found himself after his unfortunate marriage seemed to require that he make some effort to find a permanent connection with a regular salary. A few of his "job-hunting" letters were seen by some from whom a little more understanding might have been expected; I think I am justified in saying they were the sort of letters a temporarily straitened English gentleman might have written in an effort to make a profitable connection in the business world of the day before yesterday. Their tone was all wrong, of course.

Kleiner's description of Lovecraft's employment letters is apt, but I do not agree that Lovecraft had nothing to gain from a salaried job. For one thing, working for pay is one of those things like being in love, or serving in the armed forces, or being in a storm at sea, or having a surgical operation. One can learn a lot about it by reading, but no amount of reading will tell one what it is like so well as actually experiencing it. Since a job is part of the experience of nearly all men and of most women in present-day America, never to have worked for pay leaves one with a distorted, fragmentary view of the world. Nor would a job have necessarily interfered with Lovecraft's story-writing, since he devoted only a fraction of his waking time to fiction anyway.

Still, he had the qualifications of an editor and some practical experience in editing amateur publications. With a little seasoning, he might have made an excellent editor. A modest success at such a job would have obviated the need for ill-paid ghosting and eliminated much of the busy-work with which he filled his days.

Moreover, Lovecraft's fiction is flawed by lack of convincing characters and plausible dialogue. These result from his lack of human contacts: his isolation from everybody save a small circle of kindred and congenial friends. In weird fiction, characterization and dialogue are not of first importance; but any story in which characters and dialogue are well done is better than one, otherwise equal, in which they are done badly or not at all.

Another feature of Lovecraft's fiction, derived from his detached, secluded life, is a certain bloodless impersonality. He shows little interest in or sympathy for his characters. Practically speaking, his leading characters neither eat nor drink. On the rare occasion when they have to do with women, they usually come to grief. Here, too, more worldly experience would have helped Lovecraft in his fiction. Since he would not voluntarily associate with people of background and outlook markedly different from his own, he would have had to be coerced into doing so by the demands of his job.

Had he become an editor, Lovecraft might never have achieved a status like that of the late John W. Campbell. But such a job might have given Lovecraft himself some much-needed status, self-confidence, and worldly experience as well as income.

For the terms of 1923–24 and 1924–25, Sonia had been chosen president and Lovecraft, editor of the United Amateur Press Association. At the end of his 1924–25 term, he refused to serve again. He continued to attend meetings of the Blue Pencil Club and to complain of the torrent of mail from other amateurs; but thereafter he gave less time to amateur journalism.

After other members of the "Lovecraft UAPA" also refused to serve, Edgar J. Davis was persuaded to become president and Victor E. Bacon, editor. But, lacking Lovecraft's magnetic appeal to other amateur writers, this faction soon expired. Conventions and publications ceased after 1925. Lovecraft was never reconciled to the other UAPA faction, which he called the "Erford pseudo-United"[17] after one of its leaders, J. F. Roy Erford.

Lovecraft continued to interest himself in the politics of the National Amateur Press Association and to send an occasional essay to the amateur magazines, but he never held another elective amateur office. When asked in the summer of 1925 to be chairman of NAPA's Bureau of Critics, he refused, being at that time in a highly neurotic state. In the 1930s, however, he sometimes served on this bureau.

During the last years of his life, Lovecraft was still serving as "executive judge" of the NAPA and recruiting new members. He was still fussing over the amateurs' perversity in spending their energy on feuds and intrigues instead of on perfecting their literary styles, never realizing that such organizations attract people to whom feuds and intrigues are a main pleasure of life.

As far as Lovecraft's most significant work—his stories—is concerned, the time devoted in those years to amateur journalism was time wasted on a hobby that most people would have long since outgrown or at least downgraded to a minor, leisure-time interest.

But Lovecraft could never fully commit himself to his professional career, because of his cherished pose as a "gentleman dilettante."

While Lovecraft lived with Sonia in Brooklyn, most of his writing was ghosting. Besides the never-ending stream of commissions from Bush and occasional odd jobs from other would-be writers, he got some from Houdini, who treated the Lovecrafts to tickets to his show at the old Hippodrome on January 15, 1925.

The escape artist, a crusader against Spiritualist mediumship, exposed the tricks of countless mediums. Among other commissions, Houdini suggested a collaboration among himself, Lovecraft, and Eddy, for a book to be called *The Cancer of Superstition*. To slay the dragon of occult fakery once and for all, Houdini was to furnish the basic ideas. Lovecraft was to prepare outlines of the chapters, and Eddy was to write the actual book with Lovecraft's editorial help.

Lovecraft prepared an outline of twelve chapters, Eddy wrote a chapter, and Lovecraft corrected it. Then Houdini fell ill of cancer and died, on October 31, 1926. Lovecraft considered Houdini to have presented "one of the worst instances of misdirected intellect," because, although "an accomplished man with talent and intelligence," he was satisfied to be "merely a clever showman."

Lovecraft and Eddy struggled through two more chapters, failed to find a publisher, and dropped the project. They had discovered, as have others, that the public will pay vast sums to be bunked but practically nothing to be debunked.

Lovecraft wrote one story in 1924: "The Shunned House." A little over 10,000 words in length, it showed Lovecraft's growing tendency to write longer tales. It is a good yarn, although—as Wright complained when Lovecraft sent it to *Weird Tales*—too slow and wordy at the start. It also uses too many of Lovecraft's subjective adjectives like "horrible" and "obscene." Lovecraft thought that both the slow build-up and the adjectives were needed to create a spooky atmosphere, which he considered the principal point of a weird tale. In this story, however, Lovecraft made able use of the local color that he knew best.

Lovecraft based "The Shunned House" on a real house and a legend. The house was the Stephen Harris mansion at 135 Benefit

Street, Providence, where Lillian Clark had lived before Susie Lovecraft's death. This is a large, boxy, yellow clapboard house on the
east or uphill side of Benefit Street, a couple of blocks north of
Angell Street. There is a vacant lot on one side and a row of
similar big old wooden houses on the other.

The Stephen Harris house has two main stories and an attic
under a low-pitched roof. In addition, because of the slope of the
hill, the cellar opens on Benefit Street at sidewalk level. The en-
trance to the living quarters of the house is by a stair on the south
side. Two huge elms on Benefit Street shade the house from the
afternoon sun and, when in leaf, practically hide the western façade
from view. In Lovecraft's time, the house had stood vacant for years
and become seedy and dilapidated. Since then, it has been fixed up
and occupied.

The house was built in 1764, and in 1866 it received its present
number. Its site had been a graveyard, whence the human remains
were removed to North Burial Ground. There was a story that the
bones of a deceased French couple were inadvertently left behind
and still repose beneath the house. Stephen Harris's wife, it was
said, went mad upon the deaths of her children and screamed in
French from an upstairs window.

The legend used by Lovecraft was "The Green Picture" in
Charles M. Skinner's *Myths and Legends of Our Own Land* (1896).
This little tale tells of a house in Schenectady, New York, where
mold forming a human silhouette appeared on the floor of the
cellar and returned no matter how often it was scrubbed away.
Some said that a vampire buried under the cellar was trying to
leave its grave but was bound there by a spell.

"The Shunned House" starts with one of Lovecraft's rambling,
philosophical openings:

> From even the greatest of horrors irony is seldom absent.
> Sometimes it enters directly into the composition of the events,
> while sometimes it relates only to their fortuitous position among
> persons and places.

The narrator goes on to tell of the "William Harris house" on
Benefit Street:

> In my childhood the shunned house was vacant, with barren,
> gnarled and terrible old trees, long, queerly pale grass and night-
> marishly misshapen weeds in the high terraced yard where birds

never lingered. . . . The small-paned windows were largely broken, and a nameless air of desolation hung round the precarious panelling, shaky interior shutters, peeling wall-paper, falling plaster, rickety staircases, and such fragments of battered furniture as still remained.[18]

The narrator has an uncle, Elihu Whipple, M.D., thought to have been based upon Dr. Franklin Chase Clark. An antiquarian, Whipple has amassed a file of data on the house, and the narrator explores this file.

Then follow thousands of words of the history of Providence, of the house, and of the Harrises who lived there. Into his tale Lovecraft adroitly works real historical events, such as the hurricane of 1815. All who dwell in the house become anemic and sickly; they die early unless they move away. There are a mad woman screaming in French and, before her time, a French dabbler in the occult buried beneath the house.

The narrator and his uncle spend a night in the cellar with apparatus for destroying the malign entity which, they believe, causes these afflictions. The entity turns out to be a gelatinous thing, which sends out a gaseous emanation. This emanation can engulf and absorb anybody, body and soul, so that the victim's consciousness somehow lives on as part of the entity. This unwholesome fate befalls the uncle. . . .

Wright at *Weird Tales* rejected "The Shunned House" on the ground that its beginning was too slow and wordy. But Lovecraft refused to abridge it at Wright's request.

Wright remained as editor of *Weird Tales* for fifteen years. Despite his nervous disorder and a low budget, which forced him to take much inferior copy, he achieved such signal results that today we speak of a *Weird Tales* school of writing.

Wright published many standard ghost, werewolf, and vampire tales built on trite, worn-out formulas. He did this partly because of lack of money and partly because he thought he had to run some trash to draw immature readers. For the same reason, he used garish covers showing nude heroines writhing in the lustful grip of sorcerers, ghouls, and other menaces. Despite the covers, the magazine was as sexually pure within as even the puritanical Lovecraft could have desired.

Weird Tales published a variety of imaginative fiction, some of excellent quality. It printed straight science fiction and heroic fantasy like Robert E. Howard's stories of Conan, the mighty prehistoric barbarian adventurer. Here appeared the early work of several writers, like Robert Bloch, Tennessee Williams, and Ray Bradbury, who went on to literary fame and fortune. Wright paid most of his writers half a cent a word (the bottom pulp-magazine rate) but the more eminent ones a cent or a cent and a half. Lovecraft got the highest rate after 1927.

During the 1920s, when Lovecraft was gaining popularity, the most popular writer for *Weird Tales* was not Lovecraft but Seabury Quinn, who contributed voluminously to the magazine throughout its life. His stories were competent but repetitious and formula-ridden; the term "hack writer" fits Quinn precisely.

Appropriately for a man who wrote of ghoulies and ghosties, Quinn's business related to undertaking. He edited a trade journal in the field and at other times worked as a traveling salesman for undertaker's equipment. On a business trip to New Orleans, his contacts there, wishing to show him the town, took him to a fancy bordello. When the girls discovered that their visitor was Seabury Quinn of *Weird Tales*, their favorite magazine, they felt so honored by his presence that they offered him one on the house.

The magazine staggered between profit and loss, but Henneberger, Wright, and Sprenger stuck to it. In 1930, they launched a companion magazine, *Oriental Stories*, which lasted a little over three years. Changing its name to *Magic Carpet* failed to make it profitable.

Magazines meant as competitors to *Weird Tales* were *Tales of Magic & Mystery* (1927), *Strange Tales* (1931–33), and *Strange Stories* (1939–41). They usually ran for only a few issues, and none approached *Weird Tales* in viability.

These periodicals formed part of the throng of pulp magazines that proliferated in the United States during the 1920s and 30s. All were printed on cheap wood-pulp paper in the standard "pulp size" of 6½ by 10 inches. Advertisements from the back pages of *Weird Tales* read: FALSE TEETH. PILES: DON'T SUFFER NEEDLESSLY. BRINGS SOOTHING WARMTH TO VITAL GLAND IN MEN PAST 40. MAN CAN NOW TALK WITH GOD.

Lovecraft and other critics often used the term "pulp" to mean low-grade, mass-produced fiction appealing to barely literate minds. Sometimes, such a description would be fair. On the other hand, most pulp stories showed qualities that sometimes seem in short supply today. They are written frankly to entertain and not to express the author's soul, or demonstrate his cleverness, or convert the reader to some cause. They are well-organized, intelligible, and fast-moving. They are written in clear, straightforward English. Hence they can often still be read with pleasure.

From 1933 to 1938, Mrs. Margaret Brundage had a near-monopoly of painting cover illustrations for *Weird Tales*. In her dozens of pictures of naked heroines menaced by fiends and monsters, she used her own daughters as models. Lovecraft tore the covers off his copies so as not to be embarrassed by carrying such lubricous scenes about. Wright never designated one of Lovecraft's stories as the subject for a cover picture, perhaps because there were practically no women in Lovecraft's tales to be personated by the shapely Misses Brundage.

The near-disappearance of pulp magazines in the Second World War drastically reduced the market for the American short story. In fact, today's science-fiction magazines are almost the last stand of this fictional form. After 1945, the paperback novel usurped the place in popular fiction formerly held by the pulp magazines.

In 1938, pressed for cash, Henneberger, Wright, and Sprenger sold control of their Popular Fiction Publishing Company to William J. Delaney and T. Raymond Foley, publishers of *Short Stories*, which in its day was the leading competitor of *Adventure Magazine*. The editorial offices were moved to New York. Two years later, when Wright's health worsened, his new employers summarily fired him, and he soon died.

Editing of *Weird Tales* was assigned to a middle-aged Scotswoman, Dorothy McIlwraith, who had been editing *Short Stories* and continued to do so. Although an experienced editor, Miss McIlwraith never showed Wright's touch with the fantastic. She bought stories that were "weird" only in a narrow, literal sense of the word, so that the magazine lost its attractive variety. The magazine puttered along for another decade but perished in 1954. Although anthologists have mined its crumbling pages ever since, for the last twenty years no market just like *Weird Tales* has been available to writers of fantasy.

For all his undoubted gifts, Wright's policies towards Lovecraft were erratic. Wary of any startlingly new idea, he was wont to reject a story on its first submission, ask to see it again later, and buy it the second time. Writers learned that, when Wright rejected a story, the thing to do was to put it away for a while and submit it again, unaltered, with a note saying that it had been revised in accordance with Wright's suggestions. Having forgotten the details of the first submission, Wright was likely to buy it. He bought many stories from Lovecraft after rejecting them one or more times.

After Lovecraft died, Miss McIlwraith also bought several of Lovecraft's stories, once rejected. This was the fate of "The Shunned House."

Before Lovecraft came to New York to live, Kleiner, Long, and McNeil had formed a habit of meeting weekly at their respective abodes in rotation. When Lovecraft arrived, he was soon enrolled in the group. So was Sam Loveman, who appeared in August, 1924, on another job hunt and found a berth in selling rare books. Other additions were George Willard Kirk, a bookseller; Herman C. Koenig, an electrical engineer; Arthur Leeds, a columnist and writer of adventure stories; and James Ferdinand Morton.

Morton was an early campaigner for Negro rights, and his words on the subject infuriated the white-supremacist Lovecraft. Once Morton defended intimacy with Negro women in terms that suggested that he had himself enjoyed such intimacy. Lovecraft burst out: "Any white man who would do such a thing ought to have the word NEGRO branded on his forehead!"

Noticing that the names of all the original members began with K, L, or M, someone suggested calling the group the Kalem Club. So they did; but Lovecraft called them simply "the Gang." Later members (despite their names) were Vrest Orton, a Vermonter on the staff on Mencken's *American Mercury*; and Wilfred Blanch Talman, a journalist, writer, and editor, interested in his Dutch ancestry and active in the Holland Society of New York. In the autumn of 1924, Talman entered Brown University as a freshman; two years later he transferred to Columbia and graduated with the class of 1928.

The club continued to meet, usually on Wednesday nights, in

different members' quarters, although a disproportionate number of meetings took place at the Longs' because of the Longs' bountiful hospitality. The members sat up far into the night, discussing art, science, politics, literature, esthetics, philosophy, and anything else they thought about. Art, literature, and esthetics were their main concerns; literary members often read their manuscripts aloud. Lovecraft sometimes persuaded Morton to read Lovecraft's stories, because he admired Morton's professional delivery.

Such loosely organized discussion groups of intellectuals have flourished wherever numbers of such people were to be found, as in large cities and university towns. For instance, in the 1930s, three great British fantasy writers—C. S. Lewis, J. R. R. Tolkien, and Charles Williams—belonged to the Inklings at Oxford. Because of the special orientation of its members towards fantastic and imaginative fiction, however, the Kalem Club may be considered the world's first science-fiction fan society.

These meetings were Lovecraft's greatest pleasure in New York. He rarely missed one. He did not dominate the conversation; but when he did speak, said Kirk, it was like "an encyclopedia falling open and speaking up to you."[19]

Although Lovecraft never threw his weight around and was never lavishly hospitable like the Longs, he drew the other club members together by that same mysterious magnetism that he showed in the UAPA. He was unfailingly considerate. Other members, finding McNeil dull, tended to dodge meetings at his place. But Lovecraft always went lest he hurt McNeil's feelings.

When Lovecraft left New York, the club fell into desuetude. It met but rarely, usually only once or twice a year when Lovecraft visited the city.

Several times, Lovecraft met Hart Crane, then working for advertising agencies in New York. A friend of Loveman, Crane had made a minor poetic reputation and was now working on a long poem, *The Bridge*. This work, which appeared in 1930, exhibits dazzling poetical techniques but is full of such far-fetched metaphors that at least one rereading is needed to grasp what the poet is driving at.

Crane and Lovecraft tolerated each other but did not become intimate. On September 14, 1924, Crane wrote his mother:

I have been greeted so far by his [Loveman's] coat tails, so occupied has Sambo been with numerous friends of his here ever
since arriving; Miss Sonia Green [*sic*] and her piping-voiced husband, Howard Lovecraft (the man who visited Sam in Cleveland
one summer when Galpin was also there), kept Sam traipsing
around the slums and wharf streets until four in the morning
looking for Colonial specimens of architecture, and until Sam
tells me he groaned with fatigue and begged for the subway!

Lovecraft reported to his Aunt Lillian that Loveman was "too
easily exhausted to make a good explorer." Lovecraft knew of
Crane's homosexuality and alcoholism but took an attitude of pity
that a gifted man should suffer such ruinous weaknesses:

Poor Crane! A real poet & man of taste, descendant of an ancient
Connecticut family & a gentleman to his finger-tips, but the slave
of dissipated habits which will soon ruin his constitution & his
still striking handsomeness![20]

In 1931, Crane went to Mexico on a Guggenheim fellowship,
under which he was supposed to produce a poetic masterpiece on
Latin American themes. He produced nothing but went on spectacular binges. He also had his first heterosexual love affair, with a
woman friend who was getting a divorce. In 1932, they were returning by ship to the United States when Crane, who had made
and broken countless good resolutions, went on further sprees, gave
up, and jumped overboard.

As always, Lovecraft read voraciously. His favorite authors remained Poe, Dunsany, and Machen; but he also admired the early
stories of Robert W. Chambers and many of those of Algernon
Blackwood and M. P. Shiel. He considered their work uneven,
writing: "Blackwood has absolutely no style except by accident now
and then . . ."

Lovecraft had some acquaintance with modern realistic novelists, whom he read as a duty rather than for pleasure. Of Upton
Sinclair's *The Jungle*, he said: "These excited sociological harangues
are not art—propaganda is never art. . . . Sinclair is fluent, though,
and he might be an artist if he worried less about the poor oppressed
underdog and all that sort of thing." Sinclair Lewis, likewise, he
considered "A didactic essayist, not an artist. . . ."[21]

He spoke highly of two recent non-fiction books: Charles
Fort's *The Book of the Damned* (1919) and Margaret Alice Mur-

ray's *The Witch Cult in Western Europe* (1921). His appreciation, however, was not what the authors would have hoped for. He admired the books as stimuli for the writing of weird fiction, not as statements of fact. From a scientific point of view, he considered Fort's eccentric cosmological ideas as nonsense.

Miss Murray's theory was that the great European witch panic of the sixteenth and seventeenth centuries had been a struggle between Christianity and a vast pagan cult surviving underground from pre-Christian times. Lovecraft viewed this theory with temperate skepticism. He thought that such cults might have existed but that Miss Murray had grossly exaggerated their size and importance.

Along with reading, museum-haunting, and foregathering with his friends, Lovecraft enjoyed walking. He explored Prospect Park in Brooklyn, the New York Zoological Park in the Bronx, Flushing, Jamaica, and, in New Jersey, Elizabeth. He visited the Poe cottage and the Van Cortland mansion.

One night, he and Kirk offered to walk Kleiner home from Morningside Heights in Manhattan to Bushwick in Brooklyn—a distance of about ten miles. They got to within three blocks of Kleiner's home when Lovecraft found the going too much even for his iron endurance. So he and Kirk went home by rapid transit.

Lovecraft also explored Greenwich Village at night, in the years when the section was full of speakeasies, and gunfights among bootleggers and hijackers were commonplace. Kleiner recalled:

> . . . at least once, while stumbling around among old barrels and crates in some dark corner of this area, Lovecraft found a doorway suddenly illuminated and an excited foreigner, wearing the apron that was an almost infallible sign of a speakeasy bartender, enquiring hotly what he wanted. Loveman and Kirk went in after Lovecraft and got him safely out.[22]

Lovecraft had an ambivalent attitude towards New York. Like many another, he found it both fascinating and repellent. In September, 1924, he could still write of the Manhattan skyline: "Would that I could express the magick of the scene!"

Thenceforth, however, his hostile remarks came oftener. He complained of the "crude foreign hostility," "nasty cosmopolitanism," "plague of foreigners," and "vulgar trade spirit & plebeian hustle of NYC," and the "slithering human vermin in the subway." Sneers and invective against foreigners and ethnics in general and Jews in particular became more intense.

In one of his explorations, Lovecraft stumbled into an Orthodox Jewish section of Brooklyn along Rivington Street:

> This place was a revelation, for no other slum I had ever seen is just like it. Here exist assorted Jews in the absolutely unassimilated state, with their ancestral beards, skull-caps, and general costumes— which make them very picturesque, and not nearly so offensive as the strident, pushing Jews who affect clean shaves and American dress.[23]

In trying to explain why he found these people less obnoxious than the more assimilated types, Lovecraft aired an erroneous theory then current among Anglo-American gentiles. This theory was that most Jews of Russian and Polish origin were not "real" Jews but descendants of the Khazars, a Tatar nation that once ruled an empire in southeastern Russia, between the Volga and the Dnieper rivers. In the seventh century, the Khaqan of the Khazars and most of his subjects were converted to Judaism. Based on commerce, their empire was comparatively enlightened. In fact, the Khazars became too civilized for their own good, for in the tenth century the more backward Russians overthrew them.

In the 1920s, few Anglo-Americans had ever seen a Tatar and therefore found them easy to imagine as dreadful people. Anglo-American gentiles reasoned that, if Jews were unlikable, the "Tatar Jews" (as they were called) must be much worse. These "Asiatic Tatar-Mongoloids"[24] were blamed for the Bolshevik Revolution and other distressing events. It was predicted that, when the grip of the "Tatar Jews" on Russia was broken, the Russians would adopt a moderate democratic regime.

The Khazars in fact have left only a small body of descendants, the Krimchaks, who combine Judaism with Mongoloid race and a Turko-Tatar language. They dwell in the Crimea, unless war and Stalin's deportations have removed or destroyed them, and have mixed little if at all with other Russian Jews.

Lovecraft's growing antagonism to New York was by no means unique. The unsuitability of New York as a lasting abode has been an American cliché for at least a century. When Marquand's fictional George Apley goes there about 1909, he writes his wife:

> Although we are Americans, we all seem like strangers in a foreign city. I do not like to think that it is setting the style for the future. If it is, I believe that the world is going mad, that we are reaching the end of an era.[25]

From July, 1924, on, troubles piled up on the Lovecrafts. First, Sonia's hat shop failed. At about this time, a bank failure cost her her securities, so that by the time she had paid off her debts she was down to a few hundred dollars.[26] The indomitable woman quickly got a temporary job, but in September she had to sell her piano. The Rev. George T. Baker of St. Gabriel's Church bought it for $350.

On October 20th, after a day of feeling poorly, Sonia was seized while resting in bed by "sudden gastric spasms." Lovecraft took her to a hospital and brought her things next day. During her ten-day stay, he made daily visits, read aloud to her, and played chess with her. Sonia was an enthusiastic chess player and usually beat her husband, who had little interest in the game. During her illness, Lovecraft wrote "The Shunned House."

On October 30th, Sonia returned to the apartment. Her trouble had been diagnosed as a "nervous breakdown." This is understandable in view of the fact that, through business and financial disasters, she had tried not only to carry a full-time job but at the same time to support, coddle, and keep house for her gifted but unemployable husband.

It was arranged for Sonia to convalesce at a farm near Somerville, New Jersey, run by a family named Craig. Lovecraft went to visit her on November 10th and continued on by train to Philadelphia. There he put up at the YMCA and spent two ecstatic days in antiquarian exploration. "Philadelphia is marvellous! I am entranced beyond words!" he wrote.

Since it did not seem that the Lovecrafts could maintain the costly apartment at 259 Parkside Avenue, they considered moving. It was not certain where they would live or even whether they would continue to live together. Sonia, who could turn her hand to anything, considered getting "congenial lodgment in exchange for light services."

During Sonia's absence, Lovecraft began to learn to do his own housekeeping. Hitherto he had always had a woman to do it for him. In those days, a strict division of labor by sex was still widely observed in American households, although the distinction was beginning to break down. An ordinary American male had to overcome no small psychological discomfort to bring himself to do such "women's work" as cooking, cleaning, dishwashing, and bed-making. A husband helping with the dishes was a common figure of fun in cartoons.

Whatever went on within him during this time of debacle, Lovecraft gave the outward impression of taking a fatalistic attitude towards the breakup of his home. Like one of his own ineffectual narrator-heroes, he helplessly watched the approach of doom. He wrote of "the impending dissolution of this establishment in a maze of poverty and uncertainty" and "Let us eat, drink, and be merry . . . for tomorrow we disintegrate!" He sighed: ". . . at my age [thirty-four!] one has very few interests, and these are all bound up in the past—one's own past, or the past of one's race and civilisation."[27]

Annie Gamwell visited the Lovecrafts in August. Later, hearing of their impending move, Lillian Clark came to Brooklyn in December and helped with house-hunting.

Meanwhile, Sonia had been offered a department-store job in Cincinnati. Lovecraft thought that, if they left New York, Providence would be preferable. But Sonia realistically pointed out that, to live, one or the other must have a job, and the only job in sight was that in Cincinnati:

> I wanted Howard to make his home with me there, but he said he would hate to live in a midwestern city, he would prefer to remain in New York where at least he had some friends. I suggested that he have one of them come to live with him in our apartment, but his aunts thought it wiser for me to store and sell my furniture and find a studio room large enough for Howard to have the old (and several dilapidated) pieces he had brought from Providence. . . .
>
> He prized these old pieces from his R. I. home, very much. Since there was not enough room for my own modern furniture and his old . . . pieces, too, to which he clung with morbid tenacity, to please him I parted with some of my own highly prized pieces. These, I sold for a pittance so that he might surround himself with as much of his own home atmosphere as was possible.[28]

Sonia showed a touch of understandable bitterness, both for the loss of her furniture and for Lovecraft's readiness to let his aunts think for him. Even Lillian Clark seems to have thought he was carrying his fetishism for heirlooms to extremes. Next year, when he was feeling desperate, he wrote her defending his fixation:

Yes—on paper it is easy to say that "possessions are a burden", & that it is wisest to have nothing, but merely to live in a valise or trunk . . . & so on. . . . fine theory indeed! But in actual fact it all depends on the person. Each individual's reason for living is different . . . i.e., to each individual there is some one thing or group of things which form the focus of all his interests & nucleus of all his emotions; & without which the mere process of survival not only means nothing whatever, but is often an intolerable load of anguish. Those to whom old associations & possessions do not form this single interest & life-necessity, may well sermonise on the folly of "slavery to worldly goods"—so long as they do not try to enforce their doctrines on others. They are lucky—chance has been kind to them! But to others who are so constituted as to require tangible links with their background, it is useless to preach such ideals & hypotheses. Nature has given their nervous systems other needs; & to advise them to burn their goods for freedom's sake is as silly as to advise them to cut off their legs in order to escape the burden of buying trousers. It so happens that I am unable to take pleasure or interest in anything but a mental re-creation of other & better days—for in sooth, I see no possibility of ever en-countering a really congenial milieu or living among civilised people with old Yankee historic memories again—so in order to avoid this madness which leads to violence & suicide I must cling to the few shreds of old days & old ways which are left to me. Therefore no one need expect me to discard the ponderous furniture & paintings & clocks & books which help to keep 454 [Angell St.] in my dreams. When they go, I shall go, for they are all that make it possible for me to open my eyes in the morning or look forward to another day of consciousness without screaming in sheer despera-tion & pounding the walls & floor in a frenzied clamour to be waked up out of the nightmare of "reality" to my own room in Providence. Yes—such sensitivenesses of temperament are very in-convenient when one has no money—but it's easier to criticise than to cure them. When a poor fool possessing them allows him-self to get exiled & *sidetracked* through temporarily false *perspec-tive & ignorance* of the world, the only thing to do is to let him cling to his pathetic scraps as long as he can hold them. They are life for him.[29]

To judge from this frantic letter, Lovecraft was not only stuck in the teddy-bear stage of maturation but had no intention of leaving it. When faced with a problem, he tended, instead of reso-lutely attacking it, to plead that he was a person of a special kind—an "aged antiquarian" or a man with "sensitiveness of tem-perament"—and therefore utterly unable to cope with the problem.

This tendency, to duck problems by egocentric rationalizations and self-pitying verbalizations, was as much a part of his nature as his brown eyes.

When Lovecraft spoke of being "sidetracked through temporarily false perspective," he obviously referred to Sonia's idea of married life in New York. But the real author of his false perspectives and ignorance of the world—as far as one can pin the cause on any individual—was not Sonia but his mother.

After some hunting, the Lovecrafts found a large studio room that Lovecraft liked, at 169 Clinton Street, Brooklyn, a few blocks from Borough Hall. They had to sleep on a couch, since Lovecraft would not tolerate a bed in the room where he worked. Lillian Clark stayed in another room in the same building until she returned to Providence.

Then, on the last day of 1924, Sonia departed for Cincinnati.

Twelve

GUNNAR IN THE SNAKE PIT

It was the city I had known before;
The ancient, leprous town where mongrel throngs
Chant to strange gods, and beat unhallowed gongs
In crypts beneath foul alleys near the shore.
The rotting, fish-eyed houses leered at me
From where they leaned, drunk and half-animate,
As edging through the filth I passed the gate
To the black courtyard where the man would be.[1]

LOVECRAFT

The year and a quarter following Sonia's departure was the low point in Lovecraft's life. His depression and misanthropy reached near-suicidal strength, while his behavior showed him at his worst. His spells of passivity and impracticality and his habit of frittering away his time and talents were at their greatest. His phobias, prejudices, and homesickness reached maniacal intensity.

Despite everything, Lovecraft kept up a front of reserved, gentlemanly self-possession, which fooled most of his kith. Frank Long, who knew him best at this time, told me that he had seen no neurotic or psychotic symptoms. Lovecraft was always himself; at his most depressed, he fell back on his detached, materialistic philosophy, that nothing really mattered on a cosmic scale. Once when he was riding on the subway with Sam Loveman and a young woman "gave him the eye," he told Loveman:

"My one desire is to remain inconspicuous and unnoticed. If I could render myself invisible, I would gladly do so. I avoid the ordinary run of human beings and have imbibed much of the philosophy of good old Bishop Berkeley, who denied the existence of matter and even the actuality of life itself. Nothing really exists for me. Dreams provide me with a solution to the fantastic ambiguity that we choose to call life. . . . You, Samuelus, place too much stress and importance on human beings and, since this is so, you suffer. Make yourself impersonal and impervious to the mob. Deny not only contact with them, but with their existence. Books and old Colonial houses are safest; they hold well their sinister and mysterious secrets. Mistrust everything except the past or antiquity."

I am told that it is characteristic of the schizoid personality to meet disturbing experiences with a seeming objective detachment. To perceive Lovecraft's inmost feelings, behind his façade of lofty indifferentism, one must turn to his letters to his aunts.

Sonia's job in Cincinnati did not turn out well. According to her, the other employees took umbrage at the hiring of an outsider and ganged up on her. After a few weeks, her nerves gave way and she entered a Doctor Beyer's private hospital. She rested there and then took up her job again but was soon back in the hospital. This time, in mid-February, 1925, she gave up her post and returned to Brooklyn.

After holding a temporary job designing hats for a month, Sonia went to Saratoga Springs for a long rest. She stayed at the house of a woman physician, for whose child she acted as governess.

In early June, Sonia again returned to Brooklyn. She, too, had begun to dislike life in New York. Lovecraft wrote:

The turmoil and throngs of New York depress her, as they have begun to do me, and eventually we hope to clear out of this Babylonish burg for good. I find it a bore after the novelty of the museums, skyline and bolder architectural effects has worn off, and hope to get back to New England for the rest of my life—the Boston district at first, and later Providence, if I ever get the money to live there as befits a member of my family.[2]

Nobody could keep Sonia down for long, and by mid-July she had another job in prospect. But alas for Lovecraft's yearning for Yankeeland! The job was in a shop in Cleveland, to which she departed on August 20th. Lovecraft again refused to go with her to the howling wilderness of Ohio.

During this year, Lovecraft went his individualistic way. Not having Sonia around—save for brief visits every fortnight or so—to stuff him with expertly cooked food, he starved himself back to his former gauntness. By June he triumphantly announced that he was down to 146 pounds.

His daily dinner consisted of a quarter of a loaf of bread, a quarter of a can of baked beans (eaten cold), and a large piece of cheese. Cost: eight cents; a gourmet's nightmare but otherwise adequate to support life. When his aunts worried about his malnutrition, he assured them that between his austere diet and his long walks, his health was excellent. And so his physical health seems to have been through 1925.

He often went out to restaurants when invited by members of the Gang. He loved Italian food but gave an unusual reason for this preference: that Italian restaurateurs were kind to their cats. He also let his friends introduce him to Spanish and Arab restaurants. He proudly reported that he was living on $5.00 a week, with fifteen cents a day for food.

Before she left for Cincinnati on the last day of 1924, Sonia had taken Lovecraft shopping for clothes. She bought him a new suit, overcoat, hat, and gloves. Exasperated by his ancient little change purse, she also bought him a billfold.

Lovecraft was dubious at first. Looking at himself in the mirror, he said: "But, my dear, this is entirely too stylish for Grandpa Theobald; it doesn't look like me. I look like some fashionable fop!"[3]

Thieves rented the room next to his at 169 Clinton Street. On Sunday, May 24th, while Lovecraft slept the day away, they picked the lock between the next room and his dressing alcove. They stole the new summer suit that Sonia had bought him and both of his older winter suits. They stole his new overcoat, a wicker suitcase belonging to Sonia, and a radio that he was storing for

Loveman. He was left with one old suit, two old topcoats (one light and one heavy), and an odd jacket and pair of trousers in their last stages of decrepitude.

Lovecraft was crushed, then furious, especially as he had just paid to have his suits altered to fit the lean figure he had attained.

Sonia said: "I really think he was glad when the new suit and coat were later stolen; he had the old ones to resume." But from the many angry passages in his letters, I do not believe this. Ten months later, when he had bought some new clothes, he was still fuming over the incident:

And if any —— —— thief touches *this* outfit; why, by ——, I'll smash his —— —— —— for him with one fist while I pulverise his —— —— —— —— —— with the other, meanwhile kicking him posteriorly with both feet in their most pointed shoes and manner![4]

Another letter to his Aunt Lillian shows that he was by no means indifferent to clothes:

I think I have developed an eye for the difference between the clothing a gentleman wears and that which a gentleman doesn't. What has sharpened this sense is the constant sight of these accursed filthy rabbles that infest the N.Y. streets, & whose clothing presents such systematic differences from the normal clothing of real people along Angell St. & in Butler Ave. or Elmgrove Ave. cars that the eye comes to feel a tremendous homesickness & to pounce avidly on any gentleman whose clothes are proper & tasteful & suggestive of Blackstone Boulevard rather than Borough Hall or Hell's kitchen. Belknap wears the right sort, & so does Kirk, Loveman usually does, tho' his taste is not perfect. But Morton, Kleiner, Leeds & McNeil are frankly impossible. And so, pining for the sight of a Swan Point carful of regular men, I have resolved to dress like Butler Ave. or not at all. Confound it, I'll be either in good Providence taste or in a bally bathrobe!! Certain lapel cuts, textures, & fits tell the story. It amuses me to see how some of these flashy young 'boobs' & foreigners spend fortunes on various kinds of expensive clothes which they regard as evidences of meritorious taste, but which in reality are their absolute social & aesthetick damnation—being little short of placards shrieking in bold letters: "I *am an ignorant peasant*", "I *am a mongrel gutter-rat*", or "I *am a tasteless & unsophisticated yokel*". . . . Better far to wear the frayed & tattered rags of something with taste, than to sport the newest & freshest suit whose cut & texture bear the ineffaceable stigmata of plebeianism & decadence.[5]

Aside from the snobbery and provinciality of this letter, it shows a lively interest in appearance. Even if Lovecraft would have rather worn old clothes in good taste than new ones in bad, he was quite willing to be a "fashionable fop"—in a conservative way—if he could have afforded it.

If, after the loss, he professed not to mind, he was merely making a virtue of necessity. There was nothing unique in this. Most people, finding that they can change themselves and their circumstances only a little, strive to make up for their shortcomings by proclaiming that whatever they are or have is good. If one has intellect, intelligence is the greatest virtue; if one has mighty muscles, brawn is worth more than brains. If one has eminent ancestors, distinguished lineage is the thing; if one has risen from obscurity, the self-made man is the one to admire. If one has lots of energy, one's ideal is briskness and vigor; if like Lovecraft one is easygoing and dilatory, leisureliness is gentlemanly. If one is an Old American, Old Americans are the salt of the earth. Members of other groups do likewise: "We are God's chosen people." "Black is beautiful." All is self-serving rationalization.

Lovecraft did not remain ungarmented. On July 1st, 1925, Sonia had returned from Saratoga but had not yet left for Cleveland. Dining out, the Lovecrafts saw a window display of clothing across the street. After dinner, Sonia bought Lovecraft a new $25 summer suit, about which he waxed enthusiastic.

As the weather cooled in October, Lovecraft set out on his own to find a new winter suit. Showing unexpected skill at bargaining, he got a $34.50, dark-gray, two button suit for $25. He fussed and fumed over the fact that it was one of "the despised & new-fangled two-button type" instead of the three-button kind he was used to, in which the top button was left unbuttoned and was hidden by the roll of the collar. He was sure he would be uncomfortably aware of the lack of the invisible button. But, learning that only two-button suits were being made that year, he for once let common sense prevail.

Still not fully equipped, he set forth the next week for a suit of cheaper grade for hard use. After trying many shops in Brooklyn, he went to a cheap-clothing section around Fourteenth Street and Seventh Avenue in Manhattan. Here he found

. . . indescribable scum pulling one into holes in the wall where flamboyant monstrosities ululate their impossibility beneath price-cards of $4.95, $6.50, $10.00 . . . $18.00 . . . puffy rat-faced vermin hurling taunts when one does not buy and airing spleen in dialects so mercifully broken that white men can't understand them . . . craziness in cloth hanging in futuristic attitudes. . . .[6]

At last, a factory remnant shop sold him a decent brown suit, with extra trousers, for $11.95. Arthur Leeds had shown him many tricks, such as patronizing factory remnant shops, or buying a straw hat at the end of the straw-hat season, for living on next to nothing.

Lovecraft had been pleased to find that the landlady at 169 Clinton Street, Mrs. Burns, was British. He was less pleased to learn that she had the British habit of underheating the house. She was also wont to turn off the hot-water heater during hours when few were likely to bathe or shave. When Lovecraft got an electric heater, she vetoed use of the appliance because of the electric bills.

So the shivering Lovecraft undertook to buy a kerosene heater. From the production he made of the choice, purchase, and installation of the heater, one would have thought he was launching a space ship. Once he had the heater, however, he could at least warm his canned beans, stew, and spaghetti. He could also heat water for shaving at odd hours.

In the fall, the light in Lovecraft's dressing alcove went out of commission. Lovecraft could do nothing about it himself, and Mrs. Burns was always promising to have it fixed but never did so. At last Sonia, on one of her New York visits the following January, whistled up an electrician, who repaired the light.

From April through July, Lovecraft was bothered by mice. He set traps and caught several. When he caught one, he threw away trap and all:

Since writing you I have caught *two* more invaders, in each case disposing of them trap and all. Traps are only 2 for 5¢, & it does not pay to bother with repulsive details when one can avoid them at 2½¢ per experience![7]

To discard the traps rather than touch the little corpses was Lovecraft's privilege—even though, on his scale of living, nickels counted. But his excuse does not sound quite like "a drinker of foemen's blood from new-picked skulls." A few years later, however, he admitted that

> . . . I make no pretence at all of coming anywhere near the type I
> admire. . . . You are perfectly right in saying that it is the weak
> who tend to worship the strong. That is my case exactly. . . . No
> doubt I place an exaggeratedly high emotional valuation on those
> qualities which I least possess. . . .[8]

Lovecraft had long lived on Clinton Street when he discovered, with mingled horror and fascination, that he had Orientals
as housemates. A more enterprising writer would have gone out of
his way to make acquaintance of these folk, to learn about their
exotic thoughts and ways. Lovecraft preferred to keep shyly aloof
and to dream fantasies wherein they played the sinister rôles proper
to the Orientals of fiction:

> . . . once a *Syrian* had the room next to mine and played eldritch
> and whining monotones on a strange bagpipe which made me
> dream ghoulish and indescribable things of crypts under Bagdad
> and limitless corridors of Eblis beneath the moon-cursed ruins of
> Istakhar. I never *saw* this man, and my privilege to imagine him in
> any shape I chose lent glamour to his weird pneumatic cacophonies.
> In my vision he always wore a turban and long robe of pale figured
> silk, and had a right eye plucked out . . . because it had looked
> upon something in a tomb which no eye may look upon and live.
> In truth, I never saw with actual sight the majority of my fellow-
> lodgers. I only *heard* them loathsomely—and sometimes glimpsed
> faces of sinister decadence in the hall. There was an old Turk
> under me, who used to get letters with outré stamps from the
> Levant. Alexander D. Messayeh—Messayeh—what a name from
> the *Arabian Nights!*[9]

Lovecraft continued his antiquarian walks. He explored the
parks and haunted the museums. He frequented bookshops for bar-
gains; he was delighted to get an omnibus volume of Bulwer-Lytton
for ten cents.

On January 24, 1925, he went with Morton, Leeds, Kirk, and
Ernest Dench of the Blue Pencil Club to Yonkers, to see a total
eclipse of the sun, beginning at 9:12 A.M. They had a fine view of
the corona, but Lovecraft nearly froze to death. "God!" he wrote,
"Will I ever forget that eclipse expedition. . . . I was just about all
in for the rest of the winter by the time I staggered back. . . ."

About March, Lovecraft and some of his friends descended on
the Capitol Book Shop on Broadway, where they had their
silhouettes snipped out by a Negro silhouettist who signed himself
"Perry." Lovecraft, whose silhouette appears in this book, praised

the art but rewarded the artist with one of his racial jibes: ". . . certainly is clever for the work of a fat buck nigger!"

He began exploring farther afield. In April, he and Kirk took an excursion to Washington, where one of Lovecraft's correspondents served as a guide. This was Edward Lloyd Sechrist, an anthropologist of the Smithsonian Institution. Automobile transportation was furnished by Mrs. Anne Tillery Renshaw, one of Lovecraft's revision clients, who ran the Renshaw School of Speech.

They saw the usual sights: the White House, the Capitol, the Washington Monument, Mount Vernon, the Fairfax Court House, Arlington, and the rest. Lovecraft was pleased to find that the people looked less "repulsive and mongrel"[10] than those in New York. He became so absorbed in the local varieties of Colonial architecture that he nearly missed his homeward train.

In July, Lovecraft followed the newspaper reports of the famous "Monkey Trial"—the Scopes evolution trial in Dayton, Tennessee. William Jennings Bryan, who had served as a volunteer prosecuting attorney in the case, died a few days after the trial. Despite the vast gulf between his outlook and Bryan's, Lovecraft sympathized with Bryan, who, like himself, was born into an uncongenial time:

> Unfortunate soul! He meant well, dense as was his ignorance; & I have no doubt but that his alarm at the expansion of human thought was a profound, altruistic, & genuinely frantic passion. His compact little mind was hardened into a certain primitive type of American pioneer psychology, & could not bear the strain of national cultural development. Life must have been a hell to him as all the securities of his artificial world cracked one by one under the pressure of time & scientific discovery—he was a man without a world to live in, & the strain proved too much for mortal body to bear. Now he is at rest in the eternal oblivion which he would have been the first and loudest to deny. Requiescat in pace!

On September 9th, on $2.00 sent him by Lillian Clark, Lovecraft made a boat trip with Loveman and the Longs up the Hudson to Newburgh, New York. In the same month, he took a hike in the Palisades with Morton's hiking club, the Ramblers. He noted with amusement that, while he did his hiking in his ordinary second-best clothes, the Ramblers were fitted out in Great North Woods style, with breeches, boots, and canvas packs.

Another time, one of his aunts gave him the fare for a steamboat ride up the Hudson to Albany. Sometimes he had to turn down invitations to visit out-of-town friends, like Morton in New Jersey, for want of the few nickels needed for fare.

The day after the trip to Newburgh, Arthur Leeds treated Lovecraft to a showing of the silent German motion picture *Siegfried*, with a Wagnerian orchestral accompaniment. The movie's unabashed Nordicism delighted Lovecraft:

> As for the film—it was an ecstasy & a delight to be remembered for ever! It was the very inmost soul of the immortal & unconquerable blond Nordic, embodied in the shining warrior of light, great Siegfried, slayer of monsters and enslaver of kings. . . . The musick, too, was of ineffable inspiration. Insensible as I am to musick in general, I cannot escape the magic of Wagner, whose genius caught the deepest spirit of those ancestral yellow-bearded gods of war & dominion before whom my own soul bows as before no others— Woden, Thor, Freyr, & the vast Alfadur—frosty blue-eyed giants worthy of the adoration of a conquering people![11]

Lovecraft attended the meetings of the Kalem Club and the Blue Pencil Club. One fringe member of the Kalem Club was an actor, "the dainty Wheeler Dryden." Dryden was one of Charlie Chaplin's two English half-brothers and, according to Lovecraft, "a good egg, though just a bit of a sap." Dryden and Lovecraft argued religion, with Dryden defending God against Lovecraft's attacks. Out of his depth, poor Dryden was reduced to bleating: "But I say, you know, I don't claim that God is a nice old gentleman with long whiskers!"[12]

Lovecraft now began to realize one of the hazards of a writer's life. I have mentioned that writers, living away from New York City and from arty places like Taos and Carmel, tend to live solitary, reclusive lives, because there are so few colleagues with whom they can talk shop.

On the other hand, in New York or at an artists' colony, there are all too many colleagues with whom to socialize. There are also fringers who, with the least encouragement, will haunt the writer's abode, drink his beer, tell the stories of their lives, talk of the great works they will some day create, and generally waste his time. For self-employed men and scholars, time is the most precious thing they have.

Lovecraft tried to escape this predicament. Kirk (who also

lived for a while at 169 Clinton Street) and Loveman were always eager for "an afternoon of empty dawdling around in bookstalls and cafeterias" or for a long evening of talk.

Lovecraft employed stratagems "to get rid of the daily droppings-in and cafeteria loafing." He pretended to be out—even reading in his alcove with the curtains drawn, so that no crack of light should show beneath his door. He received friends in bathrobe and slippers, apologetically explaining that he was just going to bed. He was politely taciturn until they gave up trying to get interesting talk out of him. He reported progress:

> In this calling my evenings my own, to read in or do what I please in, I am achieving a sense of balance, freedom, and regained individual personality which I have long lacked. I had been asked to spend that evening around the Fourth Avenue and Downing Street slums with the gang, and would have felt myself compelled by courtesy to do so a couple of months ago. Now, however, I am severely and relentlessly my own master; and politely countered the well-meant invitation with the statement that my own affairs might make it impossible, great as would be my regret, and so on.

He turned down an invitation from Loveman to go to Washington again, much as he wanted "to see a real white man's town,"[13] because, if he let Loveman pay his fare (being unable to afford his own) he could not then decently avoid Loveman's constant company.

He resolved to reduce, not only his socializing, but his correspondence as well:

> . . . I think I shall stay up tonight in order to make up time lost in social amenities. . . . I may have to neglect correspondence & permit letters to pile up a bit—but this will do no harm now. . . .
>
> I hope to write some more stories shortly—but I must get rid of my superfluous amateur letter-writing. Any incubi or responsibilities detract disastrously from one's creative imagination. . . .
>
> I must keep my programme freer of outside events in order to preserve an equilibrium for writing, but politeness impels me to submit to many social demands till I can devise a diplomatic means of diminishing them.
>
> It's hard to keep my days to myself! Kirk just telephoned & invited me so urgently for Saturday night that I couldn't find any way of giving a polite refusal![14]

In trying to back off from his friends, Lovecraft labored under difficulties. His habit of sleeping while others worked and working during others' playtimes made him an easy target for interruptions. His personal magnetism continued to draw callers, since they found him delightful company and his code of courtesy-at-all-costs kept him from repelling their approaches. Finally, a lonely, isolated man for the first time found himself the center of a circle of congenial, devoted, admiring friends, in whose adulation he loved to bask.

It was the same with his vast correspondence. Paul Cook said that

> I frequently pointed out to him that this could be only a detriment to his literary work. He would acknowledge this fact and resolve to cut various correspondents off his list, or at least to shorten his letters to them. But a chance remark in a letter would start in motion a train of thought and the result would be a sizable manuscript. . . . All of his correspondents, like myself, enjoyed getting his letters, but some of us groaned to see how the man was using up his energy, and he had only so much, on these private letters, which, after all, amounted to very little, when he should have been working on such creative writing as would give him the place he deserved in literature.

Lovecraft never reduced his weekly letters to Lillian Clark, some of which ran to more than forty pages. At the end of 1925, he was complaining as loudly as ever about his glut of correspondence.

After Sonia's departure, Lovecraft kept at his job-hunting but in a dwindling and desultory fashion. After all, he had tried everywhere he could think of in vain.

In May, 1925, Arthur Leeds and an associate named Yesley worked up a scheme for marketing short trade-journal articles, some of which—mainly about real estate—Lovecraft was to write. Lovecraft wrote six of the articles, and at least one, for which he was to have had $3.50, was placed. But then the scheme fell through.

Lovecraft vainly answered at least two classified advertisements in the *New York Times* for commercial writers. He earned a few dollars now and then by doing clerical jobs for his friends, such as typing, or addressing envelopes for Kirk's catalogue of books. He overcame his disdain for typing long enough to retype several of his old stories for *Weird Tales*. Some, like "The Outsider" and "The Terrible Old Man," he sold at this time.

In telling his Aunt Lillian of Loveman's struggles to get a book of poetry published, he said: "I am too old & cynical & world-weary to be interested in books of my junk—I wouldn't go to the bother of typing the stuff unless I knew it would bring financial returns." This was just a defense. There is every reason to think that a professionally published book of his stories—often discussed but never realized—would have delighted him.

In December, he got an offer from a British literary agency to act as their American representative. After canvassing his friends and getting conflicting advice, he turned the offer down. While I doubt if he would ever have made a good literary agent, the experience would have been an education for him and would have given him needed contacts in the publishing world.

For a whole year, Morton kept a job offer dangling before Lovecraft. Morton had become engaged to a lady of mature years, Pearl K. Merritt. Needing more money, he heard that the city of Paterson, New Jersey, was considering establishment of a municipal museum. Morton promptly went to New Jersey, passed a civil-service test, and got the job of curator. He married Miss Merritt and moved to Paterson.

There was no museum yet. The Library Corporation of Paterson had bought an old house and a barn, under a contract that let the aged owner live in the house for the rest of his life. Meanwhile the collections, occupying a room of the library, were to be stored in the renovated barn. Eventually, the city hoped to build a proper building.

In the spring of 1925, Morton foresaw that he would need an assistant and thought of Lovecraft. Lovecraft was amenable, being a born museum curator if any man ever was. Setting up this institution, however, could not be hurried. Throughout 1925, Lovecraft reported that the museum job was still hanging fire.

Lovecraft thought at first that he might like Paterson, a town well equipped with Colonial antiquities. A closer view of its grimy industrial sections disillusioned him, for he had become allergic to the mere sight of the hated "aliens." He said that "a mongrel-Italian & Slav element is indicated by the physiognomies of the repulsive rabble." He blamed greedy manufacturers for "importing dreary hordes of inferior Syrians, Jews, Poles, & Southern Italians whose sluggish minds & broken spirits cause them to work for starvation wages till aroused by agitators."[15]

Slowly, the museum took shape. In April, 1926, when Lovecraft returned to Providence, the assistant curatorship was still a good possibility. Had he stayed longer in New York, the job would probably have been his.

Morton presided over his museum for fifteen years, building up a fine mineral collection. In 1941, when he was seventy, the Mortons bought a house in New Hampshire to retire to. Then, on October 7th, Morton was killed by an automobile.

In March, 1926, Lovecraft did obtain a temporary job, at $17.50 a week, from Loveman's employers, the booksellers Dauber & Pine. Lovecraft addressed the envelopes in which 10,000 catalogues were to be mailed out. The job lasted about three weeks. Lovecraft hated the work, but at least it could no longer be said that he had *never* earned a pay check.

In the summer of 1925, Lovecraft turned out three stories: "The Horror at Red Hook," "He," and "In the Vault." They belong in the middle rank of his stories, and all shed light on Lovecraft. He wrote "The Horror at Red Hook," of 7,500 words, at the end of July, 1925.

In a village in Rhode Island, "a tall, heavily built, and wholesome-looking pedestrian" has a nervous seizure, causing him to run screaming until he trips and falls. He is Thomas F. Malone, a detective of the New York Police Department, taking a rest cure after a shattering experience. Malone is of Irish birth, a graduate of Dublin University and a poet in his spare time, with "the Celt's far vision of weird and hidden things, but the logician's quick eye for the outwardly unconvincing. . . ."

Lovecraft had come a way since he dismissed all Irishmen as irrational bigots. Thomas Malone is not only the hero of the story; he is also one of Lovecraft's very few *heroic* heroes.

Malone is assigned to work in the Red Hook district of Brooklyn, which Lovecraft describes from personal knowledge. According to Sonia, he was stimulated to write the story by the rage he felt at the misbehavior of a crowd of ruffians who invaded a restaurant where he was eating:

Red Hook is a maze of hybrid squalor near the ancient waterfront opposite Governor's Island, with dirty highways climbing the hill from the wharves to that higher ground where the decayed lengths of Clinton and Court Streets lead off toward Borough Hall. . . . The population is a hopeless tangle and enigma; Syrian, Spanish, Italian and negro elements impinging upon one another, and fragments of Scandinavian and American belts lying not far distant. It is a babel of sound and filth, and sends out strange cries to answer the lapping of oily waves at its grimy piers and the monstrous organ litanies of the harbour whistles. . . .[16]

A fat old scholar, Robert Suydam, who lives alone in a tumble-down house, becomes the center of a cult of sinister, slant-eyed Orientals. Malone identifies these ominous Easterners as Kurdish Yezidis or devil-worshipers, who have illegally entered the country.

(The real Kurds, descendants of the ancient Medes, are big, ruddy, wholly Caucasoid men, and the Yezidis are a peaceable, well-behaved sect despite their peculiar theology. But Lovecraft had never seen a Kurd, and in 1925 a writer could still get mileage out of the sinister idea of "devil-worship.")

Suydam marries a well-connected young woman and sets out for his honeymoon on a Cunard ship. Suydam and his bride are mysteriously slain. A gang of "swart, insolent ruffians" from a freighter boards the ship and are inexplicably allowed to carry off Suydam's corpse.

Rumors of a vast demonic ceremony, to include human sacrifice, cause the police to raid the Red Hook section. In the process, Malone is dragged down into a subcellar by a "sucking force not of earth or heaven." He finds a Walpurgis night of sorcery, with all the demons of earthly mythologies—Satan, Lilith, Moloch, satyrs, and other spooks—cavorting. In a climax of horror. . . .

The story has action and color; its main fault is that Lovecraft never logically thought out his plot. Incident piles on incident without necessary connection.

In later stories, Lovecraft built his fantasies more carefully. Just after composing this story, he wrote Clark Ashton Smith: "I have always thought that weird writing is more effective if it avoids the hackneyed superstitions & popular cult formulae." Nonetheless "The Horror at Red Hook," with its conventional medieval devils invoked by their worshipers' spells, contains much "hackneyed superstition." But thenceforward, Lovecraft edged away from these well-worn themes and towards more original concepts.

In early August, feeling bored and imprisoned, Lovecraft took a long journey by ferry boat and streetcar to Elizabethtown, New Jersey, to admire its Colonial relics. Sitting in Scott Park, he wrote out his next story, "He." This 4,000-word short story is not outstanding among Lovecraft's works, since it suffers from one of his worst cases of adjectivitis.

Nevertheless, its opening paragraphs are often quoted for their autobiographical quality. Into them Lovecraft poured his feelings about New York:

> My coming to New York had been a mistake; for whereas I had looked for poignant wonder and inspiration in the teeming labyrinths of ancient streets that twist endlessly from forgotten courts and squares and waterfronts equally forgotten, and in the Cyclopean modern towers and pinnacles that rise blackly Babylonian under waning moons, I had found instead only a sense of horror and oppression which threatened to master, paralyze, and annihilate me. . . .
>
> But success and happiness were not to be. Garish daylight showed only squalor and alienage and the noxious elephantiasis of climbing, spreading stone where the moon had hinted of loveliness and elder magic; and the throngs of people that seethed through the flumelike streets were squat, swarthy strangers with hardened faces and narrow eyes, shrewd strangers without dreams and without kinship to the scenes about them, who could never mean aught to a blue-eyed man of the old folk, with the love of fair green lanes and white New England village steeples in his heart.
>
> So instead of the poems I had hoped for, there came only a shuddering blackness and ineffable loneliness; and I saw at last a fearful truth which no one had ever dared to breathe before—the unwhisperable secret of secrets—the fact that this city of stone and stridor is not a sentient perpetuation of Old New York as London is of Old London and Paris of Old Paris, but that it is in fact quite dead, its sprawling body imperfectly embalmed and infested with queer animate things which have nothing to do with it as it was in life. Upon making this discovery I ceased to sleep comfortably; though something of resigned tranquillity came back as I gradually formed the habit of keeping off the streets by day and venturing abroad only at night. . . . With this mode of relief I even wrote a few poems, and still refrained from going home to my people lest I seem to crawl back ignobly in defeat.

Then begins the tale proper. In one of his nocturnal rambles, the narrator meets a stranger, wearing a wide-brimmed black hat and a black cloak, like the "mystery man" who was a stock figure in the old silent-movie serials.

The mysterious stranger, the "he" of the story, takes the narrator to his home. He proves to be an elderly man in eighteenth-century garb, who talks of an ancestor who got magical secrets from the Indians and paid them off in poisoned rum. His speech becomes more and more archaic: he says "sartain" and "larning." He shows the narrator a vision, through a window, of the landscape in aboriginal times, then in Colonial times, and then in the future:

> For full three seconds I could glimpse that pandemoniac sight, and in those seconds I saw a vista which will ever afterward torment me in dreams. I saw the heavens verminous with strange flying things, and beneath them a hellish black city of giant stone terraces with impious pyramids flung savagely to the moon, and devil-lights burning from unnumbered windows. And swarming loathsomely on aerial galleries I saw the yellow, squint-eyed people of that city, robed horribly in orange and red, and dancing insanely to the pounding of fevered kettle-drums, the clatter of obscene crotala, and the maniacal moaning of muted horns whose ceaseless dirges rose and fell undulantly like the waves of an unhallowed ocean of bitumen.[17]

The sight of this futuristic rock festival makes the narrator scream with horror. These shrieks attract the ghosts of the Indians, whom the mysterious stranger's ancestor had poisoned, and who come for revenge. The "ancestor" is the stranger himself, kept alive by magic. . . .

In September, Lovecraft wrote "In the Vault." Only a little over 3,000 words long, it has a tightly logical structure. It is thus an advance on the rather formless, haphazard plots of Lovecraft's earlier stories. Lovecraft said he got the idea from "an interesting old fellow in Massachusetts,"[18] meaning the amateur publisher Charles W. Smith.

This simple but well-knit little ghost story tells of a crude, callous Yankee village undertaker named George Birch. Finding that he must fit a long corpse into a short coffin and not wishing the expense and trouble of making another coffin, Birch cuts off the corpse's feet to make it fit. The tale tells of the corpse's revenge.

In August, Lovecraft had an idea for another story, which he tentatively called "The Call of Cthulhu." He wrote an outline but put it aside. He did not write the actual story until the following year, when he had returned to Providence.

Wright bought "The Horror at Red Hook" and "He" for *Weird Tales* but, fearing another commotion like that over "The Loved Dead," found "In the Vault" too gruesome. Six years later, however, Wright bought "In the Vault" for $55 and ran it without repercussions in the April, 1932, issue.

During the following months, Lovecraft mentioned other stories he hoped to write but never did:

> . . . I mean to give several of my contemplated phantasies an eastern—probably Bagdad setting.
>
> I also 'fell' for one of the ancient pottery lamps whose cheapness is due to the limitless quantities lately excavated—a Grecian affair of about 500 B.C. It sits before me now, enchanting in its glamour, & has already suggested at least one weird story plot to my imagination; a plot in which it will figure as an *Atlantean* rather than Hellenic survival.
>
> Lost worlds have always been a favourite theme of mine, & I shall treat of them more than once before I lay down my fictional pen for ever. . . . I mean to do some interplanetary stuff, but mine shall not violate any known fact or law of celestial science as known at the present time.
>
> I'd like to write a tale of the digging of a Westminster St. subway —or a Providence-Pawtucket subway—& the incidental discovery of broken Corinthian columns bespeaking the forum of some unknown Roman town at the head of Narragansett Bay. A trireme under Cn. Pomponius Falco during the war against the Mediterranean pirates in Cicero's time is hurled by a storm thro' the pillars of Hercules & into the vast Atlanticus. At length it reaches a pleasant bay inhabited by copper-skinned barbarians, & after a treaty is drawn up, a town is built on the side of a pleasant hill & named MVSOSICVM—as the settlers interpret the name *Mooshassuck*, which they hear from the barbarians.[19]

When it came to writing, however, Lovecraft veered off in another direction. In November, W. Paul Cook asked Lovecraft to write "an article . . . on the element of terror & weirdness in literature, but I [HPL] shall take my time about preparing it. Meanwhile I hope to get aloof & composed enough to do some writing on my own hook."

Cook was a quiet, self-effacing little man even more devoted to amateur journalism than Lovecraft. He had served as president both of NAPA and of UAPA and as editor of the latter. From his homes in New Hampshire and Massachusetts he issued distinguished amateur magazines, first *The Monadnock Magazine* and then *The Vagrant*.

In 1925, Cook was winding up his *Vagrant* and wanted Lovecraft's essay for the first issue of an ambitious new journal, *The Recluse*. Lovecraft titled his piece "Supernatural Horror in Literature" and began research. There were, he found, many important stories in the genre of which he had heard but which he had never read. He settled down to fill these gaps in his knowledge. Despite his brave words about giving his fiction priority, he let Cook's article completely absorb his time and attention.

The article proved a bigger job than he had thought. By January, he was writing letters, justifying the task as "excellent mental discipline" and "an admirable excuse for my absenting myself from engagements." He predicted that he would finish the task in "two or three weeks," but he was still at it when he left New York in April. In July, he finished typing the final draft, although "the job nearly killed me."[20]

"Supernatural Horror" had taken practically all of Lovecraft's writing time for eight months. And for what? So that Cook could print it, free, in an amateur periodical to be seen by a few hundred other amateurs. So far from being "mental discipline," it was a piece of frivolous self-indulgence on Lovecraft's part.

In 1927, Cook did get out *The Recluse*. The single issue was so heavily slanted towards imaginative fiction that it may be called the first science-fiction fan magazine. Cook meant to issue another one, but the second issue was stillborn because his wife died and he left New England.

To a professional writer, devoting two thirds of a year to unpaid hobby writing would seem stark mad. But Lovecraft never really became a professional. He belonged to a milieu and a tradition in which "amateur" was a term of praise. Instead of "beginner," "tyro," or "bungler," it meant "a gentleman who does something for love, not for vulgar money." Cook, who had much the same attitude, admiringly described Lovecraft:

> And Lovecraft *was* an amateur. He never wrote a line with the publisher or the public in view. He had refused to alter a story when if changed to suit an editor, it would have been accepted and paid for. If his work as done according to his own inclinations would sell, it was well and good. If not, he had the satisfaction of refusing to subordinate his art to mammon. If he had thought it fitting to keep his stories short, he could have sold everything he cared to write. But his art grew, or his ideas of his work expanded, and he needed larger and larger canvasses, until it was practically impossible to find a market for his later work.[21]

Lovecraft's ideal of amateurism belonged to a fading tradition in lands across the sea. On the other hand, in a world of organization men with plastic personalities, there is much to be said for an unregenerate individualist who stubbornly sticks to Machiavelli's dictum: "Follow your own course and let the people talk." There is a bit of suppressed Don Quixote in many of us.

Still, if anyone insists on playing the Knight of the Rueful Countenance in real life, he need not complain when he is knocked base-over-apex by a windmill. Quixotry is a costly game, and he who plays it must expect to pay the price.

At nearly 30,000 words, "Supernatural Horror in Literature" was the longest piece that Lovecraft had written. It begins with the resounding assertion, with some psychological truth: "The oldest and strongest emotion of mankind is fear, and the oldest and strongest kind of fear is fear of the unknown."[22] It was certainly true for Lovecraft, whose fear of the unknown caused him to miss many opportunities. It made him shrink timidly from new places, new contacts, and new kinds of work.

Lovecraft traces fictional horror from such ancients as Pliny the Younger and Apuleius to the Gothic novel and thence to Lovecraft's contemporaries like Machen, Blackwood, Dunsany, and M. R. James. Covering a huge field, the article is a good, workmanlike job, which in other hands might have served as a master's thesis.

According to the late Thomas O. Mabbott, Lovecraft, in "Supernatural Horror," solved a problem in the interpretation of Poe. In "The Fall of the House of Usher," Lovecraft argued that

Susan, Howard, and Winfield Lovecraft, 1891.

The Phillips home at 454 Angell Street, Providence.

H. P. Lovecraft in his twenties.

Sonia Haft Greene, 1921.

H. P. Lovecraft in his forties.

Frank Belknap Long and
H. P. Lovecraft, 1931.

H. P. Lovecraft, 1934.

Lovecraft's boarding house at 169 Clinton Street, Brooklyn.

10 Barnes Street, Providence.

Quinsnicket Lake, with Lovecraft's favorite ledge.

66 College Street, Providence.

Robert E. Howard

Annie E. P. Gamwell

Robert H. Barlow

Clark Ashton Smith in his fifties.

Silhouette of H.P. Lovecraft,
by Perry.

H. P. Lovecraft as drawn by Virgil Finlay.

Roderick Usher, his sister Madeleine, and the house all shared one common soul.

In one of his last stories, "At the Mountains of Madness," Lovecraft solved another problem in Poe. This was the identity, in the poem *Ulalume*, of "Mount Yaanek." Readers had long been puzzled by Poe's location of this mountain "in the realms of the boreal pole." By "boreal pole," said Lovecraft, Poe meant the *south* magnetic pole, towards which the wind Boreas blows. Hence Mount Yaanek was the volcano Erebus in Antarctica.[23]

Nonetheless, "Supernatural Horror in Literature" is a compilation of the sort that any professor of English literature could do. I wish that Lovecraft had spent that time on his unwritten story of the lamp from Atlantis. Many scholars could have written "Supernatural Horror," but only Lovecraft could write a Lovecraftian story.

The overriding factor in Lovecraft's last year in New York was his declining mental condition. The passions and prejudices he had brought from Providence, instead of fading as do most people's on immersion in a wider world, grew to manic intensity. Providence, instead of receding to a gentle memory of youth, became an obsession. Lovecraft became as homesick as the most callow boarding-school boy on his first night away from home. Cook reported:

> I saw Lovecraft only once during his New York experience. I had only an hour in the city that time and we had but a short chat. I had sensed his mental turmoil from his letters, and when I saw him his unhappiness was painfully manifest.

Lovecraft became obsessed with trivia. In his letters to Lillian Clark, he rambled on for pages about his struggles with oil heaters, lighting fixtures, alarm clocks, mousetraps, and coat buttons.

He urged his aunts not to let his subscription to the *Providence Evening Bulletin* expire: "The more I see of other papers, the better I like the *Bulletin*." When about to answer a help-wanted ad, he wrote: "Here's hoping for an early fortune, which I shall spend in buying 454 [Angell Street] & the barn, tearing down Angell Court & putting back the stone wall. . . ."

His aunts suggested that, if he was so eager to see Providence, why not come for a visit? He replied:

As to trip—as I told AEPG, I couldn't bear to see Providence again till I can be there for ever. . . . But a temporary glimpse would be like that of a distant mariner swept by a storm within sight of his own harbour, then washed away again into the illimitable blackness of an alien sea.[24]

His snobbery became aggravated. He admired Galpin's wife, whom he met as she passed through New York in August, not only for her own charm but also because she was "descended from the most ancient Norman nobility domiciled in Ireland." He likewise took to Wilfred Talman because Talman was "tall, lean, light, & aristocratically clean-cut." He esteemed Kleiner because, outside of Kleiner's job, "he is absolutely the gentleman dilettante," never commercializing his poems or the fancy lettering that was his hobby.

He was surprised when an acquaintance named Hancock revealed a habit of borrowing things and not returning them, despite the fact that "he comes of one of the most aristocratic families in England!" But when the coal miners went on strike in September, he wrote: ". . . it is unfortunate that society ever allowed itself to become so interdependent that it must hang on the whims of a pack of dirty peasants."[25]

He took refuge in his Georgian dreams and poses and in his philosophy of indifference and futility:

As for me—I have retired conclusively from the present age. In a cosmos of aimless chaos & upon a planet of futility & decay, nothing but fancy is of any importance. Time & space are the sheerest incidentals; & when one lived in a decadent & disillusioned age which has nothing of moment to say, it becomes a man of sense to stop wasting his time on contemporary fumbling, & to turn back to a period whose utterances have something in them to which his own psychology responds. . . . I belong back with the Georgians in point of time, & in point of space take most readily to the English or Neo-English rural realm—the meadow, the wood, the farm, & the village—when I am not roaming the universe at large in quest of unique horrors.[26]

He felt that his powers were failing:

There are many things I wish to write, but every now & then I have the feeling of the aging workman that perhaps my hand has lost what little cunning it ever possessed. When my stuff is done it always disappoints me—never quite presenting the fulness of the picture I have in mind—but since a crude fixation of the image is better than nothing, I plug along & do the feeble best I can.

His feeling towards New York City became black hatred. He wrote of the "mongrel modernity" of this "alien desert" and his need to get away from "the nightmare rookeries of this Babylonish metropolis," filled with "herds of evil-looking foreigners."[27]

His ethnic phobias reached genocidal frenzy. A new suburban reservoir to supply the New York water system brought an outburst against the city as "ruthless in wiping out whole villages of real people to keep alive the stinking mongrel vermin of this chaotic metropolitan mess!" Immigration, drastically curtailed in 1924, was not restricted enough:

> I certainly hope to see promiscuous immigration permanently curtailed soon—Heaven knows enough harm has already been done by the admission of limitless hordes of the ignorant, superstitious, & biologically inferior scum of Southern Europe & Western Asia.[28]

It is hard to be patient with one who reviles others as "biologically inferior scum," when most of these scum are at least facing reality, meeting their obligations, and supporting themselves and their families, none of which Lovecraft was doing. Of his ethnic targets, Negroes came off the worst:

> Of course they can't let niggers use the beach at a Southern resort—can you imagine sensitive persons bathing near a pack of greasy chimpanzees? The only thing that makes life endurable where blacks abound is the Jim Crow principle, & I wish they'd apply it in N.Y. both to niggers & to the more Asiatic types of puffy, rat-faced Jew. Either stow 'em out of sight or kill 'em off—anything so that a white man may walk along the streets without shuddering & nausea![29]

Even the most praiseworthy Negro became a butt of Lovecraft's ridicule. When Lillian Clark praised her maid Delilah, Lovecraft replied that "She certainly is a valuable nigger, & ought to bring a good $900 or $1000 in any fair market north of Savannah. . . . I wish I could present you with a deed of sale to such a prime piece of property for Christmas, but these pesky abolitionists have wrought havoc with the trade. . . ."[30] Mention of a Negro woman lawyer brought sarcasm:

> As for the sable barristress L. Marian Poe—well, so long as she doesn't meddle wiv de white folks, Ah reckon she won' do no harm. . . . Now I suppose Delilah will try to enter professional life—possibly medicine or theology or statesmanship.

To millions of white Americans of Lovecraft's generation, the mere sight of a Negro playing a role traditionally belonging to upper-class whites—exercising authority over white men, practicing a learned profession, enjoying a genteel sport or pastime, or even displaying unwonted intelligence and ambition—caused profound psychological discomfort and aroused resentment and rage.

In making such verbal distinctions as "real people" versus "stinking mongrel vermin," or "people, Poles, & niggers,"[31] Lovecraft was doing exactly what the primitive tribesman does by calling his fellow-tribesmen "real human beings." The implication is that anybody outside the tribe is not really human and is therefore fair game, to be robbed, killed, or eaten with impunity.

To us of the 1970s, it seems strange that a man, emotionally low-keyed, kind and generous to a fault with friends and acquaintances, interested in the ancient and the exotic, and priding himself on an objective, dispassionate outlook, should develop such venomous hatred for people who had never harmed him, merely because he disliked their appearance, accents, and other superficialities. In most scientific matters, moreover, Lovecraft was a hard-headed, skeptical materialist, giving short shrift to Charles Fort, Atlantis, Elliot Smith's heliocentric theory, and all occultisms. Yet he fell hook, line, and sinker for the pseudo-scientific Aryanist cult and used it to rationalize his ethnic hatreds.

August Derleth tried to clear Lovecraft of charges of ethnic prejudice. He was not *really* a racist and an anti-Semite, said Derleth; he just had some quirks about foreigners because they had made changes in his beloved Providence.[32] This was merely Derleth's effort to whitewash his idol.

It is not surprising that Lovecraft should have started with this viewpoint, since before the First World War it was widespread among Old Americans. It was something Old American children were brought up to believe in, along with Protestant Christianity, nationalism, capitalism, and the roundness of the earth. If not universal, this Old American chauvinism was at least respectable. Nobody dreamed of hiding it as discreditable. Henry Adams's biographer explains:

> The anti-Semitism bred in the nationalist and clerical cloaca of Bismarck's Germany, uniting with that of Russia and eastern Europe, overflowed into France and finally into the United States

when the harried waves of refugees from mob violence appeared in outlandish beard and forelock and shabby gabardine. When the newcomers succeeded in the gold-bug jungle their success seemed to fastidious Puritan moralists like Henry James a vulgar parody of capitalist society. Doubtless it often was, for it lacked the graceful draperies of proper family connections, of a discreetly shared religion, of old school ties, and of unobtrusive manners.

All the latent antiforeignism and racism of the time against the south European immigrant and the Oriental came to a head in the Jew as the master image of the enemy of Anglo-Saxon supremacy. . . . by 1894 Brahmin leadership turned discreetly to the new Immigration Restriction League of Boston, whose mission was to save the nation from mongrelization.

As for "unobtrusive manners," persons making a transition from one cultural pattern to another, as by going to live in a foreign land, often give an ill-mannered impression because they do not yet know how they are expected to behave in their new surroundings. It may take them two or three generations to master all the subtleties of gesture and language, so that the newcomers can put their best feet forward.

Militant Anglo-Saxonism slowly declined during the 1920s, 30s, and 40s. It was still rife in the 1920s and has not completely vanished even yet. Between the two world wars, writers and intellectuals, helped by Hitler's antics, led the retreat from Old American chauvinism. The fact that Lovecraft clung to these views with such intensity, when other American intellectuals were abandoning it, calls for explanation.

Posthumous psychoanalysis is at best conjectural. Still, there is evidence for the unconscious drives that gave Lovecraft this belligerently tribal attitude. As a child, he was rejected by his peers; as an adult, he had many failures. His stay in New York was a shattering barrage of failures. He had tried, by marrying outside his Old American milieu and moving to the metropolis, to become an urbane cosmopolite and failed. He had tried to adapt himself to strange surroundings and failed. He had tried to become a wage-earner and failed. He had failed as a husband and family head. Evidently he had tried to effect too many changes in his life all at once.

Now, xenophobia—fear and hatred of strangers—is a common defense against one's own failures and shortcomings. The xenophobe consoles himself with the thought that at least he is better that *those* bastards.

Furthermore, like most intellectual introverts, Lovecraft was a stranger in his own world. He himself said: "I am always an outsider."[33] He blamed his own uneasiness, in contacts with ordinary Americans, on the presence among them of ethnics and aliens. He defended his vulnerable ego by railing against "aliens" and saying: "I hate any foreign influence"; but in point of fact, *he* was the alien. He would have felt completely at home only in a milieu wholly populated by H. P. Lovecrafts, and no such society exists.

He did qualify his xenophobic sentiments:

> As I have always said, missionaries are infernal nuisances who ought to be kept at home—dull, solemn asses without scientific acumen or historical perspective; & cursed with an eternal blindness to the obvious fact that different lands, races, & conditions naturally develop & demand different cultural standards & usages & different ethical & social codes.[34]

In other words, foreigners were all right in their foreign lands and should be left alone to go their own exotic ways. Lovecraft's ideal seems to have been a world neatly and permanently divided by watertight compartments into races, cultures, and nations. Any intermixture bothered him, since to him such groups were immiscible, like oil and water. The fusion of two patently different groups seemed to him a violation of the laws of nature, and to him a violation of natural law was the ultimate horror. The idea of the Melting Pot enraged him. His attitude was a little like that of the hero's mother in Santayana's *The Last Puritan:*

> Mrs. Alden . . . froze at the touch of difference. Superior power and distinction were insufferable: if she could not imitate them she denied them. And the least degree of coarseness or simplicity beneath her own offended her also. . . . Beyond the pale there could be nothing but outer darkness—an alien, heathen, unintelligible world, to be kept as remote as possible. . . . And she supposed that if occasionally that dreadful outer world became troublesome, it would be necessary to make war on it to teach it a lesson: but by far the best thing was to ignore it altogether.[35]

Despite all the dangerous nonsense that Lovecraft wrote and uttered about ethnics, we must not forget the contrast between these theoretical fulminations and his attitudes towards real individuals. Frank Long, who thinks I over-stress Lovecraft's ethnocentrism, writes me:

> This may be hard for you to believe. But during the entire NY period, in all the meetings and conversations I had with him, he never once displayed any actual hostility toward "non-Nordics"— to use the term to which he was most addicted—in my presence, either in the subway or anywhere else. . . . If one of them had been in distress he would have been the first to rush to his or her aid. Emotionally he was kindliness personified. It was all rhetorical —the kind of verbal *overkill* that so many of the hippie underground-press writers engaged in in the sixties. It was a sickness in him, if you wish—the verbalization part—but it wasn't characteristic of him in a deep, basic way. . . . In all the conversations I had with Howard he never used terms like "Kike" "dago" "Spic"— even "Nigger." It was almost always "Negro." And seemingly it was only in his letters to Mrs. Clark that what he said was *monstrous*, bad as some of his comments to other correspondents were.

Wilfred Talman also insists that he has not "the slightest recollection of his [Lovecraft's] ever having made an anti-Semitic statement orally or in a letter. Nor do I remember anything he ever said knowingly to wound a listener." The probable explanation is that Lovecraft, while still harboring his old nativist attitudes, had come to realize that, among educated Americans, such attitudes were more and more coming into disfavor as outmoded and inhumane. Therefore he kept quiet about them, save with his aunts and a very few intimates.

As a result of the pressures upon him, Lovecraft came close to a major psychotic breakdown. In January, 1926, he wrote his Aunt Lillian:

> The mass of contemporary Jews are hopeless as far as America is concerned. They are the product of alien blood, & inherit alien ideals, impulses, & emotions which forever preclude the possibility of wholesale assimilation. . . . The fact is, that an Asiatic stock broken & dragged through the dirt for untold centuries cannot possibly meet a proud, play-loving warlike Nordic race on an emotional parity. They may want to meet, but they can't—their inmost feelings & perspectives are antipodal. Neither stock can feel at ease when confronted by the other. . . . East versus West—they can talk for aeons without either's knowing what the other really means. On our side there is a shuddering physical repugnance to most Semitic types, & when we try to be tolerant we are merely blind

or hypocritical. Two elements so discordant can never build up one society—no feeling of real linkage can exist where so vast a disparity of ancestral memories is concerned—so that wherever the Wandering Jew wanders, he will have to content himself with his own society till he disappears or is killed off in some sudden outburst of physical loathing on our part. I've easily felt able to slaughter a score or two when jammed in a N.Y. subway train. . . . The line is clearly drawn, & in New York may yet evolve into a new colour-line, for there the problem assumes its most hideous form as loathsome Asiatic hordes trail their dirty carcasses over streets where white men once moved, & air their odious presence & twisted visages & stunted forms till we shall be driven either to murder them or emigrate ourselves, or be carried shrieking to the madhouse. Indeed, the real problem may be said to exist nowhere but in New York, for only there is the displacement of regular people so hellishly marked. It is not good for a proud, light-skinned Nordic to be cast away alone amongst squat, squint-eyed jabberers with coarse ways & alien emotions whom his deepest cell-tissue hates & loathes as the mammal hates & loathes the reptile, with an instinct as old as history—& the decline of New York as an American city will be the inevitable result. Meanwhile all one can do is to avoid personal contact with the intruding fabric—ugh! they make one feel ill-at-ease, as though one's shoes pinched, or as though one had on prickly woollen underwear. Experience has taught the remnants of the American people what they never thought of when the first idealists opened the gates to scum—that there is no such thing as the assimilation of a stock whose relation to our own history is so slight, whose basic emotions are so antithetical to ours, & whose physical aspect is so loathsome to normal members of our species. Such is New York's blight. Our own New England problem, though less violently repellant on the surface, is yet of discouraging magnitude; for where New York is swamped with Asiatics, our own streets are flooded with scarcely less undesirable Latins—low-grade Southern Italians & Portuguese, & the clamorous plague of French-Canadians. These elements will form a separate Roman Catholic culture hostile to our own, joining with the Irish—who in a highly unassimilated state, are the pest of Boston. Many of these stocks could be assimilated—such as the Nordic Irish of Eastern Ireland & such of the French-Canadians as are of Norman extraction—but the process will be very slow. Meanwhile separation & mutual hostility must continue, though there is much less of that shuddering, maddening physical aversion which makes New York a hell to a sensitive Nordic. . . . Outside the N.Y. & N.E. belt other racial & cultural problems occur. The hideous peasant Poles of New Jersey & Pennsylvania are absolutely unassimilable save by the thinnest trickling stream, whilst the Mexicans—half to three-quarters Indian—form a tough morsel in the southwest. . . . In general,

America has made a fine mess of its population, & will pay for it in tears amidst a premature rottenness unless something is done extremely soon. . . . In excluding the swarms of Mediterranean & Asiatic vermin that now ooze & creep over all the landscape we could have avoided most of that very sense of intolerable repulsion which a foreign name now creates in us. . . . In nations, as in society, *congeniality* is the all-important principle. As for me, I'm sick of Bohemians, odds & ends, freaks, & plebeians—C. M. Eddys & satellites & miscellany &c. They amuse for a while, but begin after a time to get frightfully on one's nerves. People get on one's nerves when they harbour different kinds of memories & live by different kinds of standards & cherish different kinds of goals & ideals. The only company for a regular conservative American is that formed by regular conservative Americans—well-born, & comfortably nurtured in the old tradition. That's why Belknap [Long] is about the only one of the gang who doesn't irritate me at times. He is *regular*—he connects up with innate memories & Providence experiences to such an extent as to seem a real person instead of a two-dimensional shadow in a dream, as more Bohemian personalities do. But my recent campaign of emancipation is now a success, & I shall henceforeward have around me none save such as are pledged to an undivided following of the conservative Anglo-Saxon tradition. It is well, for in chaotic heterogeneity there would never have been peace for me. All effort on my part would have been paralysed, since no effort would have seemed worth my exerting, if it could not earn me a place among those of my own mental type, free from common or alien social contacts & influences. And even if one cannot find a niche in congenial society, one can at least be *alone*, & that is enough for me. To be clear of irritant & hostile social fabrics is the thing—for otherwise, faced by a life of exile in hateful chaos, a bullet through the brain is the only solution.[36]

A few points about this frenzied rant may be mentioned. For one, Lovecraft speaks of "we" or "one" or "white men" or "regular conservative Americans," who are supposed to feel "shuddering physical repugnance" towards "loathsome Asiatic hordes," "hideous peasant Poles," and other out-groupers, and "intolerable repulsion" at the sound of foreign names. He assumed that he spoke for the rest of the Old Americans. In fact, only a dwindling minority of Americans felt that way at the time; the rest mingled with immigrants and ethnics without any special feeling for or against them. So Lovecraft really spoke for himself alone.

His dogmata about the implacable hostility between East and West, the uncrossable cultural gulf separating Europe and Asia, the unassimilability of non-Europeans, and so on, is bosh. There have been plenty of such assimilations. Syrians, for example, formed the main trading class in western Europe at the time of the fall of the West Roman Empire but a few centuries later had disappeared by assimilation.

Finally, Lovecraft's insistence that "non-Aryans" had nothing in common with Aryans, harbored utterly different ideas and ideals, and could never be congenial with them, is the nonsense of a man who had traveled very little and known very few "non-Aryans" well. One who has known people of many different cultures and colors learns that, once the barriers of language and etiquette are overcome, congeniality is more a matter of common interests than of ancestral memories.

Lovecraft was getting to the point where not just ethnics but nearly everybody got on his nerves. He made an exception for Long, apparently because Long, like himself, was an Old American, somewhat unworldly, and with similar ideas of the code of the gentleman —although Long never shared Lovecraft's ethnic phobias and soon came around to more realistic views.

Alarmed by Lovecraft's outburst, Lillian Clark took him to task. He reassured her about his behavior towards his friends:

> Incidentally don't fancy that my nervous reaction against alien N.Y. types takes the form of conversation likely to offend any individual. One knows when & where to discuss questions with a social or ethnic cast, & our group is not noted for *faux pas's* or inconsiderate repetitions of opinion. I don't think I fail to appreciate the genius & good qualities of the entire assemblage, for every member of which I entertain unaffected respect.[37]

By the winter of 1925–26, Lovecraft began hinting broadly that he would like to be asked back to Providence:

> As for the matter of permanent locations—bless my soul! but SH would only too gladly coöperate in establishing me wherever my mind would be most tranquil & effective! What I meant by 'a threat of having to return to N.Y.' was the matter of industrial opportunity, as exemplified in the Paterson possibility; for in my lean financial state almost any remunerative opening would constitute something which I could not with any degree of good sense or propriety refuse. Now if I were still in N.Y., I could perhaps bear such a thing with philosophical resignation; but if I were back home, I could not possibly contemplate the prospect of leaving again. Once in New England, I must be able to stick there. . . .

Throughout his New York sojourn, Lovecraft continued to use "home" to mean Providence. Morton assured him that the museum job would soon be open. "But," said Lovecraft, "if I once saw New England again, with her hilly streets leading down to the sea, & her avenues of ancient elms, & her clustered gambrel roofs, & her white steeples rising over centuried church-yards, I could never bring myself to venture outside her confines."[38]

If one asks why he did not simply return to Providence, a possible answer is the line in "He," wherein the narrator "refrained from going home to my people lest I seem to crawl back ignobly in defeat." The return to Providence would be such a defeat, and in two years Lovecraft had suffered enough defeats for a lifetime.

By this time, according to Sam Loveman, Lovecraft was carrying a bottle of poison. When he talked of suicide, he was probably not bluffing. Frank Long's mother wrote to the aunts, warning them that anything might happen if something were not done about Lovecraft's mental condition.

In March, Lillian Clark wrote to Lovecraft, urging a visit to Providence, where a small apartment on Waterman Street would be available. Lovecraft replied with qualified enthusiasm:

> Well!!! All your epistles arrived & received a grateful welcome, but the third one was the climax that relegates everything else to the distance!! Whoop! Bang! . . .
>
> And now for your invitation. Hooray!! Long live the State of Rhode-Island & Providence-Plantations!!! But I'm past the visiting-point. Even if my physique is flourishing, my nerves are a mess—& I *could never board a train away from Providence toward New York again.* . . . I'm not eager for ignominious returns via the smaller orifice of the trumpet; but if you & AEPG think it's perfectly dignified for me to slip back toward civilisation & Waterman St., I'm sure I couldn't think of anything else for one who is an integral part of Rhode Island earth. Only last night I dreamed of Foster. . . . But as to details—I'm all in favour of letting you & AEPG do *all* the planning, if you don't mind, & of sending my things ahead of me.
>
> Now about migrations—there is no question of disillusion involved. I don't expect to live in a seventh heaven of happiness anywhere, & only want to drag out my last few days in some quiet backwater where the general environment isn't too obtrusively offensive. There is no question of illusion or disillusion about

Providence—I know what it is, & have never mentally dwelt anywhere else. When I look up from my work it is Angell St. I see
outside the windows, & when I think of going out to buy anything
it is Westminster St. that comes to my eyes. . . . I have no emotional as apart from intellectual conviction that I am not in Providence this moment—indeed, psychologically speaking, I *am* & always
will be there. . . .

But as I have said before; if all hands think Boston or Cambridge a more appropriate haven, I am not disposed to pit against
their judgments an opinion from a mind whose ghastly rashness &
idiocy of 1924 brought about this New York move. . . . I am essentially a recluse who will have very little to do with people wherever he may be. I think that most people only make me nervous—
that only by accident, & in extremely small quantities, would I
ever be likely to come across people who wouldn't. . . . My life
lies not among *people* but among *scenes*—my local affections are
not personal, but topographical & architectural. . . . I will be dog-
matic only to the extent of saying that it is New England I *must*
have—in some form or other. Providence is part of me—I *am*
Providence. . . .[39]

This combination of gentle arm-twisting and cries for help
brought results. At the end of March, Lillian Clark wrote Lovecraft
that half of a double house at 10 Barnes Street was available for
rent. If he liked, he and she could live there. He responded instantly:

Whoopee! Bang!! 'Rah!! For God's sake jump at that room
without a second's delay!! I can't believe it—too good to be true!

Sonia had changed jobs, but her new job was in Cleveland, too.
Now she came to Brooklyn and took efficient charge of packing up
for her husband and arranging for trucking his goods to Providence.
He realized that he had taken a tremendous lot from Sonia and
given but little in return. His conscience nipped him, and he did
not deny the abjectness of his own part:

I have never beheld a more admirable attitude of disinterested &
solicitous regard; in which each financial shortcoming is accepted
& condoned as soon as it is proved inevitable, & in which acquiescence is extended even to my statements (as determined by my
observation of the effect of varying conditions on my nerves) that
the one *essential* ingredient of my life is a certain amount of quiet
& freedom for creative literary composition. . . . A devotion which
can accept this combination of incompetence & aesthetic selfishness
without a murmur, contrary tho' it must be to all expectations

originally entertained; is assuredly a phenomenon so rare, & so akin to the historic quality of saintliness, that no one with the least sense of artistic proportion could possibly meet it with other than the keenest reciprocal esteem, respect, admiration, & affection—as indeed it was met at first, when manifested under less trying circumstances & with far less comprehension of the chronicle of failure stretching ahead. . . . SH fully endorses my design of an ultimate return to New England, & herself intends to seek industrial openings in the Boston district after a time. . . .[40]

Despite this praise, there is reason to think that Lovecraft's feelings towards Sonia were ambivalent. In later years he rarely mentioned her, or any other woman for that matter—as if he lived in one of those English men's clubs on whose premises no lady's name was ever supposed to be uttered.

On one of the few later occasions when he did mention Sonia, he complained that she had "driven" him. In fact, Sonia had filled the rôles of husband, wife, and mother in the family, while he had been a marital cipher—a "kept man" and a difficult child. These facts can hardly have failed to wound his tender self-esteem. The more enterprising, efficient, generous, and self-sacrificing Sonia was, the more the contrast between them must have rankled.

By April 15th, everything was packed and shipped. The Gang held a farewell meeting for Lovecraft; two of them gave him books. On the 17th he departed for Providence.

Sonia had meant to go with him, but an appointment to discuss a prospective new job kept her in New York for the time being. She followed Lovecraft to Providence later.

Thirteen

CTHULHU ALIVE

I never can be tied to raw, new things,
For I first saw the light in an old town,
Where from my window huddled roofs sloped down
To a quaint harbour rich with visionings.
Streets with carved doorways where the sunset beams
Flooded old fanlights and small window-panes,
And Georgian steeples topped with gilded vanes—
These were the sights that shaped my childhood dreams.[1]

LOVECRAFT

Lovecraft took a novel with him to read on the train to Providence but became so excited by the sight of New England through the window that he could not read.

Arriving late on April 17, 1926, he settled into his new home. This was a large, wooden, Victorian double-duplex house at 10–12 Barnes Street, three blocks north of the Brown University campus. Lovecraft and his aunt were to occupy part of the half of the house numbered 10. Lovecraft took the lower floor and Lillian Clark, who had not yet moved in, the upper. Annie Gamwell was at this time living elsewhere in Providence as companion to a blind woman.

A few days later, Lovecraft was still unpacking and sorting with the help of Lillian Clark's maid Delilah. W. Paul Cook dropped in and found that Lovecraft

> . . . was without question the happiest man I ever saw—he could have posed for an "After Taking" picture for the medical ads. . . . His touch was caressing as he put his things in place, a real love-light shone in his eyes as he glanced out of the window. He was so happy he hummed—if he had possessed the necessary apparatus he would have purred.[2]

Lovecraft's accounts of his homecoming were filled with rapture:

> . . . the train sped on, and I experienced silent convulsions of joy in returning step by step to a waking and tri-dimensional life. New Haven—New London—and then quaint Mystic, with its colonial hillside and landlocked cove. Then at last a still subtler magick fill'd the air—nobler roofs and steeples, with the train rushing airily above them on its lofty viaduct—*Westerly*—in His Majesty's Province of RHODE-ISLAND & PROVIDENCE-PLAN-TATIONS! GOD SAVE THE KING!! . . . I fumble with bags and wraps in a desperate effort to appear calm—THEN—a delirious marble dome outside the window—a hissing of air brakes—a slackening of speed—surges of ecstasy and dropping of clouds from my eyes and mind—HOME—UNION STATION—PROVI-DENCE!!!! Something snapped—and everything unreal fell away. There was no more excitement; no sense of strangeness, and no perception of the lapse of time since I last stood on that holy ground. . . . What I had seen in sleep every night since I left it, now stood before me in prosaic reality—precisely the same, line for line, detail for detail, proportion for proportion. Simply, I was home—and home was just as it had always been since I was born there thirty-six years ago. There *is* no other place for me. My world is Providence.

He added that "my wife will be here either steadily or off and on, according to business arrangements now in progress."[3] He dropped in on the Eddys:

> The first we knew of it was when our doorbell rang one night . . . and there stood Lovecraft! Gaunt and thin he looked. . . . and his hands were as cold as ice when he extended them in a friendly handshake!

Lillian Clark's move was delayed for several weeks by a bout of neuralgia. After she moved, Sonia arrived to make some perma-nent arrangement. Sonia recalled:

Then we had a conference with the aunts. I suggested that I would take a large house, secure a good maid, pay all the expenses and have the two aunts live with us at no expense to them, or at least they would live better at no greater expense. HP and I actually negotiated the rental of such a house with the option to buy it if we found we liked it. HP was to use one side of it as his study and library, and I would use the other side as a business venture of my own. At this the aunts gently but firmly informed me that neither they nor Howard could afford to have Howard's wife work for a living in Providence. That was that. I now knew where we all stood. Pride preferred to suffer in silence; both theirs and mine.[4]

It was all right for Lovecraft to live on his wife's earnings in New York; but in Providence, where they were known and had a social position to keep up, it would never do. For that matter, a proper married woman with an able-bodied husband ought not to work for pay at all.

It would be interesting to know Lovecraft's feelings while these women engaged in a tug-of-war over him. But in all his letters for this period, he is discreetly silent about these matters. Evidently, while at first inclined to go along with Sonia's proposals, he swung round and accepted—if only by remaining silent—his aunts' point of view. In New York, he had poured praise upon Sonia for her "marvellously magnanimous" attitude. He proclaimed that, after all she had done for him, he would never desert her:

> I hope she won't consider the move in too melancholy a light, or as anything to be criticised from the standpoint of loyalty and good taste.

> SH's attitude in all such matters is so kindly & magnanimous that any design of permanent isolation on my part would seem little short of barbaric, & wholly contrary to the principles of taste which impel one to recognise & revere a devotion of the most unselfish & uncommon intensity.[5]

He had, moreover, urged Sonia to come to Providence. Yet, when it came to the crunch, he did in effect give her the air. Loveman said: "Her treatment by HPL was, whether conscious or unconscious, cruel." One can see why Lovecraft did not discuss this episode.

Perhaps Lovecraft's yielding to his aunts was not simply infirmity of purpose but was the outcome of a wish on his own part. His remark of a year before, about living in Providence "if I ever get the money to live there as befits a member of my family," implies that he shared his aunts' feeling about the seemly way for a Phillips to dwell on that sacred soil.

Such a man would have either to support a wife or do without one. To be a kept man would dishonor the family name. Since Lovecraft could not support Sonia or even pay his share of their joint expenses, he quietly let his aunts shoo her away. Thus he evaded both the responsibilities of marriage and any feelings of guilt for not having met them.

On Lovecraft's side, his position was not easy. This was long before Women's Lib. The popular feeling, that the man of a family must make all, or at least most, of the family's earned income was much stronger then than now.

Lovecraft had never pretended to be other than he was. Sonia had taken the initiative in their courtship, although he had tried to warn her of what she was getting into. And, if the episode left him looking hardly heroic, his stature would not have become greater if he had gone on letting Sonia support him.

Five years later, Lovecraft wrote to Derleth: "My one venture into matrimony ended in the divorce-court for reasons 98 per cent financial." This estimate ignores other weighty factors, such as his topomania (his fantastic attachment to a particular place), his xenophobia, and his sexual repression. Still, it is just possible that these other obstacles might have been overcome if Lovecraft had been able to make a decent living. In the last year of his life, he wrote a more balanced account:

> I am very much in favour of a harmonious wedded state, but mistook superficial for basic congeniality. Small similarities did not, as expected, grow greater; nor did small differences, as expected, grow less. Instead, the reverse process occurred in both cases— aided no doubt by the financial insecurity which is ever the foe of domestic adjustment. Aspirations and environmental preferences diverged increasingly, until at length—albeit without real blame or even bitterness on either side—the Superior Court of Providence County was permitted to exercise its corrective and divorcive functions, and the Old Gentleman was reënthroned in dour celibate dignity.[6]

Sonia set forth her side of the debacle in an article written after Lovecraft's death for a Providence newspaper:

I believe he loved me as much as it was possible for a temperament like his to love. He'd never mention the word, "love." He would say, "My dear, you don't know how much I appreciate you." I tried to understand him and was grateful for any crumbs from his lips that fell my way. . . . I saw in Howard a Socratic wisdom and genius. I had hoped in time to humanize him further, to lift him out of his abysmal depths of loneliness and psychic complexes by the true, wedded love. I am afraid my optimism and excessive self-assurance misled us both. (His love of the weird and mysterious, I believe, was born of sheer loneliness.)

I had hoped in other words, that my embrace would make of him not only a great genius but also a lover and husband. While the genius developed and broke through the chrysalis, the lover and husband receded into the background until they were apparitions that finally vanished.[7]

Poor strenuous, generous, managerial, loving Sonia! The moral would seem to be: girls, don't marry a man with the idea of "making a man of him" or otherwise drastically changing his nature. It won't work. Take him as he is or not at all.

Once settled in Providence, Lovecraft went back to his old routine. He ate sparingly, stayed up most of the night, and slept most mornings. He spent his time reading, writing, and walking. And, except for his later travels, that is essentially how he spent the rest of his life.

He said: "If I could get plenty of good revision to do, I'd never write another tale for these cheap commercial caterers. It ruins one's style to have a publick of tame-souled half-wits hanging over one's head as one writes." He assumed that his style was something rare and precious, which would be "ruined" by adaptation to commercial requirements. Actually, his style leaves much to be desired. Heavily influenced by Poe, much of it is of the kind that is nowadays viewed as turgid, verbose, and overwritten, with many sentences of Teutonic length. In later years he improved it somewhat.

Lovecraft passed some of his revision orders on to Clifford Eddy, who had been acting as Houdini's booking agent. Houdini had taken the place of David Bush as Lovecraft's most demanding and best-paying ghosting client. When Houdini played in Providence, early in October, 1926, he invited Lovecraft and the Eddys to his show and afterwards took them to supper with his wife Beatrice.

Houdini paid Lovecraft $75 for an article exposing the fallacies of astrology. He wanted Lovecraft to write another for him on witchcraft and to come to Detroit to collaborate. Dreading another exile, Lovecraft put Houdini off. The next he heard, Houdini had been stricken with his terminal illness.

One of Lovecraft's new correspondents was a burly, blond youth of Sauk City, Wisconsin: August William Derleth (1909–71). A freshman at the University of Wisconsin, Derleth was of German extraction and, he said, ultimately descended from an emigré French nobleman, the Comte d'Erlette. Having literary ambitions, he wrote Lovecraft in July of 1926. Thenceforth, the two kept up a weekly correspondence for the next decade.

Other correspondents told Lovecraft that the Kalem Club had held a meeting to honor their departed member. Lovecraft was flattered that they missed him, but he modestly disclaimed their praise:

> The truth is, that I am really most emphatically non-intellectual, if not almost positively anti-intellectual. I abhor mathematics, take no interest in feats of mental sprightliness, have no especial quickness of apprehension, and am certainly not at all distinguisht for holding in my head the many simultaneous threads of a complex matter. . . . It is true that I admire and respect intellect tremendously, but not true that I possess it.

He wrote that "New York was a nightmare" and that "America has lost New York to the mongrels, but the sun shines just as brightly over Providence and Portsmouth and Salem and Marble-head—I have lost 1924 and 1925, but the dawn of vernal 1926 is just as lovely as I view it from Rhodinsular windows!"[8]

On long walks, he found that he did not know Providence so well as he had supposed. He discovered that it had "the most hellish slums ever imagined by mankind," inhabited by "slug-like beings . . . which crawl about and wheeze in the acrid smoke which pours from passing trains. . . . or from secret nether altars."[9]

He explored Mount Pleasant, Davis Park, and Federal Hill, "and was astonished by the great Italian churches." The Benedict Monument to Music in Roger Williams Park moved him to ecstasy:

> All visible objects—the hushed and tenantless greensward, the piercing blue of sky and water, the gleaming and half-erubescent whiteness of the towering temple itself—combin'd with the back-ground of trans-lacustrine forest and the warmth and magick of

mid-spring to create an atmosphere of induplicable fascination, and even of a kind of pagan *holiness*.[10]

Despite his vow never again to quit Rhode Island, September found him back in New York, staying at Kirk's apartment. He attended a meeting of the revived Kalem Club and had a brief visit with Sonia, in town from Cleveland. Despite his protests, she insisted on treating him to the fare to Philadelphia for another antiquarian trip.

In October, he and Annie Gamwell made a bus tour of the ancestral areas of western Rhode Island: the Fosters and Moosup Valley. They looked up ancestral houses and distant relatives:

> The only flaw in the picture is a recent social-ethnic one—for FINNS, eternally confound 'em, have bought the old Job Place's house! This Finnish plague has afflicted North Foster for a decade, but has hardly secured a real foothold in Moosup Valley, only two families marring the otherwise solid colonialism. They are seldom seen or heard—but it does make me crawl to think of those bovine peasants in the house where my great-uncle's wife was born—and tramping about the antient Place graveyard![11]

That fact that Finns, while speaking a non-Indo-European language, were largely Nordic in racial type did not spare them. A letter that Lovecraft wrote to Long in August, in fact, contains one of his most egregious outbursts against ethnics, in a tirade to which Hitler could hardly have taken exception:

> And of course the New York Mongoloid problem is beyond calm mention. The city is befouled and accursed—I come away from it with a sense of having been tainted by contact, and long for some solvent of oblivion to wash it out! . . . How in Heaven's name sensitive and self-respecting white men can continue to live in the stew of Asiatic filth which the region has become—with marks and reminders of the locust-plague on every hand—is absolutely beyond me. . . . There is here a grave and mighty problem beside which the negro problem is a jest—for in this case we have to deal not with childlike half-gorillas, but with yellow, soulless enemies whos repulsive carcasses house dangerous mental machines warped culturelessly in the single direction of material gain at any cost. I hope the end *will* be warfare—but not till such time as our own minds are fully freed of the humanitarian hindrances of the Syrian superstition imposed upon us by Constantinus. . . .
> . . . in New England we have our own local curses . . . in the form of simian *Portuguese*, unspeakable *Southern Italians*, and jabbering *French-Canadians*. Broadly speaking, our curse is *Latin*

just as yours is *Semitic-Mongoloid*, the Mississippian's *African*, the Pittsburgher's *Slavonic*, the Arizonian's *Mexican*, and the Californian's *Chino-Japanese*.[12]

At least, Lovecraft was impartial towards non-Anglo-Saxons. He hated them all. I may note that to accuse a foreigner of "jabbering"—one of Lovecraft's favorite pejoratives—is merely a way of saying that the accuser does not understand his tongue. Ignorance of a foreign language, while pardonable, is hardly a legitimate subject for pride.

Lovecraft now talked less of the superiority of the Nordic over other Caucasoid stocks and more about the incompatibility of cultural patterns. He clung to his ethnic phobias, when most American intellectuals were giving them up, rather like Cotton Mather in his old age, grumbling that nobody seemed to take witchcraft seriously any more.

Lovecraft told Clark Ashton Smith that he had not read James Branch Cabell's *The Silver Stallion*, adding:

Irony *used* to interest me when I was younger & more impressed by the hollowness of the things it castigates. . . . I infinitely prefer Dunsany to Cabell—he has a genuine magic & freshness which the weary sophisticate seems to lack.

Even Dunsany, he thought, "doesn't write the stuff now that he wrote twenty years ago." Of Dunsany's stories, he preferred the earliest: those in *The Gods of Pegāna* (1905) and seven more volumes that appeared up to 1919. Lovecraft's basic objection to Dunsany's later work was that Dunsany had become addicted to humor. Although by no means devoid of humor in letters and conversation, Lovecraft deprecated it in fiction. He thought it spoiled whatever uncanny effect a story might have, and the weird effect was what Lovecraft most prized.

The stories that Lovecraft admired most were those that gave him a *frisson* by their effect of weirdness. This effect, he maintained, was best produced by "a strong impression of the suspension of natural laws & of the presence of unseen worlds or forces close at hand." He no longer much enjoyed H. G. Wells's science fiction, because his "fantasy is too calculated & scientific, & an undercurrent of social satire impairs their convincingness."

Among Poe's works, he did not rate "The Pit and the Pendulum," highly because its horrors were "too patently physical."[13] He considered "The Fall of the House of Usher" the best of Poe's works.

He was not unfamiliar with modern realistic fiction; in fact, he called Theodore Dreiser "a great artist" despite the clumsiness of his prose. But the things that Dreiser wrote about did not interest Lovecraft. Neither could he get absorbed in "the sentimentality of Dickens, the heroic bombast of Dumas, or the mawkishness of Victor Hugo." Real fantasy like that of Dunsany and Clark Ashton Smith, he said, "has a truth & dignity & a major place in aesthetics which . . . sentimental terrestrial romance does not."[14]

Lovecraft's favorite story by Machen was *The Hill of Dreams* (1907). This short novel tells of an English country boy, the son of a minister. The hero, who has poetical leanings, goes to the city, struggles and struggles, becomes a drug addict, goes mad, and kills himself. The story is one of a type, popular in the nineteenth and early twentieth centuries, about the hypersensitive artist hated and persecuted by the Philistines of a cruel, crass world. *The Hill of Dreams* contains autobiographical elements; although Machen himself, while he had a struggle, lived to a ripe old age.

The part that Lovecraft especially liked was a dream sequence, wherein Machen's protagonist imagines himself back in Roman Britain. Lovecraft loved atmosphere, even when much prettified as in this case, and *The Hill of Dreams* is drenched in atmosphere. But it is not for those who like something to happen in their fiction. To Lovecraft, however, action fiction belonged to a literary "underworld."[15]

Lovecraft acknowledged one other master fantasist: Walter de la Mare, whose novel *The Return* (1911) appealed to him. This tells of a man whom the spirit of a long-dead French sorcerer tries to possess. But the spirit succeeds only in part; it remolds the man's appearance to resemble that of the sorcerer but fails to possess his mind. So the man awakens to find that he has another man's face, to the understandable dismay of his wife.

Lovecraft felt that his own work was deteriorating:

> My *technique*, I think, is better than it was when I was young; but one always suspects that despite the *mechanical* improvement there may be a parallel slackening of the tension & vitality of one's work as one slips out of intense & wondering youth into stolid & cynical middle age.[16]

In response to a column titled "Why I Like Providence" in the *Providence Sunday Journal*, Lovecraft wrote a long letter to that paper, pleading for the preservation of Colonial buildings, the rehabilitation of old structures, and the banning of skyscrapers:

> These remarks are impelled by the tidal wave of building replacement in which our city is just now immersed; . . . No one, it is true, can be sorry to witness or anticipate the end of such Victorian pests as Butler Exchange, Infantry Hall and the unspeakable Superior Court House; but when a well-balanced Georgian structure like the old Butler mansion next the Arcade is removed, it would seem to be time to inquire whether the change be a real civic necessity or a mere expression of crude, restless commercial adventurism. . . .
>
> Treasures like these are too precious to lose without a struggle, and deserve all the efforts and finance which can be brought to their aid against the encroachments of boom-town "Babbitry." Any mushroom oil centre can have bright lights, skyscrapers and apartment blocks, but only a well-loved seat of centuries of pure taste and gracious living can have the urn-topped, ivied walls, the gabled and steepled vistas, the unexpected twists of cobbled court and alley, and all the manifold touches of elder landscape which mean Providence to those real natives who have grown up in it and cherish its every mood and aspect, summer and winter, sun and rain.[17]

When Lovecraft wrote, Victorian architecture and furnishings were considered the very nadir of taste; "Victorian monstrosity" was a cliché. Since then, Victorian buildings have risen in public esteem. Outstanding examples are being preserved. In time, perhaps, Victorian relics will come to be deemed as precious as Colonial relics were in Lovecraft's day. But Lovecraft never took an objective view of these tides of taste. Because the eighteenth century was *his* century, its works were, by definition, forever superior.

In May, Henneberger proposed that he try to sell a collection of Lovecraft's stories. This was the first of a number of such proposals, but none ever bore fruit.

In the 1920s, small, specialist, semi-professional publishers of science-fiction books did not exist, nor did paperbacks. Paperbacked "dime novels" had been popular with juvenile readers in America before the First World War but had gone out of use in the United States. The Second World War, with its shortages of paper and shipping space, revived paperbacks.

In Lovecraft's time, the only book market was offered by publishers of cloth-bound books. Then and now, such publishers usually consider short-story collections only by established writers. To publish such a collection by an unknown writer means a probable loss of money. An obscure writer who does a good novel can usually sell it, but he can only rarely sell a short-story collection.

During the summer of 1926, Lovecraft embarked upon one of his greatest spurts of fictional production. The period from September, 1926, to July, 1927, saw the writing of six stories, including some of his major works.

In September and October he wrote "The Call of Cthulhu," which he had outlined before leaving New York. A 12,000-word novelette, the story marked an advance in Lovecraft's fiction.

In earlier tales, Lovecraft had brought in elements that later formed part of the so-called Cthulhu Mythos. The term denotes the fictional background of about a dozen of his stories built around a single fictional setting and set of assumptions.

The Cthulhu Mythos stories do not form a consistent whole, because Lovecraft never worked out his assumptions in detail. Each story is an independent unit, sharing elements with other stories but not completely consistent with them.

In "Nyarlathotep" (written 1920), Lovecraft first introduced Nyarlathotep himself. In "The Nameless City" (1921) he brought in Abdul Alhazred and his cryptic couplet. In "The Hound" (1922) he mentioned Abdul's *chef d'oeuvre*, the accursed *Necronomicon*. In "The Festival" (1922) he placed on stage the *Necronomicon* (along with other occult books, real and imaginary) and let his narrator quote some of its Nietzschean prose. "The Festival" also introduces the imaginary New England towns of Kingsport and Arkham, fictional doublets of Marblehead and Salem respectively, and Arkham's Miskatonic University.

Lovecraft's stories use the Cthulhu Mythos concepts in varying degrees. Sometimes they are central to the story; sometimes they are barely mentioned. There is, therefore, disagreement as to which stories ought to be classed with the Mythos. (The name "Cthulhu Mythos" was never used by Lovecraft but was invented after his death. He sometimes spoke playfully of these stories as his "Cthulhuism or Yog-Sothothery.")

"The Call of Cthulhu" is a main story of the group. It was the first to make full use of the basic concept that Lovecraft, according to Derleth, once described thus:

> All my stories, unconnected as they may be, are based on the fundamental lore or legend that this world was inhabited at one time by another race who, in practicing black magic, lost their foothold and were expelled, yet live on outside, ever ready to take possession of this earth again.[18]

The stories assume that a race of supernatural—or at least super-human—powers, the Great Old Ones or Ancient Ones, once ruled the earth. In some stories, they are transcendental beings of quasi-divine powers; in others, they are visitors or invaders from another planet. In some cases, they have been paralyzed by impersonal cosmic forces; in others, they have been defeated, restrained, or banished in struggles with other extraterrestrial beings. The Ancient Ones, however, strive to resume their earthly dominion. Rash mortals tamper with the restraints upon the Great Old Ones, who thereupon begin terrifyingly to manifest themselves. Sometimes the Old Ones are vulnerable to magical spells, sometimes to more material weapons, and sometimes to nothing that mortal men can use against them.

Like most of Lovecraft's tales, "The Call of Cthulhu" is told in the first person. It begins:

> The most merciful thing in the world, I think, is the inability of the human mind to correlate all its contents. We live on a placid island of ignorance in the midst of black seas of infinity, and it was not meant that we should voyage far. The sciences, each straining in its own direction, have hitherto harmed us little; but some day the piecing together of dissociated knowledge will open up such terrifying vistas of reality, and of our frightful position therein, that we shall either go mad from the revelation or flee from the deadly light into the peace and safety of a new dark age.

After more talk of "strange survivals" from "forbidden eons," the story proper gets under way:

> My knowledge of the thing began in the winter of 1926–27 with the death of my granduncle, George Gammell Angell, Professor Emeritus of Semitic languages in Brown University, Providence, Rhode Island.[19]

The great-uncle with the good old Rhode Island name dies suddenly at ninety-two after being "jostled by a nautical-looking negro" in the streets of Providence. As Angell's heir and executor, the narrator examines his effects. Among them is a slab of baked clay, the size of a small book, bearing unknown writing and a bas-relief of a grotesque figure. While roughly humanoid, the figure has a scaly body, long claws, wings, and a head with a face of tentacles like those of an octopus.

Two years before, a nervous young artist named Wilcox had given the professor this object, based upon things he had seen in his dreams. He told Angell of dreams "of great Cyclopean cities of Titan blocks and sky-flung monoliths, all dripping with green ooze and sinister with latent horror." In these dreams, Wilcox heard a voice speaking in an unknown tongue, of which he could make out only the words "*Cthulhu fhtagn.*"

Lovecraft explained these jumbles of letters by saying that they were an attempt to present sounds of non-human vocal organs, which could not be accurately spelled. He said that "Cthulhu" could be equally well represented as "Khlûl-hloo" (*û* as in "full") or "tluh-luh."[20]

In 1908, a police inspector from New Orleans, John R. Legrasse, brought to an anthropological conference a statuette of a similar squid-headed monstrosity, resembling an image used by a degenerate Eskimo cult. Legrasse had broken up a meeting of a similar cult, practicing human sacrifice. A captured cultist named Castro explained:

> There had been eons when other Things ruled on the earth, and They had had great stone cities. Remains of Them . . . were still to be found as Cyclopean stones on islands in the Pacific. They all died vast epochs of time before man came, but there were arts which could revive Them when the stars had come round again to the right positions in the cycle of eternity. They had, indeed, come from the stars, and brought Their images with Them.
>
> These Great Old Ones, Castro continued, were not composed altogether of flesh and blood. They had shape—for did not this star-fashioned image prove it?—but that shape was not made of matter. When the stars were right, They could plunge from world to world through the sky; but when the stars were wrong, They could not live. But although They no longer lived, They would never really die. They all lay in stone houses in Their great city of R'lyeh, preserved by the spells of mighty Cthulhu for the glorious resurrection when the stars and the earth might once more be ready for Them.

Since They needed outside help for reanimation, They spoke telepathically to susceptible human beings and organized a cult to perform the proper rituals when the time came.

The final piece of the puzzle is the newspaper story of finding a ship with one living sailor on board. The living sailor, Johansen, was the only survivor of a party that had landed upon an unknown island raised from the sea.

The narrator goes to Norway to look up Johansen but finds that he has just died. Johansen has left a memoir, which his widow gives to the narrator. On the island, the party was attacked by Cthulhu himself, a colossal, gelatinous being. Johansen escaped. The narrator is sure that Angell and Johansen died because they "knew too much," and he fears the same fate.

"The Call of Cthulhu" is an excellent story of its kind, mostly told in straightforward, reportorial prose. Furthermore, Lovecraft for the first time assembled his concepts into a coherent whole.

On the first submission—as was his wont with startlingly new ideas—Farnsworth Wright rejected "The Call of Cthulhu." The following summer, however, he asked to see it again. Lovecraft sent it in with two other stories and one of his defeatist letters. He berated conventional interplanetary stories like Burroughs's tales of John Carter (which he had loved as a youth), with its stalwart human hero in love with a beautiful extraterrestrial princess:

> If I were writing an "interplanetary" tale it would deal with beings organised very differently from mundane mammalia, and obeying motives wholly alien to anything we know upon Earth—the exact degree of alienage depending, of course, on the scene of the tale; whether laid in the solar system, or the *utterly unplumbed* gulfs still farther out. . . . I have merely got at the edge of this in *Cthulhu*, where I have been careful to avoid terrestrialism in the few linguistic and nomenclatural specimens from Outside which I present. All very well—but will the readers stand for it? That's all they're likely to get from me in the future—except when I deal with definitely terrestrial scenes—and I am the last one to urge the acceptance of material of doubtful value to the magazine's particular purpose.

Despite Lovecraft's negative salesmanship, Wright bought the story for $165. It appeared in *Weird Tales* for February, 1928.

According to a list that Lovecraft included in a later letter, the tale that followed "The Call of Cthulhu" was "Cool Air" (3,500 words). This trifle is straight horror with a little science fiction, in patent imitation of Poe's "The Facts in the Case of M. Valdemar."

The narrator tells how, living in a boarding house in New York, he comes to know a fellow-boarder, Doctor Muñoz. This elderly Spanish physician lives in a room kept cold by a refrigerating machine. In time the machine breaks down. Muñoz dies and at once disintegrates into what Poe, in his similar story, called "a nearly liquid mass of loathsome—of detestable putrescence." Muñoz has really been dead for eighteen years but has been kept going by advanced medical techniques and by the cold.

On a visit to Boston, Lovecraft had seen a section of very old houses at the North End. He heard of tunnels connecting their cellars, presumably for the use of smugglers in Colonial times, and this tale provided the germ of "Pickman's Model," of 5,000 words.

"Pickman's Model" is more a conventional *Weird Tales* story than most of Lovecraft's work. The narrator tells his friend Eliot about the eccentric Bostonian artist, Richard Upton Pickman. His experience with Pickman has left him a nervous wreck, unable to enter the Boston subway. Now Pickman has disappeared.

The artist, says the narrator, set up his studio in a cellar under one of the old North End houses. There he painted horrible pictures of feasting ghouls. A particularly ghastly one has a photograph tacked to it, showing the monstrous subject of the painting. It causes the narrator (like so many Lovecraftian heroes) to scream and flee: ". . . by God, Eliot, *it was a photograph from life.*"[21]

The story stands in the middle rank of Lovecraft's tales, or a little below, because it telegraphs its punch too early. On a subsequent visit to Boston, Lovecraft was dismayed to find that the ancient houses on which he had based his story had all been demolished in a real-estate development.

Later in 1926, Lovecraft wrote two more short stories: "The Silver Key" and "The Strange High House in the Mist." "The Silver Key" (5,000 words) is another story set in Lovecraft's Dunsanian dream-world; or rather, it is the story of Randolph Carter when he can no longer go thither in dreams:

> When Randolph Carter was thirty he lost the key of the gate of dreams. Prior to that time he had made up for the prosiness of life by nightly excursions to strange and ancient cities beyond space, and lovely, unbelievable garden lands across ethereal seas; but as middle age hardened upon him he felt those liberties slipping away

little by little, until at last he was cut off altogether. No more could his galleys sail up the river Oukranos past the gilded spires of Thran, or his elephant caravans tramp through perfumed jungles in Kled, where forgotten palaces with veined ivory columns sleep lovely and unbroken under the moon.

It was typical of Lovecraft to define middle age as starting at thirty. Carter's friends try to convince him of the importance of the real world:

> So Carter tried to do as others did, and pretended that the common events and emotions of earthly minds were more important than the fantasies of rare and delicate souls.[22]

Brooding on "how shallow, fickle, and meaningless all human aspirations are," Carter tries religion, science, occultism, travel, and writing, to no avail. He finds only "pain, ugliness, and disproportion . . . poverty and barrenness." Lovecraft goes on for pages about how Carter suffers from "the hollowness and futility of real things."

At last Carter remembers an heirloom in the form of a large silver key. He goes back to a boyhood haunt near Arkham and by means of a key becomes a boy again and disappears from the real world. The narrator thinks that Carter has used the key to get back into his dream-world:

> I shall ask him when I see him, for I expect to meet him shortly in a certain dream-city we both used to haunt. It is rumored in Ulthar, beyond the River Skai, that a new king reigns on the throne of Ilek-Vad, that fabulous town atop the hollow cliffs of glass overlooking the twilight sea wherein the bearded and finny Gnorri build their singular labyrinths. . . .

As in most of Lovecraft's later stories, the writing is highly skilled. But Randolph Carter is Lovecraft's alter ego, and the author has indulged in an orgy of self-pitying narcissism. He fancies that his possession of a "rare and delicate soul" entitles him to a life of perpetual esthetic rapture, beyond the needs of common clods.

Lovecraft once castigated his early fantasy "The White Ship" as "utterly mawkish and namby-pamby." It seems to me that this criticism belongs more justly to "The Silver Key," which many readers of *Weird Tales* disliked.

"The Strange High House in the Mist" (3,800 words) is laid in Kingsport, the scene of "The Terrible Old Man." Lovecraft got the idea of the cliffs in the story from his visit with Sonia to Magnolia. On one of these crags, overlooking the sea, is a cottage, impossible to reach from the seaward side unless one can fly. The only door of this house is on the seaward side, and that wall of the house is flush with the face of the cliff.

A philosopher, Thomas Olney, spends a summer at Kingsport "with stout wife and romping children." Curious about the strange house, Olney worms his way through the woods behind it and knocks on its windows. A black-bearded man in antique costume helps him over the window sill and receives him hospitably. The man tells Olney tales of Atlantis, the Other Gods, and similar wonders.

There is a peculiar knock on the door overlooking the sea. In come Neptune, with a train of tritons and nereids, and "the gray and awful form of primal Nodens, Lord of the Great Abyss."[23] This is an Elder God alluded to elsewhere in the Cthulhu Mythos. Nodens helps Olney into the huge shell in which he rides and takes him off for a spin. Olney returns home the next day but has left a part of his soul in the strange high house, so that he is never quite the same again. This charming little fable overlaps both the Dunsanian and the Cthulhuvian series.

Both tales were sent to Wright with the second submission of "The Call of Cthulhu," but Wright rejected both. As before, he later had second thoughts and bought both. For "The Strange High House in the Mist" he paid $55.

In November, 1926, Lovecraft began a dream-fantasy in his Dunsanian style. He wrote Derleth:

> Many tales I have destroyed as below even my most charitable standard, & I'm not sure but that this fate awaits the long fantasy I am concocting at this moment.

As he got further into the story, he became gloomier about it:

> It remains to be seen how successful this bizarrerie can be when extended to novel length. I am now on page 72 of my dreamland fantasy, & am very fearful that Randolph Carter's adventures may have reached the point of palling on the reader; or that the very plethora of weird imagery may have destroyed the power of any one image to produce the desired impression of strangeness. . . . It will probably make about 100 pages—a small book—in all & has small likelihood of ever seeing the light of day in print.[24]

His pen raced, and he finished the story about the end of January, 1927. At 38,000 words "The Dream-Quest of Unknown Kadath" was the longest thing he had written.

Lovecraft thought that it "isn't much good; but forms useful practice for later and more authentic attempts in the novel form." Frank Long would have to come to Providence to see it, because "the typing of manuscripts of this length is utterly beyond the powers of a feeble old gentleman who loses interest in a tale the moment he completes it."[25]

Lovecraft never did type this novella. Fortunately, his amateurish attitude towards his writings did not deprive us of this remarkable, if flawed, narrative. After Lovecraft's death, Barlow turned over the manuscript to Derleth, who published it.

The story as we have it is a rough draft, never revised. There is no telling whether Wright would have bought it for *Weird Tales*. If, however, Lovecraft had lived until the appearance of the magazine *Unknown* in 1939, "The Dream-Quest of Unknown Kadath" would, with polishing, seem to have been a natural for it.

The story recounts the adventures of Randolph Carter, Lovecraft's scholarly Bostonian bachelor, in the dreamland of his early Dunsanian stories. This dreamland exists in another dimension, more or less coextensive with the waking world. The tale begins:

> Three times Randolph Carter dreamed of the marvellous city, and three times he was snatched away while still he paused on the high terrace above it. All golden and lovely it blazed in the sunset, with walls, temples, colonnades and arched bridges of veined marble, silver-basined fountains of prismatic spray in broad squares and perfumed gardens, and wide streets marching between delicate trees and blossom-laden urns and ivory statues in gleaming rows; while on the steep northward slopes climbed tiers of red roofs and old peaked gables harbouring little lanes of grassy cobbles. . . .
>
> When for the third time he awakened with those flights still undescended and those hushed sunsets still untraversed, he prayed long and earnestly to the hidden gods of dream that brood capricious above the clouds on unknown Kadath, in the cold waste where no man treads. But the gods made no answer and shewed no relenting, nor did they give any favouring sign when he prayed to them in dream, and invoked them sacrificially through the bearded priests of Nasht and Kaman-Thah, whose cavern-temple with its pillar of flame lies not far from the gates of the waking world. . . .
>
> At length, sick with longing for those glittering sunset streets and cryptical hill lanes among ancient tiled roofs. . . . Carter re-

solved to go with bold entreaty whither no man had gone before, and dare the icy deserts through the dark to where unknown Kadath, veiled in cloud and crowned with unimagined stars, holds secret and nocturnal the onyx castle of the Great Ones.

In light slumber he descended the seventy steps to the cavern of flame and talked of this design to the bearded priests of Nasht and Kaman-Thah. And the priests shook their pshent-bearing heads and vowed it would be a death of his soul. . . . There were, in such voyages, incalculable local dangers; as well as that shocking final peril which gibbers unmentionably outside the ordered universe, where no dreams reach; that last amorphous blight of nethermost confusion which blasphemes and bubbles at the centre of all infinity—the boundless daemon sultan Azathoth, whose name no lips dare speak aloud, and who gnaws hungrily in inconceivable, unlighted chambers beyond time amidst the muffled, maddening beating of vile drums and the thin, monotonous whine of accursed flutes; to which detestable pounding and piping dance slowly, awkwardly, and absurdly the gigantic Ultimate Gods, the blind, voiceless, tenebrous, mindless, Other Gods whose soul and messenger is the crawling chaos Nyarlathotep.[26]

Undismayed by the warnings of the priests, Carter "boldly descended the seven hundred steps to the Gate of Deeper Slumber and set out through the Enchanted Wood." There he takes counsel with his old friends the small, furry zoogs. He goes on to Ulthar and consults the old priest Atal, who accompanied Barzai the Wise on the latter's ill-fated ascent of Hatheg-Kla. When neither Atal nor the Pnakotic manuscripts nor the Seven Cryptical Books of Hsan tell him how to get to unknown Kadath, he gets Atal drunk and is directed to Mount Ngranek on the southern isle of Oriab. (If the accompanying map is not completely consistent with the stories, neither are the stories consistent with one another.)

Carter has many more adventures, with night-gaunts, moon monsters, dholes, ghouls, gugs, and ghasts. (Names like "zoogs" and "gugs" give the story a juvenile flavor; Lovecraft might have changed them on revision.)

Carter climbs Mount Ngranek and penetrates the inaccessible plateau of Leng—which, it seems, is not part of the waking world as it was in "The Hound," but a dreamland version of Tibet. At last Carter arrives before Nyarlathotep himself, in his castle atop unknown Kadath. Nyarlathotep tells him:

"For know you, that your gold and marble city of wonder is only the sum of what you have seen and loved in youth. It is the

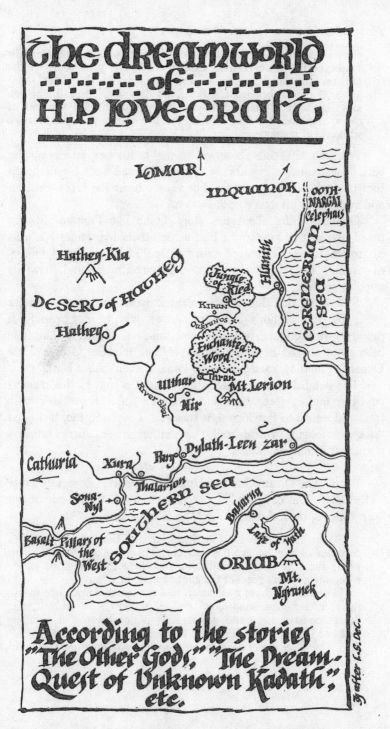

Map of H. P. Lovecraft's dream-world (by Jack Gaughan).

glory of Boston's hillside roofs and western windows aflame with sunset; of the flower-fragrant Common and the great dome on the hill and the tangle of gables and chimneys in the violet valley where the many-bridged Charles flows drowsily. These things you saw, Randolph Carter, when your nurse first wheeled you out in the springtime, and they will be the last things you will ever see with eyes of memory and love."

Nyarlathotep sends Carter on his way to his magical city on the back of a shantak, a gigantic, scaly, horse-headed bird. Nyarlathotep tries to double-cross the seeker, but Carter turns the tables on him and awakens in his own proper Boston.

Opinions differ about this story. Some like Professor St. Armand regard it as Lovecraft's best work; others like James Blish, as his worst. Lovecraft himself called it "pallid, second-hand Dunsanianism."[27] The story lacks plot and characterization and shows its unpolished state.

Still, I find that this eerie, surrealistic dream-narrative carries me along by the author's sheer power of invention. Lovecraft is prodigal with original, colorful, and amusing concepts. This tale belongs to a class of dream-narratives that includes George MacDonald's *Phantastes* and *Lilith* and Lewis Carroll's *Alice* books.

The parallel between Randolph Carter's search for his magical city and finding it to be his own Boston, and Lovecraft's exile from and return to Providence, is touching. Lovecraft, too, had been "sick with longing" for his native city, although some may find such sentiment incomprehensible.

After "The Dream-Quest of Unknown Kadath," Lovecraft wrote "The Colour Out of Space," a 12,000-word novelette and one of the best stories of the Cthulhu group. The tale begins:

> West of Arkham the hills rise wild, and there are valleys with deep woods that no axe has ever cut. There are dark narrow glens where the trees slope fantastically, and there thin brooklets trickle without ever having caught the glint of sunlight. . . .
> The old folk have gone away, and foreigners do not like to live there. French-Canadians have tried it, Italians have tried it, and the Poles have come and departed. It is not because of anything that can be seen or handled, but because of something that is imagined. The place is not good for imagination, and does not bring restful dreams at night. . . .[28]

The narrator explains that this section contains a "blasted heath," a slowly expanding circular sterile area. With the help of one of the few remaining old-timers, he ferrets out the story.

In 1882, a meteorite fell in the center of the area. It was a most peculiar meteorite, made of a leathery substance, which baffled the laboratories of Miskatonic University, and which shrank and disappeared.

Then mysterious ills beset all life in the neighborhood. Plants and animals became deformed and died. Members of the nearest farm family one by one went mad and died. The extraterrestrial visitor that came with the meteorite, it transpires, is a gaseous being of an unearthly color. . . .

The story is told in a straightforward, flat narrative style without purple patches. But the reader can easily imagine himself in one of those hilly areas of southeastern New England, where all but a few of the farms have been given up and the country has gone back to second growth.

In 1904, a young inventor named Hugo Gernsback arrived in New York City. Born in Luxemburg and educated in Germany, he set up an Electro Importing Company and four years later brought out a magazine called *Modern Electrics*. This was the first of a series of magazines published by Gernsback, such as *The Electrical Experimenter* and *Science and Invention*. In some of these magazines, Gernsback ran science-fiction stories, written either by himself or by imaginative writers of the time.

Gernsback believed that science fiction should interest and ground young people in science. To him, science-fiction stories ought to prophesy devices that might some day really come into use. Gernsback invented the word "television" long before the apparatus of that name became a reality.

In 1926, Gernsback started the first magazine exclusively devoted to science fiction: *Amazing Stories*. Two years later, Gernsback failed, lost control of *Amazing*, but was soon back with another magazine, *Wonder Stories*. A few years later, he lost control of that, too.

During these years, like many publishers operating on a shoestring, Gernsback was liberal with promises to contributors but often neglected to pay them what he had promised. Fletcher Pratt, who worked for Gernsback on *Wonder,* used to translate European science-fiction novels to run as serials. When several instalments of such a novel had been published, Pratt would coerce Gernsback into paying him what he owed by threatening not to complete the translation.

Doubting that Farnsworth Wright would like "The Colour Out of Space," Lovecraft sent it to *Amazing Stories.* In June, 1927, he learned that it had been accepted. The story duly appeared in the September issue.

Getting paid for it, however, presented a problem. After Lovecraft wrote many dunning letters, the magazine sent him a check for $25 the following May. This was fifth of a cent a word—a ridiculous price.

Thereafter, Lovecraft referred to Gernsback as "Hugo the rat." He generally refused to send any more stories to magazines other than *Weird Tales,* although some paid better, because, he said, he deemed them too "commercial." Probably he had been soured by his experience with Gernsback.

During 1927, Lovecraft spoke of other stories that he meant to write. One was a book-length novel laid in a "more naturalistic setting, in which some hideous threads of witchcraft trail down the centuries against the sombre & memory-haunted background of ancient Salem." In April he wrote:

> Just now I'm making a very careful study of *London* by means of maps, books, & pictures, in order to get background for tales involving richer antiquities than America can furnish. . . . a minute following of the town's historic growth from a thatched Celtic village on piles. . . . What I write will probably begin in Roman times. . . .[29]

On the night of October 31st, Lovecraft had a dream of ancient Rome. He had been reading a translation of *The Aeneid,* and this combined with Hallowe'en produced the following dream:

> It was a flaming sunset or late afternoon in the tiny provincial town of Pompelo, at the foot of the Pyrenees in Hispania Citerior. The year must have been in the late republic, for the province was still ruled by a senatorial proconsul instead of a praetorial legate of the Augustus, and the day was the first before the Kalends of November. The hills rose scarlet and gold to the north of the little

plain, and the westering sun shone ruddily and mystically on the crude new stone and plaster buildings of the dusty forum and the wooden walls of the circus some distance to the east. Groups of citizens—broad-browed Roman colonists and coarse-haired Romanized natives, together with the obvious hybrids of the two strains, alike clad in cheap woollen togas—and sprinklings of helmeted legionaries and coarse-mantled, black-bearded tribesmen of the circumambient Vascones—all thronged the few paved streets and forum; moved by some vague and ill-defined uneasiness. I myself had just alighted from a litter, which the Illyrian bearers seemed to have brought in haste from Calagurris, across the Iberus to the southward. It appeared that I was a provincial quaestor named L. Caelius Rufus, and that I had been summoned by the proconsul, P. Scribonius Libo, who had come from Tarrago some days before. The soldiers were the fifth cohort of the XIIth Legion, under the military tribune Sex. Asellius. . . .

The conference concerns the Very Old Folk of the hills, "little yellow, squint-eyed" people[30] who yearly kidnap some of the locals for use in their sinister ceremonies. This year none of the villagers has vanished, giving rise to the belief that the Very Old Folk are up to something particularly hellish.

After much debate, Scribonius Libo dispatches the cohort, with the narrator, to break up the impending Sabbat. There are sinister drum beats in the hills. The lights go out, the air gets cold, colossal leaping forms appear, the legionaries go mad with terror. . . .

For over a year, Lovecraft toyed with the idea of making a story out of this dream. At last, in February, 1929, he told Frank Long that Long was welcome to use the dream, since Lovecraft had lost interest in the idea.

So Long wrote a novella, "The Horror from the Hills." He placed Lovecraft's dream in a modern frame and brought in a fourth-dimensional entity, Chaugnar Faugn, as one of the Great Old Ones responsible both for the destruction of the Roman cohort and for dire doings in the modern world. Long did a competent job, but one cannot help regretting that Lovecraft did not carry out his original plan.

In 1927, Lovecraft was encouraged to learn that "The Horror at Red Hook" would be reprinted in an anthology, *Not at Night!* He edited and wrote a preface to a book of mediocre verse, *White Fire,* by a fellow-amateur, John Ravenor Bullen. The work was a "nightmare," but an admirer of Bullen paid for it.

Cook at last brought out *The Recluse,* with Lovecraft's treatise on "Supernatural Horror in Literature." Lovecraft thought of expanding the work to book length, as his pen pal Robert E. Howard urged, but never did so.

Farnsworth Wright talked of publishing a collection of Lovecraft's stories. In 1927, however, Wright published a book containing a short novel of oriental occult menace, *The Moon Terror* by A. G. Bird, padded out with short stories by Wright and others. He had a terrible time selling the whole printing and was still advertising *The Moon Terror* years later. The poor performance of *The Moon Terror* killed the plan for a Lovecraft collection.

Lovecraft's ghosting kept him busy. He acquired two new clients, one of whom was a former dentist, journalist, and United States consul named Adolphe de Castro. De Castro (born Danziger) had been a collaborator of Ambrose Bierce and had been trading on the fact ever since Bierce's disappearance in Mexico in 1913. (There is, however, a story that at their last meeting, Bierce speeded de Castro's departure by breaking a walking stick over his head.) De Castro was described as a genial fellow of some charm and erudition, but a bit of a faker. It is probably not a coincidence that the garrulous captive cultist in "The Call of Cthulhu" is named Castro.

The other client was Mrs. Zealia B. Reed, an attractive widow in her early thirties, supporting herself and her son in the Midwest by journalism and story-writing. Samuel Loveman put her in touch with Lovecraft. Both de Castro and Mrs. Reed gave Lovecraft plenty of work, but both proved hard to collect from.

When Lovecraft's criticisms of Mrs. Reed's modest literary talents discouraged her, he wrote long, chatty letters to cheer her up. He told her of his fantastic, scientific, and poetical phases; ". . . now, at thirty-seven, I am gradually headed for pure antiquarianism and architecture, and away from literature altogether!"

Pseudonyms, he said, were a matter of taste. One could become jealous of one's own pseudonym, which one had to stick to once it became established:

> My only general objection to pseudonyms is that they tend to imply a sort of self-consciousness or self-dramatisation on the user's part, which is somewhat foreign to the process of impersonal, disinter-

ested artistic creation. They imply that the user stands off and thinks of himself as an author, instead of being so wrapped up in his aesthetic vision that he never regards himself as a person at all.[31]

From a man who in his youth had used a dozen pseudonyms, this is significant advice.

Lovecraft also urged upon Mrs. Reed his own anti-commercial, art-for-art's-sake view of literature. Nobody, he said, could write anything "worth while" or having any "depth" from commercial motives. The only valid motive for writing

> . . . is a kind of heightened vision which lends strange colours to the universe, and which invests the pageant of life with a mystic glamour and veiled significance so poignant and potent that no eye may behold it without a resistless wish to capture and preserve its essence; to hold it for future hours, and to share it with those who can be made to see it with kindred perspective.

One should be able to get such a feeling from the sight of "roofs and spires, groves and gardens, fields and terraces, shaven lawns and the rippling of lillied meres." In other words, if one reacts emotionally as Lovecraft did to pretty scenery, and if one wants to write as Poe, Dunsany, and Machen did, well and good; if not, forget it.

To a genius who could overcome all obstacles, or to one who had an independent income, this might have been good advice. To a young woman of modest talents, trying to make a living by her typewriter, it was terrible advice. Lovecraft was always telling Zealia "to write *literature* as opposed to the wearisome pap and patent bourgeois-fodder, of the best-selling popular novelists,"[32] when in fact such talent as she had was for turning out "bourgeois-fodder."

Lovecraft's friends got similar counsel. He said that he wrote "for my own edification exclusively, since it improves & crystallises my dreams to get them down on paper." "An author really ought to be financially independent," he said, adding: "I have more respect for the honest plumber or truck-driver who writes to please himself in his spare time, than for a literary hack who extinguishes his own personality in a servile acquiescence to the puerile & artificial demands of an ignorant herd." Derleth should "forget the fashion altogether & write what is in him." The enthusiasm for sex in fiction during the 1920s was "a transient phase of cultural decadence."[33] (Lovecraft should have lived to the 70s!)

Lovecraft's remarks on literature reflect on his judgment of other human affairs. He had an enormously high intelligence; but, because of his reclusive, bookish personality and his peculiar up-bringing, his maturation in emotion and judgment was much re-tarded.

The childish, immature, or naïve mind tends to divide phenom-ena into a few classes, to draw hard-and-fast distinctions among these classes, and to pass sweeping, extreme judgments upon the members of each class. As one matures, one comes to see that classes are human artifacts, useful but not to be taken too seriously, and that—especially among human beings—members of any class show infinite diversity and must be judged on their individual merits.

As Lovecraft classified men into simple groups by nations, races, and cultures and exaggerated the distinctions among them, so he divided fiction into a small class of "real literature" that "has any depth" and a much larger class of "popular trash" and "hack work." He assumed that a few connoisseurs like himself appreciated the first class, while the second appealed only to the "ignorant herd." He theorized that "real literature" was produced only by a few geniuses who, like Dunsany, did not have to sell their copy for a living.

This was an immature view of fiction. Writing comes in many forms, aimed at different readerships. There is no reason to set aside one small fraction of the total as "real, worth-while literature" and dismiss all the rest as "popular trash."

Moreover, no one person's judgment settles the value of a composition. "Great literature" is not necessarily what you or I or Lovecraft enjoy, but what so many have enjoyed over the centuries that the work is still popular long after it was written. Even then, one cannot be sure. Shakespeare went through an eclipse in the late seventeenth century, and a survey taken then would have eliminated him as a major writer.

If his ideas of great literature left Lovecraft open to criticism, he also had sensible things to say on the subject. Art, he told Mrs. Reed, "is at bottom *a treatment* of life rather than life itself," and therefore "we cannot justly take factual reality as an absolute criterion of fictional availability. . . . What fiction demands is a fragment of reality typical and universal enough to arouse myriad associations in the reader and suggest the hovering nearness of things even outside and above reality. . . ." Real people are too impossibly complex and contradictory to present in full in fiction; ". . . it is the writer's business to untangle all these complexities, divine the element of drama (almost always based on *conflict*) in them, and set forth this bit of cosmic symmetry in perfect language."[34]

The "all for love" plot, he added, is silly, because in real life other factors are more important. Marriage and children, he noted, do not solve problems; they create them, and a good story would take the struggle with these problems into account.

Lovecraft was in a position to know.

Fourteen

RECUSANT SPOUSE

There is in certain ancient things a trace
Of some dim essence—more than form or weight;
A tenuous aether, indeterminate,
Yet linked with all the laws of time and space.
A faint, veiled sign of continuities
That outward eyes can never quite descry;
Of locked dimensions harbouring years gone by,
And out of reach except for hidden keys.[1]

LOVECRAFT

In his post-New York phase, Lovecraft was anything but a hermit or recluse. The friends he had made in New York saw to that. All summer and fall of 1927, his friends kept dropping in. On June 7th, he took James Ferdinand Morton to

> . . . the Violet Hill, Manton Ave. quarry, on the land of the Providence Crushed Stone & Sand Co. Well, said Co. is a dago named Mariano de Magistris, on whose land I've had a pathetic drop-in-the-bucket mortgage for the past twenty years! Every Feb. & Aug. the guy sends in a small cheque, but never pays up—so I've come to regard him as something of an institution, and feel a very proprietary interest in his rocky freehold. . . . I'd stand a good chance of losing my modest thou. if I ever had to foreclose.[2]

In mid-July, Donald Wandrei came and was whirled away on tours of Newport, Salem, and other scenic spots. Lovecraft showed Wandrei one of his favorite spots to sit and write: Quinsnicket Park, north of Providence.

Quinsnicket Park included a hill and a small lake with an overhanging ledge. Lovecraft liked to sit on the ledge, overlooking the lake in its dell. Later, Quinsnicket Park was incorporated into the much larger Lincoln Woods State Park.

While Wandrei was in Providence, Morton and the Long family appeared. Doctor Long drove them all on a tour to Newport in his new Essex but suffered acute boredom during the literary-antiquarian discussions. At length Lovecraft found him an electrical-appliance shop, where he could listen to the Dempsey-Sharkey fight on the radio.

Next day, when the Longs had left, Lovecraft, Morton, and Wandrei went to de Magistris's quarry for more mineral specimens:

> . . . we were received with ceremonious hospitality by the Dago owner. The good old Roman set all his men to hunting specimens, and his sportily Americanised son took us all home in his snappy new roadster—to say nothing of chugging back and fetching the geologist's hammer which Mortonius forgot. That's what I call real Latin courtesy![3]

What's this? Lovecraft (despite his use of "Dago") praising an Italian, when for years Italians had been jostling Poles for second place on his ethnic hate list, right behind the Jews! De Magistris, though just an ordinary Italo-American small contractor, turned out to be a decent, obliging human being. So Lovecraft perforce made some small adjustment in his attitudes.

Lovecraft still ranted against New York for its "stinking, amorphous hybridism" and "the mongrel & misshapen foreign colossus that gibbers and howls vulgarly and dreamlessly on its site."[4] Nonetheless, while the sharp boundary that he drew around his in-group never dissolved away, he began, little by little, to push this boundary outward, admitting one ethnos after another within its circuit.

While Wandrei and Morton were still in Providence, W. Paul Cook and H. Warner Munn, the latter a young aspirant writer, arrived on July 12th in the latter's car. Lovecraft engaged his visitors in one of his more curious entertainments: sitting until 2:30 A.M.

on tombstones in the cemetery of the Episcopal Cathedral of St. John.

At the end of July, Lovecraft set out on one of the tours that thenceforward formed his major recreation. He visited Cook in Athol, Massachusetts,

> . . . & was taken by him on some glorious side-trips to scenic & historic regions. . . . At West Brattleboro we called on the poet Arthur Goodenough, who is a quaint, old-fashioned farmer living obscurely among his ancestral hills.[5]

Lovecraft reached Goodenough's house in a reserved mood. Nine years before, Goodenough had published, in Charles W. Smith's *Tryout*, a poetic eulogy called *Lovecraft—an Appreciation*. The fourth stanza read:

> *Who would deny thee bays? I make no doubt*
> *That laurels from thy very temples sprout;*
> *The printed page that makes us weep—or laugh*
> *Conveys more meaning than a photograph!*

The grotesque metaphor of Lovecraft's temples sprouting herbage led Lovecraft to suspect that Goodenough was making fun of him. Acquaintance soon convinced Lovecraft that Goodenough had meant his praise. As they left, he told Cook: "Why, the man is genuine!"

Cook replied: "Howard, you are yourself genuine, although different from Arthur."[6]

Traveling by bus and stopping at YMCAs, Lovecraft continued on to Portland, Maine, where he visited Longfellow's houses; to the White Mountains, where he enjoyed a cogwheel railroad ride up Mount Washington; to Portsmouth and Newburyport; to Haverhill, where he saw Charles W. Smith; to Gloucester, Salem, Marblehead, and home to struggle with a stack of revision orders.

His visits were not over. In October, Wilfred Talman arrived from New York. Talman took Lovecraft to the library and gave him a preliminary course in heraldry.

Lovecraft was inspired to do a little genealogical research of his own. He was delighted to find a collateral ancestor, a silversmith named Samuel Casey, who in Colonial times had been condemned to be hanged for counterfeiting. Casey was sprung from jail by an armed mob of friends and fled the country. Lovecraft never took genealogy so seriously as one might have expected. Tongue in cheek, he wrote Long:

> No—I haven't found any Jews yet, though you'll surely hear of 'em if I do. After admiting all these Celts I'm willing to admit anything north of the Sahara. Did I mention the Egyptian priest Ra-ankh-Khamses, who voyaged to the Cassiterides on a Phoenician ship in the time of Psammeticus and was cast on the green shores of Quernas near the site of modern Queenstown? It is known to every schoolboy that he wed Cathlin, daughter of Fian the Bold, and if it is true that their son Fian the Terrible was the ancestor of the Ui Nialls, then of course I am an Ægyptian of the old priestly line! Then, of course, there is the Cro-Magnon Glwkhlghx, whose triumphs over the Little People on the plains of Dordogne are frescoed in a thousand caves. . . .[7]

Lovecraft read Spengler's *Decline of the West* and concluded that the "Aryan race" was nearing decadence, mainly because of the sentimental preservation of the "unfit." He urged birth control for all, to keep the morons from outbreeding the "better classes," who would practice it anyway, and to "save the fundamental biological quality of the race!"[8] This idea, common at the time, had a germ of truth but also premature, oversimplified ideas of the workings of heredity.

He was enthusiastic about E. R. Eddison's great fantasy novel, *The Worm Ouroboros*. This tale is one of the foremost examples of the sub-genre sometimes called "heroic fantasy" or "swordplay-and-sorcery fiction." It may have appealed to Lovecraft because its heroes are swaggering, larger-than-life versions of English country gentlemen, with no inhibitions about kicking the common clods out of their way, or killing them if they get above themselves.

He also read some of Marcel Proust's novels and admired the minute (to some, even tedious) detail by which Proust built up his atmosphere.

In the late 1920s, the trend of Lovecraft's thought continued towards a more genial, tolerant, broad-minded view, with fewer of his previous prickly prejudices. He admitted that there was something to be said for times other than his beloved eighteenth century:

> If I could create an ideal world, it would be an England with the fire of the Elizabethans, the correct taste of the Georgians, and the refinement and pure ideals of the Victorians.

He lost faith in Prohibition, writing Derleth:

> I'm beginning to doubt its value myself, though I was originally an
> enthusiastic advocate of it. If anything could totally get rid of
> liquor, it would be a good thing—but the question is whether the
> present attempt has produced any results comparable to the harm in-
> flicted.

August Derleth went about Sauk City in a bathrobe and
screwed a monocle into his eye. He said he did this to lend atmosphere to the stories he was writing about a British detective, Solar
Pons, modeled on Sherlock Holmes, but the likelier motive was to
shock the staid Midwestern burghers of Sauk City.

Lovecraft gently chided his young friend, recalling his own
youthful affectations, and predicted that Derleth would soon tire of
these antics. This was quaint advice from one of the world's leading
poseurs, but Lovecraft had already shed many of his affectations.

He amiably argued religion with Derleth, commenting on Derleth's parental faith:

> It seems to me—an atheist of Protestant ancestry—that Catholicism
> is really an admirable faith for those artists whose taste is wholly
> Gothic and mystical without any mixture of the classic or the in-
> tellectual.[9]

Derleth also took seriously the alleged phenomena of occultism,
Spiritualism, and extrasensory perception; he was hospitable to
tales of hauntings and premonitions. For years, Lovecraft pointed
out weaknesses and fallacies in Derleth's arguments for supernatural
phenomena.

In November, 1927, Lovecraft began a major work, "The Case
of Charles Dexter Ward." This fantasy tells of the magical revival of
persons long dead and the sorcerous evocation of beings from Outside which, if successful, may have dire world-wide effects. Like
Randolph Carter, Charles Dexter Ward is another fictional doublet
of Lovecraft himself.

Laid in Providence, the story is saturated with local color and
history:

> His home was a great Georgian mansion atop the well-nigh pre-
> cipitous hill that rises just east of the river, and from the rear win-
> dows of its rambling wings he could look dizzily out over the
> clustered spires, domes, roofs and skyscraper summits of the lower

town to the purple hills of the countryside beyond. Here he was born, and from the lovely classic porch of the double-bayed brick façade his nurse had first wheeled him in his carriage. . . .

This describes the Halsey mansion at 140 Prospect Street, built in 1801. At one period, when this house had stood empty for a time, it was reputed to be haunted by a piano-playing ghost and to have an inexpungible bloodstain on the floor.

Charles Ward is a very Lovecraftian character. "When he was larger his famous walks began; first with his impatiently dragged nurse and then alone in dreamy meditation." In adolescence, Charles is "tall, slim, and bland, with studious eyes and a slight stoop, dressed somewhat carelessly, and giving a dominant impression of harmless awkwardness rather than of attractiveness."[10]

Ward becomes an antiquarian, so devoted to his studies that he forgoes college rather than curtail them. He is especially interested in his ancestor Joseph Curwen, who came to Providence in 1692 and had the enviable ability to stay the same age for fifty years at a stretch.

Curwen, it transpires, was a dabbler in alchemy and the black arts. After he had, for decades, terrified his neighbors by strange sights and sounds from an isolated farmhouse, a posse was formed in 1770 to root him out.

Ward discovers the old Curwen house, on Stamper's Hill not far from his home. There he finds a portrait of Joseph Curwen, which closely resembles Charles Dexter Ward, and a cache of Curwen's papers.

To the alarm of his parents, Ward undertakes occult researches and himself changes, looking and sounding more and more like Curwen.

He buys the old Curwen farmhouse in Pawtuxet and moves his occult apparatus thither. Fearing for their son's sanity, the elder Wards call in a physician, Dr. Marinus Willett, who investigates Ward and his two curious confederates.

Graves are robbed. Willett learns that the gang have methods of re-creating and revivifying dead persons, if they have only a few of the "essential salts" of the corpse to start with. The senior Ward and Willett go to the farmhouse in young Ward's absence and to their horror . . .

The story is less central to the Cthulhu Mythos than "The Call

of Cthulhu," since the only certain connection is the mention of
the entity Yog-Sothoth in the spells. In later stories, Yog-Sothoth is
a Great Old One. The plotting of "Charles Dexter Ward" is looser
than in some of Lovecraft's best stories.

At 48,000 words, "The Case of Charles Dexter Ward" was the
longest story that Lovecraft ever composed. On December 1st, he
wrote Derleth that he was about to start typing it.

In fact, he never typed the story at all. After he had sworn not
to do any more ghosting for de Castro, December found him ghosting
for de Castro. When he finished that job in January, 1928, Mrs. Reed
asked him to revise "The Curse of Yig."

Meanwhile, Donald Wandrei had offered to type "The Case of
Charles Dexter Ward." Lovecraft agreed, but Wandrei found the
manuscript so crowded with changes as to be almost indecipherable.
The resulting typescript was so full of errors that it required a new
draft.

Lovecraft put the manuscript aside and never did address himself to the task. In 1940, after Lovecraft's death, Derleth and Wandrei
had a manuscript professionally typed from the original. In 1941,
an abridged version of the story appeared in two installments in
Weird Tales. Derleth and Wandrei then printed the whole story in
their second volume of Lovecraftiana, *Beyond the Wall of Sleep*
(1943).

The incredible thing is that, when Lovecraft sounded out
publishers about a collection of his shorter stories and found them
uninterested, some said they would like to see a book-length novel.
He had "The Case of Charles Dexter Ward" in his files all the time
but did nothing with it.

In 1927, Lovecraft learned of a new fantasy magazine, *Tales of
Magic and Mystery*. He sent in several manuscripts, of which the
magazine accepted "Cool Air." The story was printed in the issue
of March, 1928; but this, the fourth issue, proved the next to the
last. Lovecraft was probably never paid.

Visiting relatives in Oklahoma, Zealia Reed heard a horror story
about snakes from her sister's mother-in-law. Back in Kansas City, she
turned this idea into a story, "The Curse of Yig," and sent an outline or sketch to Lovecraft for criticism. He wrote the story, which
appeared under Zealia's by-line in *Weird Tales* for November, 1929.

Zealia got $165, of which she paid Lovecraft $15.50. Except for the local color, which Zealia furnished, the story was practically all by Lovecraft.

"The Curse of Yig" tells of a pioneer couple, Walker and Audrey Davis, who come to Oklahoma to homestead. The woman comes upon a mass of baby rattlesnakes and kills them. Alarmed, Davis tells her that now they will fall under the curse of Yig, the Indians' snake god. Davis gets his wife so worked up with his talk of Yig's vengeance that, in the dark, she mistakes him for the snake god. . . .

The winter months of 1928 saw Lovecraft swamped with revision. Although he spoke of de Castro as "an unctuous old hypocrite, whose story ruined my winter," he nevertheless revised the story in question, "The Last Test." De Castro also urged upon Lovecraft the revision of his reminiscences of Ambrose Bierce. Lovecraft read the manuscript, found it much padded, and resolved not to undertake the task unless paid in advance. De Castro then prevailed upon Frank Long to edit the manuscript and to write an introduction to it.

For a year after Lovecraft's return to Providence, Sonia worked in New York for less than she could have had elsewhere, to be near her husband. In mid-1927, she got an offer from Chicago that was too good to refuse. After half a year, disliking Chicago, she gave up that position. In December she appeared in Providence for a winter vacation. She and Lovecraft went on an antiquarian walk in Providence, but Lovecraft almost collapsed from the cold. Sonia had to help him home and revive him by rubbing his extremities.

Planning to start another millinery shop, she pressed Lovecraft to come to New York in spring for the opening. In April, 1928, Lovecraft went—not, it would seem, eagerly, for he wrote: "I may be obliged to go to New York next week." Sonia had taken an apartment at 395 East Sixteenth Street in Brooklyn and recovered what was left of her furniture. Her new shop was around the block from her apartment. Lovecraft praised the excellent taste she had shown in the shop and in the apartment. He helped her with the announcements and advertisements.

The shop opened on April 28th, and Lovecraft's visit stretched on into June. It was, however, not the usual conjugal reunion. As Sonia described it:

> That spring I invited Howard to visit me and he gladly accepted, as a visitor only. To me, even his nearness was better than nothing. The visit lasted throughout the summer but I saw him only during the early morning hours when he would return from jaunts with Morton, Loveman, Long, Kleiner, some or all of them.[11]

In plain language, Lovecraft refused to resume marital relations even when sexual intercourse would have been perfectly legal and moral. We can only guess at the reasons: his anti-sexual tabu, sexual inadequacy, fear of sexual inadequacy, or fear of being trapped in New York again.

This was hard on Sonia, a normal, full-blooded woman. While she was too moral for adultery, platonic marriage was not her style at all. If she thought her husband had come "gladly," his letters imply otherwise. A few days of trying to work in New York, he said, had brought him

> ... to the verge of what would be a complete breakdown if I did not have a staunch and brilliant colleague—my young "adopted grandchild" Frank B. Long—on whom to lean for coöperation and assistance in getting my tasks into shape. . . .

> Nothing but strong domestic pressure could ever have induced me to waste a spring in this accursed metropolitan pest-zone. . . . this time my wife really thought it only right for me to transfer a little of the domestic background to her present scene of action. Impartially reflecting, I could not help conceding the essential justice of the opinion; hence decided that the least I could do would be to conquer my anti-metropolitan repugnance for a season and avoid that depressing household inharmony which forms the theme of so many works of fiction!

In other words, a sojourn in New York was better than a family row. In Lovecraft's view, being married was fine if one did not have to live with one's mate. Sex was a sordid business, which irrepressible animal instincts might force upon young people but which ought not to interest middle-aged couples like the Lovecrafts. Ten days later, Lovecraft wrote in the same general vein but more cheerfully:

> The wife had to camp out here for quite a spell on account of business, and thought it only fair that I drop around for a while. Not having any snappy comeback, and wishing to avoid any domestick

civil war, I played the pacifist. . . . and here I am. The g. d. burg looks about the same to me—no novelty or kick to it. I can stand it better now that I have a real home back in the States.[12]

He complained that all big cities bored him after a while, but he certainly kept busy during this sojourn. He and Sonia went on long antiquarian walks. When not with Sonia, Lovecraft commuted between her apartment and that of the Longs, who drove him to West Point and to Lake Mahopac.

Lovecraft and Long formed a partnership for ghosting, which continued for three or four years. They ran advertisements in *Weird Tales* and the *New York Times,* which brought in about fifteen clients, half of them would-be poets. Lovecraft got one substantial manuscript from a would-be author, but it proved so hopeless that he sent it back unrevised rather than accept money from a dub who could never make it.

The Kalem Club had more or less dissolved, lacking the magnetism of Lovecraft's presence to draw the members together. A few old-timers, however, were rounded up for several meetings.

Lovecraft planned a southern trip. With widening horizons, his desires expanded: "If I can ever get hold of any real cash, I shall certainly obtain a modest Ford. . . ." "I'd relish seeing Oxford myself—as an antiquarian—to say nothing of the rest of Old England. I vow I'll get to London some day, if my next move has to be to the poor house." Aware that to realize these ambitions would cost money, he said he would even write for the confessions magazines if he could earn the thousand dollars per sin of which he had heard.[13]

On June 16, 1928, Lovecraft borrowed a suitcase from Sonia and set out on a round of travels. First, Vrest Orton drove him to his family's home in Vermont for the weekend. Lovecraft was delighted with the archaism of the country life:

> The trip has been a marvelous pleasure & mental stimulation, for it has brought me magically close to those basic & surviving wellsprings of early-American life which we in cities, & in southern New England generally, are accustomed to regard as extinct. Here life has gone on in the same way since before the Revolution—the same landscape, buildings, families, occupations, & modes of thought & speech.[14]

If Lovecraft had ever worked as a chore boy on a farm, he might have been less romantically nostalgic about that life. Walter

J. Coates, publisher of the amateur magazine *Driftwind*, came from North Montpelier to Orton's house to meet Lovecraft. Cook dropped in with page proofs of Lovecraft's "The Shunned House," which he planned to publish as a book.

On the 18th, Lovecraft caught buses to Athol, Massachusetts, where he stayed with Cook. On the 29th, he went to North Wilbraham, Massachusetts, where he had an invitation from the veteran amateur journalist, Edith Dowe Miniter. Mrs. Miniter lived with her cousin, Evanore Beebe. The latter was a stout squiress of seventy, who drove about in a buggy and controlled local politics. She was "fit to be tied" when Lovecraft shoveled sugar into his coffee, leaving an undissolved mass in the bottom. Lovecraft was delighted to find such antiquities as lard-burning lamps and cat ladders, placed inside chimneys to enable cats to get from one floor to the other. He also had his first glimpse of a wild deer.

These journeys cost Lovecraft little outside of bus fares, because his hosts insisted on giving him bed, board, and entertainment. His friends later thought that this trip was one of the happiest times of his life.

After a week at North Wilbraham, Lovecraft wandered around Massachusetts by bus and trolley car and went to Albany, New York. Thence he took a Hudson River boat to New York, where he exchanged suitcases with Sonia.

Failing to get Lovecraft to accept his husbandly rôle, Sonia had sublet her apartment to an elderly couple and taken a single room elsewhere. Lovecraft therefore had to stay at a hotel. Since resumption of life with Lovecraft was plainly not in the cards, Sonia did not need four spacious rooms.

July 11th found Lovecraft in Philadelphia again, whence he traveled on to Baltimore, Annapolis, and Washington. He took a train to the Shenandoah Valley, where he visited the Endless Caverns:

> For over an hour I was led spellbound through illimitable gulfs and chasms of elfin beauty and daemonic mystery—here and there lighted with wondrous effect by concealed lamps, and in other places displaying awesome grottoes and abysses of unconquered night; black bottomless shafts and galleries where hidden winds and waters course eternally out of this world and all possible worlds of mankind, down, down to the sunless secrets of the gnomes and night-gaunts, and the worlds where web-winged monsters and fabulous gargoyles reign in undisputed horror. . . .[15]

Back in Providence, Lovecraft buckled down to "The Dunwich Horror," a 17,500-word novelette based upon a tale he had heard a month before while staying at Miss Beebe's house in Massachusetts. This story combined a New England background with the fully developed Cthulhu Mythos. It begins:

> When a traveller in north central Massachusetts takes the wrong fork at the junction of the Aylesbury pike just beyond Dean's Corners he comes upon a lonely and curious country. The ground gets higher, and the brier-bordered stone walls press closer and closer against the ruts of the dusty, curving road.[16]

The story tells of the decadent Yankees of Dunwich and of the singular Whateley family. This consists of old Wizard Whateley, who owns a battered copy of the *Necronomicon*; his daughter Lavinia, a deformed albino woman; and her son by an unknown father, Wilbur, who reaches a man's size and maturity at the age of ten. All the Whateleys have repulsive, chinless faces.

Twice a year, on Hallowe'en and May Day, the Whateleys repair to a stone circle in the hills—a kind of mini-Stonehenge, attributed to the Indians—to perform nameless rites. Mysterious thunderlike noises are heard from the hilltop at such times, and on one such occasion Lavinia was impregnated.

Lovecraft used two New England phenomena. His "stone circle" is derived from several crude stone structures found in New England. Archaeologists generally credit them to early colonists or to the Amerinds, although many local antiquaries prefer to speculate about Druids, Norsemen, or other exotic visitors.

The most impressive of these structures is Mystery Hill, near North Salem, at the southern end of New Hampshire. On this site once stood a whole village, made of slabs of stone piled up in dry walls or formed into the walls and roofs of half-buried huts. A huge slab with a rectangular groove in its upper surface is called the "sacrificial table." Lovecraft is not known to have visited any of these megalithic sites; but he may have, and in any case he probably read about them.

The other phenomenon is the "Moodus noises," said to have been heard off and on for three centuries around the village of Moodus, in south-central Connecticut. These sounds, resembling explosions, are often attributed to some obscure seismic cause.

Wizard Whateley, the story tells, is converting his upper story into a kind of pen. His cattle keep vanishing, but he buys more with antique gold pieces.

Old Whateley dies, and his daughter Lavinia disappears. Now eight feet tall, Wilbur Whateley takes his *Necronomicon* to the library of Miskatonic University to compare it with the Latin version there. The librarian, the septuagenarian Dr. Henry Armitage, observes the passage—sounding like a piece out of Nietzsche—that Whateley is transcribing:

> Nor is it to be thought, that man is either the oldest or the last of earth's masters, or that the common bulk of life and substance walks alone. The Old Ones were, the Old Ones are, and the Old Ones shall be. Not in the spaces we know, but *between* them, They walk serene and primal, undimensioned and by us unseen. *Yog-Sothoth* knows the gate. *Yog-Sothoth* is the gate. *Yog-Sothoth* is the key and guardian of the gate. Past, present, future, all are one in *Yog-Sothoth*.

Months later, Whateley breaks into the library to steal the book but is attacked by the watchdog. When Armitage and two other professors reach the scene, the dog has torn the clothes off the mangled Whateley.

Below the waist, Whateley is covered with black fur. He has legs like a flesh-eating dinosaur, an eye on each hip, and a tail. A score of tentacles, with bloodsucking mouths, protrude from his belly. When he dies, he dissolves into a puddle of fetid slime. "When the medical examiner came, there was only a sticky whitish mass on the painted boards, and the monstrous odour had nearly disappeared."

Amateur Freudians have pointed to the sexual symbolisms of Lovecraft's "sticky whitish mass" and other themes: Whateley's anatomy, wherein "Below the waist . . . all human resemblance left off and sheer phantasy began"; the "long greenish-grey tentacles with red sucking mouths" that issue from the creature's abdomen; Lovecraft's use of caves and tunnels as symbols of fear; and his theme of degeneracy resulting from miscegenation.

These, they say, reflect Lovecraft's fear of sexual intercourse. One such critic says that these themes "are explorations of his own subconscious, which retains its tremendous power despite the faultiness of his style and construction and the seeming narrowness of his mind." One of Lovecraft's later correspondents, J. Vernon Shea, analyzed the problem. Lovecraft's

. . . writings were deeply influenced by Arthur Machen. Machen, the son of a clergyman, had an upbringing similar to Lovecraft's, and his writings are full of a repressed sexuality. His story, *The Novel of the White Powder*, in which the protagonist upon taking a drug is reduced to a loathsome white slime, has been interpreted as an adolescent's masturbation fantasy (Lovecraft achieved a similar effect in his *Cool Air*), and other stories like *The Great God Pan* and *The White People* hint at sexual orgies of which Machen dared not write. Machen finally sublimated his repressions by translating Casanova's *Memoirs*, but no such course was available to Howard. Although almost any other writer of fantasy would have had the followers of Cthulhu . . . participating in ineffably nasty orgiastic rites, the prim Howard foreswore any mention of sex. The reader has to use his imagination to intuit what upset Howard so terribly. Like Machen, like Hawthorne, H.P.L. could not bear to bring himself to deal directly with sexual problems in his stories. . . .

Curiously, Lovecraft seems never to have rebelled against his mother's standards of morality.

True, some Freudians carry symbolism to dubious extremes, finding sexual organs in anything elongated or hollow. But, in view of Lovecraft's history and attitudes, inferences like the foregoing are plausible.

On the other hand, Lovecraft had an imagination of exceptional power. It threw together all sorts of startling concepts, of which those with apparent sexual symbolism formed only a minor part. Lovecraft himself thought:

. . . it is amusing to speculate on what future psychologists would make of one's stories. No doubt they would find a deep significance in Klarkash-Ton's escapes from the terrestrial scene, in Two-Gun Bob's orgies of slaughter, & in my own intimations of cosmic outsideness & excursions to bygone centuries in crumbling & witch-haunted Arkham.[17]

While Wilbur Whateley is gasping out his life on the library floor at Miskatonic U, the thing in the upper story of the Whateley house has broken out and is ravaging the countryside. It stamps houses flat and devours cattle and people. Invisible, it has many legs, which leave footprints like those of a herd of elephants. Armitage obtains Whateley's diary, which tells of Whateley's occult education:

Today learned the Aklo for the Sabaoth, which did not like, it being answerable from the hill and not from the air. . . . The upstairs looks it will have the right cast. I can see it a little when I make the Voorish sign or blow the powder of Ibn Ghazi at it. . . .

The words "Aklo" and "Voorish" come from Machen's novel *The White People*, which speaks of the "Aklo letters" and "a wicked voorish dome."

Armitage and two intrepid fellow-professors track the monster to the hill with the stone circle. They make the creature visible by squirting the powder of ibn-Ghazi at it. . . .

"The Dunwich Horror" is one of Lovecraft's best stories, powerfully imaginative and suspenseful. Lovecraft's use of phonetic respelling to indicate dialect ("I vaow afur Gawd, I dun't know what he wants nor what he's a-tryin' to dew") is, however, excessive by modern standards. Nineteenth-century writers like Kipling did much of this, but contemporary writers are taught to use respelling very sparingly. One reason is that many modern readers have learned to read by sight-reading methods and hence are baffled by unfamiliar combinations of letters.

A few years ago, "The Dunwich Horror" was made into a motion picture with the same title. While not bad fun, the movie came nowhere near the original in force. Typically, Hollywood turned Wilbur Whateley into an ordinary young man and furnished him with a young lady to provide the obligatory fornication scene. Unexplained sequences and trick camera effects were piled one on another until even the most alert viewer must have been confused.

Wright bought "The Dunwich Horror" for $240, the largest literary check that Lovecraft had ever received. Yet, after Lovecraft finished this tale, he wrote no more original fiction for over a year and a half, in spite of the fact that he was enjoying some small signs of success. The British anthologist Christine Campbell Thompson chose three stories for anthologies appearing 1927–31 under the imprint of Selwyn & Blount, Ltd., of London. "The Horror at Red Hook" was published in *You'll Need a Nightlight*; "Pickman's Model" in *By Daylight Only*; and "The Rats in the Walls" in *Switch on the Light!* "The Call of Cthulhu" was reprinted in *Beware After Dark!* (1929), edited by T. Everett Harré for the Macauley Company.

For some of these appearances, Lovecraft received small sums: $15 in one case. In other cases, the money all went to *Weird Tales*, which had bought all rights. Belatedly, Lovecraft began to think about these matters: "It seems to me that Wright said something once about the 'rights' to my stories, but I was too poor & negligent a business man to pay much attention."

Lovecraft's friends encouraged him to try to market a collection of his stories. (An "anthology" contains stories by various writers; a "collection," stories by a single writer.) Derleth recommended Vanguard Press, which had published some of Derleth's work. Orton volunteered to try to sell the collection.

Lovecraft hesitated. Besides his plans for an anthology, Wright had spoken of publishing a collection of Lovecraft's tales. Therefore, said Lovecraft:

> I must, though, give Wright the first chance with the collection of tales. He continues to express a wish to handle it, & he has—despite all his limitations—been at all times so considerate & honourable in his dealings with me, that the least I can do is to give him the initial option. . . .[18]

One could always count on Lovecraft to act in a gentlemanly way. But nothing came of Wright's book-publishing plans.

Not even these events persuaded Lovecraft to write more stories for a long time. For one thing, his ghosting business was active if not always profitable. Since he could not say "No!" to an insistent client, he was always busy; he told Derleth: "Don't know when I'll get time for another tale." The shrinkage of his capital spurred him to keep trying harder; but, since he would not haggle with or dun his clients, they continued to take advantage of him. Hence, although he worked hard, he never quite made a living at his ghost-writing.

Despite his efforts to avoid working for de Castro, he let de Castro talk him into editing another short story: "The Electric Executioner," published in *Weird Tales* in 1930. An old lady in Washington, D.C., Elizabeth Tolridge, persuaded Lovecraft to revise her masses of mediocre verse. She became one of his incessant correspondents, sending him bales of clippings.

Despite his apparent success with "The Dunwich Horror" and the anthologies, Lovecraft was discouraged with his prospects. In verse, he conceded to Miss Tolridge that "my own poetic possibilities were wrecked" by excessive imitation of "Mr. Pope, Dr. Young, Mr. Thompson, Mr. Addison, Mr. Tickell, Mr. Parnell, Dr.

Goldsmith, Dr. Johnson, & so on. My verse lost every vestige of originality & sincerity, its only care being to reproduce the typical forms & sentiments of the Georgian scene amidst which it was supposed to be produced."

This imitativeness, he lamented, carried over into his prose: "There are my 'Poe' pieces & my 'Dunsany' pieces—but alas— where are my *Lovecraft* pieces? Only in some of my more realistic fictional prose do I shew any signs of developing, at this late date, a style of my own. . . ."

He sent Miss Tolridge samples of his own poetry, saying: "In all these verses you will note with ironic amusement that I freely use all the archaisms, inversions, & poeticisms against which I so constantly warn others! This is because I do not try at all to be a poet in any serious sense. My verse is simply antiquarianism & nothing more."[19]

That Lovecraft should, early in his career, have imitated Poe, Dunsany, and the Georgians is not surprising. Most writers start by imitating predecessors. Hence many contemporary writers have gone through a Hemingway period, or a Faulkner period, or even a Lovecraft period. If all goes well, in time they assimilate these influences; as Lovecraft advised his clients, they learn to "be themselves."

With Lovecraft, this process was greatly delayed. First, it was displaced by his ten lost years of sickly reclusiveness, so that he only began his serious writing at twenty-seven. Then it was further retarded by his Imp of the Perverse: his archaism, his affectations, and his snobbery.

The Imp blinded him to the advances in literary techniques since Poe's time. It led him to despise practical considerations as "bourgeois" and beneath a gentleman's notice. Now, late in the day, he began to realize how costly his earlier attitudes had been.

Moreover, as he came to a more realistic view of his writing, this very self-awareness made him conscious of his earlier imitativeness and stylistic extravagance. Hence he became more and more self-critical.

Of late I've been acquiring an increasing dissatisfaction with my products—especially the earlier ones—so that I'm almost glad Wright seems to have given up the book idea. There is a quality of cheap melodrama—extravagance, floridity, unrestraint—in my style, which needs ironing out, although it has decreased since my "Hypnos" & "Hound" period.

In later years, Lovecraft not only condemned his earlier tales but often said that he repudiated all but the latest. Lacking a successful writer's egotism, Lovecraft was easily cast down by adverse criticism. When he realized the faults of his own work, the knowledge crushed him.

As a result of the pressure of revision work and excessive self-criticism, Lovecraft's fictional output remained low for the rest of his life. After "The Dunwich Horror," he averaged only a little more than one story a year, not counting collaborations and revisions. To try to meet his readers' rising demands, Wright reprinted, without pay, many of Lovecraft's earlier tales and published many of his poems.

In some ways, Lovecraft developed. In politics, he was still a conservative nativist who supported Hoover against Al Smith. The latter, he thought, represented "the decadent & unassimilable hordes from Southern Europe & the East. . . ."[20]

He drew back further, however, from Prohibition. Hearing that Farnsworth Wright had drinking spells, he said that, considering what Wright must suffer, "I feel tempted to unearth a local bootlegger . . . & send Brother Farnsworth a case of synthetic brilliancy!"[21]

His esthetic views broadened. The stream-of-consciousness technique pioneered by James Joyce, he said, might strike the naïve as "senseless incoherence"; but there was something to be said for it. Extreme forms of it, he thought, "transcend the limits of real art," but "are destined to exert a strong influence upon art itself."[22]

Sonia complained that after Lovecraft's return to Providence: "Our marital life . . . was spent on reams of paper washed in rivers of ink." After the visit in the spring of 1928, "For the next several months we again lived in letters only." Lovecraft wrote almost daily.

He was perfectly willing and even satisfied to live this way, but not I. I began urging a legal separation, in fact, divorce. But during this period of time he tried every method he could devise to persuade me how much he appreciated me and that divorce would cause him great unhappiness; and that a gentleman does not divorce his wife unless he has cause, and that he had no cause for doing so. I told him I did everything I could think of to make our marriage a success, but that no marriage could ever be such, in letter-writing only; that a close propinquity was necessary for a true marriage. Then he would tell me of a very happy couple whom he knew, where the wife lived with her parents, in Virginia, while the husband lived elsewhere for reasons of illness, and that their marriage was kept intact through letters. My reply was that neither of us was really sick and that I did not wish to be a long-distance wife "enjoying" the company of a long-distance husband by letter-writing only.

In late 1928, Sonia paid Lovecraft another visit. She

> . . . told him that while I found it impossible to remain his wife any longer I wanted him to know that I would still be his friend if he cared for such friendship; that he ought to divorce me and find and marry a young woman of his own background and culture, live in Providence and try to live a normal life and be happy.
> "No, my dear, if you leave me I shall never marry again," he would reply. "You don't realize how much I appreciate you," he would assure me again and again. "But your way of demonstrating your affection is so unheard of!" I would reiterate again and again.[23]

At last Lovecraft yielded. On March 25, 1929, he went to a lawyer's office to sign a divorce agreement, with Eddy as a witness. Lovecraft applied for a divorce on grounds of desertion and obtained a preliminary decree. Actually, Lovecraft had deserted Sonia, who had to live where she could earn a living for both. But the law assumed that the man of the family was the wage-earner and therefore defined his residence as the family's legal domicile.

Lovecraft later explained that marriage was all right provided the couple had similar tastes, ambitions, ideas, emotions, and ideals, but it took at least two years of cohabitation to prove this identity. Therefore he approved Rhode Island's liberal divorce laws and Judge Ben Lindsey's idea of "companionate marriage." He thought that the chances of a happy marriage for "a strongly individualised, opinionated, and imaginative person" like himself "damn slender."

> And if he has the general temperament that usually goes with such a mental makeup, he will not be apt to consider a haughty celibacy any great price to pay for this ethereal inviolateness. Independence, and perfect seclusion from the futile herd, are things so necessary to a certain type of mind that all other issues become subordinate when brought into comparison with them. . . . And yet I didn't find matrimony such a bugbear as one might imagine. With a wife of the same temperament as my mother and aunts, I would probably have been able to reconstruct a type of domestic life not unlike that of Angell St. days, even though I would have had a

different status in the household hierarchy. But years brought out basic and essential diversities in reactions to the various landmarks of the time-stream, and antipodal ambitions and conceptions of value in planning a fixed joint milieu. . . . I could not exist except in a slow-moving and historically-grounded New England backwater —and the hapless sharer of the voyage found such a prospect, complicated as it was by economic stress, nothing short of asphyxiation! . . . A bird as old as that is past the age of weaving new kinds of nests, and had better not try it.

Evidently, the "wife" whom Lovecraft wanted was not a mate in the sexual sense but a surrogate mother, who would flutter round him, coddle him, and relieve him of all chores, errands, and responsibilities. In trying to put the best face on his own marital failure, Lovecraft understated Sonia's remarkable adaptability and ignored her generous offer to continue supporting him in Providence. He also exaggerated his chances of maintaining his "independence" and "seclusion" and of reviving a bygone style of life with any kind of wife whatever, when he could not even support himself.

Moreover, he assumed that most men of his mental type would not have minded celibacy. From all indications, few males in their thirties are so indifferent to sex as HPL professed to be.

For three years, Sonia held jobs in and around New York. She and Lovecraft occasionally corresponded. In 1932 she went to Europe. She wrote: "I was almost tempted to invite him along but I knew that since I was no longer his wife he would not have accepted." Probably so; but it is a pity that she did not at least extend the invitation. A trip to Europe was one of the keenest of Lovecraft's thwarted desires. She said:

However, I wrote him from England, Germany and France, sending him books, and pictures of every conceivable scene that I thought might interest him.

When I visited the Cheshire Cheese Restaurant in London I sent him a replica of the beer stein out of which Dr. Johnson drank, and other souvenirs including a picture card of the corner . . . in which the table and chairs stood that Dr. Johnson and his cronies and Boswell sat and drank and talked [at]. . . .

Upon my return to the U.S.A. I became quite ill. Upon recuperating I took a trip to beautiful Farmington, Conn. I was so enchanted with this beautiful Colonial built city that I wrote to

Howard at once to join me there which he did. . . . Yes, I believe I must have still loved Howard very much, more than I cared to admit even to myself. For, although in my travels I met many eligible men, some of them offering honest proposals of marriage, none appealed to me after a period of eight years, during which time I could not help but compare what to me appeared as the inadequacy of other men when compared in point of intellect, with Howard. . . . When Howard and I parted for the night, I said "Howard, won't you kiss me goodnight?" His reply was "No, it is better not to."

At that time I was doing some historical research work for the Brooklyn Children's Museum. Among several pieces I was delegated to do one called "Roger Williams Speaks out for Liberty before the New England Divines." Much of the research was done in the Fifth Ave. and Forty-Second St. Library in N.Y.C. But when I told HP what I had been doing along this line and would like more data, he graciously led me to the Hartford Library and at once got busy inquiring for original books and hauling down tomes for me from the shelves. . . . In parting for the night, I no longer asked for the kiss. I'd learned my lesson well.[24]

That was her last sight of Lovecraft. The museum work was a temporary job, to tide Sonia over between positions in millinery. In 1933, she went back to that business as a merchandise buyer. People who saw her then described her as much less glamorous than the gorgeous creature whom Lovecraft had married. In her fifties, she had put on weight, and she dressed and did her hair plainly.

At the end of 1933, Sonia took ship to California, where she decided to stay. Before leaving, she burned a trunkful of Lovecraft's letters.

During the next two years, she held several jobs in Los Angeles and San Francisco. In 1935, she was dating a California state senator when, at a lecture with him, she met a slender, erect, silver-haired man with courtly manners: Dr. Nathaniel Abraham Davis, a widower with grown children. He called upon her next day and, after some sparring, bluntly asked her:

"Are you gentile or Jew?"

Smiling, she replied: "What difference does it make to you?"

"Please tell me; it is important!"

"What are *you?* Gentile or Jew?"

"I am a Jew!"

"So am I," said Sonia.

Davis rose, clasped his hands together, and cried: "Thank God!"[25] He proposed on their next date, and they were married the following day.

Davis was a Brazilian Jew, sixty-eight years old, of Portuguese descent. He had led a wide-ranging career. Having uncles (the Uesci brothers) in the shipping business, he traveled on their ships and took a medical degree in Australia. He had practiced as an obstetrician in Melbourne before moving to California. Unable to afford to go through an internship to qualify as a physician in California, he became the dean of a small college.

Davis was religious; he got Sonia to serve kosher food, to attend the temple regularly, and to join Hadassah. He was also a poet, full of mysticism and idealism. He believed in reincarnation and Rosicrucianism and ran a one-man international peace organization, the Planetaryan.

Although Davis was, among other things, a professor of economics and foreign trade, he had little more sense about money than Lovecraft. He was always being lured into buying land and losing his investment. After he and Sonia were married, he gave his earnings to her and they managed better.

Davis's college closed down, and he had to hunt for a job. This was not easy for a man nearing seventy. He got one as a bookseller but was let go after a while on account of age. He got another post as a newspaper reporter for Hearst but lost this when the union refused, again on grounds of age, to admit him. Sonia went back to work to support them.

For seven years, Sonia lived with Davis in (she said) blissful happiness. Then Davis came down with cancer. He died in 1945 after a painful three-year siege.

Sonia continued to work, rejecting more proposals of marriage, until she, too, grew old. She retired to the Diana Lynn Lodge in Sunland, California, where she died, aged eighty-nine, on December 26, 1972. She had certainly led a full life.

Fifteen

FOOTLOOSE CONNOISSEUR

Eternal brood the shadows on this ground,
Dreaming of centuries that have gone before;
Great elms rise solemnly by slab and mound,
Arch'd high above a hidden world of yore.
Round all the scene a light of memory plays,
And dead leaves whisper of departed days,
Longing for sights and sounds that are no more.[1]

LOVECRAFT

After a trip to Boston with Sam Loveman, early in 1929, to view antiquities, Lovecraft in mid-April set out upon another spring tour. He had learned that "vicarious travelling is pretty pallid beside the real thing."

First he stopped at Vrest Orton's house in Yonkers. In New York, the Gang and the new friends whom he met through Orton showered him with invitations. In return for Orton's hospitality, Lovecraft revised some stories for his host.

A well-connected young man, Orton proposed to get Lovecraft a job in New York, as he had already done for Wandrei. With a suppressed shudder, Lovecraft declined. He would have welcomed a business connection that let him live in Providence. But since his background and aptitudes practically limited him to the publishing business, and since publishing was concentrated in New York, his chances of getting a post such as he had in mind were never bright.[2]

Lovecraft spent a week at Orton's and another at the Longs'. His feelings towards New York were mixed: "What irony that most of my closest friends live in a town I can't endure." On the other hand: ". . . the place is not so hateful when one knows one is not chained to it, & has Providence to greet him. . . ." In his later years, he nostalgically remembered his sojourn in New York, with

> . . . its long informal sessions at various rendezvous—the complete disregard of the clock—the quaint familiar landmarks—the spirited weekly meetings—the then burning issues and the no less burning arguments—the bookshops and the tours of exploration—surely they glow with a golden light in the perspective of eleven long years.[3]

At the end of his New York visit, he left for the South. He had expected to get only as far as Philadelphia, but a timely check from a ghosting client stretched his trip to Fredericksburg, Richmond, and Williamsburg. He wrote: "It is my first real saturation with the solid & ancient civilisation of the South—the only one I feel able to regard as equal to that of New England." He especially liked Richmond because, unlike "hideously foreignised" Baltimore, it had "only 3% foreigners." He was pleased to find that attacks of homesickness, which used to make travel a painful pleasure, were weakening.

Lovecraft visited St. John's Church in Richmond, where, at the beginning of "the treason against His Majesty's lawful government," Patrick Henry spoke his "cheaply melodramatic words. . . . The pew from which he spoke is still preserved & marked with a tablet, but as a loyal subject of the King I refused to enter it." He complacently noted the caste status of "niggers" in the South but at the same time praised "a delightful mulatto sexton—very intelligent" who "shews visitors around the building."[4]

En route home, Lovecraft went up the Hudson Valley and spent several days exploring the ancient small towns like Hurley and New Paltz. Having missed a bus connection, for the first (and as far as I know the only) time in his life he hitched a ride. A friendly Standard Oil truck driver took him from Hurley to Kingston.

In Kingston, he visited another pen pal, Bernard Austin Dwyer. Along with a cheap suitcase, Lovecraft carried a satchel of black enameled cloth, containing stationery, his diary for the year, copies of *Weird Tales,* and a small telescope for examining scenic and architectural details. In a park in Kingston, he left the case on a bench while he climbed a hill and returned a few minutes later to find it gone. When he got home, he replaced this equipment and carried a similar bag on subsequent trips.

Leaving Dwyer, Lovecraft went on to Albany and thence to spend a week with Cook in Athol. Cook drove him to Providence and there stocked up on books from a shop run by Clifford Eddy's uncle.

Now quite a gadabout, Lovecraft made two more journeys in 1929. In August, the Longs vacationed at Onset, Massachusetts, and invited Lovecraft to join them. More and more avid for new experience, he enthusiastically noted:

> The Onset excursion ended up with a sort of climax—my first aëroplane ride. Quite an exhilarating experience, which I want to repeat. In a hydro-aëroplane which ascended high over the head of Buzzard's Bay & gave one a sense of cosmic independence from the map-like world & blue & green beauty spread out below.[5]

The Longs urged Lovecraft to swim. He used to say he had never learned to swim for fear of being paralyzed by the cold, but at last they persuaded him. He appeared in a bathing suit of the vintage of 1910, with trousers down to the knees, and for a few yards swam a decorous breast stroke without apparent ill effects.

On August 28th, Lovecraft and his younger aunt, Annie Gamwell, took a bus trip to western Rhode Island to look up ancestral sites around Moosup Valley and the Fosters. They spent the day hunting down gravestones of Howards, Lyons, Phillipses, Whipleys, and Whipples. Lovecraft copied epitaphs, such as that on the tombstone of his great-great-grandfather Asaph Phillips:

> *The sweet remembrance of the just*
> *Shall flourish when they sleep in dust.*[6]

Lovecraft pronounced himself "the compleat rural squire."[7] He is not the only man to have thought that he had the instincts of a man of property without the property.

Lovecraft continued ghosting. In April, de Castro's book on Bierce appeared and sold poorly. De Castro grumbled that it would have fared better had Lovecraft been willing to rewrite it. In July, de Castro paid Lovecraft in advance (as Lovecraft had demanded in the first place) to revise the book. This kept Lovecraft busy for the next two months, but so far as I know the rewritten version was never published.

Lovecraft also took on another substantial ghosting job. In January, 1929, Maurice Moe sent him the manuscript of *Doorways to Poetry*, a book on poetical appreciation, which Moe hoped to publish as a textbook. Lovecraft not only undertook the revision but refused to be paid, explaining: "it goes against the grain for a gentleman to charge money for a favour extended to a friend."[8] Lovecraft began this revision in July and was still working on it in September. This book, too, was apparently never published.

Early in 1929, a Dr. Lee Alexander Stone, M.D., who had been superintendent of a branch of the Chicago Public Health Service, hired Lovecraft to write a piece on crime in Chicago. Lovecraft wrote the article but failed to get paid. After a year and a half of polite dunning, he wrote the man:

Sir:
In the matter of your persistently unpaid revision bill—concerning which you so persistently withhold all explanations despite repeated inquiries—I have decided, at the risk of encouraging sharp practices, to forego the use of a collecting agency and make you a present of the amount involved.

This is my first encounter with a hopelessly bad bill, and I believe I may consider the sum ($7.50) as not ill spent in acquiring practical experience. I needed to be taught caution on accepting unknown clients without ample references—especially clients from a strident region which cultivates commercial expansion rather than the honour customary among gentlemen.

Meanwhile I am grateful for so concrete an answer to the popular question, "Is Chicago a Crime-Ridden City?"

With such consideration as is appropriate to the situation, and trusting that my small gift may prove of financial aid to you, Believe me, Sir,

Yr. most obedient hble. Servt.,
H. P. LOVECRAFT

Later in 1929, Lovecraft wrote articles for Dr. Woodburn Harris, a physician campaigning against Prohibition in Chicago. He rewrote a story by Zealia Reed, "The Mound," assimilating it to the Cthulhu Mythos. Based upon tales that she had heard in Oklahoma, the story deals with the discovery of an underground civilization in caverns below the earth. Before starting this task, he wrote Elizabeth Tolridge:

> Yes—everything pertaining to the Mayan & Aztec civilisations is interesting, & I fancy I shall use the theme more than once. Indeed —my next revision job will give me a chance to practice, since it will require the introduction of this theme in such a way as to involve wholly original composition on my part.[9]

As things turned out, he did not get back to original work for months, and the stories on Meso-American themes (other than his work on "The Mound") were never written. When "The Mound" was first submitted to *Weird Tales*, Wright rejected it as too long (28,000 words), and it did not see print until after Lovecraft and Wright were dead.

Lovecraft's feeble efforts to merchandise his writings continued. After Wright rejected "The Strange High House in the Mist," he asked to see it again. But, said Lovecraft, "it is too late. I let Cook have it for *The Recluse*, & it would be in very poor taste to ask him for its return—thus implying that he can have only such things as nobody else wants."

Cook, however, had his own troubles; his wife died early in 1930. When it was plain that Cook would never issue another *Recluse*, Lovecraft sent "The Strange High House" to Wright, who published it in his issue of October, 1931.

Lovecraft spoke of submitting stories rejected by Wright to the straight science-fiction magazines. But he found such ungentlemanly peddling repugnant: "As for me, I have a sort of dislike of sending in anything which has been once rejected, so for the present I fancy I'll wait till I have something new. . . . I don't like to push my things forward. Silly attitude, no doubt, but old men will be old men!"

During his spring visit to New York, Lovecraft got an interview with an assistant editor of *Red Book Magazine*, "but it merely convinced me that nothing of mine is adapted to this type of magazine." He brushed off his failure to achieve book publication: "As for a collection of my junk,—such has often been broached, but has never eventuated, & I don't care greatly whether it ever does or not."

Unsuccessful writers and other artists often say that they care not whether the multitude appreciates their work; they create merely to express themselves. They are probably making a virtue of necessity, defending their egos against the humiliation of failure. When fame and fortune do come to artists, most of them embrace these rewards as eagerly as those made of commoner clay.

In Lovecraft's case, the depression into which every rejection threw him implies that he was not so indifferent to worldly success as he professed. He admitted as much. When, in 1935, Loring & Mussey asked whether he had anything for them to publish, he wrote a friend that he did not think the inquiry would come to anything, since four other publishers had turned down collections of his stories. Nevertheless:

> I'm shooting along a few tales just on the general principle of leaving no stone unturned. I'd hate to think, later on, that I *might* have had a book published *if* I'd responded to the request.[10]

Evidently, he would really have been delighted to see his name on the spine of a professionally published book, his protests to the contrary notwithstanding.

In verse, Lovecraft's talent briefly blazed up. At last he began to get away from Addison, Dryden, and Poe as models. In 1925, he composed a graceful light jingle of eleven quatrains, A *Year Off*:

> Had I a year to idle through,
>   With cash to waste and no restriction,
> I'd plan a programme to outdo
>   The wildest feats of travel fiction.
>
> On steamship guides I'd slake my thirst,
>   And railway maps would make me wiser—
> America consider'd first
>   To please the local advertiser.

He tells of all the places to which he would plan journeys:

> Beyond, the Pullman rates I'd get
>   For Kiao-chau and Yokohama,
> Arranging passage thro' Thibet
>   To dally with the Dalai Lama. . . .

Thus might I scheme—till in the end
The year would slip away unheeded,
My money safe with me to spend,
And the wild outing scarcely needed![11]

He tried to break out of his eighteenth-century poetic mold: "In the few metrical attempts I make, I try like hell to get rid of this tendency [to use stock phraseology]—which as you probably know, I once had in a very acute form owing to my lifelong predeliction for 18th-century style."[12]

In the late 1920s, the poet Edwin Arlington Robinson rose to fame. His *Sonnets, 1889–1927* appeared in 1928, and there is reason to think that Lovecraft was influenced by Robinson's verse. A reference to "Robinson" in one of his letters probably means the poetical, Maine-born subway inspector and customs-house clerk, who shared Lovecraft's anti-commercialism and wrote: "Business be damned."

Lovecraft wrote one poem, *The Messenger*, about November, 1929, with tongue in cheek. Bertrand K. Hart, literary editor of the *Providence Journal*, had in his column praised "The Call of Cthulhu" in Harré's anthology. Hart noted that Lovecraft had located the artist Wilson at 7 Thomas Street, in a house where Hart once lived. In revenge, Hart "threatened to arrange with the local ghouls & wraiths to send a monstrous visitor to my [Lovecraft's] doorstep at 3 A.M. . . . ." In response, Lovecraft wrote;

The Thing, he said, would come that night at three
From the old churchyard on the hill below;
But crouching by an oak fire's wholesome glow,
I tried to tell myself it could not be.
Surely, I mused, it was a pleasantry
Devised by one who did not truly know
The Elder Sign, bequeathed from long ago,
That sets the fumbling forms of darkness free.

He had not meant it—no—but still I lit
Another lamp as starry Leo climbed
Out of the Seekonk, & a steeple chimed
Three—& the firelight faded, bit by bit.
Then at the door that cautious rattling came—
And the mad truth devoured me like a flame![13]

Lovecraft heard that a row of old brick warehouses along South Water Street, at the foot of College Hill, were to be razed. Outraged, he lamented: "Their doom is a source of the greatest pain & disgust to me, although I well know that it cannot be averted."[14] On December 7, 1929, he composed a poem in twelve quatrains, *Brick Row:*

> It is so long they have been standing there—
> Red brick, slant roofs, above the harbour's edge;
> Chimneys against a fragment of salt air,
> And a green hill ascending ledge by ledge. . . .
>
> So if at last a callous age must tear
> These jewels from the old town's quiet dress,
> I think the harbour streets will always wear
> A puzzled look of wistful emptiness. . . .[15]

One may question the likening of these boxy, utilitarian structures to "jewels," but Lovecraft's hostility to change was indiscriminate. He would have kept every building built before, say, 1830. The poem, published in the *Journal*, drew praise from readers but failed to save the warehouses; of which, however, a few still stand between South Water and South Main streets.

In January, 1930, Lovecraft wrote a series of sonnets on weird themes. He composed thirty-three in about a week. *Weird Tales* bought ten for $35, while the *Providence Journal* purchased five more. Others appeared in amateur journals.

In poetry, Lovecraft (who rightly called himself "essentially a prose writer") was far surpassed by Robert E. Howard, August Derleth, and Clark Ashton Smith. Nonetheless, this cycle of sonnets was a real achievement. I have quoted parts of these sonnets as headings to Chapters III, XII, XIII, and XIV. Here is one, *The Bells*, complete:

> Year after year I heard that faint, far ringing
> Of deep-toned bells on the black midnight wind;
> Peals from no steeple I could ever find,
> But strange, as if across some great void winging.
> I searched my dreams and memories for a clue,
> And thought of all the chimes my visions carried;
> Of quiet Innsmouth, where the white gulls tarried
> Around an ancient spire that once I knew.
>
> Always perplexed I heard those far notes falling,
> Till one March night the bleak rains splashing cold
> Beckoned me back through gateways of recalling

To elder towers where the mad clappers tolled.
They tolled—but from the sunless tides that pour
Through sunken valleys on the sea's dead floor.[16]

Lovecraft called the series *Fungi from Yuggoth*, his name for a supposed trans-Neptunian planet in the Cthulhu Mythos stories. When Pluto was discovered in 1930, Lovecraft reminded his friends that, in a sense, he had predicted it.

Fungi from Yuggoth showed that Lovecraft indeed possessed a modest poetical talent. But in poetry as in other departments of life, he got started in the wrong direction and only late in the day perceived his error. After the *Fungi*, he wrote but little poetry.

Lovecraft's correspondence grew larger than ever. One pen pal was an old lady in Boston who claimed descent from Mary Easty, hanged as a witch in Salem in 1692. Delighted, Lovecraft hoped to get from her some traditions that he could use in his fiction. His witch descendant, however, proved an erratic informant, who claimed prophetic powers and wanted to know where "Dunwich" and "Arkham" were, since she could not find them on maps.

In August, 1930, Lovecraft began corresponding with another *Weird Tales* writer, Robert Ervin Howard (1906–36). Although they never met, Lovecraft, Howard, and Clark Ashton Smith became the Three Musketeers of *Weird Tales*, constantly contributing to the magazine and incessantly corresponding.

Howard spent nearly all his life in Cross Plains, in the center of Texas. He was the only child of a frontier physician. Frail and bullied as a boy, he built himself up by heroic exercise into a two-hundred-pound mass of muscle, becoming an accomplished boxer and rider and a sports fanatic. He had a withdrawn, irascible father and (like Lovecraft) a monster-mother—an over-loving, possessive woman who discouraged his normal interest in girls.

A voracious reader and a voluminous and versatile writer, Howard was a poet of some stature. His colorful, clanging verse, if not quite so brilliant as Smith's, is much more readable than most of Lovecraft's.

Howard missed college for lack of money. After odd jobs like soda-jerking and surveying, he plunged into full-time free-lance writing. After a few years (1926–29) of meager earnings and many rejections, he began to do well at it. He was the only real professional fiction-writer of the three, since Smith considered himself mainly a poet and Lovecraft, a ghost writer. In his short life, Howard wrote more fiction than Smith and Lovecraft combined. His nearly two hundred stories included fantasy, science-fiction, Western, sport, historical, and oriental adventure stories.

For seven years, Lovecraft and Howard kept up a voluminous correspondence. They argued over the races of man, the migrations of tribes, and the rise and fall of civilizations. Being of largely Irish ancestry, Howard was as pro-Irish as Lovecraft was pro-English. Sometimes their exchanges became sharp.

When Howard wished that he had been born a barbarian or on the frontier, Lovecraft accused him of romanticism, sentimentality, naïveté, and of being "an enemy to humanity." Howard retorted that Lovecraft's idealization of the eighteenth century was just as romantic and naïve. Lovecraft accused Howard of exalting the physical side of life over the intellectual; Howard replied that he merely took a balanced view, sports and exercise being as necessary to him as antiquarianism was to Lovecraft. When Lovecraft praised Mussolini and Fascism, Howard, to whom personal liberty was the prime political principle, denounced Mussolini (then bombing and gassing the Ethiopians) as a butcher and Fascism as despotism, enslavement, and a front for the financial oligarchy.

Howard comes off better in these arguments than Lovecraft. He seems far to surpass Lovecraft in warmth, breadth, balance, worldly wisdom, and common sense. His fatal weakness transpired only later.

Howard's major fictional creation was the Hyborian Age of the Conan stories. This is an imaginary prehistoric era of about 12,000 years ago, between the sinking of Atlantis and the beginnings of recorded history. Conan the Cimmerian is a gigantic barbarian adventurer, combining the qualities of Herakles, Sindbad, and James Bond.

In planning his Conan stories, of which he wrote over two dozen, Howard composed an essay, "The Hyborian Age." This set forth the pseudo-history of Conan's world, although Howard declared it was not a serious theory of human prehistory. He gave his kingdoms and characters names from Classical, oriental, Norse, and other histories and mythologies, such as Dion, Valeria, Thoth-Amon, Asgard, and Turan.

About the end of September, 1935, Howard sent a copy of "The Hyborian Age" to Lovecraft, requesting Lovecraft, when he had read it, to forward it to the fan Donald A. Wollheim. Lovecraft sent the manuscript on with a covering letter:

Dear Wollheim:—
Here is something which Two-Gun Bob says he wants forwarded to you for The Phantagraph, and which I profoundly hope you'll be able to use. This is really great stuff—Howard has the most magnificent sense of the drama of "History" of anyone I know. He possesses a panoramic vision which takes in the evolution and interaction of races and nations over vast periods of time, and gives one the same large scale excitement which (with even greater scope) is furnished by things like Stapledon's "Last and First Men."
The only flaw in this stuff is R.E.H.'s incurable tendency to devise names too closely resembling actual names of ancient history —names which, for us, have a very different set of associations. In many cases he does this designedly—on the theory that the familiar names descend from the fabulous realms he describes—but such a design is invalidated by the fact that we clearly know the etymology of many of the historic terms, hence cannot accept the pedigree he suggests. E. Hoffmann Price and I have both argued with Two-Gun on this point, but we make no headway whatsoever. The only thing to do is to accept the nomenclature as he gives it, wink at the weak spots, and be damned thankful that we can get such vivid artificial legendry. . . .
Best wishes—

Yours most sincerely,
HPL[17]

Despite Lovecraft's criticism, there is much to be said for Howard's nomenclature. Whereas Howard's made-up names are unpleasing, those borrowed from ancient sources convey the glamour of antiquity without being too difficult for the modern reader, who, having been taught to read by sight-reading methods, boggles at any name more exotic than "Smith."

Wollheim published part of "The Hyborian Age" in his *Phantagraph*. In 1938, Wollheim, Forrest J. Ackerman, and three other fans published the entire essay in a mimeographed booklet, *The Hyborian Age*.

For several years, Lovecraft feuded with Ackerman. Born in California in 1916, Ackerman has made a lifelong career of being a science-fiction fan while supporting himself as a magazine dealer, an editor, and a literary agent among other things.

In 1932, when Ackerman was in high school, Clark Ashton Smith published in *Wonder Stories* a tale called "Dweller in Martian Depths." This gruesome story tells of human explorers on Mars who encounter a monster. This creature apparently subsists on explorers' eyeballs, being furnished with appendages for extracting them. Ackerman wrote to Charles Hornig's *Fantasy Fan*, berating the story on the ground that a weird horror-fantasy had no place in a science-fiction magazine. Lovecraft replied:

> As for Ackerman's ebullition, I fear he can hardly be taken seriously in matters involving the criticism of imaginative fiction. Smith's story was really splendid, except for the cheap ending on which the Editor [of] Wonder Stories insisted. Ackerman once wrote me a letter with a very childish attack on my work—he evidently enjoys verbal pyrotechnics for their own sake and seems so callous to imaginative impressions.

The quarrel filled the column for the first six issues of the fan magazine. Ackerman's remarks evidently got under Lovecraft's skin, for during the next three years his allusions to Ackerman were enlivened by such terms as "habitual pest," "superficial Smart-Aleck," "insolent young brat," "pompous little joke," "little louse," and "insubstantial oaf."

By 1937, however, Lovecraft had left such juvenile sniping behind. He said of Ackerman: "I'm sure he must be a bright & delightful kid underneath the surface! . . . mellowing into something very different from the enfant terrible of three years ago. . . . I haven't a thing in the world against him!"

Lovecraft analyzed the qualities that made for literary success, advising Zealia Reed:

> With me the chance of producing anything profitable in the course of serious artistic work is so slim as to be almost negligible; whereas you, on the other hand appear to resemble that more fortunate group (like Booth Tarkington or Sinclair Lewis) whose serious interests happen to come closer to the popular (and therefore remunerative) field. . . .

A "superlatively great artist," he said, could expect to make a modest living from his art, while "the veriest idiot and ignoramus" like Edgar Rice Burroughs might, by luck, win a fortune.

Usually, though, the successful commercial writer (outside the dime-novel class) stands somewhere midway in merit—with a moderate cleverness of thought and a fairly glib technical assurance. . . . What really determines his success is a third and wholly different thing—an unexplainable and imponderable rapport with the mental and emotional processes of the larger reading public—which has no relation to literary skill and is found equally among the greatest geniuses and the dullest dolts. . . . But when popular sympathy is slight or nonexistent—as it is with me—there is no use expecting more than the meagrest material profit except through rare accident.

Convinced that he would never make his fortune by writing, Lovecraft said he "would jump with almost indecent avidity at any really steady job short of the absolutely ridiculous." He was sure he could earn more that way than by "the nerve-draining and ill-paying ordeal of revision."

He even wished that he could write in the popular vein. Hearing that Derleth had sold a detective story, he said: "I wish I could do it—I'd a thousand times rather write detective tales than revise—but I'm afraid I haven't the knack."[18] Actually, he was better qualified to write whodunits than many who have written them. But his self-doubt and lack of enterprise kept him from even trying.

For a while, Lovecraft held a job in Providence that by his earlier standards was not far short of the "absolutely ridiculous." He sold tickets for the late night show at a second-run movie theater. He sat in his cubicle with a book open before him. When the last show was under way, he left, stopped for a bite at the all-night Waldorf Restaurant, and hiked back up College Hill, to spend the rest of the night working.

Lovecraft mentioned his job seldom in conversation and, as far as I know, never in letters. It was not the sort of work a gentleman would have done. From the few facts that I have been able to track down, I judge that he held the job some time during 1928–30.

Apparently, Lovecraft never hunted a job in the 1930s. By then, however, the Great Depression was under way, and jobs were scarce for even the most personable and accomplished job-seeker.

In 1928, Vrest Orton moved from New York to his native Vermont and founded the Stephen Daye Press in Brattleboro. He urged Lovecraft to come to Brattleboro, too, as his editor. Lovecraft demurred on the ground of climate. In his Poesque period, he had put his thoughts on New England winters into verse:

> I remember the season,
>   It dawn'd on my gaze;
> The mad time of unreason,
>   The brain-numbing days
> When winter, white-sheeted and ghastly, stalks onward
>   to torture and craze.[19]

For several years, Orton sent Lovecraft small jobs of casual editing, mostly proofreading. He believed that he would in time have prevailed upon Lovecraft to move to Brattleboro. In 1932, however, Orton sold his publishing company and went back to New York, ending that possibility.

Lovecraft became more than ever insistent upon a writer's need for tradition, roots, and identification with one locale. In western Rhode Island, Lovecraft felt:

> . . . one's own hereditary blood-stream coursing through the scene as through the veins of some vast and exquisite organism. . . .

> Home is one's ideal setting if one is to develop one's best attributes, & New York is no place for a white man to live. . . . A man belongs where he had roots—where the landscape & milieu have some relation to his thoughts & feelings, by virtue of having formed them. A real civilisation recognises this fact—& the circumstance that America is beginning to forget it, does far more than does the mere matter of commonplace thought & bourgeois inhibitions to convince me that the general American fabric is becoming less & less a true civilisation & more & more a vast, mechanical, & emotionally immature barbarism de luxe.[20]

This is certainly not true for all writers. Some, like Derleth, have succeeded by sticking close to their native heaths; others have done equally well by roaming the wide world.

Lovecraft still played the rôle of a haughty, aristocratic, monied esthete:

> The only reason for a gentleman to do anything except what his fancy dictates, is that he can best sustain his illusions of beauty and purpose in life by falling harmoniously into the pattern of his ancestral feelings. The *individual*—feudal, proud, aloof, unfetter'd,

and dominant—that is all that matters, and society is of use to him only so far as it enlarges the pleasures he might enjoy without it.

The future aristocracy, represented in his time by the Fords and the Rockefellers, would, he thought, "be one of wealth, splendour, power, speed, quantity and responsibility alone; for, having been erected on the basis of acquisiton and industry," it would embody "the crude ideal of *doing* as opposed to the civilised ideal of *being*."[21] The true gentleman—a vanishing breed—should simply exist and let the world come to him.

The machine age, Lovecraft warned, would soon ruin the South as it had the Northeast. "Nothing good can be said of that cancerous machine-culture. . . ." While he had enjoyed his airplane ride, "I'd hate to see aëroplanes come into common commercial use, since they merely add to the goddam useless speeding up of an already over-speeded life; but as devices for the amusement of a gentleman, they're oke!"

Lovecraft cited several leading thinkers—Ralph Adams Cram, Joseph Wood Krutch, James Truslow Adams, John Crowe Ransome, T. S. Eliot, and Aldous Huxley—who were likewise warning of the dire social results of mechanization. Lovecraft thought that "It will take generations for the machine age to build up enough stable illusions to found a new fabric of satisfying tradition." Meanwhile, "All one can do at present is to fight the future as best he can."[22]

Lovecraft's neophobia—fear of the new—is a common human quality. Human beings like change but also stability. No change bores them; too much makes them uneasy. When young, they tend to favor more change than when they are older and have built up habits, associations, and affections for things as they have been.

In many ways immature, Lovecraft was prematurely old in his attitude towards change. At thirty-eight, he said: ". . . as far as my temperament is concerned, I was born an old man." He suffered from "future shock" long before Alvin Toffler invented the term. He illustrates, in extreme form, Bertrand Russell's dictum: "Science, while it has enormously accelerated outside change, has not yet found any way of hastening psychological change, especially where the unconscious and subconscious are concerned. Few men's unconscious feels at home except in conditions very similar to those which prevailed when they were children."[23]

He still fumed over the "flood of alien, degenerate, and un-assimilable immigrants." While claiming to "venerate the principle of aristocracy" and calling himself an antidemocrat, he preferred moderate, liberal policies in government. It would seem that he wanted the government to treat him in a libertarian, permissive way while ruling the ethnics with a heavy hand. One is reminded of a remark of Walter Lippmann about H. L. Mencken: that he "seems to think that you can have a privileged, ordered, aristocratic society with complete liberty of speech. That is as thoroughgoing a piece of utopian sentimentalism as anything could be."

Lovecraft was doubtful about censorship, wishing there were some way "to distinguish between authentic art—or science—& commercial pornography. . . ."[24]—a problem that still baffles the keenest legal minds. He deprecated the rages that some older persons flew into over the treatment of sex in the arts. Their feelings, he said, must have been warped by the unhealthy Victorian preoccupation with sex. As for himself:

> I hardly ever use the telephone, although there's one in the quiet house where I room. I take more pleasure in barriers interposed between myself & the modern world, than in links connecting me with it. I like to remain abstract, detached, neutral, indifferent, objective, impersonal, universal, & non-chronological. . . . The whole ideal of modern America—based on speed, mechanical luxury, material achievement, & economic ostentation—seems to me ineffably puerile. . . .

He realized his self-contraditions:

> I am, you see, a sort of hybrid betwixt the past and the future—archaic in my personal tastes, emotions, and interests, but so much of a scientific realist in philosophy that I cannot abide any intellectual point of view short of the most advanced.

He did not, however, count himself especially ill-used by fate: "Lucky is he whose temperament and opportunities permit him to live largely in historic imagination—as is likewise he who happens to be placed where the processes of change are most gradual & least noticeable."[25]

He backed off a little from his earlier opinionatedness: "I am not so free with opinions as I used to be, having outgrown the stage of cracker-barrel senate. . . ." "I often smile ruefully at some of the emphatick dogmatisms and indignations of my early Klei-comolo period."[26]

Early in 1930, Lovecraft was struggling with his revision work to scrape together money for his next trip. His work included the grading of term papers for the Renshaw School of Speech in Washington.

In April he left, going directly to South Carolina. From Columbia, he wrote that he had found a veritable "paradise":

> But what a place! A *real civilisation*, with pure American people, a sense of leisure & repose, & a vast amount of opulent (tho' not antiquarian) beauty. Why in Heaven's name does *anybody* live in the North—except from compulsion or from sentimental attachment?[27]

He spent several days in Charleston, full of energy, working up a tan, and ecstatic over Colonial remains. He stayed at the YMCA and saved laundry bills by washing his own shirts and underwear in the washbasin. He cut his own hair with a gadget that enabled him even to trim it in back, with the help of two mirrors. He breakfasted on a cheese sandwich, coffee, and ice cream and hunted down Italian restaurants for dinner. With alarm he noted that his weight had gone *up* to 142 pounds.

In dress, he encountered a problem. He tried to buy fresh detachable collars in Richmond but found that shops no longer carried them. He had to await his return to New York to renew his supply. All his life, he had worn detachable collars, but in the 1920s shirts with the collars attached began to oust the older type. His friend Cook told of the change:

> I had never known the comfort of a negligee shirt nor the time-saving value of the collar-attached device. Howard happened to be with me on the day that I had laid in a stock of negligee shirts and filled the waste basket with white collars. He was truly perturbed. Why should I deliberately lower myself a notch in the social scale when there was no need of it, and when, indeed, it was costing me money? Why not try soft white collars if stiff ones were definitely out? At least, why not wear a neckband shirt and then collars could be varied. . . . I tell this incident only as an illustration of how consistent Howard was in his feeling for *class*.

In mid-May, Lovecraft reached New York and visited the Longs. At Loveman's apartment, Lovecraft again met "that tragically drink-raddled but now eminent" poet, Hart Crane, whose poem *The Bridge* had brought him acclaim. When Crane was sober, Lovecraft found him "a man of great scholarship, intelligence, & aesthetic taste, who can argue as interestingly & profoundly as anyone I have ever seen. Poor devil—he has 'arrived' at last as a standard American poet . . . yet at the very crest of his fame he is on the verge of psychological, physical, & financial disintegration, & with no certainty of ever having the inspiration to write a major work of literature again."[28] Events confirmed Lovecraft's judgment.

At the beginning of June, revision checks forwarded to Lovecraft enabled him to go up the Hudson to visit Dwyer in Kingston, then eastward to see Cook in Athol. For some months, Cook had been in bad shape from a combination of his chronic appendicitis and a nervous breakdown, with hallucinations and threats of suicide. Now, for a while, he was better again.

In July, Lovecraft went to Boston for the NAPA convention. The program included a trip by boat up the Charles River, enlivened by the rescue of a drunk who had fallen into the water near the Harvard Bridge.

In August, Lovecraft visited the Longs on their summer vacation at Onset. They drove him about Cape Cod. At the end of his visit, he signed up for a $12 rail excursion to Quebec.

In *la belle Province*, Lovecraft noted "typical old-time French farmhouses—genuine outgrowth of the historic native building tradition." The sight of the city of Quebec, with its frowning citadel on the cliff above the St. Lawrence, took his breath away:

> Quebec! Can I ever get it out of my head long enough to think about anything else? Who cares for Paris or Antipolis now? Never have I beheld anything else like it, and never do I expect to! . . . All my former standards of urban beauty are superseded and obsolete. I can scarcely believe that the place belongs to the waking world at all.
>
> . . . it is a dream of city walls, fortress-crowned cliffs, silver spires, narrow, winding, perpendicular streets, magnificent vistas, & the mellow, leisurely civilisation of an elder world. . . . all combine to make Quebec an almost unearthly bit of fairyland.[29]

After three days of sight-seeing, Lovecraft took the train for Boston. There he made a boat trip to Provincetown, at the tip of Cape Cod:

. . . the sail—my first experience on the *open sea*—was well worth the price of the excursion. To be on limitless water out of sight of land is . . . to have the fantastic imagination stimulated in the most powerful way. The uniformly blank horizon evokes all sorts of speculations as to *what may lie beyond*.

So much for Lovecraft's alleged fear of the sea. Now an enthusiastic traveler, he sympathized with Derleth when Derleth complained of being "marooned" in flat, bucolic Wisconsin. Lovecraft said:

No wonder I am on the move nowadays, making up for lost time. But the hell of it is, that although I now have the *health* to travel, I no longer have the *cash*; so that I have to content myself with these all-too-brief & all-too-seldom jaunts. I don't know whether I'll ever get to the Old World—though I'd hate to die without ever seeing England.[30]

Alas! lost time is never found again. Lovecraft's visit to Quebec, however, affected his outlook. For years he had railed at the French-Canadians as part of the "alien hordes" polluting New England. At the same time, he had wary words of praise for French culture, as "undoubtedly *superior* to our own." In 1929, he wrote:

I hate a jabbering Frenchman with his little affectations & unctuous ways, & would defend the English culture & tradition with my last drop of blood. But all the same I can see that the French have a profounder culture than we have. . . .[31]

Lovecraft's tone changed after Quebec:

The good point about the French in Quebec is that they have dwelt immemorially on the same soil amidst the same conditions and traditions. That is what makes a civilisation! . . . No, the French are not bad; and after seeing Quebec I can never again think of Central Falls and Woonsocket and Fall River as wholly foreign.[32]

He even had a kind word for the Catholic Church in Quebec, as a force for social cohesion.

During 1930, Lovecraft was amused when some of his correspondents took his imaginary *Necronomicon* seriously and refused to believe that it did not exist. Mention of his fiction in William Bolitho's book column in the *New York World* encouraged him. He was less pleased by Bolitho's bracketing him with "the amiable hack

Otis Adalbert Kline." Kline, who ran a literary agency and acted as Robert E. Howard's agent during Howard's last years, also wrote science fiction, including several novels in imitation of Edgar Rice Burroughs's Martian and Venerian tales.

Despite these signs of literary recognition, Lovecraft felt that he was unequal to the fiction he wanted to write. He wished "to capture those elusive & indefinable sensations tending to create illusions of disordered dimensions, realities, & time-space elements, which all sensitive & imaginative people possess to a greater or less degree. . . . Poe tried to, but lacked the especial temperament. I try to, & have the temperament to know what I'm trying, but I lack the skill to convey anything of value to the reader." He lamented:

> Yes—I wish I had the energy & inspiration to write some of the myriad tales that are floating around in my head, but I'm not good for much in winter! . . . Much as I love my native New England soil, I may have to migrate some day—to some city like Charleston, S.C., St. Augustine, Fla., or New Orleans. . . .[33]

Before leaving on his 1930 trip to Charleston, Lovecraft completed a longhand draft of his next story. He took the draft with him and read it to Long in New York. Calling it "The Whisperer in Darkness," he went home determined to type it but did not complete the job until the end of September, 1930.

Reaching New York from Charleston, Lovecraft found an inquiry from Clifton Fadiman, then an editor for Simon & Schuster. Fadiman asked whether Lovecraft had any novels for sale. Lovecraft answered in his self-deprecating style and got a reply:

May 23, 1930

Dear Mr. Lovecraft:—
Thank you very much for your letter of the 21st. I am afraid that you are right in that our interest in a collection of short stories would not be very vivid.
I hope, however, that you will buckle down and do that novel you speak of. If it is good, its subject matter [the weird] will be a help rather than a hindrance.

Sincerely yours,
CLIFTON P. FADIMAN
SIMON & SCHUSTER, INC.

Lovecraft said he might someday try the novel, but he never did. Neither did he do anything with "The Case of Charles Dexter

Ward." He defended his otiosity by a pose of disdainful, pessimistic indifference: "And concerning a collection of my stuff—I may try some publisher some time, though I don't feel the least haste in the matter." "I don't think that novel scheme amounts to much—it is probably part of a general attempt to stir up possible MSS for consideration, though the number actually adopted will be slight."[34]

"The Whisperer in Darkness," 26,000 words long, was one of Lovecraft's best stories. A scholarly recluse named Henry W. Akeley, living in retirement in Vermont, writes to the narrator, Albert N. Wilmarth, an instructor at Miskatonic University. Wilmarth has noted the rumors and newspapers stories that accompanied the floods in Vermont in November, 1927. These accounts told of curious cadavers in the swollen rivers:

> They were pinkish things about five feet long; with crustaceous bodies bearing vast pairs of dorsal fins or membranous wings and several sets of articulated limbs, and with a sort of convoluted ellipsoid, covered with multitudes of very short antennae, where a head would ordinarily be.

Wilmarth tells of rumors of similar creatures lurking in the hills of Windham County, in southeastern Vermont. Akeley writes that these oversized winged prawns have been persecuting him, although he defends his house with guns and dogs. They spy upon him and vice versa. He has even obtained a phonograph record of their speech.

Akeley sends Wilmarth photographs of the tracks of the creatures, showing footprints like crabs' claws. The aliens, however, are made of "a type of matter totally alien to our part of space," so that they cannot be photographed. According to Akeley, these beings come from Yuggoth (Pluto) by flying "on clumsy, powerful wings which have a way of resisting the ether. . . ." Scientifically, this is wildly impossible; but Lovecraft often furnished his extra-terrestrials with improbable wings.

The phonograph record includes a dialogue between a human voice and a buzzing, mechanical-sounding imitation of human speech. In cryptic language, the voices discuss Nyarlathotep and other Great Old Ones. Speeches end with a refrain of "Iä! Shub-Niggurath! The Black Goat of the Woods with a Thousand Young!" Shub-Niggurath, one of the Old Ones, is a kind of fertility goddess.

Lovecraft got his habit of ending made-up names in -*ath* and -*oth* from Dunsany, who did it often (Zaccarath, Sacnoth). Dunsany probably got it from the Bible and similar sources, for -*oth* is a common feminine plural ending in Hebrew. Lovecraft explained how he chose names:

> To a large extent they are designed to suggest—either closely or remotely—certain names in actual history or folklore which have weird or sinister associations connected with them. Thus "Yuggoth" has a sort of Arabic or Hebraic cast, to suggest certain words passed down from antiquity in the magical formulae contained in Moorish & Jewish manuscripts.

More letters from Akeley imply that the Things are closing in. Then comes a different letter, retracting all he had said against the Yuggothites. It seems they are really benign, wanting only peaceful coöperation.

The Yuggothites, it transpires, extract human brains and put them into metal cylinders, which can be plugged in to enable the brain to sense and communicate. In this canned form, chosen human beings are sent all over the universe.

At Akeley's urging, Wilmarth comes to Vermont. He finds Akeley sitting bundled up in a darkened living room, supposedly suffering from asthma. In a faint, whispering voice, Akeley tells Wilmarth the secrets of the cosmos. Wilmarth narrates:

> I found myself faced by names and terms that I had heard elsewhere in the most hideous of connections—Yuggoth, Great Cthulhu, Tsathoggua, Yog-Sothoth, R'lyeh, Nyarlathotep, Azathoth, Hastur, Yian, Leng, the Lake of Hali, Bethmoora, the Yellow Sign, L'mur-Kathulos, Bran, and the Magnum Innominandum— and was drawn back through nameless aeons and inconceivable dimensions to worlds of elder, outer entity at which the crazed author of the *Necronomicon* had only guessed in the vaguest way.

These names form a roster of the entities of the Cthulhu Mythos. Some of them we have met. Bethmoora was lifted from Dunsany's story of that name; others originated as follows.

As the Cthulhu Mythos took form, Lovecraft encouraged other writers to write stories in his framework. Several did. Sometimes they borrowed Lovecraft's sinister deities, unknown places, and blasphemous books; sometimes they made up their own.

For example, Clark Ashton Smith invented the *Book of Eibon* or *Liber Ivonis*; Derleth, the *Cultes des Goules* by the "Comte d'Erlette" (his own ancestor); Long, the entity Chaugnar Faugn and Dr. John Dee's translation of the *Necronomicon;* and Howard, the *Unaussprechlichen Kulten* by "Friedrich Wilhelm von Junzt." In 1932, the last-named title caused a dispute. It was supposed to mean "unspeakable cults," but Wright decided that *unaussprechlich* meant "unpronounceable" (for some of Lovecraft's names, not a bad description). The argument was referred to one of Wright's illustrators, the gnomish, German-born C. C. Senf. *Unaussprechlich* was correct, reported Senf.

When fellow-writers sent him manuscripts of Cthulhu Mythos stories, Lovecraft in turn borrowed names and concepts from them. Tsathoggua was invented by Clark Ashton Smith, for instance, in his fantasy "The Tale of Satampra Zeiros"; the Eltdown Shards, by Richard F. Searight, a correspondent of Lovecraft who sold two stories to *Weird Tales*. Lovecraft got Hastur, Hali, and the Yellow Sign from the stories of Robert W. Chambers and Ambrose Bierce.

In "The Whisperer," Akeley tells Wilmarth: "It's from N'kai that frightful Tsathoggua came—you know, the amorphous, toad-like god-creature mentioned in the Pnakotic Manuscripts and the Necronomicon and the Commoriom myth-cycle preserved by the Atlantean high-priest Klarkash-Ton." This was Lovecraft's little in-joke, "Klarkash-Ton" being his nickname for Smith.

N'kai, also, was an underground realm in the Reed-Lovecraft collaboration, "The Mound." Kathulos was the wicked Atlantean sorcerer in Robert Howard's novel *Skull-Face*. Bran was an ancient British divinity and also the hero of several stories by Howard about the ancient British Picts.

Wilmarth evades an attempt to drug him. Prowling the house at night, he realizes that Akeley's brain is in one of the metal cylinders, and that the "Akeley" he saw must have been a disguised alien. . . .

While the earlier stories of the Cthulhu Mythos can mostly be classed as fantasies, "The Whisperer" is science fiction. Lovers of imaginative fiction have long sought to define "science fiction" and "fantasy" and to draw a hard-and-fast distinction between these two branches of the genre.

I divide fiction into two main genres: realistic fiction and imaginative fiction. Realistic fiction consists of stories that could have happened: tales of ordinary people doing realistic things in a known setting, either in the present or in the known past. Imaginative fiction comprises stories that could not have happened, being laid in the future, or on another world, or in the prehistoric past of which no details are known.

Imaginative fiction can be subdivided into science fiction and fantasy. In science fiction, the story is based upon a scientific or pseudo-scientific assumption, such as travel in interstellar space or in time, or the effect of a new invention or discovery, or the prediction of a future world.

In fantasy, on the other hand, the story is based upon a supernatural assumption, such as the existence of gods, demons, ghosts, or other supernatural beings, or magic that works.

Whereas Lovecraft's Dunsanian stories are fantasy, the Cthulhu Mythos stories fall on or close to the border between science fiction and fantasy. Some can be classed as either or as both, since there is no sharp boundary. "The Colour Out of Space" is mainly a fantasy, since Yog-Sothoth is evoked and banished by magical spells. "The Whisperer in Darkness," however, is science fiction; the powers of the aliens, while unearthly, are still limited by natural law. "The Call of Cthulhu" falls on the boundary.

Like other Ancient Ones and Elder Gods, Cthulhu is called a "god," but the term does not mean what it does in traditional religions. Lovecraft's "gods" are not, like Zeus or Yahveh, concerned with the morals and manners of human beings. They do not undertake to reward the good and punish the wicked. Their powers, though vast, are ruled by natural law. They are absorbed in their own affairs and are no more interested in the petty concerns of men than men are with those of mice, and they have no more compunction about destroying men who get in their way than men have about slaying mice.

This fictional attitude has been called the "mechanistic supernatural." It presents a cosmos that, while inhabited by superhuman entities, is basically amoral, merciless, and indifferent to man's fate. Fritz Leiber has neatly defined Lovecraft's rôle in this concept:

Perhaps Lovecraft's most important single contribution was the adaptation of science-fiction material to the purpose of supernatural horror. The decline of at least naive belief in Christian theology, resulting in an immense loss of prestige for Satan and his hosts, left the emotion of supernatural fear swinging around loose, without any well-recognized object. Lovecraft took up this loose end and tied it to the unknown but possible denizens of other planets and regions beyond the space-time continuum. This adaptation was subtly gradual. At first he mingled science-fiction material with traditional sorcery. For example in *The Dunwich Horror*, the hybrid other-dimensional entity is exorcised by recitation of a magic formula, and magical ritual plays a considerable part in the story. But in *The Whisperer in Darkness*, *The Shadow Out of Time*, and *At the Mountains of Madness*, supernatural horror is evoked almost entirely by recital of the doings of alien cosmic entities, and the books of sorcerous ritual have become merely the distorted, but realistic, histories of such entities, especially with regard to their past and future sojourns on Earth.[35]

Although *Weird Tales* was not doing well, Wright bought "The Whisperer in Darkness" for $350 and published it in his issue of August, 1931.

With "The Whisperer" out of the way, Lovecraft went off on one of his tangents. To preserve his impressions of Quebec, he began in October, 1930, to write a "travelogue" of the region. This became a book-length treatise, entitled:

A DESCRIPTION OF THE TOWN OF QUEBECK, IN NEW-FRANCE
Lately Added to His Britannick Majesty's Dominions

By H. Lovecraft, Gent., of Providence, in New-England.

This is a work of 75,000 words, with many maps and sketches. Half of it is a history of New France, from its discovery by Cartier in the 1530s down to the nineteenth century. Lovecraft indulged in his archaisms ("mixt," "extream," "joyn'd") and his unrepentant Toryism. In telling of the American Revolution, he always speaks of the British as "us" and of the Americans as "the rebels" or "the enemy."

The remaining half is an amazingly detailed description of Quebec City and its environs. With its spelling modernized and its partisanship toned down, it would have made an excellent official guidebook. But Lovecraft never even typed the work, let alone submitted it to a publisher, although it took three months in which he could easily have written a salable novel. He finished it, "solely for my own perusal and for the crystallisation of my recollections," on January 14, 1931.

When Talman asked him why he did not try to sell his voluminous travelogues, he said it was no use; his style was "one to which the modern world of trade is antipodally alien and even actively hostile." He had simply done what he felt like doing. The amateur spirit could hardly be carried further.

Through 1930, Lovecraft's health was good, except that towards the end of the year he suffered from a tic in his left eye. Sometimes this forced him to the hated typewriter.

He wrote: "Winter is the one enemy against which I have no defence but flight; & much as I love old New England I fear I shall have to shift my headquarters southward some day. . . . I may yet end up among the colonial antiquities of Charleston, Savannah, St. Augustine, or New Orleans—or perhaps Bermuda or Jamaica." He spoke thus all the rest of his life, but he never moved. Too strong were inertia and the comfort of living with a devoted aunt.

His spirit was stoical rather than happy. He did not mind his loss of belief in immortality, he said, because "Even an ordinary life-span gives most people all the boredom they can stand, & if they had immortality they would eventually find it unendurable. . . . I'm sure I don't want anything more than non-existence when I round out a few decades more." He professed indifference to worldly success: "No—I shan't give up writing phantasy, although I think I shall have fewer & fewer readers as time passes. Fortunately I don't give a hang whether or not anybody reads what I write."[36] The reasons why he did not kill himself to escape life's "burthensome quality" were

. . . strongly linked with architecture, scenery, and lighting and atmospheric effects, and take the form of vague impressions of adventurous expectancy coupled with elusive memory—impressions of certain vistas, particularly those associated with sunsets, are avenues of approach to spheres or conditions of wholly undefined delights and freedoms which I have known in the past. . . .

At the same time, he thought:

. . . for the average person there is a need for personal anchorage to some system of landmarks. . . . Religious people seek a mystical identification with a system of hereditary myths; whereas I, who am non-religious, seek a corresponding mystical identification with the only immediate tangible external reality which my perceptions acknowledge—i.e. the continuous stream of folkways around me.

He added: "One does not have to take these traditions and folkways seriously . . . and one may even laugh at their points of naivete and delusion—as indeed I laugh at the piety, narrowness, and conventionality of the New-England background which I love so well and find so necessary to contentment."[37]

Having fixed his landmarks, Lovecraft's next need, to feed his sense of adventurous expectancy, was travel. "Some day I must see the old world," he wrote, "even if I go broke in the process." Along with Carcassonne, "I wish very much to see . . . Nuremberg, Ratisbon, Rothenburg, & other European towns where the mediaeval order of things remains virtually unchanged by the centuries."[38]

Such travel, however, would have to be on his own terms, with an element of uncertainty, spontaneity, and suspense. A rigid itinerary would spoil it: "I wouldn't pay a half-dollar to see even London . . . on a Cook's tour schedule!"

Still, he did what traveling his straitened means allowed. Living on $15 a week, he said he had "become a miser in everything except 'bus fare and YMCA room rent and guide books."[39] He preferred buses to trains, not only because they were cheaper but also because, he thought, they tended to run through more scenic country. He usually bought a round-trip ticket at the start of a trip, to be sure of getting home.

Lovecraft continued to advise his young friends to avoid affectations and to fit harmoniously into their backgrounds, while not altogether following his own advice. He chided Derleth for his monocle, his alpaca overcoat, and his bathrobe for street wear:

> . . . in adolescence—as I have said before, I acquired the dignified old man complex and did my best to emulate my revered grandfather's sartorial scheme. But as I got along in my twenties, my perspective began to open up; and I realised how absurd it was to attach any especial imaginative significance at all to the way I looked. . . . This neat dressing of later life is really a bid for inconspicuousness rather than for self-assertion. A gentleman has a certain sense of harmony in the scene around him . . . and costume naturally becomes one of the minor accessories of that general harmonised scheme. . . . Much as I would feel vaguely at ease in a suit of knee-breeches, velvet coat with silver buttons, great silver shoe-buckles, three-cornered hat, and so forth, I know damn well that after having it on five minutes I would forget all about it and read or scribble along just the same as if I were in my regular

junk. . . . . besides feeling like an ass if anybody caught me in the stuff. . . . It's simply a matter of common sense to avoid arousing hostility and ridicule when absolutely nothing can be gained thereby.

Lovecraft might claim to have shed his dignified-old-man pose; but in this same letter, written when he was forty, he still called himself "Grandpa" and "an old gentleman." Now, why this persistent affectation of senescence? Most people find that age comes soon enough without anticipating it. True, there was playfulness in Lovecraft's poses. Many were assumed with tongue in cheek and twinkle in eye. Still, the persistence of the old-age pose suggests a deeper motive.

Like most people, Lovecraft put a high value on "harmoniousness" in conduct—that is, on acting in ways that his peers would approve. He said that, while he would not care what a proletarian or a "conventional and bigoted Victorian" thought about him, "I certainly would dislike to be a common butt of contempt or ridicule on the part of persons approximately like myself. . . ."

By such persons, he meant intellectual New Englanders. Lovecraft, however, did not lead the conventional life of persons of his own age and status. He did not hold a job, date the girls, or engage in sports. His style of life did evoke some contempt and ridicule among his neighbors. One of them said to me:

"Sure, I remember Lovecraft. I used to see him walking the street with his head down and his shoulders hunched in that funny way. We kids thought he was some kind of nut."[40]

The pretense of age may have been a defense against the scorn of his peers. If he were old enough, people would not expect him to hold a job, date the girls, or engage in sports. Of course, everyone knew that his elderliness was just a pretense, but it comforted him. If he constantly thought of himself as aged, he need not brood on his failure to meet conventional standards.

Lovecraft remained implacably anti-modernist in outlook. Spelling reformers, for instance, were

. . . curst money-minded provincials who are doing their vilest to corrupt our civilisation on this continent and substitute a damn'd bastard machine-and-speed worship. . . . I refuse to adopt the encroaching civilisation of mongrel Mechanamerika.[41]

World events, however, began to force changes upon his antiquated social and political outlook. During 1930, the Great Depression deepened. Unemployment remorselessly rose. The economic decline did not bottom out until 1933 and did not begin to reverse its course until around 1937, the year of Lovecraft's death.

Propagandists for Communism and Fascism agreed that democratic capitalism was finished. Soon, they cried, people would be forced to choose between Communism and Fascism. During those dismal years, democratic capitalism seemed to perform so badly as to make Communism and Fascism look almost attractive by contrast.

Between 1928 and 1930, Lovecraft lost faith in Republican conservatism. He accepted the predictions of the downfall of democratic capitalism, although he was not sure what form of government should succeed it; he leaned towards Fascism. In any case, he was sure that the government would be more authoritarian, with more economic control, than conservative American opinion then deemed tolerable:

> Sovietism and capitalism and fascism will meet in a curious triangular paradox to solve the enigma of a culture in which constant machine overproduction will have destroyed the law of supply and demand and made the individual's relation to the economic fabric an arbitrary, unstable, and difficultly determined problem.

> . . . communism really is the logical form of government toward which a machine age heads, unless checked in time by very drastic methods . . . which will ensure a more widespread diffusion of the means of life without interrupting the existing civilisation & the arts founded on individual thought & feeling. The principle of *Fascism* is the one which looks best to me. Democracy is simply a joke.

Elsewhere he described "a politically & economically socialistic state" as "the inevitable state of tomorrow."[42] He had certainly moved away from Harding Republicanism; but his movements were erratic, not yet showing his ultimate political direction.

Still a Tory Loyalist, he favored having New England secede from the United States (as it nearly did in 1810) and unite with Canada. Then:

> . . . our towns would soon be the seat of the choicest English-Canadian life and culture. . . . and it might be possible to get rid of most of our foreigners by subsidising their emigration to the

more highly industrialised area of neo-America. . . . What wouldn't I give to see the old flag go up again over the white belfry of Providence's 1761 Colony-House, whence it was treasonably lower'd on the 4th of May, 1776! God save the King!

Although Lovecraft had given French-Canadians the status of "real human beings," blacks were still beyond his pale:

Now the trickiest catch in the negro problem is the fact that it is *really twofold*. The black *is* vastly inferior. There can be no question of this among contemporary and unsentimental biologists— eminent Europeans for whom the prejudice-problem does not exist. *But*, it is *also* a fact that there *would be* a very grave and very legitimate problem *even if the negro were the white man's equal*.

This problem, he said, was that two dissimilar races, of different traditions and folkways, would have great difficulty in living together, because of the inevitable hostility that would arise between them, until they became completely merged or "mongrelised."

In discussing the Negro question, however, a new note creeps in. Lovecraft may be wrong in thinking that scientists agreed that Negroes were "vastly inferior"; they did not agree and still do not. He may exaggerate the difficulties of assimilation. At least, he shows some sympathy for the blacks instead of contempt and hatred: "No one wishes them any intrinsic harm, and all would rejoice if a way were found to ameliorate such difficulties as they have. . . ."[43] He suggested, among other proposals, setting aside certain states for them.

While Lovecraft still pontificated far beyond his knowledge on the nature of human races and the fate of mankind, he showed a growing awareness of the hollowness and superficiality of his earlier dicta. Of his early belief in forcing moral purity on the masses, he said: "I smile at some of the bigoted middle-aged carpings I used to pull off in the old Kleicomolo days!" His files held "*Conservatives* so pompous and silly that I wouldn't permit a cold-blooded non-amateur to read them for any amount of money."[44]

He was, belatedly, beginning to grow up.

Sixteen

BAFFLED BARD

I have seen Yith, and Yuggoth on the Rim,
And black Carcosa in the Hyades.
And in the slimy depths of certain seas
I have beheld the tomb where lieth Him
Who was and who shall be; and I have flown
Astride the shantak and the byakhee
Where Kadath in the Cold Waste terribly
Bears up her onyx-castled crest unknown.[1]

CARTER

During his last six years, Lovecraft traveled more than ever. He made more friends and his outlook became more mature and realistic. His literary techniques advanced. At the same time, his literary output dwindled and his efforts at publication became more discouraging.

He was oppressed by a growing conviction of failure. The reclusiveness that he had cultivated so long, he saw to have been an error:

> I was virtually an invalid—a nervous wreck with a thousand subsidiary weaknesses—in childhood, & never really got on my feet physically until I was thirty. Nor was my emergence from hermitage ever very complete. I did, surely enough, break away from belated juvenility enough to travel independently so far as waning

finances allowed; & to meet different people in person where previously I had conversed only through correspondence—but this
long-deferred semi-introduction to the world did not "take" as
thoroughly as it might have done had I been chronologically
younger. The era of expansion and late-dawn was a relatively brief
one, & was followed by a sort of slow drift back to the hermit
pattern of my early days. Vistas faded & contracted, & the glitter
of adventurous expectancy receded farther & farther—till at length
I saw the wider horizons fall off one by one. Before I knew it, I
was virtually back in my shell. Came to hate New York, whither I
had moved, like poison; & was back in Old Providence in 2 years
& 3 months from the time I started out. Old age tells—you can't
be flexible & expansive when the chill of the thirties gets into
your bones.[2]

This is partly true and partly rationalization. In 1931, when he
wrote the above, Lovecraft was getting around more and meeting
more people than ever before. But, while his mobility and sophisti-
cation were rising, his expectations were rising even faster, so that
he seemed to himself to be going backward. His talk of "the chill of
the thirties" is nonsense. Some men past forty have successfully
made a complete change of career, as by moving from business to
medicine, from the ministry to anthropology, from soldiering to
writing, or from law to acting.

He became disillusioned with his favorite historical milieux: ancient Rome, Georgian England, and Colonial America:

I realise that the Romans were an extremely prosaic race;
given to all the practical & utilitarian precepts I detest, and without
any of the genius of the Greek or glamour of the Northern barbarian.

Except in certain selected circles, I would undoubtedly find my
own 18th century insufferably coarse, orthodox, arrogant, narrow,
& artificial. . . . What I look back upon nostalgically is a dream-
world which I invented at the age of four from picture books &
the Georgian hill streets of Old Providence.[3]

A history of Dartmouth College, which he edited, changed
"my picture of the 18th century life in the Connecticut Valley—
where the people were evidently cruder & more fanatically pious,
even down to the Revolutionary period, than I had suspected before."

A sense that time was fleeting oppressed him:

Latterly I am appalled at the shortness of time in relation to the
things I need to get done—years slip by, yet my programme gets

nowhere—hence I am trying to develop a policy of conservation which shall squeeze a few more senile products out of me.[4]

He never, though, economized on letter-writing or on non-commercial outpourings like the travelogue of Quebec. He also wrote in praise of leisureliness, defended laziness, and excused idleness. To commend inactivity and then complain because one does not get things done is a case of wanting to eat one's cake and have it.

Regrets for missed opportunities became poignant. He wished he had gone to college: "I know I'd have been immeasurably better off—less awkward, retiring, & ill-adjusted—had my early health permitted me to follow a standard educational course with accompanying social activities."

He wished he had done something more with his physique. Derleth, who resembled a blond gorilla, implied that he would have preferred to look like some delicate esthete. Lovecraft answered: "Bless my soul, but I wish I *did* look like the sort of person who might have played football in his long-departed heyday!"[5] He appraised himself thus:

> Whatever "suffering" I have undergone is largely in the form of a dull falling short of aspirations, a general sense of futility in the universe, & a steady decline in worldly fortunes.

> . . . I need a business manager—or would if my junk were important enough to be a ponderable commodity. My lack of all practical calculative sense is such as to suggest the absence or early excision of a whole definite group of cells from my aged grey matter![6]

Sonia might have made him an excellent manager, but he had sent her away.

For this period, we can estimate Lovecraft's earnings and expenses from information scattered through his letters. Within a margin of error of about $150, I believe that he spent an average of close to $1,470 a year.[7]

I think he earned about $300 a year from original writings. This includes money received from Farnsworth Wright, who usually paid him a cent and a half a word for original work, his share of "Through the Gates of the Silver Key," and his $595 for the two tales sold to *Astounding Stories*. I assume that he got $5.00 each for the five poems he sold to Wright and a total of $50 for several appearances in anthologies.

There remain two other sources of income: Lovecraft's interest on and amortization of the quarry mortgage and his earnings from ghost-writing. About the mortgage, we know for sure only that at the time of Lovecraft's death, his invested capital was worth $500. His capital in the early 1920s had been around $12,000 or $13,000, but he had evidently dipped liberally into it. We do not know when and how fast it dwindled, save for his remark in 1927 about "losing my modest thou. if I ever had to foreclose."[8]

It looks as though his annual deficits, which he made up out of capital, were much larger in the early 1920s, when he was a freer spender and his earnings were negligible, than in the 1930s, when he had learned many tricks of thrift and was precariously established as a writer and reviser. If we assume that his capital was $1,000 in 1931 and $500 in 1936, he must have run an annual deficit of about $100. If that is near the truth, his annual income on the mortgages in the 1930s, at 6 per cent, must have averaged about $45.

The biggest unknown is Lovecraft's earnings from ghosting. These evidently did not make up the difference between his expenses on one hand and his income from mortgages and original writings on the other. If his income from original writings and interest on capital totaled $345, that leaves a gap between income and outgo of $1,125, to be filled by revision work and drafts on capital. If his deficits averaged $100 a year, he must have made about $1,025 from revision. To be realistic, let us say that his ghosting brought him between $900 and $1,200.

While this is only the roughest kind of estimate, it is consistent with what else is known about Lovecraft. Even though his capital was nearly gone at his death, he was in no danger of actual starvation, since his aunt could always tide him over. Annie Gamwell died in 1941, leaving a little over $10,000 in cash and securities. Had Lovecraft survived her, he would have come into this money and been able to limp along for many additional years.

One of Lovecraft's new friends was his fellow-fantasist, the Rev. Dr. Henry St. Clair Whitehead (1882–1932). Whitehead was an Episcopal minister of Dunedin, Florida, the pastor of the Church of the Good Shepherd. A middle-aged bachelor, athletic but with a tendency to ulcers, he lived with his aged father and was active in local boys' organizations.

Whitehead wrote boys' novels, religious works, and stories for *Weird Tales*. Most of his weird stories were laid in the Virgin Islands, where he had long dwelt. Many deal with such Afro-American occult beliefs as voodoo and jumbees (Virginese for zombies).

Whitehead corresponded with Lovecraft. In January, 1931, Whitehead began a story from an idea that Lovecraft gave him and urged Lovecraft to complete the story as a collaboration.

Lovecraft, however, had sworn off collaboration, on the ground that "it's a drag on both authors concerned so that the result is below the level which either might have attained alone." In particular, he declined Whitehead's offer "because of inability to do justice to the West Indian locale he has seen fit to choose. I am the sworn enemy of armchair exoticism, & believe in writing about things one personally knows—except of course in the case of Dunsanian phantasy or cosmic infinity."[9]

Besides, Lovecraft had begun a story on his own, "about a hellish Antarctic horror." He finished his tale in February but fretted that "the typing is a nightmare looming darkly ahead!"

Lovecraft finished his job, despite "the hated clicking of this damned machine-age spawn,"[10] and named the story "At the Mountains of Madness." It is a 42,000-word science-fiction story in the Cthulhu Mythos framework. Despite an overly long, slow build-up, it is perhaps the best of his longer stories.

The narrator, a professor at Miskatonic University, hopes by making public his tale to discourage other Antarctic expeditions. He fears that they will find things that it is better for men not to know, or that they will stir up some world-wide disaster.

He tells how his recent expedition set out, with sled dogs and airplanes. In Antarctica, they find a range of mountains higher than the Himalayas. An advance party camps in the foothills of these mountains, where they discover a cave full of fossils. Among these fossils are fourteen strange, leathery things, eight intact and six fragmentary.

The perfect specimens are eight feet long and barrel-shaped, with feet at one end and a cluster of tentacles at the other. They also have membranous wings folded into the grooves along their sides. Then the radio of the advance party falls silent.

Another group, including the narrator, flies to the site of the camp and finds all the men and dogs dead, save one of each, both of whom are missing. While other members of the party work on the camp, the narrator and one other man fly up into the mountains. They alight at a colossal ruined city of the Ancient Ones, who were similar to the giant winged sea cucumbers.

Reliefs on the walls give the history of the race. Coming to earth from a distant star in pre-Cambrian times, they had created gigantic ameboid servants, called *shoggoths* in the *Necronomicon*. They used the shoggoths to build their cities, but sometimes the shoggoths revolted. In time, both the Old Ones and the shoggoths disappeared.

Clues tell the men what happened to the advance party. The frozen Old Ones were still alive. When thawed out, they regained consciousness but were attacked by the frantic dogs. In the ensuing fracas, all the men and dogs were killed, and the Old Ones took one specimen of each for study. They are somewhere in the maze of passages—and, it seems, some of the shoggoths survived. . . .

It is a gripping, well-wrought tale, even though, like other stories of lost cities and lost races on earth, it has been dated by the progress of aërial exploration. One passage sheds light on Lovecraft's changing attitudes. The narrator and his companion find the remains of some of the surviving Old Ones, who have met the shoggoth and now lie headless and covered with slime. The narrator says:

> Poor devils! After all, they were not evil things of their kind. They were men of another age and another order of being. Nature had played a hellish joke on them . . . and this was their tragic homecoming. They had not even been savages—for what indeed had they done? That awful awakening in the cold of an unknown epoch—perhaps an attack by the furry, frantically barking quadrupeds, and a dazed defense against them and the equally frantic white simians with the queer wrappings and paraphernalia . . . poor Lake, poor Gedney . . . and poor Old Ones! Scientists to the last—what had they done that we would not have done in their place? God, what intelligence and persistence! . . . Radiates, vegetables, monstrosities, star spawn—whatever they had been, they were men![11]

Here Lovecraft, once the most ethnocentric and anthropocentric of men, turns over a new leaf. The Old Ones were hardly Anglo-Saxon Protestants; but, since they have qualities he respects, he welcomes them as fellow civilized beings. It took him longer to view the different races and tribes of man in the same equable light.

Lovecraft struggled through the transcription of his novel, sent the typescript off to Wright, and set out on his spring trip. In June, 1931, Lovecraft was devastated by Wright's rejection of the story, although he knew when he submitted the tale that it might fail because of its length. Wright would have had to run it as a serial; and his policy, as Lovecraft knew, was against serials, which he seldom had enough cash on hand to pay for. The position of *Weird Tales* was always precarious; hence Wright was timid about novelties and over-sensitive to readers' reactions. One bad blunder could end his magazine. But still, Lovecraft was outraged: "Confound Wright for turning down the tale I half killed myself typing!"[12]

Early in 1931, G. P. Putnam's Sons, aware of Lovecraft's slowly growing reputation, asked him if he had something for them to publish. He sent them a collection of short stories and novelettes. As Vanguard Press and Simon & Schuster had done, Putnam's considered the collection but, in July, decided against it. Lovecraft's prospects with book publishers were not enhanced by his habit of submitting battered, tattered old typescripts that had already been the rounds of a dozen friends and editors.

The rejection of "At the Mountains of Madness," combined with Putnam's turn-down, convinced Lovecraft that he might as well stop storytelling:

> I honestly think I'll quit writing altogether—or at least, quit trying to do more than occasionally jot down a few notes for my own edification. There is no demand whatever for serious work in the weird. I am confirmed in this attitude by the polite rejection my stuff has just received from Putnam's—who asked to see it in the first place.
>
> I am so dissatisfied with any production of mine that I have almost decided to write nothing further. In no case have I come near conveying the mood or image I wish to convey; & when one has not done this at 41 there is not much use in wasting time on further attempts. . . .
>
> I shall have rather a hard time landing my Antarctic story—indeed, rejections are so numerous lately that I think I'll stop writing for a while & use the time in revision.[13]

Lovecraft admitted that he was easily discouraged. He praised Derleth for his resilience:

> I envy you your persistence in the face of rejections—for under similar circumstances I acquire a sort of distrust for the merit of my stuff, & a concomitant disinclination to write more. Just now, for example, the effect of the combined Wright & Putnam rebuff is to cause me to abandon original attempts & undertake several revisory endeavours.[14]

Evidently, for success as a free-lance writer in one's own lifetime, talent is not enough. As noted in Chapter 7, one must also have energy, egotism, resilience, persistence, and hard-boiled realism. Unfortunately for people like Poe and Lovecraft, their great talent or genius was developed, as it were, at the expense of the other qualities. The greater their genius, the less they could exploit it in a rational way.

Lovecraft's view of his own work became ever more severe. He dismissed the widely admired "Outsider" as "a rotten piece of rhetorical hash with Poesque imitativeness plastered all over it." He thought he must drastically change his style:

> All my tales, except for perhaps one or two, dissatisfy me profoundly on close analysis; and I have about decided to call a halt unless I can manage better than I am doing. . . . The trouble with most of my stuff is that it falls between two stools—the vile magazine type subconsciously engrafted on my method by W. T. association, and the real story.
>
> As for my fiction—whether or not there's anything potentially in it, I know that it needs a damn thorough overhauling. It is excessively extravagant & melodramatic & lacks depth & subtlety. . . . My style is bad, too—full of obvious rhetorical devices & hackneyed word & rhythm patterns. It comes a long way from the stark, objective simplicity, which is my goal—yet I find myself tongue-tied when I attempt to use a vocabulary & syntactical pattern other than my own.

Lovecraft was not the only writer to find that his fiction tended to fall into a certain type, pattern, and tone; that, when he tried to write in an utterly different vein, his inspiration dried up and left him with "writer's block." He explained why he did not write action stories:

> I am essentially a static, contemplative, and objective person; almost a hermit in daily life, and always preferring to observe rather than

to participate. My natural—and only genuine—form of imagination is that of passive witnessing—the idea of being that of a sort of floating, disembodied eye which sees all manner of marvellous phenomena without being greatly affected by them. I am constitutionally unable to see anything interesting in mere *motions* and *events*. What absorb me are *conditions, atmospheres, appearances,* and things of that kind.[15]

This explains why most of Lovecraft's stories have passive, ineffectual "heroes," who are acted upon rather than acting and who usually lose their heads and panic in crises. Evidently, he thought of himself as an anti-hero and, like most fiction writers, put some of that imagined personality into his stories. This self-image, while a long way from the bellowing, blood-drinking berserker that he had liked to fancy himself in his twenties, may have done the real Lovecraft an injustice.

During his depressed period of late 1931, Lovecraft started a story laid in Florida but dropped it in favor of more ghosting. One difficulty in writing in a weird story about a warm country, he said, was that, to him, heat was so benign that it was hard to imagine any real menace in the tropics.

At the beginning of May, 1931, Lovecraft set out again for the South. There he contrasted the "mongrel bedlam" of New York with the Southern

. . . civilisation of such depth & tenacity that one feels himself in a *real nation*—as he can never feel in the industrialised, foreignised, & quickly-changing North. The same condition—amongst the French—exists in ancient Quebec; but we have lost it in New England. On an inexpensive coach-line one sees how profoundly the old Southern attitude has affected even the lower middle classes— all of whose forebears, of course, have dwelt in Virginia for three centuries. There is an instinctive courtesy & friendliness of a sort unknown to the North, & the long trips are occasionally diversified by the conversational remarks—civil & meant to be interesting—of utter strangers.

A pair of traveling musicians, a singer and a blind guitar player, entertained the busload, and the passengers cheerfully joined in singing without "the silly Puritan reticence & pseudo-dignity of the corresponding Yankee classes."[16]

After stops at Charleston and Savannah to admire their antiquities for a second time, Lovecraft went on to St. Augustine. There he enjoyed the ostrich and alligator farms and the old Spanish fort. He proceeded by bus to Dunedin, on the Gulf Coast north of St. Petersburg, to visit Whitehead. The warmth invigorated him. He loved the climate of Florida, although he did not care for the flat, boggy landscape and the lack of antiquities outside of St. Augustine.

Lovecraft had never before paid much attention to birds. If anything, the fact that bird-lovers tended to be cat-haters rather prejudiced him against them. The only time he was ever left speechless in an argument was when a bird-loving lady of Providence berated him as ally of bloodthirsty cats. In Florida, however, he was fascinated by the birds, from pelicans on down.

He liked Whitehead immensely and read his own stories aloud to the local boys' club. Whitehead lent him a white tropical suit and insisted that he take it with him when he left.

Timely revision checks enabled Lovecraft to go by bus and train to Key West, where he noted the Latin American influence, with movies in Spanish. Spanish Colonial architecture, like the French, began to intrigue him. "The local Cubans," he noted, "are very picturesque—& not even nearly so squalid as our Federal Hill Italians."

Lovecraft did not mind this "foreignism" because Key West, like Quebec, was "a really *old* & naturally developed town." Indeed, he found it "enchanting."[17] Had he had the money, he would have gone on to Cuba.

Although he had bought a cheap straw hat, he had taken to going hatless—for him, an orgy of informality, since "men of my age in the north stick to the traditional headgear." He enjoyed drifting without a definite schedule, laughing at the careful plans made by Morton for a trip to Nova Scotia:

> . . . for I wouldn't have more than a shadow of a kick from any trip whose moves were perfectly known in advance. The whole thrill of travel lies in the element of surprise & *unexpectedness*— suggesting as it does the quality of adventurous liberation.[18]

Back in New York in July, he noted that, whereas he formerly had no sense of time, his travels had taught him to be punctual. His friend Brobst testifies that, in the 1930s, Lovecraft was always on time.[19]

Wilfred Talman, who had a good job, had a quirk of buying lots of clothes and then tiring of them and giving them away. He gave

Lovecraft a mouse-colored Palm Beach suit, although Lovecraft hesitated to accept it because "it has a pattern, & is thus possibly too youthful for an old man." He finally took the suit but declined a light-gray winter overcoat to replace the 1909 overcoat he still wore. It "was so youthful that its appearance on me would have been even worse than that of my present archaeological reliques. . . ."[20]

He met a friend of Loveman, Leonard Gaynor, who worked for Paramount Pictures and showed an interest in Lovecraft's fiction. The chance of a movie sale was probably small, but Lovecraft preferred not to risk disappointment by following it up: ". . . in cold fact nothing of mine could ever be suitable for his purposes. Cinemas want *action*—whereas my one specialty is *atmosphere*."[21]

On July 15th, Lovecraft went on an automobile pleasure ride to Westchester County, whither he had been invited by a young friend named Allan B. Grayson. Grayson's mother drove. In Ardesley, they called upon a cousin of the Graysons. He wrote:

> This cousin—a now elderly gentlewoman—has become a sort of semi-recluse & eccentric as a result of excessive parental supervision in youth; it having been her father's design to keep her closely secluded till he could find her an husband among the German nobility. This latter he did not succeed in doing—hence died leaving a browbeaten & no longer attractive daughter in middle age, unfitted for the world by reason of early seclusion. After his death, the daughter was promptly married, for her money, by a commonplace, semi-rustic, & none too grammatical neighbour—& there the couple now live; elderly & eccentric, in the midst of scenic loveliness & architectural opulence. They keep no servant & have closed all but three rooms of the great house—dwelling like campers & wearing the most shapeless & nondescript apparel.[22]

One need not read very hard between the lines to see that Lovecraft realized the parallel between the unfortunate gentlewoman and himself.

For the rest of the year, Lovecraft stayed in New England except for short trips to Boston, Plymouth, and Hartford. In Hartford he arranged a $50 job of proofreading, for Orton's company, on a book about Dartmouth College. (This was the book that changed his view of Colonial times.) Otherwise he settled down to ghosting and revising, writing letters, reading, and strolling.

He argued science and religion with his correspondents. To

Moe, he said that the trouble with the Victorian Age was that all the first-class brains went into science, leaving none for the arts; hence the vagaries of Victorian taste. With Catholic Derleth he was polite about religion. But when, early in 1931, Frank Long flirted with Catholicism, Lovecraft went after him hammer and tongs: "that incredible & anti-social anachronism called the Popish church. . . . Popery fosters everything effeminate & repugnant." Although on other occasions he admitted religion to have some practical social value, he now declared: "I hate & despise religion" because, he said, it lied about basic, scientifically established facts.[23]

Lovecraft was still hostile to "foreign influences"; but, except for the black races (the Negroids, Australoids, and Melanesians), he had dropped his racial arguments. He now based his nativism on cultural grounds:

No anthropologist of standing insists on the uniformly advanced evolution of the Nordic as compared with that of other Caucasian and Mongoloid races. As a matter of fact, it is freely conceded that the Mediterranean race turns out a higher percentage of the aesthetically sensitive, and that the Semitic groups excel in sharp, precise intellection. It may be, too, that the Mongolian excels in aesthetick capacity and normality of philosophical adjustment.

These groups, however, were still condemned to mutual hostility, because:

Nothing but mischief can be caused by sentimentalists who try to pretend that different cultures can understand and like one another. . . . Actually, as Spengler shows, cultures are profoundly rooted, prodigiously unique, and externally hostile things—whose differences are *far greater* than is commonly suspected. . . . What we mean by Nordic "superiority" is simply *conformity to those character-expectations which are natural and ineradicable among us.* . . . We do not call [Italians] inferior, but simply admit that they are *different* beyond the limits of easy mutual understanding and cultural compatibility. . . . And don't forget that we affect alien groups just as they affect us. Chinamen think our manners are bad, our voices raucous, our odour nauseous, and our white skins and our long noses leprously repulsive. Spaniards think us vulgar, brutal, gauche. Jews . . . honestly think we are savage, sadistick, and childishly hypocritical. . . . What's the answer? *Simply keep the bulk of all these approximately equal and highly developed races as far apart as possible.* Let them study one another as deeply as possible, in the interest of that intellectual understanding which makes for appreciation and tolerance. But don't let them mix too freely. . . .

While still ethnocentric, this attitude is more sophisticated than his puerile early Nordicism or Aryanism; he was no longer proclaiming his low opinions of non-Anglo-Saxons as objective facts. Moreover, since cultures do differ in customs, manners, and morals, and xenophobia is an almost universal human trait, Lovecraft's argument is not entirely without foundation. Still, to justify his own feelings, he exaggerated the differences among different cultures and the difficulties of adaptation and assimilation. He did not foresee the homogenizing effect on the world's cultures of industralization and urbanization, and the dampening down of inter-ethnic hostility by the tremendous spread of higher education and international travel.

At times, Lovecraft even showed skepticism towards ethnic stereotypes: ". . . the superficial conception of various racial & national heritages is often amusingly at variance with the actual facts." He disclaimed his former misanthropy: "Refusal to *overvalue* people, in the mass, is no indication whatever that one *hates* or *despises* people. I'm sure I don't."[24]

In politics, he spoke of the inevitability of some kind of Socialism. Forced to choose between Fascism and Communism, he preferred Fascism. Democracy worked only on a small scale and in the United States had become a mere "hoax," a front for plutocracy. The "civilised ends" for which a government could be expected to work were physical security, an opportunity to learn and to express one's opinions, an atmosphere favorable to art and science, and "a sense of congenial placement." Even Communism would be tolerable if it could do these things, but up to then it had not.

He added: "Much may be learned from Soviet Russia, though no one would like to see the complete system of that country . . . adopted. . . ."[25] A few years before, when Lovecraft was still politically ultraconservative, E. Hoffmann Price had urged the same view of the Soviet Union upon him.

Lovecraft opposed censorship. This caused him difficulties when he tried to look with a friendly eye upon Fascism. He became resigned if not reconciled to change:

Certainly, the changes in America (& for that matter, elsewhere) resulting from mechanisation are not by any stretch of the optimistic fancy to be welcomed. All that can be said for them is that they are absolutely inevitable. Everything in modern existence is a direct & absolute corollary of the discoveries of applied steam

power & of large-scale application of electrical energy; & there is
no possible way to unmake a discovery once it has been stumbled
upon. . . . Actually, no one way of life as naturally evolved is
very much better or worse than any other. What we hate is simply
change, as such. And very naturally & reasonably, since most of the
zest of life comes from illusions depending on stable backgrounds
& continuity in traditions & folkways. . . .

Here Lovecraft anticipates Toffler's theory of "future shock."
As usual, Lovecraft's "we" is simply H. P. Lovecraft. Many relish
change and do not depend for "zest in life" or "stable backgrounds
and continuity in traditions and folkways." Others prefer a mixture
of stability and change. If we arranged people according to their
like or dislike of change, Lovecraft would stand at the "dislike" end
of the scale, while faddists who demand constant change for its
own sake would line up at the opposite end.

Towards his writing, Lovecraft was even more apologetic. He
was ashamed of much he had penned in his twenties. He wished he
could write realistic fiction for the money, but he could not. Action
stories were popular but had no real art; hence a magazine like
Argosy could never "become a market for *me*." He thought himself
too old to become versatile like Derleth. Actually, he could write
excellent action and suspense fiction, but he had convinced himself
that all such stories were "cheap pulp stuff," and that the only
fiction with any real "art" depended on atmosphere.

He still preached a humorless, art-for-art's-sake view of fiction:
"To have the reader in mind is absolutely fatal" to true art. "Art
demands that one write what is within one, and nothing more or
less." And ". . . anything that is *whimsical* is basically tawdry, in-
sincere, & the very opposite of the authentically weird."

Derleth advised J. Vernon Shea, a young correspondent, to get
some sexual experience to help his writing. Lovecraft assured Shea
that, on the contrary, sexual experience was not necessary to authorship. "Indeed, I can't see any difference in the work I did before
marriage & that I did during a matrimonial period. . . ." Perhaps
this tells more about Lovecraft's marriage than it does about the
craft of fiction.

Lovecraft was, however, careful to distinguish between his attitudes towards sex in fact and in fiction: "I detest all sexual irregularities *in life itself*,"[26] but he was not at all shocked by their

realistic portrayal in art. This was indeed a change from the day when he castigated Cook for running that story of an artist's model.

Lovecraft cherished an interest in pronunciation and dialects. For years he discussed regional variations in letters to Miss Tolridge and to Shea. His knowledge, however, remained superficial. He never, apparently, read the good books then available on the phonetics of American English, such as those of John S. Kenyon and George P. Krapp. Thus he miscalled the General American final and pre-consonantal *r* (as in *farmer*) a "rolled *r*." He voiced the common error that speakers of the proletarian New York dialect transposed the *er* and *oi* sounds, pronouncing "Ernest Boyd" as "Oinest Bird."[27] (Actually, they tended to use a single intermediate sound, between *oi* and *er*, in both words.)

In 1925, Wright had rejected Lovecraft's story "In the Vault" as too horrible. In the summer of 1931, Derleth persuaded Lovecraft to let him retype "In the Vault," whose manuscript had become tattered. Lovecraft, thanking Derleth, remarked that, since the story had already been rejected by three editors, "I doubt if it would do much good to send it again to Wright—I hate the cheapening involved in persistent peddling."[28] Derleth, however, sent "In the Vault" to Wright anyway. In October, Wright bought it for $55.

The sale encouraged Lovecraft to start another story. As an experiment, he began this new story in a style quite different from his usual one.

He made three such starts but bogged down each time. In November, he gave up his experiments and wrote the story in his natural style. Called "The Shadow Over Innsmouth," it came to 26,000 words. Combining elements of several earlier stories, "The Shadow Over Innsmouth" is not Lovecraft's best; but it is still—despite Lovecraft's blunder of putting the climax in the middle—a good, rousing yarn and central to the Cthulhu Mythos.

The narrator is a college undergraduate who, in Lovecraftian style, is "celebrating my coming of age by a tour of New England—sightseeing, antiquarian, and genealogical—and had planned to go directly from ancient Newburyport to Arkham, whence my mother's family was derived. I had no car, but was travelling by train, trolley and motor-coach, always seeking the cheapest possible route."[29]

His economy lands him in the decaying seaport of Innsmouth, of which he has heard sinister rumors. Innsmouthers are descended from a Captain Marsh, who in the 1840s brought back a strange wife from a South Sea island. They have the fishy "Innsmouth look," with receding foreheads and chins, bulging eyes, and scaly skins.

The narrator checks in at the ratty Gilman House and seeks out one of the few natives who is not one of Them. This is a nonagenarian drunkard who, plied with whiskey, tells the tale of Obed Marsh.

The doughty captain, it seems, found an island where the natives got fish and gold in return for human sacrifices to a race of aquatic humanoid beings, minions of Cthulhu. The sea-dwellers have interbred with the islanders. Their offspring begin life fully human but later acquire the sea-dwellers' ichthic appearance. In time they go back to the sea, where they live forever. Marsh's wife was one of these hybrids.

The narrator arouses the suspicions of the natives, who try to break into his hotel room. He climbs out the window, and for many pages the story is a good escape-and-pursuit narrative, despite Lovecraft's belief that he could not write action. The narrator gets away; although, being a Lovecraftian hero, he swoons like the heroine of a Victorian novel at the sight of something shocking. But then, in pursuing his genealogical studies, he learns that he, too, is a Marsh. . . .

Lovecraft took a poor view of the story:

> I don't think the experimenting came to very much. The result, 68 pages long, has all the defects I deplore—especially in point of style, where hackneyed phrases have crept in despite all precautions. Use of any other style was like working in a foreign language—hence I was left high & dry. . . . No—I don't intend to offer "The Shadow Over Innsmouth" for publication, for it would stand no chance of acceptance. I shall probably use it as a quarry. . . .[30]

Derleth offered to type the story and, when the offer was declined, hectored Lovecraft into typing it himself. Lovecraft sent Derleth the typescript, calling it "my own verbose & doubtful swansong . . . as a sort of grand finale to my present prose period."

Derleth urged Lovecraft to try the story on *Weird Tales*, but some of Lovecraft's other correspondents offered criticisms. These so discouraged Lovecraft that he filed the story away, mourning:

> As for writing on my part, I believe I am finished for good. Unfavourable estimates of my recent work have destroyed my own

confidence in it, & I do not find myself able to get on paper what I really want to express.[31]

He said: "It almost amuses me to reflect that I once thought I was on the road toward becoming able to write stories!" He was "virtually withdrawing from the professional arena," because "It is distinctly possible that I am written out. . . ." He now wrote with a ten-cent mechanical pencil, because pens tired his hand and "the very sight of a typewriter petrifies me." "Not only does it dry up all the founts of thought & imagination, but it makes me acutely nervous & gives me a headache. . . ."[32]

In order to write again, he would have to "get the whole loathsome picture of tradesmen & hagglers out of my head." "The only thing that sets me writing is complete freedom from all restrictions & from all thought of any critical standards or readers other than myself."

He was "always too close to the point of nervous exhaustion to be otherwise than retarded by the experience of repeated rejections."[33] When Derleth urged him to buck up and not let a few turndowns bother him, he plaintively replied:

> As for my own latter-day attitude toward writing & submitting—I can see why you consider my anti-rejection policy a stubbornly foolish & needlessly short-sighted one, & am not prepared to offer any defence other than the mere fact that repeated rejections *do* work in a certain way on my psychology—rationally or not—& that their effect is to cause in me a certain literary lockjaw which absolutely prevents further fictional composition despite my most arduous efforts. I would be the last to say that they ought to produce such an effect, or that they would—even in a slight degree —upon a psychology of 100% toughness & balance. But unfortunately my nervous equilibrium has always been a rather uncertain quantity, & it is now in one of its more ragged phases . . . I feel tremendously ungrateful in not availing myself of the generous encouragement & offers you have made, & could hardly blame you if you were to wash your hands of the old man as an altogether bad job—yet I feel sure that you realise how keenly I appreciate your interest & coöperation, & how much I regret having to seem stubborn, stupid, & a prey to second childhood's whims.

August Derleth was a young man of infinite energy and just that sort of "100% toughness and balance" of which Lovecraft spoke. Lovecraft envied him these qualities: "It must be great to be a superman—but have pity on mere mortals!"[34]

Actually, compared to the disappointments suffered by most writers, the rejections sustained by Lovecraft were so few as to be laughable, were we not describing a tragic situation. He would give up after one or two abortive attempts. (The present writer has sold pieces after a dozen or more rejections.)

What Lovecraft suffered from were not "second childhood's whims" but the compulsions and tabus laid upon him in his first childhood, many of which he never escaped. Thus, when Lovecraft's writing technique was at its height and his ideas as strikingly original as ever, his peculiar psychology—his feeble self-image, his anti-commercialism, his "professional amateurism"—combined to thwart such success as he might yet have achieved.

For all his self-conscious despair, Lovecraft did write a story in January, 1932: a 15,000-word novelette called "The Dreams in the Witch House." The story may have been suggested by a "House of Wonder," with walls and floors at odd angles, which Lovecraft and Sonia had visited at Coney Island nine years earlier.

Walter Gilman, an undergraduate at Miskatonic University, rooms in an ancient house in Arkham. This house had once harbored Keziah Mason, a witch who had fled from Salem during the witch panic of 1692. Gilman lives in Keziah's odd-angled room; he studies non-Euclidian calculus and quantum physics. He also dabbles in the *Necronomicon* and other occult works, in hope of finding formulae for gaining access to unknown dimensions.

Literal-minded critics have protested that there is no such thing as "non-Euclidean calculus." Of course there isn't, since Euclid flourished nearly two thousand years before calculus was invented by Newton and Leibniz. Lovecraft, I am sure, knew this and merely used the term as science-fiction writers often use pseudo-scientific terms, to "give artistic verisimilitude to an otherwise bald and unconvincing narrative."

Gilman has disturbing dreams, in which he sees the witch and the crone's familiar, called "Brown Jenkin." This creature resembles an oversized rat with a head of human shape and feet like human hands. The pair whisk Gilman off to their own dimensions, where everything looks like clusters of cubes and other geometrical figures.

There are rumors in Arkham of an impending Sabbat, with child sacrifice. Suspecting that Keziah means to involve him in this,

Gilman becomes more and more distraught. He talks of moving or of consulting a nerve specialist, but with Lovecraftian fecklessness he passively awaits his doom. . . . It is a good story, highly original and imaginative, tying the supposed seventeenth-century Salem witch cult in with the Cthulhu Mythos.

Lovecraft was in no hurry to sell the story. When Derleth urged him to let him at least type it, Lovecraft replied: "I wouldn't let you waste your time typing it for the world. . . ." About the beginning of May, Lovecraft got a client, whose work he had revised, to type "The Dreams in the Witch House" in lieu of payment.[35] He proposed to send it on the circuit of his friends, asking for criticism, before deciding whether to try it on Wright.

Derleth was first on the list; Clark Ashton Smith, second. A blunt and censorious critic, Derleth said harsh things about the story. Lovecraft then decided that "The whole incident shews me that my fictional days are probably over," and asked Derleth to return the manuscript forthwith.

For months, the story gathered dust. Then Derleth, who wanted a complete file of Lovecraft's writings, borrowed it again to type out his own copy. While he had the original, about the end of 1932, he showed it to Wright. The latter promptly bought it for $140 and printed it in his issue of July, 1933. Lovecraft refused to sell the radio dramatization rights, fearing the "vulgarisation" of the piece in the process of adaptation.[36]

In May, 1932, Lovecraft set out upon his next major journey. After stopping at the Longs' in New York, he went on to Washington, Roanoke, Knoxville, Chattanooga, Memphis, Vicksburg, Natchez, and New Orleans. He savored every moment of the way: Lookout Mountain, sunset on the Mississippi, and the antiquities of Natchez.

Lovecraft's fellow *Weird Tales* writer Edgar Hoffmann Price was living in New Orleans. Price was among other things a West Pointer, a U. S. Cavalry officer in the First World War, an amateur orientalist, and a skilled automobile mechanic. Having just lost his job to the Depression, Price was trying to keep afloat by writing stories for the pulps.

Never having met or corresponded with Price, Lovecraft "wasn't about to butt in and introduce myself." He wrote, however, to Robert Howard in Texas, telling him of his journey.

Howard had previously urged Lovecraft to visit him in Texas, promising a tour of the historic sites of the Lone Star State. He was bitterly disappointed that Lovecraft arrived in New Orleans at a moment when Howard was broke, carless, and unable to join him.

Howard therefore telegraphed Price, telling him where to find Lovecraft. The uninhibited Price at once telephoned Lovecraft, went to Lovecraft's hotel, and took Lovecraft to his own quarters. Lovecraft called the visit "the longest call I have ever paid—or ever expect to pay—in my life"

> . . . a call lasting 25½ hours without a break, from the middle of a Sunday [June 12th] evening to close upon midnight Monday. Price had a room in the Vieux Carré, & now & then his roommate would brew tea or coffee, or prepare a meal. . . . Nobody seemed to get sleepy, & the hours slipped away imperceptibly amidst discussions & fictional criticisms. Later calls lasted 10 hours or so each—& I was in touch with Price until I left.[37]

Price, too, described the meeting:

> My first sight of HPL was in the lobby of a third class hotel on St. Charles Street, in New Orleans, early in June of 1932. He wore a baggy and threadbare suit, snuff-colored, and neatly patched in several places. . . . The eyes I saw were dark brown, animated, intense, and entirely normal, without any of the weirdness I had expected.
>
> For the rest, he carried himself with enough of a slouch to make me underestimate his height as well as the breadth of his shoulders. His face was thin and narrow, longish, with long chin and jaw. He walked with a quick stride. His speech was quick and inclined to jerkiness. It was as though his body was hard put to it to keep up with the agility of his mind. . . .
>
> I was somewhat tense myself, not so much from the prospect of going to meet a fabulous character pictured as having uncanny eyes, as from the yarns I had heard: to wit, that he was an insufferably strait-laced Puritan, and that one had to guard one's speech and especially avoid any reference to drinking or habits which he deemed vices. But after a moment or so, I knew that this was neither a ghoul nor a blue-nose, but a friendly and human person, despite his seeming to be an animated dictionary.
>
> He was not pompous, and he was not pretentious—quite the contrary. He merely had the knack of using formal and academic diction for the most casual remark. We had not walked a block before I realized that no other way of speech could be truly natural for HPL. Had he used locutions less stilted, and taken to speaking as others did, *that* would have been an affectation. . . .

As a matter of courtesy, I had hidden some five cases of home brew (this was in 1932 [when Prohibition was still in force]) and a keg of raisin wine. His taste for coffee simplified the refreshment problem. Rather than "taste"—passion. He drank cup after cup, and I made pot after pot. Into each cup he stirred four heaping spoonsful of sugar. For twenty-eight consecutive hours during which we chatted at a giddy tempo, he drank coffee.

And he ate. His long face glowed when I mentioned the big kettle of chile con carne I'd cooked the day before his unexpected arrival. There were other delicacies in the refrigerator, but at the mention of chile, he unleashed a classical allusion in which "nectar" and "ambrosia" featured, and went on to say that the more highly spiced a dish, the better. . . .

Twenty-eight hours we gabbled, swapping ideas, kicking fancies back and forth, topping each other's whimsies. He had an enormous enthusiasm for new experience: of sight, of sound, of word pattern, of idea pattern. I have met in all my time only one or two others who approached him in what I call "mental greed." A glutton for words, ideas, thoughts. He elaborated, combined, distilled, and at a machine gun tempo.

He neither smoked nor drank, and, judging from all his conversation and letters, women did not exist as far as he was concerned. But excepting these, his tastes and interests approached the universal. . . .

During these twenty-eight hours, some of the Vieux Carré crowd came in, people I was sure he would deem lewd, bawdy, and sottish. They came up gaily, and with bottles. To sidetrack this outrage, as I feared he would consider it, would have been awkward, and in a sense, a belittlement rather than a mark of consideration to my guest of honor. I feared, too, that the crowd would at the best be boresome to a person of HPL's taste and background, if not offensive.

The way it turned out, . . . He not only met the visitors with a fine good fellowship and cordiality which belied all the reports I had heard of his intolerance in some respects, but he met them more than half way. And when he took the floor, they listened to this odd, this unique, this bookish, this pedantic Puritan from Providence. He held their attention from the first. His assurance and poise relieved and delighted me. . . .

This was an evening of many phases. One of my favorite HPL stories was, and still is, *The Silver Key*. In telling him of the pleasure I had had in reading it, I suggested a sequel to account for Randolph Carter's doings after his disappearance. My interest in his story stimulated him, and his appreciative response in turn stimulated me, so that before the session was over, we had seriously resolved to undertake the task. Some months later, I wrote a six thousand word first draft.

HPL courteously applauded, and then literally took pen in hand. He mailed me a 14,000 word elaboration, in the Lovecraft manner, of what I had sent him. I had bogged down, of course. The idea of doing a sequel to one of his stories was more fantastic than any fantasy he has ever written. When I deciphered his manuscript, I estimated that he had left unchanged fewer than fifty of my original words: one passage which he considered to be not only rich and colorful in its own right, but also compatible with the style of his own composition. He was of course right in discarding all but the basic outline. I could only marvel that he had made so much of my inadequate and bungling start. What I had done, in effect, was to prod him, by that start, into creating something. . . .

HPL commemorated, in that story, our twenty-eight hours of getting acquainted. The wrought-iron censers he mentions in the opening of the novelette were in my apartment at 305 Royal Street; so also the Adam fireplace, and the antique Boukhara and Persian carpets hanging on the walls.

We had a lot of fun in our collaboration. In grandiose whimsy, we decided that we'd do many collaborations, to capitalize on what he called my speed of composition. Instead of sharing the byline, we would create a new fiction star: Etienne Marmaduke de Marigny, whose output would, conservatively estimated, amount to a million words a month. We designed Moorish palaces, custom built cars, and all manner of luxuries for Etienne Marmaduke de Marigny to buy with his prodigious income, such as an automatic ice-cream freezer and dispenser offering a choice of two thousand flavors, and a wine cellar of equal versatility. HPL was broad-minded, more so than earlier accounts could have had him. I readily consented to excluding an oyster bar and anything else pertaining to seafood. Out of deference to HPL's sensibilities, I skipped concubines entirely.[38]

From New Orleans, Lovecraft returned homeward. While he was in New York, a telegram from Annie Gamwell informed him that Lillian Clark, long semi-invalided by neuritis and arthritis, had collapsed and was not expected to live.

Lovecraft caught a train to Providence and found his aunt in a coma. Two days later, on July 3, 1932, she peacefully died at seventy-six.

For two months, Lovecraft stayed home except for a few short excursions. The ship lines sailing to Newport had a rate war, reducing their fares to fifty cents. Lovecraft took advantage of this to make three trips to Newport. There he found a place on the cliffs where he could sit and write in scenic solitude. He also went to Newbury-port for a total eclipse of the sun.

He signed up for a ten-dollar rail excursion from Boston to Montreal and Quebec. He urged Cook to come with him. Cook declined, foreseeing an ordeal of "Sleep, if at all, in your seat. Train crowded to the last seat. Noisy, squalling brats, shrill-voiced women and liquorish men. Grab a dried-up sandwich or a stale cup of coffee now and then. . . ." Privately, Lovecraft thought it just as well that Cook refused. For all his plaints about lack of energy, Lovecraft, when sight-seeing, galloped about at a rate that exhausted his companions. Cook reminisced:

> Early the following Tuesday morning [September 6th], before I had to go to work, Howard arrived back from Quebec. I have never before nor since seen such a sight. Folds of skin hanging from a skeleton. Eyes sunk in sockets like burnt holes in a blanket. Those delicate, sensitive artist's hands and fingers nothing but claws. The man was dead except for his nerves, on which he was functioning. That evening he had a dinner appointment in Somerville with a woman for whom he was doing some revision, and he had plans for things he wanted to do during the day. I was scared.[39]

Cook lost his temper and berated his friend for his folly. He took Lovecraft to a restaurant for a proper breakfast, then to a room in his rooming house, where he bullied Lovecraft into spending the day asleep. After a second meal, he finally sent Lovecraft on his way.

The client in Somerville, Massachusetts, was a stout, auburn-haired divorcée, Hazel Drake Heald (1896–1961). In 1932, Clifford Eddy's wife Muriel had gotten up a New England Writers' Club and had thus come to know Mrs. Heald. Hazel had a story, "The Man of Stone," with an adequate plot but amateurish execution. Mrs. Eddy put her in touch with Lovecraft, who visited Somerville to revise this and other stories.

Lovecraft completely rewrote "The Man of Stone," putting in touches of the Cthulhu Mythos. Laid in the Adirondacks, it concerns a backwoods occultist who gets from the *Book of Eibon* a formula for turning people to stone. He uses it on a man whom he suspects of being his wife's lover, and in revenge the wife. . . . "The Man of Stone" appeared under Hazel Heald's by-line in *Wonder Stories* for October, 1932.

Lovecraft revised several other tales for Mrs. Heald. One is "The Horror in the Museum," about a waxwork museum. One exhibit is a gigantic, spidery, tentacled monstrosity called Rhan-Tegoth and the remains of a man who has been sacrificed to it. The monstrosity turns out to be not made of wax after all.

Another, "Winged Death," tells of a scientist who causes the death of a rival scientist by having him bitten by a tsetse fly infected with sleeping sickness. The victim's spirit takes possession of another fly of the same kind. "Out of the Eons" is a story of a strange mummy from a Pacific isle. It recounts a legend of the people of the lost continent of Mu and their Yuggothian god Ghatanothoa, the mere sight of whom literally petrifies the viewer. "The Horror in the Burying Ground" tells about hauntings in a New England village populated by degenerates, drunkards, and half-wits. All four appeared, as by Hazel Heald, in *Weird Tales*.

Hazel had Lovecraft to dinner with romantic accessories like candlelight. She confided to Muriel Eddy that, being lonely, she would like to know Lovecraft better and asked her help in furthering the relationship.

Lovecraft, however, had been all through this and was not having any more. His visits to Somerville tapered off. Although he continued to work with Hazel, he was always too busy to make the journey to Somerville or even to come to the Eddys' when Muriel Eddy invited the pair.

In the election of 1932, Lovecraft abandoned the Republican party for good, calling it "hopelessly obsolescent." Of the leading candidates, he most favored the program of Norman Thomas, the Socialist; but, holding that a vote for Thomas would be wasted, he came out for Franklin D. Roosevelt.

Lovecraft was impressed by Technocracy, which flourished in 1932 and which he called "of tremendous importance."[40] An engineer named Howard Scott launched this movement. Scott proposed to solve the crisis of democratic capitalism by putting the government into the hands of a kind of soviet of engineers (as Thorstein Veblen had advocated a decade before) on the dubious assumption that engineers were more trustworthy and less self-interested than other men. Technocracy spawned several books and a number of articles but faded away after Roosevelt's election.

Soon after the election, Lovecraft was cast down by the news that Henry Whitehead, his host of the previous spring in Florida, had died on November 23d. Whitehead's death was the first of several such losses among the writers of *Weird Tales*, which, together with Wright's dismissal and death, began the decline of the magazine.

After his Canadian trip, Lovecraft stuck to his anti-commercial resolution. He dabbled in amateur journalism, "which I can't quite bring myself to forego." Although Cook's project of publishing "The Shunned House" had fallen through, Lovecraft refused to try the story on Wright again because "I don't feel like hawking my product to editors who feel as coolly toward them as does Satrap Pharnabazus."[41]

Harold S. Farnese, dean of the Los Angeles Institute of Musical Art, wrote to Lovecraft proposing a joint project: a Cthulhuvian operetta in one act, called *Fen River* and laid on the planet Yuggoth. As a starter, Farnese had already set two of Lovecraft's *Fungi from Yuggoth* sonnets, *Mirage* and *The Elder Pharos*, to music. Lovecraft replied with mingled enthusiasm and self-doubt:

> I really feel quite overwhelmed by the force of the implied compliment! If I were able to do justice to such an enterprise, there is nothing I would rather attempt—for despite a profound ignorance of music, I am acutely sensible of its marvellous power, and keenly appreciative of its ability to enhance the effect of allied forms of expression. But over against this looms the fact that I have *no experience whatever in dramatic composition*—and how is a frank novice to evolve anything capable of correlation with the score of an accomplished composer? . . . I would like enormously to co-operate if I thought I could—for the picture of those swampy rivers choked with noxious weeds and trickling sluggishly through sunless tangles of grotesque and gigantic trees, or lapping at cave-riddled cliffs of basalt carven with non-human hieroglyphs, is one which surely catches poignantly at my imagination!

Farnese kept urging. He had already assembled a cast of characters, including Yurrengarth (tenor), Yannimaid (soprano), Chlorander (tenor), Nickelman (baritone or bass), Aril (mezzo-soprano), Serac the priest (baritone), Terrete the ferryman (bass), and "people of the swamp village."

As he thought the project over, Lovecraft shrank from the prospect of writing a lot of dialogue, which he considered inimical to his weird effects. In the end, he recoiled in a paroxysm of humility. It was "too big an order for one absolutely without experience." "I don't believe I'm equal to writing it, anyway." "I'd only make an ass of myself if I tried anything so ambitious & sustained." "It's better not to attempt anything too ambitious, & I fancy the wiser course is to let Farnese find another collaborator."[42]

One may wonder what Lovecraft had to lose by going in with Farnese, how he expected to get experience if he did not start somewhere, and why he was so sure that he would be no good at librettos. But, along with all his other tabus and inhibitions, the fear lest he "make an ass of himself" was perhaps the operative factor. He had failed at many things. These failures had battered his sensitive ego until, despite his posture of cool detachment, he could not bear to expose himself to any more such blows. He would play safe henceforth, doing only what he knew he could do.

That meant hack jobs such as writing a brochure on European travel, which he did in December. He intended to write fiction only as an occasional solitary amusement. He thought his style had been "more or less influenced by the cheap & tawdry methods & moods of commercial writing" and was "full of awkwardnesses and crudities" and "hackneyed rhetorical devices."[43]

He did not, however, intend to let his manuscripts be changed by some "pachydermatous mob-caterer who knows & cares nothing for genuine quality. . . ." "Commercial writing & I have absolutely nothing in common." "The whole weary business of catering to the childish whims of an ignorant canaille is ineffably repulsive & infuriating to me. . . ." When Price twitted him with refusing to change his stories out of mere laziness, he replied:

> Probably you are right in saying that some reluctance to change work is due to indolence—but oddly enough, I have a certain respect for that form of indolence. To begin with, I do not very seriously reprehend any sort of laziness. All work is really vain, & the lazy man is often the wisest in the long run. . . . Undeniably, I have a contempt for any performance of *hard work* when the object is not *intrinsic excellence.* . . . What I really want is *any* kind of a non-literary job paying $15.00 per week or more—plus enough unworried leisure to write with excellence as a sole object, & with no thought of audience or professional markets.

He said he would work at "*anything*—elevator man, pickaxe artist, night-watchman, stevedore, what the hell—*except writing.*"[44]

But I have no evidence that Lovecraft ever sought a salaried job after 1930. Nor do I know whom he expected to recognize the "intrinsic excellence" of his unsold writings.

Lovecraft talked a lot about "genuine quality" or "intrinsic excellence" in fiction, blandly assuming that such things existed. In fact, such concepts are just vaporous abstractions, with no more objective reality than elves. Everybody is entitled to define them as he pleases; but, as the psychologist Thouless pointed out, "It is as easy to define unicorn as to define rhinoceros."[45] Brilliant as he was, Lovecraft spent much of his life, in effect, arguing learnedly about the anatomy of unicorns and the culture of elves.

Lovecraft explained why he could not write realistic fiction:

> . . . I simply haven't anything to say in any field outside the unreal. I have not a keen sensitiveness for the drama of actual life. Academically I appreciate its importance & I can admire the artistic skill which captures & utilises it; but it does not interest me enough to make me want to get it down on paper myself.

An equally compelling reason was:

> I fear no one can be a genuinely great realist without doing an obnoxious amount of nosing & gossiping. That sort of thing is instinctively repulsive & abhorrent to me. . . .

While "it is hard to say that all realists are bounders," nonetheless: "Long and I have often tried to settle the question as to whether one may at the same time be a successful realist & a gentleman, & our conclusions have generally tended toward the negative side." Lovecraft believed in "being a gentleman first & a specifick artist second if at all."[46]

Seventeen

THWARTED THINKER

The cloudless day is richer at its close;
A golden glory settles on the lea;
Soft, stealing shadows hint of cool repose
To mellowing landscape, and to calming sea.[1]

LOVECRAFT

The Longs invited Lovecraft to New York, starting the day after Christmas, 1932. Lovecraft went for a week. Loveman now had an apartment big enough to display his collection of curios, antiques, and art objects. He gave Lovecraft two of these: a Mexican Indian stone statuette and an African flint knife with an ivory handle.

Back home, Lovecraft settled down to ghosting, nagged by a growing fear of destitution. Now that Lillian Clark was gone, Lovecraft had to pay the whole $40-a-month rent on his part of 10 Barnes Street. This expense was eating into his pathetic remaining capital at an alarming rate.

Amid his financial worries, he turned his attention to an overdue task. Lovecraft was generally averse to collaboration, because "any hampering element arrests my own imagination." He may not have seriously meant his badinage with Price in New Orleans, about a sequel to "The Silver Key."

Price, however, did. At the end of September, 1932, Lovecraft received Price's 6,000-word first draft of the projected sequel. He sent Price a letter glowing with praise but confided to Derleth: "I couldn't very well escape that collaboration; since Price sent his original share before I could gracefully escape, & seemed so eager to go ahead that refusal would have been boarish."

It took Lovecraft six months to get around to the sequel, "Through the Gates of the Silver Key"; but then a flood of ghosting work descended upon him. This included an 80,000-word novel to revise and a client in Hartford to help with antiquarian research on the local Athenaeum.

Lovecraft finally sent the manuscript to Price on April 6, 1933. He told Derleth that he had found the work twice as hard as original composition and, with his usual pessimism, added: "I still don't think it'll sell."[2]

Price made a few changes in the finished manuscript and sent it to *Weird Tales*. On August seventeenth, Wright returned it with what Lovecraft called a "tearful" rejection. Wright said he loved the story but was afraid to buy it, because "with business as poor as it is now, I feel that we cannot risk discouraging so many readers from buying the magazine, merely by printing a story that is so utterly alien to even their wildest dreams. . . ."[3]

As had happened before, Wright thought better of his decision. In November, Price called upon him in Chicago. After some discussion, Wright bought the story for $140. Holding that Lovecraft had done at least three quarters of the work, Price insisted on paying Lovecraft three quarters of the money, or $105.

"Through the Gates of the Silver Key" is, I think, far superior to the tale of which it is a sequel. It begins:

> In a vast room hung with strangely figured arras and carpeted with Boukhara rugs of impressive age and workmanship, four men were sitting around a document-strewn table. From the far corners, where odd tripods of wrought iron were now and then replenished by an incredibly aged Negro in somber livery, came the hypnotic fumes of olibanum; while in a deep niche on one side there ticked

a curious, coffin-shaped clock whose dial bore baffling hieroglyphics and whose four hands did not move in consonance with any time system know on this planet. . . .[4]

The four are Etienne-Laurent de Marigny, "the distinguished Creole student of mysteries and Eastern antiquities" and the executor of the will of the vanished Randolph Carter; Ward Phillips, an aged eccentric and mystic from Providence, who had known Carter; Ernest K. Aspinwall, an apoplectic-looking lawyer from Chicago and a cousin of Carter; and the Swami Chandraputra, bearded and turbaned. Aspinwall insists that the time has come to divide up the Carter estate. De Marigny and Phillips oppose this.

This swami explains that, having gone back to his boyhood, Carter then used the Silver Key to open the gateway out of earthly dimensions. He confronts the supernatural guardian of that gate, mentioned in the *Necronomicon* as "'UMR AT-TAWIL, the Most Ancient One, which the scribe rendered as THE PROLONGED OF LIFE."[5]

In a dreamlike hyperdimensional space, Carter meets the other Ancient Ones. He learns to be conscious of himself in the past, present, and future, and also of the innumerable other beings of which Randolph Carter is only one "facet."

One of these beings is the wizard Zkauba, living in the remote past on the planet Yaddith, where the civilized race is "rugose, partly squamous, and curiously articulated in a fashion mainly insect-like yet not without a caricaturish resemblance to the human outline." They have clawed limbs and tapirlike snouts. ("Rugose" and "squamous" mean "wrinkled" and "scaly.") The Yaddithites war against the "bleached viscous Dholes in the primal tunnels that honeycombed the planet."[6]

Carter takes possession of the mind of Zkauba in order to study means of returning to Earth in human form. But now he finds that the spells for this are not to be had on Yaddith. They were contained in a parchment in the box where Carter had found the Silver Key. Like Lovecraft setting out for New York with the Houdini manuscript, Carter had forgotten to take this parchment with him. Anything that happens to a writer, no matter how unpleasant at the time, can sooner or later be exploited in his writing.

All that Carter can do, then, is to travel through time and

space to Earth in Zkauba's body, find the parchment, and use it to resume his proper human form. He makes the journey by a "light-wave envelope," with the Zkauba-facet kept unconscious by a drug. But he must postpone the threatened division of his estate until he can resume his human shape.

Throughout this recital, Aspinwall sneers and snorts. He accuses the swami of wearing a mask. The swami admits this but explains that he is Randolph Carter. Shouting that the swami is just a crook and a faker, Aspinwall seizes the beard to yank off the mask. . . .

For all of Lovecraft's grousing, Price deserves credit for prodding Lovecraft into creating a good piece of entertainment. Even though the mysterious clock is never accounted for, the collaborators composed a sound, taut story.

By March, it seemed plain to Lovecraft that poverty would prevent a spring trip in 1933. "I wish I knew how people manage to acquire cash!" he lamented.

A maiden lady named Alice Rachel Sheppard dwelt in the Samuel B. Mumford house at 66 College Street. This was a cubical, yellow wooden clapboard house with a monitor top, behind the John Hay Library on the Brown University campus.

A friend of Annie Gamwell, Miss Sheppard had since 1900 taught German in the public schools of Providence. Although not of German background, she was so ardent a Germanophile that she stopped her subscription to the *New York Times* when that paper denounced Hitler.

Miss Sheppard, who occupied the ground floor of the Mumford house, told Annie Gamwell that the tenants of the upper story were leaving. Annie Gamwell proposed that she and her nephew take the upper floor at 66 College Street. The total rent would be only $40 a month (the same that Lovecraft was paying at 10 Barnes Street), which he and Annie would divide. They would get five spacious rooms. Hot and cold water and steam heat were piped in from Brown University, which owned the house.

Lovecraft was reconciled to the agonies of moving by the fact that the house was "Colonial." If it did not have an actual fanlight over the front door, it had the next best thing, a fan carving.

Lovecraft moved on May 21st to 23d and spent the next two weeks arranging his possessions and helping his aunt to move. Annie

Gamwell ate her dinners at the Fedden boarding house within a block, and Lovecraft sometimes joined her.

Once settled, Lovecraft went into rhapsodies over his new quarters:

> After admiring such [Colonial houses] all my life, I find something magical & dreamlike in the experience of actually living in one for the first time. To come *home* through a carved Georgian doorway & sit by a white colonial mantel gazing out through small-paned windows over a sea of centuried roofs & dense verdure. . . . I keep fearing that some museum guard will come around & boot me out at 6 o'clock closing time!

> Men with periwigs, knee-breeches, & three-cornered hats have actually dwelt in this abode![7]

Lovecraft was mistaken about the age of the Mumford house. While he thought it was built around 1803, it was really erected in 1825, when periwigs, knee breeches, and three-cornered hats had long vanished. Still, the house followed eighteenth-century design.

For a week or two, Lovecraft was ecstatic, and he always loved that house. He soon made friends with all the neighboring cats. These cats were given to congregating on a nearby low roof, where they sat quietly, ignoring one another in feline fashion, before going about their business. Lovecraft called this tribe the Kappa Alpha Tau fraternity, or KAT. The letters stood for *Kompsôn Ailourôn Taxis*, or Company of Elegant Cats. For the rest of his life, he filled his letters with the doings of the KAT.

On June 14th, Miss Sheppard rang the doorbell for Annie Gamwell, to invite her to the president's reception after the Brown University commencement. Hurrying to answer the ring, Annie Gamwell fell downstairs and broke her ankle.

Mrs. Gamwell spent three weeks in the hospital and came home with her leg in a cast. For two months she had a nurse and, after the cast came off in August, walked on crutches. In the afternoon, when the nurse took time off, Lovecraft had to be on deck to answer the doorbell. He had to give up a planned trip to the NAPA convention in New York in July.

Lovecraft tended to go to pieces under any exacting routine. He complained: ". . . my nerves all shot to hell as a result of my 'imprisonment.' . . . a whole year . . . has been subtracted from my existence." Not until the end of 1933 was Mrs. Gamwell able to get about without a walking stick.

While Annie Gamwell was laid up, Wilfred Talman lured Lovecraft into another unpaid writing job. Talman had become editor of the quarterly magazine of the Holland Society of New York, *De Halve Maen*.[8] The name means "The Half Moon," after the ship in which Henry Hudson discovered the river that bears his name. The 1,400-word article, "Some Dutch Footprints in New England," tells of attempts by the Dutch of early Colonial times to get a foothold in this region.

Talman wrote several stories for *Weird Tales*. One of these ("Two Black Bottles," in *Weird Tales* for August, 1927) Lovecraft revised, making changes in the dialogue that Talman disliked. Talman had his revenge with "Some Dutch Footprints," when, he said, "The quibbling in correspondence over spelling, punctuation, and historical facts before the script suited us both approached booklength proportions."[9]

During 1933, Lovecraft's political outlook changed. For a while he became an open Fascist sympathizer. Although never a complete, uncritical True Believer in Fascist doctrines, he could have been called a Fascist fellow-traveler. Likewise many American intellectuals of the time, including some of Lovecraft's young friends like Robert Barlow, became Communist fellow-travelers.

Unlike her sister Lillian, Annie Gamwell was a person of lively social instincts. A few months' exposure to his aunt's conservative business-class friends disillusioned Lovecraft with these "best people." He found them dull, stuffy, inesthetic, and unintellectual, full of "ignorance, loose thinking, blind habit, cowardly evasion," and other shortcomings.

Lovecraft's xenophobia, which had subsided, burst out again. His letters of 1933 have many examples of anti-ethnic rant. He raved about the Jews' "alien & emotionally repulsive culture-stream" and "ruthless enterprise"; about their supposed control of American newspapers through advertising, as a result of which "Taste is insidiously moulded along non-Aryan lines." He fumed at immigrants: "crawling peasants," "stinking mongrels," "ghetto bastards," and "scum and dregs of their own countries . . . the weaklings who couldn't keep on top among their own people."[10]

He made some effort to distinguish between race and culture: "Semitic blood couldn't hurt us in the least. . . ." "The trouble with the Jew is not his blood . . . but his . . . antagonistic *culture-tradition.*" But he still talked of "Aryan racial instincts," claiming that Nordics "think & feel & act in a characteristic Nordic fashion as long as the old blood remains predominant."[11]

He had not, in fact, yet escaped from his pseudo-scientific racial beliefs. He argued not only that the Aryan conquerors were Nordics (improbable) but also that they had proved their superiority by forcing their language on the conquered. No Aryans, he said, had ever given up their Aryan speech (untrue).[12]

He still professed discomfort in the presence of persons different from himself. Writing of the "Latin mongrelisation" of Providence, he remarked:

> One has to get down to Richmond to find a town which really *feels like home*—where the average person one meets looks like one, has the same type of feelings & recollections, & reacts approximately the same to the same stimuli.

He was bothered not only by the "verminous hordes of distorted aliens" in New York but also by the self-styled literati and intelligentsia to be found there, which "type also gives me a highly unpalatable mixture of discomfort & boredom. . . . I feel like an explorer amongst a queer African or Polynesian tribe . . . & am rather ill at ease unless there are a few more 'white men'—regular folk from the real America—present."[13]

Had Lovecraft ever moved south to live, he would have found most Southerners no more congenial or sympathetic than he found New Yorkers, businessmen, intellectuals, and ethnics. They would, for instance, have been outraged by his religious views. In this mental state, Lovecraft found almost everybody unpleasant company.

Having already dismissed most of his fellow-countrymen as "bourgeois," "the herd," or "the rabble," Lovecraft had found people of so many classes obnoxious that there were hardly any left to qualify as "regular folk from the real America." But in his personal contacts with people, however he may have despised them in the abstract, his courtly manners so well hid any distaste that his friends found it hard to take his misanthropic outbursts seriously.

I suspect that the basic cause of Lovecraft's misanthropy was nothing the others did or said but reflected the fact that they were getting on in the world while he was not. For all his powerful intellect, superior cultural background, inherited social status as an Old American, and monastic frugality, Lovecraft could never quite support himself. The contrast tormented him, and at times he was ready to take out his vexation on anybody.

One of Lovecraft's friends said: "Howard's monomania about race was about as close to insanity as anything I can think of." Certainly, Lovecraft's tirades on the subject suggest a dictum of the psychiatrist Searles, whom I have previously quoted. Doctor Searles says that psychotics find abstractions more real than concrete reality; they react to them more intensely than they do to reality.[14] This is not to say that Lovecraft was psychotic; but the extent to which he could get worked up over abstractions like "racial instinct" and "culture streams" implies a psychological disturbance of no small degree.

On January 30, 1933, Adolf Hitler was sworn in as Chancellor of Germany by President von Hindenburg (whom Lovecraft admired). During the next few months, Hitler converted his position into a total dictatorship.

During the summer school vacation of 1933, Alice Sheppard, Lovecraft's downstairs neighbor, went to Germany and returned full of enthusiasm. She found that "the morale & general condition of Germany are infinitely better than they were last year. Reports of 'barbarism' are incredibly magnified."

For the next year, Lovecraft's letters were full of apologies for dictators in general and Hitler in particular. Fascist dictators he said, were the only ones who could arrest the "decadence" that he saw overwhelming civilization and the "disintegration of western cultural standards." They were purifying their respective countries of "alien taints." Hitler, Mussolini, Kemal, and Stalin, he thought, were all out to cure the "rottenness" of contemporary culture.

Hitler, although "extreme, grotesque, & occasionally barbarous," was "profoundly sincere & patriotic." Although he did present a peril, "that cannot blind us to the honest rightness of the man's basic urge. . . . I know he's a clown, but by God I *like* the boy!" "Hitler is ill-informed, badly balanced, & neurotic—but he is one of those crude forces which sometimes make history. . . ."

Lovecraft disapproved of book-burning and the suppression of freedom of thought and speech: "I am far from a Nazi, & would probably get kicked out of Germany for my opinions regarding the universe, the facts of science, & the rights of free aesthetic expression—but at the same time I refuse to join in the blind herd-prejudice against an honest clown whose *basic* objects are all essentially sound despite the occasionally disastrous extremes & absurdities in his present policy."[15]

Lovecraft went on volubly about "historical & sociological forces," the "burden of Versailles," and the menace of Communism, than which Hitler was a lesser evil. Similar sentiments were then common among conservative, isolationist, Germanophilic, or racist Americans, like H. L. Mencken, Col. Robert McCormick, John Foster Dulles, and Charles Lindbergh.

At the same time, Lovecraft became an enthusiastic supporter of Franklin D. Roosevelt and his New Deal. Roosevelt, he said, was after all a gentleman. If his program was designed to help the ignorant masses, that was no more than the *noblesse oblige* of a true aristocrat towards his inferiors.

Now, how could a man support Roosevelt, call himself a liberal Democrat, praise Norman Thomas, speak of the inevitability of Socialism, and at the same time apologize for Hitler and write: "I am an unreserved fascist" and "I believe some form of fascism to be the only sort of civilised government possible under the industrial economy of the machine age"?[16]

The answer is that Lovecraft called himself all sorts of things without much regard for consistency. For instance: "I shall have to call myself a sort of cross betwixt a fascist & an old-time non-bolshevik socialist" and "Since 1931 I have been what would probably be called a *socialist*—or among the Russians, a *menshevik* as distinguished from a *bolshevik*."

Furthermore, his ideas both of Roosevelt's program and of Fascism were highly abstract, unrealistic, and unsullied by personal contact with politics. His friend E. A. Edkins wrote:

> No monk in his cell was ever more withdrawn from the excitements and occupations of ordinary life than that beaked and bony dreamer, sitting in his aerie on "The Ancient Hill". Yet such was the scope of his intellectual curiosity that he even developed an academic interest in government and a singularly romantic con-

ception of the New Deal, gorgeously complicated with Utopian ideologies that would have astonished even Mr. Roosevelt, who, in Lovecraft's opinion, was about to produce an authentic Millennium out of his presidential hat. The embroideries contributed by Lovecraft included adequate provisions for indigent gentlemen and scholars, baronial largesse for the peasantry, liberal endowments for those desiring to practise the arts and sciences, a stiff educational test for voters, and the gradual substitution of an aristocracy of intellect for the present aristocracy of wealth.[17]

Lovecraft's ideal "social fascism" resembled no form of government ever seen on earth—certainly not the European dictatorships then called "Fascistic." He advocated "affairs being administered by commissioners appointed by a dictator seated through an intelligent & educationally select electorate. . . . Ballots ought to be given only to persons who pass both an impartial intelligence test & test of economic, social, political, & general cultural knowledge; it being understood that opportunities for education must always be kept equal."

When Lovecraft described this utopia to Robert E. Howard, the latter sensibly pointed out that such an intellectually elite ruling class would, unless kept in check, prove just as oppressive as any other elite. As for the question that leaps to the mind of a modern reader—how to keep this dictator, chosen by voters of whatever IQ, from rigging elections or changing the constitution to keep himself in power forever—Lovecraft seems never to have thought of that.

From the end of 1933 on, Lovecraft's criticism of Hitler and Fascism grew ever more severe. The Nazis, he said, in forcing art to serve their own political and economic ends, were almost as bad as the Communists. Hitler might still be a lesser evil than Communism, but his "attempted regulation of Germanic culture seems to grow less instead of more rational."

In the last three years of his life, Lovecraft proclaimed himself "opposed to the Nazi tribal ideal." He spoke of "the tragedy of those new philosophies, so popular in totalitarian dictatorships, which exalt unreason & demand that scholarship be used only to serve preconceived propagandist ends." He denounced the "crazy scientific fallacies . . . such as one sees in Nazi Germany and Soviet Russia."[18] The Nazis, he concluded, were as bad as the Communists. Like most liberal Americans, he sympathized with the Republican side in the Spanish civil war of 1936–39 but was perplexed and disturbed by Stalin's purge trials of the same period.

By 1935, Lovecraft was cured of Fascistic leanings. He still upheld Roosevelt but confessed himself baffled by the problem of "how to get a decent brand of socialism." He preferred the Scandinavian evolutionary progress towards Socialism but doubted whether it would work in the United States without a *coup d'état*. This might result "in some tyrannical & arbitrary group like that imagined in Lewis's 'It Can't Happen Here.' . . . Modern politics is too much for an old man."

Besides the antics of Hitler and his Nazis, Lovecraft was swayed by Sinclair Lewis's *It Can't Happen Here* (1935); Lovecraft mentioned this novel, which he read as a serial in the *Providence Bulletin*, in several letters. Another influence was the great popularization of the biological sciences, *The Science of Life* (1929–34), by H. G. Wells, Julian Huxley, and George P. Wells. In September, 1935, J. Vernon Shea lent Lovecraft this book. Lovecraft hailed it as "by all odds the greatest single exposition of biological knowledge which I have ever seen. . . . the most important book I have read in years. . . ."[19] He kept the book over a year, reading and rereading it.

The significance here of *The Science of Life* is that the authors succinctly debunked the Aryan myth:

> First, there is no such thing as an "Aryan race." There are only groups of peoples of very various stock who speak languages of Aryan type. . . .
> Secondly, there is no such thing as a pure "Jewish race." The term *Jewish* denotes a community with a certain religious and seminational tradition, in which some community of descent is involved. But the Jews themselves are of markedly mixed origin. . . .
> Thirdly, the Nordic race, on which so much political stress has been laid, hardly exists anywhere in a state even approaching purity. In Germany, for instance, Nordic genes are very much mixed with those of Alpine, and, to a lesser extent, with those of Mediterranean provenance, and there has also been a certain infiltration of Mongolian characters from the East. . . .
> Fourthly, the Nordics have not, as is often claimed, been responsible for all the great advances in human history. The greatest advance of all, from barbarism to civilization . . . was made in the

Near or Middle East, probably by dark-haired people of Mediterranean type, certainly not by any tall and fair-haired, blue-eyed Nordic stock. . . .

Another event confirmed Lovecraft's disillusionment with Hitler and the Aryan cult. At the end of the school year of 1935–36, Alice Sheppard retired from teaching, gave Lovecraft a number of her books, and in August left for Germany. Her plan was to stay there for three years and then settle for good in Newport. In September, new tenants moved into the ground-floor apartment of 66 College Street. Although Annie Gamwell was "heartbroken" by their low social status, Lovecraft said he had "become democratic in my old age" and so did not mind them.[20]

Miss Sheppard's German idyll did not long endure. When she arrived, the Nazis' persecution of the Jews was in high gear. Totally disillusioned, Miss Sheppard soon returned to Providence, where her firsthand accounts of Nazi cruelties horrified the tender-hearted Lovecraft.

One of the most striking changes in Lovecraft in his last years was the loss of his Judaeophobia. His anti-Jewish fixation had already been blunted by his friendship with such gifted Jews as Sam Loveman, Robert Bloch, Henry Kuttner, and Donald Wollheim. By 1936, Lovecraft was urging assimilation as the solution to the so-called Jewish problem:

> The general Jewish question has its perplexing cultural aspects, but the biologically unsound Nazi attitude offers no solution. . . . What is more, it is equally silly to *belittle* even the admittedly hybrid art of Judaeo-Germans or Judaeo-Americans. It may not represent genuine German or American feeling, but it at least has a right to stand on its own feet as a frankly exotic or composite product—which may well excel much of our own art in intrinsic quality. Still more—it is equally silly to insist that the mere element of *blood* as distinguished from *culture* makes art necessarily hybrid. . . . almost any line of solution [of Gentile-Jewish hostility] is better than the arbitrary & unscientific one the Nazis have chosen. . . .

He also warned against attempts by far-right conservatives to regain power by

> . . . a shrewdly organised fascist movement based on primitive emotional appeals . . . (waving the flag, rousing nominal Christians against "Jewish intellectualism", exciting native-Americans against "Catholic-Irish-Jewish . . . democracy". . . .)

Lovecraft named Father Coughlin, William Dudley Pelley's Silver Shirts, and the Ku Klux Klan as the kind of instruments these "reactionaries" would use to achieve their ends. Now Lovecraft showed puzzled disapproval when a young friend developed Nazi ideas like those that Lovecraft had espoused a few years before:

> His pro-fascism is not to be marvelled at in view of his past Menckenian attitudes, but this new anti-Semitism of his is really curious. He never used to have it (our good friend Loveman is of Jewish origin, & —— was a prime booster of his work), & I fancy it must be an outcome of his latter-day Germanophilia—which tends to forget the older German main stream while centreing around the present eccentric regime.[21]

Lovecraft also became disenchanted with Spengler's *Decline of the West*. Spengler, he thought, carried his organic analogies—likening a culture to a living being, with youth, maturity, and old age—to an unscientific extreme.

Weeks before his death, Lovecraft attended a New Deal rally and was delighted with "the phenomenal penetration & wit," of the main speaker, Rabbi Stephen Wise: "I can well imagine the polite Nazis of Wall St. cursing him as a blasphemous non-Aryan intellectual!"[22] Altogether, Lovecraft did a remarkable turnabout in his last years.

The summer of 1933 brought its stream of visitors. On July 4th, Edgar Hoffmann Price arrived for a four-day stay, and Paul Cook appeared during the latter part of Price's visit. Price recalled:

> The following year, HPL and I met in Providence, at 66 College Street. His aunt, Mrs. Gamwell, was then in the hospital, so that there was no one to persuade us to keep sane hours. My recollection is that this time, we were on the go for thirty-four hours. . . .
> Harry Brobst, interne at a local madhouse, joined us, and we went to the cemetery just off Benefit Street, around four in the morning. . . . HPL was monologuing about Edgar Allan Poe, and Mrs. Helen Whitman he had courted; and here was the lady's house. And then—
> Of a sudden, and as though HPL's gesture had made it materialize, I was looking into a churchyard, and it seemed, was almost in it. It could have been a scene from one of his stories. In that light, and perhaps because of the sudden revelation, it seemed

something that could not belong to this earth. . . . With perfect showmanship, HPL had saved that spectacle until last and then, with perfect timing offered it to prove that Providence still had something all its own.

The following day, I made East Indian curry. Harry Brobst came over with six bottles of beer. This seemed daring, until I learned the fine distinctions HPL made. Beer was now legal. We were not violating the law of the land, he asserted by way of justifying his change of front. We drank with his blessing, though he declined to take a glass with us.

"And what," he asked, out of scientific curiosity, "are you going to do with so *much* of it?"

"Drink it," said Brobst. "Only three bottles a-piece."

I'll never forget HPL's look of utter incredulity. . . . And he watched us with unconcealed curiosity, and with a touch of apprehension, as we drank three bottles a-piece. . . .

He relished the East Indian curry, with lamb and rice. For months we had discussed the dish by mail. "Now, there is the kind for women and children, and for the great American public—a pallid, gutless, quite innocuous sauce. Then there is the blighting, blasting, searing curry in the true Indian fashion. One drop of it has been known to draw blisters from a Cordovan boot. . . ." And *that* was the kind HPL craved. He stood by as I blended it, and he sampled from time to time as it simmered on the range.

"More chemicals and acids?" I'd ask him.

"Mmm . . . this is savory, and by no means lacking in fire, but it could be more vigorous."

When he agreed that it was about right, I admitted that while I had eaten hotter curry in my time, this was certainly strong enough. . . .

There are parts of Rhode Island which have neither bus nor interurban railway service. When I learned of this, I insisted that we should visit these parts in my Model A—"Great Juggernaut," as HPL named the car. He was diffident about permitting me to serve his convenience, and tried to talk the idea down, yet I knew that once he overcame his scruples against what he termed reversing roles of host and guest, he keenly anticipated seeing corners of Rhode Island which he had never visited.

He was a good guide. Only once or twice did we have to stop and ask our way. We went to the snuff mill which had once been owned by a kinsman of Gilbert Stuart whose portraits of George Washington are often reprinted today. I would have been content with a look from the outside. There was an admission charge of fifty cents. I was dreadfully short of money, and hated to see him spend his. I knew that while he had never had the extreme ups and downs I had had, he skimped along gallantly in order to afford trips such as that to New Orleans. But he insisted. . . .

I learned finally that for years he had wanted to see the Hazard home; so we went. The place was said to have a rare and peculiar type of roof. The sight of it delighted HPL. Then daring took possession. Since we were here, we should see the interior, he proposed.

I didn't like the idea of invading a private residence, but I did not like to object. HPL took the lead. It was not until Mr. Hazard came to the door that I realized what fortitude Lovecraft had required to carry on. He was for a dreadful moment a martyr to his love of architecture and the antiquarian. He was visibly trembling, and he groped and fumbled for words. Behind that sallow, poker face was an extremely sensitive personality, appalled by the full awareness of his presumption in asking, and so near the time of the mid-day meal, for permission to inspect the home.

The Hazards, however, were gracious, setting him at ease. I think they were repaid by seeing his appreciation of, for instance, a certain newel post and baluster.[23]

Harry K. Brobst was one of Lovecraft's few personal friends in Providence from 1932 on. When Lovecraft first knew him, he was in training as a psychiatric nurse at Butler Hospital. He graduated from Brown in 1939 with a major in psychotherapy and eventually became a professor of psychology at Oklahoma State University.

About 1930, Lovecraft disagreed with Clifford Eddy on a ghostwriting job and saw less of the Eddys thereafter. In his last years, however, he had one more local friend. This was a small but brilliant youth named Kenneth J. Sterling, who lived briefly in Providence in 1936 before entering Harvard and who became a physician in New York.

After Price and Cook came Morton for a brief stopover, and then a friend of Clark Ashton Smith, a very attractive young woman named Helen V. Sully, who was studying music. Helen Sully had met the Gang in New York, and the Longs drove her to Providence. To Smith, Lovecraft wrote of the "devastating havoc" she had created among them. To her he wrote later, apologizing for the unwelcome amorous propositions that some of them had made to her. He got her quarters in the nearby boarding house and took her on sight-seeing tours. He insisted on paying for everything, even the boarding-house bill. After an expedition to Newport:

That night, after dinner, he took me to a graveyard associated with Poe. . . . It was dark, and he began to tell me strange, weird stories in a sepulchral tone and, despite the fact that I am a very matter-of-fact person, something about his manner, the darkness, and a sort of eerie light that seemed to hover over the gravestones got me so wrought up that I began to run out of the cemetery with him close at my heels, with the one thought that I must get up to the street before he, or whatever it was, grabbed me. I reached a street lamp, trembling, panting, and almost in tears, and he had the strangest look on his face, almost of triumph. Nothing was said.[24]

It would hardly seem to most single men that the way to entertain a pretty girl was to lure her to a graveyard at night and scare the wits out of her. But Lovecraft was a highly original character.

Lovecraft's second cousin, Ethel Phillips, had lost touch with Lovecraft and his aunt. Now Mrs. Roy A. Morrish, she picked up the old acquaintance and made several calls on Annie Gamwell at 66 College Street. Lovecraft was never visible, being secluded in his study. Evidently his aunt twitted him on his unsociability, for the next time Mrs. Morrish called, Lovecraft appeared and lectured the whole evening on the history of Rhode Island.

During the last week of July, 1933, Lovecraft spent several days with the Longs at Onset. Frank Long urged Lovecraft to try a plotting machine in composing stories. Several such gadgets were available, by which a would-be writer could crank out arbitrary combinations of scenes, characters, and plot elements. Lovecraft bought one called *Plot Game*; but it was made for stories of "romance-adventure," and Lovecraft found the concept "too overwhelmingly repulsive" even to try it.

In August, he was fortunate in finding an aunt-sitter, who enabled him to make his third trip to Quebec. He found himself more and more favorable towards French-Canadians, even while acknowledging their low educational standards, their prickly defensiveness towards English-speaking folk, and the tenacity with which they clung to their own ways:

> The long train ride to Quebec . . . was unusually pleasant . . . Most of the passengers were honest, simple French peasants bent on visiting ancestral soil or on grovelling at the miracle-working shrine of La Bonne Ste. Anne de Beaupré.

> Much as I hate any foreign influence, I'm damned if I don't admire these tough little frog-eaters. . . .[25]

He spent four days in Quebec. There he was also thrilled to meet an aged, blind French physician and soldier of fortune, who claimed to have been one of Theodore Roosevelt's Rough Riders and to have known Jules Verne.

After Lovecraft got back to Providence, Annie Gamwell's nurse left. Lovecraft arranged to have an electric door-opener installed, so that he did not have to be on deck all the time to answer rings.

In August, 1933, Lovecraft wrote "The Thing on the Doorstep," a novelette of a little over 10,000 words. It is on the border line between science fiction and fantasy but closer to the latter. When he had finished it in longhand, Lovecraft could not "decide whether it's any good or not." He did not force himself to type the story until the following winter.

Then he launched the story on the rounds of his friends. By August, 1934, he said he had been encouraged by their comments; but he still had not submitted the manuscript, "in order to keep as clear as possible of external criticisms & rebuffs." ". . . I don't want the effect of rejection just now."[26] Anyway, he was sure that Wright would not like the story.

Incredible as it seems to a professional, Lovecraft kept the story in his files for another year. In the summer of 1935, he finally sent it to Wright, along with another story called "The Haunter of the Dark." Wright promptly bought both.

"The Thing on the Doorstep" is in the middle rank of Lovecraft's stories: below his best but far above the *Weird Tales* average. Lovecraft paid more heed than usual to character in this story, which begins typically:

> It is true that I have sent six bullets through the head of my best friend, and yet I hope to show by this statement that I am not his murderer. At first I shall be called a madman—madder than the man I shot in his cell at the Arkham Sanitarium. . . .[27]

The narrator, Daniel Upton, tells of the former "best friend," Edward Pickman Derby. The description includes the autobiographical passage already quoted in Chapter 3: "He was the most phenomenal child scholar I have ever known. . . ."

The more normal Upton makes a living, marries, and begets

a son. He still shows Lovecraftian features, like a tendency to faint when shocked. The parallels to Lovecraft's own life are stressed in the account of Derby's young manhood:

> In self-reliance and practical affairs, however, Derby was greatly retarded because of his coddled existence. His health had improved, but his habits of childish dependence were fostered by over-careful parents, so that he never travelled alone, made independent decisions, or assumed responsibilities. It was early seen that he would not be equal to a struggle in the business or professional arena. . . .

At Miskatonic University, Derby becomes a devotee of magical lore like the *Necronomicon*. His adulthood parallels Lovecraft's:

> By the time he was twenty-five Edward Derby was a prodigiously learned man and a fairly well-known poet and fantaisiste, though his lack of contacts and responsibilities had slowed down his literary growth by making his products derivative and over-bookish. . . . He remained single—more through shyness, inertia, and parental protectiveness than through inclination—and moved in society only to the slightest and most perfunctory extent. When the [First World] war came both health and ingrained timidity kept him at home. . . . Edward's mother died when he was thirty-four, and for months he was incapacitated by some odd psychological malady. His father took him to Europe, however, and he managed to pull out of his trouble without visible effects. Afterwards he seemed to feel a sort of grotesque exhilaration, as if of a partial escape from some unseen bondage.

Derby falls in with a dissolute set at the university and dabbles in black magic. He meets a co-ed named Asenath Waite, small, dark, and pretty but for a touch of the "Innsmouth look." She comes from Innsmouth, where her father, Ephraim Waite, was notorious as a sorcerer. Asenath is an intense, strong-willed woman who claims that she can, by hypnotism, exchange personalities with others. She makes a set for Derby and marries him. Then it transpires that Asenath is using her powers to swap souls from time to time with her feckless husband. The so-called Asenath's personality is not really that of Ephraim Waite's daughter but that of sinister old Ephraim himself. . . .

Some critics have thought that Asenath is a fictionalization of Sonia Greene. There are resemblances, notably Sonia's aggressive rôle in bringing about the marriage and her tendency to "drive" her husband, as Asenath does in a more literal sense with Derby.

There are, however, many differences also. It seems reasonable to view Asenath as a composite product of Lovecraft's imagination, with touches of various women he had known: his mother, Sonia, and others.

While Lovecraft was too much of a gentleman to say so out-right, one may suspect that, by this time, he was aware that the person who had done him the most harm was his mother. His remarks about "a partial escape from some unseen bondage" confirm this idea.

For the rest of the year, Lovecraft stayed home except for brief trips to Cape Cod and Plymouth. He wrote of his longing to visit the Old World. He also hoped, he said, to make a continental tour of the United States, seeing his Western correspondents like Smith and Derleth. He would not, however, go to Chicago to see the World's Fair of 1933, the Century of Progress, even if he could afford to, because its "damned modern faddism in architecture" was so ugly that it "would give me a nausea lasting the rest of my life."[28]

At the end of the year, the Longs invited Lovecraft to New York for another visit over New Year's. Loveman gave Lovecraft an ancient Egytian *ushabti* figurine from a tomb, a Mayan statu-ette, and a wooden Balinese monkey. Lovecraft was delighted when Abraham Merritt, the Hearst editor and writer of such celebrated fantasies as *The Ship of Ishtar*, had him to dinner at the Players' Club.

On New Year's Eve, Lovecraft attended a party given by Sam Loveman and his roommate. Loveman recounted:

> My roommate, Pat McGrath, who shared the apartment and privately called Howard a "ghoul," decided on a certain New Year's eve celebration and, so, some twenty-five of our friends were invited. Included were Mrs. Grace Crane (Hart Crane's mother), who was properly appalled at the unconventional conversation of our guests, and Howard P. Lovecraft. Drinks were served and, to Lovecraft, who never even remotely tasted hard liquor, ginger-ale. Pat beckoned me into the kitchen. "Have you noticed how talka-tive Howard has very suddenly become?" I hadn't, but, as we en-tered the room where the guests were assembled, there was Love-craft, the very life of the party, talking, gesticulating, radiating smiles and laughter, rolling his verbal gymnastics with witticisms

and even indulging in a spirited aria from Gilbert and Sullivan's "Mikado"—a display of exhilarating pyrotechnics that I had never seen or heard him indulge in before. Pat whispered mirthfully into my ear, "I SPIKED HIS DRINK!"

It is said that Lovecraft forgot his inhibitions so far as to cry "Bullshit!" when someone advanced an opinion he deemed absurd. He never learned what had happened to him; a year later he was still boasting that he had never touched liquor in his life.[29]

After typing "The Thing on the Doorstep," Lovecraft did not get back to original fiction for months. He had so many orders for ghost-writing that he passed a surplus on to his friends.

He had trouble with Zealia Reed, who had now married D. W. Bishop, owner of a farm in Missouri. Zealia refused to pay the modest charges for revision, for which Lovecraft and his colleagues had billed her. According to Lovecraft's friends, she had decided that she did not need their help any more.

After some months of fruitless efforts, Zealia tried to regain Lovecraft's help. To lure him on, she began in the summer of 1934 to pay off her debt to him at a dollar a week. When, however, she tried to get him to ghost another story for her on speculation (with payment when and if the story was sold) he refused. He said he was too fully committed to other clients and was in a precarious nervous state. Then she stopped paying. According to Lovecraft, late in 1936 she still owed him $26, Frank Long $34, and Maurice Moe $11. When they dunned her, she merely became furious.

Mrs. Bishop had her own complaints. The main one was that, although she learned much about writing from Lovecraft, he insisted on trying to make her into a writer of macabre fantasies of his own kind. Her own natural talent, she learned, was for the so-called true confessions—stories of "how I lost my virtue in the tonneau of a Packard limousine but was saved by the love of a good man." Since stories of this kind were anathema to Lovecraft, Zealia never dared to tell him that she was writing and selling them.[30]

De Castro, too, tried in 1934 to inveigle Lovecraft into ghost-writing, on speculation, a treatise called *The New Way*, which presented some eccentric view of the origin of Jesus. Lovecraft referred de Castro to Moe and Price, who also turned him down.

Lovecraft got more nibbles from book publishers; from Alfred A. Knopf in 1933 and from Loring & Munsey in early 1935. Each time, he sent in a collection of stories, and each time the collection was regretfully declined. Even before the rejection by Loring & Munsey, Lovecraft was so sure of failure that he pettishly declared himself through with professional writing:

> I doubt if I shall respond to any further requests from publishers —it is obviously a futile proceeding in view of the unpopular nature of the tales. Nor do I believe I shall ever do much more writing.

He was "damned if I'll peddle" manuscripts "around to uninterested publishers." Lovecraft's friends tried to coax him out of his defeatism, but:

> His negative view of his work was destined to grow, not abate, and I [Derleth], like most of Lovecraft's correspondents, soon grew to accept it, knowing that any alteration in his perspective must come from within and could not come from outside, no matter how many of us strove to encourage him by taking matters into our own hands and selling his manuscripts . . .[31]

During 1933–34, Lovecraft devoted hard thought to fictional technique. In advising a friend on how to plot a story, he set forth an elaborate scheme of outlining and synopsizing. A first synopsis, he said, told the events of the tale in the order in which they happened. A second synopsis told the events in the order in which they were narrated. This might be quite different from the first, as when the author used flashbacks. Then followed the rough and final drafts.[32]

In one letter, Lovecraft sounded as if he had come to terms with himself. If he could not be a second Poe, at least he would not fret about it:

> While having the highest respect for the authors of realistic fiction, & envying those who are able to accomplish the successful reflection of life in narrative form, I am sadly aware through actual experiment that this is a province definitely closed to me. The fact is, that I have absolutely nothing to say where actual, unvarnished life is concerned. The events of life are so profoundly & chronically uninteresting to me—& I know so little about them as a whole— that I can't scrape up anything in connexion with them which could possibly have the zest & tension & suspense needed to form a

real story. That is, I am incurably blind to dramatic or fictional values except where violations of the natural order are concerned. Of course, I understand *objectively* what these values are, & can apply them with fair success to the criticism & revision of others' work; but they do not take hold of my imagination sufficiently to find creative expression. . . . What is more, I don't know enough about life to be an effective exponent of it. On account of my early ill-health & naturally retiring disposition my contacts with mankind—& with its varied aspects, folkways, idioms, attitudes, & standards—have been extremely limited; so that there are probably very few people outside the extreme rustic class who are more fundamentally unsophisticated than myself. I don't know what different kinds of people do & think & feel & say. . . . the would-be realist who does not know life well is perforce compelled to resort to imitation—copying what he picks up from the doubtful & artificial media of books, plays, newspaper reports, & the like. . . . Let us say that I'm called upon to portray the way one of your dashing young clubman-detectives responds to a given situation. Now I'm not a dashing young clubman-detective & never was one—nor have I ever been acquainted with any. Obviously I don't know how the hell one of them (assuming that there are such persons) would react to any given situation. . . . And this is true of so many different types of person—there are so *few* types that I really understand (& I'm not sure that I understand even them)—that I could never piece out the dramatis personae of any well-rounded work of fiction. . . .

. . . I am interested only in broad pageants—historic streams —orders of biological, chemical, physical, & astonomical organisation—& the only conflict which has any emotional significance to me is that of *the principle of freedom* or *irregularity* or *adventurous opportunity against the eternal & maddening rigidity* or *cosmic law* . . . especially the laws of *time*. Individuals & their fortunes within natural law move me very little. . . . In other words, the only "heroes" I can write about are *phenomena*. The cosmos is such a closely-locked round of fatality—with everything prearranged—that nothing impresses me as *really dramatic* except some sudden & abnormal *violation of that relentless inevitability*. . . . something which cannot exist, but which can be imagined as existing. . . . Naturally one would *rather* be a broad artist with power to evoke beauty from every phase of experience—but when one unmistakably *isn't* such an artist, there's no sense in bluffing & faking & pretending that one *is*. It being settled that I'm a little man instead of a big man, I'd a damn sight prefer to let it go frankly at that—& try to be a good little man in my narrow, limited, miniature fashion—than to cover up & pretend to be a bigger man than I am. Such pretence can lead only to futile overreaching, pompous vacuity, & ultimate loss of whatever little good I might have accomplished had I stuck to the one small province which was really mine.[33]

Lovecraft's insistence that a fiction writer should write only about what he knew personally is a counsel of perfection, which a practicing writer cannot afford to follow literally. (For that matter, Lovecraft did not always follow it.) While personal experience is an enormous help in writing about any milieu, writers do not live long enough to experience all the milieux they may wish to write about. Therefore, a practical fictioneer must pad out his own experience with what he can pick up by reading, travel, and conversation.

If—as Lovecraft implied—he did attempt to write realistic fiction, he must have completely destroyed these false starts, for no scrap of them is known to survive.

At other times, Lovecraft gave himself up to dissatisfaction and despair—the "negativism" for which Derleth twitted him:

> I myself am still irked by my inability to give form & expression to the reactions produced in me by certain phenomena of the external world . . . but at my age I know that I shall never be able to utter what I wish to utter. . . . I have something to say but can't say it.

Stories he "repudiated" included two of his most impressive works: "The Dream-Quest of Unknown Kadath" and "The Case of Charles Dexter Ward." His correspondent Robert Barlow, however, persuaded Lovecraft to lend him the longhand manuscripts, promising to type them.

Lovecraft said that his own finances were going steadily downhill: "Outgo persists, income shrinks to invisibility." The last suit he ever bought was one that he got in Athol, at a removal sale in 1928; and he still wore his 1908 overcoat. He foresaw his own doom when his remaining capital should be consumed:

> So far I've kept a goodly number of old family items around me— but when my final financial collapse occurs, there's no telling what will happen. I certainly don't wish to survive the environment created by familiar books, paintings, furniture, vases, statuary, &c. which I have had around me all my life.

He was helpless to avert this fate:

> For commercial pursuits I never had the slightest aptitude—indeed, my lack of skill in this direction amounts to a positive cerebral blank. I simply *cannot* think or calculate in terms of gain. . . . a weakness which will prove my destruction in the end.[34]

Even childhood recollections, in which he had taken such comfort, became anticlimactic when they petered out in "mediocrity & non-achievement like mine." He lashed out at Farnsworth Wright, who had paid him more for his stories than all his other editors combined, as pedantic, inconsistent, and pompous. He cared nought for his physical organism:

> As to my health—I simply don't give a god damn about it. It is a matter of perfect indifference to me whether I shuffle off to oblivion tomorrow or live to be 100—provided, in the latter case, that I can have enough cash to keep my possessions around me. If I ever speed up the grim reaper it will be simply from lack of money to live decently.[35]

He thought: "It would be better if more people forgot all about their health." A superstitious person might say that the Reaper took him at his word.

Much of Lovecraft's time during these last years was taken up with the busy-work of amateur journalism. He recruited Barlow and others into the NAPA. He let himself be saddled with the chairmanship of the NAPA Critical Bureau and received stacks of amateur journals to criticize.

He continued this activity up to his last year, even though revolted by the amateurs' behavior: "When I look over the current papers I am exasperated by the preponderance of material by chronic juveniles—hopeful perpetual beginners up to 75 years of age." "What a feud-factory amateurdom is!" When an ex-president of NAPA, Ralph W. Babcock, berated the new president, Hyman Bradofsky (whom Lovecraft supported), Lovecraft was outraged by "the incredibly insulting & absolutely unmotivated attack which he has just sent poor Hymie. . . ."[36] Actually, since all such organized hobbyism is essentially juvenile, such immature amusements as insults, feuds, plots, and hare-brained schemes are to be expected of the hobbyists.

Despite the vicissitudes of the Depression, the readership of science-fiction magazines grew through the 1930s. During most of this decade, there were four American magazines of imaginative fiction, not counting such abortive efforts as *Strange Tales*. The four were *Weird Tales*, *Amazing Stories*, *Wonder Stories* (later

Thrilling Wonder Stories), and *Astounding Stories* (later *Astounding Science Fiction*). The big expansion of the field did not begin until 1938, when *Marvel Science Stories* appeared. From 1939 to 1941, the number of magazines grew until there were over twenty.

Lovecraft took a poor view of the three "straight" science-fiction magazines, *Amazing*, *Wonder*, and *Astounding*. He was sure, with some justification, that their pages were filled with the uninspired prose of "mass-production hacks" like Otis Adalbert Kline. Lovecraft missed the notable rise in the literary quality of the magazines at the end of the decade. This improvement was largely the doing of John W. Campbell (1910–71), who in 1937 became editor of *Astounding Stories*.

Even during Lovecraft's lifetime, talented writers began to flow into the science-fiction field. One, for example, was Catherine L. Moore, whose first published story, "Shambleau," appeared in *Weird Tales* for November, 1933. Lovecraft was enthusiastic about the story and enrolled Miss Moore into his circle of correspondents. In 1940, she married another member of the circle, Henry Kuttner.

Lovecraft was equally delighted with Stanley G. Weinbaum's "A Martian Odyssey" in *Wonder Stories* for July, 1934. Weinbaum gave every sign of becoming one of science fiction's giants when he died of lung cancer on December 14, 1935.

The early 1930s also saw the first appearance of organized science-fiction fandom. The early clubs and their publications were ephemeral; but, as fast as one died, another sprang up.

Lovecraft had a central rôle in this movement because several fanzine publishers belonged to his circle. Several were also fellow-amateur journalists or were recruited into amateur journalism by Lovecraft. Their amateur journals specialized in stories of and articles about imaginative fiction and were thus pioneer science-fiction fan magazines. Publications by members of the Lovecraft circle included Barlow's *Dragon-Fly* and *Leaves*; Charles D. Hornig's *The Fantasy Fan*; and Donald A. Wollheim's *The Phantagraph*.

In 1934, William L. Crawford of Everett, Pennsylvania, launched a magazine called *Unusual Stories*, which became *Marvel Tales*. Crawford's hope was, by persuading professional writers to contribute stories free, to build up a big enough circulation among fans to convert the amateur periodical into a professional one, able to pay for its copy. The scheme did not work, then or since. After seven issues, lack of money forced Crawford to give up.

Crawford also tried, in 1936, to publish Lovecraft's *The Shadow Over Innsmouth* as a book. He got four hundred copies printed and half of these bound, of which he sold 150 before his financial collapse compelled him to quit publishing and go on the road, selling subscriptions to *The Farm Journal*. Those 150 copies were as close as Lovecraft came to having his name on a book in his lifetime. He was not much pleased by the result; still, considering the travails through which Crawford went (including having his fingers crushed in his press) the wonder was that the book appeared at all.

During his last year, Lovecraft discussed with a Western fan, Duane W. Rimel of Asotin, Washington, the possibility of a joint fan magazine. This project, however, was never realized. Lovecraft died just too early to witness the growth of science-fiction fandom into a major socio-literary movement, with a galaxy of organizations, publications, and conventions. The first World Convention was held in New York on July 2–4, 1939.

Robert Hayward Barlow (1918–51) had begun corresponding with Lovecraft in 1931. In the spring of 1934 he was a short, slight sixteen-year-old with a small chin and a bulging forehead. He suffered from eye troubles and attacks of malaria. A delicate little person of lively intellect and varied artistic talents, he was handicapped by his very versatility. He was much given to starting more things than he could finish.

Lovecraft described Barlow as a "writer; painter; sculptor; printer; pianist; marionette designer, maker, & exhibitor; landscape gardener; tennis champion; chess expert; bookbinder; crack rifle shot; bibliophile; manuscript collector; & heaven knows what else!" Acquaintances remembered Barlow as a pleasant personality and an interesting conversationalist. On first meeting him, Lovecraft called him "a splendid little chap" and "a really brilliant boy prodigy . . . but immensely mature for his age."[37]

Barlow's life was complicated, first by his family situation and secondly by his homosexual proclivities. There was probably a connection between the two. His sexual aberration, however, may not have developed until near the end of Lovecraft's life.

The family home was at De Land, Florida, seventeen miles inland from Daytona Beach. Barlow's father, Everett D. Barlow, was a retired U. S. Army lieutenant colonel and something of a mental case. Subject to moods of intense depression, he suffered from delusions of having to defend his home against the attacks of a mysterious Them. He was cracked on religion and on sex.

Robert Barlow got on badly with his father. At this time, he told his friends that he hated the colonel; although later, after his parents had been divorced, he carried on a friendly correspondence with him. Robert Barlow's mother, Bernice Barlow, spoiled and pampered her son (somewhat as Lovecraft's mother had done with him) and quarreled with her husband over the boy's upbringing.

In the spring of 1934, Barlow and his mother were at De Land while the father, in the North, recuperated with relatives from one of his attacks. In January, Robert Barlow began urging Lovecraft to come for a visit to Florida. By April, Lovecraft had planned the trip. He was, he said, doing it on a shoestring. The round-trip bus fare from Providence came to $36, and he allowed an additional $30 for all other expenses.

On the road, Lovecraft spent $1.75 a week for food: a ten-cent breakfast and a fifteen-cent dinner a day. He managed by buying cheap groceries like bread and canned beans and eating in his room by means of his own knife, fork, spoon, and can opener. He figured on a dollar a night for lodging. Sometimes he did even better, as when he got a room in St. Augustine in 1931 for $4.00 a week.

After a week's visit with the Longs in New York, Lovecraft stopped a few days in Charleston. He wrote: "One of Loveman's friends—the artist Prentiss Taylor—now lives there . . . I was supposed to look him up, but was somewhat relieved to find him out of town." He toured the U.S.S. *Constitution* before going on to De Land, arriving May 2d.

At the Barlows', the heat stimulated Lovecraft. In high spirits, he went hatless and coatless and boasted of the tan he was working up.

His one disappointment was in not being able to go on to Havana. He was consoled by a trip with the Barlows to Silver

Springs. There he had his first view of a jungle-shaded tropical river and even glimpsed wild alligators.

While Lovecraft was at De Land, he and Barlow composed a little literary spoof called "The Battle that Ended the Century." About 2,000 words long, it begins:

> On the eve of the year 2001 a vast crowd of interested spectators were present amidst the romantic ruins of Cohen's Garage on the former site of New York, to witness a fistic encounter between two renowned champions of the strange-story firmament—Two-Gun Bob, the Terror of the Plains, and Knockout Bernie, the Wild Wolf of West Shokan. . . .
>
> In round two the Shokan Soaker's sturdy right crashed through the Texan's ribs and became entangled in sundry viscera; thereby enabling Two-Gun Bob to get in telling blows on his opponent's unprotected chin. Bob was greatly annoyed by the effeminate squeamishness shown by several onlookers as muscles, glands, gore, and bits of flesh were spattered over the ringside. . . .[38]

"Two-Gun Bob" was of course Robert E. Howard, while by "Knockout Bernie" Lovecraft meant Bernard Dwyer. Over two dozen other colleagues were mentioned under pseudonyms: Frank Belknap Long as "Frank Chimesleep Short," Seabury Quinn as "Teaberry Quince," and himself as "Horsepower Hateart." Barlow printed the composition as a brochure and mailed it out to other fans and members of the Lovecraft circle. For months, Lovecraft ambiguously denied his authorship, saying: ". . . it is scarcely the sort of thing a staid old-timer would be likely to start."

The Barlows persuaded Lovecraft to stay on to the latter part of June. Mrs. Barlow remembered:

> . . . her son and Lovecraft were inseparable. They stayed up all night, and did not bother coming down for breakfast. Their days were spent rowing on the lake, playing with Barlow's cats, Cyrus, Darius, and Alfred A. Knopf. . . . And always they conversed, with Lovecraft speaking volubly and incessantly on topics as unrelated as the Abyssinian war, chemistry, and Lord Dunsany. The Barlows had built a "backwoods" cabin between Eustis and De Land. . . . Robert used it as a workshop. While Lovecraft talked, the boy bound books with the skins of snakes he had shot for that purpose.

Barlow and Lovecraft persuaded Paul Cook to send the unbound sheets of Lovecraft's *The Shunned House.* Barlow meant to bind the remaining sheets himself. Lovecraft entertained the Barlows by reading his stories aloud to them.

Once he went with Barlow and two others on a berry-picking expedition. Lovecraft professed a love of sylvan scenes, but practical woodcraft was something else. Barlow described the foray:

> We picked for over an hour, Lovecraft blundering about in the bushes, striving valiantly to keep up with us, although, being an amateur at berry-picking, he managed only half a basket by the time we had finished. So we helped him fill the basket, and started for home, H.P.L., by his own choice, bringing up the rear. When we came to the creek, I called out to him to point out where the board-bridge was; he replied that he saw it, so we went on our way.
>
> When we reached home, he was no longer with us. He came in considerably later, soaked to the skin. He had not after all, seen the plank on which he was to cross, but had plunged into the creek . . . bedraggled and woebegone, he was still first and foremost the gentleman—he apologized to my mother for losing the berries!

Despite such mishaps, Lovecraft had a wonderful time. The heat filled him with energy; he later wrote: "You ought to have seen me . . . toting bricks, digging up & transplanting trees, carrying pails of water for young orange trees, &c. . . ."[39] He beat his way back north via Charleston, Richmond, and Philadelphia, returning home on July 10th.

The rest of 1934 saw visits to Lovecraft by Morton, Price, Cook, and Cole. Lovecraft himself made local trips. At the beginning of September, he took ship to Nantucket Island. There he hired a bicycle to cover the town and examine its antiquities:

> . . . the first time in 20 years I had been on a wheel. Riding proved just as easy & familiar as if I had last dismounted only the day before—& it brought back my lost youth so vividly that I felt as if I ought to hurry home for the opening of Hope St. High School! I wish it were not conspicuous for sedate old gents to ride a bike in Providence!

He wrote an article on Nantucket, using for his title the sobriquet bestowed on the town by Daniel Webster: "The Unknown City in the Sea." He wrote a verse on the death of the kitten Sam Perkins, a favorite local feline:

> *The ancient garden seems at night*
> *A deeper gloom to bear,*
> *As if some silent shadow's blight*
> *Were hov'ring in the air.*

With hidden griefs the grasses sway,
Unable quite to word them—
Remembering from yesterday
The little paws that stirred them.[40]

Price urged Lovecraft to collaborate on another Randolph Carter story. After all, they had left poor Randolph disappearing into the strange clock. . . . But Lovecraft begged off: "I'm too near a nervous smashup to attempt anything with as much strain & forced labour as collaboration."

Lovecraft also began, in September, to complain—ominously, as things turned out—of "indigestion."[41]

In November, 1934, for all his defiant words about no more stories, Lovecraft wrote another tale. "The Shadow Out of Time" is a science-fiction novella of 27,000 words, set in the Cthulhu Mythos. It begins:

> After twenty-two years of nightmare and terror, saved only by a desperate conviction of the mythical source of certain impressions, I am willing to vouch for the truth of that which I think I found in Western Australia on the night of July 17–18, 1935.[42]

Nathaniel Wingate Peaslee, the narrator, tells how he joined the faculty of Miskatonic University and rose to full professor. In 1908, he fell victim to a kind of amnesia, in which he had no memory of his former life but seemed to have been taken over by another personality, which knew a lot about some subjects but nothing about others. Seized with horror and repulsion, his wife divorces him, and she and two of his three children refuse ever to see him again, even after he regains his normal self.

After his return to his former personality in 1913, Peaslee suffers from recurrent dreams, in which he is a member of the Great Race that ruled the earth in Triassic times:

> The Great Race's members were immense rugose cones ten feet high, and with head and other organs attached to foot-thick distensible limbs spreading out from their apexes. They spoke by the clicking or scraping of huge paws or claws attached to the end of two of their four limbs, and walked by the expansion and contraction of a viscous layer attached to their vast, ten-foot bases.

To study the past and the future, these super-limpets had mastered the secret of mental time travel. They could exchange personalities with beings of other ages, and one of them had done this with Peaslee. The captive personalities from other ages were pumped of information and, if they proved adaptable, were allowed to roam the world in atomic-powered aircraft. During his captivity, Peaslee met many other such captive minds and conversed with them:

> There was a mind from the planet we know as Venus, which would live incalculable epochs to come, and one from an outer moon of Jupiter six million years in the past. Of earthly minds there were some from the winged, star-headed, half-vegetable race of paleogean Antarctica; one from the reptile people of fabled Valusia; three from the furry prehuman Hyperborean worshippers of Tsathoggua; one from the wholly abominable Tcho-Tchos; two from the Arachnid denizens of earth's last age; . . .

> I talked with the mind of Yiang-Li, a philosopher from the cruel empire of Tsan-Chan, which is to come in 5,000 A.D.; with that of the general of the great-headed brown people who held South Africa in 50,000 B.C.; with that of a twelfth-century Florentine monk named Bartolomeo Corsi. . . .

And so on for a whole page. The "reptile people of fabled Valusia" are borrowed from Robert Howard's stories of King Kull, while the "Hyperborean worshippers of Tsathoggua" are lifted from Clark Ashton Smith.

Peaslee communicates his dreams to his colleagues. An Australian archaeologist invites Peaslee to join a dig at a mysterious ruin in the desert. Prowling the ruin at night, Peaslee comes upon evidence that the underground menace, which the Great Race had feared, is still present. . . .

It is a good story—not Lovecraft's best, but well up the scale. Furthermore, "The Shadow Out of Time" was the last major story that Lovecraft wrote.

Eighteen

GUTTERING LAMP

Lover of hills and fields and towns antique,
How has thou wandered hence
On ways not found before,
Beyond the dawnward spires of Providence?
Hast thou gone forth to seek
Some older bourne than these—
Some Arkham of the prime and central wizardries?[1]

CLARK ASHTON SMITH

For Christmas, 1934, Lovecraft and his aunt put up a Christmas tree, his first since boyhood. He listened to the British Empire Christmas broadcast on Annie Gamwell's radio. (A friend had given him a small set some time before, but he could never make it work.) When the King had finished his speech:

> . . . I turned face down the dollar bill that was tied on top of one of my gifts. . . . . I couldn't bear to see the features of one who was instrumental in the cruel tearing of these colonies from the Empire in whose fabrick they rightly belong![2]

On December 30th, Lovecraft went to New York for his year-end visit. A meeting of the Gang on January 2, 1936, drew fifteen Kalems. Barlow came from Washington, where he was in art school.

The severe winter of 1935–36 kept Lovecraft indoors, struggling with ghosting and correspondence. He worked intermittently on "The Shadow Out of Time," complaining that "I simply cannot produce anything original when my programme is crowded." He had plenty of story plots, he said, but too little time and energy to make stories of them. He refused several proposals for collaboration.

Lovecraft had finally realized his own fault of "adjectival heaviness." In his current work, he said, ". . . I am pausing now & then to cut out involuntary bits of overcolouring which insist on creeping in—references to 'monstrous & maddening arcana of daemoniac palaeogean horror' &c. &c."

When he finished "The Shadow Out of Time" about late March, he said he was "so badly dissatisfied with it that I can't bear to type it." He sent the pencilled scribble to Derleth, telling him: "Don't worry about the MS.—its total loss would entail no great harm, & I may junk it myself in the end." He hoped, he said, "to continue any revolt against revision & extensive correspondence long enough to do something on another yarn—something with an Arkham scene."[3]

Lovecraft began to take advantage of the many free lectures at Brown. In the winter and spring of 1935 he attended a poetry reading by Archibald MacLeish and lectures on the art of the cinema, on Japanese art, on the Church of Santa Sophia in Istanbul, on Albrecht Dürer, on Italian Baroque architecture, and on Benjamin Franklin.

The two Franklin lectures had a sequel. Lovecraft was always given to vivid dreams, which he later remembered in detail.

Most of Lovecraft's dreams took place in winter. He said that three quarters of them concerned the scenes and people of his childhood, "But the real scenes frequently merge into unknown & fantastic realms, & include landscapes & architectural vistas which could scarcely be on this planet. At times I also have historical dreams—with a setting in various remote periods. Occasionally—but not often—a dream of mine forms a usable fictional plot."

During his last years, Lovecraft dreamed of climbing with a group of men in medieval costume over the roofs of an old town in pursuit of a "Thing of primal evil"; of approaching a street car to find that its crew had conical faces ending in a single red tentacle; of meeting an evil clergyman in a garret full of forbidden books; of being visited by a troop of sinister young black magicians in dinner jackets; of revisiting his former home at 598 Angell Street, finding it in moldering decay and hearing dragging footsteps from his former room; of being attacked by insects that pierced his brain, giving him visions of life on other worlds; of being a surgeon of 1864, Dr. Eben Spencer, and finding another doctor performing experiments like that of the famous Frankenstein; of watching, from the battlements of a castle, a battle between hosts of phantom warriors; and of being offered a million pounds sterling by the curator of a museum for a clay bas-relief that he had just made himself. After the talks on Franklin:

These lectures so impressed me, that on the night following the second one I had a most picturesque dream involving Dr. Franklin & myself & centreing in a curious distortion of time . . . whereby an area of 1785 merged imperceptibly into an area of 1935. Franklin & I were riding horseback from Philadelphia to New York through the world of 1785—he being just return'd from France. The road was narrow & muddy, & border'd by rail fences considerably inter-twin'd with vines & briars. I had on a full green coat of old style (say of 1760) with silver buttons; a flower'd reddish waistcoat, snuff-colour'd small-cloaths, & black leather riding-boots. Glimpses I later caught of myself in windows reveal'd that I had a rather small, tightly-curl'd half-powder'd bag-wig & a black three-corner'd hat. Dr. Franklin was drest in buff, in an affectation of the Quaker fashion, & wore his own hair (now become very grey) stringing about his shoulders. He had on a broad-brimmed hat of the Quaker fashion. . . . My companion's voice was pleasant, unaffected by age, & without any offensive provincial accent. Our conversation re-lated to a horrible truth of which I had somehow become master—namely that something hideous & inexplicable had happen'd to time, & that there lay somewhere ahead of us a monstrous night-mare of machinery & decadence call'd 1935. Franklin would not believe me—but some rumour had reach'd the village of New-Brunswick, for as we rode through the cobbled streets of that place we found frighten'd crowds & heard bells tolling in all the steeples. Around Metuchen, some time later, we encounter'd a curious fog—& in Rahway we could see the spectral shapes of 1935 (new build-ings, motors, modernly drest persons) impinging on the cobble-stones, gambrel roofs, Georgian facades, & knee-breech'd inhabit-ants of 1785. . . . Half way down the Elizabethtown road the

fog vanish'd, & we were in the full world of 1935—with our horses
rearing at the bewildering streams of motors. At last Franklin re-
alised that something was gravely wrong—for he saw passers-by
staring amazedly at our costume. Once he put his mind to the
problem, he seem'd to have no difficulty in grasping what had happen'd; & so ample was his scientifick training, that he cou'd appreciate the modern uses of the electrical fire which he had so
spectacularly snatch'd from the heavens in 1752. In (modern)
Elizabeth, . . . I stopt to purchase some cloathing of 1935, donning it in the shop. Dr. Franklin, however, refused to alter his
semi-Quaker attire, & continued to receive curious stares. In Newark we left our horses at a livery stable & took the Hudson Tubes
to New-York, emerging at 33d St. . . . Here no one noticed
Franklin's costume, & we walk'd about freely—I pointing out to
the philosopher various marvels & horrors (like the Empire State
Bldg., the foreign populace, the strange conveyances, & so on) of
1935, whilst he attempted to adjust them to his previous knowledge. At times we talk'd of politicks, & I candidly blam'd him for
permitting his advocacy of just colonial reforms to extend to the
treasonable length of sanctioning that revolt against our rightful
Sovreign & Parliament which selfish, greedy & misguided provincials had instituted in 1775 & terminated with tragick & suicidal
success two (or rather, 152, for this spectre of a world of 1935 was
appallingly realistick) years ago. I had, it appear'd, been a kind of
secretary to Genl. Sir Guy Carleton of His Majesty's regulars—first
in Quebec & later (until its evacuation by our troops) in New-
York. During this rambling ciceronage & discussion, & without the
attainment of any dramatick denouement or the approximation of
any logical story plot, I began slowly to drift into wakefulness.[4]

When Lovecraft spoke of his personal feelings, the melancholy
note became stronger. He was surer than ever that his writing
days were over:

> . . . it is possible that I have wholly lost the knack of fictional for-
> mulation, & ought to cease altogether from attempting stories. I'll
> experiment a little more, though, before finally arriving at such a
> conclusion. No—this ["The Shadow Out of Time"] is the only
> thing since "The Thing on the Doorstep" which I have not de-
> stroyed. Nothing recent has really *come alive*—& I certainly don't
> want to put forth mechanical, routine bull of the sort which messes
> up the pages of WT & its still worse contemporaries.

He listed his heirlooms: "a set of a dozen teaspoons . . . 2
big tables, 4 chairs, 1 stool, & one small stand. . . . a good 18th
century nail-studded chest, a little leather box or trunk . . . a pair
of brass candlesticks. . . . A few rather interesting old *papers*. . . ."

and so on. He berated himself for not having clung to more of them:

> After all, the material objects which I so desperately cherish as lega-
> cies of bygone years are the merest drop in the bucket in compari-
> son to what many inherit. I seethe with envy when I hear of this or
> that person living in a house descended from his ancestors, or pos-
> sessing the furniture, china, silver, pewter, paintings, &c. &c. which
> his forbears knew in the 18th century. . . . Sheer indolence caused
> me to let any number of admirable reliques of every kind to slip
> through my fingers. . . . But at that, I wouldn't cherish the stuff if
> it weren't what I grew up with. *That* is the real secret of my attach-
> ment—not so much that the objects are intrinsically old or remotely
> ancestral, but that *they are the things I have always lived with ever
> since I could talk & walk.* . . . Some of them may be ugly, lacking in
> real age, trivial, & all that—but they are too closely woven into the
> pattern of my daily existence to be other than precious to me.
> . . . To these things I shall hang on as long as I can—& when I can
> no longer house them I have no wish to continue existence. . . . It
> is probably fortunate that not every one is as strongly attached as I
> to the material reliques of his early life. When such an attachment
> coexists with an inability to retain the objects in question, the sum-
> mit of tragedy is reached. I'd rather live in a hovel with my old
> stuff than in a palace without it.[5]

This illustrates what I said about Lovecraft's emotional development: that he had gotten "stuck in the teddy-bear stage"
and had never grown beyond it, like Peter Pan insisting: "I want
always to be a little boy and to have fun!"

Helen Sully wrote Lovecraft from California, complaining of
feeling "hopeless, useless, incompetent, & generally miserable." To
cheer her up, Lovecraft preached his own stoical indifferentism:
"Half our misery—perhaps more—comes from our mistaken notion
that we *ought to be happy* . . . that we . . . 'deserve' or 'have a
right to' acute happiness," whereas happiness was a transient,
ephemeral thing. The best one could reasonably hope for was the
lack of acute suffering.

Miss Sully had called Lovecraft "beautifully balanced & contented," and no doubt this was how he impressed many. To show
her how much better off she was than he, however, he confided
his true feelings:

> In actual fact, there are few total losses & never-was's which
> discourage & exasperate me more than the venerable Éch-Pi-El. I
> know of few persons whose attainments fall more consistently short

of their aspirations, or who in general have less to live for. Every aptitude which I wish I had, I lack. Everything which I wish I could formulate & express, I have failed to formulate & express. Everything which I value, I have either lost or am likely to lose. Within a decade, unless I can find some job paying at least $10.00 per week, I shall have to take the cyanide route through inability to keep around me the books, pictures, furniture, & other familiar objects which constitute my only remaining reason for keeping alive. And so far as *solitude* is concerned, I probably capture all medals. In Providence I have never seen a congenial mind with which I could exchange ideas, & even among my correspondents there are fewer & fewer who coincide with me on enough points to make discourse enjoyable except on a few specialised points. The newer generation has grown away from me, whilst the older is so fossilised as to form very meagre material for argument or conversation. In everything—philosophy, politics, aesthetics, & interpretation of the sciences—I find myself alone on an island, with an atmosphere almost of hostility gathering around me. With youth, all the possibilities of glamour & adventurous expectancy departed—leaving me stranded on a shelf with nothing to look forward to. . . . The reason I have been more "melancholy" than usual in the last few years is that I am coming to distrust more & more the value of the material I produce. Adverse criticism has of late vastly undermined my confidence in my literary powers.

He escaped from this melancholy, he told her, by rational analysis. There was nothing to be angry at, since his failures were the result of his own limitations and bad luck, not the malignity of an evil world. With youth, good looks, talent, and versatility, Helen was a thousand times better off than he. "So . . . for Tsathoggua's sake cheer up!"[6]

On June 5, 1935, having mailed an old pair of pants ahead for use in the palmetto thickets of Florida, Lovecraft departed to visit the Barlows, arriving on the 9th. This time, the elder Barlow was present.

Young Barlow had warned HPL to stay off the subjects of sex and religion in his father's presence, but apparently there was no trouble between Lovecraft and the eccentric colonel. In fact, Lovecraft and the colonel sang duets of turn-of-the-century popular songs, and the Barlow family urged Lovecraft to stay on and on for months. They even invited him to remain through the following winter, but he felt that he had to get back to his books and files to do any serious work.

They took him on a rowboat trip along Black Water Creek, giving him another view of a tropical river. The combination of high temperatures and hard outdoor work filled Lovecraft with energy and high spirits: "I have contributed unskilled labour to this project, & have single-handed (canst imagine Grandpa actually *at work?*) cut a roadway . . . through the palmetto wilderness from the landing to the previous cabinward cart-path."[7]

Reviving his boyhood skill of typesetting, Lovecraft helped Robert Barlow to print a collection of poems by Frank Belknap Long, *The Goblin Tower*. They kept the job secret in order to surprise Long.

As usual, Barlow was full of ambitious plans. He would bind into books the sheets of *The Shunned House* that Cook had printed. He would print an edition of the Lovecraft sonnet cycle, *Fungi from Yuggoth,* and other poems.

About the poems, Lovecraft first urged his young friend "not to waste his time on such trivialities." When Barlow persisted, Lovecraft said that he preferred to suppress most of his early poetry, which "I'd pay blackmail to keep out of sight today." In any case, Lovecraft besought Barlow to eliminate all of Lovecraft's once cherished archaisms, like "doom'd."[8]

Neither the bound edition of *The Shunned House* nor the volume of poetry, however, materialized. Cook sent Barlow the unbound sheets of the former. Barlow managed to bind about a dozen sets into books, which he sold for $1.00 each. The rest were still unbound when Barlow left Florida for good a year later and abandoned them.

At the end of August, Lovecraft set out for home. In Washington, he called on Elizabeth Tolridge. He had shirked this chore before—for lack of money, he told her; because he feared boredom, he confided to others. This time, "Aunt Liz" had no chance to bore, because another old lady did all the talking.

In New York, a heavily tanned Lovecraft impressed Long as looking much younger. Lovecraft arrived home three months and nine days from setting out.

Lovecraft spent the autumn of 1935 quietly, with occasional trips around New England. His friend Cole, in Boston, took him on several, including a journey on September 21st to Wilbraham, Massachusetts (Lovecraft's "Dunwich").

On October 8th, Lovecraft made an excursion with his aunt to New Haven. For over seven hours, while Annie Gamwell visited an old friend, he prowled the town, admiring Colonial relics and waxing enthusiastic over the architecture of the Yale quadrangle.

At the year's end, Lovecraft made his annual visit to the Longs in New York. He met the pulp writers Arthur J. Burks and Otto Binder and the fan (later writer and editor) Donald A. Wollheim. He saw "good old Seabury Quinn" for the first time since 1931.

Lovecraft attended a dinner of the American Fiction Guild, where he "saw a good many of the cheap magazine hacks whose names are familiar to the reading proletariat." He rather deplored the commercial success that Frank Long and Donald Wandrei had achieved with their stories, being sure that it would make "cheap magazine hacks" of them, as he thought it had of E. Hoffmann Price and C. L. Moore. "And to think they were once lit'ry guys!"[9] he mourned.

Save for the pause in Florida, Lovecraft in 1935 attended to his ghost-writing. Price again urged a collaboration upon him, proposing that, when the story was sold, all the money be used to finance a trip to California for Lovecraft. Often as Lovecraft had spoken of a Far Western trip, he begged off: the story would not sell; the money should not be squandered on transportation for an "uninteresting old crank."

Adolphe de Castro also kept after Lovecraft to work on his treatise *The New Way*. Although he had often resolved not to work any more for de Castro, Lovecraft could not hold out against any determined favor-seeker. He said he had "rashly promised to help" de Castro on his nonsense, since he hated "to let the old chap down. . . . He is really very generous & likeable."[10] So Lovecraft agreed, against his better judgment, to give the work a light editing without charge. He found it so full of historical errors that he advised de Castro to rewrite it as a novel.

During 1935, Lovecraft and his young correspondent Robert Bloch, in Milwaukee, engaged in a fictional jape. Early in the year, Bloch wrote a short story, "The Shambler from the Stars" (*Weird Tales*, September, 1935). The narrator tells how he corresponded with an unnamed "mystic dreamer in New England."

From this recluse he learned of the *Necronomicon* and other books of forbidden lore. After a fruitless search for these sinister volumes, the narrator comes upon a copy of Ludvig Prinn's *De Vermis Mysteriis*, or "mysteries of the worm," for which Lovecraft furnished the title.

The narrator takes the book to Providence to show the "mystic dreamer." The latter excitedly reads one of the spells aloud. Thereupon an invisible, tentacled Thing enters, seizes the dreamer, and bleeds him dry.

Bloch asked Lovecraft's permission to destroy him thus. Lovecraft carped at being portrayed as smoking a pipe but otherwise approved. Bloch deleted the pipe and got a release:

> Providence, R.I.
> April 30, 1935
>
> To Whom it May Concern:
>   This is to certify that Robert Bloch, Esq., of Milwaukee, Wisconsin, U.S.A.—reincarnation of Mijnheer Ludvig Prinn, author of DE VERMIS MYSTERIIS—is fully authorized to portray, murder, annihilate, disintegrate, transfigure, metamorphose, or otherwise manhandle the undersigned in the tale entitled THE SHAMBLER FROM THE STARS.
>
> [signed] H. P. Lovecraft[11]

The document was attested by Abdul Alhazred, Friedrich von Junzt, Gaspard du Nord (translator of the *Livre d'Eibon*), and the Tcho-Tcho Lama of Leng, in specious imitations of their native scripts.

The next November, Lovecraft demolished Bloch in a story, "The Haunter of the Dark" (10,000 words; *Weird Tales*, December, 1936). The protagonist is "Robert Blake," an artist and writer from Milwaukee. Living in Providence, Blake becomes fascinated by a huge old deserted church, which the author modeled on the real St. John's Catholic Church. Blake learns that an evil cult, the Starry Wisdom, once used this church as its headquarters.

Breaking into the church, Blake finds a cache of mildewed occult books, including such sinister volumes as the *Necronomicon* and the *Cultes des Goules*. He discovers a strange object, the Shining Trapezohedron, which is "a window on all time and space,"[12] originally made on Yuggoth. He also disturbs a malignant entity lurking in the steeple. . . .

In this story, the Italians of Federal Hill, led by one of their priests, appear on the side of good. During a violent storm at night, the entity prepares to emerge, but it cannot stand light. When electrical power fails, the people come out with candles and lanterns to keep the Thing at bay.

Some years later, Bloch wrote a third story of the series, "The Shadow from the Steeple" (*Weird Tales*, September, 1950). A Dr. Ambrose Dexter investigates the Shining Trapezohedron, with ominous results.

Twice more, Lovecraft was persuaded to break his rule against collaboration. One correspondent was William Lumley, "who claims to be an old sailor who has witnessed incredible wonders in all parts of the world, & to have studied works of Elder Wisdom far stronger than your *Cultes des Goules* or my *Necronomicon*." Lumley talked Lovecraft into rewriting a story of his, "The Diary of Alonzo Typer."

The result was an average *Weird Tales* story of a man who, driven by "some unfathomable urge" to explore "unholy mysteries," moves into a mysterious house near Attica, New York. There he finds a cellar bedight with cryptic glyphs, a locked iron door through which come menacing sounds of shuffling and slithering, and finally a Thing sent from "the dreadful, eon-old and forbidden city of Yian-Ho" to destroy him. Elements of the Cthulhu Mythos are dropped in, such as the planet Yaddith, the *Livre d'Eibon*, and "Iä, Shub-Niggurath!"

Lovecraft not only rewrote the story but also insisted that Lumley keep all of the $70 it brought, because Lumley "needs encouragement."[13] The tale appeared in *Weird Tales* for February, 1938, under Lumley's name alone. In gratitude, Lumley sent Lovecraft a copy of Budge's translation of the Egyptian *Book of the Dead*.

In January, 1936, Lovecraft's young friend Kenneth Sterling persuaded Lovecraft to collaborate on "In the Walls of Eryx," the only conventional interplanetary story in which Lovecraft had a hand. Lovecraft was conservative on space travel. He thought an unmanned moon rocket possible before many years. Manned space travel he considered not impossible but improbable, because "there are no good reasons for desperate attempts involving heavy sacrifice," unless "before the end of the existing civilisation some wholly new principle might enable men to reach the moon, & possibly Mars & Venus."

The narrator of this story searches the jungles of Venus for a kind of power crystal found there, which is worshiped by the Venerian "man-lizards." He gets lost in a transparent maze. . . .

Sterling had already sold three stories to *Wonder Stories*. Judging from style, Lovecraft put much less of his own writing into "In the Walls of Eryx" (*Weird Tales*, October, 1939, under a joint by-line) than into the Lumley story. Thereafter, the demands of a medical education ended Sterling's literary career.

In 1935, Lovecraft also lent his efforts to a fannish project. A young fan in Brooklyn, Julius Schwartz, worked as a science-fiction literary agent and edited a fan periodical, *The Fantasy Magazine*.

Early in 1935, Schwartz conceived the idea of a round-robin story. He planned to have five writers write sections of the tale in this order: (1) Catherine L. Moore, (2) Frank Belknap Long, (3) Abraham Merritt, and (4) H. P. Lovecraft; for the fifth and concluding section, Schwartz considered Clark Ashton Smith and Edmond Hamilton. Both of these, however, begged off.

The story was called "The Challenge from Beyond." Miss Moore wrote the opening and Long the next section. When the manuscript reached Merritt, he balked, saying that Long had strayed too far from the original assumptions. Merritt said he would not contribute anything unless Schwartz discarded Long's part and let Merritt write the second section instead.

Awed by Merritt's prestige, Schwartz gave in. Lovecraft was indignant at Merritt's "unsportsmanlike" behavior. Long, furious, quit the project.

The manuscript reached Lovecraft on his 1935 trip to Florida, and he wrote his section while stopping at Charleston on his return journey. In New York, he persuaded Long to drop his grudge and take the last place in the lineup. Schwartz had meanwhile enlisted Robert E. Howard to write the fourth section. The composite tale was published in *The Fantasy Magazine* for September, 1935.

Not surprisingly, the story is an amusing *curiosum* rather than a literary masterpiece. About 6,000 words long, it opens with C. L.

Moore's account of George Campbell, camping out in the Canadian woods and finding a worn cube of quartz with mysterious powers. Merritt's second section merely builds up the atmosphere further: "He felt a chill of spirit, as though from contact with some alien thing."[14]

The third or middle section, which was now Lovecraft's, entailed the most active plotting. Lovecraft conceived that the civilized inhabitants of the distant planet Yekub, in the form of giant centipedes, had sent these quartz cubes hither and yon through the universe. When natives of the planets on which these devices come to rest examine them, the centipedes swap minds with them. So George Campbell finds himself in the body of a centipede. When he sees himself in a mirror, in true Lovecraftian style he faints.

The next section was Howard's. When Campbell comes to, he is no longer a wishy-washy Lovecraftian anti-hero but a Howardian super-hero—a Conan among centipedes. He snatches up a sharp implement, kills the head centipede questioning him, and dashes through the building. He slays right and left until he can seize the luminous globe, which the centipede-folk worship. Thus he makes himself emperor of the planet.

The last section was by Long. While Campbell in his centipede body goes on to glory, his earthly body proves uncontrollable by the Yekubian mind that has entered it. It becomes a drooling idiot and dies.

Early in 1936, Lovecraft engaged in one more piece of fannish writing. This was a little sketch or essay called "A History of the Necronomicon." In pseudo-learned style, this seven-hundred-word spoof begins:

> Original title *Al Azif*—*Azif* being the word used by Arabs to designate that nocturnal sound (made by insects) supposed to be the howling of demons.
> Composed by Abdul Alhazred, a mad poet of Sanaa, in Yemen, who is said to have flourished during the period of the Ommiade Caliphs, circa A.D. 700. He visited the ruins of Babylon and the subterranean secrets of Memphis and spent ten years in the great southern desert of Arabia—the Roba El Khaliyeh or "Empty Space" of the ancients and "Dahna" or "Crimson Desert" of the modern Arabs, which is held to be inhabited by protective evil spirits and monsters of death. Of this desert many strange and un-

believable marvels are told by those who pretend to have penetrated it. In his last years Alhazred dwelt in Damascus, where the *Necronomicon (Al Azif)* was written, and of his final death or disappearance (A.D. 738) many terrible and conflicting things are told. He is said by Ebn Khallikan (twelfth century biographer) to have been seized by an invisible monster in broad daylight and devoured horribly before a large number of fright-frozen witnesses. Of his madness many things are told. He claimed to have seen the fabulous Irem, or City of Pillars, and to have found beneath the ruins of a certain nameless desert town the shocking annals and secrets of a race older than mankind. He was only an indifferent Moslem, worshipping unknown Entities whom he called Yog-Sothoth and Cthulhu.

An account follows of the various editions of the *Necronomicon*, with its suppressions by the authorities. Then a summary:

1. Al Azif written circa A.D. 730 at Damascus by Abdul Alhazred.
2. Translated into Greek as *Necronomicon*, A.D. 950 by Theodorus Philetas.
3. Burnt by Patriarch Michael A.D. 1050 (i.e., Greek text) . . . (Arabic text now lost).
4. Olaus translates Greek into Latin, A.D. 1228. . . .

Wilson H. Shepherd, a fan in Alabama, published the little jape as a leaflet in 1938. It has several times been reprinted, usually as "The History and Chronology of the Necronomicon."

Lovecraft dashed off the essay without checking his facts, for the work contains errors. For example, the real Olaus Wormius lived in the sixteenth and seventeenth centuries, not in the thirteenth. Nevertheless, Lovecraft's scholarly quotations and references convinced many that the work existed, and they plagued librarians and booksellers by asking for it. An index card for the book was smuggled into the files of the Yale Library. A waggish bookseller, Philip C. Duschness of New York, listed a copy of the Latin edition in his Catalogue No. 78 at $375.

Once the *Necronomicon* almost materialized. In the later 1930s Manly Wade Wellman, then a pulp writer and later a professor in North Carolina, entered a little basement bookshop in New York, where books teetered on sagging shelves and dust lay thick over all. A little old woman, who looked as if she had just laid aside her broomstick, asked him what he wanted. Joshing, Wellman replied:

"Do you by any chance have a copy of the *Necronomicon*?"

"Why, yes, heh heh," cackled the crone, "right—about—here!"[15]

It was a false alarm—she had not heard him aright—but it gave Wellman quite a turn.

Although, in 1935, Lovecraft said that he could not thenceforth give much time to amateur journalism, he did make one more sizable contribution. Maurice Moe persuaded him to write a 15,000-word article on Roman architecture for Moe's journal. Lovecraft sent Moe the only draft. When it became plain that Moe would not publish the work, Lovecraft asked for it back, because Hyman Bradofsky wanted it for his *Californian*. In December, 1935, Lovecraft groaned: "I suppose I'll have to type it."

As things turned out, he was spared the effort, because Moe had lost the manuscript. This article is one of the three substantial pieces of writing by Lovecraft—letters aside—known to have been lost.

He once ghost-wrote a story, for an unnamed client, about Clark Ashton Smith's toad-god Tsathoggua. When the client sent the story to *Weird Tales*, Wright rejected it, and the story has not been heard of since.

Lovecraft also told a chance acquaintance, whom he met on the streets of Providence, that he had

> . . . written a story about a true incident. At one time there was a young woman, a chambermaid in the hotel on Benefit Street, who left and married into wealth. Sometime afterward, she returned to visit the hotel as a guest. When she found herself discourteously treated and snubbed, she departed but put a "curse" on the hotel, on all those who had humiliated her, and on everything concerned with the hotel. In short order, ill luck apparently befell all and the hotel itself burned down. Furthermore, it had never been possible, somehow, for anyone to rebuild on the site. Even on the day H. P. Lovecraft told us the story, the place where the hotel had stood was still a vacant lot.
>
> Lovecraft finished the story and, without making his usual carbon copy, made only one draft, which he then mailed to the publisher. His story never appeared in print. It was lost in the mails.

Of his own work, Lovecraft wrote: "I'm pretty well burned out in the lines I've been following . . . that's why I'm experimenting around for new ways to capture the moods I wish to depict." The "sincere artist," he thought, should depend not upon plot and incident but upon mood and atmosphere. The best weird tales were those in which the narrator was a passive spectator, as he often is in dreams. But the spirit of the times, Lovecraft thought, was averse to such work:

> Fantasy is the expression of subjective instead of objective life— moods instead of events—& the sort which I write represents moods coloured by tradition. This is wholly against the modern taste. Today the demand is for reality—& if not objective reality, then the sort of mood-analysis which excludes tradition & deals more with raw emotional psychological complexities than with sheer constructive imagination.[16]

He still maintained his art-for-art's-sake stand: "Good writing can have no motivation save the author's desire for expression & harmonic utterance. . . ." A commercial market led a writer "to debase his style in compliance with low-grade editorial demands." The writer, therefore, should derive his income from some source other than writing. "If I can't get cash without twisting my writing, I'll willingly starve. . . . I don't know of any reason for remaining alive except to try to do the only thing which to me seems worth doing."[17]

For all his changes of front in his last years, Lovecraft never wavered in his anti-commercialism. If anything, even as he became more friendly towards ethnic groups, he became more dogmatically opposed to the competitive business spirit.

"All good work," he wrote, "must come from the subconscious," without regard for markets. The clientele of the pulp magazines was "a hopelessly vulgar & stupid rabble." "Commerce is more or less averse to all the arts. . . . the rabble & tradesmen . . . hate all good literature." "The profit motive is of no significance whatever in any work remotely connected with the genuine arts."[18]

He admitted that his point of view was not only impractical but even inimical to his own survival. In arguing about the reprinting of old stories in *Weird Tales*, he said:

> If this is "poor business", then I say damn business! Academically, I can see your side of the matter—but the contrary view is rooted deep in my basic philosophy of life. I can never countenance commercialism as an ultimate object, nor feel any lasting or genuine sympathy for its methods. It is of course necessary that every individual be provided with food, clothing, & lodging, but I can never accustom myself to the idea of acquisition as a primary ob-

ject. That is, I can never think of the expenditure of effort in direct terms of profit. With me, objects are (1) the creation of something of intrinsic excellence if possible, & (2) the supplying of genuine needs. If my own survival cannot be ensured as an incidental to the pursuit of these objects, then I feel that something is wrong. Just what to do about it I cannot tell—but the acknowledgment of the difficulty does not alter my basic instincts & emotions. . . . the fact remains that I am always at a lethargic standstill except when acting from one or the other of the motives which seem valid & rational to me—the creation of something as good as I can make it, & the performance of a service which needs performing.

Lovecraft was not, as he liked to think, being objective and impersonal. There is no objective measure of "intrinsic excellence"; it resides in the eye of the beholder. Ideas of excellence differ, even among cultivated, knowledgeable people.

Likewise, whether one is "performing a service which needs performing" or "supplying a genuine need" is subjective; for who shall judge which needs are "genuine"? People differ widely over the correct "need" in every contingency of life. So Lovecraft's statement actually demands the right to do whatever Lovecraft feels like doing. If the world will not support him in return, something is wrong with the world.

To be sure, Lovecraft's intentions were altruistic. But the modern world has no place for free-lance saints. It is not set up to care for those who, though physically and mentally able, lack the normal drives towards self-preservation and self-advancement.

In the spring of 1936, Lovecraft heard that Maurice Moe planned to attend the Bread Loaf Writers' Conference in Vermont. This is the oldest writers' conference of its kind in the nation.

A common-sense view of writing as a profession is that, for a beginning writer with native talent, a moderate use of books on "how to write," courses on writing, and writers' conferences can be helpful. If nothing else, they may teach the tyro to avoid some of the mistakes that Lovecraft made in his career.

To Lovecraft, however, anything so realistic, practical, or as he would say "commercial" was unacceptable. Of writers' conferences he said: "I haven't much use for 'arty' atmospheres, & distrust every influence which makes anybody think of himself as 'a writer' instead of as simply *a balanced individual member* of society. My ideal is *the gentleman of broad interests*—philosophic, scientific, historical, civic, literary, aesthetic, recreational, &c.—*in his own hereditary setting;* with the practice of the arts as a mere spontaneous & non-self-conscious adjunct to the general process of living." Despite the good repute of Bread Loaf, Lovecraft said that even "if anybody gave me the cash to go there I'd probably spend it on a trip to Charleston or St. Augustine!"[19]

In his last months, Lovecraft developed an interest in economic theory. Whether a study of economics would have given him a less feudal-aristocratic view of business and commerce, we shall never know.

Mournfully, Lovecraft continued to write that Wright's rejection of "At the Mountains of Madness" "did more than anything else to end my effective literary career," and ". . . everything since 'Mts of Madness' has been . . . a failure. . . . I simply lack whatever it is that enables a real artist to convey his mood. . . . I'm farther from doing what I want to do than I was 20 years ago."[20]

Nevertheless, the end of 1935 brought encouragement. Julius Schwartz persuaded Lovecraft to let him try to sell "At the Mountains of Madness." Soon Schwartz reported that he had sold the novel to *Astounding Stories* for $350. When Schwartz deducted his 10 per cent commission, there was $315 left for Lovecraft.

At about the same time (October, 1935), Donald Wandrei obtained the manuscript of "The Shadow Out of Time," which Barlow had typed. Wandrei sent the story to F. Orlin Tremaine, the editor of *Astounding Stories.* Tremaine bought this one, too, for $280, all of which went to Lovecraft.

When the stories appeared, Lovecraft carped loudly at Tremaine's editing of his spelling, punctuation, and paragraphing. Still, $595 was the most that Lovecraft had ever received for his writings in so short a time. He became almost cheerful: ". . . the occurrence is distinctly encouraging, & may start me on a new period of intensive writing." "I must let Schwartz . . . peddle other things of mine."[21]

At home, Lovecraft struggled with his files and records. He realized that he had been so careless in lending books and manuscripts that now he did not know where most of them were. "There is always a certain peril in lending—but weird books are so hard to get that an owner feels uncomfortably selfish if he refuses to take a chance & share his good luck with fellow-enthusiasts."

More than ever obsessed by the past, he played a bizarre nostalgic game with his aunt: ". . . imagining the calendar turned back to 1898 or 1900 or 1902 or so, & conversing as one actually would in that period . . . mentioning the shops, plays, songs, car lines, news, sights, surroundings, & daily activities then flourishing, & excluding all anachronistic idioms & allusions."[22]

In January, 1936, after Lovecraft's return from New York, another hard winter closed down. To aggravate Lovecraft's hibernal misery, he came down with grippe or influenza. He also complained of eye trouble and "bum digestion." "My eyes give out occasionally without warning—producing a sort of vortex-like vision which summarily calls a halt to the day's labours."

Then, when his own grippe let up in February, leaving "me weak as a rag,"[23] Annie Gamwell caught a more severe case. On March 17th, she was taken to a hospital. She spent two weeks there and another fortnight in a convalescent home, not returning to 66 College Street until late April.

Lovecraft's eye trouble may have been the result of simple failure to get an eye examination and new glasses. The digestive trouble, however, was something else. Months later, long after January's virus had departed, Lovecraft still complained of digestive trouble, calling it "grippe."

It was, in fact, a cancer of the colon. By blocking his intestinal tract, it gave him ever-increasing constipation. In February, 1937, over two years after his disfunction had first appeared, he wrote: "Shall very shortly see what a physician has to say,"[24] implying that he had not yet consulted one.

Doctors tell me that, even in the 1930s, if Lovecraft's disease had been diagnosed early—say, in 1935—he would have had a fair chance of undergoing successful surgery. Boston was and is one of the world's leading medical centers.

Lovecraft's failure to consult a doctor sooner can be explained on several grounds. One is his poverty, although I am sure that Annie Gamwell would have been more than willing to help her only nephew. Another factor is that, in the 1930s, the idea of regular physical and dental examinations, on general principles, was not so widespread as it now is.

Most inhibiting, however, were Lovecraft's habits. He took a perverse pride in a passive, fatalistic attitude towards his physique, and up to the time in question he had gotten away with it. He still had all his own teeth, despite his habits of gorging on sweets and seeing the dentist only at five-year intervals.

In April, 1936, Robert Barlow invited Lovecraft to Florida once more. Lovecraft declined: "My aunt's illness, the lamentable state of the treasury, & the utter disorganisation of my writing programme (which renders absence from my library a vast handicap) all unite to frown upon the idea of carefree migration." He also turned down an invitation from the Longs.

He complained of unanswered letters, jobs in amateur journalism fobbed off on others, borrowed books yet unread, and recurrent eye trouble. He wrote: "My own programme is totally shot to pieces, & I am about on the edge of a nervous breakdown. I have so little power of concentration that it takes me about an hour to do what I ordinarily do in five minutes. . . ."[25] Instead, he hoped that Barlow would come north to visit him.

The winter and spring of 1936 passed quietly. Lovecraft's amateur-journalist friend, Anne Tillery Renshaw, gave him a major ghosting job: to write, from her notes and rough drafts, a textbook for her Renshaw School of Speech in Washington, to be called *Well Bred Speech*.

At first, Lovecraft proposed merely to give the manuscript a light editing; but Mrs. Renshaw wrote: "Don't you dare send my ms. home!" She wanted the full treatment. Lovecraft soon discovered that he had to disabuse Mrs. Renshaw of some quaintly obsolete ideas, as that language originated in divine revelation, or that English was descended from Hebrew. When asked what his charges would be, he replied: "Rates can be discussed later—I fancy that any figure you would quote (with current precedent in mind) would be satisfactory."

Mrs. Renshaw had expected to have her book ready for the printer in the winter of 1936. But Lovecraft took longer and longer. His client extended the deadline to May 1st and then to September

1st. Mrs. Renshaw's letters, at first delighted with his help, became less so as time dragged on.

Despite having worked for sixty hours at a stretch, Lovecraft did not send in the manuscript until September 19th. He asked Mrs. Renshaw, when she had read it, to return it for final polishing. The price had not yet been set, but Lovecraft told friends that he hoped for $200. Mrs. Renshaw paid him $100.

Instead of returning the manuscript, Mrs. Renshaw made her own drastic cuts in the text and rushed it off to the printer. The book appeared before the end of the year. It would be a pleasure to report that, after all that work, Lovecraft had produced something of permanent value. But, academically speaking, *Well Bred Speech* was a disaster. This little book is disorganized, superficial, amateurish, and worthless.

In the introductory section on language, Lovecraft still confuses the language and the race of peoples like the so-called Aryans. The chapter on "Sentences to Correct" is hopelessly muddled. In the pronunciation section, Lovecraft recommends such rare or obsolete pronunciations as "inDISoLUble," "conCENtrate," and "Pro-FEEL" (for "profile").[26] There is no indication that either Mrs. Renshaw or Lovecraft had read any modern scientific work on phonetics. Lovecraft owned a copy of William Russell's *Orthophony; or, the Cultivation of the Voice in Elocution* (1869), and probably relied upon this grossly obsolete text as his authority.

Besides his failing health, I suppose that Lovecraft had been betrayed by one aspect of his gentleman complex. This was the idea that any gentleman of broad culture was *ipso facto* better qualified to deal with a technical subject than some grubby specialist. A well-bred, well-read man like himself, with wide experience in writing and editing and an old hobby interest in the evolution and pronunciation of English, knew all he needed to know on the subject. He was mistaken.

Lovecraft continued his lecture-going. He heard talks on modern art, on Plato, on ancient Greece, on Gilbert Stuart, on the silver-smiths of Colonial Rhode Island, on Chinese civilization, on Mayan ruins, and on the speed of light. He attended Rhode Island's Tercentenary celebration:

On May 4th the Rhode Island Tercentenary exercises opened with a parade in colonial costumes which started at the college gate . . . & proceeded down the hill to the ancient market house, where it was joined by Gov. Green in a coach actually surviving from the 18th century. The detachment then proceeded to the 175-year-old colony house in North Main St., where was held a mock-session of that rebel legislature of May 4, 1776, at which the seditious delegates treasonably disavowed the rightful authority of King & Parliament. In this session—conducted 160 years before— the part of each rebel legislator was taken by some lineal descendant; Gov. Green representing his ancestor Col. Arnold, who presented the original draught of the treasonable resolution. . . . The costuming was so good, & the addresses (text preserved in full in minutes of the original 1776 meeting) so well delivered, that one might well imagine . . . the years to have dissolved away. . . . It was all I could do to keep from crying down the rebel proposers of treason, or from applauding those loyal deputies who urged the reasonable arbitration of existing troubles without recourse to illegal secession. At the end of the session the deputies chanted the newly-adopted formula "God save the United Colonies"—but I, loyal to the past & to my hereditary sovereign, murmured without change the familiar rightful syllables—GOD SAVE THE KING![27]

In dabbling in genealogy, Lovecraft was pleased to learn that he was descended from John Field, an Elizabethan astronomer who introduced Copernicanism to England. He also discovered that he was a sixth cousin of Robert Barlow and a tenth cousin of James Morton.

Lovecraft read George Santayana's *The Last Puritan*, just published, and was delighted by its "truly remarkable dissection of the sterile genteel culture which dominated New England in the 19th century . . . now in its death throes."

Lovecraft's friend Paul Cook, after a long series of nervous and physical breakdowns, quit New England in late 1935 and went to East St. Louis, Illinois, where he worked on a local newspaper. Lovecraft saw him no more.

In July, 1936, Lovecraft was staggered by the death of Robert E. Howard. For all of Howard's talent, energy, and physical prowess, the gods in assembling him somehow left out the cog that provided a love of life. As early as 1923, he began toying with the idea of suicide.

This is common among adolescents, but with Howard the idea

grew. His letters mention his "gloominess" and "black moods." He said: "My father is a man and can take care of himself, but I've got to stay on as long as my mother is alive." In poems he brooded:

> *I am weary of tide breasting,*
> *Weary of the world's behesting,*
> *And I lusted for the resting*
> *As a lover for his bride.*

The mutual devotion of Howard and his mother is a textbook Oedipus complex. With his bossy, overbearing father, Howard's relations might be called love-hate, alternating furious quarrels with emotional reconciliations.

Whatever conflicts were boiling in Howard's subconscious, money was not a major problem. Howard's circumstances were never easy, since word rates were low and payment often late, and since his mother's illnesses cost a lot. Still, at one time he made the largest income (a little over $2,000 a year) in Cross Plains— even more than the town banker, and that in the depths of the Depression.

Howard began to show paranoid delusions of persecution. He owned several pistols, his favorite being a Colt .38 automatic; and he took to carrying a pistol against "enemies," who were probably imaginary. He said, with some truth: "These people around here think I'm crazy as hell, anyway."[28] Neighbors kept asking when he was going to quit fooling around with stories and get down to work, when he was working longer hours and making more money than most of them.

In the 1930s, Mrs. Howard's health declined. On the hot morning of June 11, 1936, hopelessly ill with cancer, she was in a terminal coma. When Howard learned this, he went out, got into his car, and shot himself through the head. He died eight hours later, at the age of thirty. He had hinted in letters of this intention, and Doctor Howard had long known of it and dreaded it. Lovecraft wrote to Price:

It seems incredible—I had a long normal letter from him written May 13. He was worried about his mother's health, but otherwise seemed perfectly all right. . . . Nobody else in the gang had quite the driving zest & sponteneity of Brother Conan. . . . That bird had gifts of an order higher than the readers of his published work

could suspect, & in time would have made his mark in real literature with some folk-epic of his beloved southwest. . . . It's hard to
describe precisely what made his stories stand out so—but the real
secret is that *he was in every one of them*, whether they were ostensibly commercial or not. . . . He was almost alone in his ability
to create real emotions of fear & of dread suspense. . . . And this
is the giant whom Fate had to snatch away while hundreds of in-
sincere hacks continue to concoct phony ghosts & vampires & space-
ships & occult detectives!

Howard's special talent, said Lovecraft, was "the description
of vast megalithic cities of the elder world, around whose dark
towers and labyrinthine nether vaults lingers an aura of prehuman
fear and necromancy which no other writer could duplicate."[29]
But Howard had an even bigger Imp of the Perverse than Lovecraft's.

Through 1936, Lovecraft made little effort to market his stories.
When queried about this, he loftily replied: "As to lack of *push*
—in my day a gentleman didn't go in for self-advertising, but
left that to the little parvenu egotists."

Lovecraft still confused "gentleman" in the sense of "a man
of superior manners, morals, culture, and taste" and the word
in the older sense of "a man of property." Practice of any art,
such as painting, music, drama, fiction, or verse, takes the form
of either the private amusement of the artist, or entertainment, or
propaganda. In Lovecraft's ideals, art should be the artist's amusement; but to create such art requires an income from another
source. This Lovecraft lacked, although he acted as if he thought
he ought to have it as a reward for his gentlemanly virtues.

That leaves art as entertainment and as propaganda, although
a work of art can be both at once. Since Lovecraft's art was not
propaganda, it was perforce entertainment—a branch of show business. In entertainment, some self-promotion is necessary if the
artist wants his just reward, without worrying about being thought
a "little parvenu egotist."

The fact that Schwartz, acting as his literary agent, had sold
"At the Mountains of Madness" compelled Lovecraft at long last
to give thought to agents. He noted that, of the only two agents
he knew, Otis Adalbert Kline and Julius Schwartz, Kline was the
better established, with wider contacts.

Schwartz wanted to sell a collection of Lovecraft's stories, headed by "The Colour Out of Space," to a British publisher. Lovecraft said to go ahead and try. During the summer, while Schwartz was working on this project, Lovecraft sent Wright the manuscripts of "The Thing on the Doorstep" and "The Haunter of the Dark," "as a mere formality before letting Schwartz have them for some British reprinting project."[30] Wright promptly bought them.

Lovecraft never made a hard-and-fast agenting agreement with Schwartz, nor did he encourage others who showed interest in his works. When Leo Margulies became the publisher of *Wonder Stories* (renamed *Thrilling Wonder Stories*) and queried Lovecraft, the latter doubted "if he would care for anything of the sort I write." When Derleth proposed marketing a Lovecraft collection, Lovecraft urged him not to spend "too much energy on the project."[31]

In October, Wilfred Talman said that he would like to act as agent for Lovecraft's stories. Lovecraft wrote:

> I have no idea that he could succeed any better than anybody else, but because he is an old friend I think I ought to let him try (so far as the American market is concerned) ahead of Schwartz or any other professional. . . . After he has tried all his potential markets and failed (as he undoubtedly will!) I might possibly let Schwartz try & fail likewise.

Instead of taking on Kline, the most experienced agent he knew of, or Schwartz, who had actually sold one of his stories, Lovecraft gave the job to the inexperienced Talman "because he is an old friend." After one agent had exhausted the field without result, Lovecraft assumed that another would be willing to send the same manuscripts around to the same publishers a second time. Nothing came of Talman's agenting efforts, although—considering Lovecraft's invincible will-to-failure—it is unlikely that any other agent could have done more for him then.

Lovecraft's attitude was patently unprofessional; but then, he never considered himself a professional. Professionalism and its ways were to him all part of the "commercialism," which he now hated and despised as heartily as he had once hated ethnics and other *bêtes noires*. The whole idea of rationally plotting and resolutely pursuing the course most likely to bring him material success repelled him as ungentlemanly and "tradesmanlike."

This anti-commercialism is connected with Lovecraft's Socialism. He became a Socialist neither because he had been converted to Marxist doctrines (he had not), nor because his heart bled for the downtrodden, but because of his experience with American business. It was not that he loved the working class, although he had shed much of his earlier snobbery and sincerely wanted a just society. It was that he hated capitalism, the "American business system." He hated it because it had punished him, by poverty and neglect, for being unable or unwilling to adopt its own hustling, aggressive, calculative, competitive, hard-boiled, egocentric, opportunistic spirit. He preferred, he said, to live in "backwaters," finding them "a thousand times more attractive than any spot where the ugly processes & vulgar ideals of gain remain paramount," even though he admitted the "narrowness & bigotry"[32] of such places.

The summer of 1936 passed quietly. Maurice Moe and his son Robert arrived on July 18th for a two-day visit. On July 28th came another visitor. Lovecraft wrote Mrs. Renshaw:

> One evening as I came home from a writing session on Prospect Terrace . . . I found a youthful guest parked in the living-room & surrounded by a profusion of bags & baggage. . . . Little Bobby Barlow, my Florida host of '34 & '35, arrived for an indefinite stay & requiring a maximum of guiding, conversation, & time-consuming attention in general! Ædepol! The kid took a room at the boarding-house across the garden, but despite this degree of independence was a constant responsibility. He *must* be shewn this or that museum or book-stall . . . he *must* discuss some new fantasy or chapter in his future monumental novel. . . . & so on & so on. What could an old man do—especially since Bobby was such a generous & assiduous host himself last year & the year before? Well— I did a lot of work in the small hours after the kid had retired to his trans-hortense cubicle (& then he thought it funny that Grandpa didn't get up till noon!), but what headway could such stolen snatches make against a schedule congestion which had things already half shot to hades?

Never having worked for a living, Barlow had no notion of what he was costing his host in working time; while Lovecraft, a gentleman if it killed him, could not bring himself to ration his hospitality, especially since he had suggested the visit.

Barlow's home had broken up. Bernice Barlow left her erratic husband and moved to Leavenworth, Kansas, where she had kin. The Barlows were presently divorced; the colonel remarried and lived to 1952. Robert Barlow planned to join his mother in Leavenworth and enter the Kansas City Art Institute. Lovecraft wrote:

> During his visit I also had another unexpected guest—old Adolphe Danziger de Castro, one-time friend of Ambrose Bierce & later a revision client of mine. . . . Old 'Dolph, now 77, is the same amiable charlatan as ever. . . . He tried to wish some insanely unprofitable revision jobs on me—but the obviously hopeless state of my programme enabled me to put him off without offending him. Meanwhile Bobby Barlow & I shewed him around the town, & derived considerable enjoyment from his pompous reminiscences of the great. On one occasion we sat on a tomb in a hidden hillside churchyard just north of here & wrote rhymed acrostics (at Barlow's suggestion) on the name of Edgar Allan Poe—who 90 years ago wandered through that selfsame necropolis whilst on visits to Providence.[33]

On September 1st, Barlow left for Kansas. As winter closed down, Lovecraft, ignoring the growing discomfort from his "indigestion," kept working away. He bought two sets of walnut drawers in which to store books and papers. Intrigued by tales of the "desert of black blood" in New Mexico, he thought of writing a story laid in Mexico and the southwestern United States. He planned to ask Price's help in getting the local color right and began to study Spanish colonial history.

He was fascinated by the idea of defeating time, which he wished to portray in its "horrible & mysterious essence." For several years he had toyed with the idea of a book-length novel. His friend Edkins wrote:

> Just before his death Lovecraft spoke to me of an ambitious project reserved for some period of greater leisure, a sort of dynastic chronicle in fictional form, dealing with the hereditary mysteries and destinies of an ancient New England family, tainted and accursed down the diminishing generations with some grewsome variant of lycanthropy. It was to be his *magnum opus*, embodying the results of his profound researches in the occult legends of that grim and secret country which he knew so well, but apparently the outline was just beginning to crystallize in his mind, and I doubt if he left even a rough draft of his plan.[34]

In October, Talman urged Lovecraft to start such a novel, so that he could present a sample and a synopsis to William Morrow and Co. The editors there had turned down a collection of Love-craft's shorter stories but showed a lively interest in a book-length tale of this type. Lovecraft gave various excuses for not under-taking the task. In February, he finally confessed that the state of his health made it impossible, writing: "If I ever get through this damned mess, & the firm still feels receptive, we may be able to talk more to the point."

In October, also, Lovecraft attended a meeting of the Sky-scrapers, a local society of amateur astronomers, which met under the auspices of Brown University. In January, he got a request from a publisher for a series of articles on popular astronomy. Realizing that he had fallen behind in the march of science, he began brushing up on the subject.

He still struggled with correspondence, vowing to reduce it but then lamenting: ". . . how the hell can one get out of epis-tolatory obligations without being snobbish & uncivil?"

For Christmas, his young correspondent Willis Conover sent him a human skull from an Indian burial mound. Lovecraft called it a "fitting gift"[35]; but neither he nor the donor realized just how fitting it was.

In the election of 1936, Lovecraft stood for Roosevelt, while Annie Gamwell and her business-class friends were equally strong for Alfred M. Landon. One of the friends left a sunflower-shaped Landon button for Lovecraft, who reported that he came "damn near having a family feud on my hands!" over politics. On October 21st, he went to the state capitol to glimpse "the only first-rate, forward-looking leader in the United States"—Franklin D. Roose-velt.

At the same time, several of his young leftist friends bom-barded him with Communist literature: John Strachey's *The Capi-talist Crisis*, R. Palme Dutt's *Fascism and Social Revolution*, and even copies of *The New Masses*. Lovecraft took it good-naturedly: "Do you kids think you can make a communist out of your grandpa!"[36] Starting the Strachey book, he admitted his ignorance of economics and resolved to repair that lack. He proposed to begin with H. G. Wells's *The Health, Wealth, and Happiness of Mankind*.

He was still for gradual social change in a reformist or Socialist direction. He thought the Marxian exaggeration of class consciousness and economic class conflict "a vicious principle." "I condemn it in the rich or well-born snob—& I condemn it equally in the penniless or labouring snob." He looked forward to the day when a gentleman would be ranked as such purely on his culture, regardless of his wealth or his occupation.

He protested that, despite his attacks on modernistic art and architecture, he did not oppose all progress. He was all for comfort. Beauty, however, needed associations connected with a particular style. A structure must be not only physically but also psychologically comfortable. "We must not be left homesick & bewildered in the midst of an alien world of strange forms. . . ." So, furnishings must be physically comfortable, esthetically harmonious, and visibly related to "previous familiar examples of the same thing." A Frank Lloyd Wright building or a piece of geometrical furniture might be abstractly beautiful, but they would not do for "the man with an historic sense & with a strong feeling of group-continuity."[87] Some contemporary architects and psychologists agree.

In his personal life, Lovecraft saw no escape from ever-deepening poverty. He thought that poverty had one ironic advantage: it protected a "dead-broke old nonentity" like himself against designing women. He sadly wished that he could visit the Old World "& immerse myself still more deeply in the stream of history."[88] He wished he could afford the Model T Ford that Price had offered for sale in California for $15. He liked speed, as friends who had driven him discovered; for ordinary transportation, however, he would be satisfied to putter along at thirty m.p.h. (Considering his mechanical ineptness, it is probably lucky that he was never turned loose in middle age with a car.)

He had learned some lessons about human relations. During his low periods in the late 1920s, he had found all human contact irksome if the other party did not have the same interests, feeling, and prejudices as he and agree with him on everything. Naturally, he never found such a companion. Now he took a more realistic view:

> This general comprehension of separate worlds & their workings is usually as sound a basis of congeniality as that rarer & perhaps wholly non-existent phenomenon of an *identity* of private universes. At least, what makes me feel cordial & at ease toward anyone is not so much an identity of tastes & beliefs & perspectives, as

an assurance that my own tastes & beliefs & perspectives are not re-garded as insane, incomprehensible, or non-existent![39]

He even overcame his lingering ethnocentrism to say some-thing kindly about a Negro. He wrote Elizabeth Tolridge: "You are surely lucky to have the coöperation of the dusky Alice (whom Barlow recalls most pleasantly—& whose pension I hope can be successfully arranged). . . ."[40]

He vehemently castigated his earlier self and apologized for the opinions of his youth. His long autobiographical letter of February 3, 1924, to Edwin F. Baird had fallen into the hands of his admirer Conover, who wished to publish it. Lovecraft vetoed the publication:

> Well—about that damn letter—I gape with mortification at its egotistical smugness, florid purple passages, ostentatious exhibi-tionism, ponderous jauntiness, & general callousness. It wouldn't be so bad if I had written it at 23—but at 33! What a complacent, self-assured, egocentric jackass I was in those days! All that gabble about the shaping & development of—the world's most perfect cipher! Well—the excuse, if any, is this: that the invalidism & se-clusion of my earlier years had left me, at 33, as naive & inexperi-enced & unused to dealings with the world as most are at 17 or 18. As you see by the letter, I had only just burst out of the shell of retirement, & was finding the external world as novel & fascinating as a kid finds it. I was drunk with a sense of expansion, as it were—fascinated by new scenes (I'd just been to New Hampshire, Salem, Marblehead, New York, & Cleveland for the first time) & allured by the will o' the wisp of literary success (first WT placements the year before—& the future rosily imagined)—so that my whole psy-chology was that of a belated adolescence, with the usual egotism, pompous writing, jauntiness, & show-off tendencies of the callow. It is hard for me to recapture the mood of that far-off age—but very obviously, I thought I was quite a guy. . . . Well—the one consolation is that I'm not quite as effervescently sappy a dub in '37 as I was in '24. I may be bad enough now—but at least, the years have been able to focus my sense of proportion a bit, so that I would scarcely be capable of quite such an orgy of blah as this nauseous spouting which the past has yielded up.[41]

Lovecraft explained the faults of his self-education:

As the years progressed, my advance in knowledge & discrimination was sadly one-sided & ill-proportioned—this to some extent because of the semi-invalidism which interrupted & curtailed my formal education (I missed college altogether) & kept me to some extent out of the most active contact with the practical world. In some things I was flagrantly & conspicuously the reverse of precocious—retaining unreal, bookish, & thoughtlessly conventional ideas about all sorts of surrounding realities & institutions far into chronologically adult life. I analysed & investigated only what interested me—thus leaving vast fields untouched, & accepting the traditional delusions & prejudices of my environment (a socially, politically, & economically conservative one) regarding the facts & issues in such fields.

Lovecraft's experience argues against the educational movement, which surfaces every few years, that would encourage students to study whatever they please, without required courses. Lovecraft explained his change of political views:

All this from an antiquated mummy who was on the other side until 1931! Well—I can the better understand the inert blindness & defiant ignorance of the reactionaries from having been one of them. I know how smugly ignorant *I* was—wrapped up in the arts, the natural (not social) sciences, the *externals* of history & antiquarianism, the *abstract* academic phases of philosophy & so on—all the one-sided standard lore to which, according to the traditions of the dying order, a liberal education was limited.[42]

Lovecraft was over-severe with his self-education. What he had needed in his twenties was not so much the social sciences (which are not really very scientific) as practical experience in buying and selling, being hired and fired, commanding and obeying. He needed to learn his way around that vast world of commerce and industry, which he later found so repulsive but without which there would be no millions of readers for the works of literary men.

In late 1936, Lovecraft's eye trouble seems to have cleared up. But his "digestive trouble" grew. In the winter of 1937, he complained in addition of swollen feet. This was an affliction of long standing, which he blamed on the cold. There was no trip to New York, although the Longs again invited him.

By mid-February, his "grippe" forced him to type his letters. He probably suspected the nature of his illness. In a letter to Derleth of February 17th, after speaking of his renewed interest in astronomy, he said: "Funny how early interests crop up again toward the end of one's life."

Lovecraft grew rapidly weaker. He lost weight and had difficulty retaining his food. He spent days in bed, propped up on pillows, trying to write letters and post cards with a pencil or dictating them to his aunt.

Within a day or two after the writing of the above letter to Derleth, Annie Gamwell summoned Dr. William L. Leet. Doctor Leet found Lovecraft sitting in the bathtub in water, because it seemed to ease his pain. The doctor put him on medications and got him to keep a record of his food intake.

A specialist, who examined Lovecraft on March 2d, confirmed the suspicion that he had cancer. On March 10th, Lovecraft entered the Jane Brown Memorial Hospital. Since the cancer had already spread throughout his trunk, the specialist advised against an operation. (The time for surgery had been a year and a half earlier.) Lovecraft could no longer take food by mouth; he was fed intravenously and sedated with morphine.

Emaciated, distended with gas and fluid, and often in great pain, Lovecraft still charmed the nurses by his gentle politeness and stoical courage. He died early on the morning of March 15th.

His death certificate gave the causes of death as "carcinoma of intestines, chronic nephritis." "Nephritis"—inflammation of the kidneys—may be due to any of several causes. Some sources say that his kidney malfunction was merely a secondary effect of his cancer; others imply that it was an independent ailment of long standing. This question can hardly be settled now.

At noon on March 18th, a funeral service was held at the chapel of the undertakers Horace B. Knowles & Sons. Four persons attended: Annie Gamwell; her old friend, Miss Edna W. Lewis; Lovecraft's second cousin, Ethel Phillips Morrish; and his amateur-journalist friend from Boston, Edward H. Cole. The Eddys meant to go but arrived as the hearse was driving off.

Lovecraft was buried in the family plot in the Swan Point Cemetery. No stone marked his grave, but his name was inscribed on the central shaft, which already bore the names of his parents. He was forty-six and a half years old. Paul Cook remembered him as "one of the truest gentlemen and staunchest friends I have ever known."[43]

Nineteen

POSTHUMOUS TRIUMPH

Outside the time-dimension, and outside
The ever-changing spheres and shifting spaces—
Though the mad planet and its wrangling races
This moment be destroyed—he shall abide
And on immortal quests and errands ride
In cryptic service to the kings of Pnath,
Herald or spy, on the many-spangled path
With gulfs below, with muffled gods for guide.[1]

CLARK ASHTON SMITH

Lovecraft had made out a will on August 12, 1912. This will left everything to his mother; or, if she predeceased him, to his aunts; or, if one of them predeceased him, to the surviving aunt. This, in effect, left Annie Gamwell as his sole heir. The inventory of his estate listed only:

Three (3) promissory notes dated February 1, 1911, balance due thereon cannot be determined, if any, secured (sic) by mortgage deed of real estate recorded in Office of Recorder of Deeds of City of Providence, State of Rhode Island in Mortgage Book No. 305 at page 482[2]

This remnant of Lovecraft's investment in Mariano de Magistris's quarry business was valued at $500. No value was assigned to his literary estate.

Before his death, Lovecraft had named Robert Barlow his literary executor. While common in the literary world, the office of literary executor has no legal standing. The literary executor is merely someone whom the testator recommends as qualified to tidy up his writings: to sell rights yet unsold, to arrange for completion and publication of works in progress, and so on. The executor may take this person's advice but is not bound by it.

When Derleth proposed the sale of a Lovecraft collection, HPL had conveyed to Derleth the right to publish a number of his stories. Some of these were already in public domain, and others have since lost their copyright protection.

On January 29, 1941, four years after Lovecraft's death, Annie Gamwell died. Her will left to August Derleth and Donald Wandrei, "in equal shares, all royalties that I may receive from the book entitled, 'The Outsider and Others,' by H. P. Lovecraft, said book being published by Arkham House, Sauk City, Wisconsin, 1939."[3] Everything else was to be divided equally between her friend Edna W. Lewis and Lovecraft's second cousin, Ethel Phillips (Mrs. Roy A.) Morrish.

In recent years, Lovecraft's bequest has been questioned on grounds having to do with Lovecraft's marriage, the validity of his divorce from Sonia, (which has been questioned), and Sonia's remarriage. I will not go into these legal arguments, which are not yet settled; save to say that, until some action is successfully brought against the Lovecraft and Gamwell wills, they may be presumed valid. That makes Annie Gamwell's heirs the owners of the Lovecraft literary estate, save for such rights as have been conveyed to others.

Soon after Lovecraft's burial, Robert Barlow appeared in Providence. He gathered a mass of Lovecraft's manuscripts and letters and departed for Kansas, promising to sort and catalogue the papers.

Months went by. Barlow deposited some of Lovecraft's letters and poems in the Brown University Library, where they formed the nucleus of the Lovecraft Collection there. But he answered letters vaguely, late, or not at all. He was busy at the Kansas City

Art Institute; his homosexuality developed further during his two years at this school.

Derleth and Wandrei, eager to get on with a Lovecraft collection, became impatient. Wandrei grew furious. Told that Barlow had betrayed his trust and stolen from Annie Gamwell, Clark Ashton Smith sent Barlow a cutting letter, saying that, because of Barlow's "unethical" conduct, Smith wanted nothing more to do with him.

Derleth and Barlow continued to coöperate, albeit not without friction. In 1938, Barlow left Leavenworth to go to California via Mexico. Before leaving, he turned his remaining Lovecraft papers over either to Derleth or to the Brown University Library and had no more to do with the Lovecraft literary estate.

When Annie Gamwell died, a Providence bookseller named H. Douglass Dana, called in to appraise the books and papers in her estate, went to the house to see them. He found a heap of Lovecraft papers overlooked by Barlow, including dozens of manuscripts, piled in front of the furnance and about to be shoveled into it. He bought the lot for $75 or less and offered them at cost (or nearly so) to Brown University. Brown hesitated but finally met his modest demand.

Barlow went to live with a family named Beck, in Lakeport, California. Two of the four Beck sons, Claire and Groo, were science-fiction fans with a printing press. In June, 1938, their Futile Press produced a printed version of *The Notes and Commonplace Book of H. P. Lovecraft*, edited by Barlow.

Barlow quarreled with members of the Beck family and left. Resolving at last to make a real career, he became interested in Mexican archaeology and for several years studied the subject in California and in Mexico. He proved to have an extraordinary gift for languages, becoming fluent not only in Spanish but also in Nahuatl, the tongue of the Aztecs. He became bitterly anti-American and pro-Indian.

In 1942, Barlow got his A.B. from the University of California and went to Mexico for good. He became an outstanding archaeologist, head of his department at Mexico City College. He and Wigberto Jiménez Moreno, between them, put pre-Columbian Mexican chronology on a sound basis.

All this time, however, Barlow energetically pursued his career as a homosexual lover. This was long before Gay Liberation, and Mexico has been if anything less tolerant of sexual deviation than the United States. On January 2, 1951, Barlow killed himself with an overdose of sedatives, because he was being blackmailed for his relations with Mexican youths.

Derleth submitted a collection of Lovecraft's stories to Charles Scribner's Sons, which had published several of his own books, and to Simon & Schuster. Both rejected the proposal; the editor at Simon & Schuster, however, suggested that Derleth and Wandrei publish the book themselves.

And so they did, calling their company Arkham House after Lovecraft's fictitious New England town. Derleth raided a bank loan that he had raised for building a house, and Wandrei scraped up a smaller sum. For their title, they chose *The Outsider and Others*, alluding not only to the story "The Outsider" but also to Lovecraft's feeling of alienation.

In 1939, Derleth and Wandrei received 1,268 copies of the book, with an elegant jacket by Virgil Finlay. This was a young artist in Rochester, New York, who had become a distinguished illustrator for *Weird Tales* and had corresponded with Lovecraft. The huge book, of xiv + 553 pages of small type, contained nearly a third of a million words. These included an Introduction by Derleth and Wandrei, thirty-six stories by Lovecraft, and Lovecraft's essay "Supernatural Horror in Literature."

At the first World Science Fiction Convention, in New York in July, 1939, the forthcoming volume was announced at a pre-publication price of $3.50. After publication, it would cost $5.00. Nowadays, a book of this description would retail at $15 to $30.

Arkham House got 150 advance orders, but the rest of the edition sold so slowly that the original printing remained in print for four years. During that time, Derleth published a volume of his own stories and a book of the stories of Clark Ashton Smith under the Arkham House imprint.

Early in their association, Wandrei suggested to Derleth that they publish a collection of Lovecraft's letters. So they wrote to all the Lovecraft correspondents they could reach, asking for the loan of their files. For years, Derleth and Wandrei were deluged with letters, which came in bulky packages and were transcribed by a typist before being returned.

The resulting mass of transcripts, totaling over two and a half million words, formed the basis for the volumes of *Selected Letters* published by Arkham House from 1965 on. Three volumes have appeared to date; two more are promised for about the time of publication of this book.

In 1942, Wandrei joined the Army. Thereafter his work for Arkham House was confined to editing the Lovecraft letters. In 1943, Derleth published a second large omnibus volume of Lovecraft, *Beyond the Wall of Sleep*. It included early, minor stories; the novels "The Dream-Quest of Unknown Kadath" and "The Case of Charles Dexter Ward"; some of Lovecraft's collaborations; sixty-five poems; and a memoir of Lovecraft by W. Paul Cook. Miss McIlwraith at *Weird Tales* had rejected "The Dream-Quest of Unknown Kadath"; so one can see why the magazine did not do better under her editorship.

After *The Outsider and Others* and *Beyond the Wall of Sleep* had gone out of print, they became collector's items. As interest in Lovecraft rose, so did dealers' prices for these books. At last accounts, they were bringing $200 to $300 a volume. Arkham House later issued these and other writings by Lovecraft in smaller volumes.

Derleth continued to publish books, not only by Lovecraft and himself but also by other writers in the genre of imaginative fiction, like Blackwood, Bloch, Howard, Leiber, Long, and Whitehead. By keeping a sharp eye on costs, he squeezed a modest profit out of Arkham House. In some years, when the company showed a deficit, Derleth made up the difference out of his earnings as a writer in other fields. Once, when Derleth was at his wit's end for $2,500 to pay his printer, Dr. David H. Keller bailed him out with a loan on an unsecured note.

After the Second World War, several science-fiction fans started similar small publishing companies. Nearly all perished within a decade of their birth, but at this writing Arkham House is still in business.

In 1945, Derleth wrote a short novel in the Cthulhu Mythos, *The Lurker at the Threshold*. This was based upon fragments by Lovecraft totaling 1,200 words, plus a few of his notes. The story was published by Arkham House as a collaboration between Lovecraft and Derleth. Derleth also published, as collaborations with Lovecraft, a number of Cthulhu Mythos stories in *The Survivor and Others* (1957) and *The Shuttered Room* (1959). In these collections, Lovecraft's contribution was merely some of the notes in "The Commonplace Book." Derleth did all the real work, elaborating and systematizing the Cthulhu Mythos.

Derleth also made considerable changes in the Mythos. Expanding upon hints in Lovecraft's writings, such as the being called Nodens, Derleth developed a whole pantheon of benign deities, the Elder Gods. These oppose the Ancient Ones and sometimes help men in their struggle with the Great Old Ones. In Lovecraft's Cthulhuvian universe, on the other hand, mankind has no powerful friends to speak of.

Derleth was criticized for exploiting Lovecraft's name in this way and for his hard-boiled, belligerent attitude towards others who wished to reprint Lovecraft stories. He demanded reprint fees even when the stories had long been in public domain. Anthologists (including the present writer), wishing to keep on good terms with Derleth for the sake of future business, usually went along with his demands.

Derleth also asserted questionable claims to the entire Lovecraft literary corpus. In 1947, hearing that Sonia Greene Lovecraft Davis was thinking of publishing some writings by Lovecraft, he threatened to sue her is she did it without his permission. Nothing came of the threat, and he and Sonia made up later; but his attitude was clear.

On the other hand, Derleth devoted much of his working life to Lovecraft, for minor financial returns. Without Derleth's herculean efforts, Lovecraft might have remained unknown to the general public forever.

Besides the "posthumous collaborations" with Lovecraft, Derleth wrote many Cthulhuvian stories of his own. These appeared in magazines from 1939 to 1957 and were collected in the Arkham House books *The Mask of Cthulhu* (1958) and *The Trail of Cthulhu* (1962). If Derleth did not have quite Lovecraft's feverish imagination, neither was he addicted to fustian Poesque rhetoric. He wrote in a clear, straightforward style with plenty of dialogue.

Other writers continued the Cthulhuvian tradition. In 1969,

Arkham House published a collection of twenty stories, *Tales of the Cthulhu Mythos*. This included stories not only by members of the old Lovecraft circle, such as Frank Belknap Long, but also by newcomers, including two British storytellers, J. Ramsey Campbell and Brian Lumley. Lovecraft's standing as a myth-maker is secure.

Robert E. Howard and H. P. Lovecraft died within a year of each other. Each death brought a spate of letters of tribute and regret to *Weird Tales* and other publications. Robert Bloch wrote that, had he known of Lovecraft's condition, he would if need be have crawled on hands and knees to reach his bedside.

Clark Ashton Smith also left the scene. For five years, Smith had been a prolific *Weird Tales* author. He had, however, no great urge to compose fiction. He viewed himself as mainly a poet and wrote stories only to earn money to care for his parents in their dotage. After they died in 1935 and 1937, he went back to poetry, drawing, and sculpture; his stories appeared only at long intervals.

The departure of its Three Musketeers dealt *Weird Tales* a blow whence it never recovered. Beginning with the issue of July, 1937, the magazine carried some Lovecraft in every one of seventeen successive issues—poetry, reprints of old stories, and stories newly bought but previously rejected. The magazine also began to suffer direct competition: first from *Unknown* (later *Unknown Worlds*) in 1939–43, and from *The Magazine of Fantasy and Science Fiction* from 1950 on. Both paid better than *Weird Tales* and thus skimmed the cream of the fantasy crop. Several former *Weird Tales* regulars like Robert Bloch, Ray Bradbury, Henry Kuttner, Frank Belknap Long, and C. L. Moore were drawn away for better-paying work elsewhere. The declining *Weird Tales* shrank to digest size and ended with the issue of September, 1954.

Thanks largely to Derleth's efforts, interest in Lovecraft grew through the 1940s. By 1950, Lovecraft was the center of a cult of admirers who praised him extravagantly and took any adverse criticism as a personal affront. Interest sagged in the 1950s but rapidly waxed in the 60s.

When, in 1945, that formidable dean of American critics, Edmund Wilson, wrote a column on horror stories for *The New Yorker*, correspondents reproached him for not mentioning Lovecraft.

Having read but not liked some Lovecraft stories, Wilson gave the fantasist from Providence a closer look. In tones of magisterial doom, he announced:

> I regret that, after examining these books, I am no more enthusiastic than before. The principal feature of Lovecraft's work is an elaborate concocted myth which provides the supernatural element for his most admired stories. This myth assumes a race of outlandish gods and grotesque prehistoric peoples who are always playing tricks with time and space and breaking through into the contemporary world, usually somewhere in Massachusetts.

Wilson describes the super-limpets of "The Shadow Out of Time" and comments:

> Now, when the horror of a shuddering revelation of which a long and prolix story has been building up turns out to be something like this, you may laugh or you may be disgusted, but you are not likely to be terrified—though I confess, as a tribute to such power as H. P. Lovecraft possesses, that he at least, at this point in his series, in regard to the omniscient conical snails, induced me to suspend disbelief. It was the race from another planet which finally took their place, and which Lovecraft evidently relied on as creations of irresistible frightfulness, that I found myself unable to swallow: semi-invisible polypous monsters that uttered shrill whistling sounds and blasted their enemies with terrific winds. Such creatures would look very well on the covers of the popular magazines, but they do not make good adult reading. And the truth is that these stories were hack work contributed to such publications as *Weird Tales* and *Amazing Stories*, where, in my opinion, they ought to have been left.
>
> The only real horror in most of these fictions is the horror of bad taste and bad art. Lovecraft was not a good writer. The fact that his verbose and undistinguished style has been compared to Poe's is only one of the many sad signs that almost nobody any more pays any real attention to writing. . . .

Wilson professes to find it "terrifying" that Prof. Thomas O. Mabbott should write: "Lovecraft is one of the few authors of whom I can honestly say that I have enjoyed every word of his stories." Then Wilson decries Lovecraft's adjectivitis: "sprinkling his stories with such adjectives as 'horrible,' 'terrible,' 'frightful,' 'awesome,' . . . Surely one of the primary rules for writing an effective tale of horror is never to use any of these words—especially if you are going, at the end, to produce an invisible whistling octopus." Wilson continued:

Lovecraft himself, however, is a little more interesting than his stories. . . . his long essay on the fiction of supernatural horror is a really able piece of work. He shows his lack of sound literary taste in his enthusiasm for Machen and Dunsany, whom he more or less acknowledged as models, but he had read comprehensively in this field—he was strong on the Gothic novelists—and writes about it with much intelligence.

Wilson credits Lovecraft with "a scientific imagination rather similar, though much inferior, to that of the early Wells. . . . But the Lovecraft cult, I fear, is on even a more infantile level than the Baker Street Irregulars and the cult of Sherlock Holmes."[4]

Brilliant but opinionated, Edmund Wilson suffered from the same literary snobbery that afflicted Lovecraft: that of dividing literature into a small class of work that he liked, which he called "real literature," and dismissing everything else as "hack work." Wilson called Somerset Maugham "second-rate" and, in another *New Yorker* article, damned the entire detective-story genre under the title: "Who Cares Who Killed Roger Ackroyd?" Since he also dismissed Dunsany and Machen and gave Tolkien's *Lord of the Rings* three rousing sneers, one suspects that he did not like any fantasy.

This is a narrow view of literature. Stories are of many different kinds, for many different purposes. They are addressed to many different readerships and can be classed as good, bad, or indifferent according to how well they appeal to their readers. We all have our preferences, but it serves no useful purpose to judge a child's fairy tale, a novel exposing conditions in the alarm-clock industry, and whodunit by the same standards. By and large, the more different genres that, when well done, one can enjoy, the more fun one can get out of reading.

In 1962, a decade after Edmund Wilson's blitz, another Wilson —Colin, a versatile British writer and critic—considered Lovecraft in a book called *The Strength to Dream* (*Literature and the Imagination*):

In some ways, Lovecraft is a horrifying figure. In his "war with rationality" he brings to mind W. B. Yeats. But, unlike Yeats, he is sick, . . . Lovecraft is totally withdrawn; he had rejected "reality"; he seems to have lost all sense of health that would make a normal man turn back halfway. . . . He began as one of the worst and most florid writers of the twentieth century, but finally developed a certain discipline and economy—although he always remained fond of words like "eldritch" and "grotesque," and such combinations as "black, clutching panic" and "stark utter horror." Two short novels, *The Shadow Out of Time* and *The Case of Charles Dexter Ward* are certainly minor classics of horror fiction; while at least a dozen stories deserve to survive. . . .

Nevertheless, it must be admitted that Lovecraft is a very bad writer. . . .

But although Lovecraft is such a bad writer, he has something of the same kind of importance as Kafka. If his work fails as literature, it still holds an interest as a psychological case history. Here was a man who made no attempt whatever to come to terms with life. . . .

All the same, Lovecraft is not an isolated crank. He is working in a recognizable romantic tradition. If he is not a major writer, he is psychologically one of the most interesting men of his generation.[5]

Although more temperate than the other Wilson, Colin Wilson misjudged Lovecraft. He credited the staunchly materialistic atheist with wishing to "undermine reality" and prove the existence of transcendental beings and powers. Taking the stories more seriously than their author did, he ignored their playful element.

Colin Wilson's criticism had a sequel. He had visited Providence and read James Warren Thomas's master's thesis on Lovecraft in the Brown University Library. Thomas had been so shocked by Lovecraft's racism that he could see nothing good in the man, like a Prohibitionist who writes about Poe but cannot get past the fact that Poe was a drunkard. Hence Thomas enlivened his treatise with such terms as "sexless misfit," "spineless and selfish creature," and "psychopathic weakling." These so outraged Derleth that he browbeat Thomas into giving up his plans to publish the thesis as a book.

After correspondence with Derleth, Wilson was persuaded to examine Lovecraft more closely. By 1967, he wrote: "I am now willing to admit that my assessment of Lovecraft in *The Strength to Dream* was unduly harsh."[6] Furthermore, he wrote a science-fiction novel, *The Mind Parasites*, with Lovecraftian angles, and Arkham House published the American edition.

In 1963, the executive editor of *Fantasy and Science Fiction* was Avram Davidson, a writer of science fiction and fantasy with a strong vein of humor. In the January issue, he considered the

Derleth-Lovecraft volume, *The Survivor and Others,* in a hilarious if wildly prejudiced review:

> THE SURVIVOR AND OTHERS is an intriguing and entertaining little goodie. Howard Phillips Lovecraft, Heaven knows, had a talent for writing which was of no mean proportion; only what he did with this talent was a shame and a caution and an eldritch horror. If he had only gotten the Hell down out of his auntie's attic and obtained a job with the Federal Writers Project of the WPA, he could have turned out guidebooks that would be classics and joys to read, forever. Only he stayed up there, muffled up to the tip of his long, gaunt New England chin against the cold which lay more in his heart than in his thermometer, living on 19¢ worth of beans a day, rewriting (for pennies) the crappy MSS of writers whose complete illiteracy would have been a boon to all mankind; and producing ghastly, grisly, ghoulish and horrifying works of his own as well—of man-eating *Things* which foraged in graveyards, of human/beastie crosses which grew beastier and beastlier as they grew older, of gibbering shoggoths, and Elder Beings which smelt real bad and were always trying to break through Thresholds and Take Over—rugous, squamous, amorphous nasties, abetted by thin, gaunt New England eccentrics who dwelt in attics and who eventually were Never Seen Or Heard From Again. Serve them damn well right, I say.
>
> In short, Howard was a *twitch*, boys and girls, and that's all there is to it.
>
> Of course, August Derleth feels different. August Derleth is an incredibly active, incredibly prolific writer who lives in Wisconsin and has written something like 811 books under his own name; the pseudonyms, who cares? In a way, August Derleth may be said to have *invented* H. P. Lovecraft, having rescued him from well-deserved obscurity in the *Weird Tales* files. . . . We all have our time-bound longings. Horace Gold [former editor of *Galaxy Science Fiction*] would love to have made love to Nefertiti. I would give lots and lots to have poured tea for Dr. Johnson. And August Derleth, I feel it in my bones, would have sold his soul to an Eldritch Horror to have collaborated with H. P. Lovecraft. And now he has.

Davidson ends: "As I say, Derleth tries hard, but he doesn't quite turn the trick, because he is as sane as they come and Lovecraft was as nutty as a five-dollar fruit-cake."[7]

Whereas Colin Wilson thought Lovecraft a bad writer with interesting ideas rooted in his neuroses, Davidson deemed him a good writer spoiled by his neuroses, which he called "unwholesome." Like Colin Wilson, Davidson, when he had looked into Lovecraft further and thought the matter over, decided that his previous judgment of Lovecraft had been unduly censorious, and that there was much to be said for Lovecraft as man and as writer.

In fact, neither was Lovecraft so peculiar nor Derleth so "normal" or "average" as Davidson once thought. Davidson's burlesques of Lovecraft's style merely show that any writer of marked individuality is a fair target for burlesque; Lovecraft was even known to burlesque himself.

Among others who have commented on Lovecraft, Vincent Starrett considered that "The best of his stories are among the best of their time." Peter Penzoldt, author of *The Supernatural in Fiction* (1952) wrote: "Lovecraft's work has both great merits and great defects. . . . He was too well read. . . . In fact he was influenced by so many others that one is often at a loss to decide what is really Lovecraft. . . ." According to Professor John A. Taylor of Washington and Jefferson College, Lovecraft was "the greatest American author of horror tales since Poe," while Isaac Asimov called him a "sick juvenile." Drake Douglas, author of *Horror!* (1966) averred:

> Lovecraft's tales are superbly written. Probably no other writer of horror—including the master Poe himself—was so successful in creating the very atmosphere of horror, fear and terror. . . . A highly literate man, Lovecraft used the English language in its most perfect and elegant form. There is no cheapness or vulgarity in his writing. . . . his writing seems almost Victorian—the leisurely, incomparably rich and elegant style of a Dickens or a Stevenson. It has been demonstrated again and again that this style of writing is by far the most effective for stories of horror. Lovecraft's are, indeed, among the best-written short stories produced in this country, and only their content—for too often, even now, the writing of horror is not considered as serious literature—prevents them from being considered as models of form and style. . . .
>
> In his chosen field, Lovecraft has no peers, with the possible exception of Poe, whom he himself called "the master," . . . we may yet see the day when Howard Phillips Lovecraft, the Rhode Island recluse, will take his proper place in American literature at the side of the revered Edgar Allan Poe.[8]

Evidently, knowledgeable persons differ about Lovecraft. Whether one likes his work or not, he is a writer to be taken seriously.

The first book of Lovecraft's stories to attain wide distribution was a paperbacked collection, which Derleth got out for the Armed

Services Editions in 1945: *The Dunwich Horror and Other Weird Tales*. After the Second World War, paperbacked reprints of Lovecraft collections appeared more and more often, until, in 1970, Ballantine Books and its affiliate Beagle Books began to issue the entire Lovecraft corpus in paperback.

During the 1950s, books of Lovecraft were published abroad in at least five foreign languages. Lovecraft's impact was greatest in France; in 1970, 300,000 copies of his paperbacks had been sold in that country.

At least half a dozen motion pictures, ranging from fair to awful, have been based upon Lovecraft's stories. "The Case of Charles Dexter Ward" was made into *The Haunted Palace* and credited in the advertisements not to Lovecraft but to Poe. "The Colour Out of Space" became *Die, Monster, Die!*, made by a British company with the setting moved to England.

James Schevill, a professor at Brown, wrote a play, *Lovecraft's Follies*, which in 1970 ran for a month in Providence. It is a surrealistic extravaganza, described as "a series of dreams of H. P. Lovecraft." It brings in Hitler, nuclear research, Hiroshima, moon rockets, Robert J. Oppenheimer, and other post-Lovecraft phenomena. Lovecraft appears on stage a few times but only to utter racist remarks, some quoted from his early amateur writings.

A trio of professors in Providence—Barton L. St. Armand and Keith Waldrop of Brown and Henry L. P. Beckwith, Jr., of the Rhode Island School of Design—held a lurk-in the night of March 15, 1970. More than 150 persons, mostly students, paraded with flashlights and lanterns about the Lovecraftian sites on College Hill. The show ended with a reading of *Fungi from Yuggoth* near the Shunned House.

Occultists have sought to climb on the Lovecraftian bandwagon. Kenneth Grant, writing in the British *Man, Myth, and Magic*, asserted that Lovecraft's "ancient sources of wisdom forbidden to man" and his sinister extra-dimensional entities really existed. Who knows? In 1971, an undergraduate at Brown, rooming at 10 Barnes Street, reported seeing HPL's ghost in the building.

To make room for Brown's new List Art Building, in August and September, 1959, the Samuel Mumford house at 66 College Street was moved two blocks north. Its address became 65 Prospect Street. It now faces the green-domed Christian Science church across the street, a fact which I am sure would have brought pungent comments from its former tenant.

What shall we think of Lovecraft? First, what of his writing? In twenty years of writing, Lovecraft wrote sixty-odd professionally published stories. (The exact number depends upon how one counts marginal cases—ghost-writings, collaborations, and vignettes.) This is a respectable output for a part-time writer, but an industrious full-time writer could have produced several times as much.

These stories fall into several classes. There are the Dunsanian fantasies, the dream-narratives, the stories of New England horror, the Cthulhu Mythos stories, and several tales that are *sui generis*. Several use the theme of the ghoul-changeling; several others, that of psychic possession. These classes are not mutually exclusive, and many of the stories straddle two or more classes. Thus "The Dream-Quest of Unknown Kadath" is at the same time a dream narrative, a Dunsanian fantasy, and a Cthulhu Mythos story, and the ghoul-changeling theme appears in it.

Lovecraft's stories nearly all fall on or close to the border between science fiction and fantasy. Earlier stories tend to be pure fantasy; later ones, science fiction, while some combine features of both. In his earlier stories, the conflict is presented as one between good and evil, paralleling the similar concept in Christianity and other theological religions. In the later stories, Lovecraft's aliens and entities are no longer good or evil in the traditional sense; they are merely self-interested, like any other organisms.

Lovecraft was a very large frog in a very small puddle, the subgenre of the macabre imaginative tale. If you agree that there is nothing *infra dignitatem* about imaginative fiction in general and about macabre fantasy in particular, then there is no reason for not considering a good writer in this genre as worthy as a good writer in any other.

Lovecraft's prose has features to which many critics object, notably his wealth of subjective adjectives like "horrible." I do not like this myself. Instead, however, of dismissing this as "bad writing," it would be more objective to say that it is a style now out of fashion. It was in vogue in the Romantic Era, roughly 1790 to 1840, and was much used by Poe and his Gothic predecessors. It is disfavored today; but fashions change, and some day it may regain its popularity.

It takes a little more effort to read this style with enjoyment, just as it does to read the archaistic prose of William Morris or E. R. Eddison, than it does to read a work in brisk, terse contemporary style. But many find the effort worth-while. Unless one is limited to the very latest thing in literature, Lovecraft can be read with much pleasure, prolix, leisurely style and all.

Some of Lovecraft's early stories, such as the "Herbert West" series, are pretty bad by almost any standard. But Lovecraft steadily improved. During the 1930s he proved himself, for all his stylistic oddities, a master storyteller. As Bernard De Voto once put it, the essential quality of a good storyteller is neither accurate observation, nor warm human sympathy, nor technical polish, nor ingenuity in plotting, helpful as all these may be. It is a peculiar vividness of imagination, enabling the writer to grip the reader's attention and drag it along with the story willy-nilly. This, I think, Lovecraft had.

One starting on Lovecraft should be warned that too many stories, read all at once, tend to tire the reader by repetition of the same fictional tricks and plot formulae. This is the case with most short-story writers. All fiction writers tend to repeat themselves.

Some foreign enthusiasts have gone overboard in calling Lovecraft one of the greatest writers of all time. I do not expect, in the foreseeable future, to see him widely ranked with Homer, Shakespeare, and Tolstoy. But he may well overtake Poe. Poe worked in more different genres than Lovecraft—he practically invented the detective story—and his influence spread further than Lovecraft's is ever likely to do.

In his non-professional writings, Lovecraft uttered much nonsense. So did Poe, such as his windy, meaningless "Eureka." One must read Poe's collected works through, including his labored, dismal attempts at humor, to appreciate how bad Poe could be at times. That, however, is the risk of fame. Posterity then insists on publishing one's juvenilia, fragments, and literary miscarriages, while the blunders and botches of lesser scriveners are decently forgotten.

Still, in the field that Lovecraft made his own, I think he stands on a level with Poe or even a shade above.

Moreover, after Lovecraft's literary faults have been taken into account, he still had a powerful imagination. His Cthulhu Mythos is an imaginative creation ranking with Lewis Carroll's Wonderland, Burroughs's Barsoom, Eddison's Zimiamvia, Baum's Oz, Howard's Hyborian Age, and Tolkien's Middle Earth. By putting his own neuroses and nightmares into fictional form, he prodded sensitive spots in his readers' psyches. He exerted wide influence among writers in his sub-genre. He turned out much good, sound entertainment; and that—unless one harbor Lovecraftian notions of art for art's sake—is the main purpose of writing fiction in the first place.

Next, consider Lovecraft's career. Here we have a horror story of another kind—a cautionary tale showing how not to be a writing man. On the practical side, Lovecraft had a genius for doing the wrong thing. In the current catch phrase, he was a loser. He took a perverse pride in being resolutely unrealistic. Unless the would-be writer really prefers a posthumous success or none at all, he should bear these lessons in mind.

He should thoroughly master his craft—all angles of it. For example, he should be a proficient touch typist. Shorthand, too (which Lovecraft scorned to learn, on the theory that it was impossible to well-educated persons), is useful.[9] He should know the business as well as the literary end of writing (record-keeping, accounting, contract and copyright law, and so on). These things are set forth in books and courses. He should be energetic, enterprising, resilient, and intensely self-disciplined. He should keep himself in good physical trim. He should not take a snobbish attitude towards writing of kinds other than his own.

Then, if he also has inborn talent, he may not spend his last years, like Lovecraft, in constant frustration, unable to achieve even modest, reasonable desires for lack of money. If Lovecraft had really not cared about money and the things that take money to buy, one could say that he was happy in his poverty. But, as we have seen, he was not at all happy about it, even though he might try to put a good face on it.

It is sometimes said that Lovecraft might have fared better if he had abandoned his ghosting for full-time writing. But, even if he had doubled or tripled his production of short stories and novelettes, he could not have sold many more than he did. His market was for many years limited to *Weird Tales*, and an editor does not like to run too many stories of one limited type.

This situation changed later. In his last years, Lovecraft's stories became more science-fictional. After his death, the literary standards of the science-fiction magazines, especially of *Astounding Stories*, rose. If Lovecraft had lived longer, he might have found a secure place in the science-fiction scene of the 1940s and later.

Lovecraft's most glaring neglect, however, was his failure to exploit the possibilities of the book-length novel. He was told again and again that, while book publishers did not want a collection of his short pieces, they would very much like to see a novel by him; but he did nothing about it. He could have written such a novel at any time during the period 1926–36, if he had given it the time that he spent on unpaid things like "Supernatural Horror in Literature" and the travelogue of Quebec. He never even typed "The Case of Charles Dexter Ward," nor did he ever start his projected New England chronicle. During this time, many less talented writers achieved book publication of novels.

Another neglect was his failure to commercialize several kinds of non-fiction writing that he did well: antiquarianism, architecture, folklore, travel, and popular science. He did write on these subjects, but only in letters and for the amateur press. He knew of the Federal Writers Project and its American guidebooks, since his friend Leeds was working for it, but he made no effort to join it. He could also have lectured professionally on these subjects. To judge from some lecturers I have heard, his high voice would not have been a fatal obstacle. Lethargy, timidity, and his anti-commercial bias kept Lovecraft from even exploring these sources of income.

Lastly, consider the man himself. He was not a "twitch"; he was a man who, as a result of congenital tendencies (his schizoid personality), compounded by an abnormal upbringing, was long delayed in maturation. He showed adolescent bumptiousness, prejudices, dogmatism, and affectations, and adolescent timidity towards new human contacts and relationships, in his thirties, more than a decade after he had ceased to be an adolescent. In some respects, such as the sexual and the monetary, he never did mature.

He was brought up in the conservative, upper-class Yankee Puritan tradition and long accepted its view of the world. Because, however, of his isolation, coddling, literary fixations, and lack of animal vitality, he acquired only the negative part of that outlook: its austerity, abstemiousness, frugality, integrity, and reserve. He missed the positive side: competitiveness, acquisitiveness, industry, enterprise, practicality, shrewdness, and self-disciplined willingness to drudge at unpleasant tasks when one's long-term interests call for it.

He caught a heavy dose of nineteenth-century American nativism, the local variety of racism or ethnocentrism. Later world events caused this attitude to seem a much worse fault than it did in the early years of this century, when it was widespread and respectable. Lovecraft's failure to make his way in the world reinforced this bias, since it provided a convenient rationalization for his failure. The "verminous foreign hordes," he felt, had cheated him of his birthright.

This view clashed with his kindness, friendliness, gentleness, courtesy, and altruism in dealing with individuals, whether Old Americans or ethnics. It was one more contradiction with which he had to struggle. It aggravated his difficulties in marriage and in living in the big city. He resolved the paradox only in his last years, by dropping nearly all his ethnic prejudices. Then, however, it was too late to make much difference in his life.

That Lovecraft had much to offer the world is shown by his posthumous success. That he failed to exploit his talents so as to get a decent living from them in his lifetime is obvious. Some infer that Lovecraft did not mind his lack of worldly success; Thomas ends his thesis:

> Thus ended a life which, one feels, had been lived for the most part—with a purposeful, single-minded defiance of the influences of modern society—precisely as Howard Phillips Lovecraft desired.

I do not believe this, although Lovecraft persuaded many of it by his façade of fatalistic calm. The stiff-upper-lip pose, however, was part of his code. When he occasionally dropped the mask, he showed his despairing unhappiness: ". . . there are few total losses & never-was's which discourage & exasperate me more than the venerable Ech-Pi-El. I know of few persons whose attainments fall more consistently short of their aspirations, or who in general have less to live for."

The qualities that barred Lovecraft from worldly success have been set forth: his self-indulgence, time-wasting, anti-commercialism, amateurishness, quixotry, and the rest. But the most fell weapon of his Imp of the Perverse, I think, was his facility of rationalizing. This is common among highly verbal, articulate people; their mental agility makes it easy.

Lovecraft knew his faults, recognizing them in Gissing's *Henry Rycroft*. Instead, however, of struggling to overcome them, he preferred to think up eloquent excuses, pretexts, justifications, and rationalizations of his contraproductive acts and attitudes, such as: "As to lack of *push*—in my day a gentleman didn't go in for self-advertising."

Lovecraft's schizoid personality made it hard for him realistically to meet the contingencies of life, while his brilliance and skill with words enabled him, instead of trying to compensate for his failings, to make virtues of them. A successful writer's career, for example, calls for intense self-discipline, and Lovecraft lacked self-discipline; but he tried to make a virtue of this very lack by proclaiming that a gentleman had no "reason . . . to do anything except what his fancy dictates."

Although Lovecraft hated his failure, I think that he must have convinced himself that is was better to fail while sticking to his peculiar code of the gentleman than to succeed by means of "tradesmanlike" acts of self-advancement. When he failed, he blamed his failure, not on his impractical code, but on defects in his writing. Between his code and his writing talent, the code, which gave him a feeling of belonging to a superior kind of being, was the more precious to him. Therefore, as Derleth noted, Lovecraft could not be argued or jollied out of his growing belief that his writing was worthless. To admit that his writing was really good would have meant admitting that the code he had lived by since boyhood had been a ghastly mistake. As Benjamin Franklin once said: "So convenient a thing it is to be a reasonable creature, since it enables one to find or make a reason for everything one has a mind to do."[10]

Lovecraft did, however, considerably change himself, shedding many of his earlier attitudes, poses, prejudices, and obsessions. Moreover, he was cut off far short of his normal life expectancy. We shall never know how he would have made out, had he been granted another twenty years. The possibilities are infinite in number. One who had made the drastic changes in outlook that he did in his forties might have undergone equally surprising metamorphoses in his fifties.

Despite his oddities, those who knew him loved him and were fascinated by him. He always tried to do the right thing. He kept learning and improving all his life; and that, it seems to me, is the best use to which a mind can be put.

His life was starred with wrong decisions at crises, beginning with his failure to finish high school. One can see why, to him, these decisions did not seem wrong at the time. As one member of the Lovecraft circle said to me, "Hindsight is a terrible thing."

Of course, we cannot tell what would have happened had he decided otherwise than he did. The results might have been better or worse, for "time and chance happeneth to them all."[11]

It is tempting, in reading of the blunders and follies of our predecessors, to imagine that, could we but go back and influence such a person at the critical moment—if we could apply some sort of psychoanalytical screwdriver to him—he would have avoided this or that error. It is probably well that we cannot.

Imagine what would have been the result of applying this treatment to the Three Musketeers of *Weird Tales*: Robert E. Howard, Clark Ashton Smith, and H. P. Lovecraft, three literary geniuses *manqué*. They might have been so thoroughly cured of their neuroses that Howard would have become a cowboy, Smith a writer of jingles for some San Francisco advertising firm, and Lovecraft a high-school science teacher. And we should have had no stories from them at all.

NOTES

(NB: When a group of letters is referred to in a note, the names of the writer and of the addressee, if they occur more than once, are omitted after the first occurrence; e.g., in Note 18 on Chapter 4, "HPL to J. F. Morton, Dec. 1926; 30 Jul. 1929; to A. W. Derleth, 20 Jan. 1927" means "letter from H. P. Lovecraft to James F. Morton, Dec. 1926; letter from H. P. Lovecraft to James F. Morton, 30 Jul. 1929; letter from H. P. Lovecraft to August W. Derleth, 20 Jan. 1927.")

One: College Hill

1. H. P. Lovecraft: *Providence,* lines 1–8, in *Fungi from Yuggoth* (1971), p. 1.
2. The address was then 194 Angell, but in the late 1890s the numbering of the houses was changed.
3. Scott (1961), pp. 59, 68; (1944), p. 319. The original psychiatric record in Butler Hospital was destroyed by a fire in 1955 and so is not available.
4. HPL to L. P. Clark, 14 Feb. 1925; Scott (1944), pp. 313f; (1961), p. 55.
5. Derleth, in HPL: *The Dark Brotherhood & Other Pieces,* p. 320; Davis: "The Private Life of Howard Phillips Lovecraft," p. 3.
6. HPL to H. O. Fischer, late Jan. 1937.
7. Davis (1969), p. 117; Cook (1941), p. 10.
8. HPL to H. V. Sully, 15 Aug. 1935; Slonim; Koki, pp. if; Walter (1959), p. 179.
9. Morton, p. 26.
10. Eisner, p. 3; address by Samuel Loveman at a meeting of the Eastern Science Fiction Assn., Newark, N.J., 2 Mar. 1952.

11. HPL to Rheinhart Kleiner, 25 Nov. 1915; to J. F. Morton, 10 Feb. 1923. In the published volumes of HPL's *Collected Letters*, Kleiner's given name is misspelled "Reinhardt."
12. HPL to J. F. Morton, 1 Mar. 1923; Davis (1949), p. 10.
13. HPL to D. Wandrei, 10 Feb. 1927; Davis (1949), *loc. cit.*
14. HPL to E. H. Price, 13 Oct. 1935; to F. B. Long, 17 Oct. 1930.
15. HPL to C. A. Smith, 16 Nov. 1926; to S. Quinn, 11 Sep. 1931; to H. O. Fischer, late Jan. 1937.
16. A. Galpin (personal communication).
17. Wade.
18. Houtain, p. 3.
19. According to one theory, this island (called Aquidneck by the Indians and still sometimes so called) reminded an early official of Rhodes in the Meditarranean; according to another, the name comes from *rodtlich Eylandken*, "little reddish island," applied to one of the islands by an early Dutch explorer.
20. HPL to W. B. Talman, 24 Mar. 1931.
21. Kimball, pp. 307f.
22. Birmingham, p. 74.
23. Marquand, pp. 10, 15.
24. Birmingham, pp. 19f; Clara L. Hess to A. W. Derleth, 18 Oct. 1948.
25. Henry L. P. Beckwith (pers. comm.); interview with Ethel P. Morrish, 5 Sep. 1972.
26. St. Armand (1966), p. 10; Scott (1961), pp. 54, 68.

Two: BENT TWIG

1. Edgar Allan Poe: *Dream-Land,* ll. 1–8.
2. L. I. Guiney to F. H. Day, 30 May 1892; 14 Jun. 1892; 25 Jul. 1892; 30 Jul. 1892 (Guiney-Day Correspondence, Library of Congress). Louise Guiney never named the Lovecrafts, but it is obvious to whom she referred.
3. HPL to J. V. Shea, 4 Feb. 1934.
4. Koki, p. 9. Koki has the date of W. S. Lovecraft's breakdown wrong as 1898.
5. Death certificate of W. S. Lovecraft; Keller (1958), p. 24.
6. Davis (1969), p. 117; (1949), p. 7.
7. Adams, pp. 384f.
8. HPL to R. Kleiner, 16 Nov. 1916.
9. HPL to J. V. Shea, 4 Feb. 1934.
10. HPL to B. A. Dwyer, 3 Mar. 1927.
11. HPL: "A Confession of Unfaith," p. 19; HPL to R. E. Howard, 30 Oct. 1931.
12. HPL: "A Confession of Unfaith," p. 20; paraphrased in HPL to E. F. Baird, 3 Feb. 1924; to R. Michael, 20 Jul. 1929; to R. E. Howard, 30 Oct. 1931.
13. Machen (1951), p. 28.

14. HPL to M. W. Moe, 5 Apr. 1931.
15. HPL to B. A. Dwyer, 3 Mar. 1927; HPL: "Some Notes on a Nonentity," p. xi.
16. Adams, p. 11; HPL to R. H. Barlow, 16 Mar. 1935; to A. W. Derleth, 9 Sep. 1931; to E. F. Baird, 3 Feb. 1924.
17. HPL to Z. B. Reed, 13 Feb. 1928; to R. Kleiner, 16 Nov. 1916; to R. Bloch, c. 1 Sep. 1933.
18. Gough, pp. 248, 260, 364; HPL to Z. B. Reed, 13 Feb. 1928; to J. V. Shea, 10 Nov. 1931.

Three: NIGHT-GAUNTS

1. HPL: *Night-Gaunts,* ll. 1–8, in *Fungi from Yuggoth* (1971), p. 125.
2. HPL to M. W. Moe, 1 Jan. 1915; to R. Kleiner, 16 Nov. 1916.
3. Cook (1943), p. 428; (1941), p. 10; interview with Ethel P. Morrish, 5 Sep. 1972.
4. HPL: *The Shuttered Room & Other Pieces,* pp. 45f; HPL to J. V. Shea, 19 Jul. 1931.
5. Koki, p. 8; Clara L. Hess, in the *Providence Journal,* 19 Sep. 1948, VI, p. 8, col. 1.
6. Davis (1948), col. 1; (1949), p. 5; HPL to A. W. Derleth, 4 Dec. 1935; to R. F. Searight, 5 Mar. 1935.
7. HPL to R. Bloch, Nov. 1933; to J. V. Shea, 23 Sep. 1933.
8. HPL (to R. Kleiner, 16 Nov. 1916) says: "I entered the highest grade of primary school," but I do not believe that the school would have let a seven-year-old, however talented, start at the fourth grade. He might, however, have started in the second. Muriel Eddy (pers. comm.) says that Annie Gamwell "owned a limestone quarry in East Providence, R.I., which she sold for financial reasons to help Mrs. Lovecraft after her husband died." Dates and details are wanting.
9. HPL to M. W. Moe, 1 Jan. 1915; Cook (1943), *loc. cit.*; HPL to R. H. Barlow, 10 Apr. 1934; to V. Finlay, 24 Oct. 1936.
10. HPL: *The Outsider & Others,* p. 217; *The Dunwich Horror & Others,* p. 281; HPL to J. V. Shea, 22 Dec. 1932.
11. HPL to B. A. Dwyer, 3 Mar. 1927; to J. V. Shea, 4 Feb. 1934.
12. HPL to B. A. Dwyer, *op. cit.*; to R. Michael, 8 Jul. 1929.
13. HPL: *The Shuttered Room & Other Pieces,* pp. 46f.
14. *Ibid.,* pp. 48–52.
15. *Ibid.,* pp. 52f.
16. HPL to B. A. Dwyer, 3 Mar. 1927; to H. O. Fischer, late Jan. 1937; to A. Galpin, 29 Aug. 1918; G. Wetzel (pers. comm.).
17. HPL to R. H. Barlow, 24 May 1935; HPL to J. V. Shea, 4 Feb. 1934; to R. Bloch, c. 1 Sep. 1933; to R. Kleiner, 16 Nov. 1916; to H. V. Sully, 4 Dec. 1935.
18. HPL to R. Kleiner, *loc. cit.*; to A. W. Derleth, 17 Feb. 1931; to A. Galpin, 27 May 1918. This clubhouse is probably that on Great

Meadow Hill, which HPL visited with Harold Munroe in the summer of 1921; see HPL to R. Kleiner, 11 Aug. 1921.

19. HPL to Z. B. Reed, 8 Sep. 1927; to E. F. Baird, 3 Feb. 1924; to R. F. Searight, 16 Apr. 1935; to M. W. Moe, 5 Apr. 1931; to R. Kleiner, 16 Nov. 1916; *Providence Journal*, 31 Mar. 1904.

Four: SPOILT GENIUS

1. H. P. Lovecraft: *Despair*, ll. 1–8, in *Fungi from Yuggoth* (1971), p. 80.

2. HPL to J. V. Shea, 4 Feb. 1934.

3. HPL to H. O. Fischer, 10 Jan. 1937. In HPL to D. W. Rimel, 23 Jul. 1934, Lovecraft alludes to "some bantam roosters I had," but without indication of when he had them. I infer it was before March, 1904, when he still lived at 454 Angell St.

4. HPL to C. A. Smith, 17 Jan. 1930; to R. Kleiner, 16 Nov. 1916; Scott (1961), p. 56; Koki, p. 20.

5. HPL to J. V. Shea, *op. cit.*; Koki, p. 21.

6. HPL: *Marginalia*, pp. 268–75.

7. HPL to A. W. Derleth, 23 Sep. 1933; to H. O. Fischer, late Jan. 1937.

8. HPL to R. Bloch, 1 Jun. 1933; Muller, pp. 5f.

9. *The United Amateur*, XVI, 4 (Nov. 1916), pp. 53–57; HPL: *The Shuttered Room & Other Pieces*, pp. 54–63. The quotations follow copy of the older version. In the later version, typographic eccentricities have largely been edited out.

10. *The Scientific American*, XCV, 8 (25 Aug. 1906), p. 135; HPL to R. Kleiner, 16 Nov. 1916; 19 Feb. 1916; Faig: *Howard Phillips Lovecraft . . .* , p. 46; HPL to K. J. Sterling, 20 Nov. 1935.

11. HPL to A. Galpin, 21 Aug. 1918; to M. W. Moe, 5 Apr. 1931; to F. B. Long, 19 Nov. 1920; W. M. S. Russell: "To Seek a Fortune," in *The Listener*, LXXX, 2060 (19 Sep. 1968), p. 365.

12. HPL to M. F. Bonner, 1 Apr. 1936; to A. T. Renshaw, 30 Mar. 1936; to F. B. Long, 3 Nov. 1930; to E. H. Cole, 30 Sep. 1923; to K. J. Sterling, Jun. 1935; to C. A. Smith, 22 Oct. 1933. In HPL to W. V. Jackson, 7 Oct. 1921, Lovecraft reported the Brownie as lost, but apparently it turned up again.

13. Koki, *loc. cit.*; HPL to B. A. Dwyer, 3 Mar. 1927. Lovecraft is apparently never listed among the graduates of the Hope Street High School.

14. HPL to E. F. Baird, 3 Feb. 1924; to R. Kleiner, 16 Nov. 1916.

15. HPL to E. F. Baird, *op. cit.*; to R. H. Barlow, 10 Apr. 1934; to H. V. Sully, 4 Dec. 1935.

16. W. Peter Sax, M.D. (pers. comm.); Everts & "Gamwell" (1973), p. 24.

17. HPL to M. W. Moe, 5 Apr. 1931.

18. HPL to J. F. Morton, Dec. 1926; 30 Jul. 1929; to A. W. Derleth,

20 Jan. 1927; to M. F. Bonner, 4 May 1936; to W. Conover, 23 Sep. 1936.
19. HPL to C. A. Smith, 15 Oct. 1927; to H. V. Sully, 4 Dec. 1935.
20. Dennis Gabor: *The Mature Society* (N.Y.: 1972), p. 58.
21. HPL to W. Conover, 23 Sep. 1936.
22. Elizabeth Akers Allen: *Rock Me to Sleep*, st. 1.

Five: HAUNTED HOUSE

1. Edwin Arlington Robinson: *Miniver Cheevy*.
2. HPL to R. H. Barlow, 8 Aug. 1933; Virginia W. (Mrs. Carlos G.) Wright to W. T. Scott, 23 Sep. 1948, quoted in the *Providence Journal*, 3 Oct. 1948, & HPL: *Something About Cats*, pp. 249f; HPL to A. Galpin, 27 May 1918. Lovecraft's condition resembles that once called "acedia" of "accidie."
3. HPL to R. Kleiner, 16 Nov. 1916; to H. O. Fischer, late Jan. 1937.
4. H. V. Wesson, p. 9; R. Knight: *Intelligence and Intelligence Tests* (Lon.: 1959), quoted in J. R. Baker: *Race* (Lon.: 1974), p. 496. HPL to F. L. Baldwin, 1934, in *The Acolyte*, I, 4 (Summer, 1943), pp. 22f.
5. HPL to B. A. Dwyer, 3 Mar. 1927.
6. HPL to A. Galpin, 21 Aug. 1918; 29 Aug. 1918.
7. W. Peter Sax (pers. comm.); W. T. Scott (1944), p. 3; (1961), p. 68; HPL to E. H. Price, 15 Feb. 1933; to A. Galpin, 29 Aug. 1918.
8. Shea, pp. 83f; *Providence Journal*, 19 Sep. 1948; 3 Oct. 1948; Clara L. Hess to A. W. Derleth, 9 Oct. 1948. In his article, Shea mistakenly listed me among those critics who "have been especially hostile toward Lovecraft and his works" (p. 82). As Shea and I have since agreed in correspondence, I should not, had I been so hostile, have spent the time on this book.
9. Cook (1941), pp. 7ff.
10. HPL to E. H. Price, 18 Nov. 1932; Scott (1961), pp. 56f.
11. HPL to V. Finlay, 24 Oct. 1936; Cook, *op. cit.*, p. 9; (1943), p. 428; HPL to A. W. Derleth, early Dec. 1927. HPL wore a size eight shoe.
12. Marquand, p. 25; HPL to M. W. Moe, 15 May 1918; to E. H. Price, 13 Jan. 1935; Talman, p. 14.
13. HPL: "Department of Public Criticism," in *The United Amateur*, XVI, 8 (May, 1917), p. 109; HPL to J. V. Shea, 22 Dec. 1932; *The Zenith* (Jan. 1921), p. 5; HPL to F. B. Long, 26 Jan. 1921; to R. H. Barlow, 10 Apr. 1934; to S. P. Lovecraft, 30 Nov. 1911.
14. HPL to J. V. Shea, 30 Oct. 1931; Wandrei (1944), pp. 368, 364; Price (1944), p. 19. Maxfield's was later sold and became a French restaurant; sold again, it is now the Far East Restaurant, redecorated in Chinese style and offering Chinese and Polynesian food.
15. "Cats & Dogs," in *Leaves* (Summer, 1937); reprinted as "Something About Cats" in *Something About Cats & Other Pieces*, pp. 3–18; HPL to J. F. Morton, Dec. 1926.

16. Starrett, p. 120; Galpin (1959), pp. 194f; HPL to R. Kleiner, 13 May 1921.
17. HPL to J. V. Shea, 4 Oct. 1931; to A. W. Derleth, 16 Jan. 1931; to R. F. Searight, 4 Nov. 1935.

Six: AMATEUR SUPERMAN

1. HPL: *New-England Fallen,* in *Fungi from Yuggoth* (1971), pp. 15–20.
2. HPL to E. H. Cole, 23 Nov. 1914; to the Gallomo, 1920.
3. HPL to R. Kleiner, 16 Nov. 1916; *The Argosy,* LXIII, 2 (Sep. 1913), pp. 478f.
4. *The Argosy,* LXXIV, 1 (Dec. 1913), p. 237; LXXVI, 2 (May 1914), p. 478.
5. *The Argosy,* LXXIV, 1 (Dec. 1913), quoted in *The Golden Atom,* No. 9 (Dec. 1940), p. 12.
6. *The Argosy,* LXXVI, 2 (May 1914), p. 477.
7. *The Argosy,* LXXVII, 3 (Oct. 1914), p. 718.
8. *All-Story Weekly,* XXIX, 1 (14 Mar. 1914), p. 223; CXIV, 3 (15 Nov. 1919), p. 528. The first quotation is also quoted in Moskowitz, p. 373; but Moskowitz has the date wrong as March 7, 1914.
9. Keffer, p. 82; Barlow (Summer, 1943). Derleth (Oct. 1958) corrected Keffer's statement that "Consul Hasting" and "Randolph St. John" were pseudonyms of HPL, attributing them to Alfred Galpin and Rheinhart Kleiner respectively. Moskowitz (p. 378) speculated that HPL used "Augustus T. Swift" to avoid another controversy; not impossible, but HPL had by then gotten into the habit of using pseudonyms on the least pretext.
10. HPL to C. A. Smith, 25 Mar. 1923; to B. A. Dwyer, 3 Mar. 1927.
11. *Providence Evening News,* 1 May 1917, p. 5; 2 Oct. 1917, p. 4; 31 Oct. 1914, p. 10.
12. HPL to M. W. Moe, 8 Dec. 1914; to A. W. Derleth, 26 Nov. 1932; *The Tryout,* VI, 7 (Jul. 1920). The Swift-Partridge conflict is told in L. S. de Camp & C. C. de Camp: *Spirits, Stars, & Spells* (N.Y.: 1966), pp. 28f. Like some other amateurs, C. W. Smith of *The Tryout* did not number his pages.
13. HPL to E. H. Cole, 9 Nov. 1914; 13 May 1918; *The Tryout,* V, 4 (Apr. 1919), pp. 13f; Wetzel (1973), p. 19.
14. *The Tryout,* III, 3 (Feb. 1917); reprinted in Wetzel (1955), p. 27. The poem is printed "With apologies to W. Raleigh, Esq., since it is an obvious parody of Sir Walter Raleigh's *The Nymph's Reply to the Passionate Shepherd,* which in turn was a parody on Marlowe's *The Passionate Shepherd to His Love*—which was also parodied in *The Tryout,* II, 11 (Oct. 1916), in *The Modern Businessman to His Love,* by Olive G. Owen.
15. HPL to E. H. Cole, 23 Nov. 1914.
16. *The Providence Amateur,* I, 1 (Jun. 1915), pp. 1ff.
17. HPL to R. Kleiner, 4 Jun. 1916; to A. Galpin, 29 Aug. 1918; *The*

Tryout, III, 3 (Feb. 1917); J. T. Dunn (pers. comm., 16 Nov. 1973); Lovecraft & Dunn; Wetzel (1973), p. 19.

18. *The Conservative*, I, 1 (Apr. 1915), pp. 2f. Lovecraft changed printers at the last moment, and the new printer apparently balked at Lovecraft's idiosyncratic spellings like "civilisation."

19. Herodotus, I, 134; Aristotle: *Politics*, VII, vii; A. J. Toynbee: *A Study of History* (Lon.: 1934), I, p. 161.

20. Hofstadter, p. 162; Marquand, p. 216.

21. Santayana, p. 29; Scott (1961), p. 101 (referring to Booth Tarkington); HPL to H. O. Fischer, 10 Jan. 1937.

22. *All-Story Cavalier Weekly*, XL, 3 (9 Jan. 1915), p. 546; ms. in the John Hay Library, Brown Univ.; Koki, pp. 30f; Thomas, pp. 19f. *De Triumpho Naturae* is dedicated to Prof. W. B. Smith of Tulane University, author of *The Colour Line* and also of *The Birth of the Gospel* (1933), wherein he sought to prove, by learned but far-fetched arguments, that Jesus was a purely mythical character like Osiris.

23. Ripley, p. 455; Gobineau, pp. 107, 126, 23ff. Gobineau also praised the Jews and the Armenians.

24. A partial exception is Dr. Carleton S. Coon, who in some of his anthropological books hints that he thinks the white or Caucasoid race is superior to the black or Negroid—but also that the yellow or Mongoloid is superior to both.

25. For Chamberlain, see William L. Shirer: *The Rise & Fall of the Third Reich* (N.Y.: 1960), pp. 152–59.

26. Chamberlain, I, p. 266. For the translator's "Teutons," Chamberlain used the scholarly term *Germanen*, which has the same connotation in German.

27. Ripley, pp. 526–29; Davis: "The Private Life of Howard Phillips Lovecraft," p. 40; HPL to R. Kleiner, 4 Dec. 1918. Ripley actually called the northerners "Teutons," but the term "Nordics" was later substituted because "Teutonic," like "Celtic" and "Semitic," is properly a linguistic, not racial, term.

Seven: WASTED WARRIOR

1. HPL: *Regnar Lodbrug's Epicedium (An 8th Century Funeral Song), The Acolyte*, II, 3 (Summer, 1944); *Fungi from Yuggoth* (1971), p. 50. Part of an incomplete translation by Lovecraft from the Latin of Olaus Wormius.

2. *The Conservative*, I, 2 (Jul. 1915), p. 4.

3. *Ibid.*, p. 5.

4. Isaacson (Jun. 1915), pp. 7f; *The Conservative*, I, 2 (Jul. 1915), pp. 9f. This and other editorials by HPL in *The Conservative* are quoted more fully in *Something About Cats*, pp. 252–77.

5. Isaacson (Opus 2), pp. 8f.

6. Fletcher Pratt: *Secret & Urgent* (N.Y.: 1939), p. 85; HPL to J. F. Morton, 26 May 1923; *The Conservative*, I, 3 (Oct. 1915), p. 5.

Lovecraft apparently did not know that in the speech of many of Pope's time, "join" and "line" did rhyme, being pronounced with a diphthong (like that heard today in New York proletarian dialect in "learn") between those now used in "join" and "line."

7. *The Conservative*, I, 3 (Oct. 1915), pp. 8, 10.
8. HPL to E. H. Cole, 23 Nov. 1914; to R. Kleiner, 28 Mar. 1915; 14 Sep. 1915.
9. HPL to R. Kleiner, 30 Sep. 1915; to A. de Castro, 14 Oct. 1934.
10. HPL to E. H. Cole, 30 Sep. 1923; to R. Kleiner, 14 Oct. 1917.
11. HPL to R. Kleiner, 25 Nov. 1915.
12. *The United Amateur*, XV, 7 (Feb. 1916), pp. 85f.
13. *The Conservative*, V, 1 (Jul. 1919), pp. 9ff.
14. Kleiner (1949), pp. 218ff; HPL to R. F. Searight, 15 Oct. 1933.
15. HPL to M. W. Moe, 18 May 1922.
16. Loveman (1936), p. 74; HPL to R. Kleiner, 8 Nov. 1917; to F. B. Long, 8 Feb. 1922.
17. HPL to A. T. Renshaw, 3 May 1922; to M. W. Moe, 18 May 1922.
18. HPL to F. B. Long, 21 Aug. 1926.
19. HPL to R. Kleiner, 23 Dec. 1917; 4 Dec. 1918; to F. B. Long, 3 Nov. 1930; Wandrei (1959), p. 125.
20. Scott (1961), p. 71; *Lord Chesterfield's Letters to His Son*, Letter xxi, 11 Dec. 1747 (old style).
21. HPL to E. S. Cole, 16 Jan. 1919; to R. Kleiner, 14 Oct. 1919; to the Kleicomolo, Oct. 1916.
22. HPL to the Kleicomolo, Oct. 1916; to R. Kleiner, 25 Nov. 1915; to M. W. Moe, 15 May 1918.
23. HPL to the Kleicomolo, 8 Aug. 1916; to R. Kleiner, 23 Feb. 1918; 14 Sep. 1919.
24. HPL to R. Kleiner, 10 Aug. 1915; to J. F. Morton, 10 Feb. 1923; to F. B. Long, 13 May 1923.
25. HPL to R. Kleiner, 23 May 1917; 23 Feb. 1918.
26. HPL to R. Kleiner, 22 Jun. 1917; 27 Aug. 1917; to M. W. Moe, 30 May 1917. Edward H. Cole (Cole, p. 14) repeats a story he heard from Dunn, Lovecraft's colleague in the Providence Amateur Press Club, that HPL tried to enlist in the British Army in 1914–15 but was extricated by his aunts. Since Lovecraft never mentioned any such episode, this is probably nothing but a garbled version of the story of HPL's abortive enlistment in the R.I. National Guard.

Eight: GHOSTLY GENTLEMAN

1. Hoffman, p. 199.
2. *The Inspiration* (Apr. 1917), pp. 3f; *The Dixie Booster*, IV, 4 (Spring, 1916), p. 9.
3. Davis (1948), p. 8, col. 2; HPL to E. Tolridge, 25 Jun. 1933; to R. Kleiner, 16 Jul. 1919; 21 Aug. 1919; *Weird Tales*, XXX, 3

(Sep. 1937), p. 341, & *Fungi from Yuggoth* (1971), p. 95; HPL to R. Kleiner, 4 Apr. 1918.

4. *The Tryout*, III, 7 (Jun. 1917), by "Lewis Theobald, Jun."; HPL: *Selected Poetry (Second Series)*, p. 15. C. W. Smith misprinted the word "amorous" as "armours." The false rhyme of lines 2 & 4 is probably another misprint.

5. *The Tryout*, VI, 1 (Jan. 1920); *The Vagrant*, Jul. 1918; *Fungi from Yuggoth* (1971), p. 82. *Laeta* appeared in *The Tryout* for Feb. 1918. In *To Phillis*, the word "and" in the sixth line is probably a misprint for "had."

6. *The Vagrant* (Spring, 1917), by "Albert Frederick Willie"; HPL: *The Doom that Came to Sarnath*, pp. 82ff.

7. Macauley, p. 43.

8. HPL: *The Outsider & Others*, pp. 6, 140; *Dagon & Other Macabre Tales*, pp. 8f; *The Doom that Came to Sarnath*, p. 22. I am not certain that "The Tomb" was written before "Dagon"; but it is the first of the two alluded to in HPL's letters.

9. HPL: *The Notes & Commonplace Book Employed by the late H. P. Lovecraft . . .* ; *Beyond the Wall of Sleep*, pp. xv–xxvii; *The Shuttered Room & Other Pieces*, pp. 97–123; HPL to R. Kleiner, 20 Jan. 1920; 7 Mar. 1920.

10. *Leaves*, II (1938); HPL: *Marginalia* p. 285; *Dagon & Other Macabre Tales*, p. 335. "Azathoth" is probably a combination of "azoth," the medieval alchemists' name for mercury, and "Thoth," the Greek version of the ibis-headed Egyptian god of wisdom, Tehuti.

11. *The Philosopher*, I, 1 (Dec. 1920), pp. 3ff; HPL: *The Outsider & Others*, pp. 7ff; *Dagon & Other Macabre Tales*, pp. 19–22.

12. Carter (1972), p. 21; HPL to A. Galpin, 14 Nov. 1918; to R. F. Searight, 31 Aug. 1933; St. Armand (1966), p. 45; Koki, p. 208.

13. HPL to A. T. Renshaw, 24 Feb. 1936; Bush, pp. 89, 122.

14. *The United Co-Operative*, I, 3 (Apr. 1920), pp. 1–6; HPL: *The Outsider & Others*, pp. 210–14; *The Horror in the Museum & Other Revisions*, pp. 3–9.

15. *The Vagrant* (Spring, 1927), pp. 188–95; HPL: *Beyond the Wall of Sleep*, p. 218; *The Horror in the Museum & Other Revisions*, p. 15.

16. HPL: *The Shuttered Room & Other Pieces*, p. 63; Clara L. Hess to A. W. Derleth, 9 Oct. 1948, quoted in HPL: *Something About Cats*, p. 249.

17. Scott (1961), p. 60; HPL to R. Kleiner, 30 Mar. 1919.

18. HPL to S. P. Lovecraft, 24 Feb. 1921; 17 Mar. 1921.

19. HPL to E. J. Davis, 12 May 1925; Scott, *op. cit.*, p. 68; Keller (1958), p. 22; *The Silver Clarion*, III, 1 (Apr. 1919), pp. 8ff.

20. *The National Amateur* (Jul. 1919); HPL: *The Shuttered Room & Other Pieces*, pp. 85–96.

21. HPL to A. T. Renshaw, 1 Jun. 1921.

22. *Pine Cones*, I, 6 (Oct. 1919), pp. 2–9; HPL: *Beyond the Wall of Sleep*, pp. 33–39; *The Doom that Came to Sarnath*, pp. 39–50.

23. *The United Co-Operative*, I, 2 (Jun. 1919, as "Lewis Theobald, Jr."), p. 8; HPL: *Beyond the Wall of Sleep*, p. 3; *The Doom that Came to Sarnath*, pp. 52f.

24. *The United Amateur*, XX, 2 (Nov. 1920), pp. 19ff; HPL: *Beyond the Wall of Sleep*, pp. 6f; *The Doom that Came to Sarnath*, pp. 57–60; HPL to R. Kleiner, 14 Dec. 1921. The ellipses (. . .) in the first paragraph of "Nyarlathotep" are mine; the rest, HPL's.

25. Hence the name "Amenhotep" means "Amen is contented." Many Bantu names begin with a palatalized *n* (=*ny* or Spanish *ñ*). For theories of the pronunciation of ancient Egyptian names, see my *Great Cities of the Ancient World*, p. 43.

26. HPL to C. A. Smith, 14 Apr. 1949; Amory, pp. 33f; HPL to R. Kleiner, 9 Nov. 1919; to E. Tolridge, 8 Mar. 1929. The letter to Smith, a decade after the event, attributes this "shock" to *A Dreamer's Tales*; but in his letters of 1919, *Time and the Gods* is the first book by Dunsany mentioned. Koki (p. 58) mistook HPL's allusion, in his article "Dunsany and His Work," to Dunsany's "eyeglass" as meaning that Dunsany had a glass eye.

27. *The Tryout*, V, 11 (Nov. 1919), pp. 11f; Wetzel (1955), III, p. 21; *The Tryout*, V, 12 (Dec. 1919), pp. 12f.

28. *The United Amateur*, XIX, 2 (Nov. 1919), pp. 30–33; HPL: *Beyond the Wall of Sleep*, pp. 24–27; *Dagon & Other Macabre Tales*, pp. 41–46; HPL to S. Quinn, 11 Sep. 1931.

29. *The Tryout*, VI, 11 (Nov. 1920), pp. 3–9; HPL: *The Outsider & Others*, pp. 19, 121; *Dagon & Other Macabre Tales*, pp. 56, 47; *The Spectator*, No. 418 (30 Jun. 1712), quoted in Fish, pp. 28f.

30. *The Tryout*, VI, 11 (Nov. 1920); VI, 5 (May 1920); HPL: *The Outsider & Others*, pp. 19, 28–31, 121; *Dreams & Fancies*, pp. 77, 61–68. The story closely follows the wording of a letter to the Gallomo of 11 Dec. 1919, in which HPL narrates the dream.

31. *The Rainbow*, II, 2 (May 1922), pp. 10ff; HPL: *The Outsider & Others*, pp. 10–13; *The Dream-Quest of Unknown Kadath*, pp. 142–50. In Lovecraft's later stories, "Innsmouth" is an imaginary New English town. Lovecraft may have forgotten that in "Celephais" he gave a place of that name an English setting.

32. *Weird Tales*, XXXII, 5 (Nov. 1938), pp. 617–26; *The Tryout*, VII, 4 (Jul. 1921), pp. 11–15; HPL: *The Outsider & Others*, pp. 113–20, 138f, 234–41; *Dagon & Other Macabre Tales*, pp. 73–85.

33. *Weird Tales*, XXXII, 4 (Oct. 1938), pp. 489–92; HPL: *Beyond the Wall of Sleep*, pp. 13ff: *The Doom that Came to Sarnath*, pp. 2–7. The ellipses are HPL's.

34. HPL to J. V. Shea, 19 Jun. 1931; HPL: *The Outsider & Others*, p. 63; *The Dunwich Horror & Others*, p. 53; Koki, p. 138; HPL to R. Kleiner, 23 Jan. 1920; to E. F. Baird, 3 Feb. 1924.

35. Houtain & Cook, pp. 6, 22; Wetzel (1953), p. 3; HPL to R. Kleiner, 10 Sep. 1920. Some writers on Lovecraft have confused the July and August meetings, treating them as one and the same.
36. *The Boys' Herald*, LXXII, 1 (Jan. 1943), pp. 6f; HPL to S. P. Lovecraft, 24 Feb. 1921; Davis (1948), col. 1.
37. Scott (1961), p. 61; death certificate of Sarah Susan Lovecraft. The letter in which HPL tells his mother of the St. Patrick's Day party, dated 17 Mar. 1921, seems to have been written on Mar. 24th but to have been misdated.

Nine: JOURNEYMAN FANTASIST

1. W. S. Gilbert: *Patience*, Act I.
2. HPL to R. Kleiner, 12 June. 1921; to W. V. Jackson, 7 Oct. 1921.
3. Inventory of H. P. Lovecraft's estate, 21 Apr. 1937, & of A. E. P. Gamwell's, 13 Mar. 1941, Probate Court of Providence.
4. Thorstein Veblen: *The Theory of the Leisure Class* (N.Y.: 1931), p. 42; HPL to R. Kleiner, 12 Jun. 1921; J. K. D. (?) to E. H. Cole, 26 Mar. 1937; HPL to A. E. P. Gamwell, 19 Aug. 1921.
5. HPL to R. Kleiner, 12 Mar. 1922; 15 Jan. 1922; *Home Brew*, No. 6; HPL: *Beyond the Wall of Sleep*, p. 75; *Dagon & Other Macabre Tales*, p. 150.
6. HPL to R. Kleiner, 30 Jul. 1921; 11 Aug. 1921.
7. S. Loveman to G. de la Ree, 16 Jul. 1973; HPL to M. W. Moe, 18 May 1922; Galpin (1959), p. 199; HPL to W. V. Jackson, 7 Aug. 1921; to R. Kleiner, 21 Sep. 1921.
8. HPL to M. W. Moe, 18 May 1922; A. W. Derleth (pers. comm., 8 Sep. 1953); E. H. Cole to A. W. Derleth, 19 Dec. 1944 (Derleth, 1945, p. 15); *The Rainbow*, I, 1 (Oct. 1921), pp. 9ff.
9. HPL: "Americanism," pp. 119f; HPL to R. Kleiner, 21 Sep. 1921; to M. W. Moe, 21 Jun. 1922.
10. HPL: "A Confession of Unfaith," p. 22.
11. *The National Amateur*, XVIII, 6 (Jul. 1919); HPL: *The Outsider & Others*, pp. 127–31; *The Dunwich Horror & Others*, pp. 121–29. Derleth (1945), p. 117, and in HPL: *Dagon & Other Macabre Tales*, p. vii, says that "The Picture in the House" was written in 1920; but in HPL to R. Kleiner, 14 Dec. 1921, HPL says he had finished it two days before.
12. When the story was reprinted in *Weird Tales* for Jan. 1924, Eduardo Lopez, by a typographical error, became "the sailor Lopex" and this misspelling has been perpetuated in later reprintings. Condra plausibly argues that Lovecraft got his information on Pigafetta and Lopez via Thomas Huxley's *Man's Place in Nature* (1863).
13. Carter: "H. P. Lovecraft: The Books"; de Camp: "Books that Never Were"; Home; *Home Brew*, Jan., Feb., Mar., Apr., 1922; HPL: *The Outsider & Others*, pp. 14–18, 242–54; *Beyond the Wall of Sleep*, pp. 45–49; *Dagon & Other Macabre Tales*, pp. 155,

160–86. The original fictitious *Book of Thoth* is sometimes confused with the medieval alchemical treatises attributed to an equally fictitious "Thoth-Hermes."

14. HPL to M. W. Moe, 18 May 1922; *Jersey City American Standard*, 20 Sep. 1859; *Chicago Tribune*, 25 Jul. 1876; *Chicago Times*, 6 May 1886, quoted in Herbert G. Gutman: "Work, Culture, and Society," in *The American Historical Review*, LXXVIII, 3 (Jun. 1973), p. 584; HPL to F. B. Long, 9 Jun. 1922; Davis (1948), cols. 1, 3; (1949), pp. 5, 7.

15. HPL to A. Galpin, 30 Jun. 1922; to F. C. Clark, 4 Aug. 1922; to J. F. Morton, 8 Jan. 1924.

16. C. A. Smith to G. Sterling, 26 Mar. 1926; C. A. Smith: *Selected Poems* (1971), p. 103.

17. HPL to M. W. Moe, n.d. (*Selected Letters*, I, p. 163, probably Oct. 1922); to A. E. P. Gamwell, 3 Oct. 1922.

18. HPL to R. Kleiner, 11 Jan. 1923; to J. F. Morton, 10 Feb. 1923; 24 Feb. 1923.

19. Cook (1941), p. 62; *Weird Tales*, II, 2 (Sep. 1923), pp. 80, 82.

20. HPL to F. B. Long, 12 May 1923.

Ten: BASHFUL LOVER

1. W. S. Gilbert: *Patience*, Act I.

2. HPL to J. F. Morton, 8 Mar. 1923.

3. HPL to F. B. Long, 24 Jul. 1923; Machen (1951), p. 193; Boswell: *Life of Dr. Johnson*, II, p. 16; HPL to A. W. Derleth, early Oct. 1932; to R. Kleiner, 14 Dec. 1921. "Boarish" is not a misprint for "boorish" but an archaism, meaning "crude, beastly."

4. *The Conservative*, No. 13 (Mar. 1923), p. 7; M. E. Eddy: *The Gentleman from Angell Street*, p. 4.

5. C. M. Eddy, Jr., p. 245; Cook (1941), p. 33; HPL to R. F. Searight, 4 Nov. 1935; HPL: *The Dark Brotherhood & Other Pieces*, p. 100.

6. Derleth (pers. comm., 8 Sep. 1953); Davis (1948), col. 3. Koki (pp. 102f) repeats a story he heard from one who allegedly got it from HPL himself: that Sonia once persuaded Lovecraft, on a visit to New York, to spend the night on her sofa rather than hunt for quarters, and that she then coerced him into marrying her by telling him that he had "compromised" her. I have found no confirmation for this tale, which seems out of character for both parties.

7. Davis, *op. cit.*, cols. 2f; HPL to L. P. Clark, 9 Aug. 1922; to C. A. Smith, 25 Jan. 1924.

8. HPL: *The Outsider & Others*, p. 85; *The Dunwich Horror & Others*, p. 52.

9. HPL to E. F. Baird, 3 Feb. 1924. The ellipses after "poet" are HPL's; the others, mine.

10. Davis (1948), col. 3.

11. M. E. Eddy (1968), p. 93; Thomas, pp. 43ff; Keller (1958), pp. 22f; A. W. Derleth (pers. comm.).
12. Gissing, pp. 42, 46, 148ff, 31.
13. E. H. Cole to A. W. Derleth, 19 Dec. 1944 (Derleth, 1945, p. 15); Shea, p. 90; HPL to J. V. Shea, 14 Aug. 1933; 4 Feb. 1944.
14. HPL to A. W. Derleth, 16 Feb. 1933; to R. H. Barlow, 30 Aug. 1936; Eric Bentley: *The Cult of the Superman* (1969), *passim*. See also Colin Wilson (1962), Chap. V.
15. HPL to J. V. Shea, 13 Oct. 1931.
16. Cook (1941), p. 13; (1968), p. 12; HPL to R. Kleiner, 23 Jan. 1920; to F. B. Long, 20 Feb. 1924.
17. Thoreau, pp. 465f; Marquand, p. 294.
18. HPL to R. Kleiner, 23 Apr. 1921; to E. H. Cole, 30 Sep. 1923; to A. W. Derleth, 14 Mar. 1933.
19. HPL to S. H. Greene, *c.* 1922 (*The Arkham Collector,* No. 9 [Winter, 1971], pp. 242–46); A. W. Derleth (pers. comm., 8 Sep. 1953); Koki, p. 155; Derleth (1948), p. 114.
20. Anne Freemantle: review of *The Marlborough House Set,* by Anita Leslie, in the *New York Times Book Review,* 6 May 1973, p. 4.

Eleven: QUIXOTE IN BABYLON

1. Edgar Allan Poe: "The Imp of the Perverse," in *Prose Tales (First Series)* (Boston: 1876–84), p. 533.
2. *Ibid.*, p. 531; HPL to F. B. Long, 21 Mar. 1924; Davis (1948), col. 4; (1949), p. 8. Lovecraft's account of the wedding and honeymoon, in the letter cited, differs in some details from Sonia's. Since Lovecraft wrote less than three weeks after the events, whereas she wrote twenty-four years later, HPL's account is probably the more accurate.
3. HPL to F. B. Long, 21 Mar. 1924; to J. F. Morton, 12 Mar. 1924; to L. P. Clark, 9 Mar. 1924.
4. HPL to L. P. Clark, *op. cit.*
5. HPL & Sonia H. Lovecraft to A. E. P. Gamwell, Mar. 1924; HPL to B. A. Dwyer, 26 Mar. 1927.
6. HPL to J. F. Morton, 6 May 1924; S. H. Davis, unpub. ms.
7. Davis: "The Private Life of Howard Phillips Lovecraft," pp. 12f; abridged in Davis (1948), col. 4, & (1949), p. 8.
8. Davis (1948), col. 6; (1949), pp. 10f.
9. Davis (1948), cols. 5, 6; (1949), p. 10.
10. Davis: "The Private Life of Howard Phillips Lovecraft," p. 39.
11. *Ibid.*, pp. 12f; Davis (1948), cols. 4, 5; (1949), pp. 8f; HPL to L. P. Clark, post card, 10 Sep. 1924.
12. HPL to E. H. Cole, 21 Jul. 1924; Davis: "The Private Life of Howard Phillips Lovecraft," p. 10; HPL to F. B. Long, 21 Mar. 1924. Ellipses after "CHICAGO" and "scenes" Lovecraft's, others mine. HPL got the expression "O gawd, O Montreal!" from an article by Ezra Pound in *The Dial* (F. B. Long, pers. comm.).

13. J. C. Henneberger to J. Frieman, 20 Oct. 1968; Davis: *op. cit.*, pp. 10f, 7; Searles, p. ix.

14. Searles, pp. 67, 62, 99.

15. S. H. Davis (1948), col. 6; (1949), p. 10; HPL to L. P. Clark, 29 Sep. 1922; to C. M. Eddy, 5 Sep. 1924; ms., John Hay Library. In the sixth paragraph of the employment letter, HPL originally wrote that he was "of pure English American Protestant ancestry" but considered changing to this to the more tactful "of cultivated native ancestry." Since neither wording is crossed out, I do not know which was used in the typed version.

16. F. B. Long (pers. comm.); *New York Times*, n.d.; HPL to L. P. Clark, 1 Aug. 1924.

17. Kleiner (1949), pp. 225f; HPL to E. H. Cole, 15 Jul. 1935.

18. HPL: *The Dark Brotherhood & Other Pieces*, p. 319; *Weird Tales*, XXX, 4 (Oct. 1937), pp. 418–36; HPL: *The Outsider & Others*, pp. 147–63; *At the Mountains of Madness & Other Novels*, pp. 222–47.

19. HPL to A. W. Derleth, 18 Mar. 1931; F. B. Long (pers. comm.); Koki, p. 121.

20. Crane, p. 187; HPL to S. Loveman, 29 Apr. 1923 (quoted in Koki, p. 120); to L. P. Clark, 18 Sep. 1925 (bis); 14 Oct. 1925.

21. HPL to A. W. Derleth, 19 Oct. 1926; 25 Oct. 1926.

22. Kleiner (1949), p. 224.

23. HPL to L. P. Clark, 29 Sep. 1924; 4 Nov. 1924; 17 Nov. 1924; 29 Nov. 1924.

24. HPL to L. P. Clark, 29 Sep. 1924. I recall editorials raising the Khazar theory in the 1920s in the *Los Angeles Times* and in the British magazine *Flying*.

25. Marquand, p. 213.

26. I think the bank failure occurred at this time; but, in Sonia's dozen fragments of autobiography, in manuscript (both in longhand and typed) in the John Hay Library, the chronology is so scrambled that I cannot be utterly sure that the failure did not occur later, around 1930.

27. HPL to L. P. Clark, 12 Nov. 1924; 11 Nov. 1924; 4 Nov. 1924; 29 Sep. 1924.

28. Davis (1948), col. 5; (1949), pp. 9f; "The Private Life of Howard Phillips Lovecraft," p. 7. Koki (p. 114) says that Sonia urged that one of the aunts come to New York to keep house for HPL, but I have not seen evidence of this and suspect that it is due to a misunderstanding by Koki of Sonia's accounts.

29. HPL to L. P. Clark, 8 Aug. 1925. Ellipses Lovecraft's.

Twelve: GUNNAR IN THE SNAKE PIT

1. HPL: *The Courtyard*, in *Fungi from Yuggoth* (1971), p. 117. The chapter title refers to the story of Gunnar in the Sigurd legend. After Sigurd's death, Gunnar is lured to the court of Atli (=At-

tila), betrayed, bound, and cast into a pit of venomous serpents. His sister Gudrun smuggles a harp to him, which he plays with his toes. This charms the serpents, until one serpent (evidently not a lover of good music; an early rock fan perhaps?) does him in. See *Volsunga Saga*, transl. by William Morris (1962), p. 219.

2. F. B. Long (pers. comm.); Loveman (1958), p. 35; HPL to M. W. Moe, 15 Jun. 1925.
3. Davis (1948), col. 4; (1949), p. 9.
4. Davis, *loc. cit.*; HPL to J. F. Morton, Mar. 1926. (This letter, in *Selected Letters II*, pp. 3f, is shown by internal evidence and comparison with other letters to have been misdated as Mar. 1925.)
5. HPL to L. P. Clark, 24 Oct. 1925.
6. HPL to L. P. Clark, *op. cit.*
7. HPL to L. P. Clark, 6 Jul. 1925.
8. HPL to F. B. Long, 13 May 1923; 27 Feb. 1931.
9. HPL to B. A. Dwyer, 26 Mar. 1927.
10. HPL to E. H. Cole, 29 Sep. 1934; to L. P. Clark, 11 Apr. 1925; 21 Apr. 1925. In the letter to Cole, HPL speaks of getting "back to the protecting rays of my oil heater." This must be a mistake, since he did not get the oil heater until the following October.
11. HPL to L. P. Clark, 27 Jul. 1925; 12 Sep. 1925.
12. HPL to R. Bloch, late 1933; to E. H. Cole, 24 Feb. 1925.
13. HPL to L. P. Clark, 28 May 1925; 20 May 1925.
14. HPL to L. P. Clark, 8 Aug. 1925; 8 Sep. 1925; 7 Nov. 1925; 14 Nov. 1925.
15. Cook (1941), p. 17; HPL to L. P. Clark, 18 Sep. 1925 (bis); 1 Sep. 1925.
16. HPL: *The Outsider & Others*, p. 101; *Dagon & Other Macabre Tales*, p. 243.
17. HPL: *The Outsider & Others*, pp. 92, 96; *Dagon & Other Macabre Tales*, pp. 230f, 237.
18. HPL to C. A. Smith, 20 Sep. 1925.
19. HPL to L. P. Clark, 30 Jul. 1925; 8 Sep. 1925; 23 Dec. 1925; 14 Nov. 1925.
20. HPL to L. P. Clark, 14 Nov. 1925; to F. B. Long, Jul. 1926; to L. P. Clark (called "unknown" in *Selected Letters II*, p. 37), 11 Jan. 1925; to F. B. Long, Jul. 1926.
21. Cook (1941), p. 38.
22. HPL: *The Outsider & Others*, p. 509.
23. Mabbott, pp. 38f.
24. Cook (1941), p. 16; HPL to L. P. Clark, 22 Oct. 1925; 26 Feb. 1926; 15 Sep. 1925; 2 Apr. 1925.
25. HPL to L. P. Clark, 23 Aug. 1925; 27 Aug. 1925; 13 Dec. 1925; 15 Sep. 1925.
26. HPL to L. P. Clark, 28 Sep. 1925.
27. HPL to C. A. Smith, 20 Sep. 1925; 9 Oct. 1925; to L. P. Clark, 22 Dec. 1925; 7 Aug. 1925.

28. HPL to L. P. Clark, 18 Sep. 1925 (bis); 13 Dec. 1925.
29. HPL to A. E. P. Gamwell, 26 Feb. 1925.
30. HPL to L. P. Clark, 7 Nov. 1925; 2 Dec. 1925.
31. HPL to L. P. Clark, 16 Feb. 1926; 18 Sep. 1925 (bis); 4 Nov. 1924; to A. E. P. Gamwell, 10 Feb. 1925.
32. Derleth: "Final Notes," pp. 305f.
33. Samuels, p. 357; HPL to L. P. Clark, 29 Mar. 1926.
34. HPL to L. P. Clark, 12 Sep. 1925. (In *Selected Letters II*, p. 25; the addressee of this letter is there called "unknown.")
35. Santayana, p. 89.
36. F. B. Long (pers. comm., 18 Jul. 1973, 22 Aug. 1973); Talman (1973), p. 14; HPL to L. P. Clark, 11 Jan. 1926. Long's parents called him "Belknap" to distinguish him from his father, but nearly all his friends called him "Frank." Talman (pers. comm.) states that, on reviewing his correspondence with HPL, he did find one very minor anti-Jewish gibe.
37. HPL to L. P. Clark, 27 Mar. 1926.
38. HPL to L. P. Clark, 22 Dec. 1925.
39. HPL to L. P. Clark, 27 Mar. 1926; 29 Mar. 1926.
40. HPL to L. P. Clark, 22 Dec. 1925.

Thirteen: CTHULHU ALIVE

1. HPL: *Background*, in *Fungi from Yuggoth* (1971), p. 134.
2. Cook (1941), p. 16.
3. HPL to F. B. Long, 1 May 1926.
4. Eddy: *The Gentleman from Angell Street*, p. 17; Davis: "The Private Life of Howard Phillips Lovecraft," pp. 25f.
5. HPL to L. P. Clark, 1 Apr. 1926; 6 Apr. 1926; 22 Dec. 1925.
6. HPL to A. W. Derleth, 16 Jan. 1931; to F. Leiber, 1936 (quoted in Scott, 1961, p. 64).
7. Davis (1948), cols. 6, 7; (1949), p. 11. For the unsettled question of the validity of HPL's divorce, see Koki, p. 211.
8. HPL to F. B. Long, 20 May 1926; 1 May 1926.
9. HPL to W. B. Talman, 23 Apr. 1926; to F. B. Long, 23 Apr. 1926 (ellipses HPL's).
10. HPL to W. B. Talman, 25 Jun. 1926; to F. B. Long, 20 May 1926.
11. HPL to F. B. Long, 26 Oct. 1926 (bis).
12. HPL to F. B. Long, 21 Aug. 1926.
13. HPL to C. A. Smith, 9 Aug. 1926; HPL to A. W. Derleth, 19 Nov. 1926; to W. B. Talman, 24 Aug. 1926.
14. HPL to F. B. Long, 26 Oct. 1926; to C. A. Smith, 16 Nov. 1926.
15. HPL to R. F. Searight, 3 Feb. 1934; to A. W. Derleth, 2 Sep. 1926.
16. HPL to A. W. Derleth, 31 Oct. 1926.
17. *Providence Sunday Journal*, 10 Oct. 1926.
18. HPL to A. W. Derleth, 16 May 1931; Derleth (1945), pp. 69f. The authenticity of the latter quotation has been questioned; it does not occur in the surviving letters from HPL to Derleth. It is said (D. W.

Mosig, pers. comm.) that, when queried on this matter, Derleth not only failed to produce the source but also became angry. The quotation may be a paraphrase from memory of something that Derleth believed HPL to have written.

19. HPL: *The Outsider & Others*, pp. 255–73; *The Dunwich Horror & Others*, pp. 130–59.

20. Although interested in dialects and pronunciations and aware of the *Linguistic Atlas of the United States and Canada*, of which the New England section was already under way at Brown University, Lovecraft, no phonetician, apparently never knew the International Phonetic Alphabet. From his remarks, I infer that he had in mind a pronunciation something like "Tlhülhü(lh)," with *t* somewhere between *c* in "cube" and *t* in "tune," *lh* a voiceless *l* like Welsh *ll*, and *ü* about as in German *dünn*. See HPL to D. W. Rimel, 23 Jul. 1924; to H. O. Fischer, 10 Jan. 1937. He originally spelled it "Cthulhul" but forgot the final *l*.

21. HPL to F. Wright, 5 Jul. 1927; *The Outsider & Others*, p. 178; *The Dunwich Horror & Others*, p. 32.

22. HPL to A. W. Derleth, 2 Aug. 1929; HPL: *The Outsider & Others*, p. 32; *At the Mountains of Madness & Other Novels*, pp. 386f.

23. HPL: *The Outsider & Others*, pp. 22–27; *Dagon & Other Macabre Tales*, pp. 260–68. In Celtic mythology, Nodens (also called Nudd, Nuada) is a god of fertility and medicine and a protector of fishermen. "Olney" is an old Rhode Island name, rhyming with "pony."

24. HPL to A. W. Derleth, 26 Nov. 1926; early Dec. 1926.

25. HPL to W. B. Talman, 19 Dec. 1926; to F. B. Long, Feb. 1927.

26. HPL: *Beyond the Wall of Sleep*, pp. 76f; *At the Mountains of Madness & Other Novels*, pp. 290ff. The last sentence of the quotation is a paraphrase of the conclusion of the prose poem *Nyarlathotep*.

27. HPL to J. V. Shea, 21 Aug. 1931.

28. HPL: *The Outsider & Others*, p. 32; *At the Mountains of Madness & Other Novels*, pp. 386f.

29. HPL to C. A. Smith, 21 Jan. 1927; to A. W. Derleth, Apr. 1927. In the second of these two letters, HPL proposes to junk his complete file of *Weird Tales*. Today such a file would be worth hundreds of dollars.

30. HPL to D. Wandrei, 2 Nov. 1927. Another narration of the same dream appears in a letter to B. A. Dwyer (Nov. 1927) in *Dreams & Fancies*, pp. 14–26. HPL compared the Very Old Folk to the Scythians. Actually, the real Scythians were not Mongoloids, as Lovecraft seems to have thought, but racially much like the modern Russians.

31. R. E. Howard to HPL, late Feb. 1931; HPL to L. P. Clark, 19 Jun. 1928; to Z. B. Reed, 28 Aug. 1927.

32. HPL to Z. B. Reed, 5 Jun. 1927; Bishop, p. 144.

33. HPL to D. Wandrei, 27 Mar. 1927; to A. W. Derleth, 16 May 1927; 22 May 1927; 20 Nov. 1927.
34. HPL to Z. B. Reed, 12 Jun. 1927.

Fourteen: RECUSANT SPOUSE

1. HPL: *Continuity,* in *Fungi from Yuggoth* (1971), p. 137.
2. HPL to J. F. Morton, 19 May 1927.
3. HPL to M. W. Moe, 30 Jul. 1927.
4. HPL to D. Wandrei, 10 Feb. 1927.
5. HPL to A. W. Derleth, 5 Sep. 1927.
6. *The Tryout,* IV, 8 (Aug. 1918); Cook (1941), pp. 4, 6.
7. HPL to F. B. Long, Dec. 1927.
8. HPL to A. W. Derleth, 26 Mar. 1927.
9. HPL to J. F. Morton, 1 Apr. 1927; to A. W. Derleth, 5 Oct. 1928; 20 Feb. 1927.
10. HPL: *The Outsider & Others,* p. 138; *At the Mountains of Madness & Other Novels,* pp. 106f. HPL's handwriting being what it was, it is possible that the word "bland" in this quotation should be "blond."
11. HPL to L. P. Clark, 29 Apr. 1928; to A. W. Derleth, 19 Apr. 1928; Davis (1948), col. 7; (1949), p. 12.
12. HPL to Z. B. Reed, 1 May 1928; to J. F. Morton, 10 May 1928.
13. F. B. Long (pers. comm., 26 Jul. 1972); HPL to L. P. Clark, 17 May 1928; to A. W. Derleth, Oct. 1928.
14. HPL to L. P. Clark, 19 Jun. 1928.
15. Cook (1941), p. 21; HPL to Z. B. Reed, 28 Jul. 1928.
16. HPL: *The Outsider & Others,* p. 292; *The Dunwich Horror & Others,* p. 160.
17. Rothovius; *The Moodus Mystery;* Colligan; Skinner, II, p. 43; Harris, II, p. 5; Shea, p. 89; HPL to A. W. Derleth, Apr. 1933.
18. HPL: *The Outsider & Others,* p. 310; *The Dunwich Horror & Others,* pp. 188f; HPL to A. W. Derleth, early Nov. 1928; Nov. 1928.
19. HPL to A. W. Derleth, 14 Mar. 1929; to E. Tolridge, 8 Mar. 1929. The stories by de Castro on which HPL worked had previously been published in the book *In the Confessional and the Following* (1893).
20. HPL to A. W. Derleth, 26 Sep. 1929; Oct. 1928.
21. HPL to A. W. Derleth, late Sep. 1928.
22. HPL to Z. B. Reed, 2 Oct. 1928.
23. Davis: "The Private Life of Howard Phillips Lovecraft," pp. 28ff (punctuation slightly edited); abridged in Davis (1948), (1949).
24. HPL to M. W. Moe, 2 Jul. 1929; Davis, *op. cit.,* pp. 29–32. On p. 40, Sonia says: "He admired Hitler, and read 'Mein Kampf' almost as soon as it was released and translated into English." There must be a mistake here, because Sonia last saw HPL in 1932, and the first published English translation of *Mein Kampf* was the much abridged one by E. T. S. Dugdale of 1933. It is unlikely that Lovecraft wrote Sonia about it, since he said (HPL to A. Galpin, Sep.

1930) that after the divorce their correspondence was limited to birthday and Christmas greetings.

25. Fragmentary unpublished reminiscences by Sonia Davis in the John Hay Library. It is alleged (Koki, pp. 210f) that Lovecraft failed to execute the document required to make his divorce final, so that Sonia's marriage to Davis was bigamous—an assertion that much distressed her when she was told of it in her last years. A recent search confirms Koki's assertion that Lovecraft's divorce was never made final (R. C. Harrall, pers. comm., 19 Jul. 1974).

Fifteen: FOOTLOOSE CONNOISSEUR.

1. HPL: *Where Poe Once Walked,* in *Fungi from Yuggoth* (1971), p. 87.
2. HPL to H. V. Sully, 17 Sep. 1934. Zealia Reed Bishop (Bishop, pp. 146f) says that, during this visit to New York, Lovecraft met her at the Longs' apartment. She describes the meeting in detail: "A tall, gaunt, black-clad figure, carrying an oblong case, glided into the room like a shadow. . . ." *Selon* Mrs. Bishop, Lovecraft promised to send "The Curse of Yig," which had been rejected by one editor, to *Weird Tales.* He asked that she give the job of revising her next story, "The Mound," to Frank Long, which she did. Frank Long says that the entire story is untrue; that she twice visited the Long apartment in New York and Lovecraft at least once in Providence, but that she never met Lovecraft at the Longs' place in New York. Long disclaims having done any revisory work on "The Mound." Zealia must, he thinks, have confused her various meetings with Long and Lovecraft and added a generous icing of fiction to the account. She made other highly improbable statements about HPL, as that he was familiar with Swahili and other native African languages (Koki, p. 259).
3. HPL to A. W. Derleth, 13 Apr. 1939; to L. P. Clark, 12 Apr. 1929; to R. Kleiner, 21 May 1936 (quoted in St. Armand, 1966, p. 65).
4. HPL to L. P. Clark, 2 May 1929.
5. HPL to L. P. Clark, 13 May 1929; to E. Tolridge, late Aug. 1929. The non-sentence is Lovecraft's.
6. F. B. Long (pers. comm.); HPL to D. W. Rimel, 4 Aug. 1935; to F. B. Long, 1 Sep. 1929; to A. W. Derleth, 4 Sep. 1929.
7. HPL to F. B. Long, *op. cit.* In researching for this book, I discovered that in 1823, Asaph Phillips's daughter Anna married Gardner Lyon, a great-grandson of my great-great-great-great-grandfather, Caleb Lyon of Woodstock, Conn. I suppose that this makes me a fifth cousin by marriage of H. P. Lovecraft. (See Albert Brown Lyons: *Lyon Memorial* [Detroit: 1905,], pp. 47, 66f, 90, 120, 298, 300, 304.)
8. HPL to M. W. Moe, Jan. 1929; to J. F. Morton, 30 Jul. 1939.
9. HPL to J. F. Morton, 26 Sep. 1930; to E. Tolridge, 26 Nov. 1929. HPL used the spellings "forego" (relinquish) and "forbear" (ancestor) where the dictionary prefers "forgo," "forebear." "Forego, forbear" properly mean "precede, abstain."

10. HPL to A. W. Derleth, *c.* 5 Jun. 1929; *c.* 24 Apr. 1929; to E. Tol-ridge, late Aug. 1929; to R. F. Searight, 5 Mar. 1935.
11. HPL: *Beyond the Wall of Sleep*, pp. 371f.
12. HPL to A. W. Derleth, 15 Dec. 1929.
13. HPL to A. W. Derleth, 23 Feb. 1930; to C. A. Smith, 3 Dec. 1929; Colman McCarthy: "Poet Edwin Robinson—He Starved for His Art," in the *Milwaukee Journal*, 5 Sep. 1973, p. 8; *Fungi from Yuggoth* (1971), p. 90. Different versions of this poem differ slightly.
14. HPL to E. Tolridge, 19 Dec. 1929.
15. HPL: *Beyond the Wall of Sleep*, pp. 409f; *Fungi from Yuggoth* (1971), pp. 88f. Lovecraft's original title was *The East India Brick Row*.
16. HPL to E. Tolridge, Jan. 1930; HPL: *Beyond the Wall of Sleep*, p. 401; *Fungi from Yuggoth* (1971), p. 125. The second line does not scan.
17. R. E. Howard to HPL, Jul. 1932; Dec. 1932; Feb. 1933; 31 May 1935; Jul. 1935; 5 Dec. 1935; 13 May 1936; HPL to D. A. Woll-heim, 7 Oct. 1935.
18. *The Fantasy Fan*, I, 2 (Oct. 1933), pp. 27f; HPL to R. H. Barlow, 11 Aug. 1933; 30 Aug. 1933; to D. W. Rimel, 13 Apr. 1934; 16 Apr. 1935; to E. H. Price, 27 Aug. 1936; to W. Conover, 10 Jan. 1937; to Z. B. Reed, 20 Mar. 1929; to A. W. Derleth, 1 Apr. 1929. In his fantasies, Lovecraft sometimes borrowed real ancient names (Menes, Kranon) in just the manner he chided Howard for doing. Smith's story was reprinted as "The Dweller in the Gulf" in the Smith collection, *The Abominations of Yondo* (Arkham House, 1960).
19. H. K. Brobst & V. Orton (pers. comm.); HPL: *The City*, in *Fungi from Yuggoth* (1971), p. 70.
20. HPL to J. F. Morton, 19 Oct. 1929; to A. W. Derleth, 6 Oct. 1929.
21. HPL to J. F. Morton, 30 Oct. 1929; 19 Oct. 1929.
22. HPL to W. Harris, 25 Feb. 1929; to J. F. Morton, 8 Nov. 1929; 19 Oct. 1929; to E. Tolridge, 10 Jun. 1929.
23. HPL to W. Harris, *op. cit.*; Bertrand Russell: *The Impact of Sci-ence on Society* (N.Y.: 1953), p. 108.
24. HPL to W. Harris, *op. cit.*; to A. W. Derleth, *c.* 23 Sep. 1929; *New York Times Book Review*, 19 Aug. 1973, p. 4.
25. HPL to A. W. Derleth, 26 Sep. 1929; to W. Harris, *op. cit.*; to E. Tolridge, 21 Feb. 1929.
26. HPL to W. Harris, *op. cit.*; to M. W. Moe, 4 Jan. 1930.
27. HPL to L. P. Clark, 28 Apr. 1930.
28. Cook (1941), p. 48; HPL to L. P. Clark, 24 May 1930.
29. HPL to A. W. Derleth, 9 Sep. 1930; to A. Galpin, Sep. 1930; to E. Tolridge, *c.* 7 Sep. 1930.
30. HPL to A. Galpin, *op. cit*; to A. W. Derleth, *op. cit.*
31. HPL to J. F. Morton, 19 Oct. 1929; to W. Harris, 9 Nov. 1929.
32. HPL to J. F. Morton, 31 Oct. 1930.

33. HPL to A. W. Derleth, 12 Jan. 1930; late Jan. 1930; 18 Feb. 1930.
34. HPL to L. P. Clark, *op. cit.*; to A. W. Derleth, 24 May 1930; to E. Tolridge, 3 Jul. 1930. Searight alluded to the Eltdown shards (the name was derived from "Piltdown") in his story "The Sealed Casket" (*Weird Tales*, Mar. 1935) but Wright deleted the allusion.
35. HPL: *The Outsider & Others*, pp. 319–58; *The Dunwich Horror & Others*, pp. 212–77; HPL to D. W. Rimel, 14 Feb. 1934; Wetzel (1958); Leiber (1944), p. 3. Robert E. Howard (to HPL, Aug. 1930) said that he had made up the name "Kathulos" and had not derived it (as some have thought) from "Cthulhu."
36. HPL: A *Description of the Town of Quebeck* . . . ; HPL to W. B. Talman, 10 Dec. 1930; to E. Tolridge, 11 Feb. 1930; 24 Apr. 1930.
37. HPL to A. W. Derleth, 27 Dec. 1930.
38. HPL to C. A. Smith, 2 Feb. 1930; to E. Tolridge, 24 Apr. 1930.
39. HPL to J. F. Morton, 19 Oct. 1929; to W. B. Talman, 10 Dec. 1930.
40. HPL to A. W. Derleth, 13 Dec. 1930. Ellipses after "junk" Lovecraft's. The man who remembered Lovecraft was a waiter at the Minden Hotel, on Waterman Street just east of the Brown campus. Friends of Lovecraft tell me that this gives an exaggerated impression of his slouch; that he actually stood fairly straight.
41. HPL to J. F. Morton, 3 Jan. 1930.
42. HPL to M. W. Moe, 18 Jun. 1930; to E. Tolridge, 20 Dec. 1930; 24 Apr. 1930.
43. HPL to J. F. Morton, 30 Dec. 1930. Lovecraft called this date "3d Day before the Kalends of Ianuarius," which (translating from the Roman to the modern calendar) means Dec. 30th. In *Selected Letters III*, the date is erroneously given as "January, 1931." For Haldeman-Julius, see my *The Great Monkey Trial*, pp. 169f.
44. HPL to M. W. Moe, 18 Jun. 1930; to H. Spink, 13 Aug. 1930.

Sixteen: BAFFLED BARD

1. Lin Carter: *Beyond*, in *Amra*, II, 47 (Aug. 1968), p. 8.
2. HPL to J. V. Shea, 21 Aug. 1931.
3. HPL to R. E. Howard, 30 Jan. 1931; to F. B. Long, 27 Feb. 1931.
4. HPL to J. V. Shea, 13 Oct. 1931; to A. W. Derleth, 31 Jan. 1931.
5. HPL to J. V. Shea, 9 Dec. 1931; to A. W. Derleth, 20 Nov. 1931.
6. HPL to J. V. Shea, 7 Aug. 1931; to A. W. Derleth, 17 Feb. 1931.
7. The estimate is summed up as follows:

Food & miscellaneous, at home:	$700
Rent:	240
Travel (including food):	300
Postage:	150
Books & magazines:	50
Clothes:	25
Dental & medical expenses:	5
	$1,470

The low figure for clothes is explained by the fact that at least two suits were given him by friends, and that for dental and medical expenses by the fact that he went to physicians and dentists only at intervals of several years.

8. HPL to E. H. Price, 19 Jun. 1935; to J. F. Morton, 19 May 1927.

9. HPL to A. W. Derleth, c. 4 Jan. 1931; 31 Jan. 1931.

10. HPL to A. W. Derleth, 13 Feb. 1931; 1 Mar. 1931; to C. A. Smith, 26 Mar. 1931.

11. HPL: *The Outsider & Others*, pp. 499f; *At the Mountains of Madness & Other Novels*, p. 90. Ellipses Lovecraft's. "Shoggoth" could not be classical Arabic, which has neither g nor o.

12. HPL to A. W. Derleth, 23 May 1931; to L. P. Clark, 22 Jun. 1931.

13. HPL to A. W. Derleth, 13 Jul. 1931; 14 Nov. 1931; to R. H. Barlow, 13 Jul. 1931.

14. HPL to A. W. Derleth, 10 Aug. 1931.

15. HPL to A. W. Derleth, 3 Aug. 1931; to J. V. Shea, 9 Dec. 1931; to C. A. Smith, 20 Nov. 1931.

16. HPL to L. P. Clark, 5 May 1931.

17. Walter (1959), p. 187; HPL to L. P. Clark, 11 Jun. 1931; 16 Jun. 1931.

18. HPL to D. W. Rimel, 1 Jun. 1934; to L. P. Clark, 16 Jun. 1931.

19. H. K. Brobst (pers. comm.).

20. HPL to L. P. Clark, 8 Jul. 1931; 16 Jul. 1931.

21. HPL to L. P. Clark, 8 Jul. 1931.

22. HPL to L. P. Clark, 16 Jul. 1931.

23. HPL to A. W. Derleth, 16 Jan. 1931; 10 Dec. 1931; 23 Dec. 1931; 2 Jan. 1932; to F. B. Long, 27 Feb. 1931.

24. HPL to J. F. Morton, 18 Jan. 1931; to J. V. Shea, 4 Oct. 1931.

25. HPL to E. Tolridge, 25 Jan. 1931; 23 Mar. 1931; 31 Aug. 1931.

26. HPL to E. Tolridge, 29 Apr. 1931; to W. B. Talman, 25 Oct. 1931; to A. W. Derleth, 13 Feb. 1931; 6 Nov. 1931; 9 Feb. 1933; to J. V. Shea, 13 Oct. 1931.

27. HPL to J. V. Shea, 9 Oct. 1931. Properly, the American r is called a "retroflexed r." The New Yorkese pronunciation of "Ernest Boyd" can be roughly represented as "Öinest Böid," in which ö represents a sound varying between the u of "up" and the ö of German *Hölle*. This dialect now seems to be dying out.

28. HPL to A. W. Derleth, 24 Sep. 1931.

29. HPL: *The Outsider & Others*, p. 360; *The Dunwich Horror & Others*, pp. 309f.

30. HPL to A. W. Derleth, 10 Dec. 1931.

31. HPL to A. W. Derleth, 21 Jan. 1932; to J. V. Shea, 13 Oct. 1932.

32. HPL to A. W. Derleth, 31 Jan. 1932; 19 Feb. 1932; 29 Feb. 1932; 25 Feb. 1932; to D. W. Rimel, 22 Jan. 1934.

33. HPL to A. W. Derleth, 29 Feb. 1932; 25 Feb. 1932; 2 Feb. 1932.

34. HPL to A. W. Derleth, 4 Mar. 1932; 11 Mar. 1932.

35. Weinberg; W. S. Gilbert: *The Mikado*, Act II; HPL to A. W. Der-

leth, 4 Mar. 1932. Lovecraft's original title was "The Dreams of Walter Gilman." The client was probably Hazel Heald.

36. HPL to J. F. Morton, 18 Jan. 1931; to A. W. Derleth, 6 Jun. 1932; to R. E. Morse, 27 Feb. 1933.

37. R. E. Howard to HPL, 1931; Jun. 1932; HPL to J. V. Shea, 13 Oct. 1932. Ellipses Lovecraft's.

38. Price (1949), pp. 278–82.

39. Cook (1941), p. 37.

40. HPL to A. W. Derleth, c. 30 Oct. 1932; to E. Tolridge, 14 Dec. 1932; to J. V. Shea, 22 Dec. 1932.

41. HPL to A. W. Derleth, early Oct. 1932; late Oct. 1932.

42. HPL to H. S. Farnese, 22 Sep. 1932; to E. H. Price, 3 Oct. 1932; to R. H. Barlow, 22 Sep. 1932; to A. W. Derleth, 12 Sep. 1932; late Oct. 1932.

43. HPL to E. H. Price, 20 Oct. 1932; to C. A. Smith, Oct. 1932.

44. HPL to E. H. Price, 20 Dec. 1932; 20 Oct. 1932; 12 Jan. 1933; 15 Aug. 1934; to R. F. Searight, 17 Mar. 1934.

45. R. H. Thouless: *Straigh & Crooked Thinking* (N.Y.: 1932), p. 174.

46. HPL to J. V. Shea, 16 Nov. 1932; 27 Oct. 1932; 22 Dec. 1932; to A. Galpin, 24 May 1933. Long soon abandoned this impractical (for a professional writer) point of view.

Seventeen: THWARTED THINKER

1. HPL: *Sunset,* in *Fungi from Yuggoth* (1971), p. 24.

2. HPL to A. W. Derleth, 14 Apr. 1933; 7 Apr. 1933.

3. HPL to E. H. Price, 25 Aug. 1933; F. Wright to HPL, 17 Aug. 1933.

4. HPL: *The Outsider & Others,* p. 40; *At the Mountains of Madness & Other Novels,* p. 398.

5. In more correct Arabic, 'Umr aṭ-Ṭawîl.

6. These "Dholes," which also occur in the dreamland of "The Dream-Quest of Unknown Kadath," are probably the same as the "Doels" of "The Whisperer in Darkness." Both are probably derived from the "Dôls" mentioned but not described in Machen's "The White People." There is no connection with the coyotelike dhole of India.

7. HPL to A. W. Derleth, early May 1933; to E. H. Cole, 9 Aug. 1933; to E. Tolridge, 8 Jun. 1933. Ellipses Lovecraft's.

8. HPL to J. V. Shea, 14 Aug. 1933. In modern Dutch, *maen* (moon) is spelled *maan.* Lovecraft misspelled the name of the magazine in his letters as *De Haelve Man.* Hudson was English but his employers and his ship Dutch.

9. Talman, p. 7.

10. HPL to R. H. Barlow, 1 Feb. 1934; to J. V. Shea, 29 May 1933; 30 Jul. 1933; 23 Sep. 1933; to R. Bloch, c. 1 Sep. 1933.

11. HPL to J. V. Shea, 30 Jul. 1933; 29 May 1933; 23 Sep. 1933; to R. H. Barlow, 1 Feb. 1934.

12. HPL to J. V. Shea, 23 Sep. 1933. Examples of replacement of Indo-European speech by those of other language families are found in Hungary, in Turkey, and in parts of North Africa that once spoke Greek or Latin but now speak Arabic.

13. HPL to J. V. Shea, 8 Nov. 1933; to H. V. Sully, 6 Feb. 1934.

14. G. de la Ree (pers. comm., quoting a letter from Samuel Loveman); Searles, p. 116.

15. HPL to J. V. Shea, 29 May 1933; 30 Jul. 1933; 14 Aug. 1933; 23 Sep. 1933; to H. V. Sully, 15 Jul. 1934; to R. Bloch, c. Aug. 1933.

16. HPL to A. Galpin, 25 Jul. 1934; to R. Bloch, *op. cit.*

17. HPL to H. V. Sully, 24 Nov. 1933; to R. H. Barlow, 1 Feb. 1934; Edkins, pp. 2f.

18. HPL to R. H. Barlow, 13 Jun. 1936; 27 Jan. 1937; to F. Leiber, 19 Dec. 1936; R. E. Howard to HPL, Jul. 1935. In the *New York Times* for 29 Mar. 1974, p. 33, the historian Joseph Farkas proposed a similar system of voting.

19. HPL to A. W. Derleth, 24 Oct. 1936; to K. J. Sterling, 16 Sep. 1936; to J. V. Shea, 5 Dec. 1935.

20. Wells, Huxley, & Wells: *The Science of Life* (Garden City, N.Y.: 1936), p. 1449; HPL to R. H. Barlow, 30 Sep. 1936; H. K. Brobst (pers. comm.).

21. HPL to A. W. Derleth, 24 Oct. 1936; to R. Bloch, 2 Feb. 1937 (name left blank because the man is still alive). One hangover from HPL's ethnocentric days, which he never outgrew, was that of dropping into a pseudo-Yiddish dialect when writing about Jewish colleagues, even when praising or defending them; e.g., in HPL to E. H. Cole, 3 Jul. 1935, about Bradofsky: "For *that* he shood go into debt & publish ah foist-class megazine!" or 21 Jan. 1936: "Oy! Vhat ah life!" That such burlesquing of ethnic ways might be offensive seems never to have occurred to him; but Old Americans were generally less sensitive in such matters then than now.

22. HPL to J. V. Shea, 24 Nov. 1934; to R. Bloch, 7 Feb. 1937.

23. Price (1949), pp. 283–86.

24. HPL to C. A. Smith, 25 Jul. 1933; to H. V. Sully, 11 Jul. 1935; Sully, p. 119. Helen Sully became Mrs. George Trimble of Auburn, California.

25. Interview with Ethel Phillips Morrish, 5 Sep. 1972; HPL to K. J. Sterling, 14 Dec. 1935; to J. V. Shea, 23 Sep. 1933; 8 Nov. 1933.

26. HPL to C. A. Smith, 26 Aug. 1933; to E. H. Price, 15 Aug. 1934; 31 Aug. 1934.

27. HPL: *The Outsider & Others*, p. 217; *The Dunwich Horror & Others*, p. 281.

28. HPL to R. H. Barlow, 14 May 1933.

29. Loveman (1958), p. 36; HPL to W. F. Anger, 28 Jan. 1935.

30. HPL to R. H. Barlow, 6 Aug. 1934; 26 Oct. 1934; 30 Nov. 1936; 11

Dec. 1936; Cook (1941), pp. 57f; Bishop, pp. 149f. Mrs. Bishop says that, when she sold the Reed-Lovecraft story "Medusa's Coil" to *Weird Tales* in 1938, for $120, "I stipulated that half this sum should be paid to Lovecraft's aunt, Annie E. P. Gamwell, since in the interval Lovecraft had died, and she was without funds." Mrs. Bishop may or may not have made this payment, but it is not true that Annie Gamwell was destitute. She had over $10,000 in cash and securities. (Probate Court of the City of Providence, Inventory of the Estate of Annie E. P. Gamwell, 24 Mar. 1941.)

31. HPL to R. H. Barlow, 24 May 1935; to A. W. Derleth, 15 Jul. 1935; Derleth (1959), p. 166.
32. HPL to D. W. Rimel, 23 Jul. 1934.
33. HPL to E. H. Price, 15 Aug. 1934. Ellipses after "cosmic law" & "inevitability" Lovecraft's.
34. HPL to A. Galpin, 28 Apr. 1934; to E. H. Price, 17 Sep. 1934; to R. F. Searight, 4 Aug. 1935; 5 Mar. 1935. Ellipses in the last quotation Lovecraft's.
35. HPL to J. V. Shea, 4 Feb. 1934; to D. W. Rimel, 16 Mar. 1934; to R. H. Barlow, 10 Apr. 1934.
36. HPL to R. F. Searight, 4 Aug. 1935; to E. H. Cole, 31 Jan. 1934; 30 Apr. 1935; 25 Mar. 1936.
37. W. L. Crawford (pers. comm.); HPL to A. W. Derleth, 19 May 1934; to D. W. Rimel, 13 May 1934.
38. HPL to H. V. Sully, 30 Apr. 1934; HPL: *Something About Cats*, pp. 165f.
39. HPL to D. W. Rimel, 10 Aug. 1934; to E. H. Cole, 1 Jun. 1935; Koki, pp. 254f.
40. HPL to E. H. Cole, 17 Sep. 1934; HPL: *Little Sam Perkins*, in *Fungi from Yuggoth* (1971), p. 52.
41. HPL to E. H. Price, 8 Oct. 1934; 17 Sep. 1934; to E. H. Cole, 17 Sep. 1934; to E. Tolridge, 6 Oct. 1934. Brian Lumley, a contemporary writer of Cthulhuvian stories, brings the clock into his tales "De Marigny's Clock" and *The Burrowers Beneath*.
42. HPL: *The Outsider & Others*, p. 400; *The Dunwich Horror & Others*, p. 370.

Eighteen: GUTTERING LAMP

1. Clark Ashton Smith: *To Howard Phillips Lovecraft*, in *Selected Poems*, p. 287.
2. HPL to E. Tolridge, 29 Dec. 1934. Ellipses after "gifts" Lovecraft's.
3. HPL to R. Bloch, c. early Mar. 1935; c. late Mar. 1935; to J. V. Shea, 10 Feb. 1935; to A. W. Derleth, 6 Mar. 1935; to E. H. Price, c. 4 Feb. 1935.
4. HPL to W. Conover, 10 Jan. 1937; to R. H. Barlow, 20 Apr. 1935. Printed, slightly abridged, in HPL: *Dreams & Fancies*, pp. 50ff. A shorter version occurs in HPL to H. V. Sully, 24 Apr. 1935.

5. HPL to A. W. Derleth, 25 Feb. 1935; to R. H. Barlow, 20 Apr. 1935.
6. J. M. Barrie: *Peter Pan*, Act I *et passim*; HPL to H. V. Sully, 15 Aug. 1935.
7. HPL to K. J. Sterling, 21 Jan. 1936; to E. H. Cole, 3 Jul. 1935.
8. HPL to E. Tolridge, 20 Dec. 1935; to R. H. Barlow, 13 Jun. 1936.
9. HPL to E. H. Price, 20 Jan. 1936; to A. Galpin, 17 Jan. 1936; to R. H. Barlow, 5 Sep. 1935.
10. HPL to E. H. Price, 21 Aug. 1935; 4 May 1935.
11. HPL: *Marginalia*, facing p. 311. In the signature of von Junzt, HPL so painstakingly imitated German longhand that "Friedrich" looks like "Fvindvuf," which one commentator (Charles O. Gray: "Nameless Cults: A History," in *The Howard Collector*, No. 17, Autumn, 1972, p. 23) actually took it to be.
12. HPL *et al.*: *Tales of the Cthulhu Mythos*, p. 192.
13. HPL to A. W. Derleth, 4 Dec. 1935; HPL: *The Horror in the Museum & Other Revisions*, pp. 159, 172. Compare the "Yian-Ho" of "Alonzo Typer" with the "Yian" mentioned in "The Whisperer in Darkness."
14. HPL to N. H. Frome, 20 Jan. 1937; to E. Tolridge, 1 Jul. 1929; HPL: *Beyond the Wall of Sleep*, p. 321; Sam Moskowitz (ed.): *Horrors Unknown* (N.Y.: 1971), p. 7. Schwartz persuaded two other groups of science-fiction authors to write composite stories for him, but these did not include Lovecraft.
15. HPL: *A History of the Necronomicon*; *Beyond the Wall of Sleep*, pp. xxviiif; Derleth: "The Making of a Hoax"; M. W. Wellman (pers. comm.); Shaw. This is an expansion of the account in HPL to C. A. Smith, 27 Nov. 1927. The name of Arabia's "Empty Quarter" were better transliterated as the Rub' al-Khali. In 1973, the science-fiction fan and writer George H. Scithers published an edition of *Al Azif* (*The Necronomicon*) in facsimile in the (fictitious) Duriac language, with a Cthulhuvian introduction by the present author (Philadelphia: Owlswick Press, 1973). Lovecraft said that he got the meaning of *azif* from a note on Beckford's *Vathek*.
16. HPL to R. H. Barlow, 17 Dec. 1935; Shaw; HPL to D. W. Rimel, 28 Sep. 1935; to K. J. Sterling, 20 Nov. 1935.
17. HPL to H. Kuttner, 16 Apr. 1936; to R. H. Barlow, 21 Oct. 1935; to R. Bloch, 2 Nov. 1935; to E. H. Price, 15 Dec. 1935.
18. HPL to E. H. Price, 16 Mar. 1936; 14 Mar. 1935; to V. Finlay, 10 Oct. 1936.
19. HPL to E. H. Price, 29 Jul. 1936; to J. V. Shea, 19 May 1936.
20. HPL to E. H. Price, 2 Feb. 1936; 12 Feb. 1936.
21. HPL to D. W. Rimel, 12 Nov. 1935; to R. F. Searight, 4 Nov. 1935.
22. HPL to R. E. Morse, 16 Jan. 1936; to A. W. Derleth, 4 Dec. 1935 (ellipses Lovecraft's).
23. HPL to E. H. Cole, 28 Jan. 1936; to A. W. Derleth, 11 Feb. 1936; 9 Apr. 1936.

24. HPL to H. O. Fischer, 16 Feb. 1937.
25. HPL to R. H. Barlow, 29 Apr. 1936; to J. V. Shea, 19 May 1936.
26. HPL to A. T. Renshaw, 24 Feb. 1936; Koki, p. 297; Renshaw, pp. 20, 22.
27. HPL to H. V. Sully, 12 May 1936; *Orthophony* was published by Fields, Osgood & Co. of Boston.
28. HPL to H. V. Sully, 26 Jul. 1936; to E. H. Cole, 15 Aug. 1936; T. C. Smith: "Report on a Writing Man," in *The Howard Collector*, I, 4 (Summer, 1963), p. 7 (copyright © 1962 by Glenn Lord); R. E. Howard to HPL, late Feb. 1931; 1931; *The Tempter*, in Robert E. Howard: *Always Comes Evening* (Arkham House, 1957), p. 80.
29. HPL to E. H. Price, 20 Jul. 1936; HPL: "Robert Ervin Howard: In Memoriam," in *Fantasy Magazine* (Sep. 1936) & Robert E. Howard: *Skull-Face & Others* (Arkham House, 1946), p. xiii.
30. HPL to W. Conover, 6 Sep. 1936; to D. W. Rimel, 27 Aug. 1936.
31. HPL to A. W. Derleth, 13 Mar. 1936; 16 Dec. 1936.
32. HPL to V. Finlay, 10 Oct. 1936; to R. F. Searight, 11 Aug. 1934; 8 Sep. 1934.
33. HPL to A. T. Renshaw, 19 Sep. 1936. All ellipses (in two quotations) Lovecraft's. "Ædepol" is a Latin interjection meaning "By Pollux!" "Trans-hortense" is a Latinistic coinage by HPL, meaning "across the garden."
34. HPL to E. H. Price, 16 Mar. 1936; Edkins, p. 6.
35. HPL to E. H. Price, 16 Mar. 1936; Edkins, p. 4; HPL to W. B. Talman, 28 Feb. 1937; to R. H. Barlow, 3 Jan. 1937 (misdated 1936); 27 Dec. 1936.
36. HPL to R. H. Barlow, 30 Nov. 1936; 3 Jan. 1937 (misdated 1936); Koki, p. 305.
37. HPL to R. H. Barlow, 11 Dec. 1936; to F. Utpatel, 11 Jan. 1937.
38. HPL to R. H. Barlow, 30 Sep. 1936; to V. Finlay, 10 Oct. 1936.
39. HPL to H. O. Fischer, late Jan. 1937.
40. HPL to E. Tolridge, 20 Oct. 1936.
41. HPL to W. Conover, 31 Jan. 1937. Ellipses Lovecraft's.
42. HPL to H. O. Fischer, 10 Jan. 1937; to R. Bloch, 7 Feb. 1937. The first quotation continues with the sentence, quoted in Chap. 6, beginning: "Yuggoth, but I'd pay blackmail . . ."
43. E. P. Morrish (pers. comm.); HPL to C. A. Smith, 5 Feb. 1937; to A. W. Derleth, 17 Feb. 1937; Cook (1941), p. 1. Koki (p. 309) says that "forty" attended the funeral. This is an error, which may have occurred in transcription.

Nineteen: POSTHUMOUS TRIUMPH

1. Clark Ashton Smith: *H.P.L.*, in HPL: *The Shuttered Room & Other Pieces*, p. 204.
2. Inventory of the estate of Howard P. Lovecraft, Probate Court of the City of Providence, May 6, 1957 [error for 1937]. The "(sic)" is in the original.

3. Will of Annie E. P. Gamwell, 10 Jan. 1940.
4. K. W. Faig, Jr. (pers. comm.); A. W. Derleth to S. H. Davis, 30 Nov. 1947 (in Talman, p. 29); Tierney (1972); E. Wilson, pp. 287–90, rewritten from a similar article in *The New Yorker*, 24 Nov. 1945. There is some uncertainty about Dana's purchase of the Lovecraft papers. The inventory of Annie Gamwell's estate lists "Library: $35.00," but I do not know if this includes the Lovecraft papers or if this represents the price paid by Dana.
5. C. Wilson, pp. 1–10.
6. Thomas (1950), pp. 43, 109, 115; *The Arkham Collector*, I, 1 (Summer, 1967), p. 17.
7. Davidson, pp. 48ff.
8. Starrett, p. 122; Penzoldt, pp. 165f; *The Arkham Collector*, I, 1 (Summer, 1967), p. 47; R. Smith, p. 4; Douglas, pp. 266f, 276.
9. K. Grant, back cover; HPL to R. E. Morse, 16 Jan. 1936.
10. Thomas, p. 180; HPL to H. V. Sully, 15 Aug. 1935; to W. Conover, 6 Sep. 1936; to A. W. Derleth, 5 Jun. 1929; Carl Van Doren: *Benjamin Franklin* (N.Y.: 1938), pp. 37f.
11. C. L. Moore (pers. comm.); Ecclesiastes, IX: 11.

BIBLIOGRAPHY

This bibliography does not attempt to include all the many published editions of writings by and about H. P. Lovecraft. The works listed here are those actually consulted in preparing this book. For the most complete Lovecraft bibliography to date, see Owings (1973).

Adams, Henry: *The Education of Henry Adams, An Autobiography*, Boston: Houghton Mifflin Co., 1918.

Adorita, Sister Mary: *Soul Ordained to Fail* (*Louise Imogen Guiney, 1861–1920*), N.Y.: Pageant Pr., 1962.

Amory, Mark: *Lord Dunsany: A Biography*, Lon.: Collins, 1972.

Baldwin, F. Lee: "H. P. Lovecraft: A Biographical Sketch," in *Fantasy Magazine*, IV, 5 (No. 29, Apr. 1935), pp. 108ff.

———: "Some Lovecraft Sidelights," in *Fantasy Commentator*, II, 6 (Spring, 1948), pp. 219f.

Banks, Ann: "Lovecraftimania at Brown," in *Brown Alumni Monthly*, Feb. 1972, pp. 22ff.

Barlow, Robert H.: Misc. papers collected by George T. Smisor (microfilm).

———: "Pseudonyms of H. P. Lovecraft," in *The Acolyte*, I, 4 (Summer, 1943), p. 18.

———: "The Wind That Is in the Grass (A Memoir of H. P. Lovecraft in Florida)," in HPL: *Marginalia*, pp. 342–50.

Barner, Marian F.: "Miscellaneous Impressions of H. P. L.," in Grant & Hadley, pp. 23f.

Bentley, Eric: *The Cult of the Superman* (A *Study of the Idea of Heroism in Carlyle and Nietzsche* . . .), Gloucester, Mass.: Peter Smith, 1969.

Bergier, Jacques: "H. P. Lovecraft, ce grand génie venu d'ailleurs," in *L'Herne* (1969), pp. 121–25.

Bertin, Eddy C.: "Colin Wilson," in *Tamlacht*, II, 2 (No. 12, n.d.), pp. 16–22.

———: "The Cthulhu Mythos: A Review and Analysis," in *Nyctalops*, I, 4 (Jun. 1971), pp. 3–6.

———: "H. P. Lovecraft Did Not Write SF, by His Own Standards," in *Nyctalops*, I, 2 (Oct. 1970), pp. 3ff.

———: "In the Trail of Lovecraft: The Followers of Cthulhu," in *Nyctalops*, I, 5 (Oct. 1971), pp. 5–12, 28.

Birmingham, Stephen: *The Late John Marquand*, Phila.: J. B. Lippincott Co., 1972.

Bishop, Zealia: *The Curse of Yig*, Sauk City: Arkham House, 1953.

Bloch, Robert: "Notes on an Entity," in *Tamlacht*, II, 2 (No. 12, n.d.), p. 14.

———: "Out of the Ivory Tower," in HPL: *The Shuttered Room and Other Pieces*, pp. 171–77.

Bradley, Marion Zimmer: "The (Bastard) Children of Hastur," in *Nyctalops*, I, 6 (Feb. 1972), pp. 3–6.

———: "Two Worlds of Fantasy," in *Haunted*, I, 3 (Jun. 1968), pp. 82–85.

Brennan, Joseph Payne: "H. P. L.: An Informal Commentary," in *Fresco*, VIII, 3 (Spring, 1958), pp. 5–8.

———: *Lovecraft: An Evaluation*, New Haven: Macabre House, 1955.

Bryant, Roger: "Necronomicon," in *Tamlacht*, II, 2 (No. 12, n.d.), pp. 10–13.

Bush, David V.: *The University of the Master Mind*, Chicago: David V. Bush, 1923.

Butman, Robert: "Modern Mythological Fiction," in *The Reader and Collector*, III, 5 (Oct. 1945), pp. 1–12; III, 6 (Jan. 1946), pp. 13–27; IV, 1 (Apr. 1946), pp. 6–39.

Caen, Michel: "Lovecraft/Cinema," in *L'Herne* (1969), pp. 182ff.

Campbell, Ramsey: "A Personal Tribute," in *Is*, No. 4 (Oct. 1971), pp. 59f.

Carter, Lin: "H. P. Lovecraft: The Books," in HPL: *The Shuttered Room and Other Pieces*, pp. 212–49.

———: "H. P. Lovecraft: The Gods," in HPL: *The Shuttered Room and Other Pieces*, pp. 250–67.

———: "HPL: The History," in Wetzel (1955), pp. 38ff.

————: *Lovecraft: A Look Behind the Cthulhu Mythos*, N.Y.: Ballantine Books, 1972.

Chalker, Jack L. (ed.): *Mirage on Lovecraft*, Baltimore: Mirage Publications, 1965.

Chamberlain, Houston Stewart: *Foundations of the Nineteenth Century*, N.Y.: John Lane Co., 1912, 2 vols.

Cole, Edward H.: "Ave Atque Vale!" in Wetzel (1955), pp. 10–17.

Colligan, Douglas: "Brawl Over a '2,000-Year-Old' Archaeological Site," in *Science Digest*, LXXIII, 1 (Jan. 1973), pp. 11–16.

Condra, Cyrus B.: "The Sailor Lopez and Kindred Musings," in *Ausländer*, No. 3 (Jun. 1966), pp. 20–24.

Cook, W. Paul: "An Appreciation of H. P. Lovecraft," in HPL: *Beyond the Wall of Sleep*, pp. 424–58.

————: "H. P. Lovecraft," in *The Olympian*, No. 35 (Fall, 1940), pp. 28–35.

————: *H. P. Lovecraft: A Portrait*, Baltimore: Mirage Pr., 1968. (Identical with Cook [1941], minus one paragraph and with different pagination.)

————: *In Memoriam: Howard Phillips Lovecraft* (*Recollections, Appreciations, Estimates*): privately printed, 1941.

Cox, Arthur Jean: "Some Thoughts on Lovecraft," in *Haunted*, II, 2 (Dec. 1964), pp. 26–30.

Crane, Hart: *The Letters of Hart Crane*, 1916–1932, N.Y.: Hermitage House, 1952.

Crawford, William L.: "Lovecraft's First Book," in HPL: *The Shuttered Room and Other Pieces*, pp. 287–90.

Davidson, Avram: Review of *The Survivor and Others*, in *The Magazine of Fantasy and Science Fiction*, XXIV, 1 (No. 140, Jan. 1963), pp. 48ff.

Davis, Sonia H.: "H. P. Lovecraft as his Wife Remembers Him," in *Books at Brown*, XI, 1 & 2 (Feb. 1949), pp. 3–13.

————: "Howard Phillips Lovecraft as his Wife Remembers Him," in the *Providence Sunday Journal*, 22 Aug. 1948, part VI, p. 8.

————: "Lovecraft as I Knew Him," in HPL: *Something About Cats and Other Pieces*, pp. 234–46.

————: "Memories of Lovecraft," in *The Arkham Collector*, I, 4 (Winter, 1969), pp. 116f.

————: Misc. unpublished autobiographical mss. in the John Hay Library.

————: "The Private Life of Howard Phillips Lovecraft," unpublished ms. in the John Hay Library.

de Camp, L. Sprague: "Books that Never Were," in *Fantasy and Science Fiction*, XLIII, 6 (No. 259, Dec. 1972), pp. 78–85.

———: "Eldritch Yankee Gentleman (Literary Swordsmen and Sorcerers, No. 2)," in *Fantastic Stories*, XX, 6 (Aug. 1971), pp. 98–106, & XII, 1 (Oct. 1971), pp. 100–8.

———: "H. P. Lovecraft and H. S. Chamberlain," in *Amra*, II, 57 (Jun. 1972), pp. 3–9.

———: "Sierran Shaman (Literary Swordsmen and Sorcerers, No. 4)," in *Fantastic Stories*, XXII, 1 (Oct. 1972), pp. 101–12.

———: "Skald in the Post Oaks (Literary Swordsmen and Sorcerers, No. 1)," in *Fantastic Stories*, XX, 5 (Jun. 1971), pp. 99–108.

———: "Sonia and H.P.L.," in Talman (1973), pp. 24–27.

de la Mare, Walter: *The Return*, N.Y.: G. P. Putnam's Sons, 1922.

Derleth, August W.: "Addenda to *H. P. L.: A Memoir*," in HPL: *Something About Cats and Other Pieces*, pp. 247–77.

———: "Arkham House: A Thumbnail Story," in *The Fossil*, Oct. 1950, pp. 240f, 247.

———: "The Arkham House Story," in *Fantastic Worlds*, I, 1 (Summer, 1952), pp. 7–12.

———: "Final Notes," in HPL: *The Dark Brotherhood and Other Pieces*, pp. 302–21.

———: *H. P. L.: A Memoir*, N.Y.: Ben Abramson, 1945.

———: "H. P. L.—Two Decades After Death," in *Fresco*, VIII, 3 (Spring, 1958), pp. 9ff.

———: "H. P. Lovecraft and His Work," in HPL: *The Dunwich Horror and Others*, pp. ix–xx.

———: "H. P. Lovecraft's Novels," in HPL: *At the Mountains of Madness and Other Novels*, pp. ix–xi.

———: "Introduction," in HPL: *Dreams and Fancies*, pp. vii–x.

———: Letter in *Haunted*, I, 3 (Jun. 1968), p. 114.

———: "Lovecraft as Mentor," in HPL: *The Shuttered Room and Other Pieces*, pp. 141–70.

———: "The Making of a Hoax," in HPL: *The Dark Brotherhood and Other Pieces*, pp. 262–67.

———: "Myths About Lovecraft," in *The Lovecraft Collector*, No. 2 (May 1949), pp. 1–4.

———: " 'New Pseudonyms' Rejected by Derleth," in *The Fossil*, LVI, 159 (Oct. 1958), p. 90.

———: "On the Lurker at the Threshold," in *The Arkham Sampler*, I, 2 (Spring, 1948), pp. 49f.

———: *Some Notes on H. P. Lovecraft*, Sauk City: Arkham House, 1959.

———: "W. Paul Cook: 1881–1948," in *The Arkham Sampler*, I, 2 (Spring, 1948), pp. 95f.

————: "Weird Tales in Retrospect," in *Inside Science Fiction*, No. 16 (No. 50, Sep. 1956), pp. 36–42.

Doris, Virginia Louise: *The Stephen Harris Mansion at ⌗135 Benefit St., Providence, R.I. . . .* , Providence: privately printed, n.d.

Douglas, Drake: *Horror!*, N.Y.: The Macmillan Co., 1966.

Duschnes, Philip C.: *Books*, Catalogue No. 78 (N.Y.).

Eddy, Clifford M., Jr.: "Walks with H. P. Lovecraft," in HPL: *The Dark Brotherhood and Other Pieces*, pp. 242–45.

Eddy, Muriel: *The Gentleman from Angell Street*, Providence: privately printed, n.d.

————: "H. P. Lovecraft Among the Demons," in the *Providence Sunday Journal Magazine*, 8 Mar. 1970, pp. 23–27.

————: "Howard Phillips Lovecraft," in Grant and Hadley, pp. 14–22.

————: *The Howard Phillips Lovecraft We Knew*, Providence: privately printed, n.d.

————: Letter in *The Magazine of Horror*, VI, 2 (No. 32, May, 1970), pp. 115f.

————: *Lovecraft Memorabilia* (unpublished ms.).

————: "Lovecraft's Marriage and Divorce," in *Haunted*, I, 3 (Jun. 1968), pp. 86–93.

————: "The Man Who Came at Midnight," in *Fantasy Commentator*, III, 3 (Summer–Fall, 1949), p. 71.

Edkins, E. A.: "Idiosyncrasies of H. P. L.," in *The Olympian*, No. 35 (Fall, 1940), pp. 1–7.

Edwards, Jay: "Lovecraftiana," in *Lethe*, No. 7 (Aug. 1947), pp. 1–5; No. 8 (Feb.–Mar. 1948), pp. 2–5.

Eitel, Elaine Gillum: *The Sense of Place in H. P. Lovecraft*, master's thesis, Lamar State College of Technology, May 1970.

Everts, R. Alain: "Ira A. Cole and Howard Phillips Lovecraft: A Brief Friendship," in Frierson, pp. 19ff.

————: "Mrs. Howard Phillips Lovecraft," in *Nyctalops*, II, 1 (No. 8, Apr. 1973), p. 45.

———— and Gamwell III, Phillips: "The Death of a Gentleman; the Last Days of Howard Phillips Lovecraft," in *Nyctalops*, II, 1 (No. 8, Apr. 1973), pp. 24f.

Faig, Kenneth W., Jr.: *Howard Phillips Lovecraft: The Early Years, 1890–1914*; unpublished paper, John Hay Library.

————: "The Lovecraft Circle: A Glossary," in *Mirage*, No. 10 (1971), pp. 27–40.

————: "Lovecraft's Providence," in *Tamlacht*, II, 2 (No. 12, n.d.), pp. 4–9.

————: "R. H. Barlow," unpublished paper, 1971, John Hay Library.

Fish, Robert Stevens: *The Oral Interpretation of the Horror Stories of H. P. Lovecraft*, master's thesis, University of Oklahoma, 1965.

Fiske, John: *Myths and Myth-Makers (Old Tales and Superstitions Interpreted by Comparative Mythology)*, Boston: Houghton, Mifflin & Co., 1901.

Frierson, Meade, III (ed.): *HPL*, Birmingham, Ala.: privately printed, 1972.

Galpin, Alfred: "Memories of a Friendship," in HPL: *The Shuttered Room and Other Pieces*, pp. 191–201.

Gissing, George: *The Private Papers of Henry Rycroft*, N.Y.: E. P. Dutton & Co., 1927.

Gobineau, Arthur de: *The Inequality of Human Races*, N.Y.: Howard Fertig, 1967.

Goodenough, Arthur: *Lovecraft—An Appreciation*, in *The Tryout*, IV, 8 (Aug. 1918). Verse.

Gough, John B.: *Sunlight and Shadow (or Gleanings from My Life Work)*, Hartford: A. D. Worthington & Co., 1881.

Grant, Donald M., and Hadley, Thomas P. (eds.): *Rhode Island on Lovecraft*, Providence: Grant-Hadley, 1945.

Grant, Kenneth: "Dreaming Out of Space," in *Man Myth and Magic*, No. 84.

Grant, Madison: *The Passing of the Great Race (or The Racial Basis of European History)*, N.Y.: Charles Scribner's Sons, 1922.

Guiney, Louise Imogen: *Happy Ending: The Collected Lyrics of Louise Imogen Guiney*, Boston: Houghton Mifflin, 1927.

————: Letters to Frederick H. Day, 1892–93, Library of Congress.

H. P. Lovecraft: A Symposium, in *The Riverside Quarterly*, 1963.

Harris, Mason: "Lovecraft and the Horror of Darkness," in *Entropy*, No. 3 (1971); No. 4 (Oct. 1971).

Harrison, Michael: "Howard Phillips Lovecraft," in *Fantasy Advertiser*, II, 4 (Nov. 1947), pp. 21ff.

Henneberger, J. C.: "Letters to Joel Frieman," in WT 50 (Oak Lawn, Ill., 1974), pp. 4, 6.

————: "Out of Space, Out of Time," in *Deeper than You Think*, I, 2 (Jul. 1968), pp. 3ff.

Hersey, Harold: "Looking Backward into the Future," in *Golden Atom*, No. 1 (1955), pp. 45–68.

Hoffman, Daniel: *Poe Poe Poe Poe Poe Poe Poe*, Garden City: Doubleday & Co., Inc., 1972.

Hofstadter, Richard: *Social Darwinism in American Thought*, Boston: Beacon Pr., 1963.

Home, William Scott: "The Lovecraft 'Books': Some Addenda and Corrigenda," in H. P. Lovecraft: *The Dark Brotherhood and Other Pieces*, pp. 134–52.

Houtain, George Julian: Editorial in *The Zenith*, Jan. 1921, pp. 2–5.

———and Cook, W. Paul (eds.): *Epgephi*, Boston: privately printed, 1920; pseudonymous account of the amateur journalistic convention of July 2–12, 1920, in Boston.

"Howard Phillips Lovecraft: Las Pesadillas de los Hombres," in *La Opinión*, Buenos Aires, 5 Aug. 1973.

"In Memoriam: Maurice Winter Moe," in *The Westminster Witness*, Jul. 1940.

Isaacson, Charles D.: "Discussions of Charles D. Isaacson," in *In a Minor Key*, Jun. 1915.

———: "Concerning the Conservative," in *In a Minor Key*, No. 2.

"James F. Morton, Museum Curator, Fatally Injured," in the *Paterson Evening News*, 7 Oct. 1941, pp. 1f.

Keffer, Willametta: "Howard P(seudonym) Lovecraft: The Many Names of HPL," in *The Fossil*, Jul. 1958.

Keller, David H.: "Lovecraft's Astronomical Notebook," in *The Lovecraft Collector*, No. 3 (Oct. 1949), pp. 1–4.

———: "Notes on Lovecraft," in *Mirage on Lovecraft*, pp. 29–35.

———: "Shadows Over Lovecraft," in *Fresco*, VIII, 3 (Spring, 1958), pp. 12–29; includes reply by Kenneth Sterling.

Kimball, Gertrude Selwyn: *Providence in Colonial Times*, Boston: Houghton Mifflin Co., 1912.

Klein, Gérard: "Entre la fantastique et la science-fiction: Lovecraft," in *L'Herne*, pp. 47–74.

Kleiner, Rheinhart: "Epistle of Mr. and Mrs. Lovecraft," in *The Brooklynite*, XIV, 2 (Apr. 1924).

———: "Howard Phillips Lovecraft," in *The Californian*, V, 1 (Summer, 1937), pp. 5–8.

———: "Howard Phillips Lovecraft," in *The Phoenix*, III, 1 (Sep. 1943), pp. 73f.

———: "A Memoir of Lovecraft," in HPL: *Something About Cats*, pp. 218–28; reprinted from *The Arkham Sampler*, I, 2 (Spring, 1948), pp. 51–61.

Koki, Arthur S.: *H. P. Lovecraft: An Introduction to his Life and Writings*, master's thesis, Columbia University, 1962.

Lacassin, Francis: "Lovecraft et les trous de la toile peinte," in *L'Herne*, pp. 106–10.

Laney, Francis T.: "The Cthulhu Mythology," in *The Acolyte*, I, 2 (Winter, 1942), pp. 6–12; reprinted in HPL: *Beyond the Wall of Sleep*, pp. 415–23.

Le Bris, Michel: "La lettre et le désir," in *L'Herne*, pp. 91–103.

Leiber, Fritz: "A Few Short Comments on the Writings of HPL," in Frierson, p. 18.

———: "Some Random Thoughts About Lovecraft's Writings," in *The Acolyte*, III, 1 (No. 9, Winter, 1945), pp. 20ff.

———: "Through Hyperspace with Brown Jenkin," in HPL: *The Dark Brotherhood and Other Pieces*," pp. 164–78.

———: "The Whisperer Re-examined," in *Haunted*, II, 2 (Dec. 1964), pp. 22–25.

———: "The Works of H. P. Lovecraft: Suggestions for a Critical Appraisal," in *The Acolyte*, II, 4 (No. 8, Fall, 1944), pp. 3ff; reprinted in slightly different form as "A Literary Copernicus," in HPL: *Something About Cats and Other Pieces*, pp. 290–303.

Lévy, Maurice: "Fascisme et Fantastique, ou le cas de Lovecraft," in *Caliban* (Annals of the Faculté des Lettres et Sciences Humaines de Toulouse), VII, 57–78.

———: *Lovecraft ou du Fantastique*, Paris: Union Générale d'Éditions, 1972.

L'Herne, No. 12, Paris: Diffusion Minard, 1969.

Long, Frank Belknap: "Some Random Memories of H. P. L.," in HPL: *Marginalia*, pp. 332–37. (See also under Schiff.)

Lovecraft, H. P.: *Ad Britannos—1918*, in *The Tryout*, IV, 4 (Apr. 1918).

———: *Ad Criticos*, in *Golden Atom*, No. 9 (Dec. 1940), p. 12; reprinted from *The Argosy*, LXXIV, No. 2 (Jan. 1914).

———: *Ad Scribam* (*Jonathan E. Hoag*), in *The Tryout*, VI, 2 (Feb. 1920).

———: "The Alchemist," in *The United Amateur*, XVI, 4 (Nov. 1916), pp. 53–57; reprinted in HPL: *The Shuttered Room and Other Pieces*. (In the later version, some of Lovecraft's typographic eccentricities were edited out.)

———: "The Allowable Rhyme," in *The Conservative*, I, 3 (Oct. 1915), pp. 3–6.

———: "Amateur Criticism," in *The Conservative*, IV, 1 (Jul. 1918), pp. 5f.

———: *The Amateur Journalist*, North Tonawanda: SSR Publications, 1955. (Vol. V of *The Lovecraft Collectors Library*, ed. by George Wetzel.)

———: "Amateur Standards," in *The Conservative*, II, 4 (Jan. 1917), pp. 3f.

———: *An American to Mother England*, in *Dowdell's Bear-Cat*, No. 16 (Nov. 1916).

————: "Americanism," in *The United Amateur*, XVIII, 6 (Jul. 1919), pp. 118ff.

————: *Amissa Minerva*, in *The Toledo Amateur*, May 1919, pp. 11–14.

————: *April*, in *The Tryout*, IV, 3 (Mar. 1918).

————: *April Dawn*, in *The Tryout*, IV, 1 (Apr. 1920).

————: Astronomical columns, "The January Sky," "The February Sky," &c., in the *Providence Evening News*, weekly from 1 Jan. 1914 to 2 May 1918.

————: "At the Root," in *The United Amateur*, XVII, 6 (Jul. 1918), pp. 111f.

————: *August*, in *The Tryout*, IV, 8 (Aug. 1918).

————: "The Bay Stater's Policy," in *The Bay Stater*, IV, 3 (Jun. 1915).

————: *Bells*, in *The Tryout*, V, 13 (Dec. 1919).

————: *Best Supernatural Stories of H. P. Lovecraft*, Cleveland: World Pub. Co., 1945.

————: *Beyond the Wall of Sleep*, Sauk City: Arkham House, 1943.

————: "Bolshevism," in *The Conservative*, V, 1 (Jul. 1919), pp. 10f.

————: *The Bookstall, an Epistle to Rheinhart Kleiner, Esq., Poet-Laureate*, in *The United Official Quarterly*, II, 2 (Jan. 1916).

————: "The Brief Autobiography of an Inconsequential Scribbler," in *The Silver Clarion*, III, 1 (Apr. 1919), pp. 8f.

————: *Britannia Victoria*, in *The Inspiration*, Apr. 1917, pp. 3f.

————: *Brotherhood*, in *The Tryout*, III, 1 (Dec. 1916).

————: *Brumalia*, in *The Tryout*, III, 1 (Dec. 1916).

————: "By Post from Providence," in *The Californian*, V, 1 (Summer, 1937), pp. 10–23. (Excerpts from letters to Rheinhart Kleiner.)

————: "The Case for Classicism," in *The United Co-Operative*, I, 2 (Jun. 1919), pp. 3ff.

————: "Chairman of the Bureau of Critics Reports on Poetry," in *The National Amateur*, LVII, 1 (5 Sep. 1934), 2d sec., p. 3.

————: "Charleston," in HPL: *Marginalia*, pp. 199–237; reprinted from a private printing by H. C. Koenig.

————: *Clouds*, in *Fantasy Commentator*, II, 6 (Spring, 1948), p. 190.

————: "Comment," in *The Silver Clarion*, III, 1 (Apr. 1918), pp. 7, 5.

————: "Concerning 'Persia—in Europe,'" in *The Tryout*, III, 2 (Jan. 1917).

————: "A Confession of Unfaith," in *Selected Essays*, pp. 19–22.

————: "The Conservative and his Critics," in *The Conservative*, I, 3 (Oct. 1915), pp. 7f.

————: *Continuity*, in *Causeries*, Feb. 1936.

————: "The Convention," in *The Tryout*, XIII, 8 (Jul. 1930).

————: "The Crawling Chaos," by "Elizabeth Berkeley & Lewis Theobald, Jun.," in *The United Co-Operative*, I, 3 (Apr. 1921), pp. 1–6. Reprinted in *Beyond the Wall of Sleep*, pp. 210–14.

————: "The Crime of the Century," in *The Conservative*, I, 1 (Jul. 1915), pp. 2f.

————: *Dagon and Other Macabre Tales*, Sauk City: Arkham House, 1965.

————: *The Dark Brotherhood and Other Pieces*, Sauk City: Arkham House, 1966.

————: *Death*, in *The Californian*, V, 1 (Summer, 1937), p. 25.

————: "Defining the 'Ideal' Paper," in *The National Amateur*, LXII, 3 (Jun. 1940), pp. 8–12.

————: "Department of Public Criticism," in *The United Amateur*, from XIV, 4 (Mar. 1915) to XXVIII, 3 (Jan. 1919).

————: "A Descent to Avernus," in *Bacon's Essays*, Summer, 1929, p. 8.

————: *A Description of the Town of Quebeck, in New-France . . .* , ms. in the John Hay Library.

————: *Despair*, by "Ward Phillips" in *Pine Cones*, I, 4 (Jun. 1919).

————: "The Despised Pastoral," in *The Conservative*, IV, 1 (Jul. 1918), p. 2.

————: *The Doom That Came to Sarnath*, N.Y.: Ballantine Books, 1971.

————: *The Dunwich Horror and Others*, Sauk City: Arkham House, 1963.

————: *Earth and Sky*, in *Pine Cones*, I, 1 (Dec. 1918), p. 1.

————: " 'Ebony and Crystal,' by Clark Ashton Smith," in *L'Alouette, A Magazine of Verse*, Jan. 1924. Review.

————: "Editorial," in *The Conservative*, I, 2 (Jul. 1915), pp. 4f.

————: "Editorial," in *The Conservative*, I, 3 (Oct. 1915), pp. 6f.

————: "Editorial," in *The United Amateur*, XXIV, 1 (Jul. 1925), pp. 8f.

————: *The Eidolon*, in *The Tryout*, IV, 10 (Oct. 1918).

————: *Fact and Fancy*, in *The Tryout*, III, 3 (Feb. 1917).

————: *The Familiars*, in Driftwind, V, 1 (Jul. 1930), p. 35.

————: *The Feast*, in *The Hub Club Quill*, XV, 2 (May 1923).

————: "Finale: Campbell's Plan," in *The Badger*, II, (Jun. 1915), pp. 17–20.

————: "For What Does United Stand?" in *The United Amateur*, XIX, 5 (May 1920), p. 101.

————: *Fungi from Yuggoth and Other Poems*, N.Y.: Ballantine Books, Inc., 1971; reprinted from *Collected Poems*, Sauk City: Arkham House, 1964.

————: *Further Criticism of Poetry*, privately printed by H. C. Koenig, n.d.; reprinted in *The National Amateur*, Dec. 1944.

————: *Germania—1918*, in *The Tryout*, IV, 11 (Nov. 1918), pp. 2–6.

————: "The Green Meadow," by "Elizabeth Neville Berkeley & Lewis Theobald, Jr.," in *The Vagrant*, Spring, 1927, pp. 188–95.

————: *Greetings*, in *The Silver Clarion*, II, 10 (Jan. 1919).

————: *The Haunter of the Dark and Other Tales of Horror*, London: Victor Gollancz, Ltd., 1951.

————: "The Haverhill Convention," in *The Tryout*, VII, 4 (Jul. 1921).

————: "Helene Hoffman Cole—Litterateur," in *The United Amateur*, XVIII, 5 (May 1919), pp. 92f.

————: "Heritage or Modernism: Common Sense in Art Forms," in HPL: *Marginalia*, pp. 161–73; reprinted from *The Californian*, Summer, 1935.

————: *A History of the Necronomicon*, Oakman, Ala.: Rebel Pr., 1938; reprinted as "History and Chronology of the Necronomicon," in HPL: *Beyond the Wall of Sleep*, pp. xxviiif; in *Mirage*, I, 6 (Winter, 1963–64), pp. 34–36.

————: *Homecoming*, in *Science-Fantasy Correspondent*, Nov.–Dec. 1936, p. 24; reprinted from *The Fantasy Fan*, Jan. 1935.

————: "Homes and Shrines of Poe," in *The Californian*, Winter, 1934, pp. 8ff.

————: *Horace, Book III, Ode IX*, a translation by "Theobald," in *Sappho—The Magazine of Verse*, I, 4 (n.d.), p. 11.

————: *The Horror in the Museum and Other Revisions*, Sauk City: Arkham House, 1970.

————: *The House*, by "Ward Phillips," in *The Philosopher*, I, 1 (Dec. 1920), p. 6.

————: *The Howler*, in *Driftwind*, VII, 3 (Nov. 1932), p. 100.

————: "Idealism and Materialism—A Reflection," in *The National Amateur*, XLI, 6 (Jul. 1919), pp. 11–18; reprinted in *Selected Essays*.

————: "In a Major Key," in *The Conservative*, I, 2 (Jul. 1915), pp. 9ff.

————: "In Memoriam: Robert E. Howard," in *Fantasy Magazine*, No. 38 (Sep. 1936), pp. 29–32.

————: "In the Editor's Study," in *The Conservative*, No. 13 (Jul. 1923), pp. 21–24.

————: "In the Editor's Study: A Remarkable Document," in *The Conservative*, III, 1 (Jul. 1917), p. 4.

————: "In the Editor's Study: Anglo-Saxondom," in *The Conservative*, III, 1 (Jul. 1917), p. 4.

————: "In the Editor's Study: The League," in *The Conservative*, V, 1 (Jul. 1919), pp. 9f.

————: "In the Editor's Study: Rudis Indigestaque Moles," in *The Conservative*, No. 12 (Mar. 1923), pp. 6ff.

————: "In the Editor's Study: Rursus Adsumus," in *The Conservative*, No. 12 (Mar. 1923), pp. 5f.

————: "Introducing Mr. John Russell," in *The Conservative*, I, 2 (Jul. 1915), pp. 8f.

————: *Iterum Conjunctae*, in *The Tryout*, III, 6 (May 1917).

————: *John Oldham: A Defence*, in *The United Co-Operative*, I, 2 (Jun. 1919), p. 7.

————: *Laeta: A Lament*, in *The Tryout*, IV, 2 (Feb. 1918).

————: *Lines for Poet's Night*, in *Pegasus*, Feb. 1924, pp. 31ff.

————: *Lines on Gen. Robert E. Lee*, in *The Coyote*, III, 1 (Jan. 1917), pp. 1f.

————: *Lines on the 25th Anniversary of the Providence Evening News, 1892–1917*, in *The Tryout*, IV, 1 (Dec. 1917), pp. 3ff.

————: "Liquor and its Friends," in *The Conservative*, I, 3 (Oct. 1915), pp. 10f.

————: "Literary Review," in *The Californian*, IV, 3 (Winter, 1936), pp. 27–33.

————: "The Literature of Rome," in *The United Amateur*, XVIII, 2 (Nov. 1918), pp. 17–21.

————: "Looking Backward," in *The Tryout*, VI, 1–6 (Jan.–Jun. 1920).

————: "Lord Dunsany and his Work," in HPL: *Marginalia*, pp. 148–60.

————: "Lucubrations Lovecraftian," in *The United Co-Operative*, I, 3 (Apr. 1921), pp. 8–15.

————: *March*, in *The United Amateur*, XIV, 4 (Mar. 1915), p. 68.

————: *Marginalia*, Sauk City: Arkham House, 1944.

————: "A Matter of Uniteds," in *Bacon's Essays*, I, 1 (Summer, 1927), pp. 1ff.

————: "Memory," by "Lewis Theobald, Jun.," in *The United Co-Operative*, I, 2 (Jun. 1919), p. 8.

————: "Merlinus Redivivus," in *The Conservative*, IV, 1 (Jul. 1918), pp. 4f; reprinted in *Something About Cats and Other Pieces*, pp. 151f.

————: "Metrical Regularity," in *The Conservative*, I, 2 (Jul. 1915), pp. 2ff.

————: Misc. letters from the John Hay Library and other sources (originals, photocopies, and microfilms).

————: *A Mississippi Autumn*, in *Ole Miss*, No. 2 (Dec. 1915), pp. 5f.

————: *Monody on the Late King Alcohol*, in *The Tryout*, V, 8 (Aug. 1919).

————: "More 'Chain Lightning'," in *The United Official Quarterly*, II, 1 (Oct. 1915), pp. 1–4.

————: "Les Mouches Fantastiques," in *The Conservative*, IV, 1 (Jan. 1918), pp. 7f; reprinted in *The Amateur Journalist*, pp. 23f.

————: "Nietzscheism and Realism," in *The Rainbow*, I, 1 (Oct. 1921), pp. 9ff; reprinted in *Selected Essays*, pp. 23–26.

————: "No Transit of Mars," in the *Providence Sunday Journal*, 3 Jun. 1906.

————: *The Notes & Commonplace Book Employed by the Late H. P. Lovecraft . . .* , Lakeport, Calif.: Futile Pr. 1938. Published in somewhat different form as "The Commonplace Book of H. P. Lovecraft, annotated by August Derleth & Donald Wandrei," in *The Shuttered Room and Other Pieces*, pp. 97–123.

————: "Notes on Interplanetary Fiction," in *The Acolyte*, I, 4 (Summer, 1943), pp. 15–18; reprinted in *Marginalia*, pp. 140–47.

————: "Notes on the Writing of Weird Fiction," in *The Amateur Correspondent*, II, 1 (May–Jun. 1937), pp. 7–10; reprinted in *Marginalia*, pp. 135–39.

————: *The Nymph's Reply to the Modern Business Man*, by "Lewis Theobald, Jr.," in *The Tryout*, III, 3 (Feb. 1917), p. 2.

————: "Observations on Several Parts of North America," in *Marginalia*, pp. 238–67.

————: *October*, in *The Tryout*, X, 7 (Jan. 1926).

————: *Ode for July Fourth, 1917*, in *The United Amateur*, XVI, 9 (Jul. 1917), p. 1.

————: *Old Christmas*, in *The Tryout*, IV, 12 (Dec. 1918).

————: "The Omnipresent Philistine," in *The Oracle*, May, 1924, pp. 14–17.

————: *On a Battlefield in France*, in *The Voice from the Mountains*, Jul. 1918, p. 11.

————: *On a Modern Lothario*, in *The Blarney Stone*, II, 4 (Jul.–Aug. 1914), pp. 7f.

————: *On a Poet's Ninety-First Birthday*, by "Lewis Theobald, Jun.," in *The Tryout*, VII, 11 (Mar. 1922).

————: *On the Cowboys of the West,* in *The Plainsman,* I, 4 (Dec. 1915), pp. 1f.

————: *On the Death of a Rhyming Critic,* in *The Toledo Amateur,* Jul., 1917, pp. 11f.

————: *On the Return of Maurice Winter Moe, Esq., to the Pedagogical Profession,* by "Lewis Theobald, Jun.," in *The Wolverine,* No. 10 (June. 1921), pp. 15f.

————: *The Outsider and Others,* Sauk City: Arkham House, 1939.

————: *Percival Lowell 1855–1916,* in *Excelsior,* I, 1 (Mar. 1917), p. 3.

————: *Phaeton,* in *The Californian,* V, 1 (Summer, 1937), p. 24.

————: *The Poe-et's Nightmare: A Fable,* in *The Vagrant,* No. 8 (Jul. 1918), p. 13.

————: *The Poet of Passion,* by "Lewis Theobald, Jun.," in *The Tryout,* III, 7 (Jun. 1917).

————: "Poetry and the Gods," by "Anna Helen Crofts & Henry Paget-Lowe," in *The United Amateur,* XX, 1 (Sep. 1920), pp. 1–4.

————: *The Port,* in *Driftwind,* V, 3 (Nov. 1930), p. 37.

————: "The President's Message," in *The National Amateur,* XLV, 6 (Jul. 1923); reprinted in HPL: *The Amateur Journalist,* pp. 7–10.

————: "The Professional Incubus," in *The National Amateur,* XLVI, 4 (Mar. 1924); reprinted in HPL: *The Amateur Journalist,* pp. 15ff.

————: *Prologue,* in *The Tryout,* III, 8 (Jul. 1917).

————: *Providence,* in *The Californian,* V, 1 (Summer, 1937), pp. 26f.

————: *Quinsnicket Park,* in *The Badger,* II (Jun. 1915), pp. 7–10.

————: "A Reminiscence of Dr. Samuel Johnson," by "Humphrey Littlewit, Esq.," in *The United Amateur,* XVII, 2 (Nov. 1917), pp. 21–24.

————: "The Renaissance of Manhood," in *The Conservative,* I, 3 (Oct. 1915), pp. 8ff.

————: "A Reply to the Lingerer," in *The Tryout,* III, 7 (Jun. 1917); reprinted in HPL: *The Amateur Journalist,* pp. 19f.

————: "Reports of Officers: President's Message," in *The United Amateur,* XVII, 6 (Jul. 1918), pp. 127f.

————: *The Rose of England,* in *The Scot,* II, 14 (Oct. 1916), p. 1.

————: *A Rural Summer Eve,* in *The Trail,* I, 2 (Jan. 1916), pp. 12f.

————: *The Rutted Road,* in *The Tryout,* X, 8 (Mar. 1926).

————: *Selected Essays*, North Tonawanda: SSR Publications, 1952. (Vol. I of *The Lovecraft Collectors Library*, ed. by George Wetzel.)

————: *Selected Letters, I*, Sauk City: Arkham House, 1965.

————: *Selected Letters, II*, Sauk City: Arkham House, 1968.

————: *Selected Letters, III*, Sauk City: Arkham House, 1971.

————: *Selected Poetry (First Series)*, North Tonawanda: SSR Publications, 1953. (Vol. III of *The Lovecraft Collectors Library*, ed. by George Wetzel.)

————: *Selected Poetry (Second Series)*, North Tonawanda: SSR Publications, 1955. (Vol. IV of *The Lovecraft Collectors Library*, ed. by George Wetzel.)

————: "The Simple Spelling Mania," in *The United Co-Operative*, I, 1 (Dec. 1918), pp. 1ff; reprinted in HPL: *The Amateur Journalist*, pp. 5f.

————: "Some Backgrounds of Fairyland," in *Marginalia*, pp. 174–83.

————: "Some Causes of Self-Immolation," by "L. Theobald, Jun.," in *Marginalia*, pp. 184–98.

————: "Some Dutch Footprints in New England," in *De Halve Maen*, IX, 1 (18 Oct. 1933), pp. 2, 4.

————: "Some Notes on Interplanetary Fiction," in *Marginalia*, pp. 140–47; reprinted from *The Recluse*, 1927, and *The Californian*, Winter, 1935.

————: *Something About Cats and Other Pieces*, Sauk City: Arkham House, 1949.

————: *The Spirit of Summer*, in *The Conservative*, IV, 1 (Jul. 1918), p. 1.

————: *Spring*, in *The Tryout*, V, 4 (Apr. 1919).

————: *The State of Poetry*, in *The Conservative*, I, 3 (Oct. 1915), pp. 1ff.

————: *Sunset*, in *The United Amateur*, XVII, 5 (May 1918), p. 90.

————: "Supernatural Horror in Literature," N.Y.: Ben Abramson, 1945; reprinted from *The Recluse*, 1927, and *The Fantasy Fan*, Oct. 1933 to Feb. 1935; reprinted in *The Outsider and Others*, pp. 509–53.

————: "The Symphonic Ideal," in *The Conservative*, II, 3 (Oct. 1916), pp. 10f; reprinted in HPL: *The Amateur Journalist*, pp. 13f.

————: "Systematic Instruction in the United," in *Ole Miss*, No. 2 (Dec. 1915), pp. 4f.

————: *Temperance Song*, in *The Dixie Booser*, IV, 4 (Spring, 1916). p. 9.

————: *The Teuton's Battle Song*, in *The United Amateur*, XV, 7 (Feb. 1916), pp. 85f.

————: "The Thing in the Moonlight," in *Bizarre*, Jan. 1941, pp. 5, 20; reprinted in HPL: *Dreams and Fancies*, pp. 94ff.

————: "Time and Space," in *The Conservative*, IV, 1 (Jul. 1918), pp. 3f; reprinted in HPL: *Something About Cats*, pp. 149f.

————: *To a Youth* (*Dedicated to Master Alfred Galpin, Jun.*), in *The Tryout*, VII, 1 (Feb. 1921).

————: *To Alan Seeger*, in *The United Amateur*, XVIII, 2 (Nov. 1918), p. 24.

————: *To an Infant* (*Dedicated to Richard Merritt Dench*), in *The Brooklynite*, XV, 4 (Oct. 1925), p. 2.

————: *To Arthur Goodenough, Esq.*, in *The Tryout*, IV, 9 (Sep. 1918).

————: *To Endymion* (*Frank Belknap Long, Jr.*), by "L. Theobald, Jun.," in *The Tryout*, VIII, 10 (Sep. 1923).

————: *To Jonathan Hoag, Esq., On His 87th Birthday*, in *Eurus*, I, 1 (Feb. 1918), pp. 5f.

————: *To Jonathan Hoag* (*Upon his 95th Birthday*), in *The Brooklynite*, XVI, 2 (May 1926), p. 1.

————: *To Miss Beryl Hoyt* (*Upon her First Birthday—February 21, 1927*), in *Justice*, Feb. 1927, p. 3.

————: *To Mr. Galpin*, in *The Tryout*, VII, 9 (Dec. 1921).

————: *To Mr. Hoag, Upon his 93rd birthday, February 10th, 1924*, in *Pegasus*, Jul. 1924, p. 33.

————: *To Phillis*, by "L. Theobald, Jun.," in *The Tryout*, VI, 2 (Feb. 1920).

————: *To Samuel Loveman, Esquire* (*On his Poetry and Drama, Writ in the Elizabethan Style*), in *Dowdell's Bear-Cat*, IV, 5 (Dec. 1915).

————: *To the American Flag*, in *The Californian*, V, 1 (Summer, 1937), pp. 27.

————: *To the Members of the Pin-Feathers on the Merits of Their Organization, and of Their New Publication, The Pinfeather*, in *The Pinfeather*, I, 1 (Nov. 1914), pp. 3f.

————: *To the Members of the United Amateur Press Association from the Providence Amateur Press Club*, in *The Providence Amateur*, I, 1 (Jun. 1915), pp. 1ff.

————: "The Truth About Mars," in *The Phoenician*, Autumn, 1917, p. 8.

————: "The Unknown City in the Ocean," in *The Perspective Review*, Winter, 1934, pp. 7f.

————: "The Vers Libre Epidemic," in *The Conservative*, II, 4 (Jan. 1917), pp. 4f.

————: "The Vivisector," by "Zoilus," in *The Wolverine*, No. 9 (Mar. 1921) to No. 11 (Nov. 1921).

————: "The Weird Work of William Hope Hodgson," in *The Reader and Collector*, III, 3 (Jun. 1944), pp. 5f; reprinted from *The Phantagraph*, Feb. 1937.

————: "What Amateurdom and I Have Done for Each Other," in *The Boys' Herald*, LXXII, 1 (Jan. 1943), pp. 6f.

————: "What Belongs in Verse," in *The Perspective Review*, Spring, 1935, pp. 10f.

————: "Winifred Virginia Jackson: A 'Different' Poetess," in *The United Amateur*, XX, 4 (Mar. 1921), pp. 48–52.

————: A *Winter Wish*, in *The Tryout*, IV, 2 (Feb. 1918).

———— and August Derleth: *The Survivor and Others*, Sauk City: Arkham House, 1957.

———— and Divers Hands: *The Shuttered Room and Other Pieces*, Sauk City: Arkham House, 1959.

———— and John T. Dunn: *Lines on Graduation From the R. I. Hospital's School of Nurses*, in *The Tryout*, III, 3 (Feb. 1917), pp. 13ff. (Credited to Dunn.)

———— and Others: *Tales of the Cthulhu Mythos*, Sauk City: Arkham House, 1969.

Loveman, Samuel: *The Hermaphrodite and Other Poems*, Caldwell, Idaho: Caxton Printers, 1936.

————: "Howard Phillips Lovecraft," in HPL: *Something About Cats and Other Pieces*, pp. 229–33; reprinted from *The Arkham Sampler*, Summer, 1948.

————: "Lovecraft as a Conversationalist," in *Fresco*, VIII, 3 (Spring, 1958), pp. 34ff.

Mabbott, Thomas Ollive: "Lovecraft as a Student of Poe," in *Fresco*, VIII, 3 (Spring, 1958), pp. 37ff.

Macauley, George W.: "Lovecraft and the Amateur Press," in *Fresco*, VIII, 3 (Spring, 1958), pp. 40–44.

————: "Lovecraftana, Extracts from H. P. Lovecraft's Letters," in *O-Wash-Ta-Nong*, III, 2 (Spring, 1938), pp. 1–4.

Machen, Arthur: *The Autobiography of Arthur Machen*, Lon.: Richards Pr., 1951.

————: *The Hill of Dreams*, Lon.: E. G. Richards, 1907; N.Y.: Knopf, 1923.

————: *The House of Souls*, N.Y.: Alfred A. Knopf, 1923.

MacNulty, Sir Arthur Salusbury: *The British Medical Dictionary*, Lon.: Caxton Pub. Co., Ltd.

Marquand, John P.: *The Late George Apley* (*A Novel in the Form of a Memoir*), Boston: Little, Brown & Co., 1936.

Michaud, Paul R.: "In Paris; Lovecraft," in the *Providence Evening Bulletin*, 29 Dec. 1970, p. 12.

"The Moodus Mystery," in *Coronet*, Feb. 1934, pp. 171f.

Moore, Wilbert E. (ed.): *Technology and Social Change*, Chicago: Quadrangle Books, 1972.

Mooser, Clare: "A Study of Robert Barlow: The T. E. Lawrence of Mexico," in *Mexico Quarterly Review*, III, 2 (1968), pp. 5–12.

Morton, James F.: "A Few Memories," in *The Olympian*, No. 35 (Fall, 1940), pp. 24–28.

Moskowitz, Sam: *Explorers of the Infinite*, Cleveland: World Pub. Co., 1963.

————: *Under the Moons of Mars* (*A History and Anthology of "The Scientific Romance" in the Munsey Magazines, 1912–1920*), N.Y.: Holt, Rinehart & Winston, 1970.

Muller, George: *The Origins of H. P. Lovecraft's Fiction*, unpub. treatise, John Hay Library, 1969.

Murat, Napoléon: "Rêve et création chez Lovecraft," in *L'Herne*, pp. 126–32.

"Old House Will Get New View," in the *Providence Sunday Journal*, 9 Aug. 1959.

Onderdonk, Matthew H.: "Charon—in Reverse, or, H. P. Lovecraft Versus the 'Realists' of Fantasy," in *Fantasy Commentator*, II, 6 (Spring, 1948), pp. 193–97.

————: "The Lord of R'lyeh," in *Fantasy Commentator*, I, 6 (Spring, 1945), pp. 103–14.

Orton, Vrest: "H. P. Lovecraft," unpublished memoir.

Owings, Mark: *The Necronomicon: A Study*, Baltimore: Mirage Pr., 1967. A spoof.

————: *The Revised H. P. Lovecraft Bibliography*, Baltimore: Mirage Press, 1973.

Penzoldt, Peter: *The Supernatural in Fiction*, Lon.: Peter Nevill, 1952.

Price, Edgar Hoffmann: "E. Hoffman [*sic*] Price Disagrees with a Too Enthusiastic Description," in *The Acolyte*, III, 4 (No. 12, Fall, 1945), pp. 31f.

————: "The Golden Days," in *Deeper than You Think*, I, 2 (Jul. 1968), pp. 13–17.

————: "Howard Phillips Lovecraft," in *The Acolyte*, II, 4 (No. 8, Fall, 1944), pp. 17ff.

————: "The Man Who Was Lovecraft," in HPL: *Something About Cats and Other Pieces*, pp. 278–89.

————: "Reminiscences of H. P. L.," in Frierson, pp. 16f.

————: "The Sage of College Street," in *The Amateur Correspondent*, II, 1 (May–Jun. 1937), pp. 6f.

Renshaw, Anne Tillery: *Well Bred Speech*, Washington, D.C., privately printed, 1936.

Rhode Island, A Guide to the Smallest State, Boston: Houghton Mifflin & Co., 1937.

Ripley, William Z.: *The Races of Europe: A Sociological Study*, N.Y.: D. Appleton & Co., 1899.

Rivais, Yak: "The bottom—At last!" in *L'Herne*, pp. 163–76.

Rothovius, Andrew E.: "Lovecraft and the New England Megaliths," in *The Dark Brotherhood and Other Pieces*, pp. 179–97.

Russell, Samuel D.: "Open Season on Lovecraft," in *Haunted*, I, 1 (Mar. 1963), pp. 9f, 17; I, 2 (Dec. 1964), pp. 38–42.

St. Armand, Barton Levy: "Facts in the Case of H. P. Lovecraft," in *Rhode Island History*, XXXI, 1 (Feb. 1972), pp. 3–19.

————: *The Outsider in Legend and Myth*, master's thesis, Brown University, 1966.

Samuels, Ernest: *Henry Adams: The Major Phase*, Cambridge, Mass.: Harvard University Pr., 1964.

Santayana, George: *The Last Puritan* (*A Memoir in the Form of a Novel*), N.Y.: Charles Scribner's Sons, 1936.

Scarborough, Dorothy: *The Supernatural in Modern English Fiction*, N.Y.: G. P. Putnam's Sons, 1917.

Schevill, James: *Lovecraft's Follies*, Chicago: Swallow Pr., 1971.

Schweitzer, Darrell: "Lovecraft on Television," in *Nyctalops*, I, 6 (Feb. 1972), pp. 12ff.

Schiff, Stuart D.: "An Interview with Frank Belknap Long," in Frierson, pp. 7–11.

Scott, Winfield Townley: *Bookman's Gallery*, in the *Providence Journal*, 18 Sep. 1948, Sec. IV, p. 8, col. 1; 3 Oct. 1948, Sec. VI, p. 8, col. 5.

————: "The Case of Howard Phillips Lovecraft," in the *Providence Sunday Journal*, 26 Dec. 1943, Sec. III, p. 6.

————: *Exiles and Fabrications*, Garden City: Doubleday & Co., Inc., 1961.

————: "The Haunter of the Dark; Some Notes on Howard Phillips Lovecraft," in *Books at Brown*, VI, 3 (Mar. 1944), pp. 1–4.

————: "His Own Most Fantastic Creation," in HPL: *Marginalia*, pp. 309–31; reprinted in slightly different form in *Exiles and Fabrications*.

————: "Lovecraft as a Poet," in Grant & Hadley, pp. 3–7.

Searles, Harold F.: *The Nonhuman Environment*, N.Y.: International University Pr., Inc., 1960.

Seeing Providence, Providence Journal Co., n.d.

Selle, W. A.: *Body Temperature (Its Changes with Environment, Disease and Therapy)*, Springfield, Ill.: Charles C. Thomas.

Shaw, Lee: "The Day He Met Lovecraft," in *Brown Alumni Monthly*, LXXII, 7 (Apr. 1972), p. 3.

Shea, J. Vernon: "H. P. Lovecraft: The House and the Shadows," in *The Magazine of Fantasy & Science Fiction*, XXX, 5 (May 1966), pp. 82–99.

Skinner, Charles M.: *Myths & Legends of Our Own Land*, Phila.: J. B. Lippincott Co., 1896, 2 vols.

Slonim, Marc: "European Notebook," in the *New York Times Book Review*, 17 May 1970.

Smisor, George: "R. H. Barlow and 'Tlalocan,'" in *Tlalocan*, III, 2 (1952), pp. 97–102.

Smith, Clark Ashton: *Selected Poems*, Sauk City: Arkham House, 1971.

Smith, Reginald: *Weird Tales in the Thirties*, Santa Ana, Calif.: privately printed, 1966.

Solon, Ben: "Lovecraft on the Doorstep," in *Haunted*, I, 3 (Jun. 1968), pp. 87f.

"Some Notes on Lovecraft," in *The Science Fiction Critic*, I, 10 (Jul. 1932), p. 2.

Spencer, Truman J.: *The History of Amateur Journalism*, N.Y.: The Fossils, Inc., 1957.

Squires, Roy A.: *Hail, Klarkash-Ton!*, Glendale, Calif.: privately printed, n.d. Post cards from HPL to C. A. Smith.

Starrett, Vincent: *Books and Bipeds*, N. Y.: Argus Books, 1947.

Stoddard, Lothrop: *The Rising Tide of Color (Against White World-Supremacy)*, N.Y.: Charles Scribner's Sons, 1922.

Sully, Helen V.: "Memories of Lovecraft, II," in *The Arkham Collector*, I, 4 (Winter, 1969), pp. 117ff.

Talman, Wilfred B.: "Lovecraft Revisted," in *Fresco*, X, 2 (Winter–Spring, 1960), pp. 48ff.

———: *The Normal Lovecraft*, Saddle River, N.J.: Gerry de la Ree, 1973.

Tenison, Eva Mabel: *Louise Imogen Guiney, Her Life and Works, 1861–1920*, Lon.: Macmillan & Co., 1923.

Thomas, James Warren: "H. P. Lovecraft: A Portrait in Words," in *Fresco*, IX, 1 (Fall, 1958), pp. 33–40.

———: *Howard Phillips Lovecraft: A Self-Portrait*, master's thesis, Brown University, 1950.

Thoreau, Henry David: *The Portable Thoreau*, N.Y.: Viking Pr., 1962.

Tierney, Richard L.: "The Derleth Mythos," in Frierson, p. 53.

————: Letter in *Nyctalops*, I, 5 (Oct. 1971), pp. 51ff.

Truchaud, François: "The Dream-Quest of Howard Phillips Lovecraft," in *L'Herne*, pp. 15–25.

Unterecker, John: *Voyager, A Life of Hart Crane*, N.Y.: Farrar, Straus & Giroux, 1969.

Versins, Pierre: "Les débuts de Lovecraft dans 'Weird Tales,'" in *L'Herne*, pp. 30–38.

Walter, Dorothy C.: "Lovecraft and Benefit Street," in Grant and Hadley, pp. 8–13.

————: "Three Hours with H. P. Lovecraft," in HPL: *The Shuttered Room and Other Pieces*, pp. 178–90.

Wandrei, Donald: "The Dweller in Darkness: Lovecraft, 1927," in HPL: *Marginalia*, pp. 362–69.

————: "Lovecraft in Providence," in HPL: *The Shuttered Room and Other Pieces*," pp. 124–40.

Warner, Harry, Jr.: *All Our Yesterdays*, Chicago: Advent Publishers, 1969.

————: "Joseph Fann and His Brothers," in *New Frontiers*, II, 1 (May 1964), pp. 8–23.

Weinberg, Robert: "H. P. Lovecraft and Pseudomathematics," in *Nyctalops*, I, 5 (Oct. 1971), pp. 3f.

————: "Robert E. Howard and the Cthulhu Mythos," in *Nyctalops*, I, 2 (Oct. 1970), p. 6.

Wesson, Helen V.: "The Phenomenon of HPL," in *The Fossil*, LV, No. 154 (Jul. 1957), pp. 1, 9–17.

———— and Sheldon Wesson: "Revenant: The Vagrant Ghost," in *The Fossil*, LV, No. 157 (Apr. 1958), pp. 45, 52–58.

West, Wallace: "Wright or Wrong?" in *Deeper than You Think*, I, 2 (Jul. 1968), pp. 8ff.

Wetzel, George T.: "The Cthulhu Mythos: A Study," in Wetzel (1955), pp. 18–27; reprinted in Frierson, pp. 35–41.

————: "The Dream-Gate and Other Matters," in *Fantasias*, No. 4, pp. 8–11.

————: "An Early Portrait of Lovecraft," in *Renaissance*, II, 2 (Mar. 1953), pp. 3ff.

————: "Genesis of the Cthulhu Mythos," in *Fantasy Commentator*, I, 12 (Fall, 1946), pp. 24–32.

————: "The Ghoul-Changeling," in *Fantasy Commentator*, III, 5 (Winter, 1951–52), pp. 131f.

————— (ed.): *HPL: Memoirs, Critiques, and Bibliographies*, North Tonawanda: SSR Publications, 1955.

—————: "Lovecraft in the Ashville [*sic*] Gazette-News," in *Renaissance*, II, 2 (Mar. 1953), pp. 12f.

—————: "A Lovecraft Profile," in *Nyctalops*, II, 1 (No. 8, Apr. 1973), pp. 18ff.

—————: "A Lovecraft Randomonium," in *Destiny*, I, 6 (Winter–Spring, 1952), pp. 11f, 29.

—————: "Lovecraft's Amateur Press Works," in *Destiny*, I, 4–5 (Summer–Fall, 1951), pp. 23ff.

—————: "The Mechanistic Supernatural of Lovecraft," in *Fresco*, VIII, 3 (Spring, 1958), pp. 54–60.

—————: "Notes on the Cthulhu Mythos," in HPL: *The Shuttered Room and Other Pieces*, pp. 278–86.

—————: "On the Cthulhu Mythos," in *The Arkham Sampler*, II, 2 (Spring, 1948), pp. 48f.

—————: "The Research of a Biblio," in Wetzel (1955), pp. 41–57.

—————: "Some Thoughts on the Lovecraft Pattern," in *Fantasy Commentator*, I, 12 (Fall, 1946), pp. 316f, 322.

Wilson, Colin: *The Outsider*, Boston: Houghton Mifflin Co., 1956.

—————: *The Strength to Dream* (*Literature and the Imagination*), Boston: Houghton Mifflin Co., 1962.

Wilson, Edmund: *Classics and Commercials: A Literary Chronicle of the Forties*, N.Y.: Farrar, Straus & Co., 1950.

Wilstach, John: "The Ten-Cent Ivory Tower," in *Esquire*, XXV, 1 (No. 146, Jan. 1946), pp. 83, 160ff.

Wood, Squire G.: *A History of Greene and Vicinity, 1845–1929*, Providence: privately printed, 1936.

INDEX